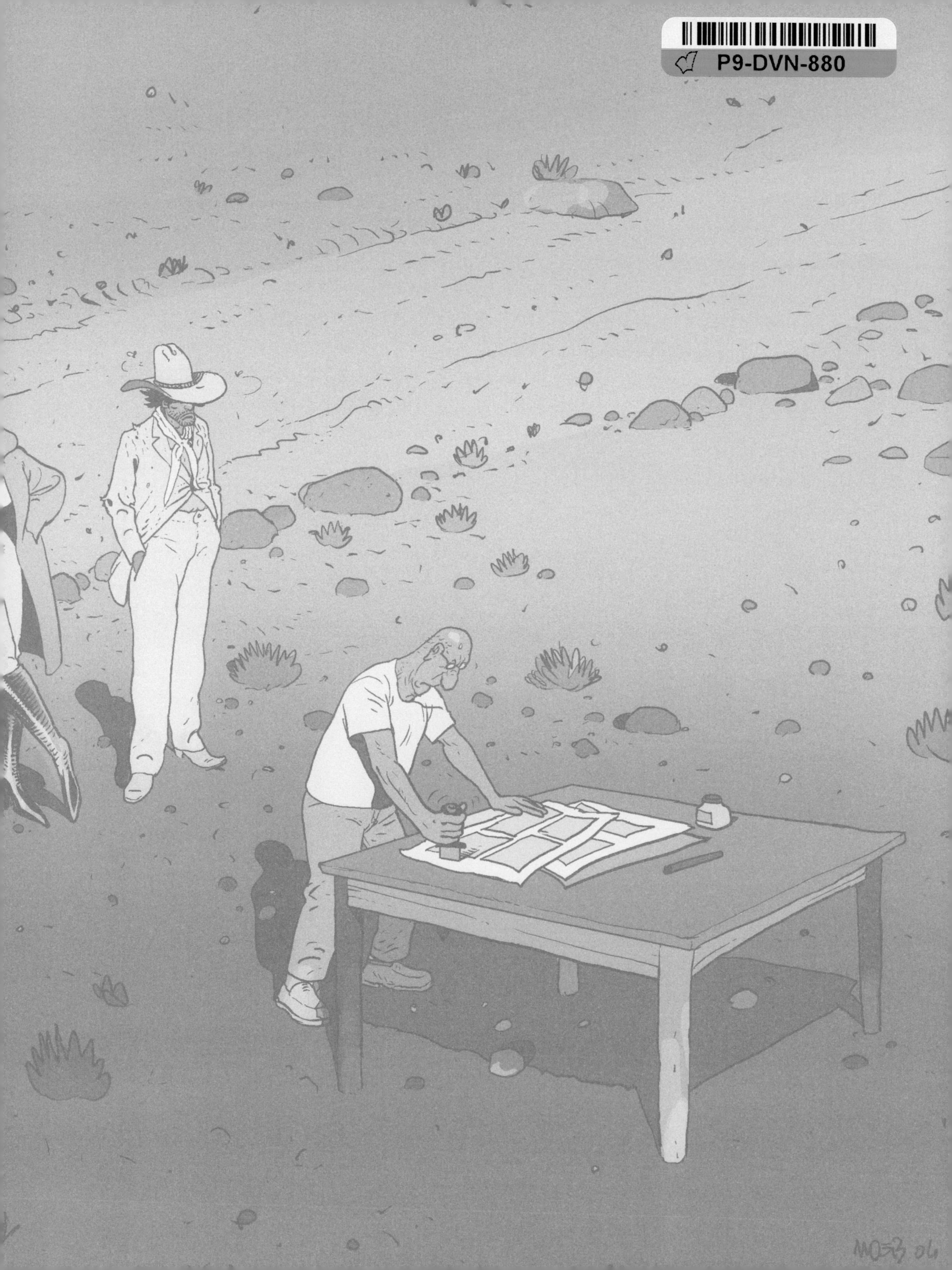
MOEB.06

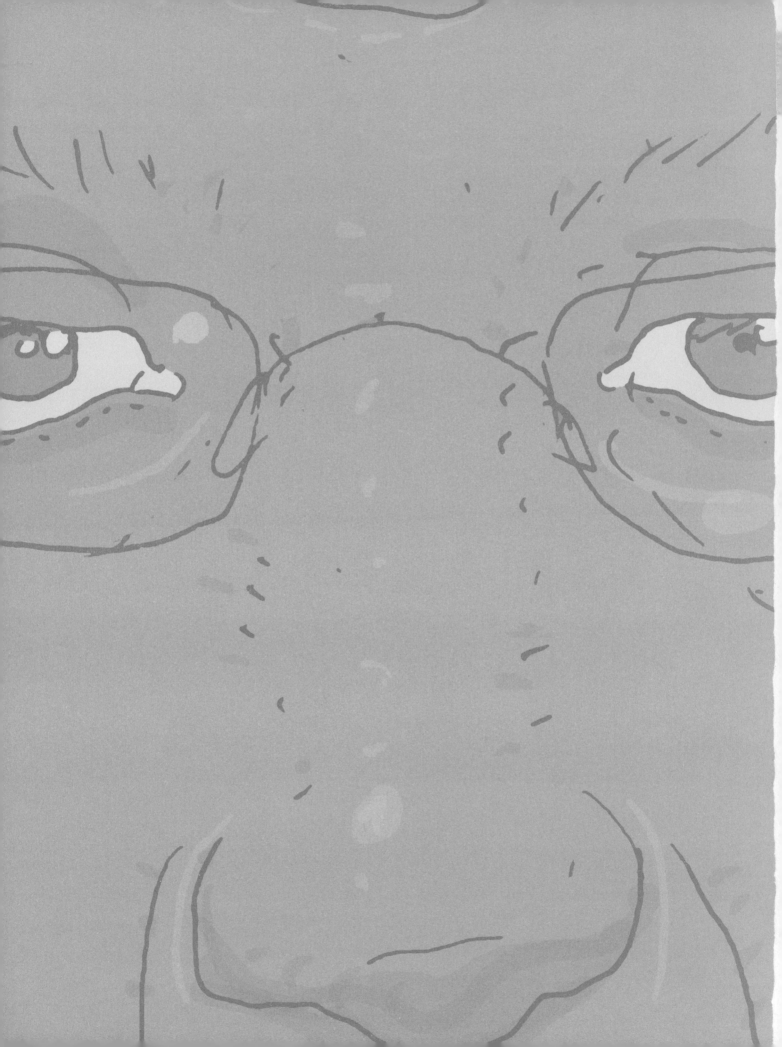

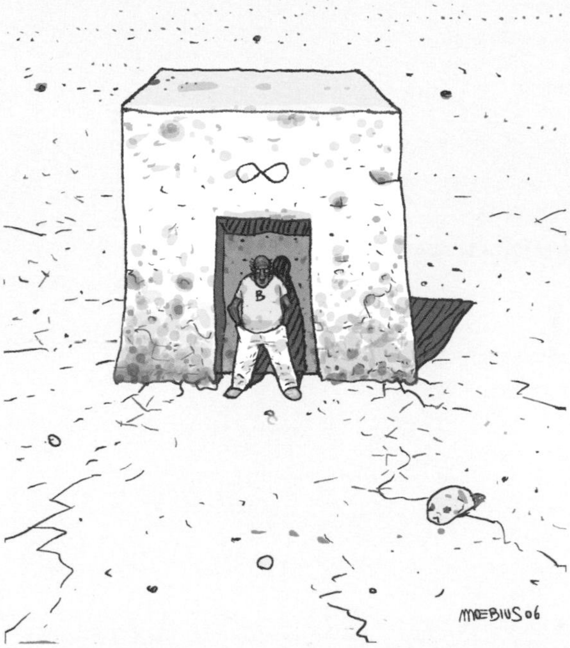
MŒBIUS 06

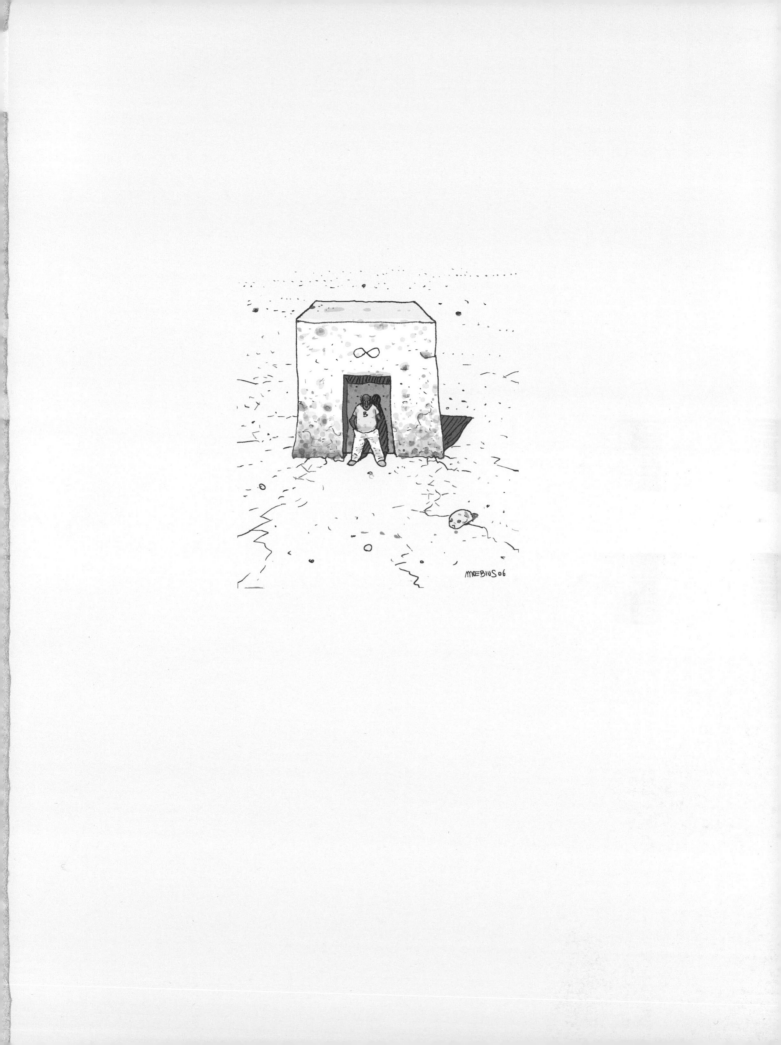

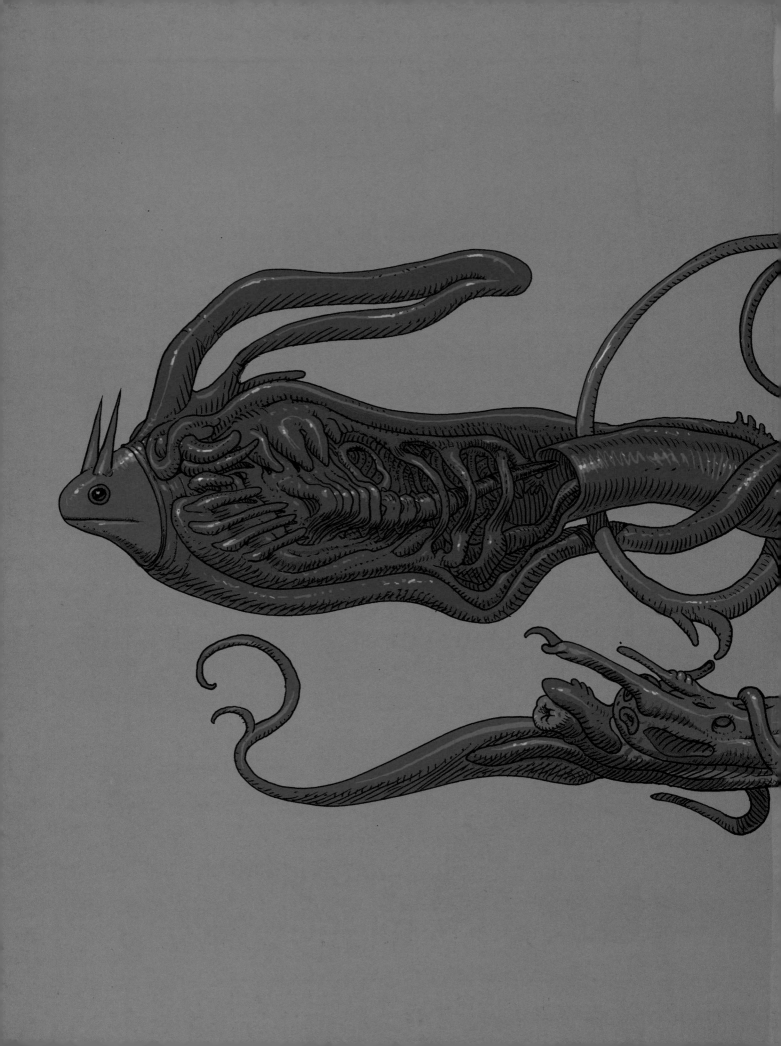

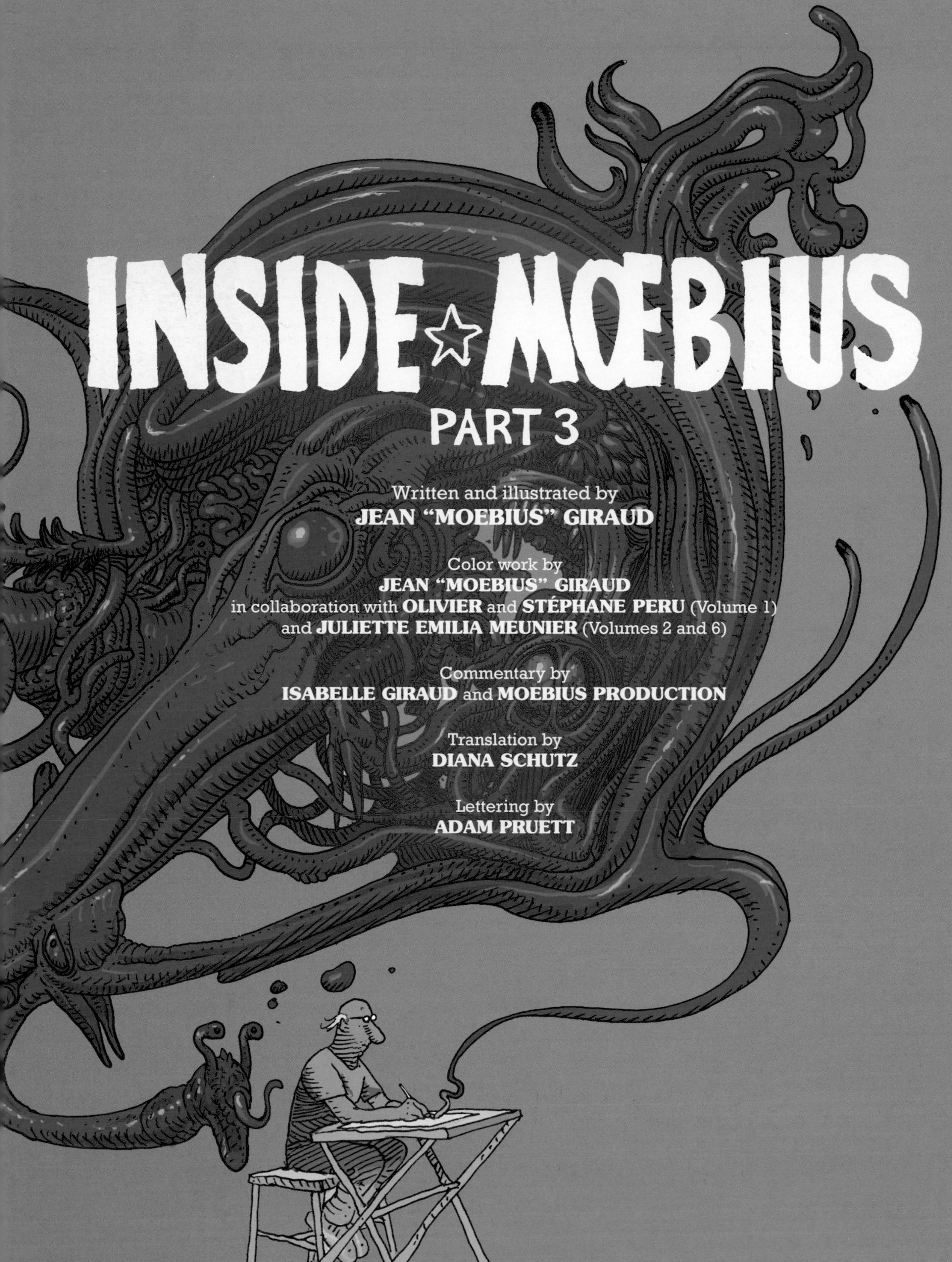

INSIDE MŒBIUS

PART 3

Written and illustrated by
JEAN "MOEBIUS" GIRAUD

Color work by
JEAN "MOEBIUS" GIRAUD
in collaboration with **OLIVIER** and **STÉPHANE PERU** (Volume 1)
and **JULIETTE EMILIA MEUNIER** (Volumes 2 and 6)

Commentary by
ISABELLE GIRAUD and **MOEBIUS PRODUCTION**

Translation by
DIANA SCHUTZ

Lettering by
ADAM PRUETT

DARK HORSE BOOKS

Publisher
MIKE RICHARDSON

Tout Inside Moebius Editor
ISABELLE GIRAUD

Dark Horse Edition Senior Editor
PHILIP R. SIMON

Dark Horse Edition Associate Editor
MEGAN WALKER

Tout Inside Moebius Designers
CLAIRE CHAMPEVAL and **NAUSICAÄ GIRAUD**

Dark Horse Edition Designers
JUSTIN COUCH with **RICK DeLUCCO** and **PATRICK SATTERFIELD**

Digital Art Technician
ADAM PRUETT

Dark Horse's *Inside Moebius* editions are based on the final French-language collection of this work, *Tout Inside Moebius*, published by Moebius Production.

MOEBIUS LIBRARY: INSIDE MOEBIUS PART 3

Published by
Dark Horse Books
A division of Dark Horse Comics, Inc.
10956 SE Main Street
Milwaukie, OR 97222

DarkHorse.com | Moebius.fr

To find a comics shop in your area,
visit the Comic Shop Locator Service at comicshoplocator.com

First edition: October 2018
ISBN: 978-1-50670-604-7

10 9 8 7 6 5 4 3 2 1

Printed in China

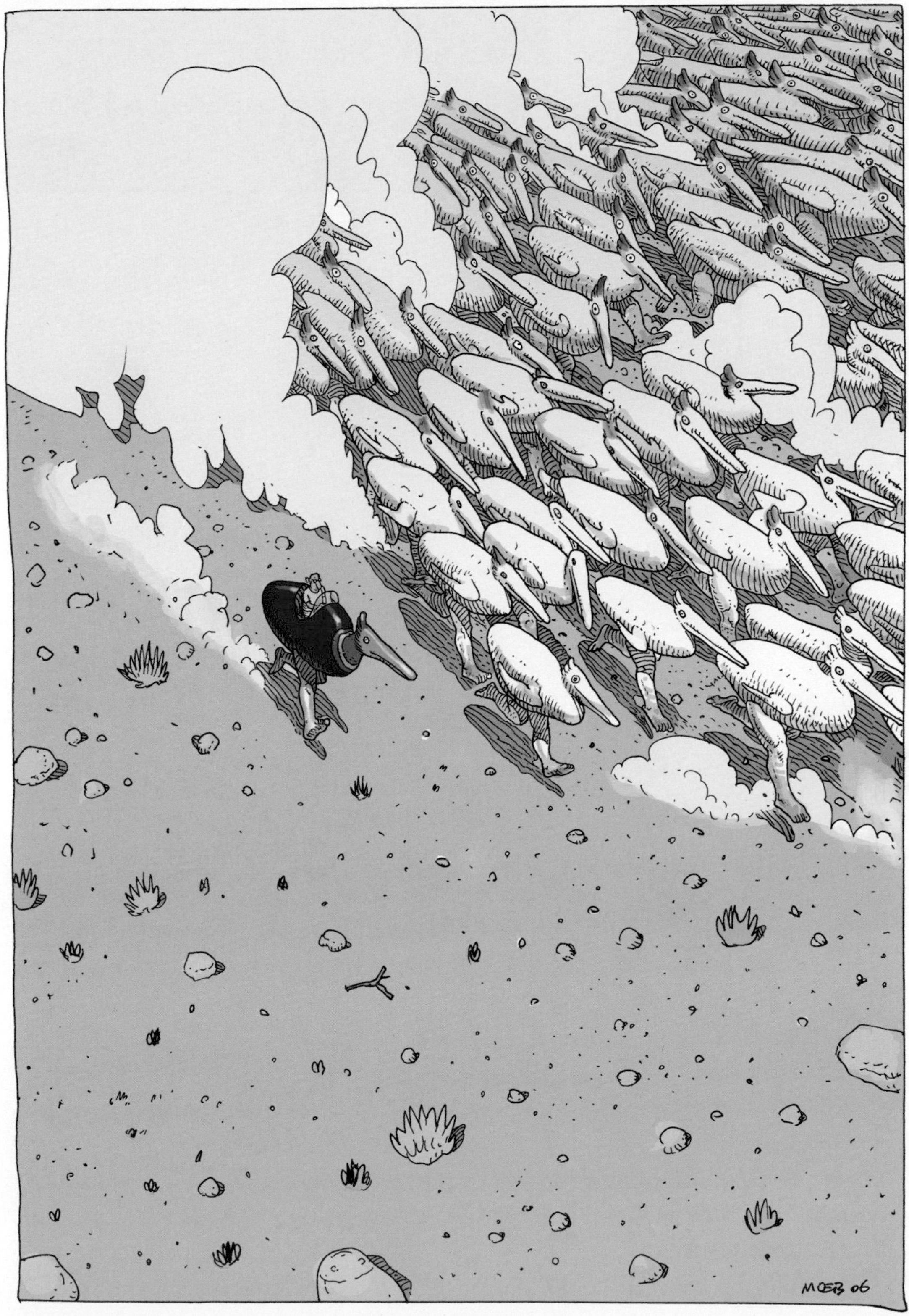
MŒB 06

FOREWORD

by Isabelle Giraud

From the Earth to the Sky, From the Sky to the Earth

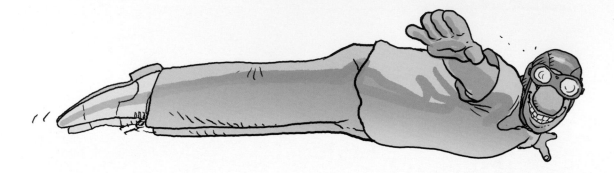

The six volumes of *Inside Moebius* were born between the years 2000 and 2009, unexpectedly emerging from the universe designed for *40 jours dans le désert B* (*40 Days in Desert B*), a book published in 2000 by Stardom.

Through the magic of art, Moebius's resolve to stop smoking weed—and thus to "weed himself out"—provided the landscape for this Desert B, at the heart of which he established a setting for psychic expression.

In *Inside Moebius*, the vast empty space of the blank page is under the total control of the author, who alone has the power to pervade it and the daring, even, to introduce himself within. Down below, at the level of the page, life takes shape exclusively under his will. Up above, at the level of the reader, Moebius well knows he must trust in this angel on high whose perceptivity will be sorely tested.

Fellow readers! Moebius has put you in a choice position. Don't hesitate to read and re-read every single panel, to flip back a few pages, to peruse the previous volumes in order to better find and understand the keys to interpreting the story.

Don't be afraid of losing yourself in the Moebius labyrinth: it's the price you pay for the gentle thrill growing between you and the master of the realm, Jean Giraud himself! *He* certainly doesn't hesitate to go the extra mile in this work—the extra *ten* miles—just to please you. He's put all his heart into: unveiling his secrets for you; introducing you to his creative dramas and joys; and ushering you through the door of his "Big Bulletproof Airtight Ego-Bunker!"

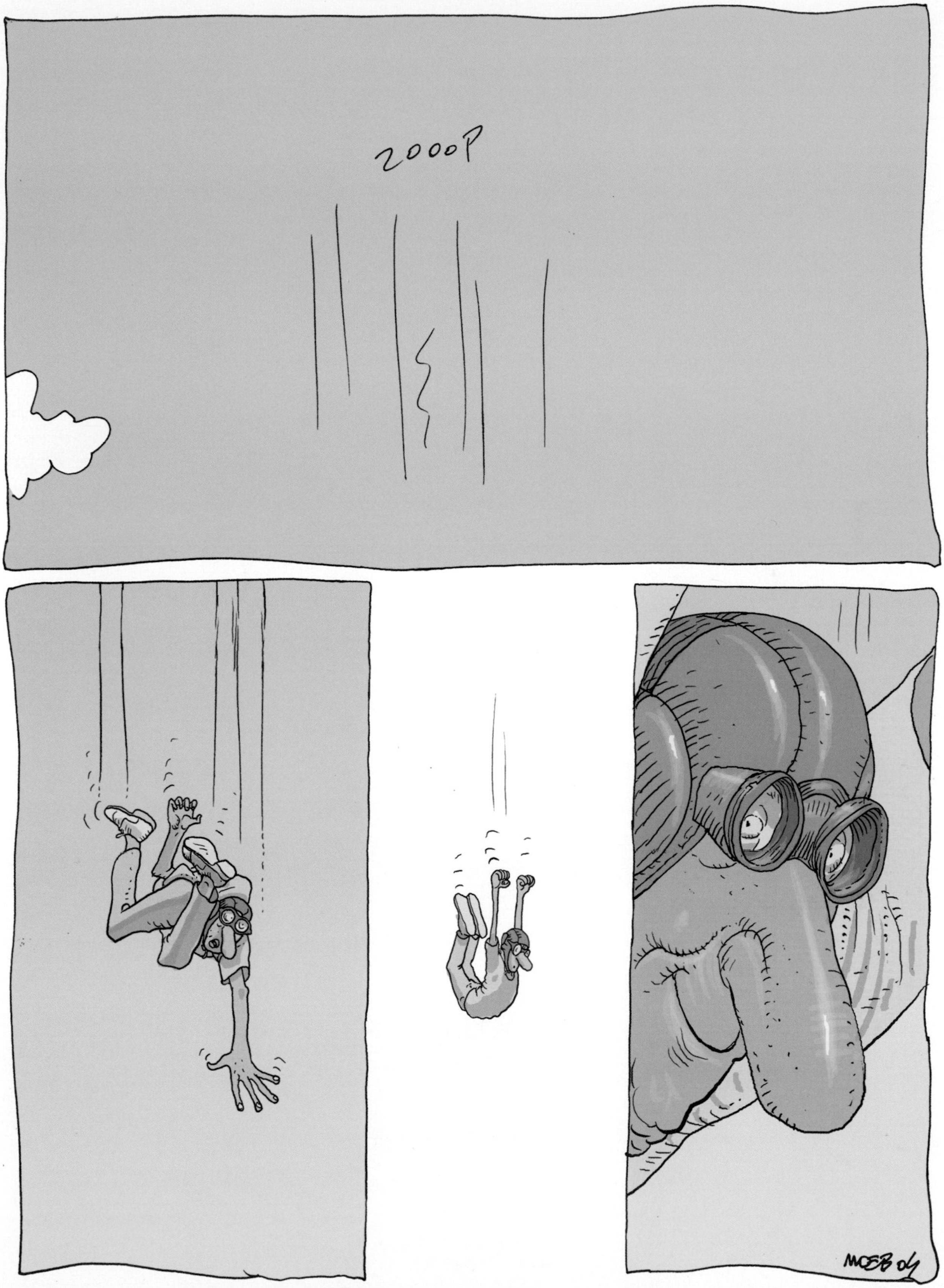
ZOOOP
MOEB 04

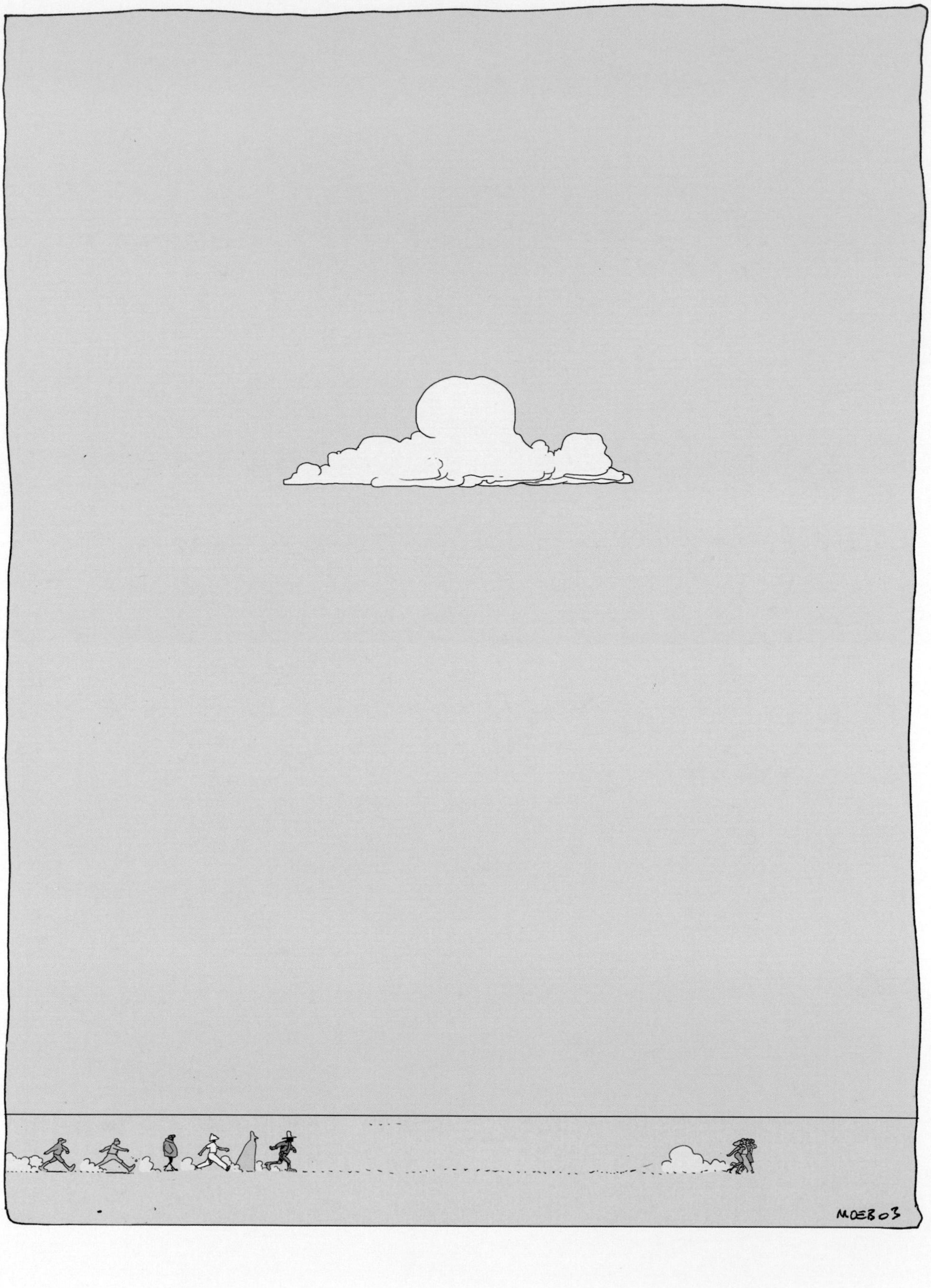
MOEB 03

Possible Vanishing Point

For its artist, *Inside Moebius* is "a discipline and a technique; it's the result of an entire study extending over years." Its primary graphic methodology is improvisation, of both line and story structure. A rigidity of form isn't necessary. The form emerges bit by bit, gaining its rhythm from the artist's own daily life. It's also a study of point of view and of the effects of perspective generally: "Simply displacing the object of perception is enough to immerse oneself in another state of consciousness." In the vast emptiness of Desert B, everything is possible. It's the ideal space for recording the never-ending to-and-fro between the exterior and interior of the self. For such a multifaceted artist, however, the question of self offers infinite answers. But never mind! It's sufficient to focus on the essential and to surround oneself with beloved characters such as Blueberry, Arzak, the Major, Malvina, Stel, and Atan.

Originally created as a journal in which the author might accurately transcribe his overall impressions of his decision to stop smoking, *Inside Moebius* quickly became "His Autobiographical Œuvre." Jean chooses to use himself as a character—the leading actor—in this adventure. He presents himself as the subject of a story in which he summons his acclaimed creations to the heart of Desert B. As a result, two parallel forces underlie the action, as the author/creator finds himself caught up not only in his "living" reality, but also with his paper creations (and, above all, with Jean Giraud himself).

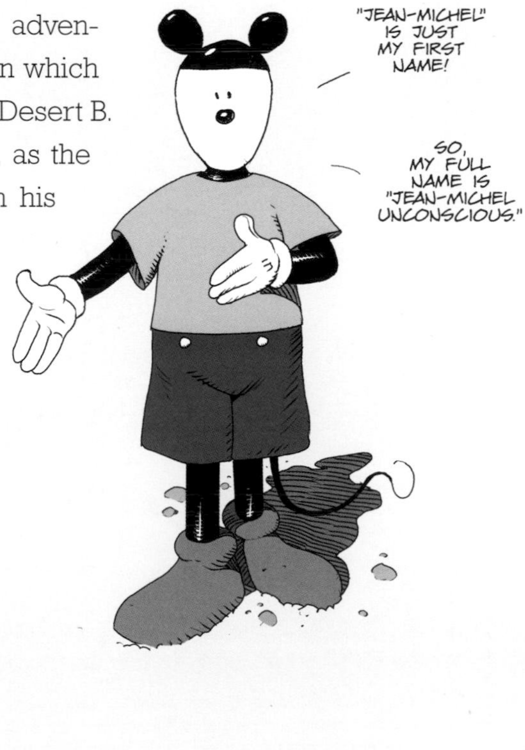
ACTUALLY, MY NAME IS "UNCONSCIOUS."
I am everywhere and nowhere!
"JEAN-MICHEL" IS JUST MY FIRST NAME!
SO, MY FULL NAME IS "JEAN-MICHEL UNCONSCIOUS."

Getting High

In Desert B, it's very easy for the author to rid himself of spatiotemporal constraints: he can simply fly off, move through designated doors, or fall asleep and wake up in the thick of a dream to begin to find meaning in what's going on. When reality becomes too difficult to bear, it "drops into art," the transcription drawing a path to elucidation. In the second volume of *Inside Moebius Part 1*, Osama bin Laden becomes a character on the page, and he reproaches the Major—himself the quintessential product of Western society—for claiming to represent *all* of humanity and for attempting to impact history by way of this myth—to which the Major responds that the collapse of the Twin Towers will fade from collective memory and the fate of the planet will transcend Earth's destiny. The Major's knowledge of an upcoming cosmocivilization helps to put things in perspective for us: fragile humans still bound to earthly events.

Almost every one of the six volumes of *Inside Moebius* either begins or ends with flight. For the author, flying symbolizes the ever-present desire to escape by way of drawing and its deliberations; to throw off gravity's shackles; to rise; to sail over the cares of earthly life. Flying allows him to access other perceptions of reality, to 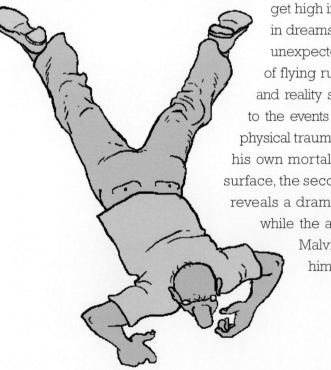 get high indeed, and to search for an answer in dreams. But as with Icarus, sometimes the unexpected precipitates his fall. His dream of flying runs up against physical constraints, and reality supersedes. In this case, in addition to the events of 9/11, Jean also suffered a major physical trauma in 2001, giving him a glimpse of his own mortality. And so, beneath its humorous surface, the second volume of *Inside Moebius* also reveals a dramatic dimension. At the story's end, while the author would prefer to keep flying, Malvina catches up with him and begs him to return home to his bunker.

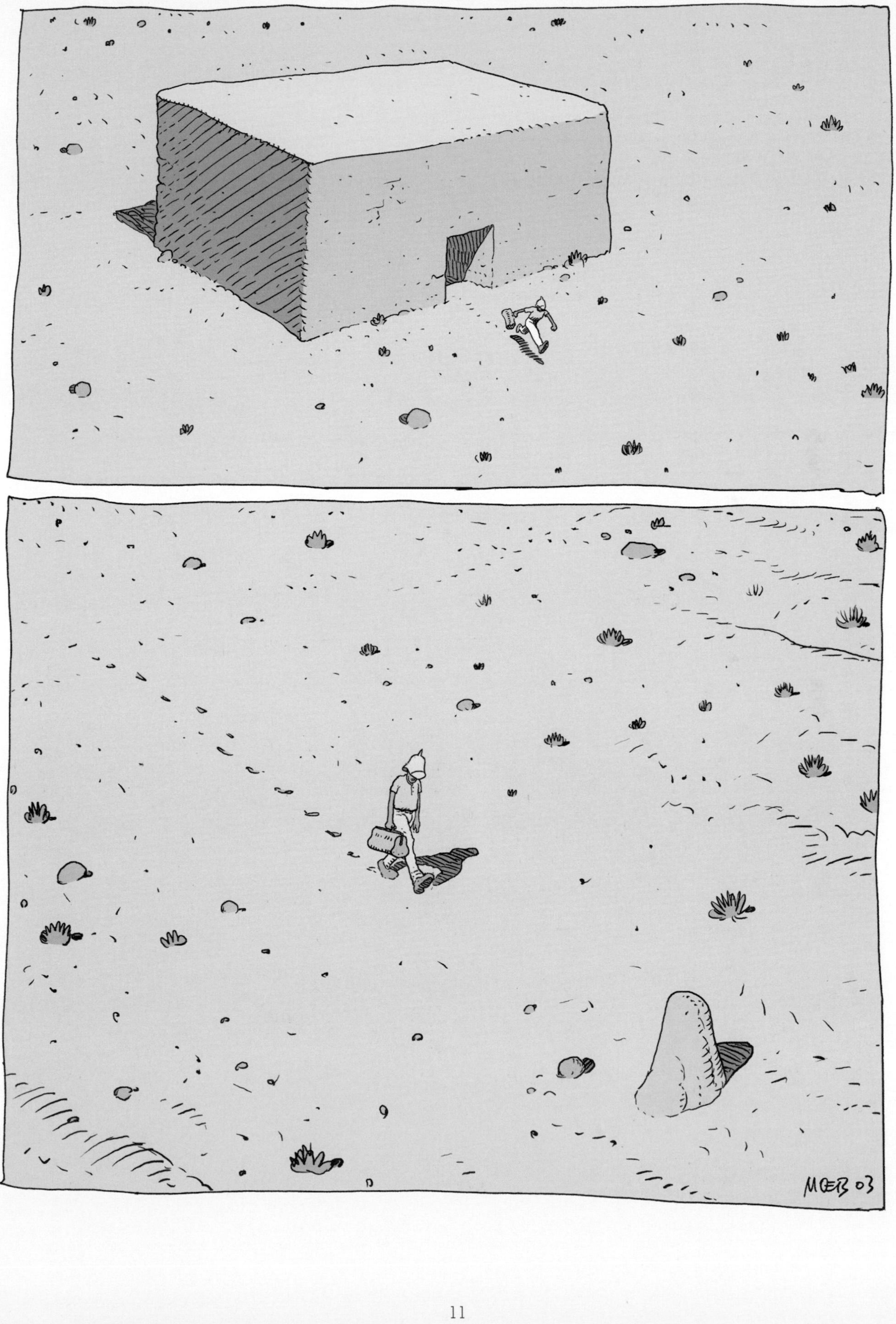
MŒB 03

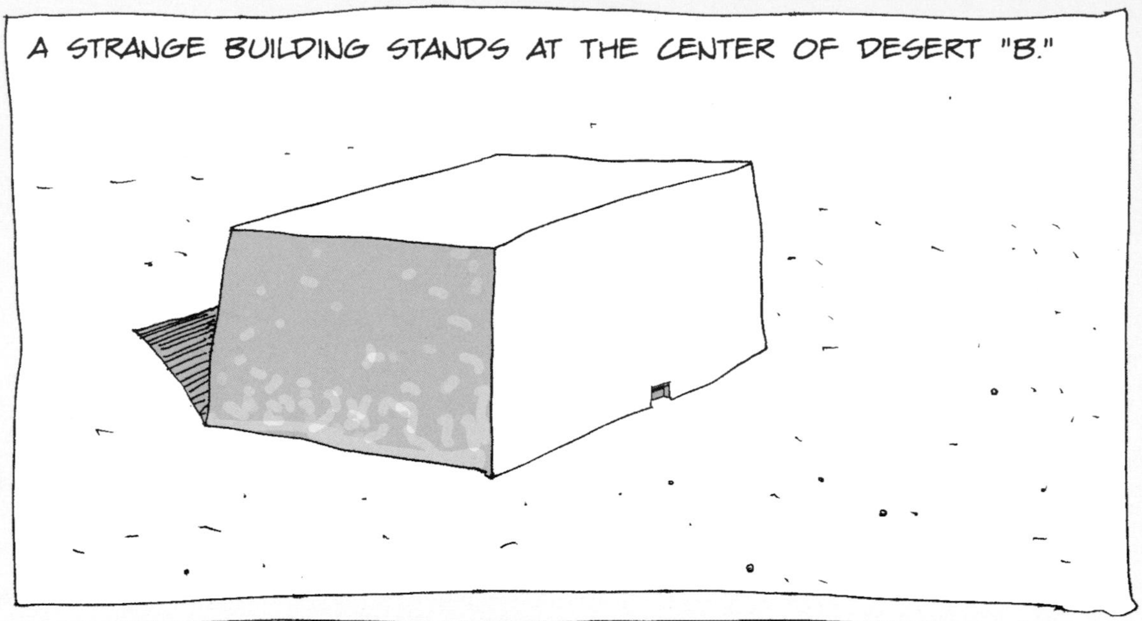
A STRANGE BUILDING STANDS AT THE CENTER OF DESERT "B."

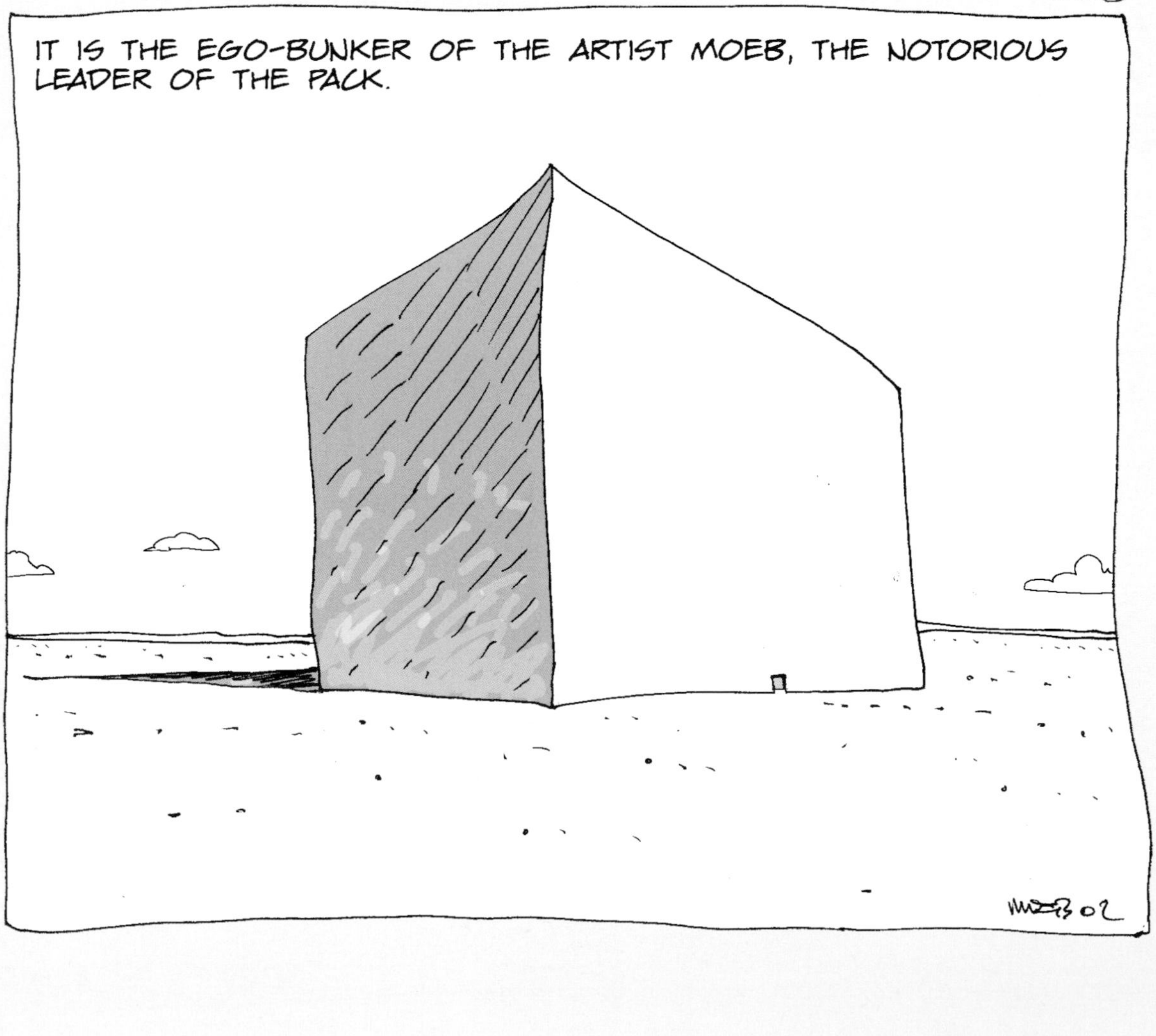
IT IS THE EGO-BUNKER OF THE ARTIST MOEB, THE NOTORIOUS LEADER OF THE PACK.

Ego-Bunker

"It all started back in that icy room of my grandparents . . ."

The Desert B bunker, that monolithic monument appearing in each of the six volumes of *Inside Moebius*, constitutes the absolute refuge: everything is decided here, in this shelter to which Moebius withdraws to make contact with another dimension. His characters also gain entry at times, either at his invitation or because they're desperate for a script. Vexed at being abandoned during the author's retreats, his characters vainly attempt pursuit to prevent him from thinking only of himself. And so they decide to track down and invade the bunker.

This sacred place, subject to all manner of transmutation, allows Moebius to change footing, to wander its infinite corridors, to go through designated doorways, to find a way out. Its interior sometimes resembles a labyrinth, other times a series of nested drawers, corridors, and doors granting passage from one dimension to another, albeit at the risk of losing oneself. The Ego-Bunker may well correspond to the ancient *tumuli*, domelike mounds constructed by Celtic tribes and flanked by a small door allowing human access to a second dimension—from our world to that of the Spirits, those beings who took on the appearance of the "Little People."

We can no doubt see a race of demigods in the figures of Arzak, Blueberry, the Major, Stel, and Atan, thanks to whom the author attains a certain spirituality of his own.

Surviving Oneself

The spatial dimension of *Inside Moebius* is augmented by the temporal. The urgent appeals of his fictional characters provide a soundtrack to the artist's life. Their number, their demands, and their jealousy of each other lead the author to abandon them, conferring instead with his own doubles—especially his 1970s counterpart—who have materialized out of the past. Finding himself face to face with an infinity of selves, the author is prevented from taking his own path . . . to the point of becoming a stranger among all these selves: the "successive" selves, "perpendicular" selves, "folded, multiplied, or divided" selves, the "parallel" selves, the "diagonal" selves . . .

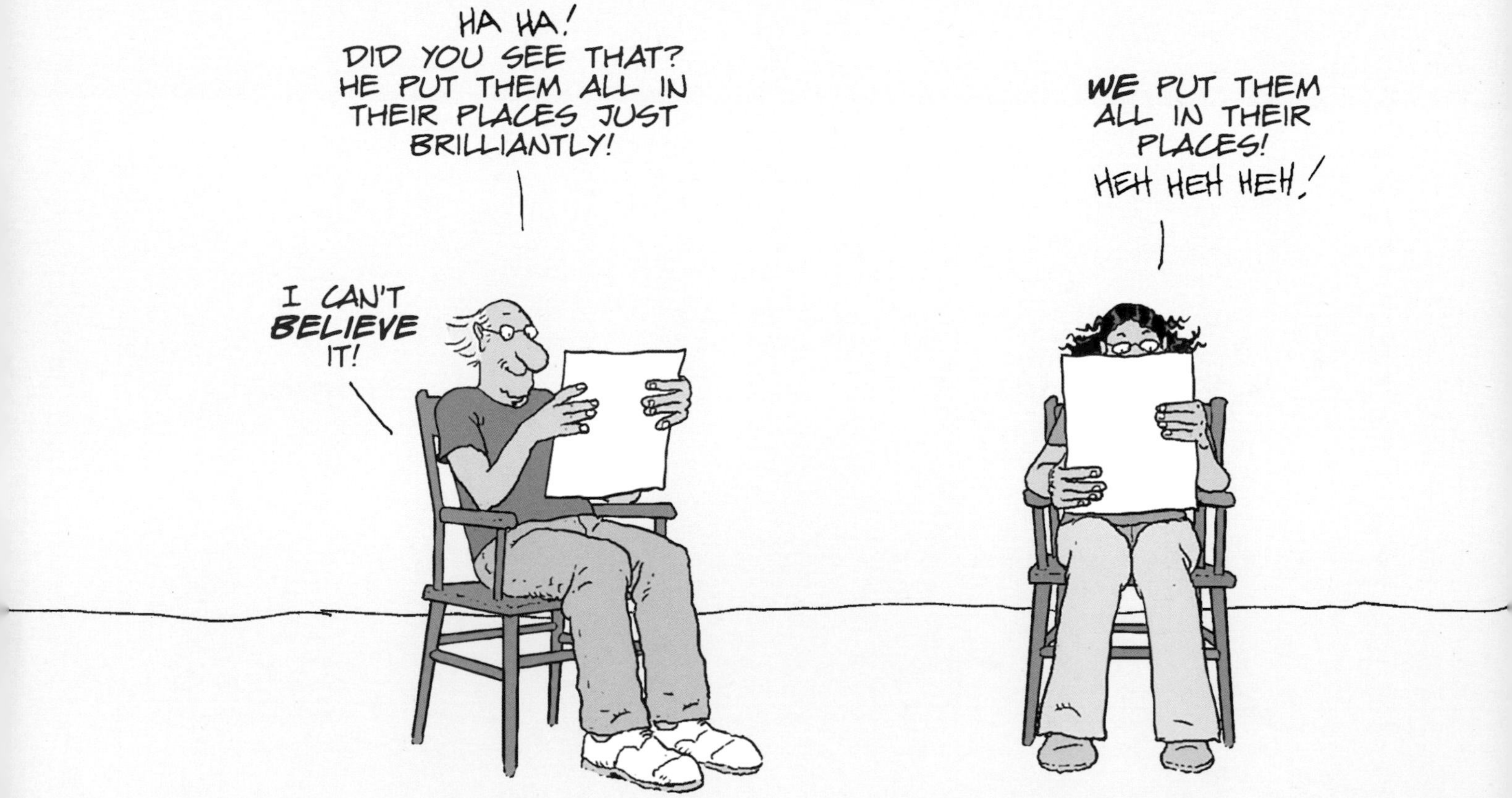
I CAN'T BELIEVE IT!
HA HA! DID YOU SEE THAT? HE PUT THEM ALL IN THEIR PLACES JUST BRILLIANTLY!
WE PUT THEM ALL IN THEIR PLACES! HEH HEH HEH!

What A Blast!

Moebius takes on existential questions about God, death, illness, and love—including self-love—and tries to find answers in dreaming. He insists, here, on the need to make time for oneself, to let oneself be absorbed—devoured even—by the unconscious in order to truly find oneself. Dreams and the unconscious are themes that recur throughout the author's entire body of work. His ultimate reference text remains *The Art of Dreaming* by Carlos Castaneda. For Moebius, there is no turning back from the effectiveness of his spiritual mentor's method of freeing oneself from all obsessions: and that is, simply, to sleep beside oneself . . .

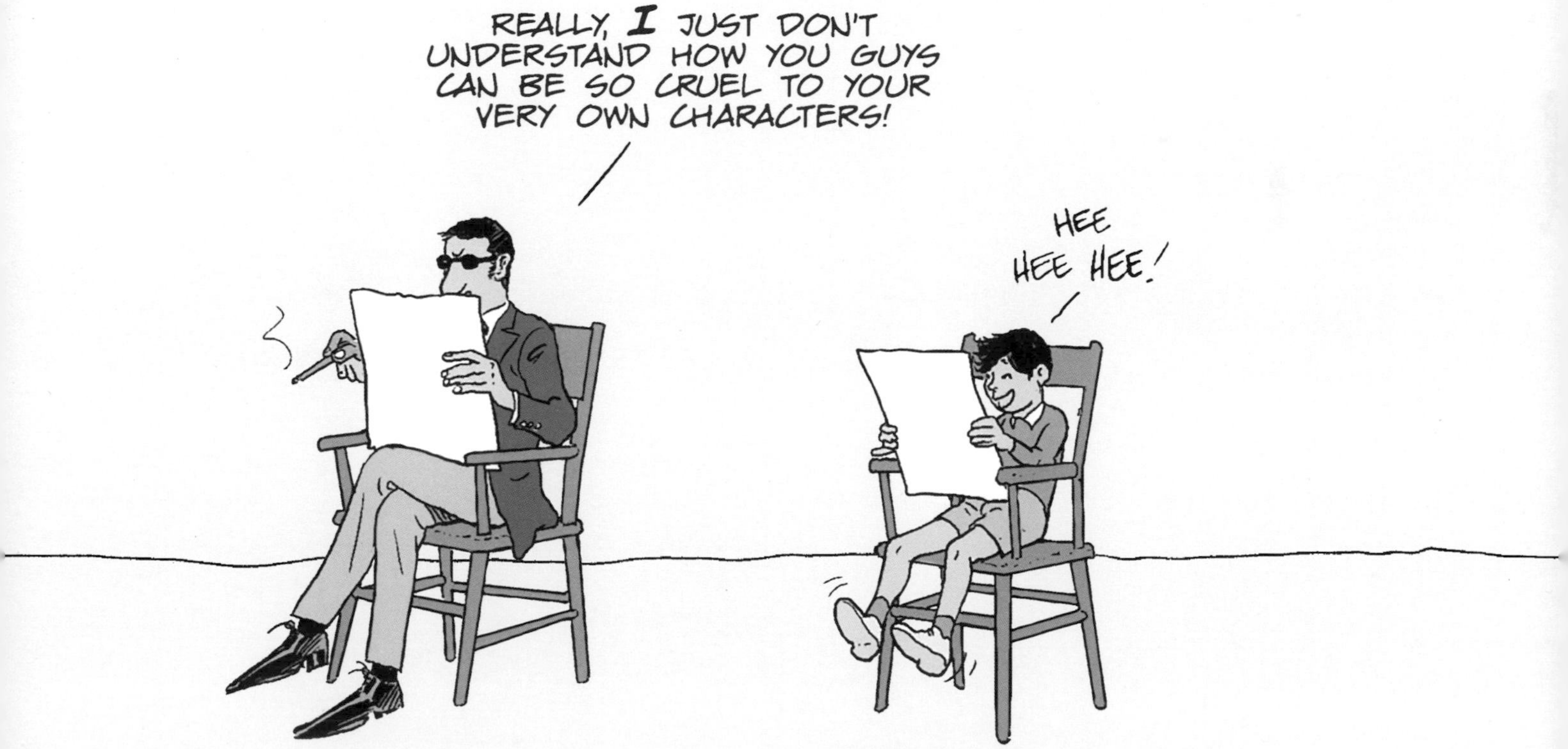
REALLY, I JUST DON'T UNDERSTAND HOW YOU GUYS CAN BE SO CRUEL TO YOUR VERY OWN CHARACTERS!
HEE HEE HEE!

A LITTLE TALK WITH ISABELLE IN 2007 . . .

This scene takes place in a small restaurant in the southern suburb of Armjourth.

Jean: Isabelle!

Isabelle: Yes, my love?

Jean: I'm asking myself all sorts of questions about the new collection of *Inside Moebius* . . .

Isabelle: Questions? What kind of questions?

Jean: This kind, for example: What sort of reception will the book have?

The young woman smiles imperceptibly.

Isabelle: You know perfectly well that no one can answer that question.

With the tip of her knife, she plays with a small, delicately textured bone of stramod that she's pushed to the side of her plate.

Isabelle: Nonetheless, I think this third one has every single quality your public expects.

Jean: My public?

The man facing her hangs his head sadly, an empty pout drawn at his lips. Behind the slender frame of his glasses, his gaze seems lost in the distance . . . Indeed . . . That was precisely the question . . .

Isabelle: Heyyy! Why the disillusion in your voice? I guarantee it's true . . . This is exactly the kind of book that will appeal to real Moebius fans.

Jean: I . . . I just don't know. I wrote and drew this story without any thought for the reader, you know. I just followed the whimsical labyrinth of my own inspiration, as free as the wind, without any plan or constraint—completely irresponsible.

Isabelle: But isn't that exactly what you did with the first two volumes?

Jean: *Uh*, in fact, yes. But—

Isabelle: Listen! It's your very *lack* of a plan—this visible deconstruction of the narrative—that gives the series so much charm!

Jean: But then, the impact of this deconstruction, that's never happened to me before! Isabelle, I appreciate your efforts to cheer me up, but—

Isabelle: Wait! I think this third book will even interest new types of readers, so long as their minds are open to humor and literary divagation.

Jean: In terms of divagation, it's true that I—

Isabelle: On the other hand, I notice that you've been especially careful with your drawing this time. It's still very simple, but you reach a level of quality in places that's comparable to *The [Airtight] Garage*!

Jean: . . . ?

Isabelle: So? Other questions?

Jean: Isabelle!

Isabelle: Yes!

Jean: Let's wrap up the questions, settle our bill, and take a romantic stroll along the Star Canal . . . It's nice out, and life is beautiful!

The couple leaves the restaurant, walking away down the seawall, hand in hand.

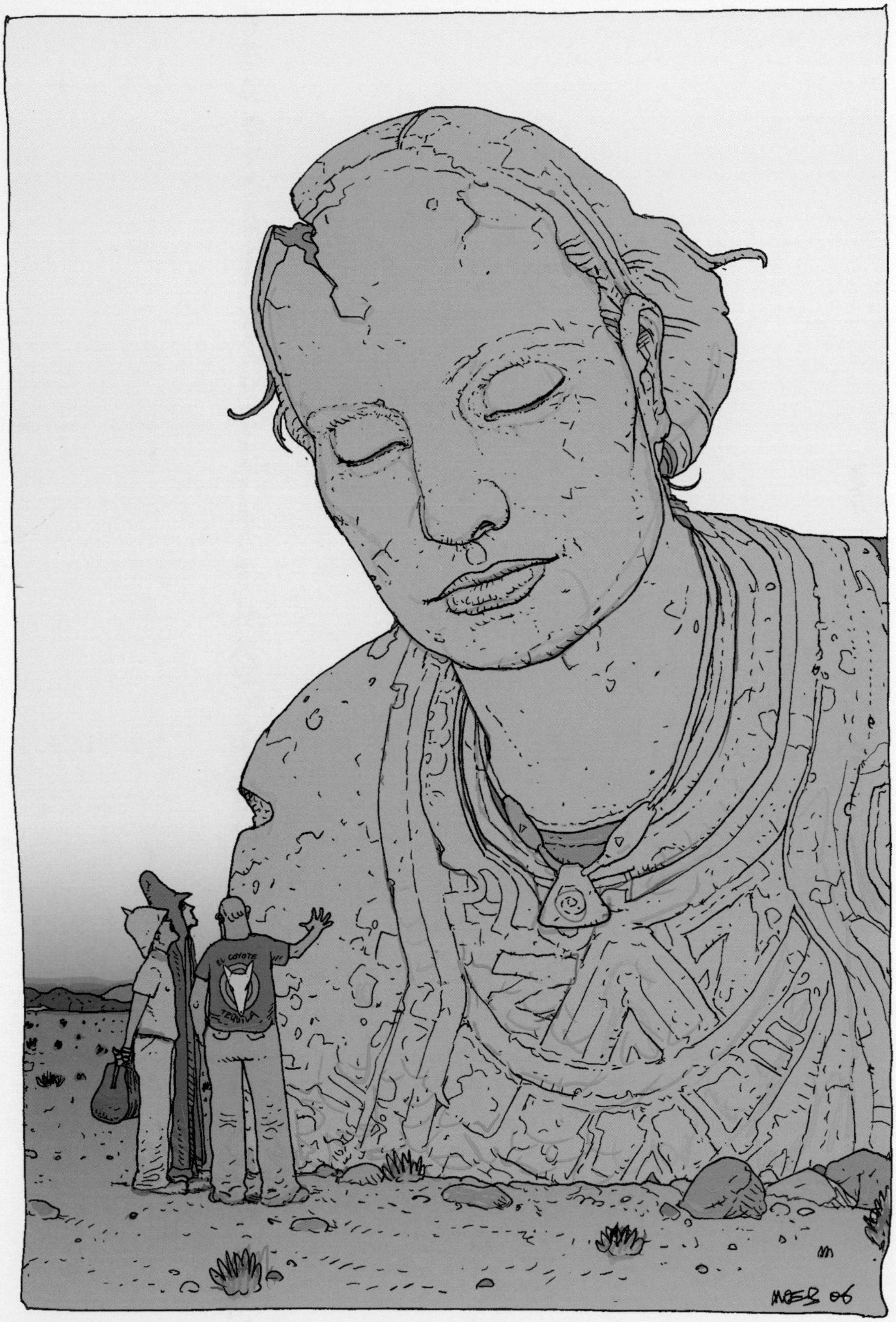
EL COYOTE
TEQUILA

INSIDE (V)

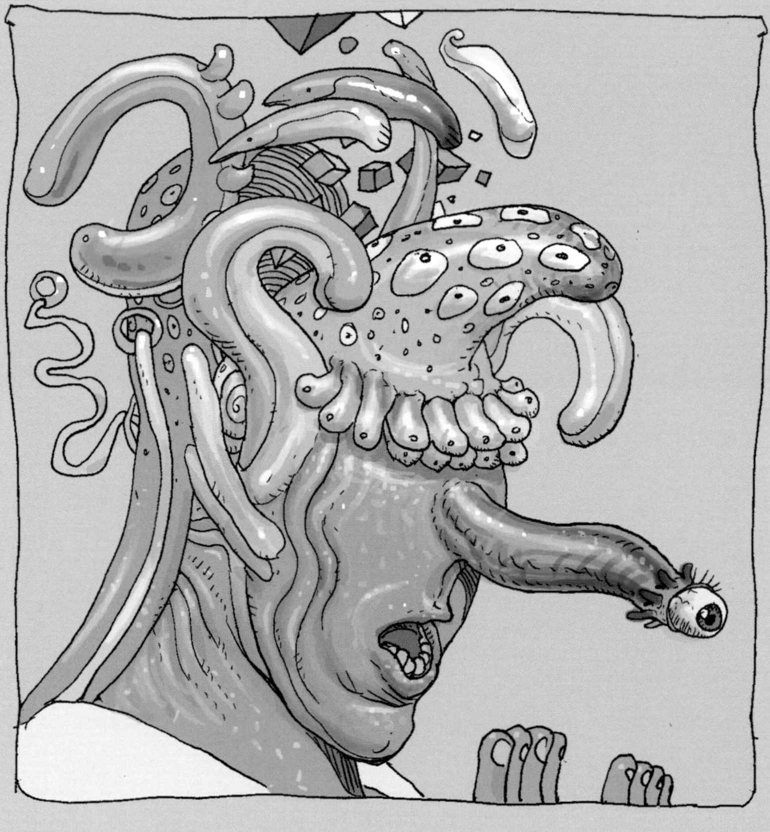

MOEBIUS
2004

INSIDE MOEBIUS

VOLUME 5

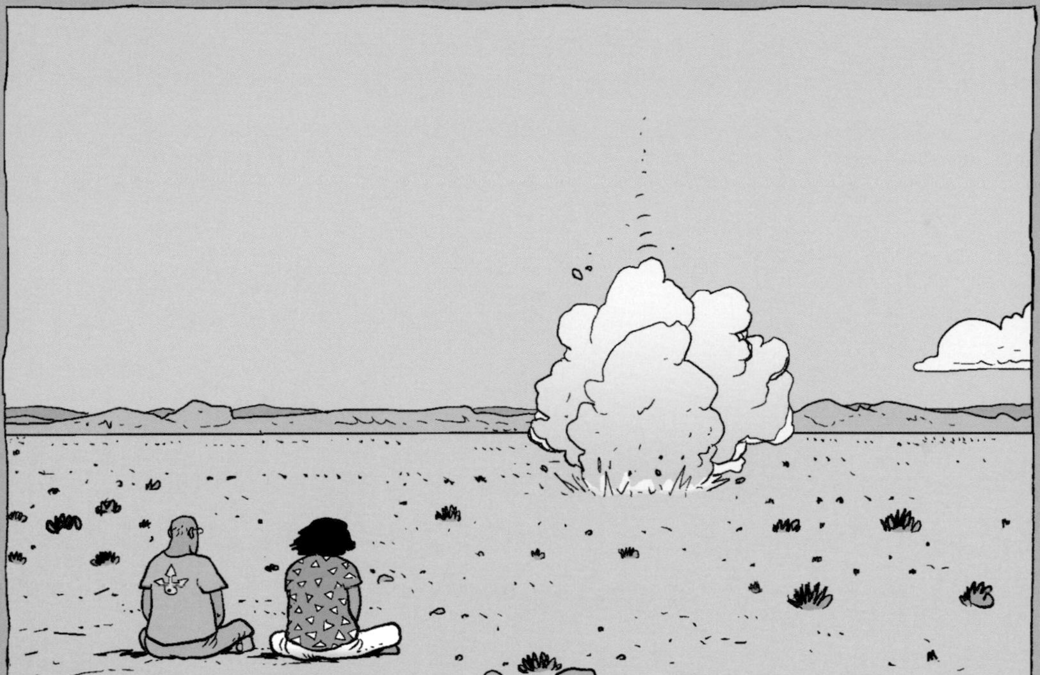
MOEBIUS

I absolutely must wake up
at the very heart of this dream!
Just like it says in the book!

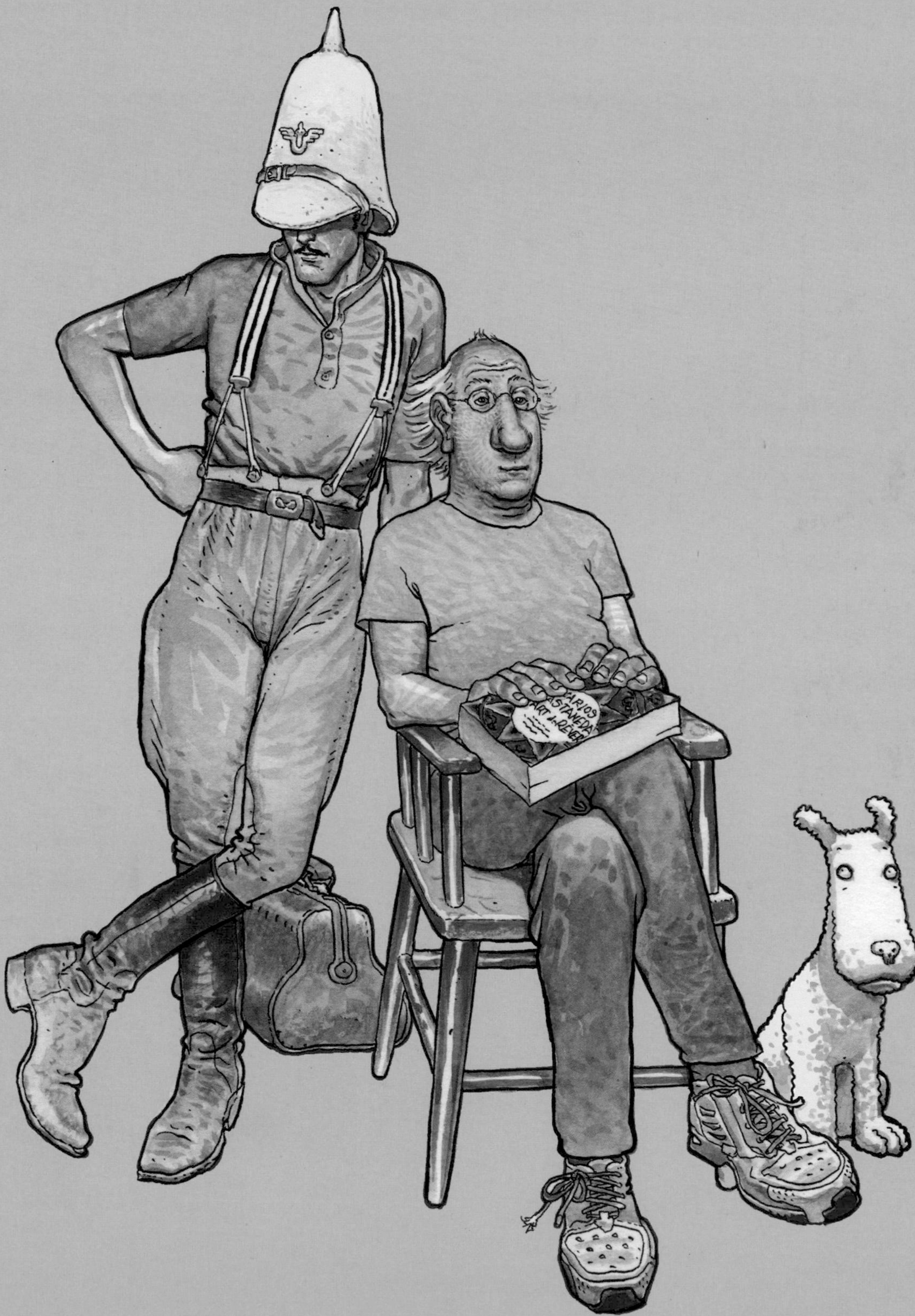
ARIOS
ASTANEDA
ART À RÊVER

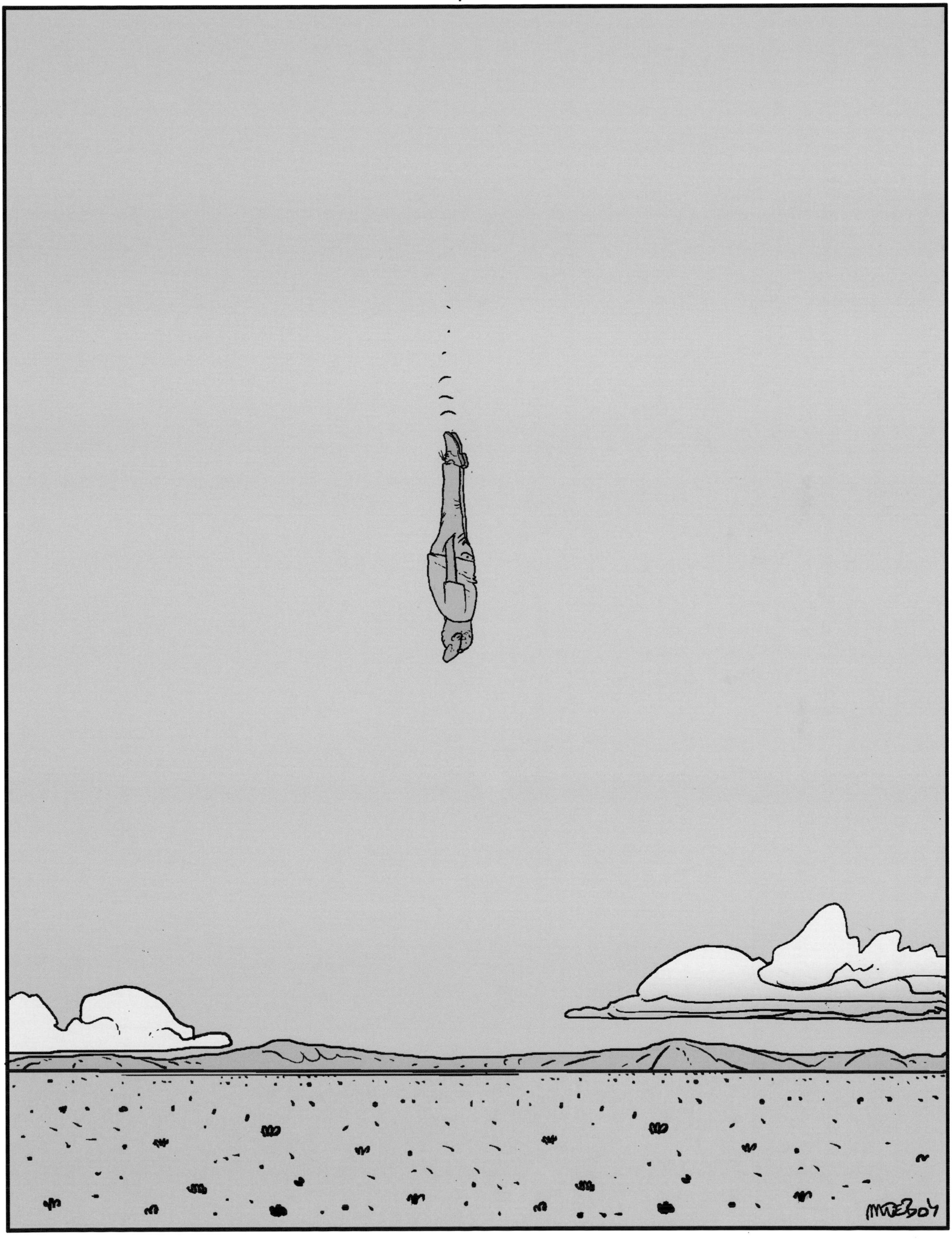

2

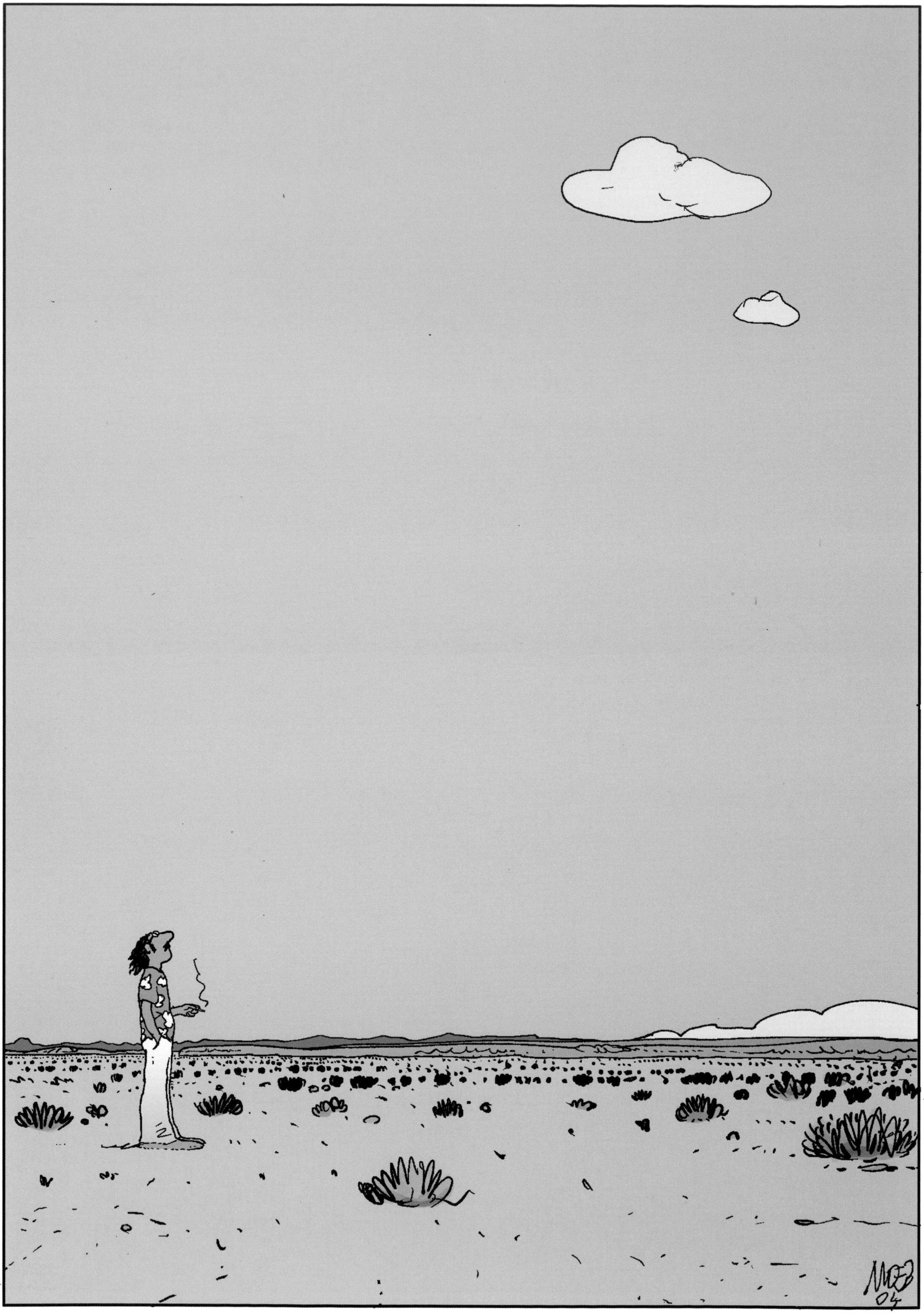

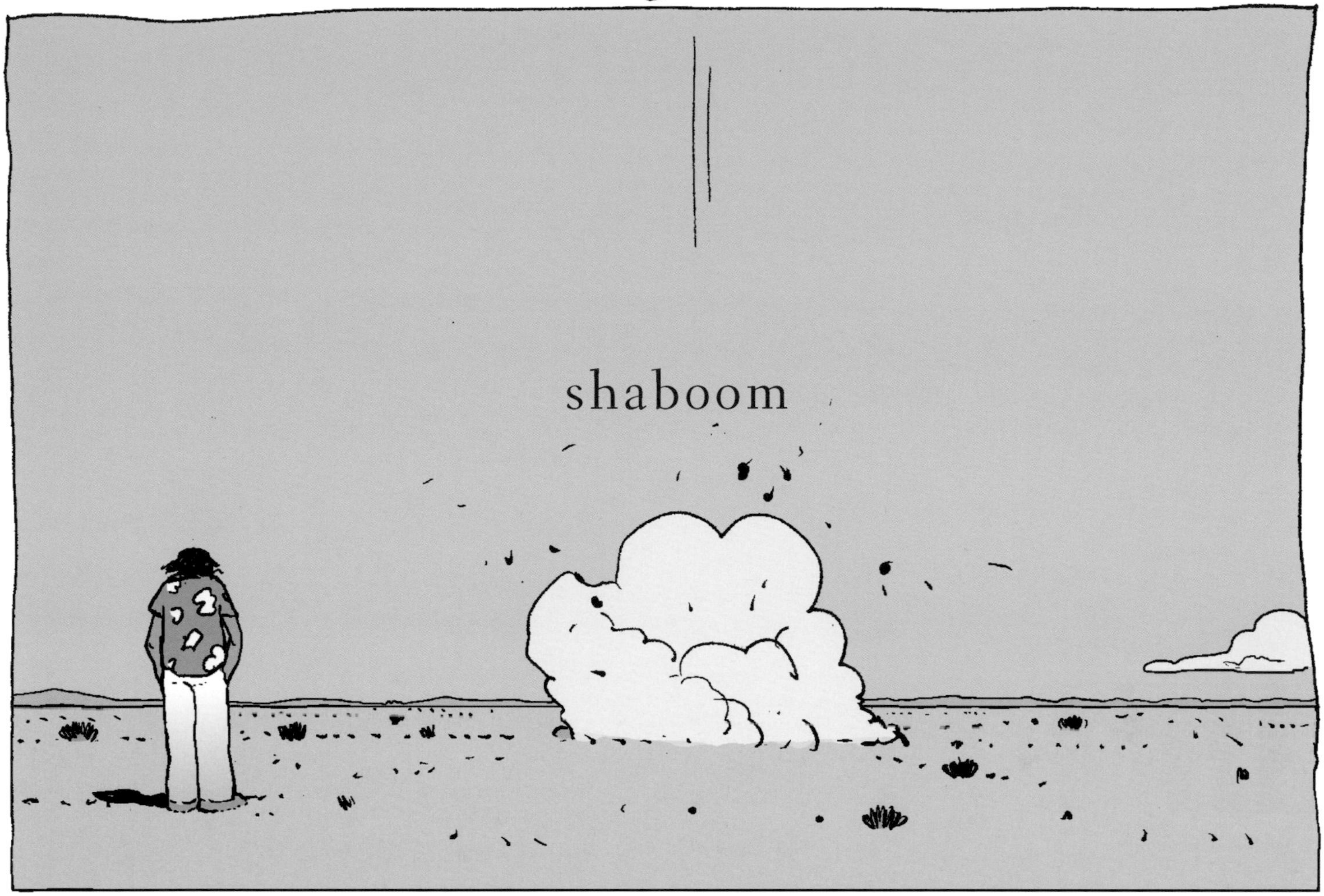
shaboom

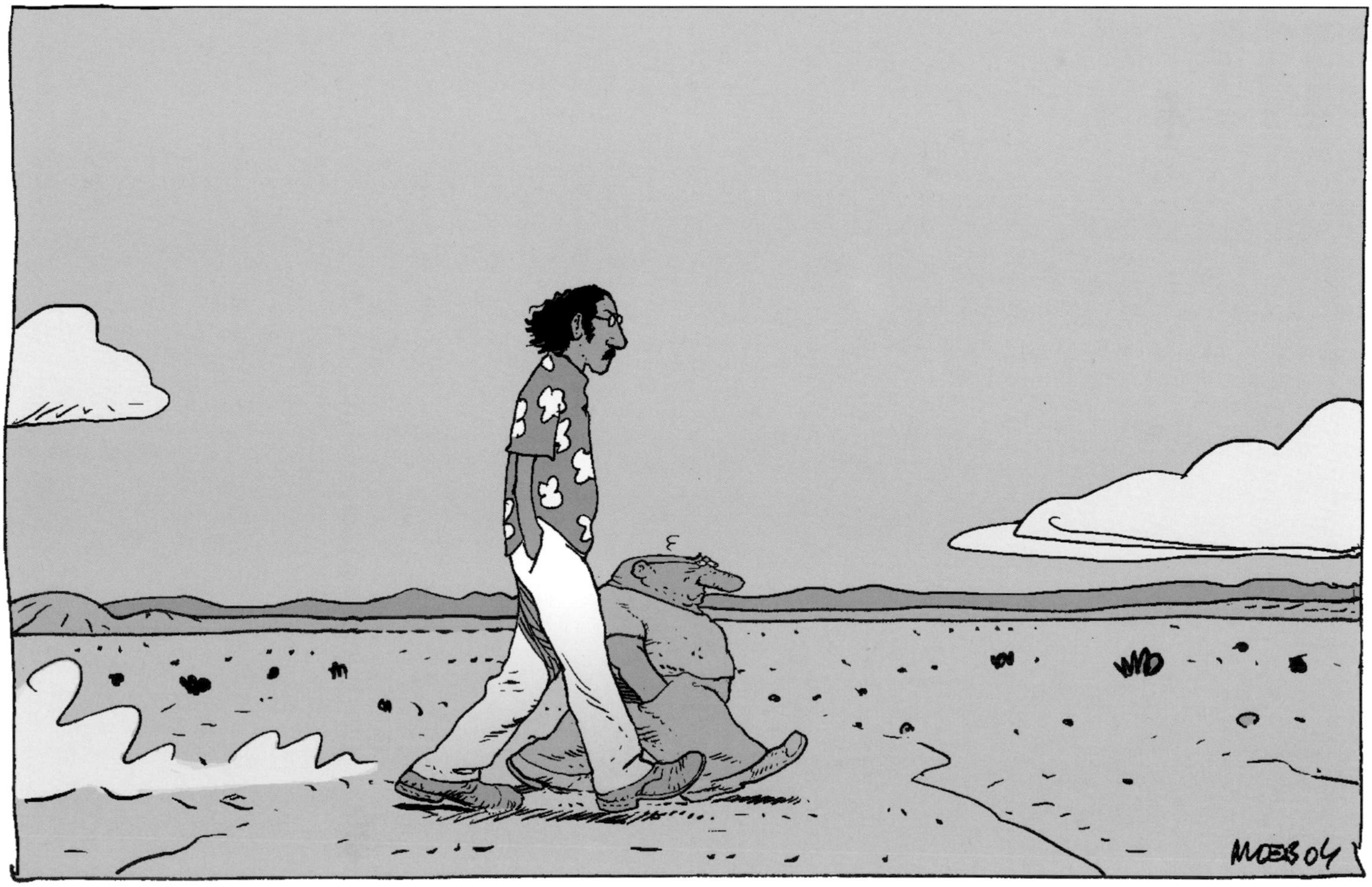

. . . I intend to take some action!

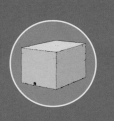

THE PATHETIC ADVENTURES OF MOEB IN DESERT "B"

BY : MOEBIUS

(INSIDE HIMSELF)

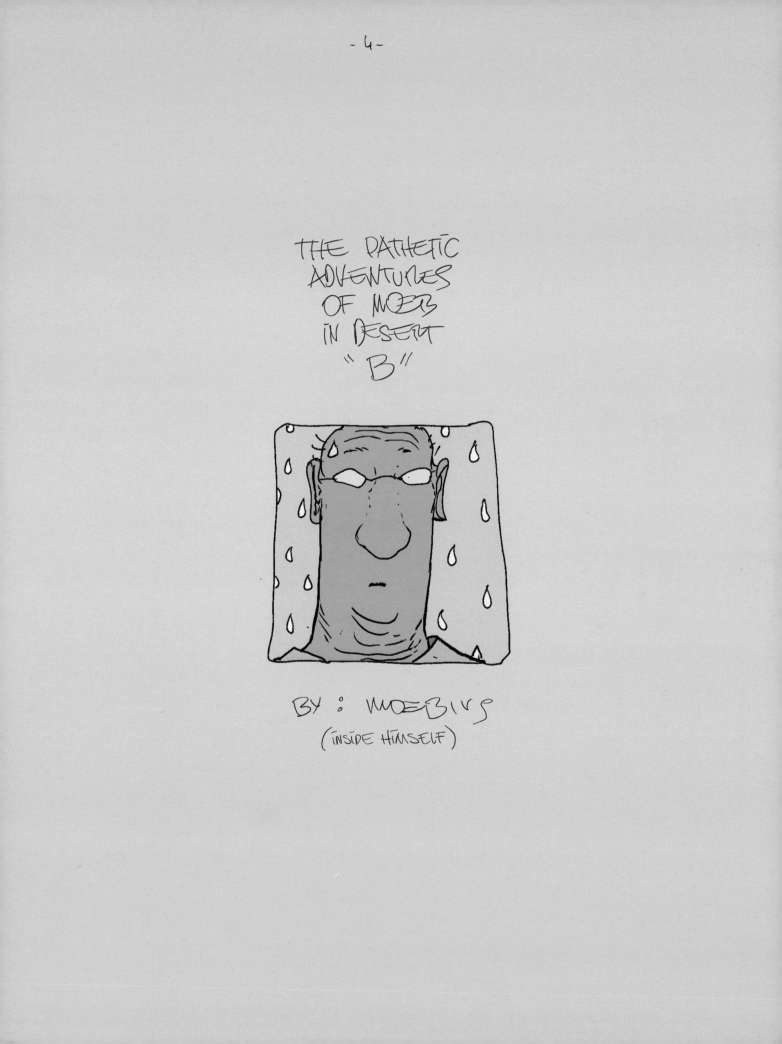

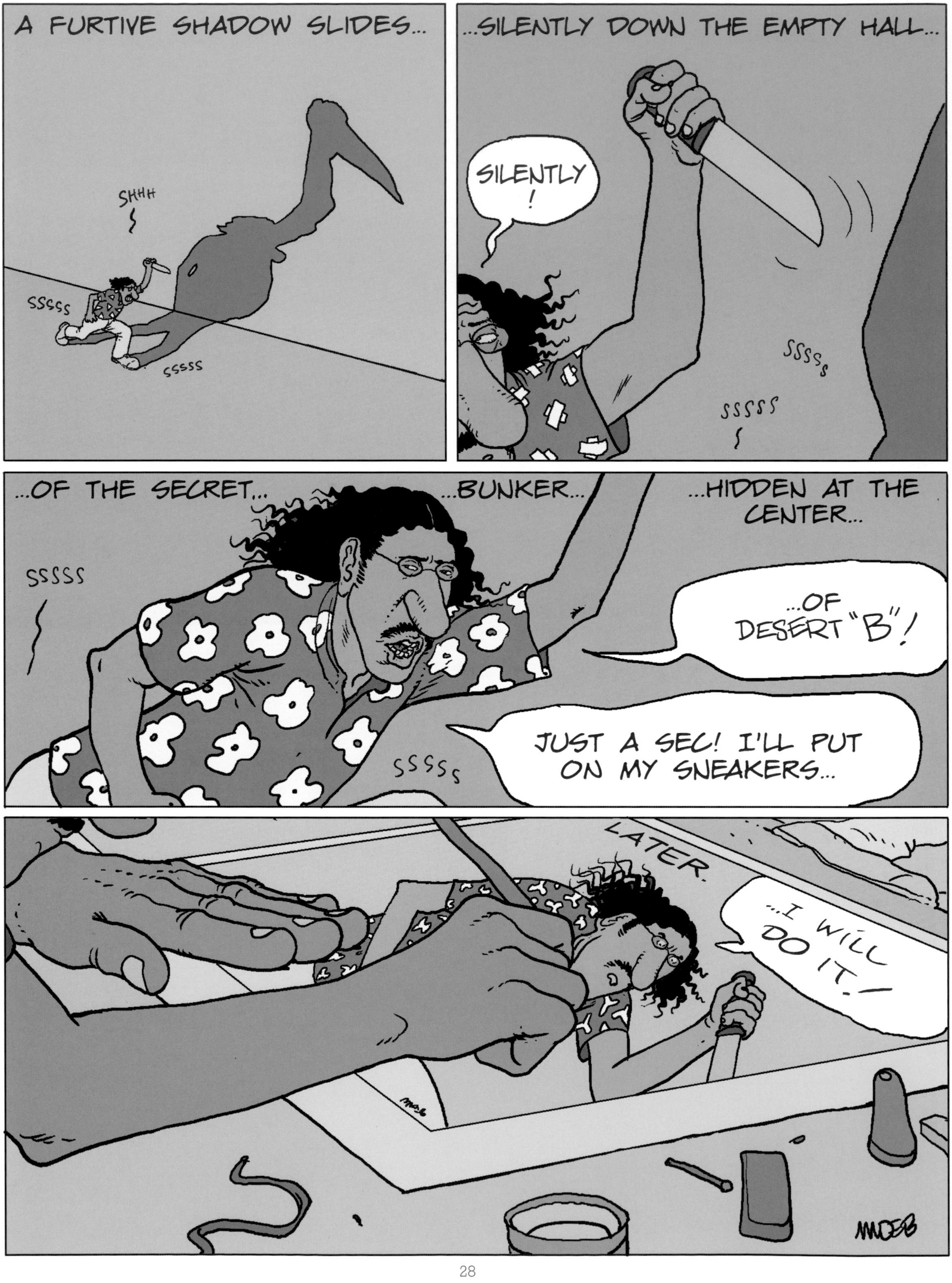
A FURTIVE SHADOW SLIDES...
SHHH
SSSSS
SSSSS
...SILENTLY DOWN THE EMPTY HALL...
SILENTLY!
SSSSS
SSSSS
...OF THE SECRET...
...BUNKER...
...HIDDEN AT THE CENTER...
SSSSS
...OF DESERT "B"!
JUST A SEC! I'LL PUT ON MY SNEAKERS...
SSSSS
LATER.
...I WILL DO IT!
MOEB

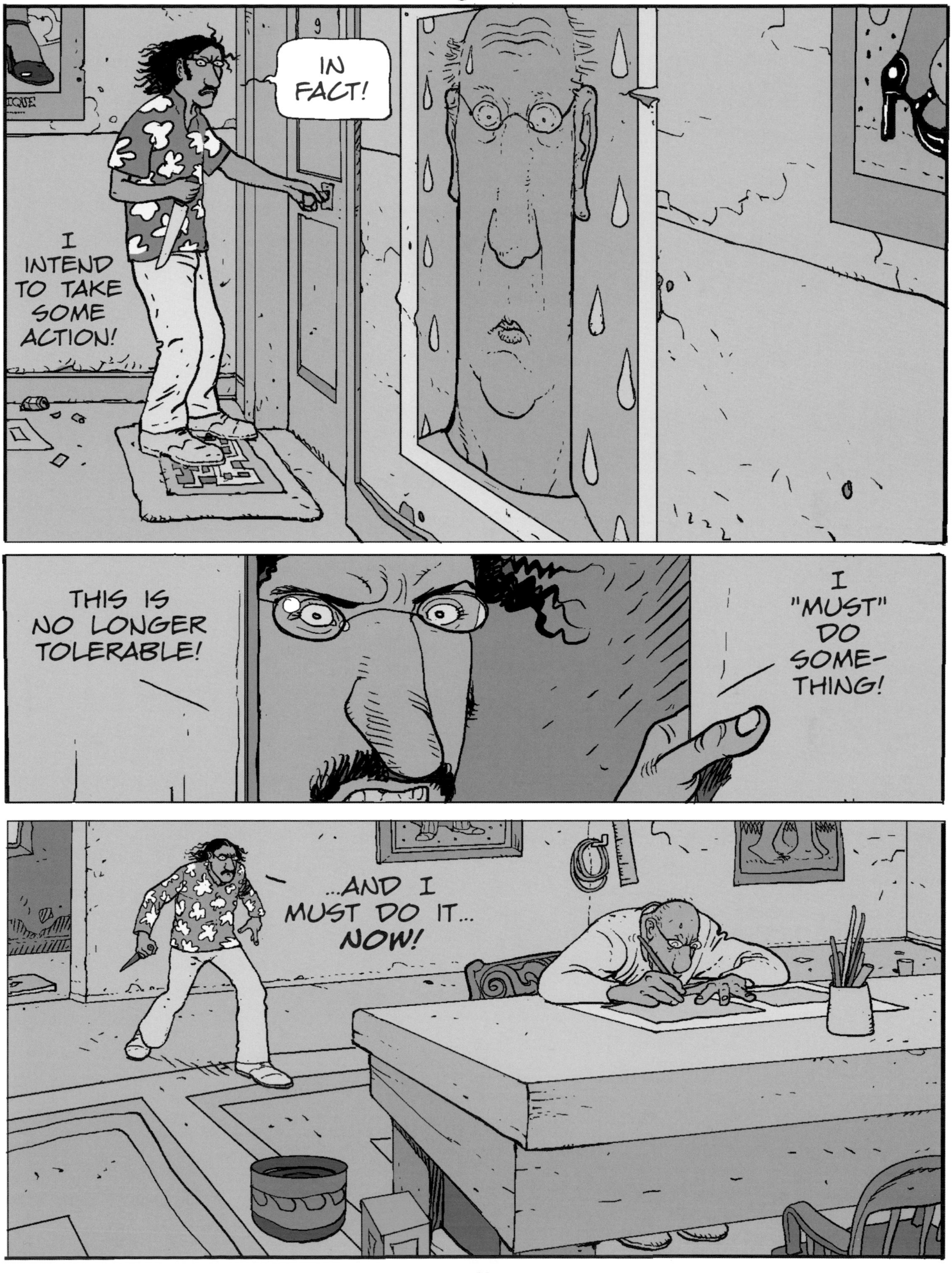
IN FACT!
I INTEND TO TAKE SOME ACTION!
THIS IS NO LONGER TOLERABLE!
I "MUST" DO SOME-THING!
...AND I MUST DO IT... NOW!

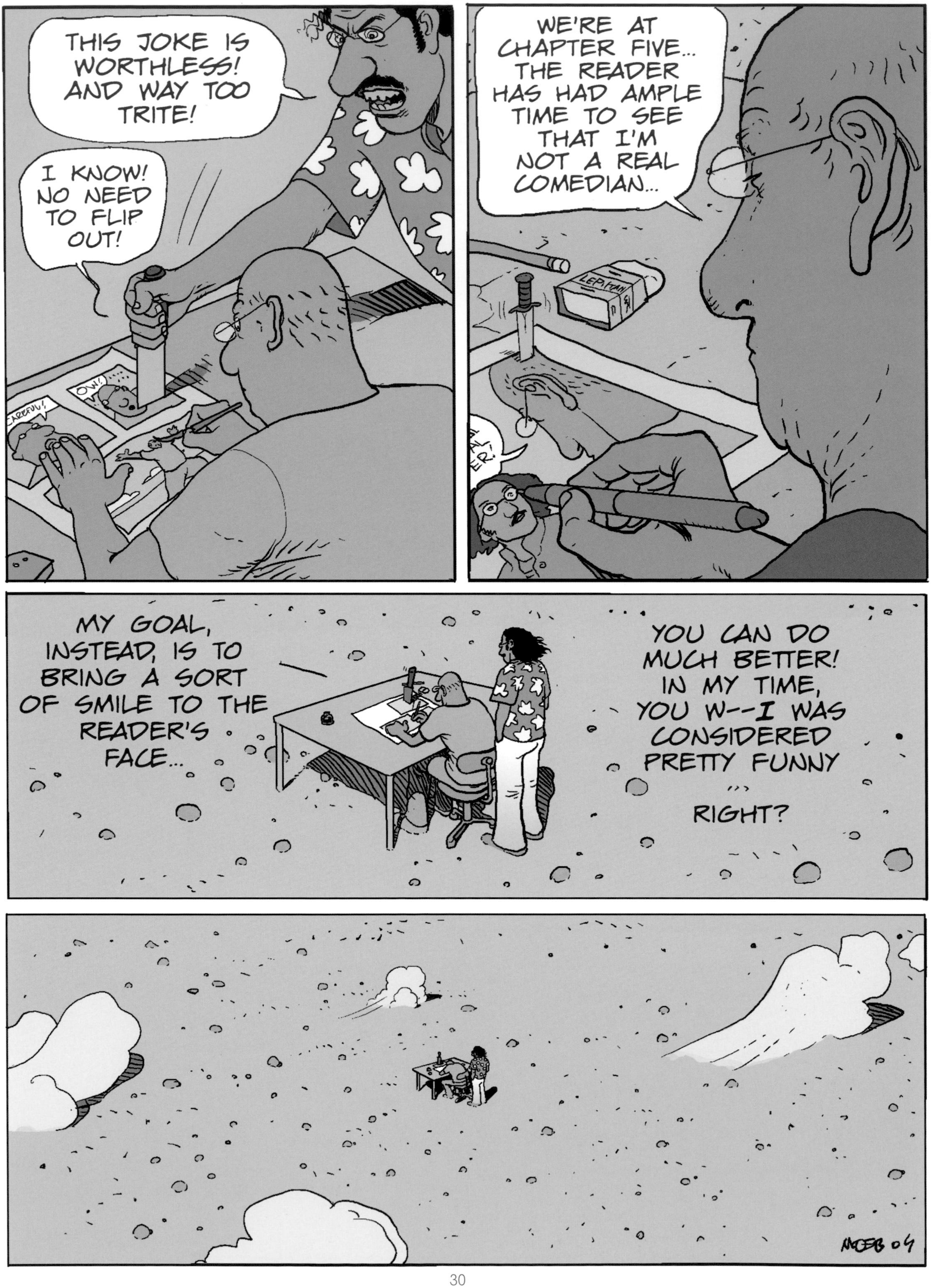
THIS JOKE IS WORTHLESS! AND WAY TOO TRITE!
I KNOW! NO NEED TO FLIP OUT!
WE'RE AT CHAPTER FIVE... THE READER HAS HAD AMPLE TIME TO SEE THAT I'M NOT A REAL COMEDIAN...
MY GOAL, INSTEAD, IS TO BRING A SORT OF SMILE TO THE READER'S FACE...
YOU CAN DO MUCH BETTER! IN MY TIME, YOU W--I WAS CONSIDERED PRETTY FUNNY
...
RIGHT?

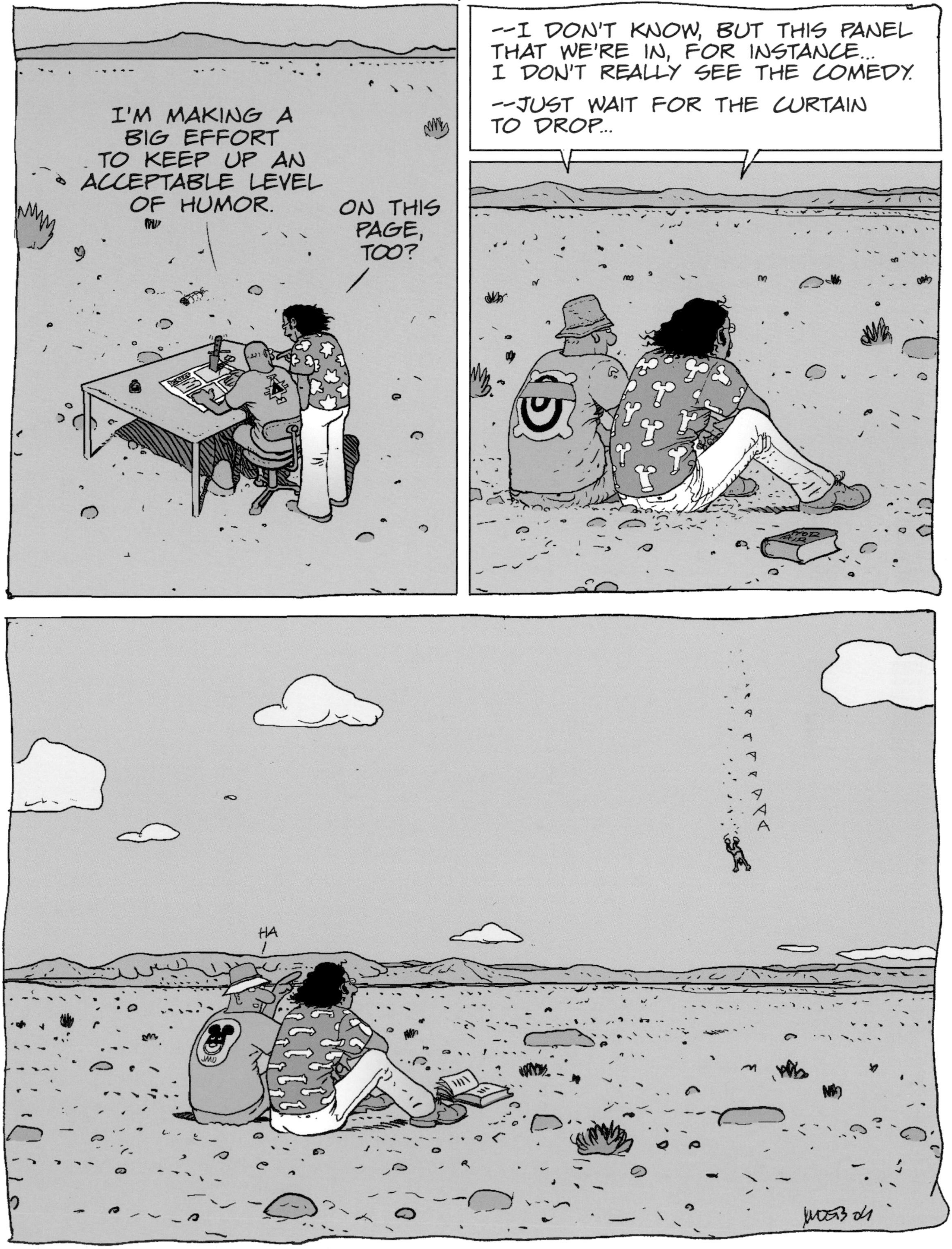
I'M MAKING A BIG EFFORT TO KEEP UP AN ACCEPTABLE LEVEL OF HUMOR.
ON THIS PAGE, TOO?
--I DON'T KNOW, BUT THIS PANEL THAT WE'RE IN, FOR INSTANCE... I DON'T REALLY SEE THE COMEDY.
--JUST WAIT FOR THE CURTAIN TO DROP...
AAAAAAAAA
HA

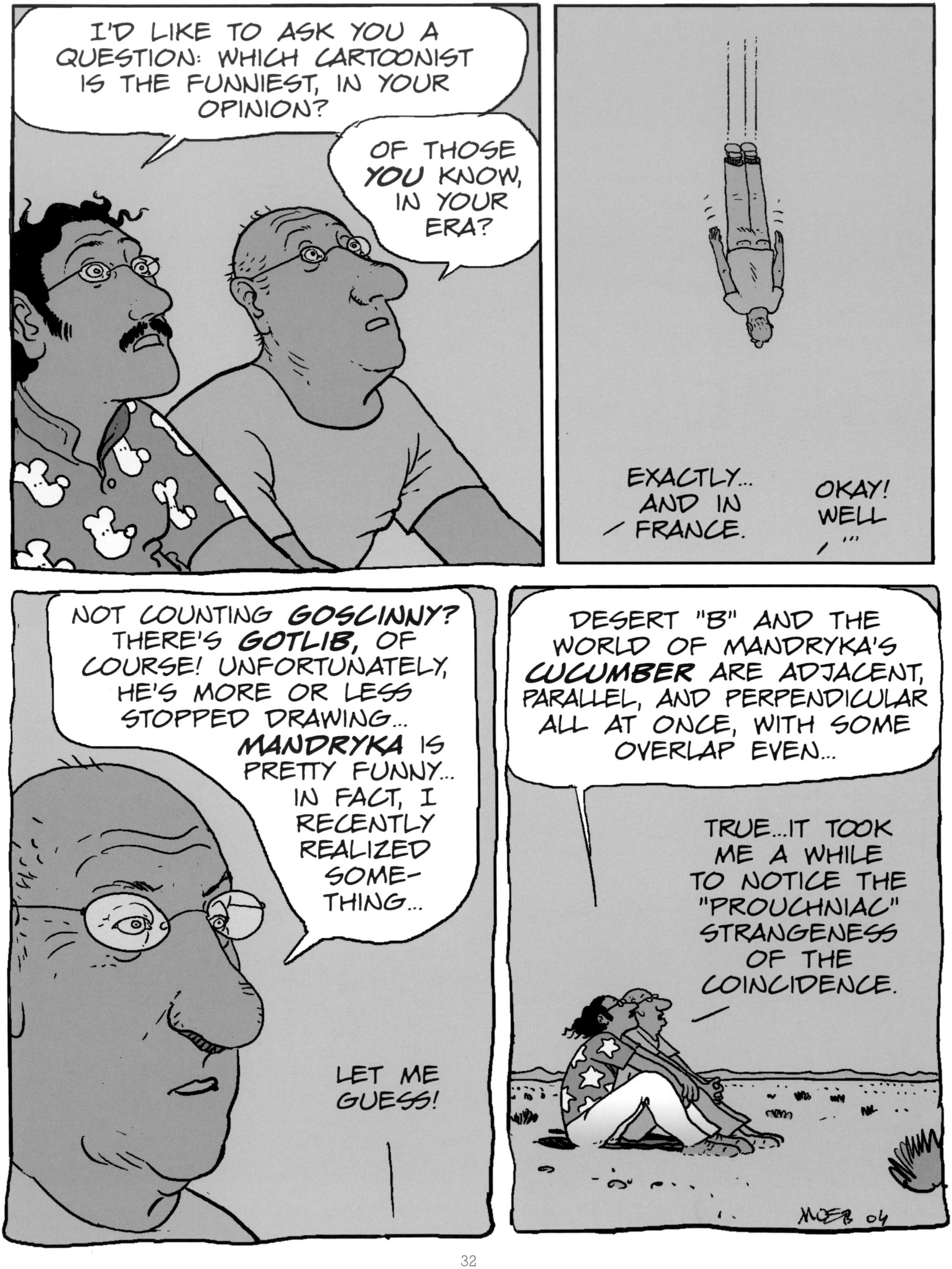
I'D LIKE TO ASK YOU A QUESTION: WHICH CARTOONIST IS THE FUNNIEST, IN YOUR OPINION?
OF THOSE ***YOU*** KNOW, IN YOUR ERA?
EXACTLY... AND IN FRANCE.
OKAY! WELL ...
NOT COUNTING ***GOSCINNY?*** THERE'S ***GOTLIB,*** OF COURSE! UNFORTUNATELY, HE'S MORE OR LESS STOPPED DRAWING... ***MANDRYKA*** IS PRETTY FUNNY... IN FACT, I RECENTLY REALIZED SOME-THING...
LET ME GUESS!
DESERT "B" AND THE WORLD OF MANDRYKA'S ***CUCUMBER*** ARE ADJACENT, PARALLEL, AND PERPENDICULAR ALL AT ONCE, WITH SOME OVERLAP EVEN...
TRUE...IT TOOK ME A WHILE TO NOTICE THE "PROUCHNIAC" STRANGENESS OF THE COINCIDENCE.
MOEB 04

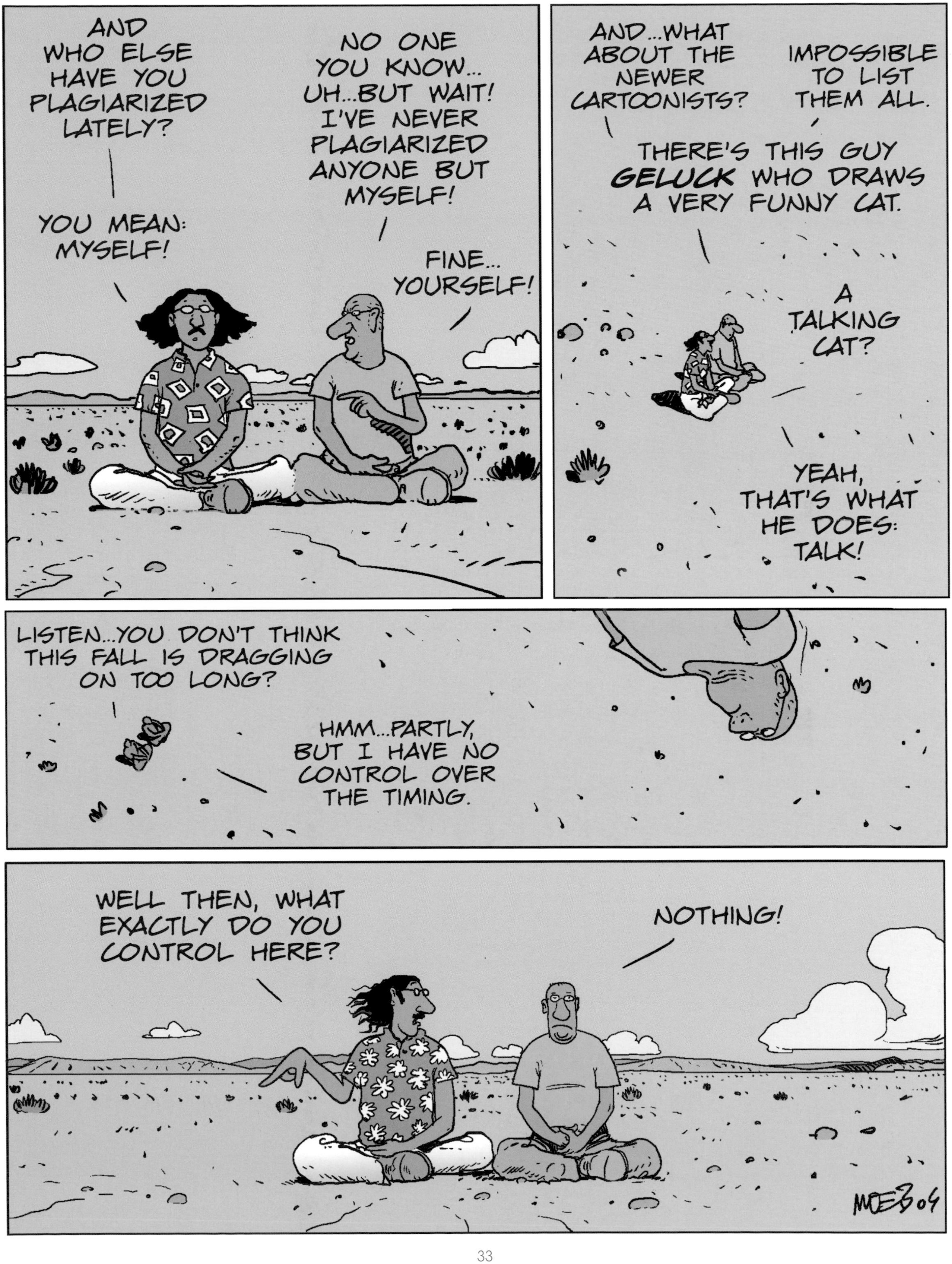
AND WHO ELSE HAVE YOU PLAGIARIZED LATELY?
NO ONE YOU KNOW... UH...BUT WAIT! I'VE NEVER PLAGIARIZED ANYONE BUT MYSELF!
YOU MEAN: MYSELF!
FINE... YOURSELF!
AND...WHAT ABOUT THE NEWER CARTOONISTS?
IMPOSSIBLE TO LIST THEM ALL.
THERE'S THIS GUY **GELUCK** WHO DRAWS A VERY FUNNY CAT.
A TALKING CAT?
YEAH, THAT'S WHAT HE DOES: TALK!
LISTEN...YOU DON'T THINK THIS FALL IS DRAGGING ON TOO LONG?
HMM...PARTLY, BUT I HAVE NO CONTROL OVER THE TIMING.
WELL THEN, WHAT EXACTLY DO YOU CONTROL HERE?
NOTHING!
MOEB 04

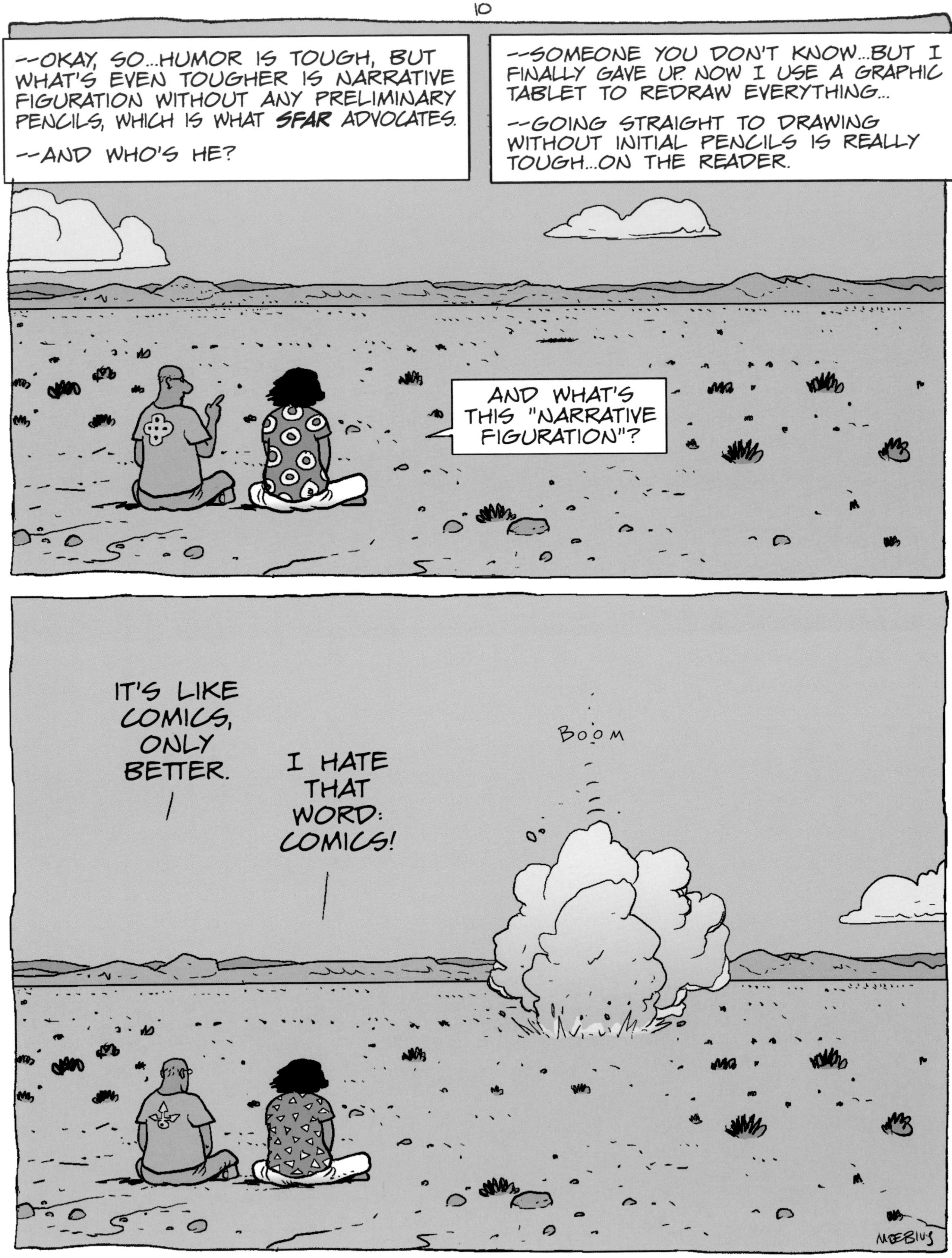
--OKAY, SO...HUMOR IS TOUGH, BUT WHAT'S EVEN TOUGHER IS NARRATIVE FIGURATION WITHOUT ANY PRELIMINARY PENCILS, WHICH IS WHAT SFAR ADVOCATES.
--AND WHO'S HE?
--SOMEONE YOU DON'T KNOW...BUT I FINALLY GAVE UP. NOW I USE A GRAPHIC TABLET TO REDRAW EVERYTHING...
--GOING STRAIGHT TO DRAWING WITHOUT INITIAL PENCILS IS REALLY TOUGH...ON THE READER.
AND WHAT'S THIS "NARRATIVE FIGURATION"?
IT'S LIKE COMICS, ONLY BETTER.
I HATE THAT WORD: COMICS!
BOOM
MOEBIUS

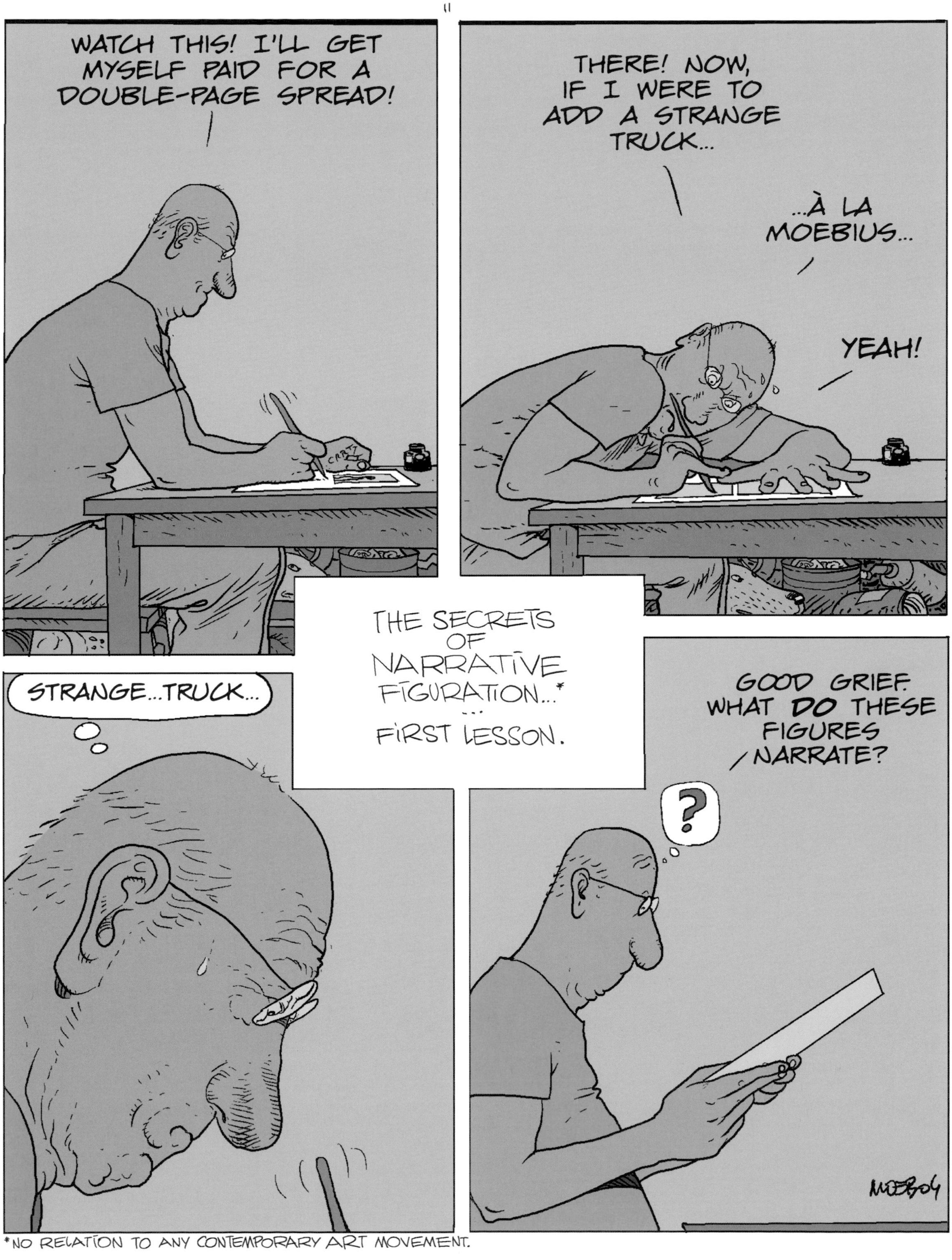
WATCH THIS! I'LL GET MYSELF PAID FOR A DOUBLE-PAGE SPREAD!
THERE! NOW, IF I WERE TO ADD A STRANGE TRUCK...
...À LA MOEBIUS...
YEAH!
THE SECRETS OF NARRATIVE FIGURATION...* ... FIRST LESSON.
STRANGE...TRUCK...
GOOD GRIEF. WHAT DO THESE FIGURES NARRATE?
?
MOEB04

*NO RELATION TO ANY CONTEMPORARY ART MOVEMENT.

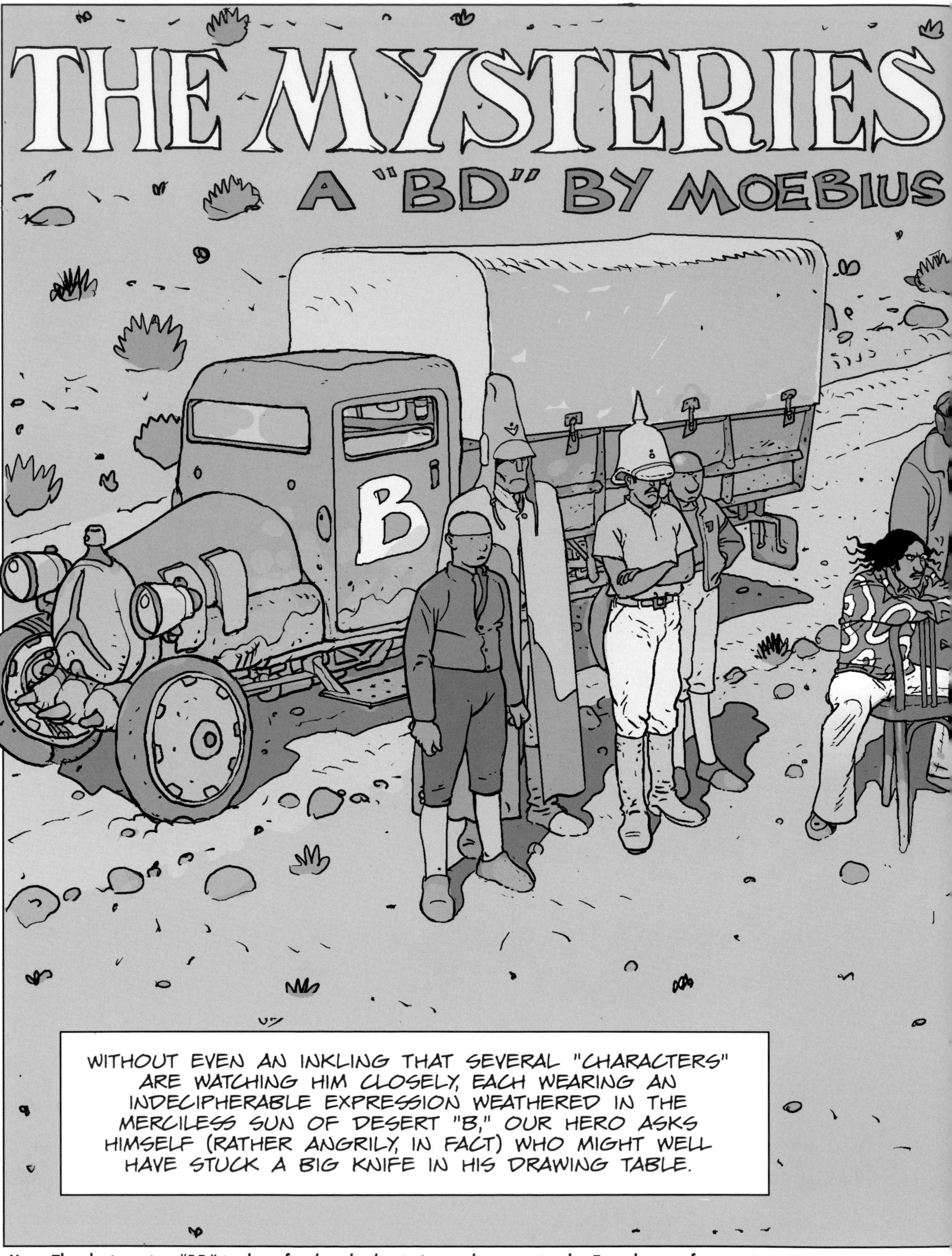
THE MYSTERIES
A "BD" BY MOEBIUS
B
WITHOUT EVEN AN INKLING THAT SEVERAL "CHARACTERS" ARE WATCHING HIM CLOSELY, EACH WEARING AN INDECIPHERABLE EXPRESSION WEATHERED IN THE MERCILESS SUN OF DESERT "B," OUR HERO ASKS HIMSELF (RATHER ANGRILY, IN FACT) WHO MIGHT WELL HAVE STUCK A BIG KNIFE IN HIS DRAWING TABLE.

Note: The designation "BD" is short for *bande dessinée*, or *drawn strip*, the French term for *comics*.

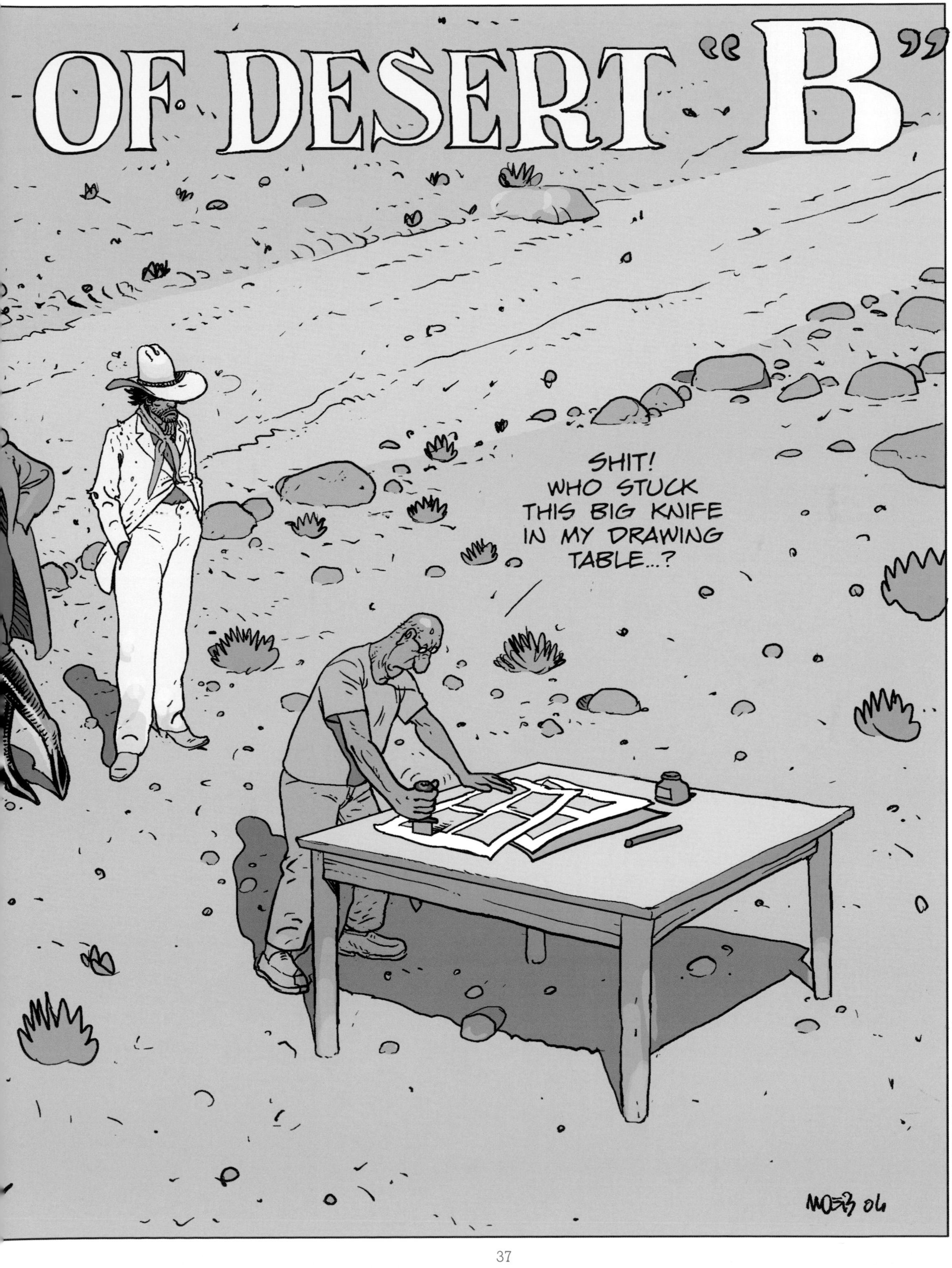
OF DESERT "B"
SHIT! WHO STUCK THIS BIG KNIFE IN MY DRAWING TABLE...?
MOEB 06

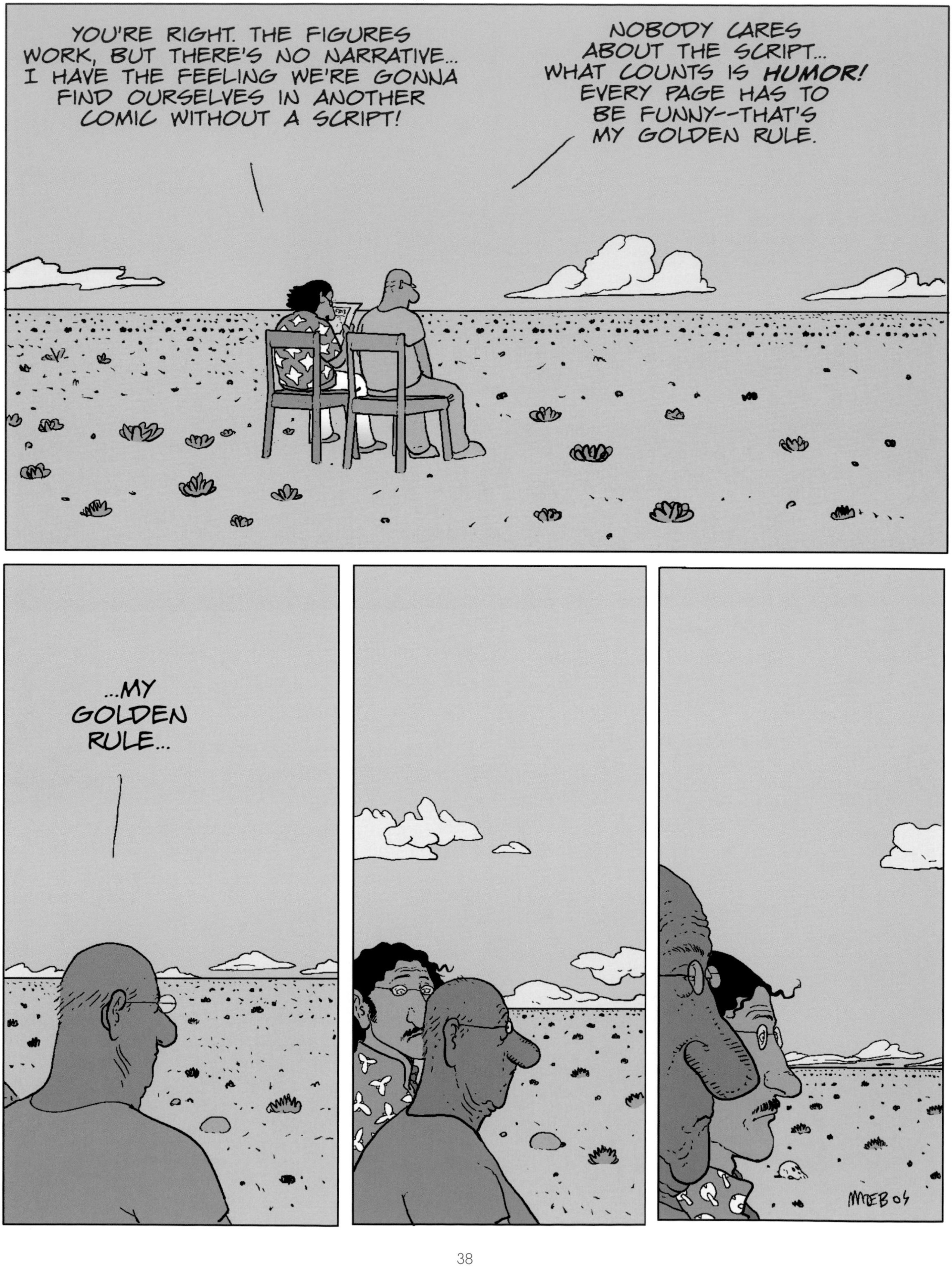
YOU'RE RIGHT. THE FIGURES WORK, BUT THERE'S NO NARRATIVE... I HAVE THE FEELING WE'RE GONNA FIND OURSELVES IN ANOTHER COMIC WITHOUT A SCRIPT!
NOBODY CARES ABOUT THE SCRIPT... WHAT COUNTS IS **HUMOR!** EVERY PAGE HAS TO BE FUNNY--THAT'S MY GOLDEN RULE.
...MY GOLDEN RULE...
MOEB 05

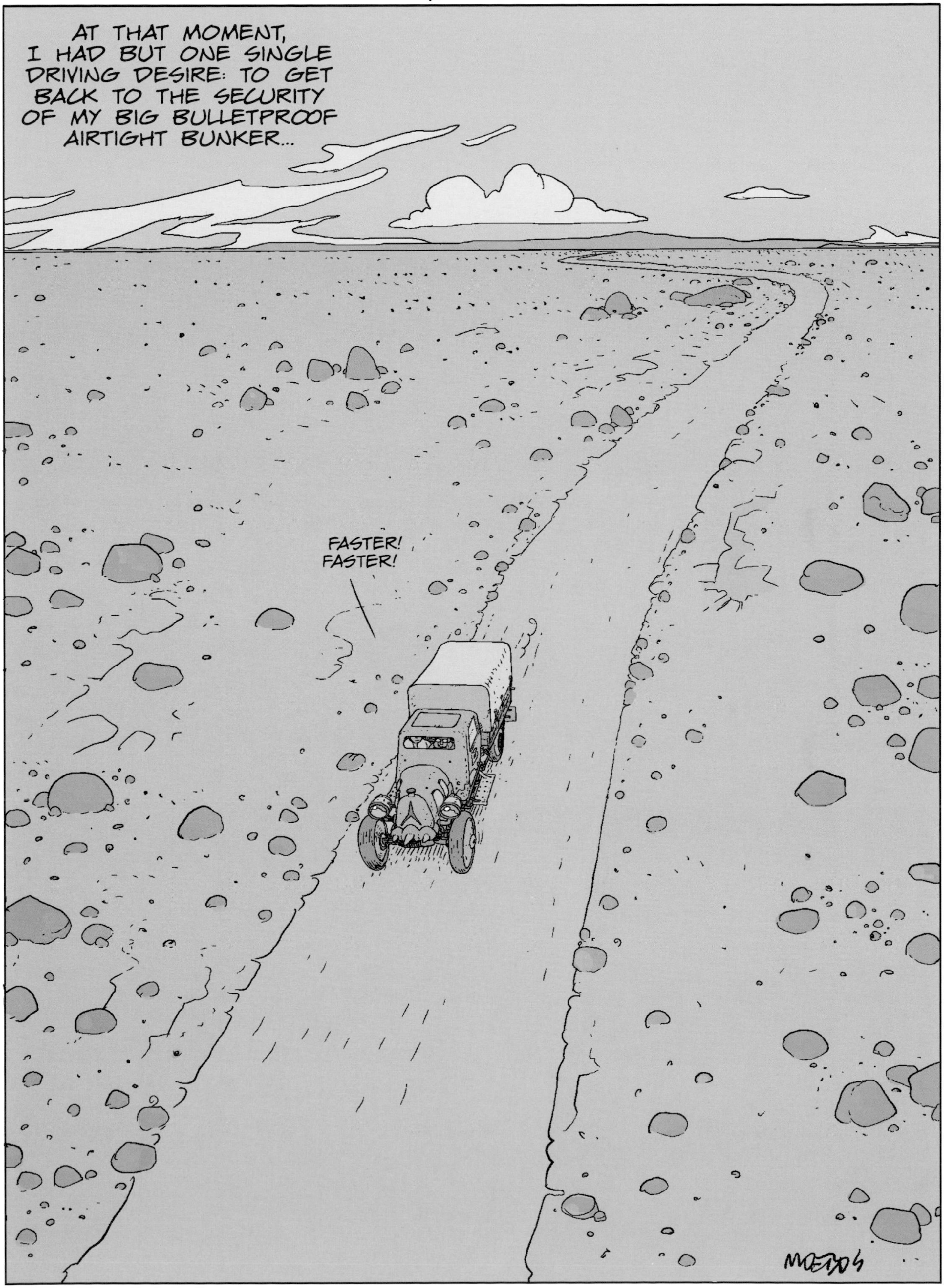
AT THAT MOMENT, I HAD BUT ONE SINGLE DRIVING DESIRE: TO GET BACK TO THE SECURITY OF MY BIG BULLETPROOF AIRTIGHT BUNKER...
FASTER! FASTER!
MOEBIUS

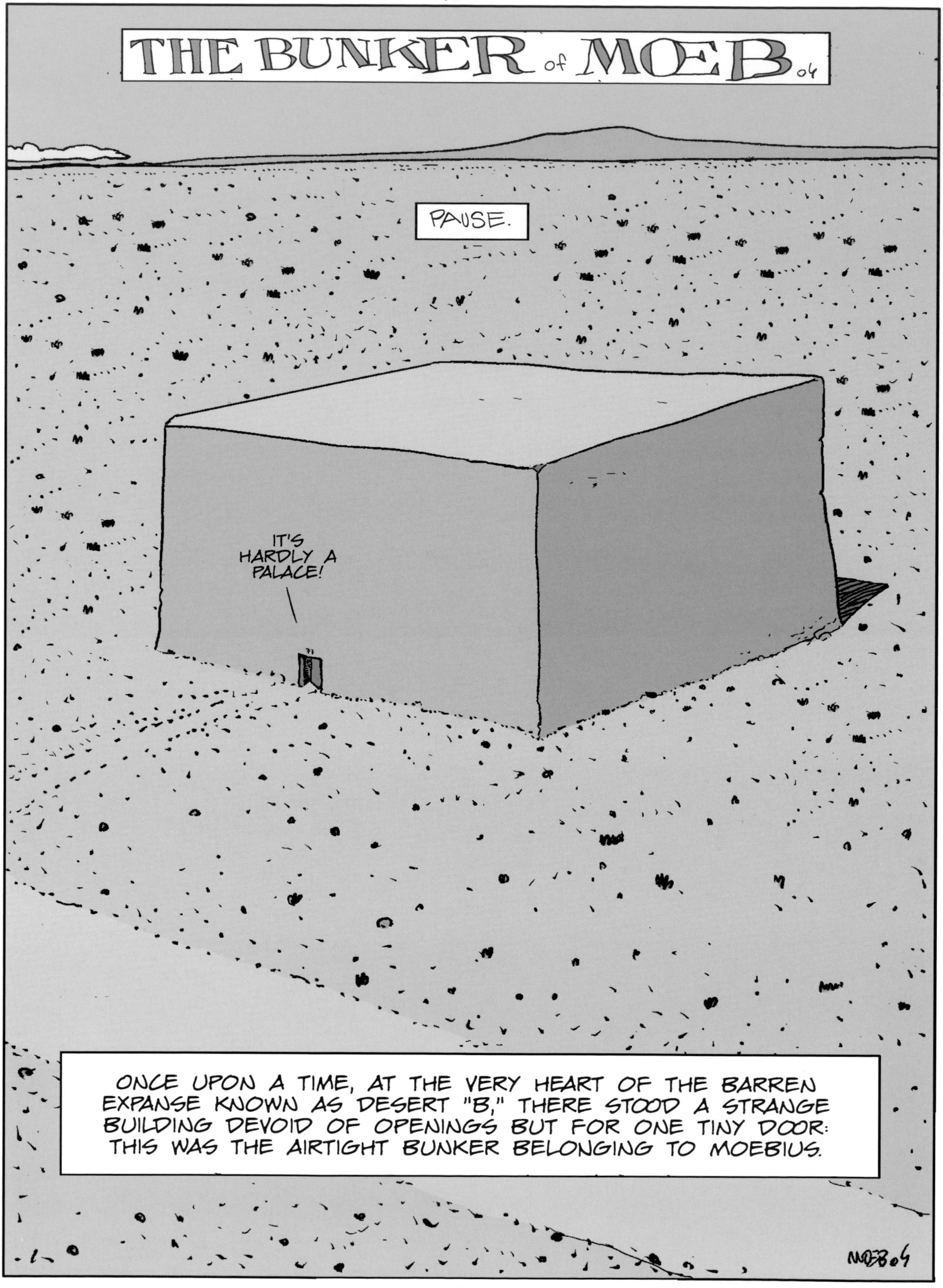
THE BUNKER of MOEB.04
PAUSE.
IT'S HARDLY A PALACE!
ONCE UPON A TIME, AT THE VERY HEART OF THE BARREN EXPANSE KNOWN AS DESERT "B," THERE STOOD A STRANGE BUILDING DEVOID OF OPENINGS BUT FOR ONE TINY DOOR: THIS WAS THE AIRTIGHT BUNKER BELONGING TO MOEBIUS.
MOEB.04

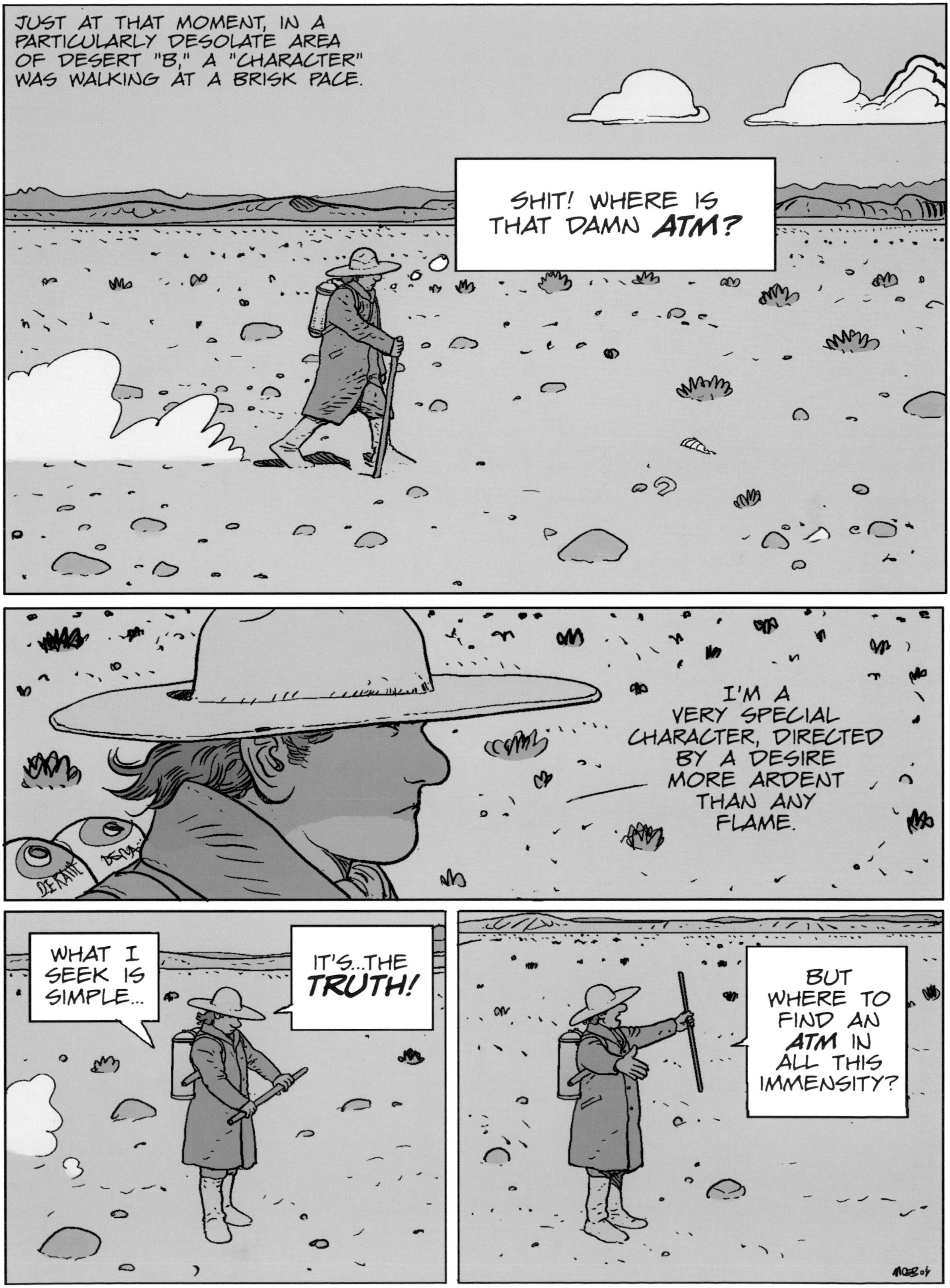
JUST AT THAT MOMENT, IN A PARTICULARLY DESOLATE AREA OF DESERT "B," A "CHARACTER" WAS WALKING AT A BRISK PACE.
SHIT! WHERE IS THAT DAMN ATM?
I'M A VERY SPECIAL CHARACTER, DIRECTED BY A DESIRE MORE ARDENT THAN ANY FLAME.
WHAT I SEEK IS SIMPLE...
IT'S...THE TRUTH!
BUT WHERE TO FIND AN ATM IN ALL THIS IMMENSITY?

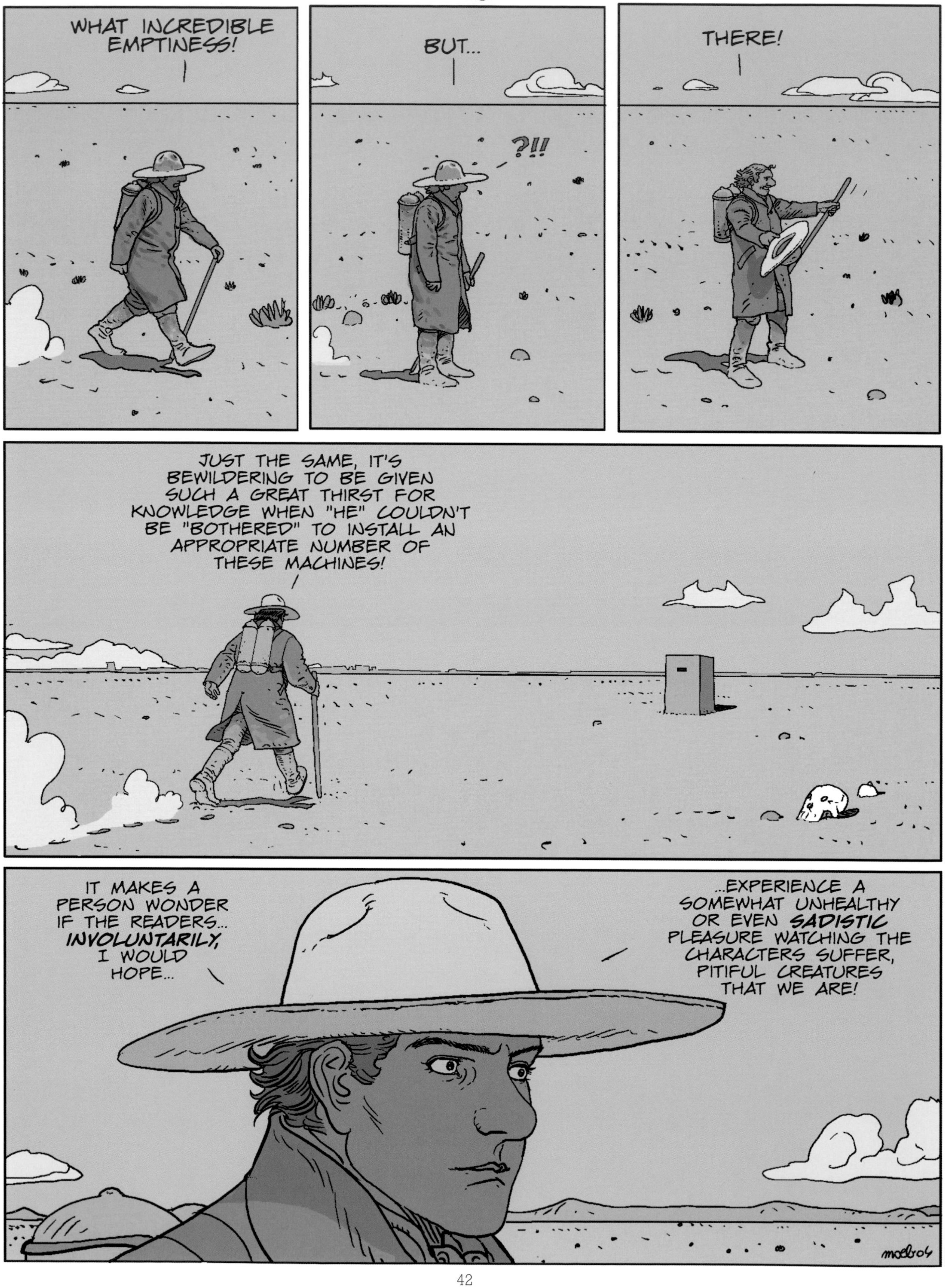
WHAT INCREDIBLE EMPTINESS!
BUT...
?!!
THERE!
JUST THE SAME, IT'S BEWILDERING TO BE GIVEN SUCH A GREAT THIRST FOR KNOWLEDGE WHEN "HE" COULDN'T BE "BOTHERED" TO INSTALL AN APPROPRIATE NUMBER OF THESE MACHINES!
IT MAKES A PERSON WONDER IF THE READERS... ***INVOLUNTARILY,*** I WOULD HOPE...
...EXPERIENCE A SOMEWHAT UNHEALTHY OR EVEN ***SADISTIC*** PLEASURE WATCHING THE CHARACTERS SUFFER, PITIFUL CREATURES THAT WE ARE!
moebius

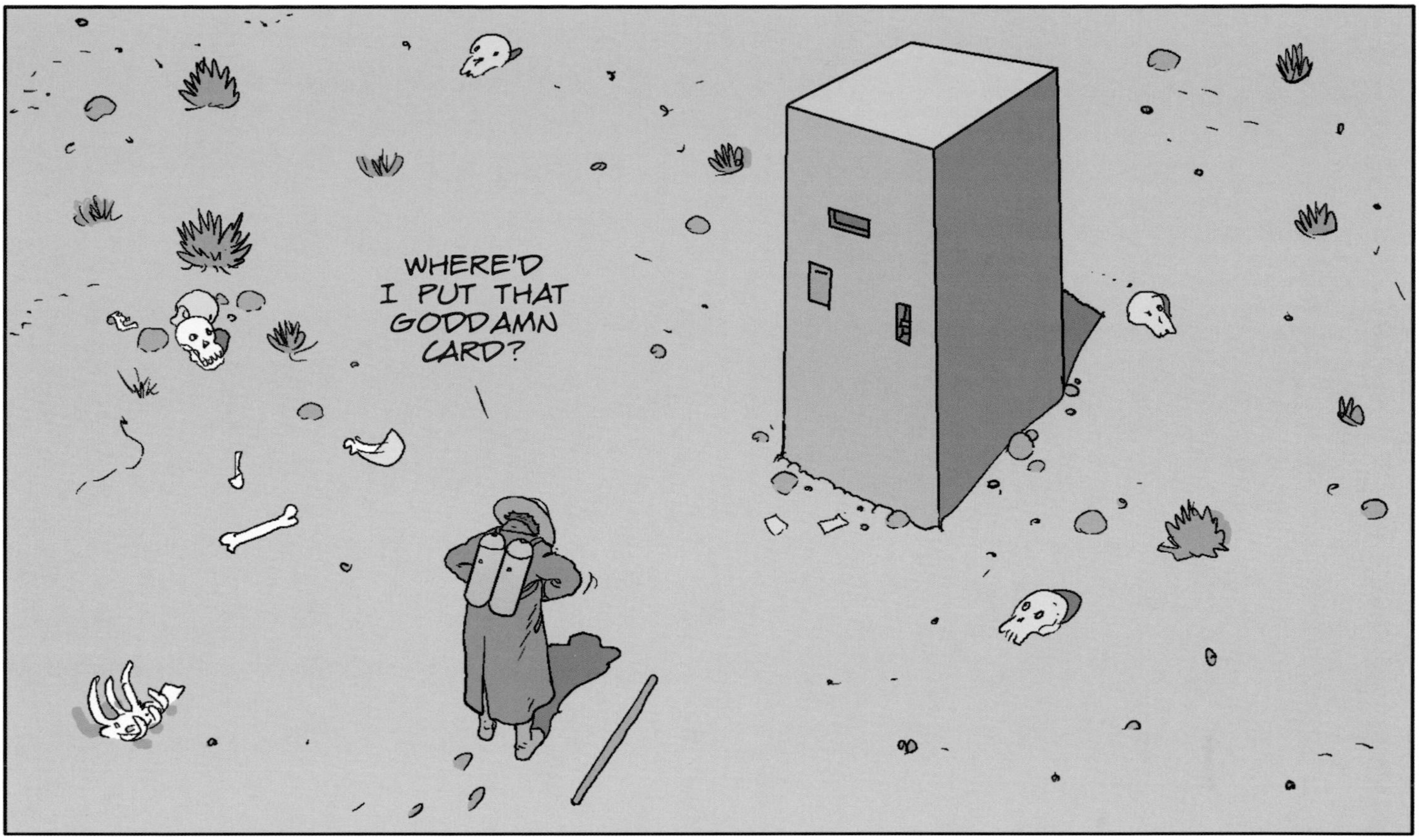
WHERE'D I PUT THAT GODDAMN CARD?

ALARMING REVELATIONS AT THE HEART OF "B"

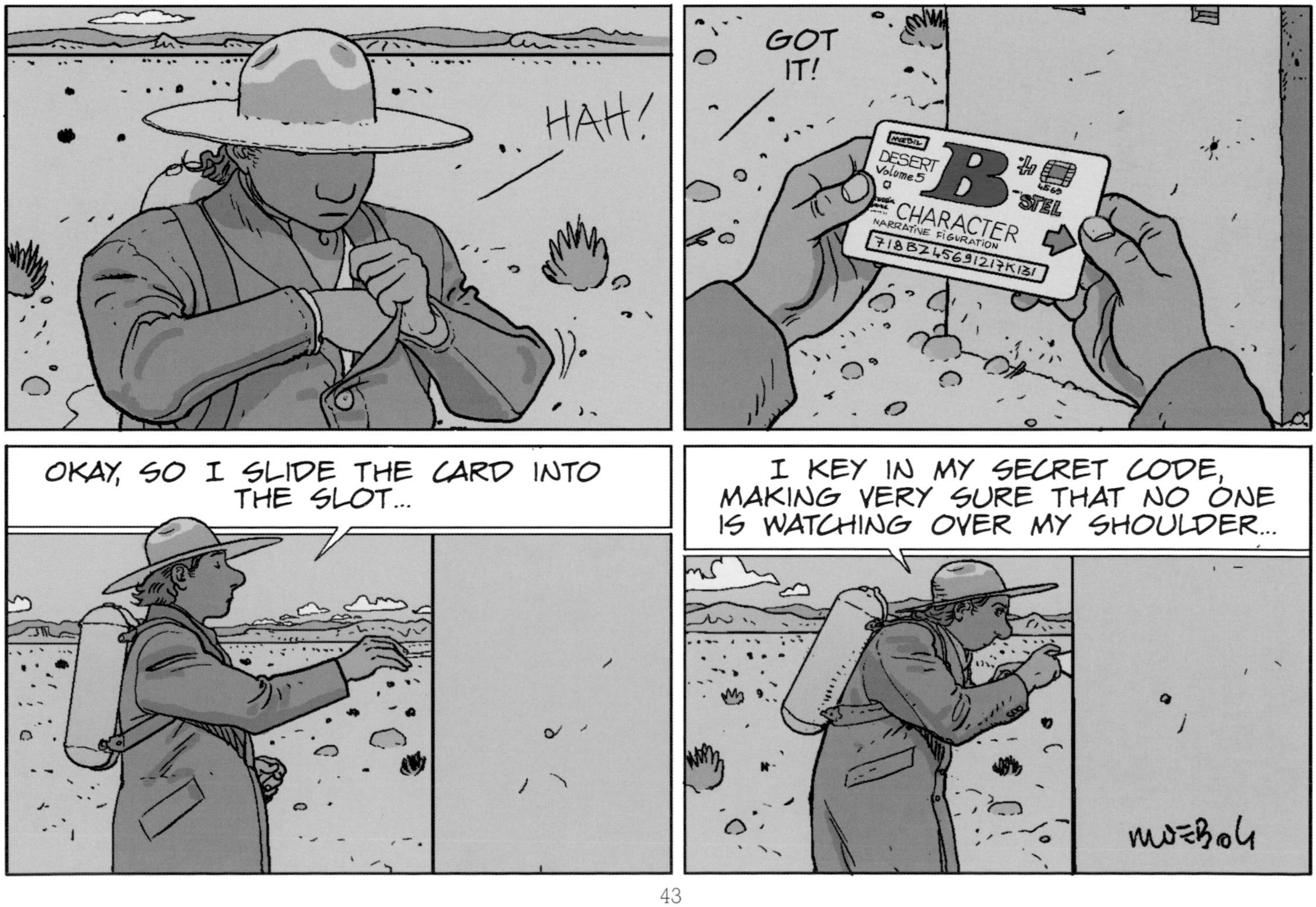
HAH!
GOT IT!
MŒBIL
DESERT
Volume 5
B
4569
STEL
CHARACTER
NARRATIVE FIGURATION
718BZ45691217K131
OKAY, SO I SLIDE THE CARD INTO THE SLOT...
I KEY IN MY SECRET CODE, MAKING VERY SURE THAT NO ONE IS WATCHING OVER MY SHOULDER...
MŒBIUS

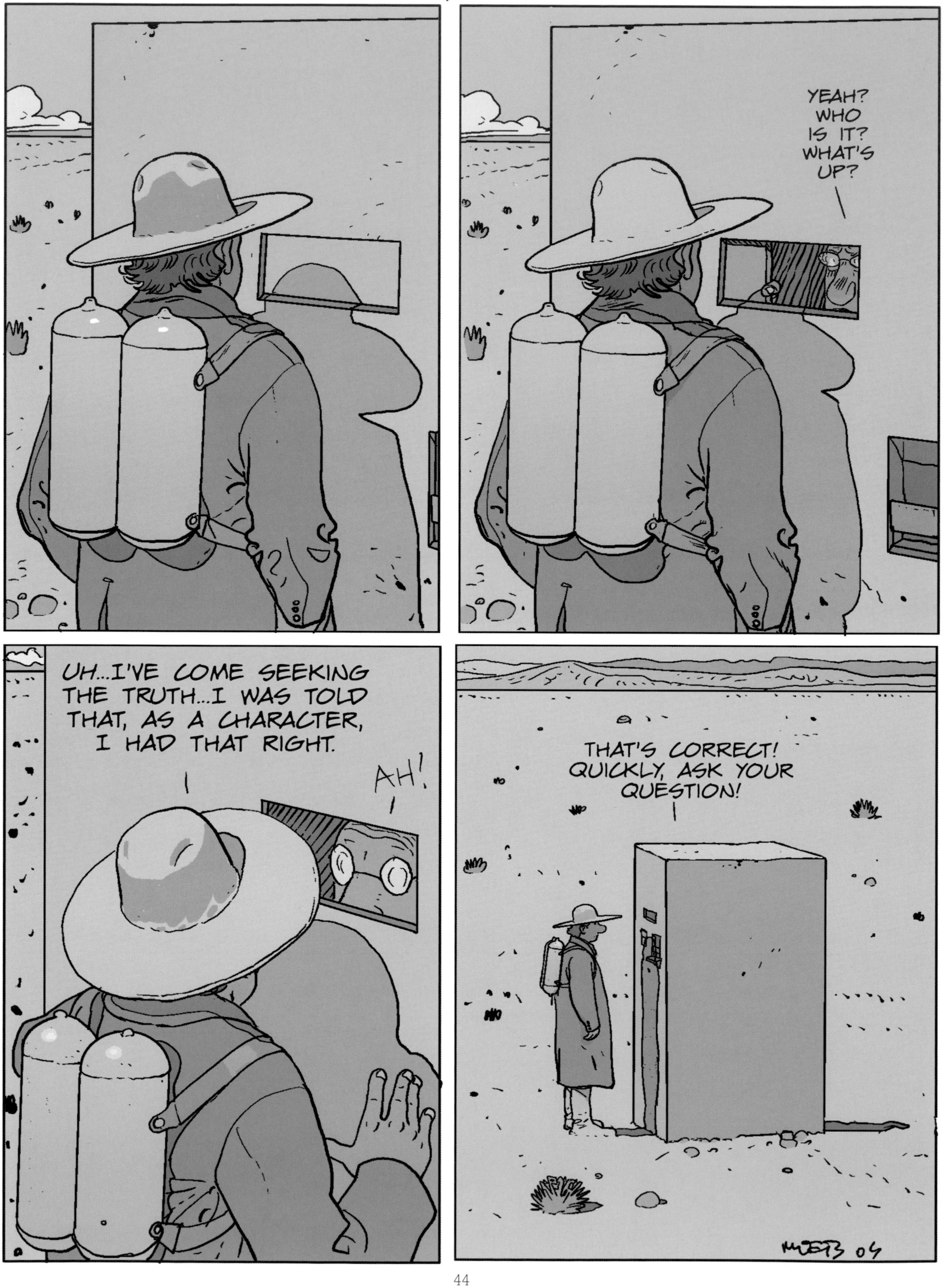
YEAH? WHO IS IT? WHAT'S UP?
UH...I'VE COME SEEKING THE TRUTH...I WAS TOLD THAT, AS A CHARACTER, I HAD THAT RIGHT.
AH!
THAT'S CORRECT! QUICKLY, ASK YOUR QUESTION!
MŒBIUS 04

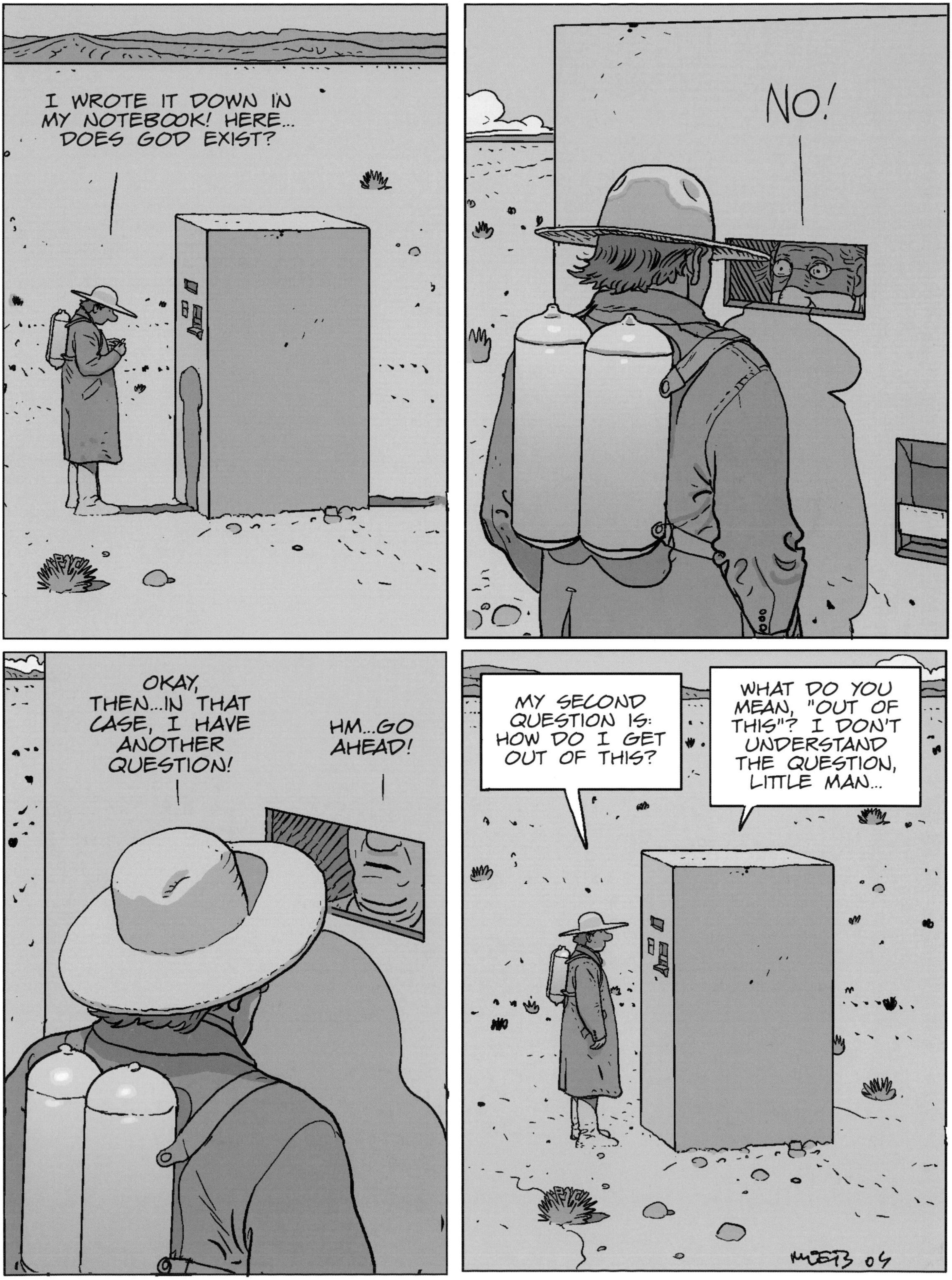
I WROTE IT DOWN IN MY NOTEBOOK! HERE... DOES GOD EXIST?
NO!
OKAY, THEN...IN THAT CASE, I HAVE ANOTHER QUESTION!
HM...GO AHEAD!
MY SECOND QUESTION IS: HOW DO I GET OUT OF THIS?
WHAT DO YOU MEAN, "OUT OF THIS"? I DON'T UNDERSTAND THE QUESTION, LITTLE MAN...

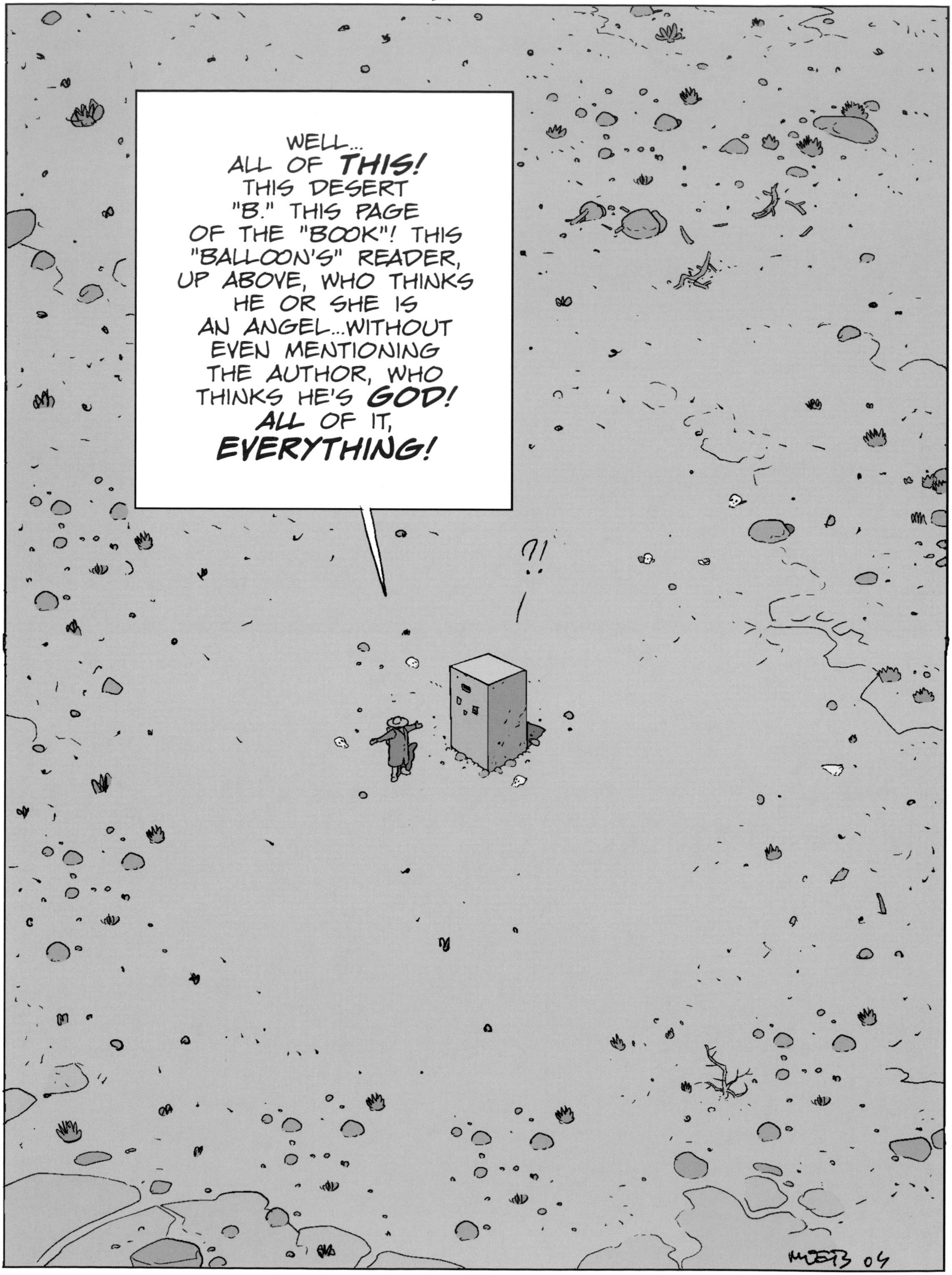
WELL... ALL OF THIS! THIS DESERT "B." THIS PAGE OF THE "BOOK"! THIS "BALLOON'S" READER, UP ABOVE, WHO THINKS HE OR SHE IS AN ANGEL...WITHOUT EVEN MENTIONING THE AUTHOR, WHO THINKS HE'S GOD! ALL OF IT, EVERYTHING!
?!

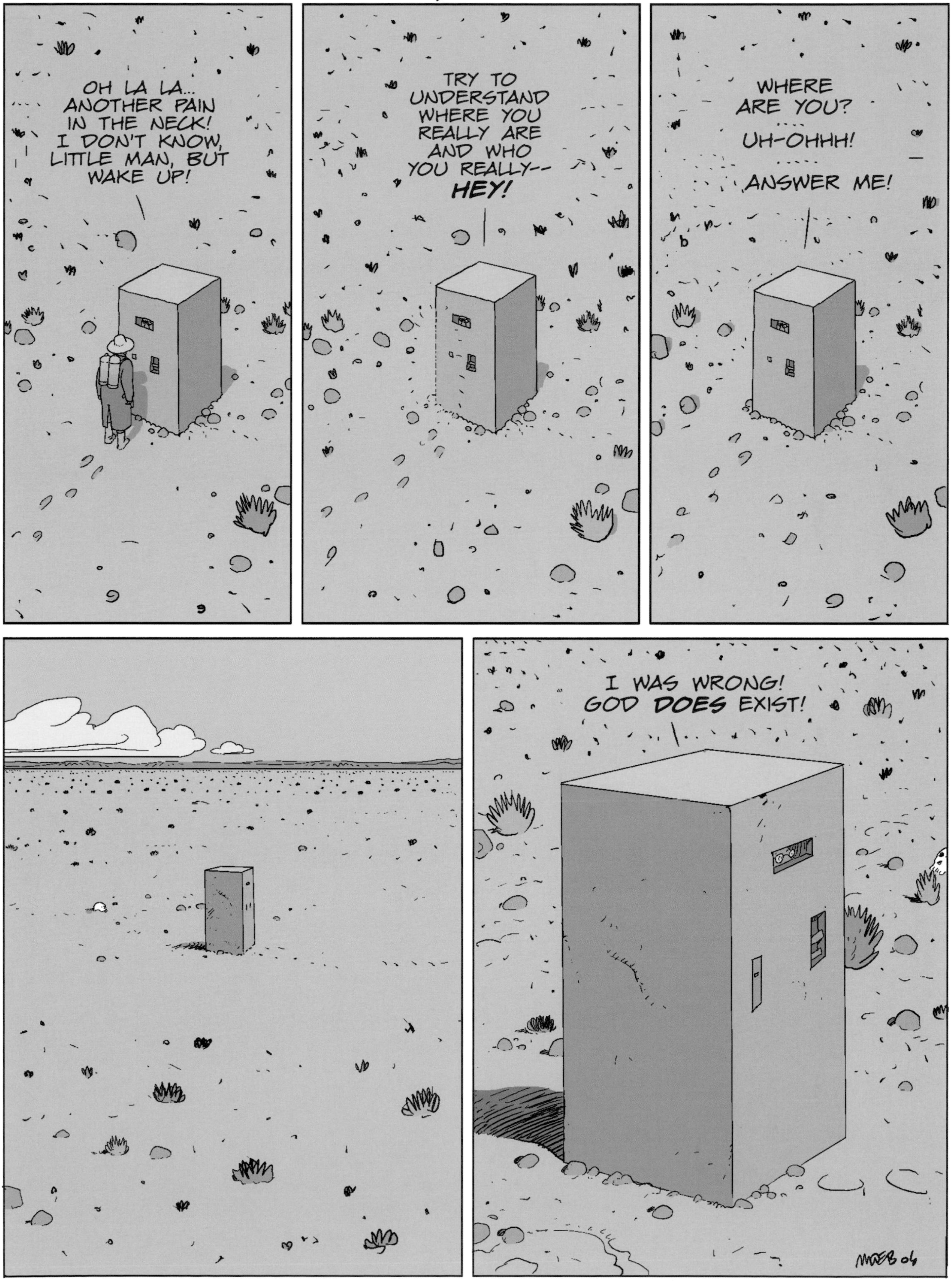
OH LA LA... ANOTHER PAIN IN THE NECK! I DON'T KNOW, LITTLE MAN, BUT WAKE UP!
TRY TO UNDERSTAND WHERE YOU REALLY ARE AND WHO YOU REALLY-- HEY!
WHERE ARE YOU? .... UH-OHHH! ..... ANSWER ME!
I WAS WRONG! GOD DOES EXIST!
MOEB 04

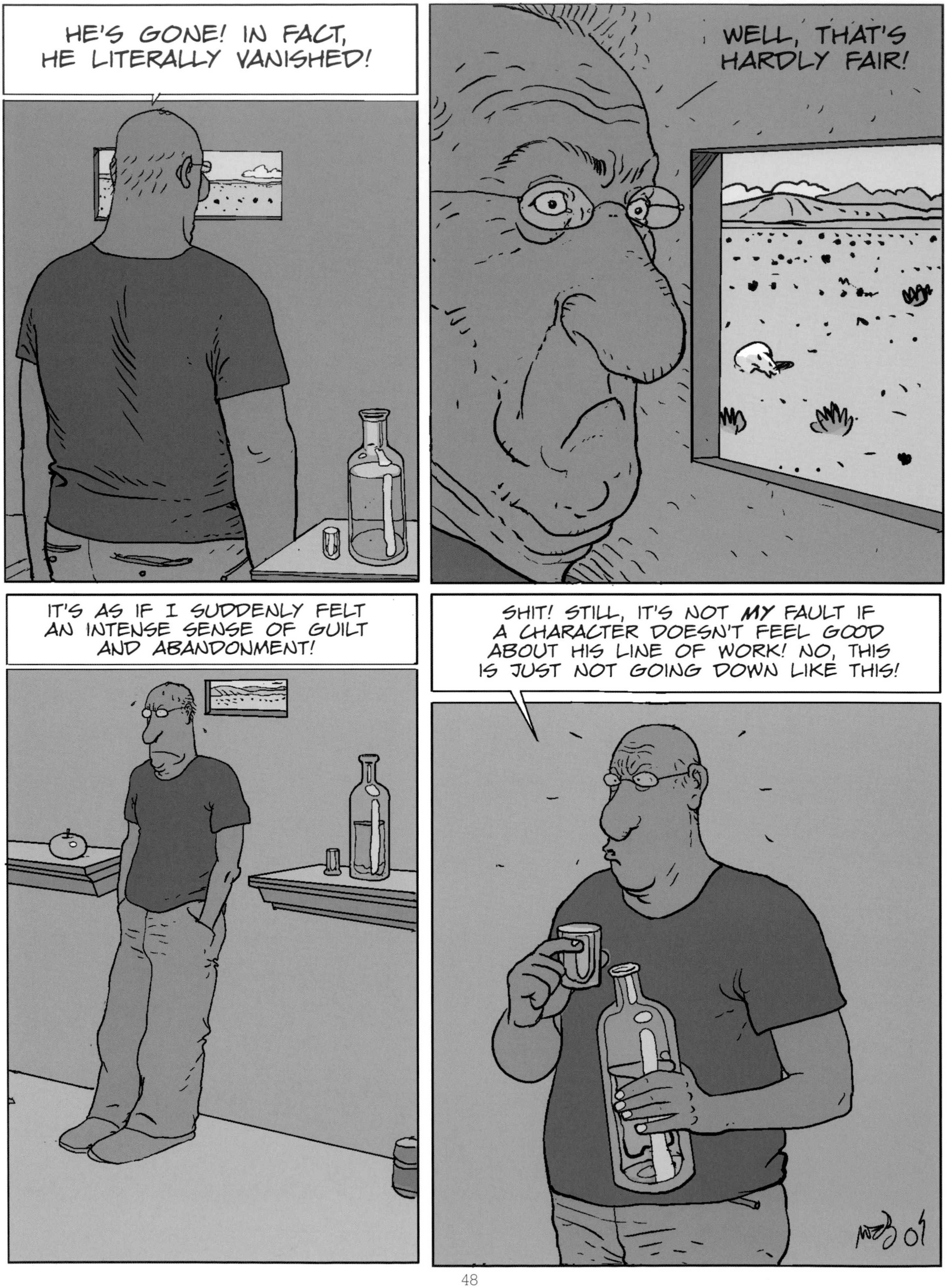
HE'S GONE! IN FACT, HE LITERALLY VANISHED!
WELL, THAT'S HARDLY FAIR!
IT'S AS IF I SUDDENLY FELT AN INTENSE SENSE OF GUILT AND ABANDONMENT!
SHIT! STILL, IT'S NOT MY FAULT IF A CHARACTER DOESN'T FEEL GOOD ABOUT HIS LINE OF WORK! NO, THIS IS JUST NOT GOING DOWN LIKE THIS!

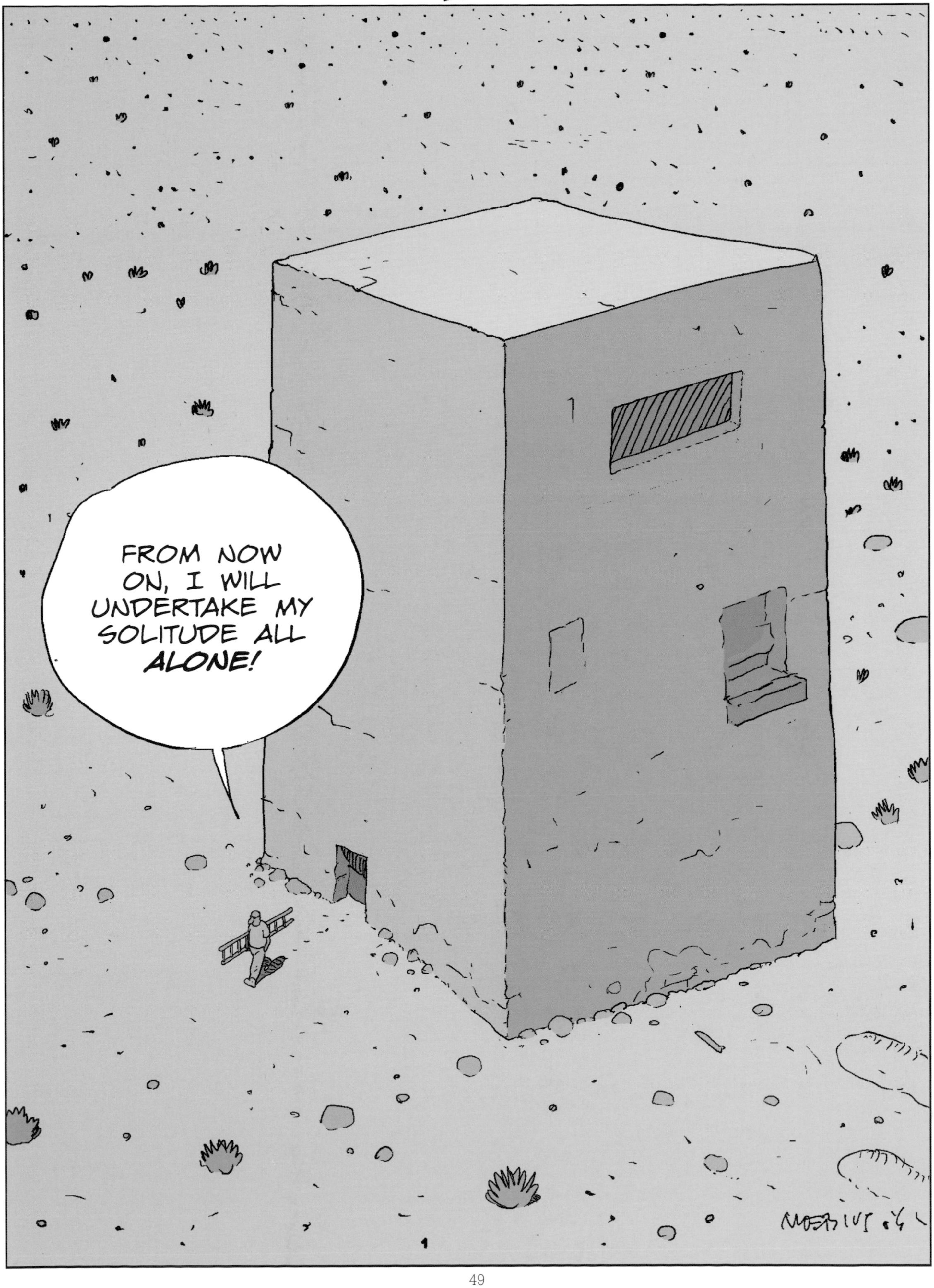
FROM NOW ON, I WILL UNDERTAKE MY SOLITUDE ALL ALONE!
MOEBIUS

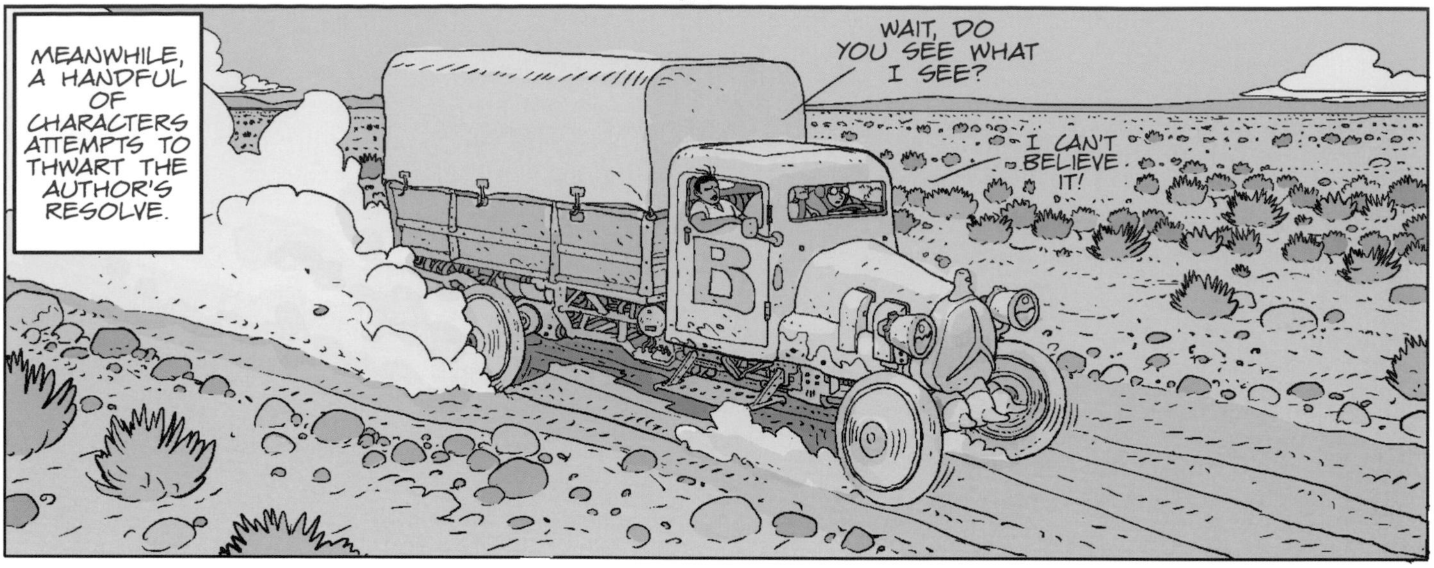

MEANWHILE, A HANDFUL OF CHARACTERS ATTEMPTS TO THWART THE AUTHOR'S RESOLVE.
WAIT, DO YOU SEE WHAT I SEE?
I CAN'T BELIEVE IT!
B

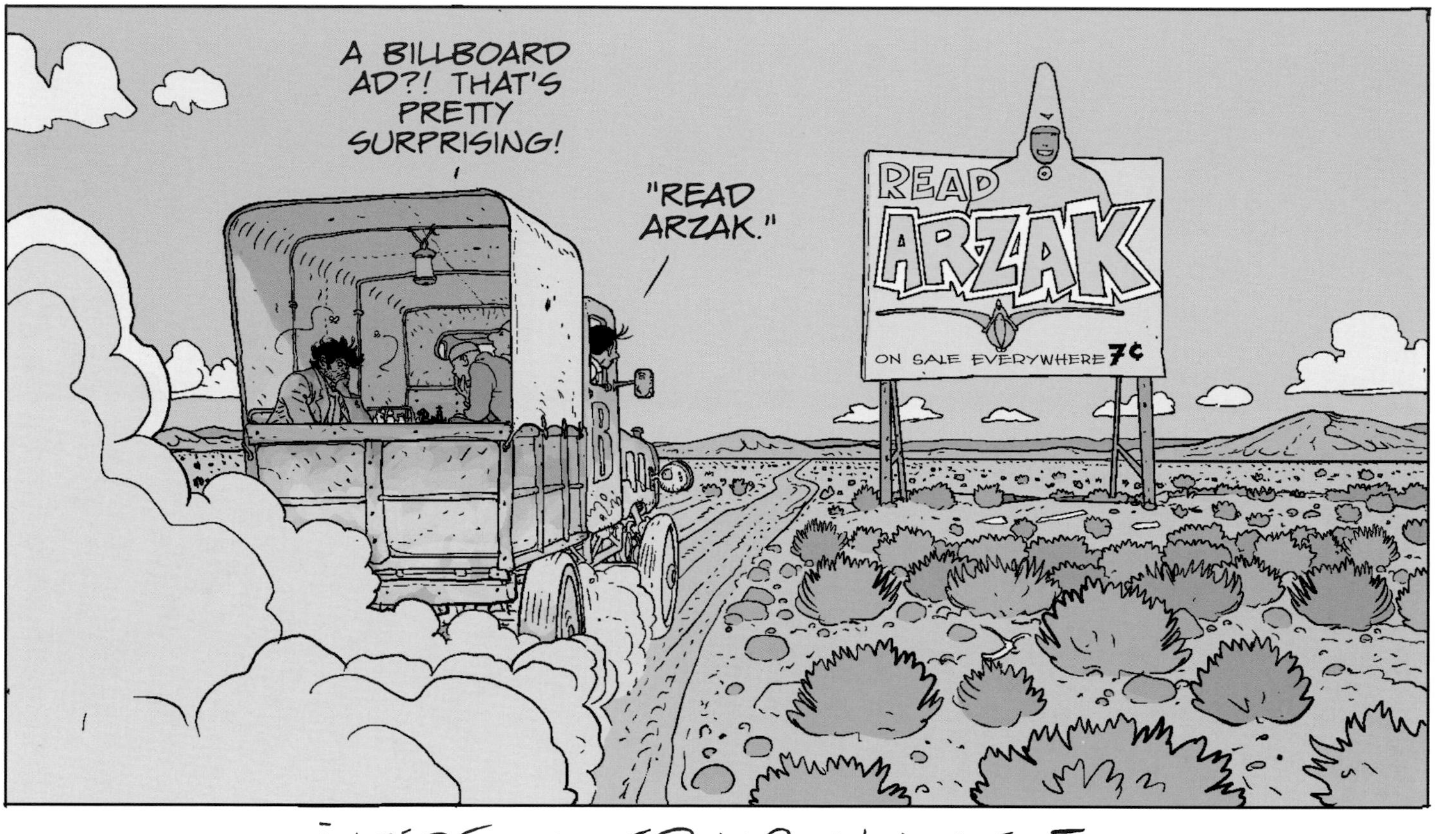

A BILLBOARD AD?! THAT'S PRETTY SURPRISING!
"READ ARZAK."
READ
ARZAK
ON SALE EVERYWHERE 7¢
B

INSIDE MOEBIUS VOLUME 5.

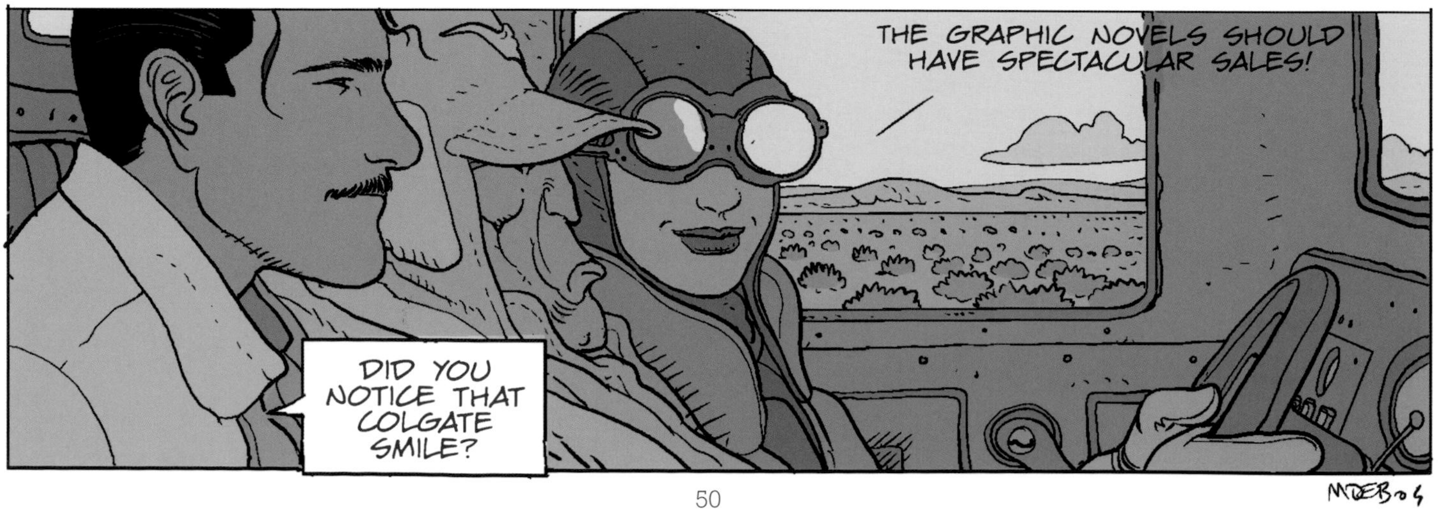

THE GRAPHIC NOVELS SHOULD HAVE SPECTACULAR SALES!
DID YOU NOTICE THAT COLGATE SMILE?

MOEB 04

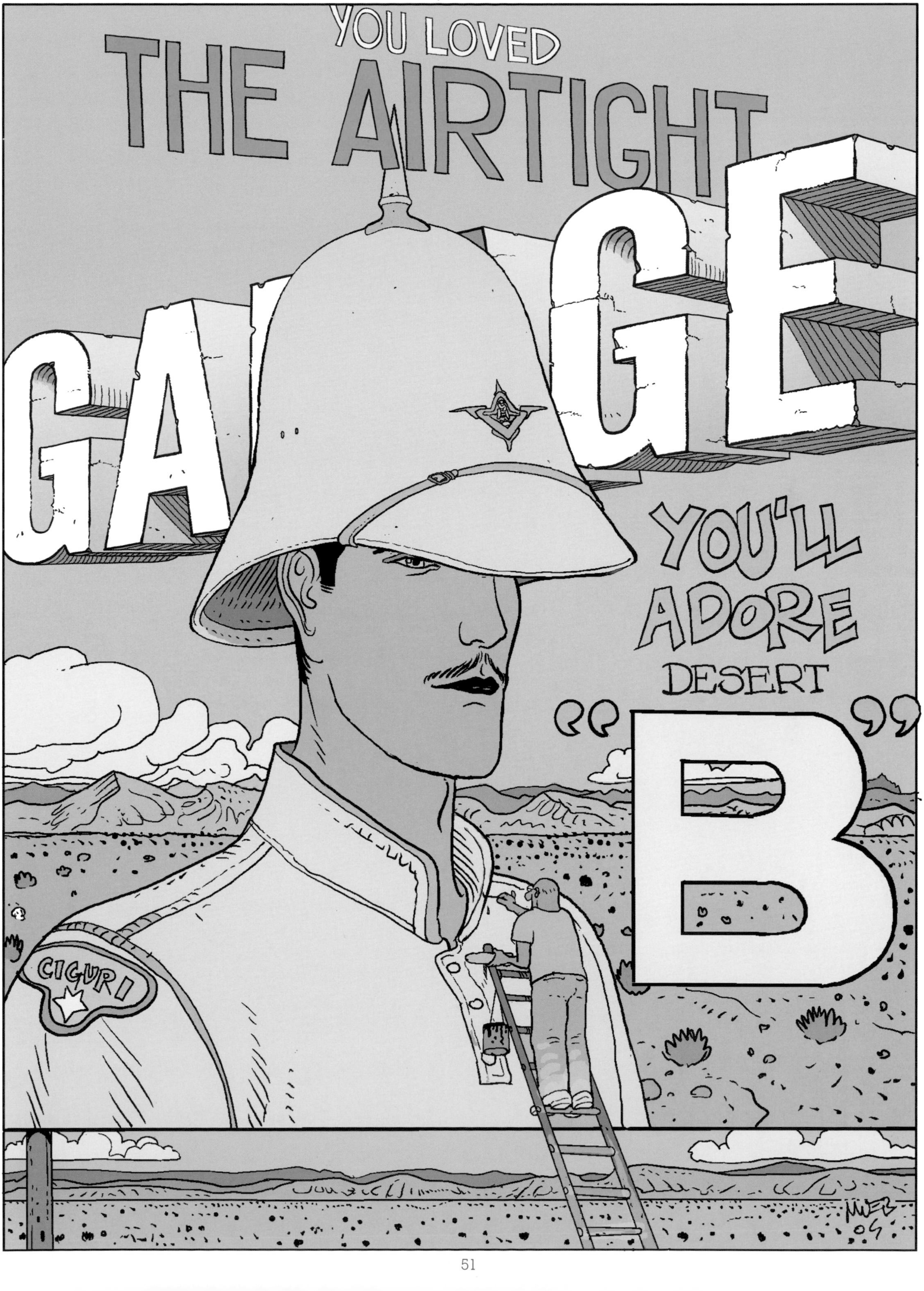
YOU LOVED
THE AIRTIGHT
GA
GE
YOU'LL
ADORE
DESERT
"B"
CIGURI
MŒB 05

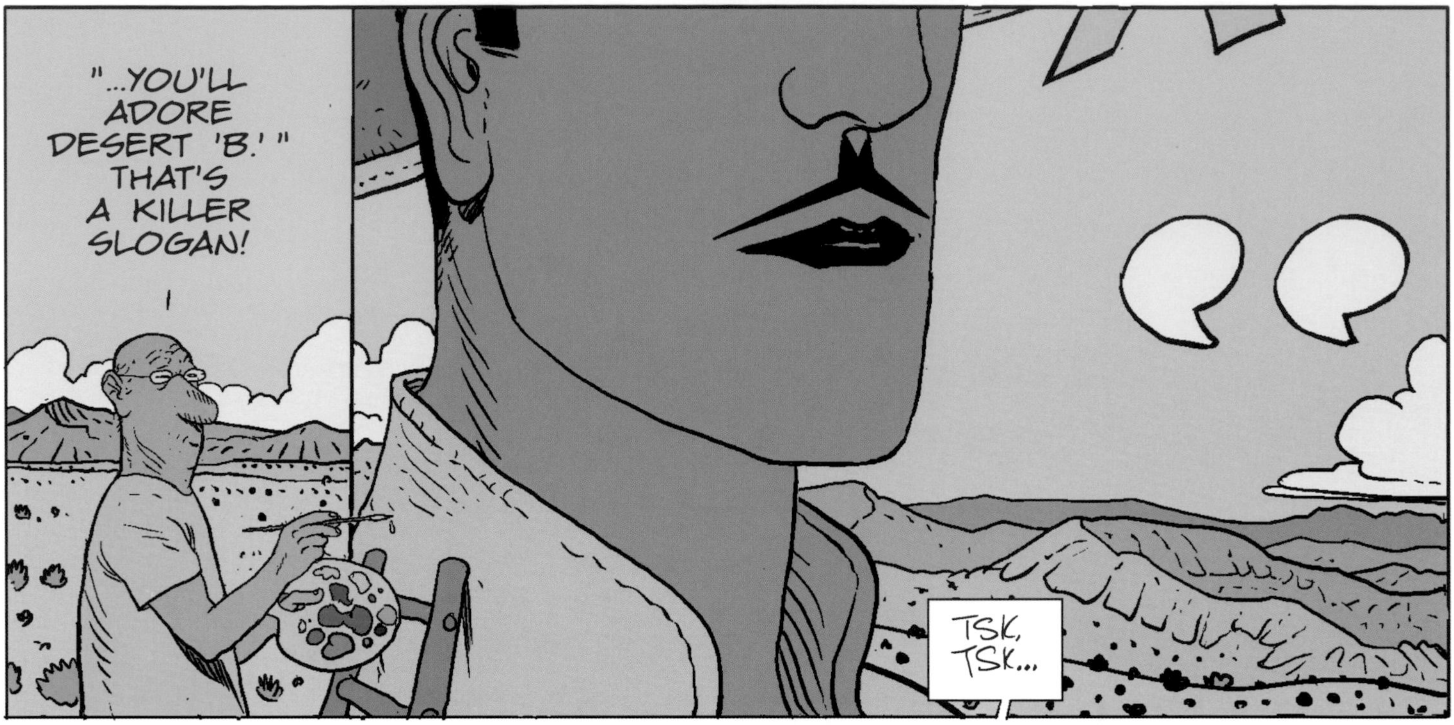
"...YOU'LL ADORE DESERT 'B.' " THAT'S A KILLER SLOGAN!
TSK, TSK...

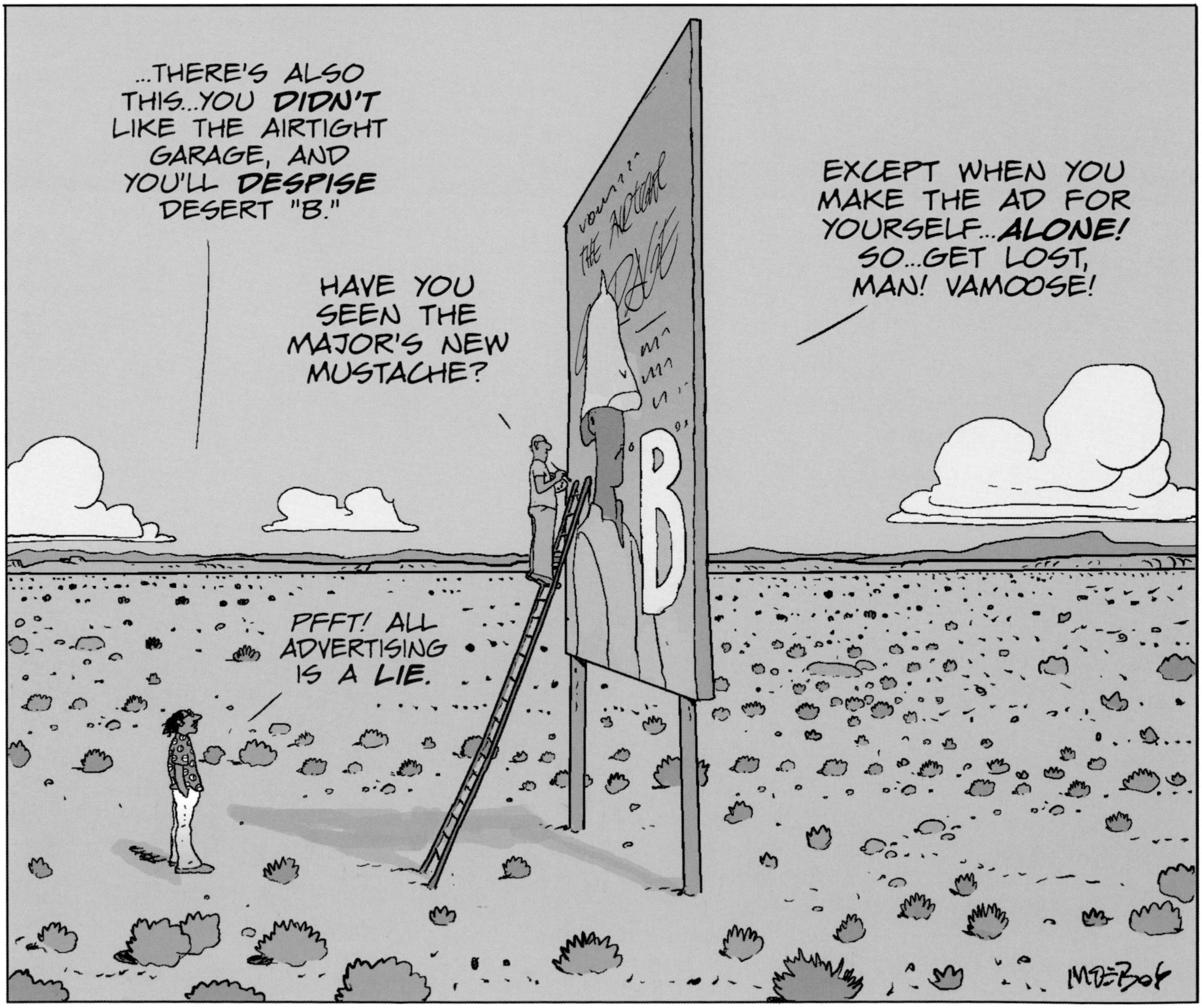
...THERE'S ALSO THIS...YOU **DIDN'T** LIKE THE AIRTIGHT GARAGE, AND YOU'LL **DESPISE** DESERT "B."
HAVE YOU SEEN THE MAJOR'S NEW MUSTACHE?
EXCEPT WHEN YOU MAKE THE AD FOR YOURSELF...**ALONE!** SO...GET LOST, MAN! VAMOOSE!
PFFT! ALL ADVERTISING IS A **LIE**.
B
MŒBIUS

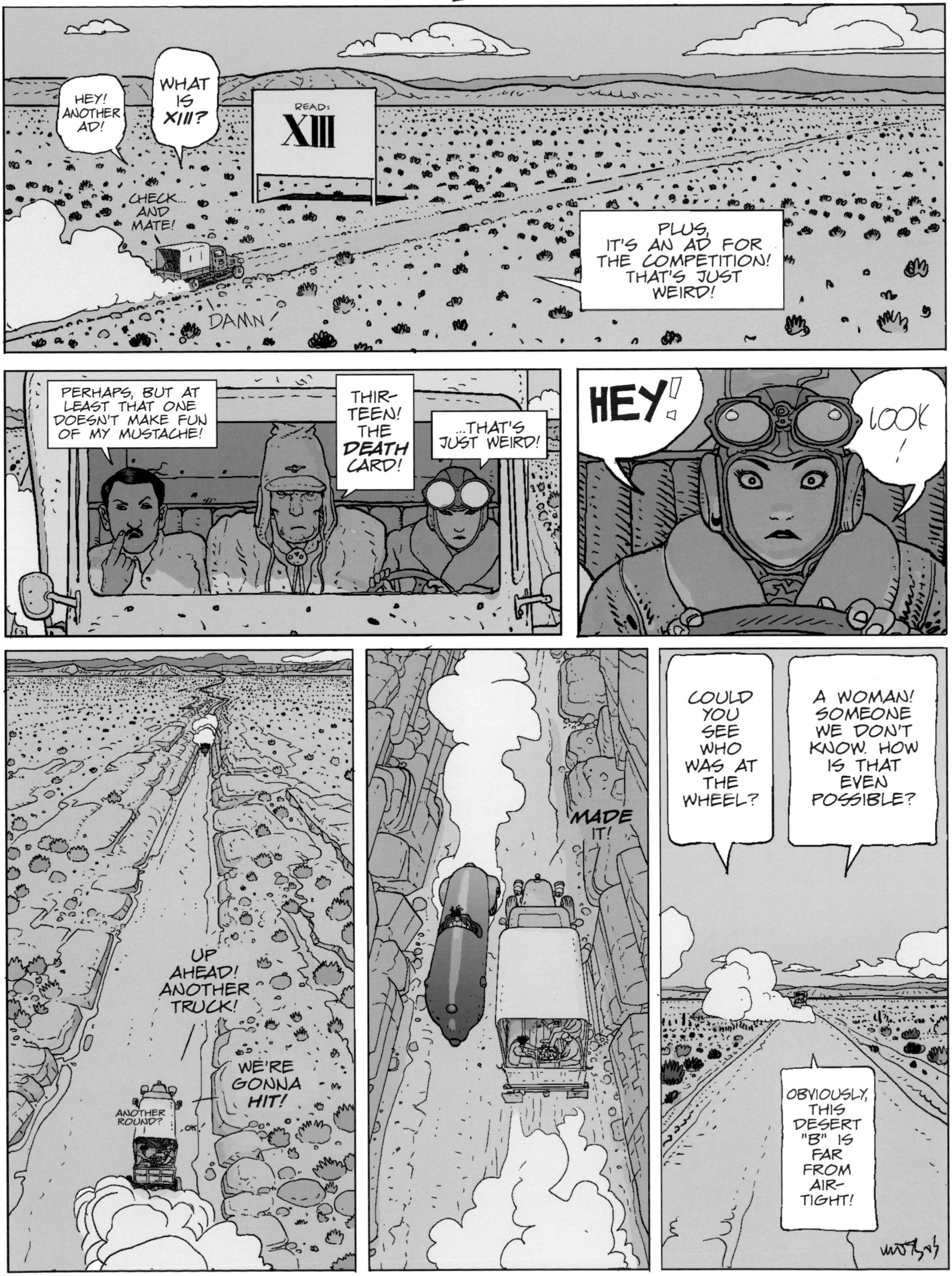
HEY! ANOTHER AD!
WHAT IS XIII?
READ: XIII
CHECK... AND MATE!
DAMN!
PLUS, IT'S AN AD FOR THE COMPETITION! THAT'S JUST WEIRD!
PERHAPS, BUT AT LEAST THAT ONE DOESN'T MAKE FUN OF MY MUSTACHE!
THIR-TEEN! THE DEATH CARD!
...THAT'S JUST WEIRD!
HEY!
LOOK!
UP AHEAD! ANOTHER TRUCK!
WE'RE GONNA HIT!
ANOTHER ROUND?
OK!
MADE IT!
COULD YOU SEE WHO WAS AT THE WHEEL?
A WOMAN! SOMEONE WE DON'T KNOW. HOW IS THAT EVEN POSSIBLE?
OBVIOUSLY, THIS DESERT "B" IS FAR FROM AIR-TIGHT!

30

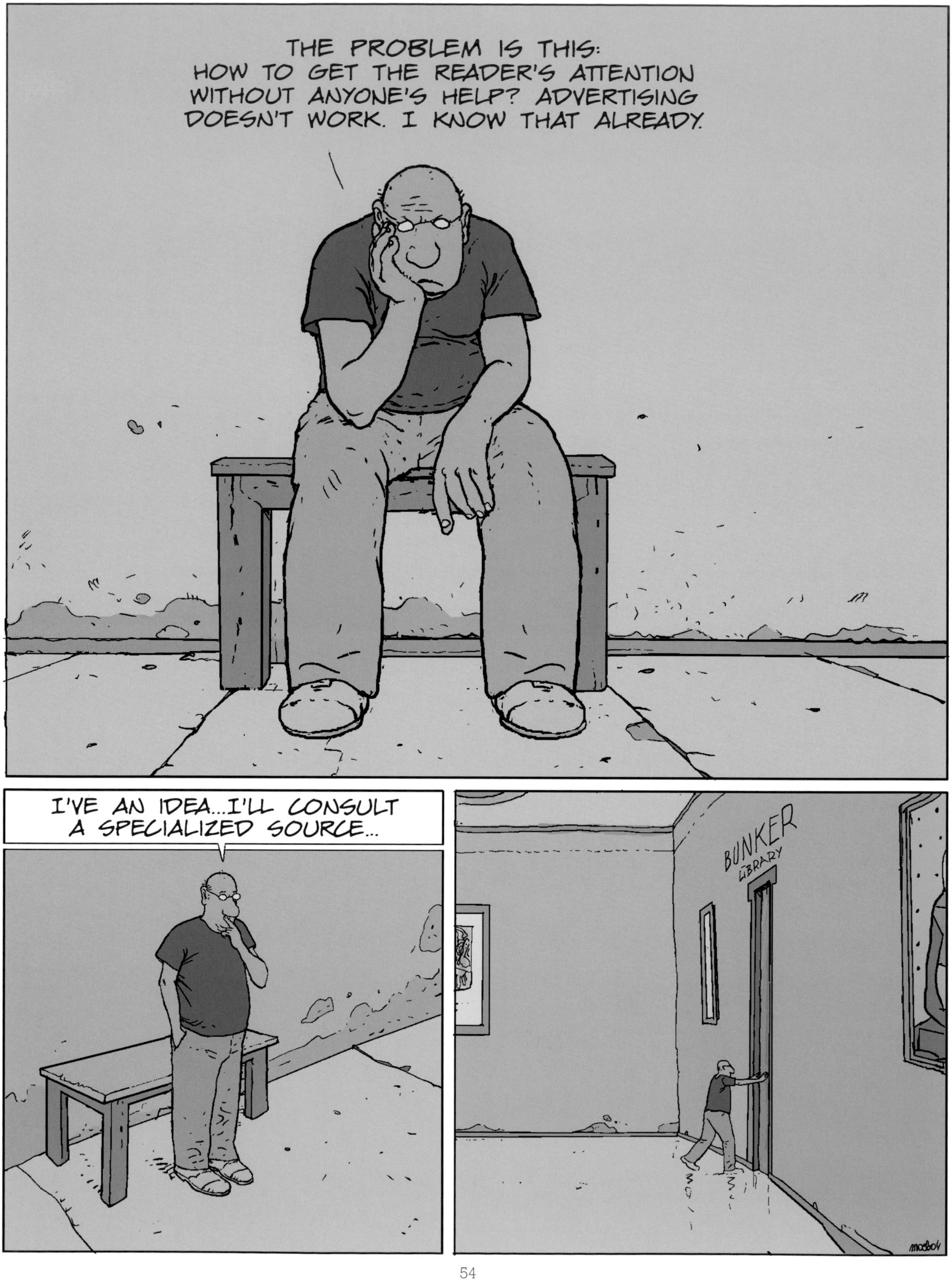
THE PROBLEM IS THIS: HOW TO GET THE READER'S ATTENTION WITHOUT ANYONE'S HELP? ADVERTISING DOESN'T WORK. I KNOW THAT ALREADY.
I'VE AN IDEA...I'LL CONSULT A SPECIALIZED SOURCE...
BUNKER
LIBRARY
moebius 04

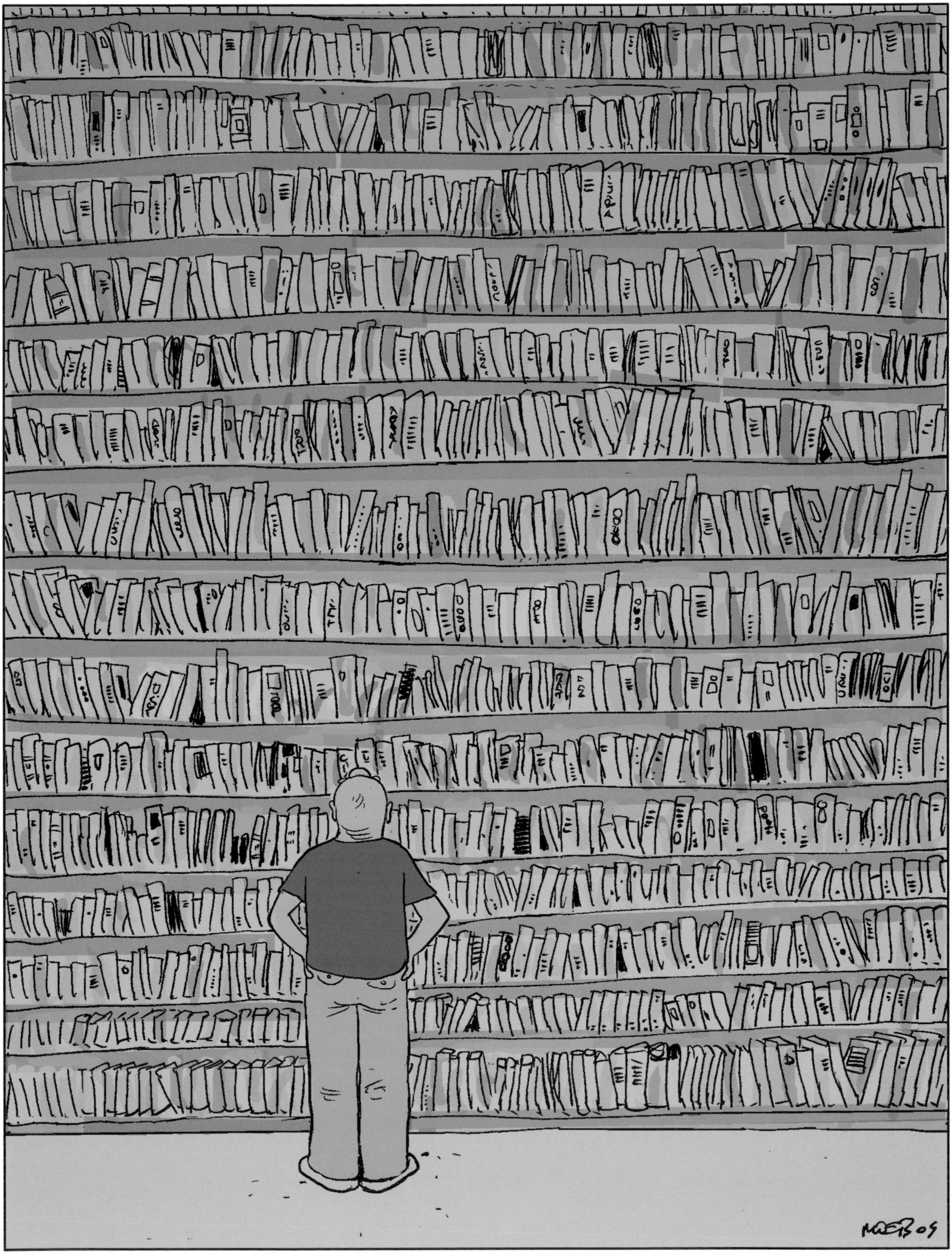

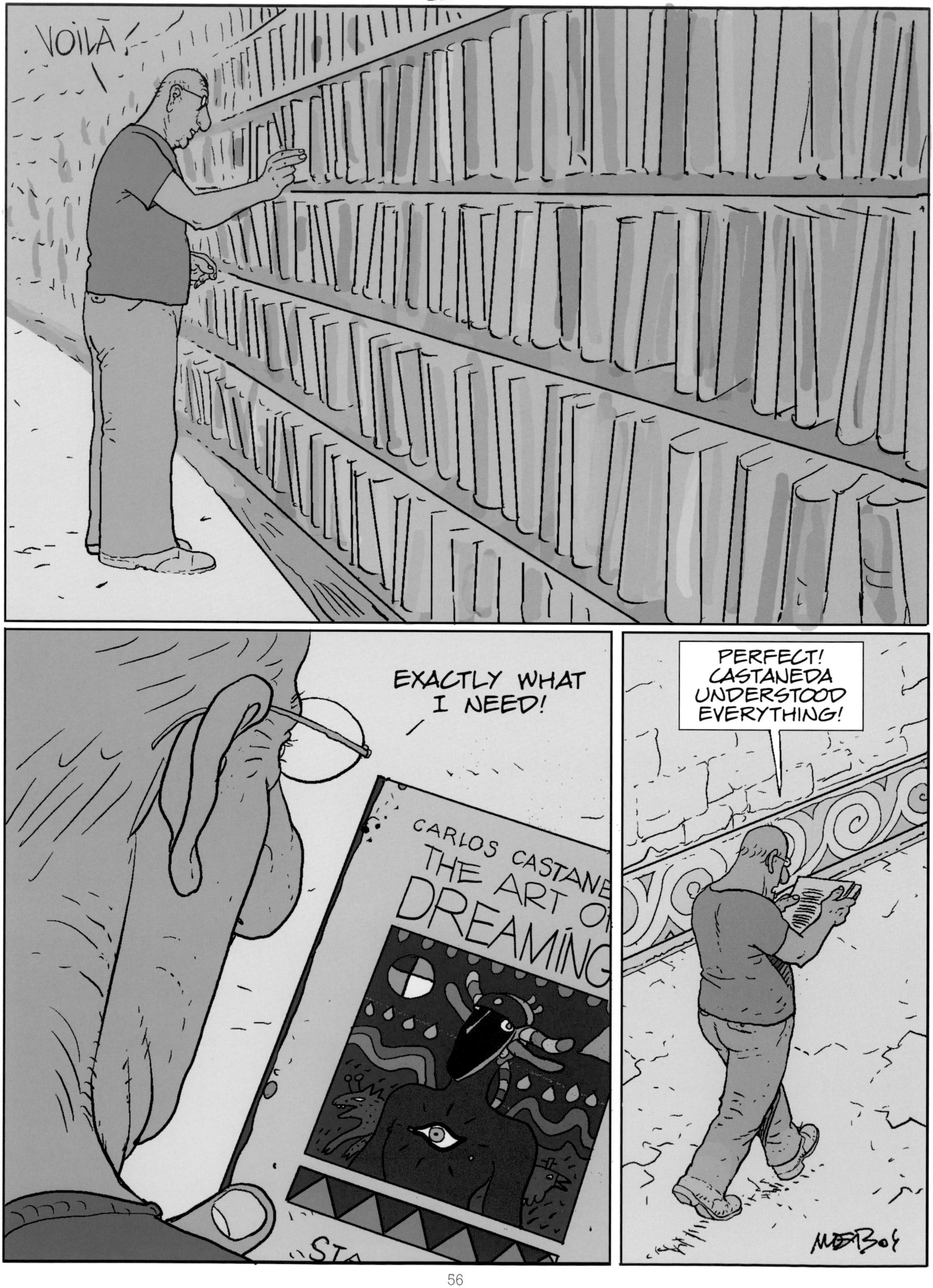
VOILÀ!
EXACTLY WHAT I NEED!
DREAMING
PERFECT! CASTANEDA UNDERSTOOD EVERYTHING!

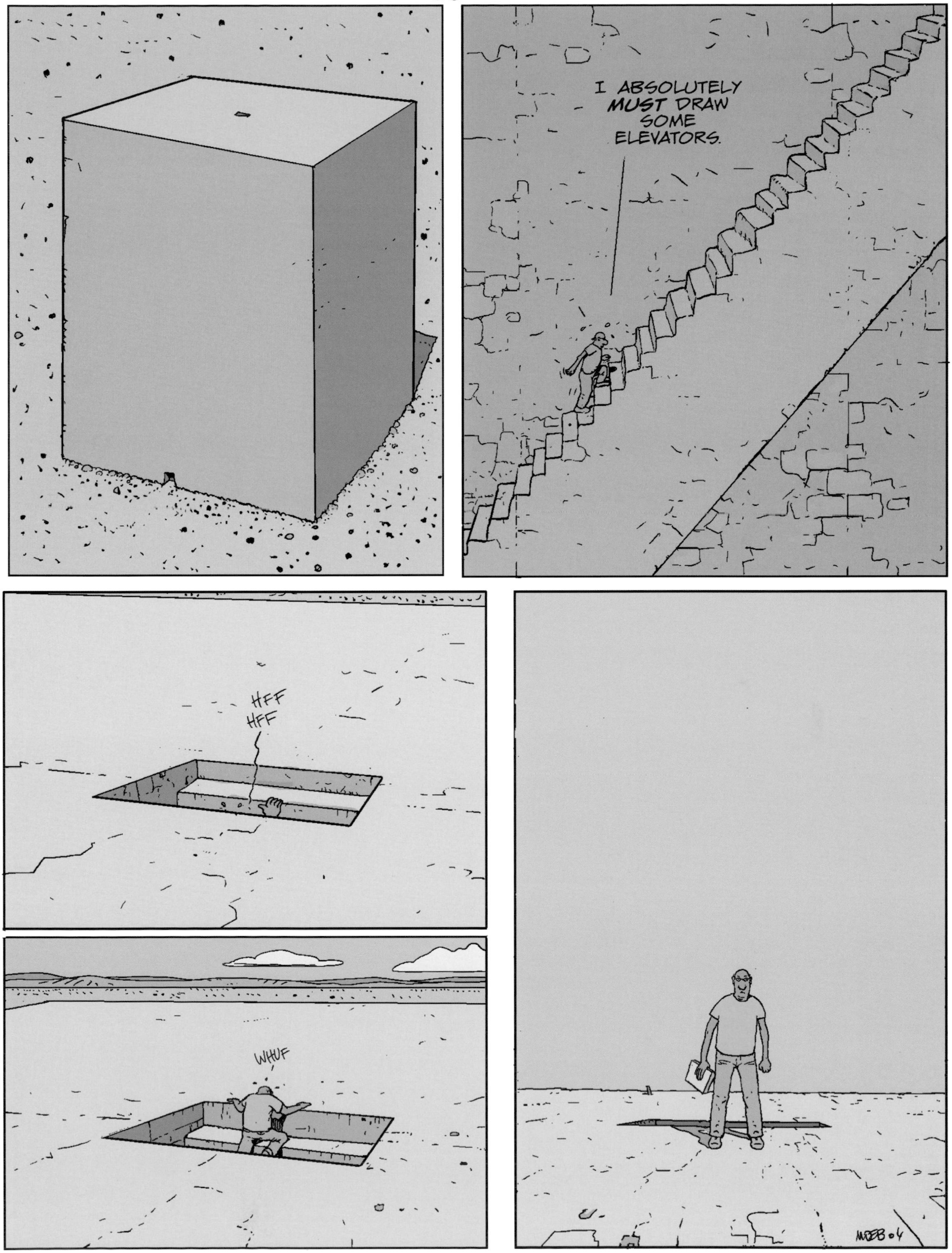
I ABSOLUTELY MUST DRAW SOME ELEVATORS.
HFF HFF
WHUF
MŒB 04

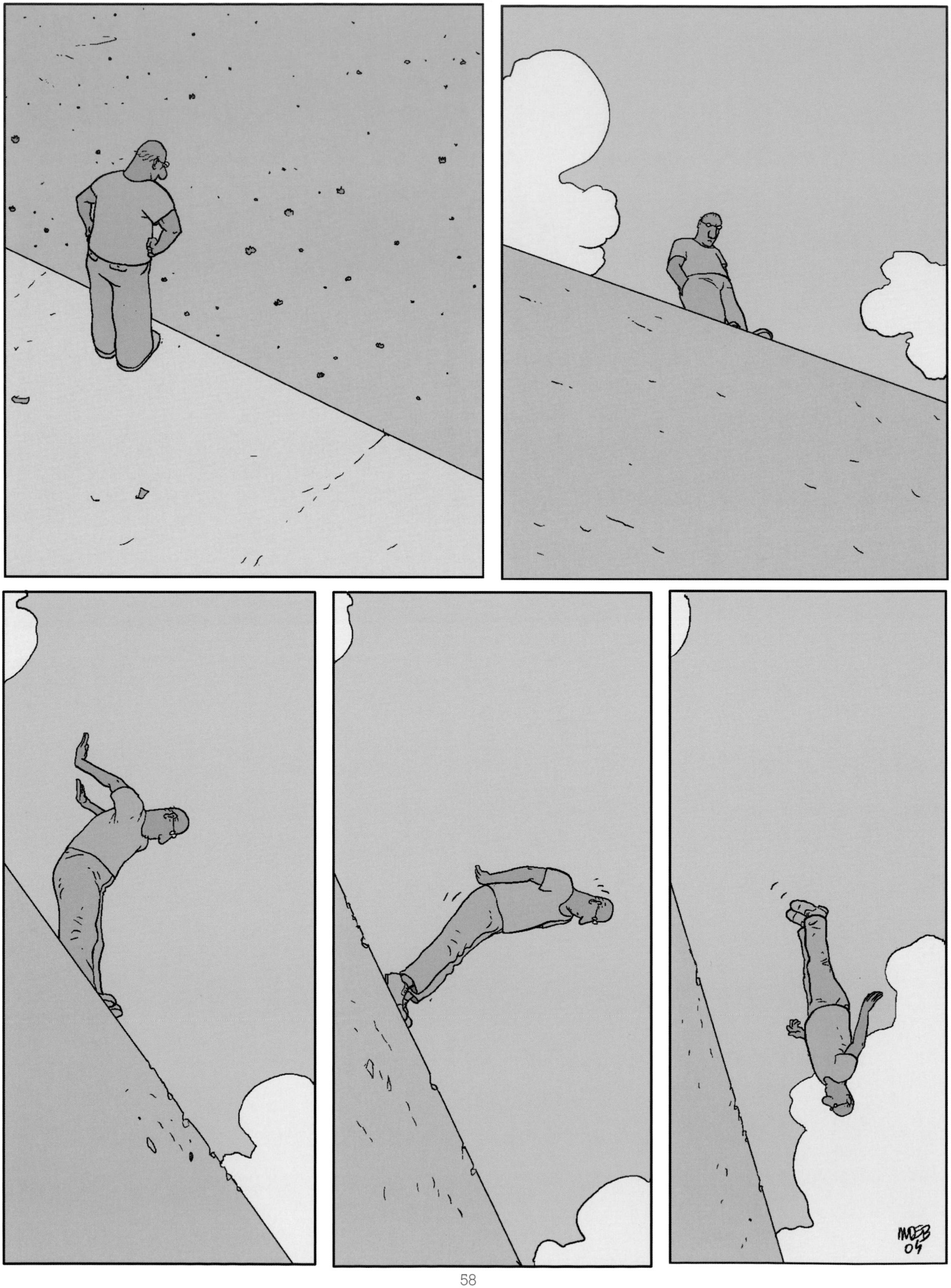
MOEB
04

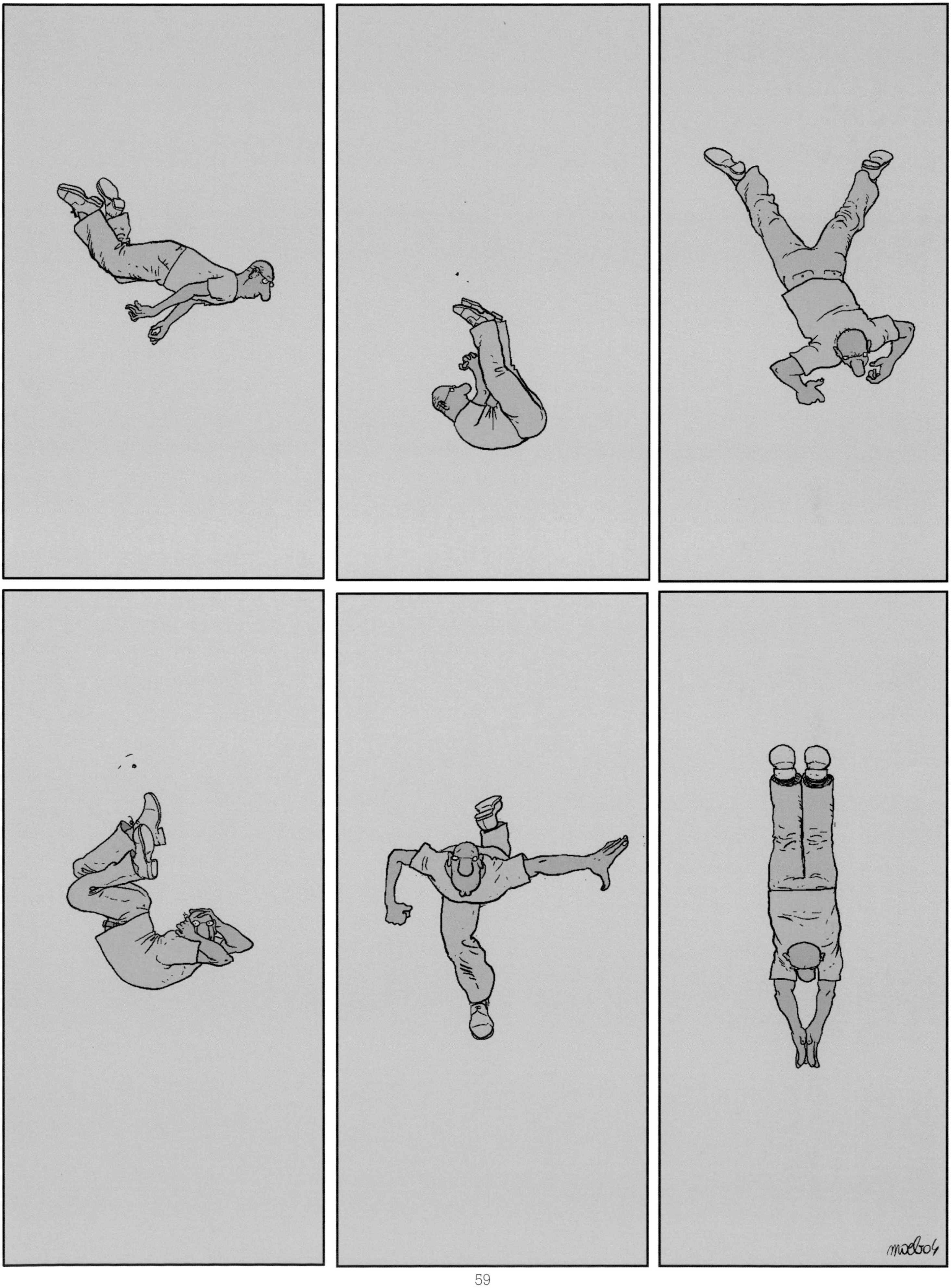

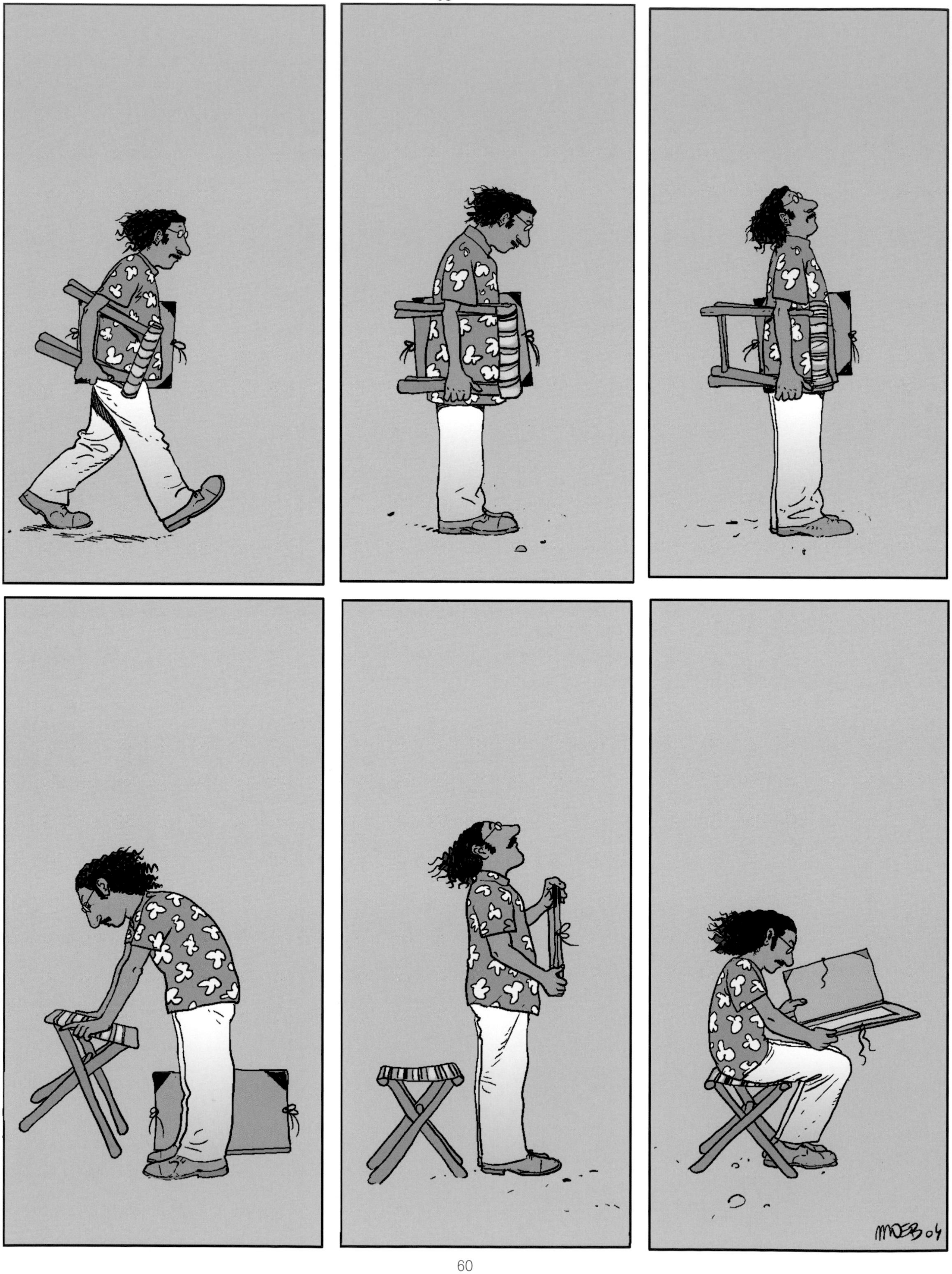
MŒBIUS 04

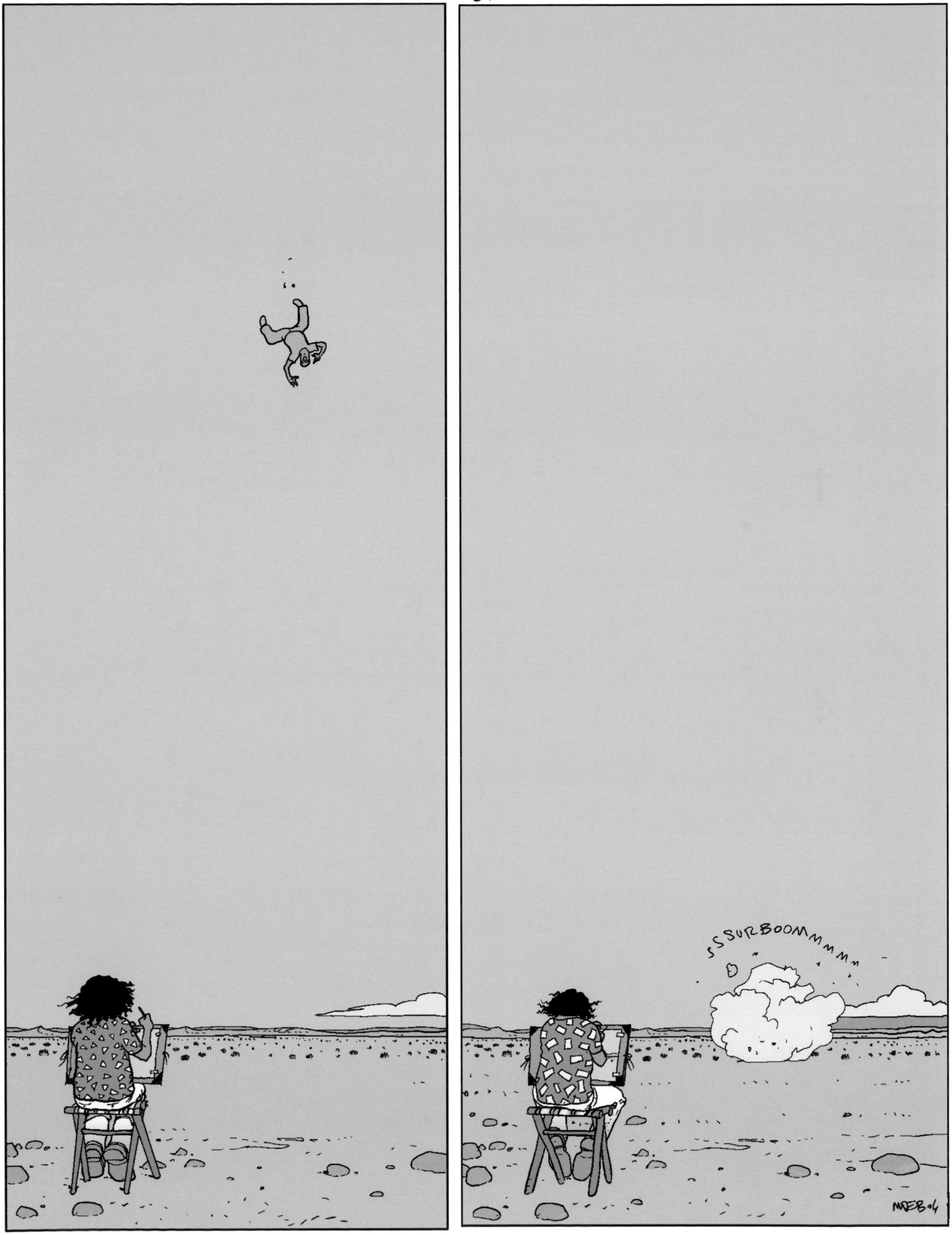

sSSURBOOMMMMM
MŒB 04

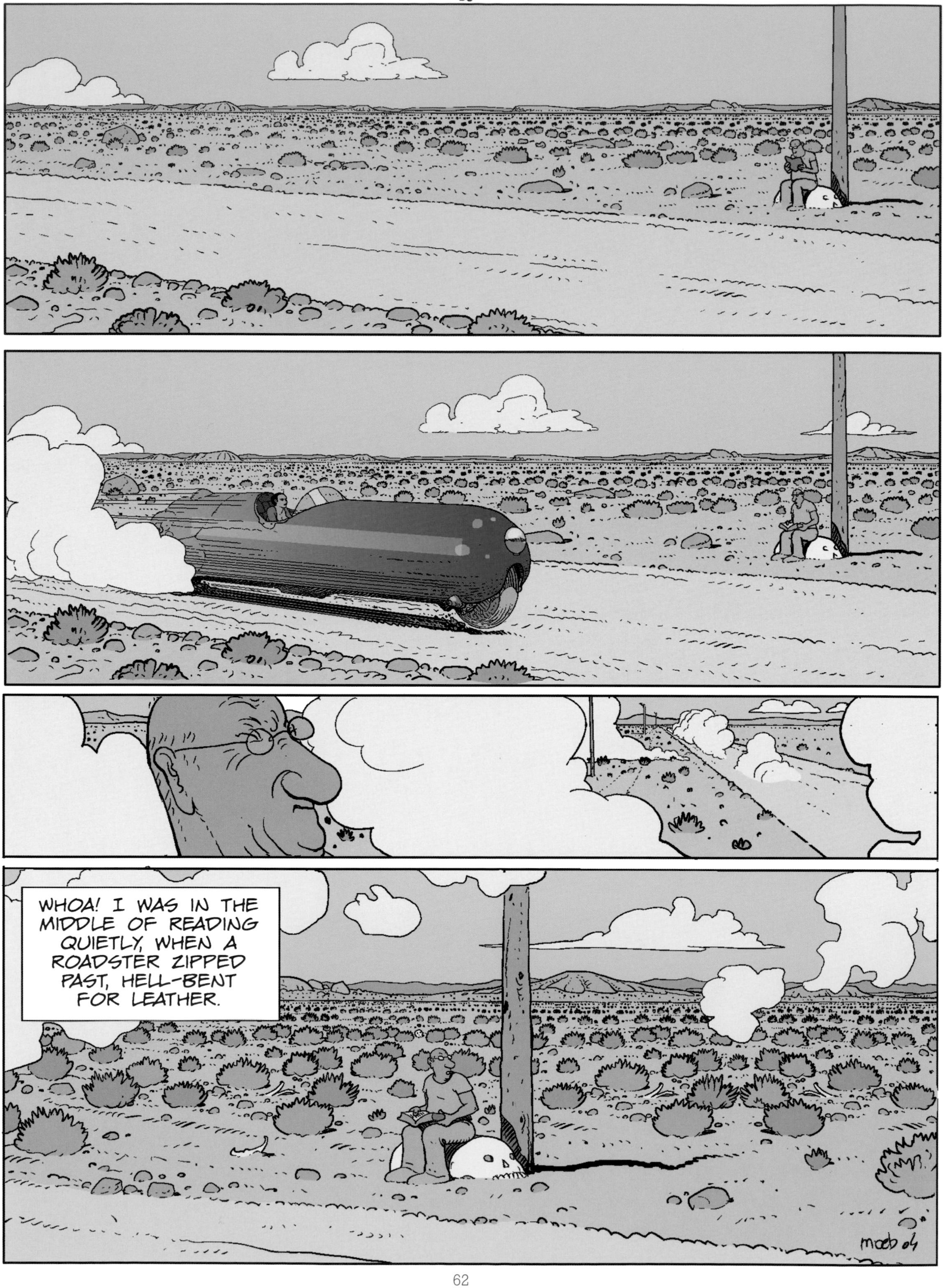
WHOA! I WAS IN THE MIDDLE OF READING QUIETLY, WHEN A ROADSTER ZIPPED PAST, HELL-BENT FOR LEATHER.

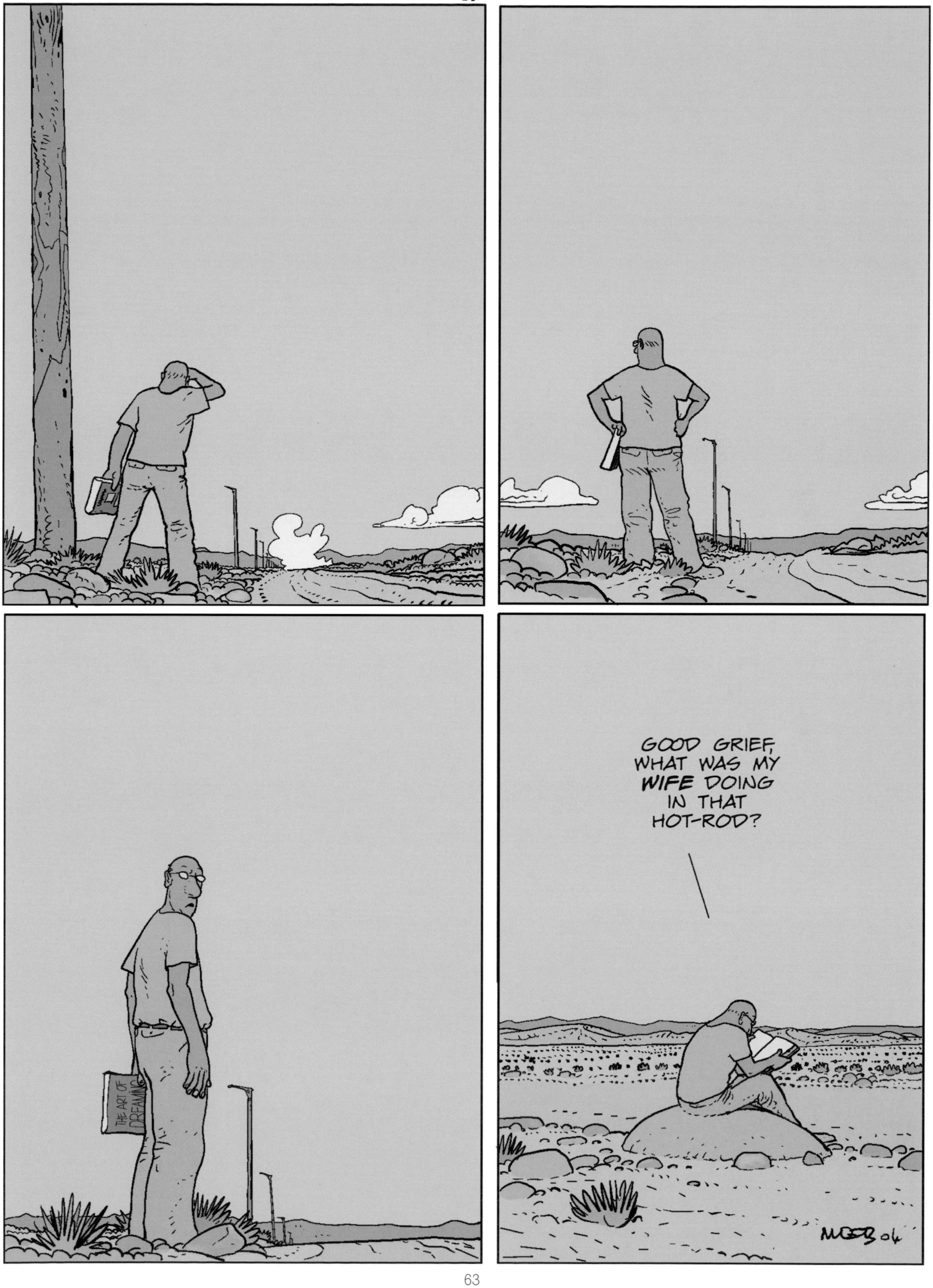
THE ART OF DREAMING
GOOD GRIEF, WHAT WAS MY **WIFE** DOING IN THAT HOT-ROD?
MŒBIUS 04

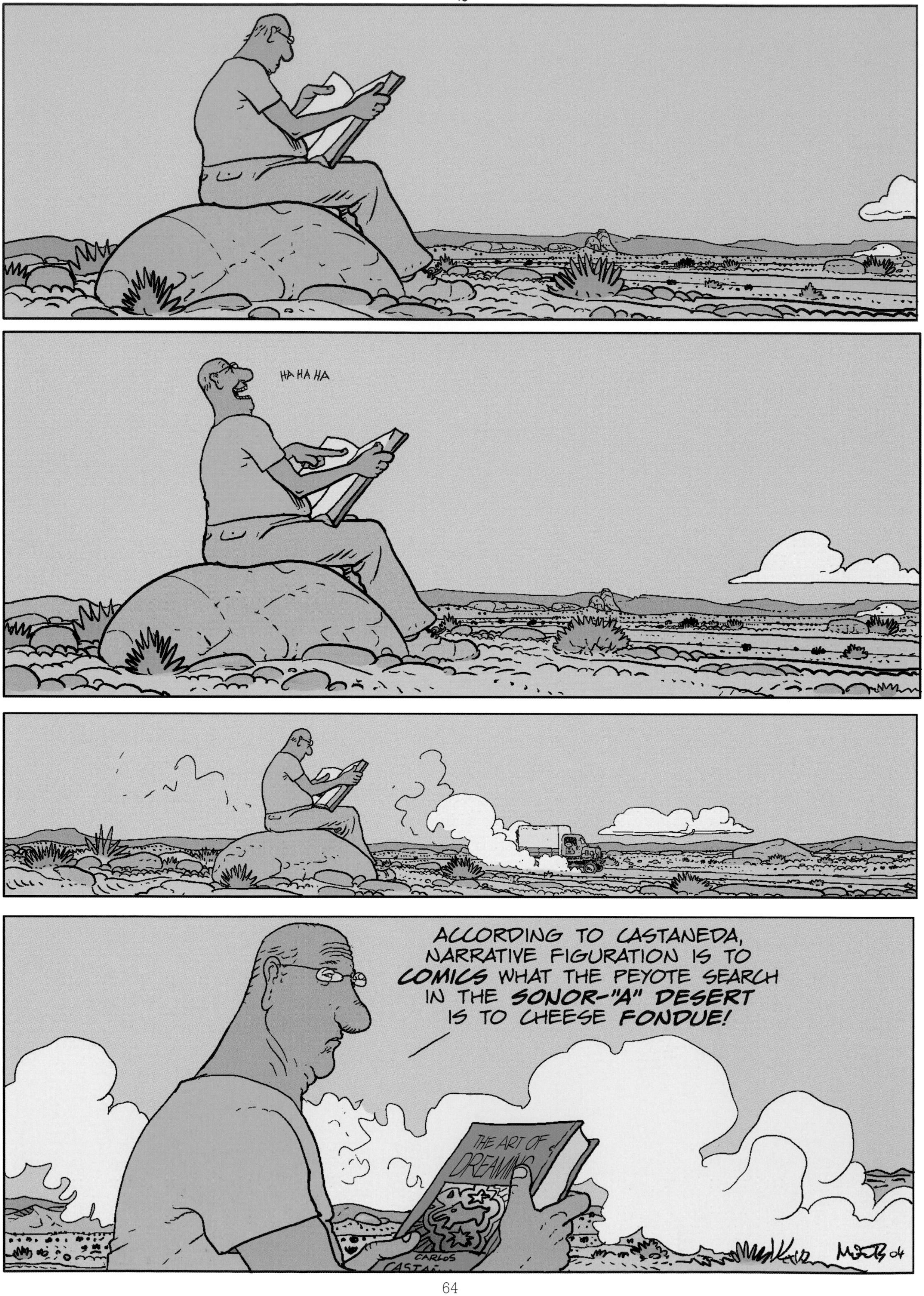
HA HA HA
ACCORDING TO CASTANEDA, NARRATIVE FIGURATION IS TO COMICS WHAT THE PEYOTE SEARCH IN THE SONOR-"A" DESERT IS TO CHEESE FONDUE!
THE ART OF
CARLOS

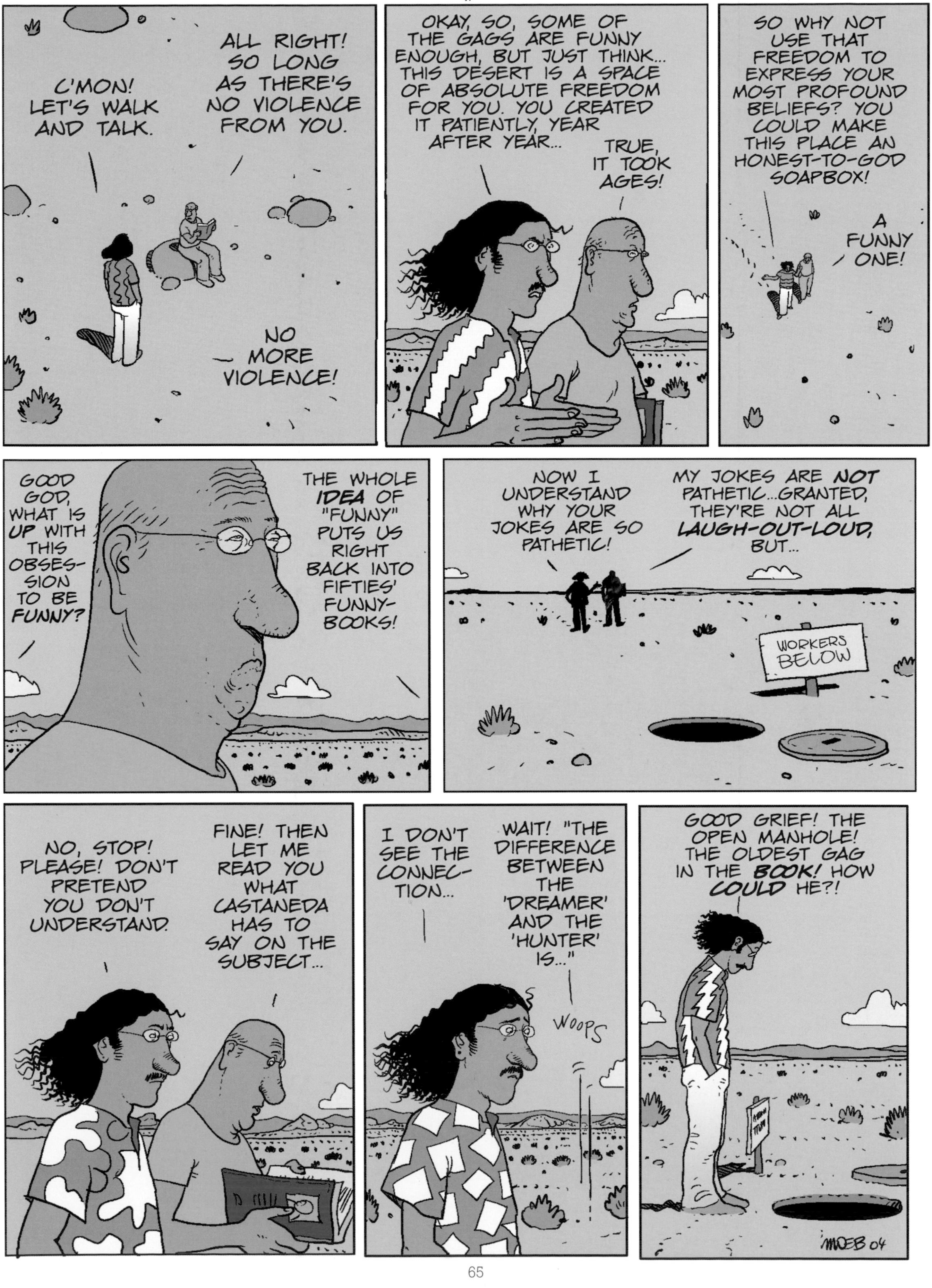
C'MON! LET'S WALK AND TALK.
ALL RIGHT! SO LONG AS THERE'S NO VIOLENCE FROM YOU.
NO MORE VIOLENCE!
OKAY, SO, SOME OF THE GAGS ARE FUNNY ENOUGH, BUT JUST THINK... THIS DESERT IS A SPACE OF ABSOLUTE FREEDOM FOR YOU. YOU CREATED IT PATIENTLY, YEAR AFTER YEAR...
TRUE, IT TOOK AGES!
SO WHY NOT USE THAT FREEDOM TO EXPRESS YOUR MOST PROFOUND BELIEFS? YOU COULD MAKE THIS PLACE AN HONEST-TO-GOD SOAPBOX!
A FUNNY ONE!
GOOD GOD, WHAT IS **UP** WITH THIS OBSES-SION TO BE **FUNNY**?
THE WHOLE **IDEA** OF "FUNNY" PUTS US RIGHT BACK INTO FIFTIES' FUNNY-BOOKS!
NOW I UNDERSTAND WHY YOUR JOKES ARE SO PATHETIC!
MY JOKES ARE **NOT** PATHETIC...GRANTED, THEY'RE NOT ALL **LAUGH-OUT-LOUD,** BUT...
WORKERS BELOW
NO, STOP! PLEASE! DON'T PRETEND YOU DON'T UNDERSTAND.
FINE! THEN LET ME READ YOU WHAT CASTANEDA HAS TO SAY ON THE SUBJECT...
I DON'T SEE THE CONNEC-TION...
WAIT! "THE DIFFERENCE BETWEEN THE 'DREAMER' AND THE 'HUNTER' IS..."
WOOPS
GOOD GRIEF! THE OPEN MANHOLE! THE OLDEST GAG IN THE **BOOK!** HOW **COULD** HE?!
MOEB 04

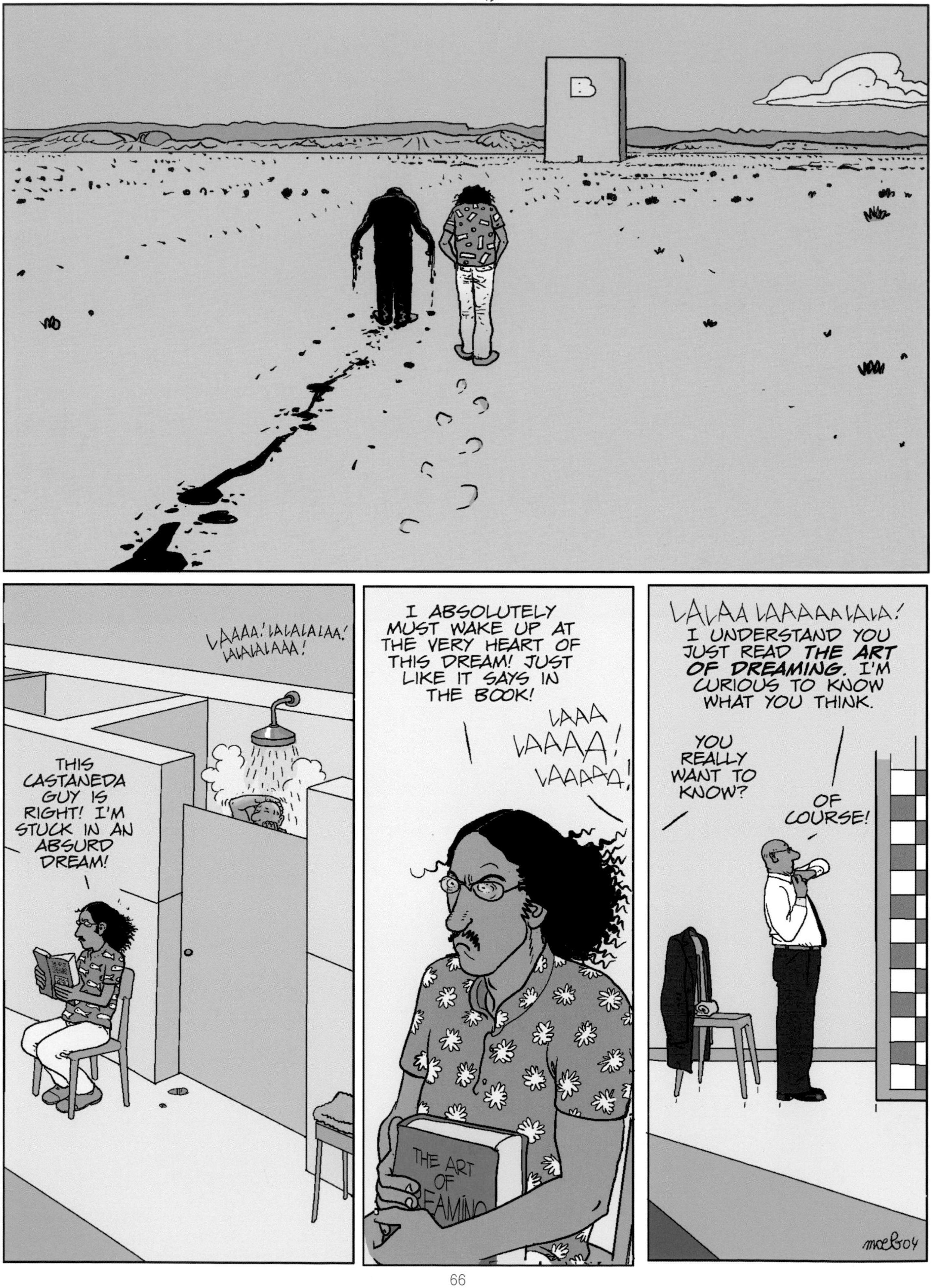
LAAAA! LALALALAA! LALALALAAA!
THIS CASTANEDA GUY IS RIGHT! I'M STUCK IN AN ABSURD DREAM!
I ABSOLUTELY MUST WAKE UP AT THE VERY HEART OF THIS DREAM! JUST LIKE IT SAYS IN THE BOOK!
LAAA LAAAA! LAAAAA!
THE ART OF
LALAA LAAAAALALA!
I UNDERSTAND YOU JUST READ **THE ART OF DREAMING**. I'M CURIOUS TO KNOW WHAT YOU THINK.
YOU REALLY WANT TO KNOW?
OF COURSE!
moebi04

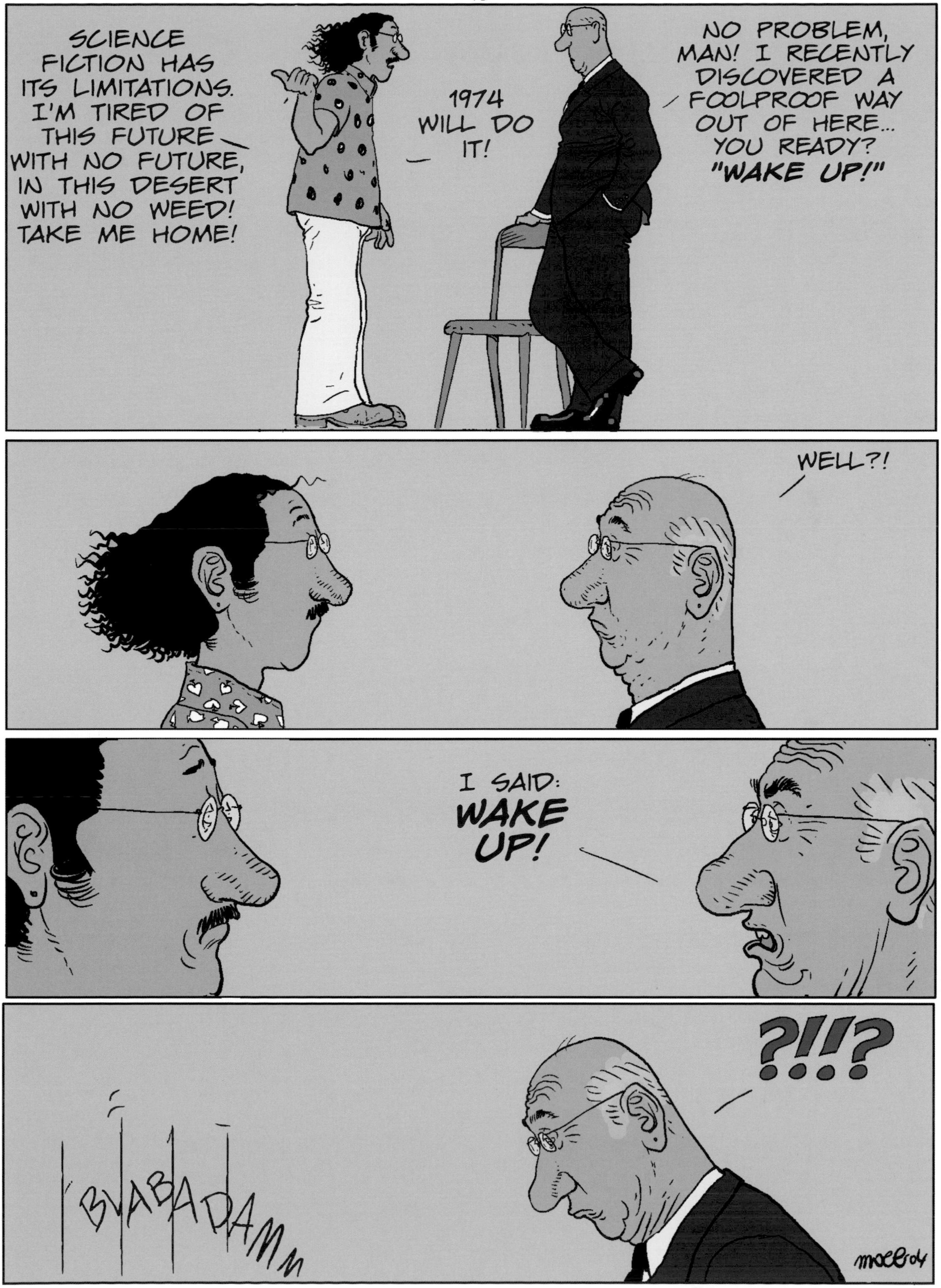
SCIENCE FICTION HAS ITS LIMITATIONS. I'M TIRED OF THIS FUTURE WITH NO FUTURE, IN THIS DESERT WITH NO WEED! TAKE ME HOME!
1974 WILL DO IT!
NO PROBLEM, MAN! I RECENTLY DISCOVERED A FOOLPROOF WAY OUT OF HERE... YOU READY? "WAKE UP!"
WELL?!
I SAID: WAKE UP!
BVABADAMM
?!!?
moebius 04

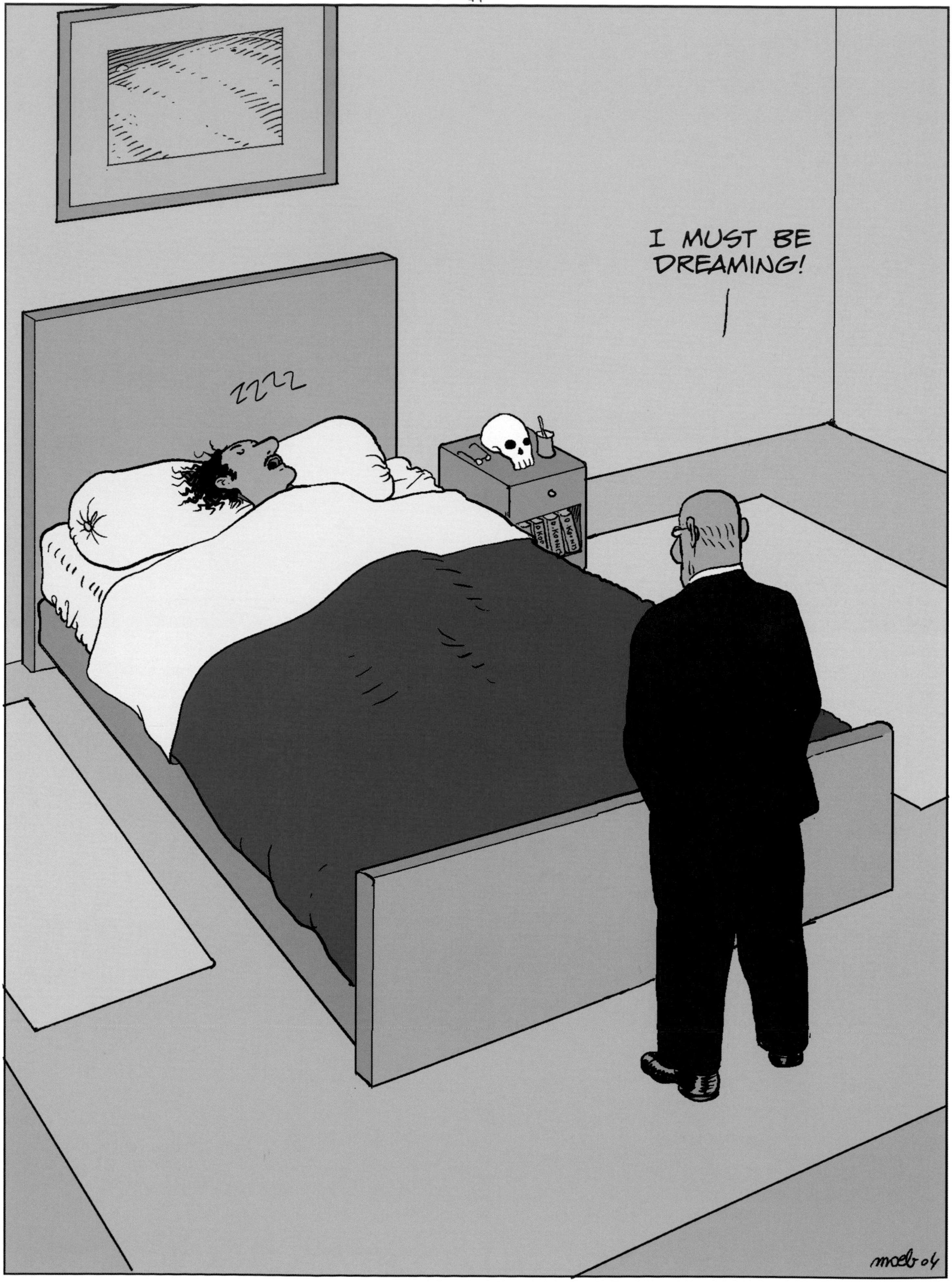
I MUST BE DREAMING!
ZZZZ

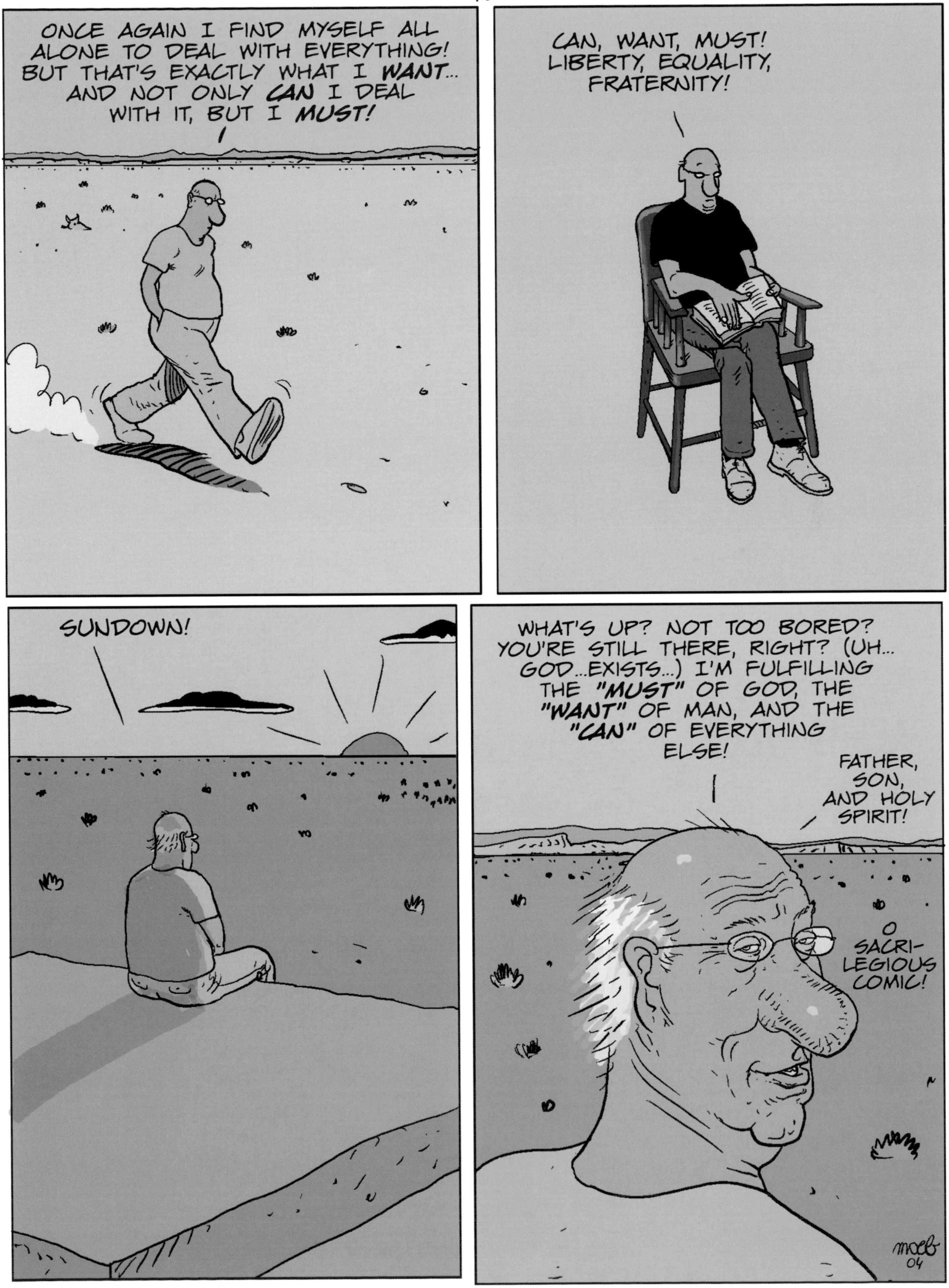
ONCE AGAIN I FIND MYSELF ALL ALONE TO DEAL WITH EVERYTHING! BUT THAT'S EXACTLY WHAT I WANT... AND NOT ONLY CAN I DEAL WITH IT, BUT I MUST!
CAN, WANT, MUST! LIBERTY, EQUALITY, FRATERNITY!
SUNDOWN!
WHAT'S UP? NOT TOO BORED? YOU'RE STILL THERE, RIGHT? (UH... GOD...EXISTS...) I'M FULFILLING THE "MUST" OF GOD, THE "WANT" OF MAN, AND THE "CAN" OF EVERYTHING ELSE!
FATHER, SON, AND HOLY SPIRIT!
O SACRI-LEGIOUS COMIC!
moeb 04

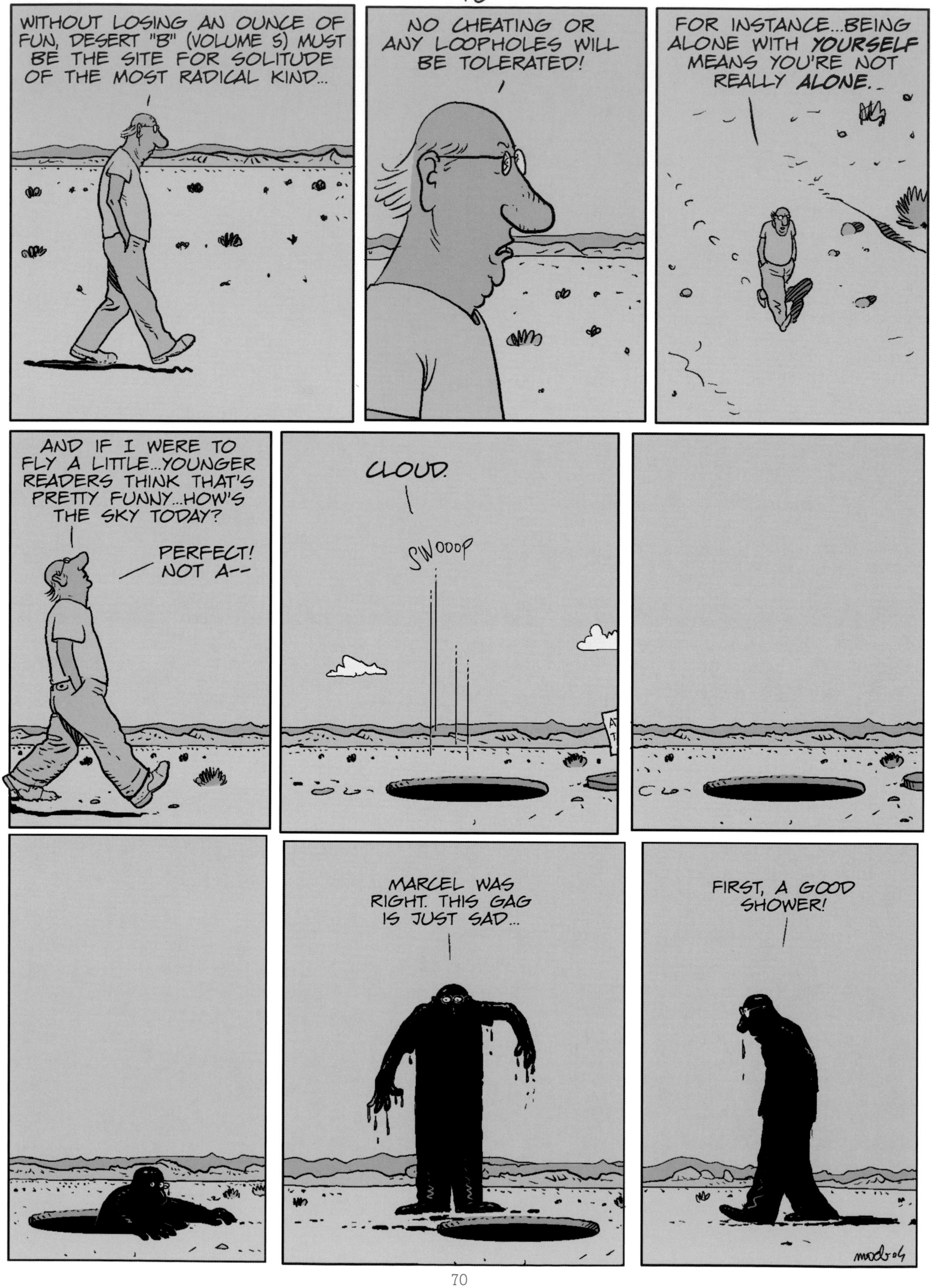
WITHOUT LOSING AN OUNCE OF FUN, DESERT "B" (VOLUME 5) MUST BE THE SITE FOR SOLITUDE OF THE MOST RADICAL KIND...
NO CHEATING OR ANY LOOPHOLES WILL BE TOLERATED!
FOR INSTANCE...BEING ALONE WITH **YOURSELF** MEANS YOU'RE NOT REALLY **ALONE**...
AND IF I WERE TO FLY A LITTLE...YOUNGER READERS THINK THAT'S PRETTY FUNNY...HOW'S THE SKY TODAY?
PERFECT! NOT A--
CLOUD.
SWOOOP
MARCEL WAS RIGHT. THIS GAG IS JUST SAD...
FIRST, A GOOD SHOWER!
modb 04

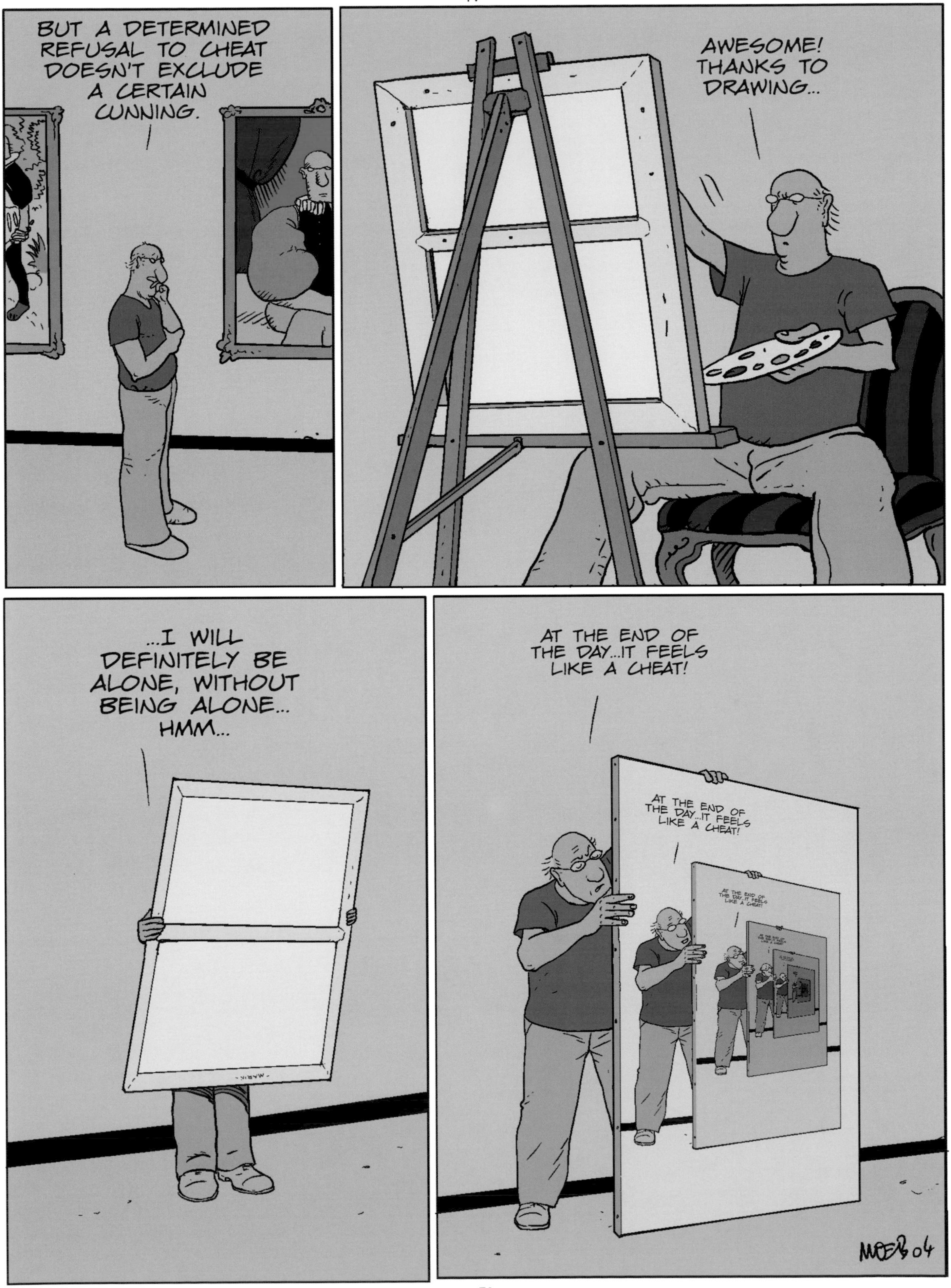
BUT A DETERMINED REFUSAL TO CHEAT DOESN'T EXCLUDE A CERTAIN CUNNING.
AWESOME! THANKS TO DRAWING...
...I WILL DEFINITELY BE ALONE, WITHOUT BEING ALONE... HMM...
AT THE END OF THE DAY...IT FEELS LIKE A CHEAT!
AT THE END OF THE DAY...IT FEELS LIKE A CHEAT!
MOEB 04

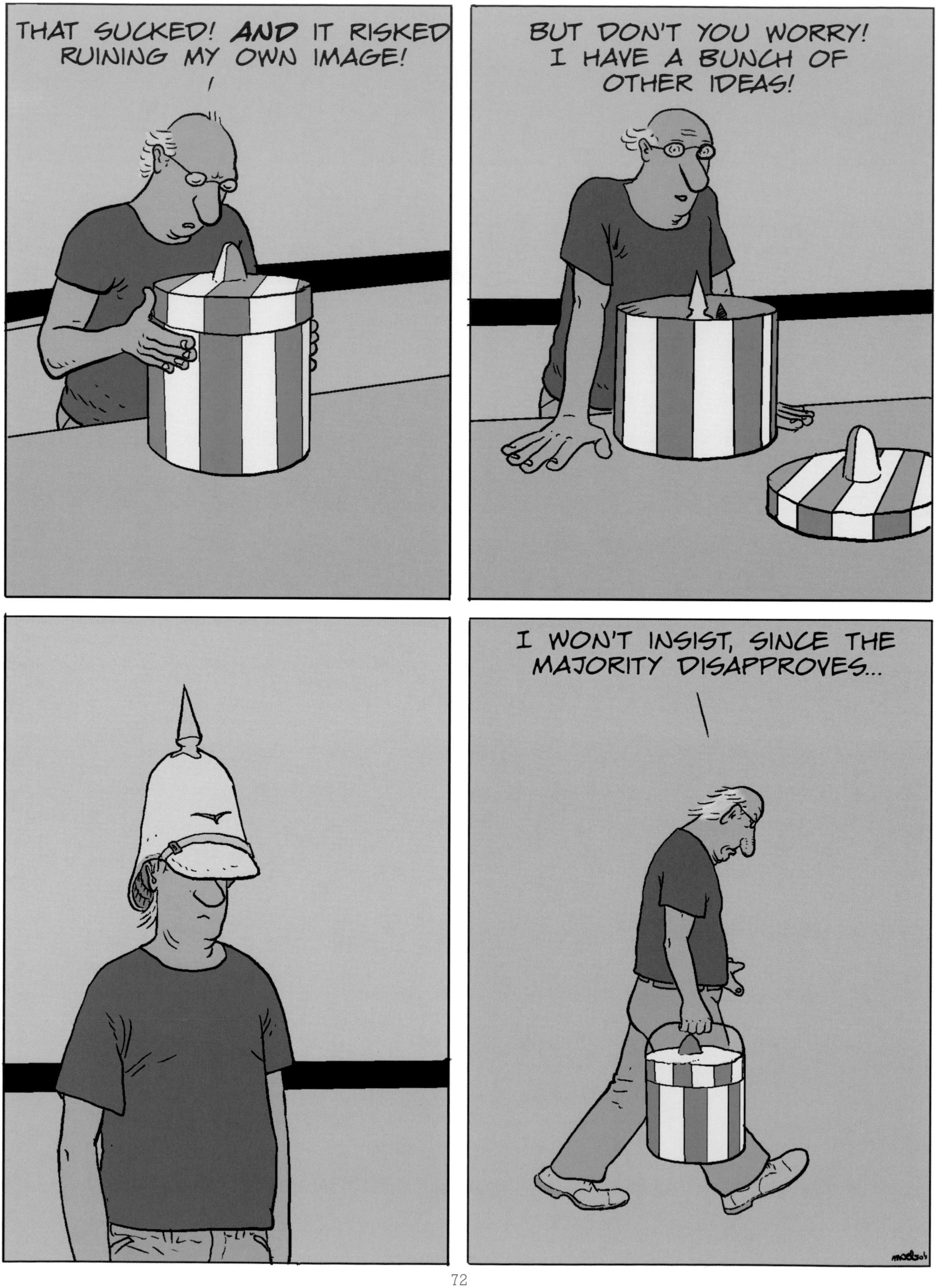
THAT SUCKED! AND IT RISKED RUINING MY OWN IMAGE!
BUT DON'T YOU WORRY! I HAVE A BUNCH OF OTHER IDEAS!
I WON'T INSIST, SINCE THE MAJORITY DISAPPROVES...

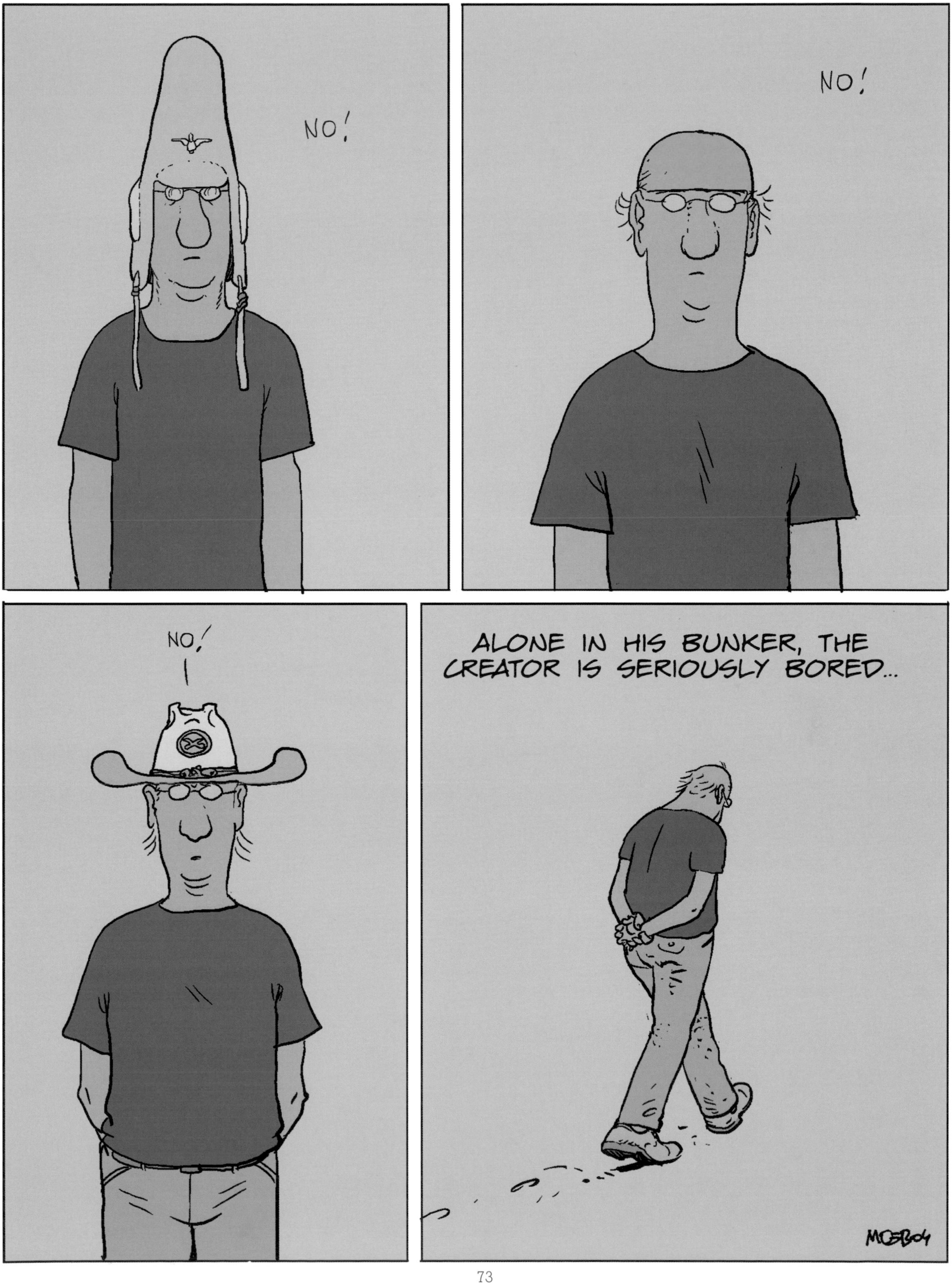
NO!
NO!
NO!
ALONE IN HIS BUNKER, THE CREATOR IS SERIOUSLY BORED...
MOEBIUS 04

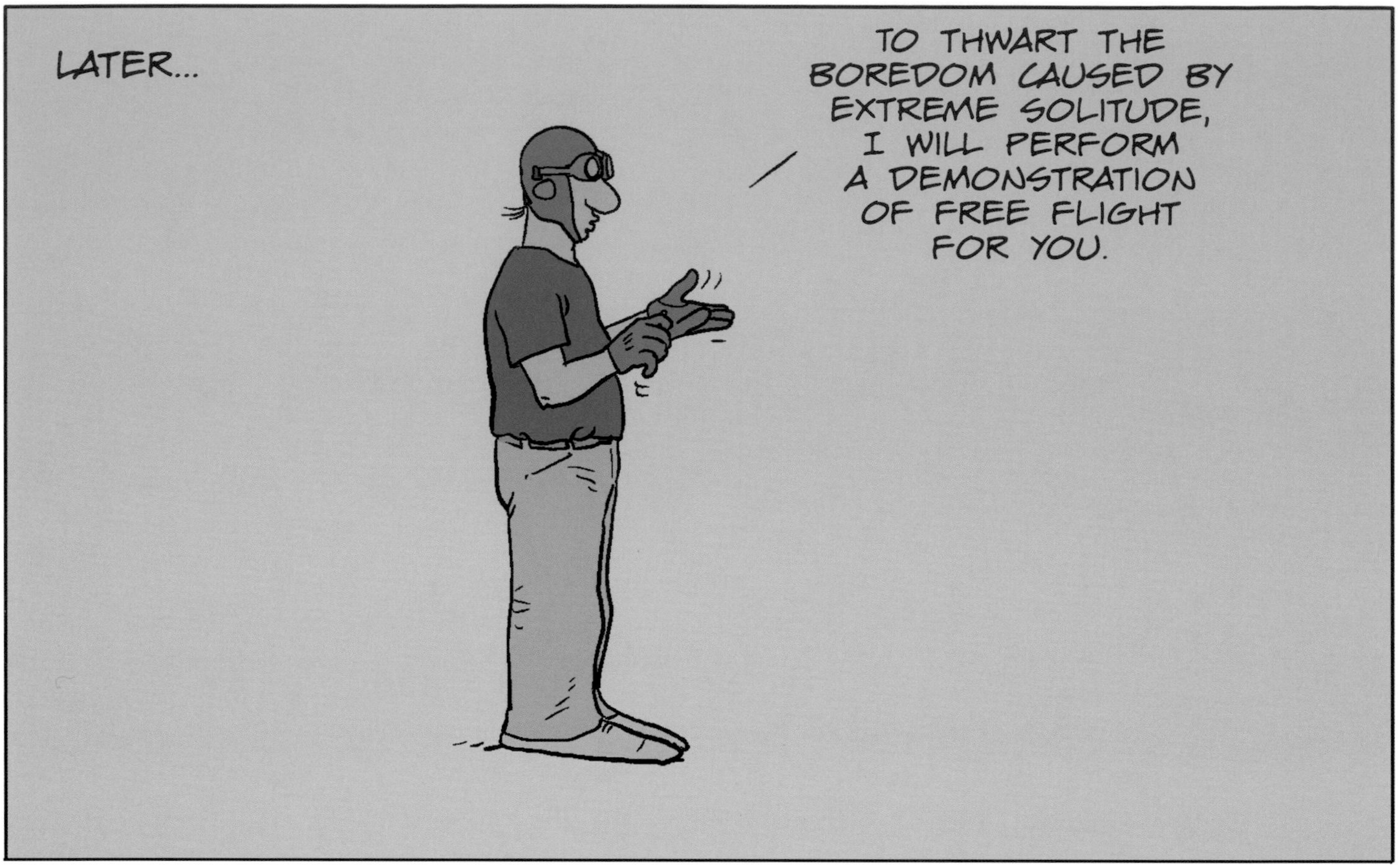
LATER...
TO THWART THE BOREDOM CAUSED BY EXTREME SOLITUDE, I WILL PERFORM A DEMONSTRATION OF FREE FLIGHT FOR YOU.

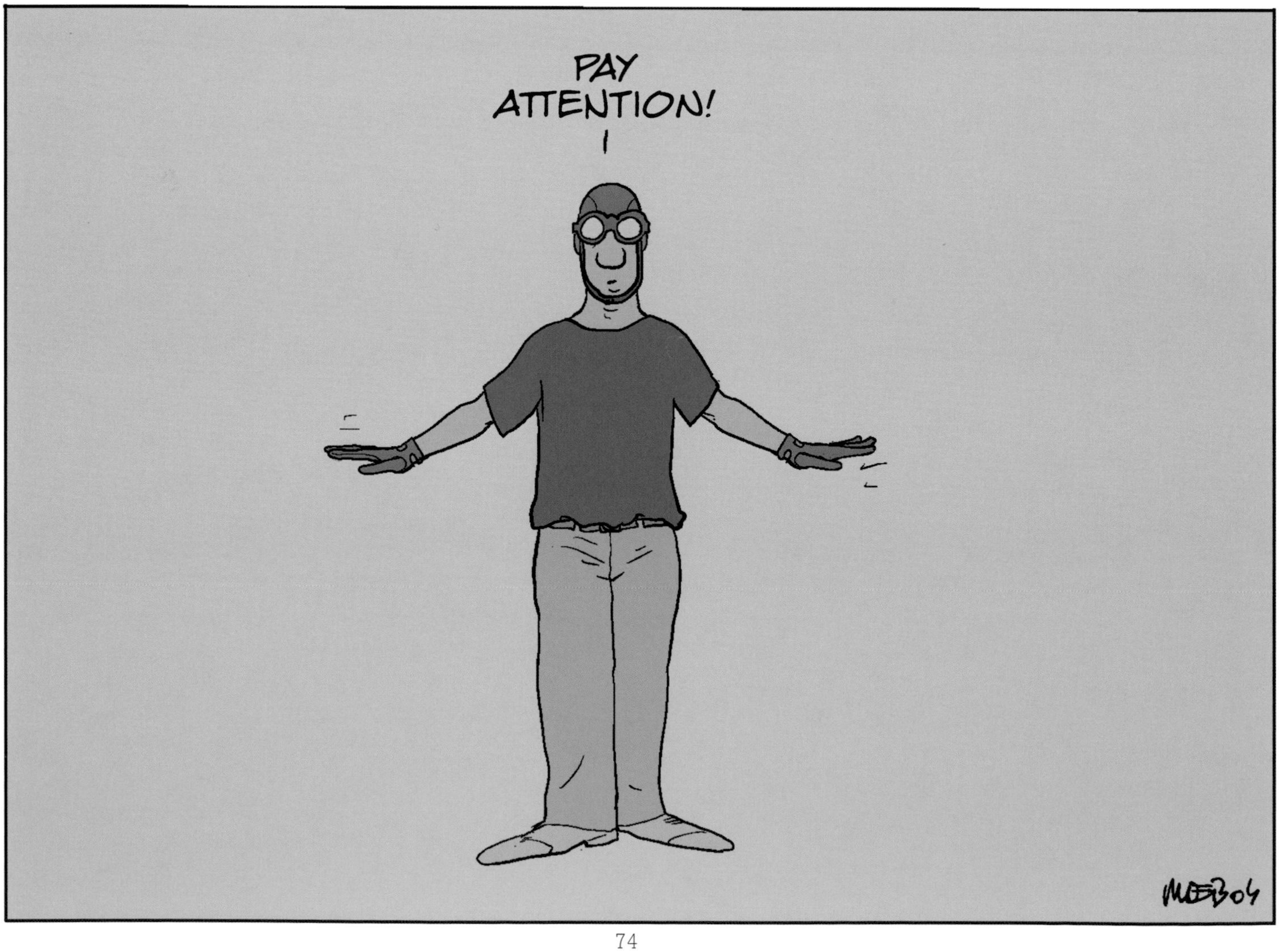
PAY ATTENTION!

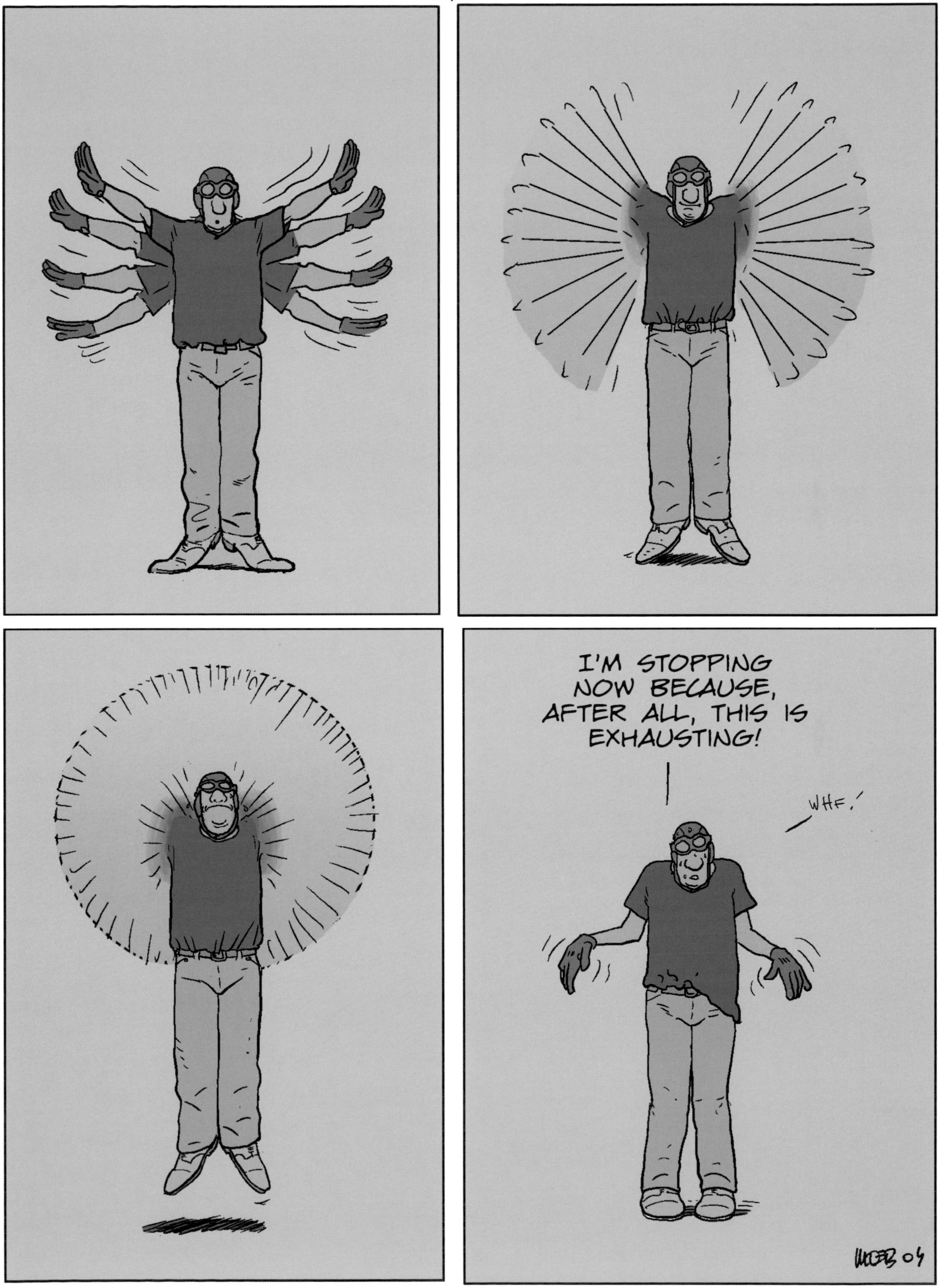
I'M STOPPING NOW BECAUSE, AFTER ALL, THIS IS EXHAUSTING!
WHF!

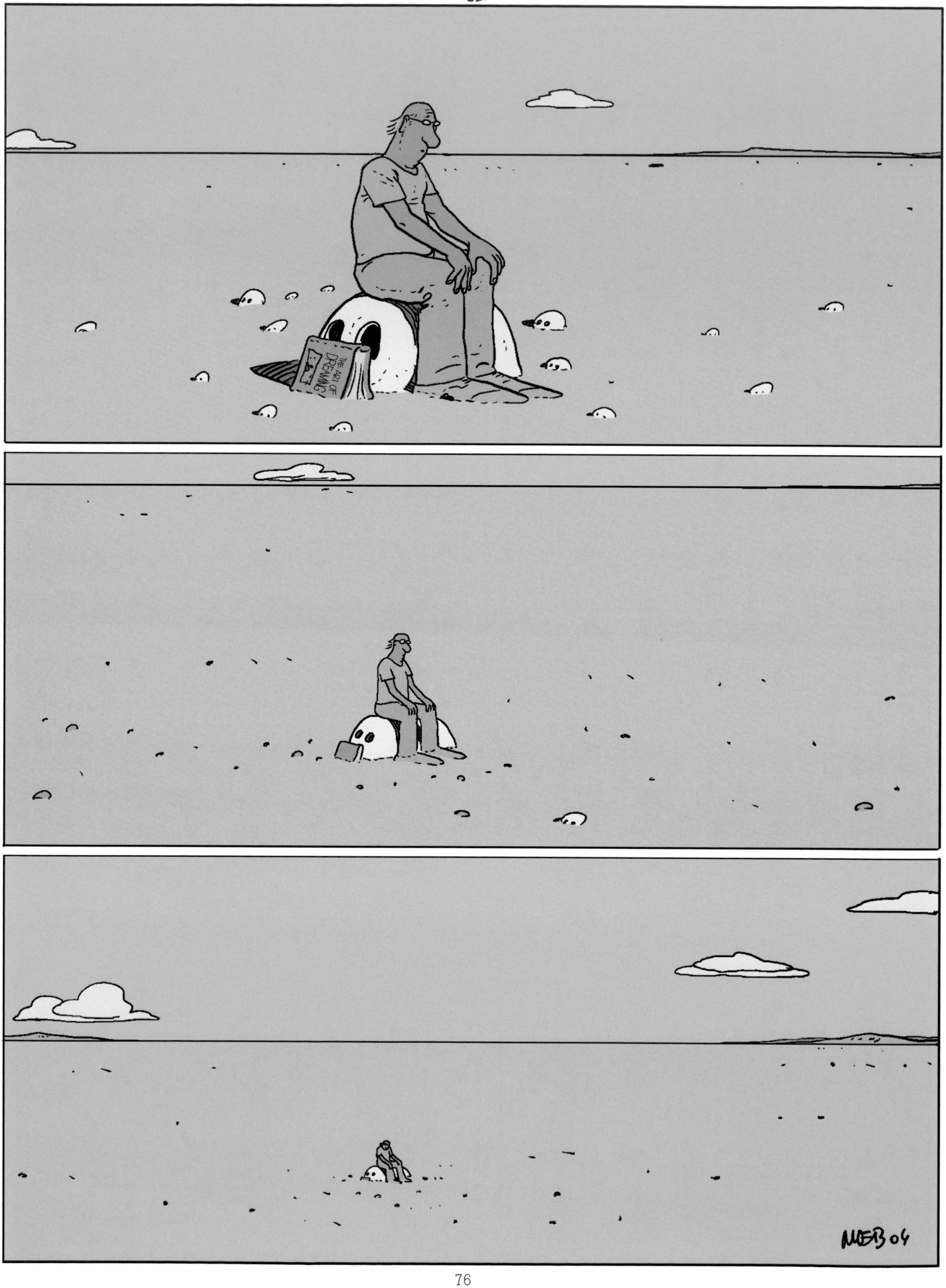
THE ART OF
DREAMING
MŒB 04

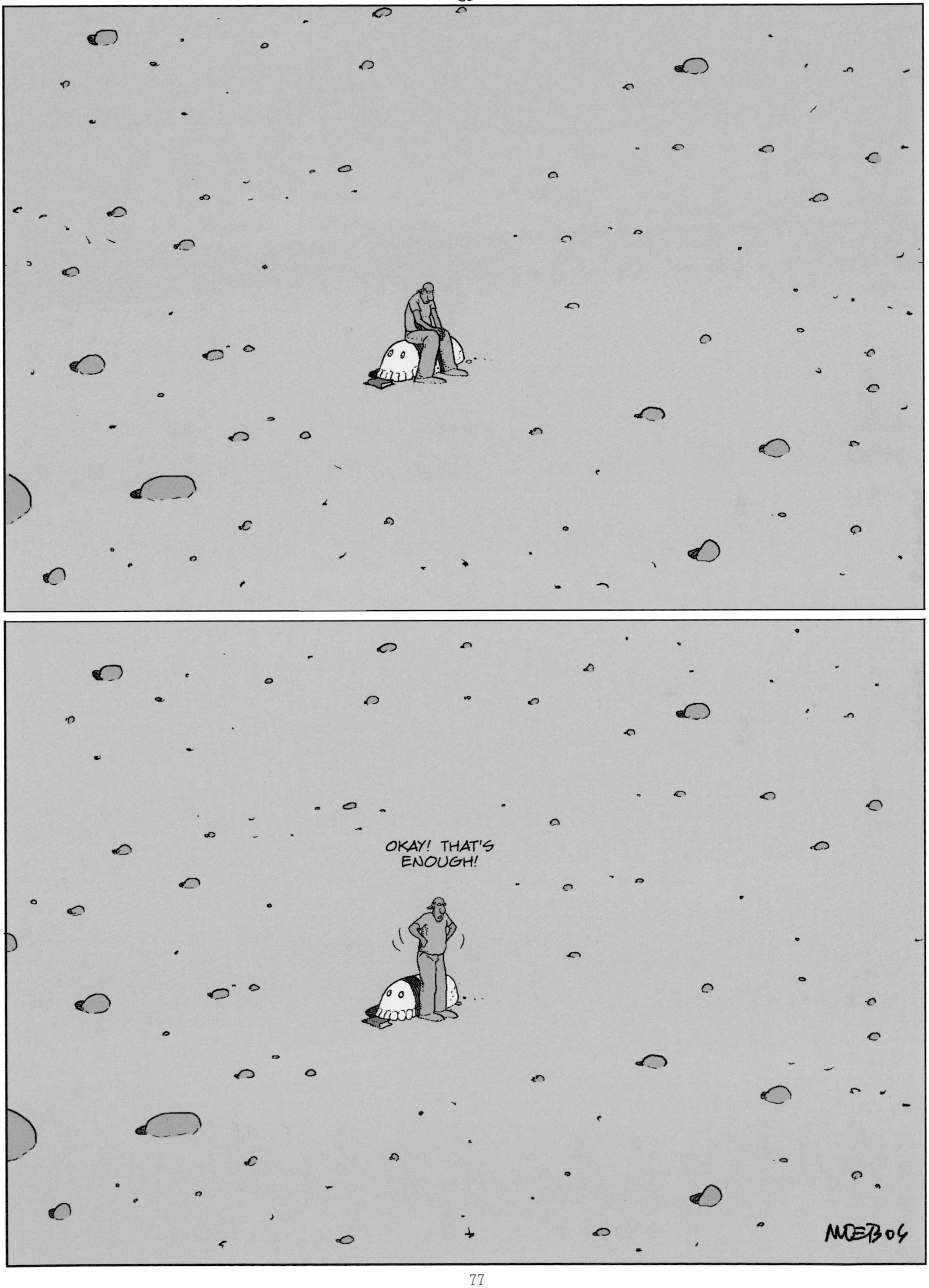
OKAY! THAT'S ENOUGH!
MOEB 04

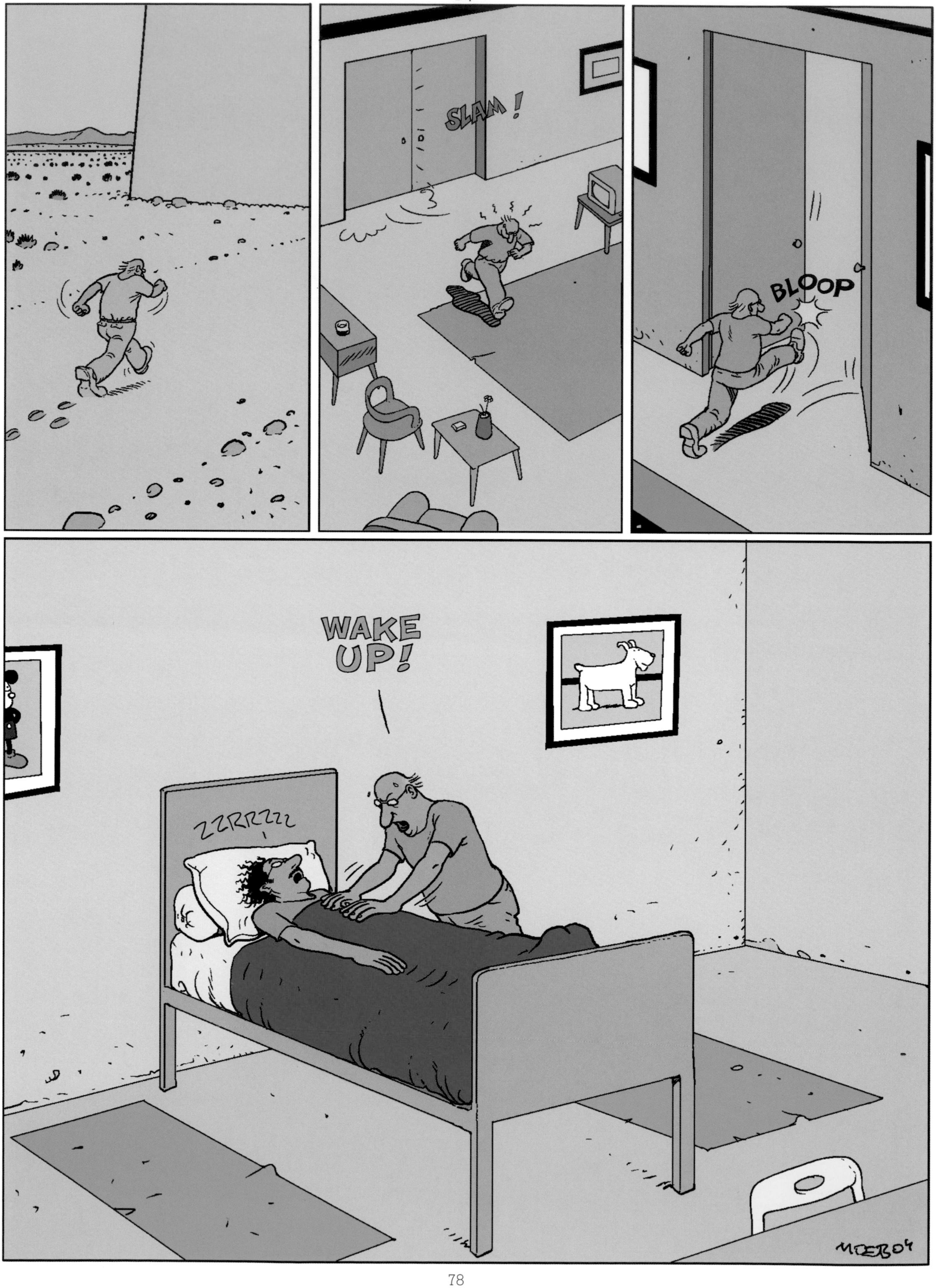
SLAM !
BLOOP
WAKE UP!
ZZRRZZZ
MOEB04

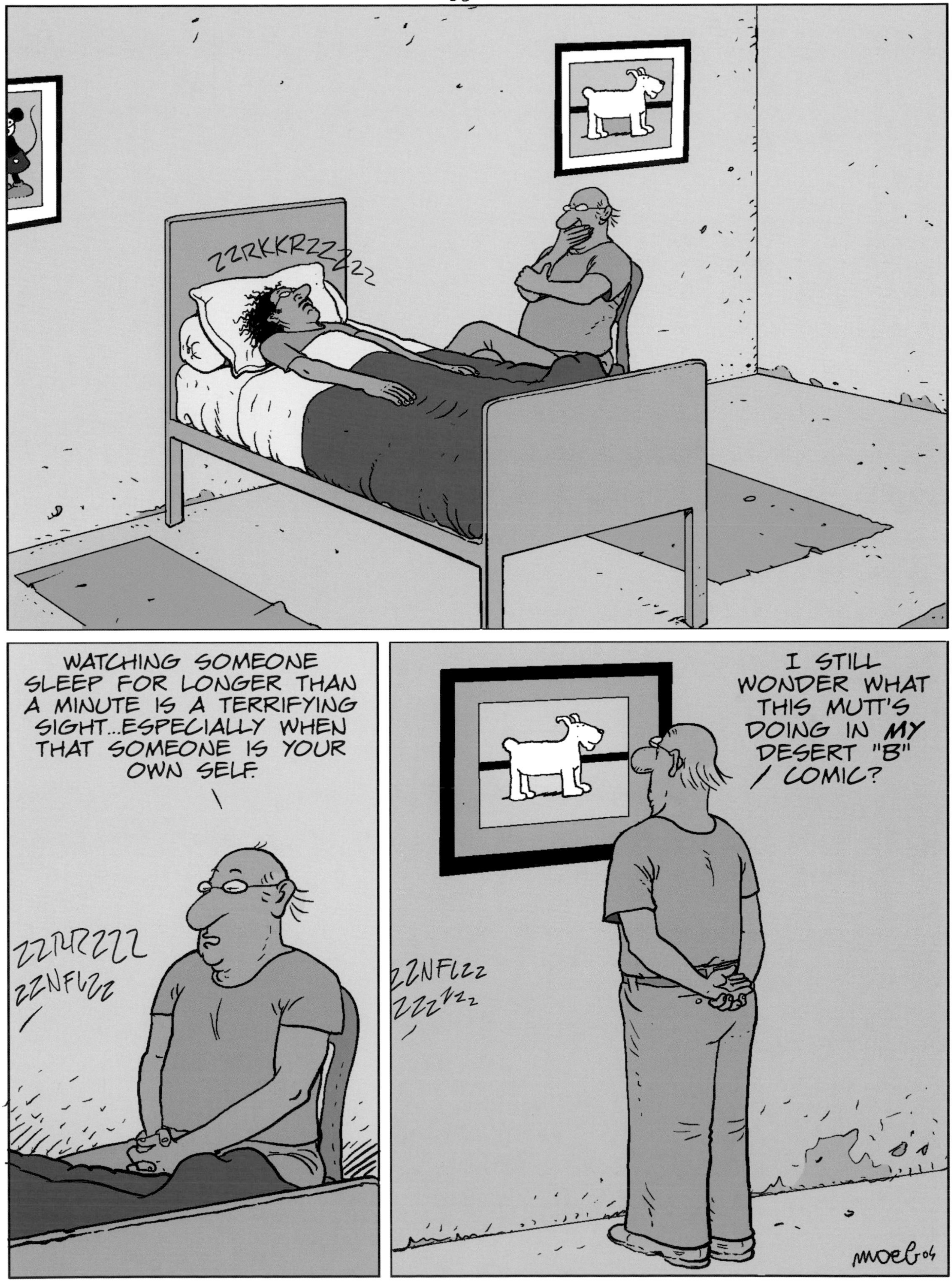
ZZRKKRZZZZZZ
WATCHING SOMEONE SLEEP FOR LONGER THAN A MINUTE IS A TERRIFYING SIGHT...ESPECIALLY WHEN THAT SOMEONE IS YOUR OWN SELF.
ZZRRZZZZ
ZZNFLZZ
I STILL WONDER WHAT THIS MUTT'S DOING IN MY DESERT "B" / COMIC?
ZZNFLZZ
ZZZZZZ
moeb 04

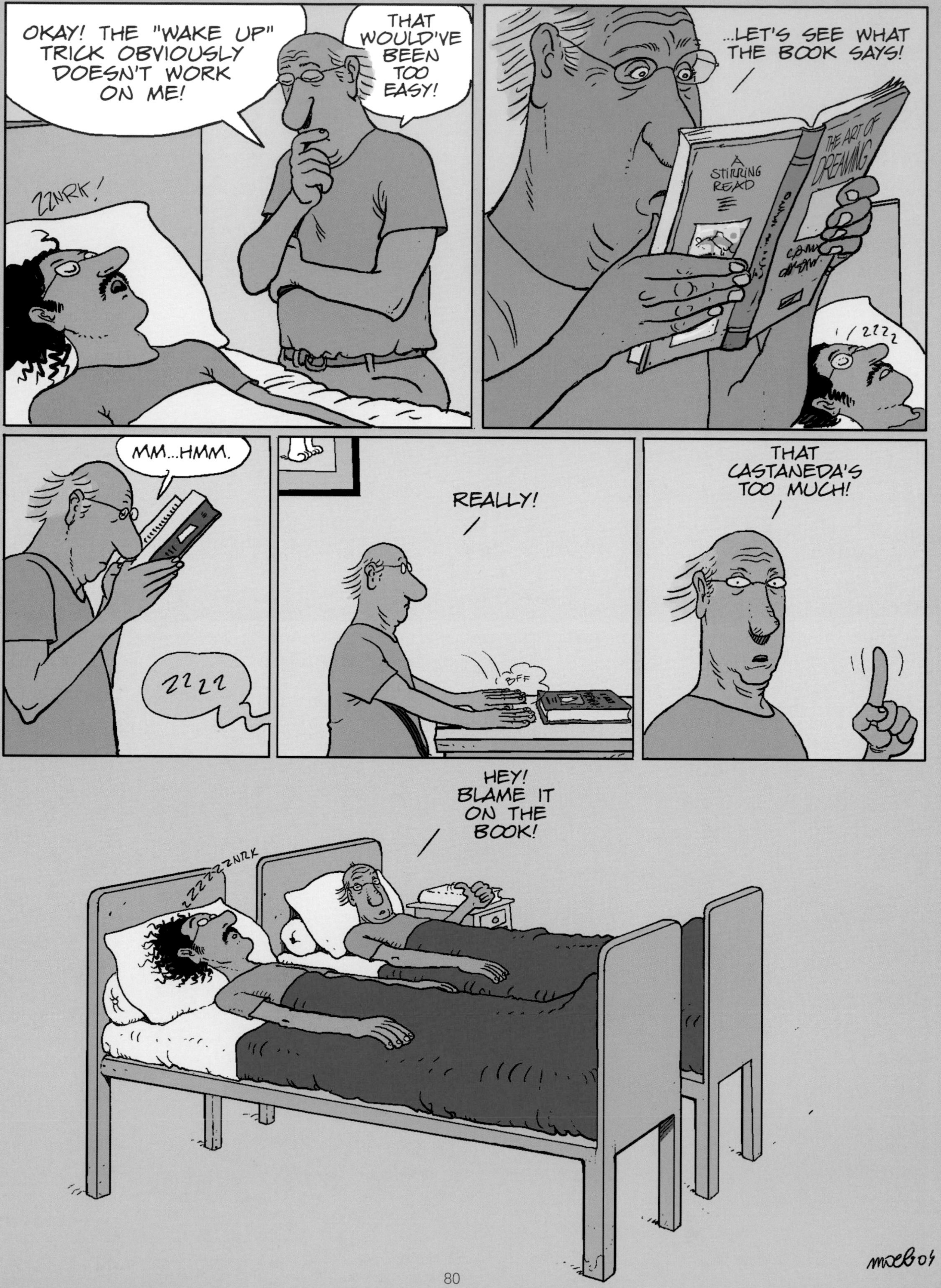
OKAY! THE "WAKE UP" TRICK OBVIOUSLY DOESN'T WORK ON ME!
THAT WOULD'VE BEEN TOO EASY!
ZZNRK!
...LET'S SEE WHAT THE BOOK SAYS!
A STIRRING READ
THE ART OF DREAMING
ZZZZ
MM...HMM.
ZZZZ
REALLY!
BFF
THAT CASTANEDA'S TOO MUCH!
HEY! BLAME IT ON THE BOOK!
ZZZZZZZNRK
moeb 04

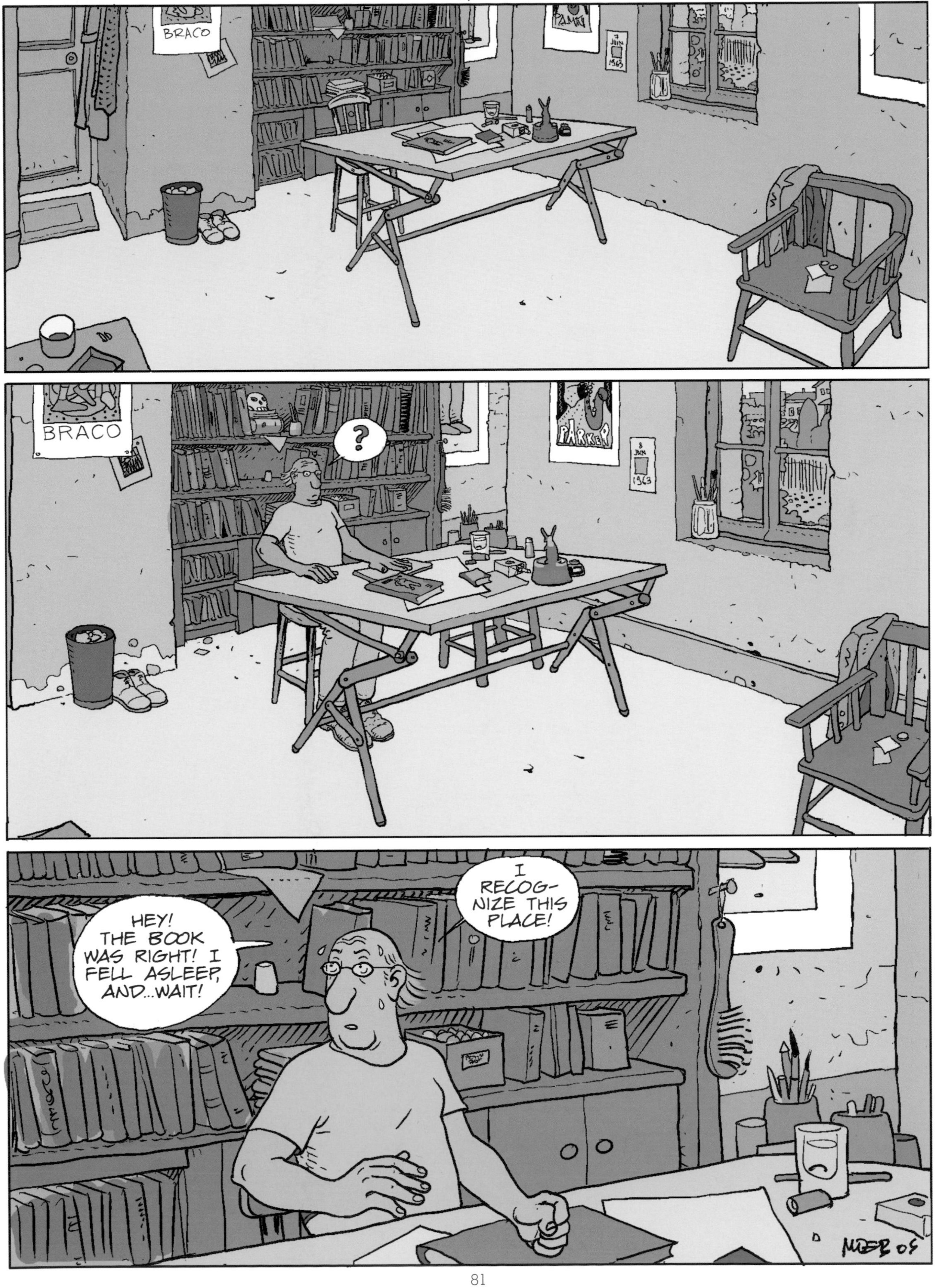
BRACO
BRACO
PARKER
?
HEY! THE BOOK WAS RIGHT! I FELL ASLEEP, AND...WAIT!
I RECOG- NIZE THIS PLACE!

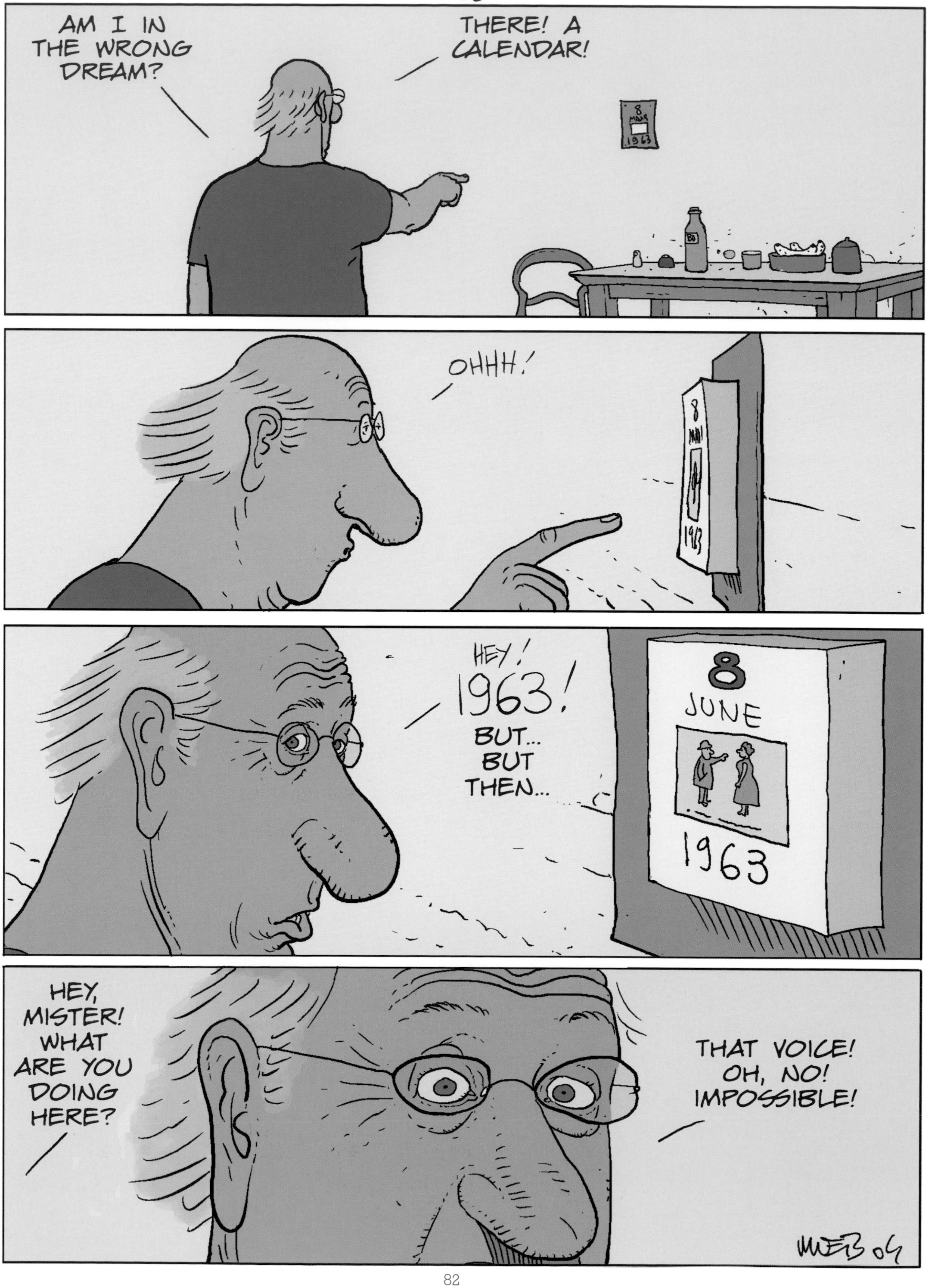
AM I IN THE WRONG DREAM?
THERE! A CALENDAR!
OHHH!
HEY! 1963! BUT... BUT THEN...
8
JUNE
1963
HEY, MISTER! WHAT ARE YOU DOING HERE?
THAT VOICE! OH, NO! IMPOSSIBLE!

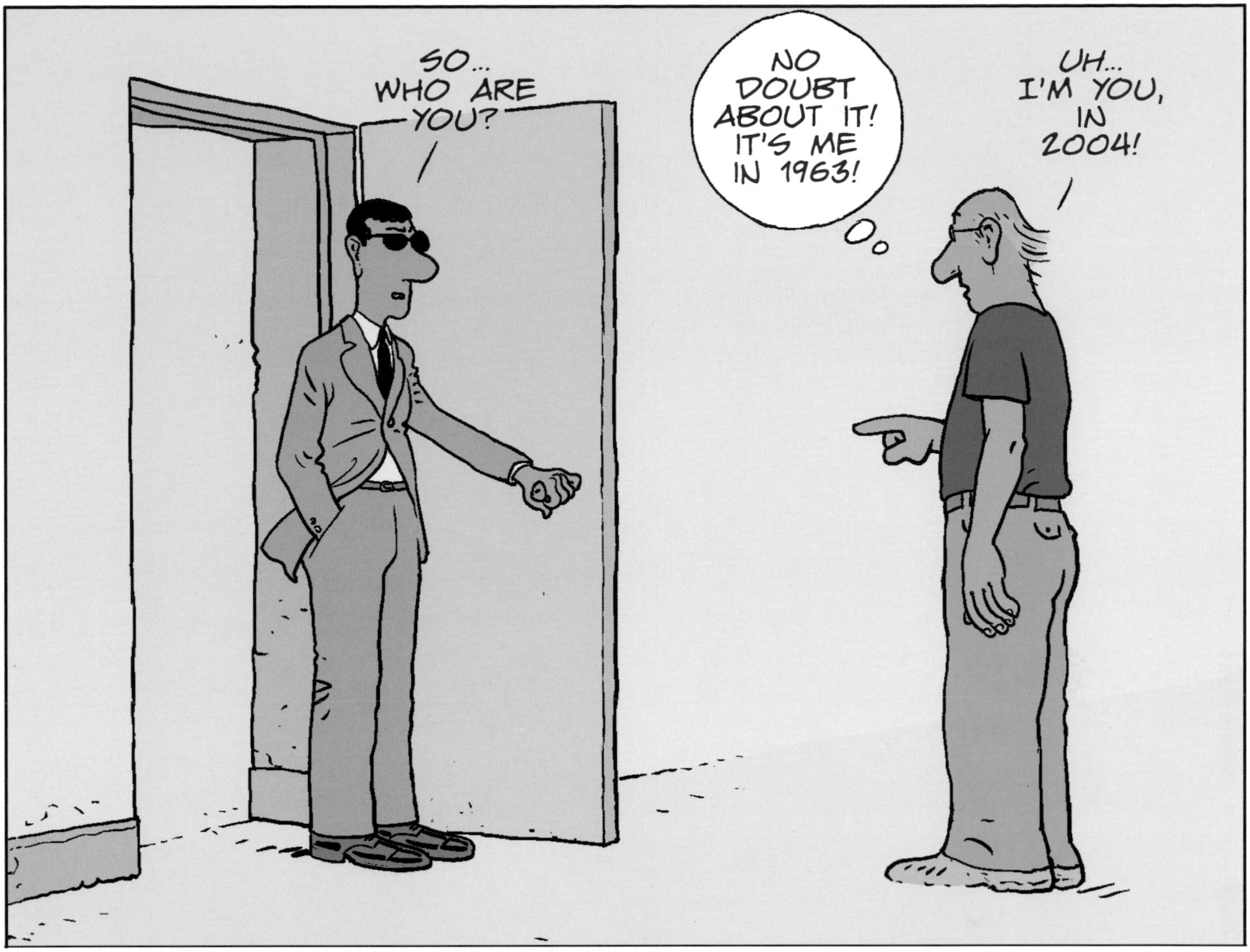
SO... WHO ARE YOU?
NO DOUBT ABOUT IT! IT'S ME IN 1963!
UH... I'M YOU, IN 2004!

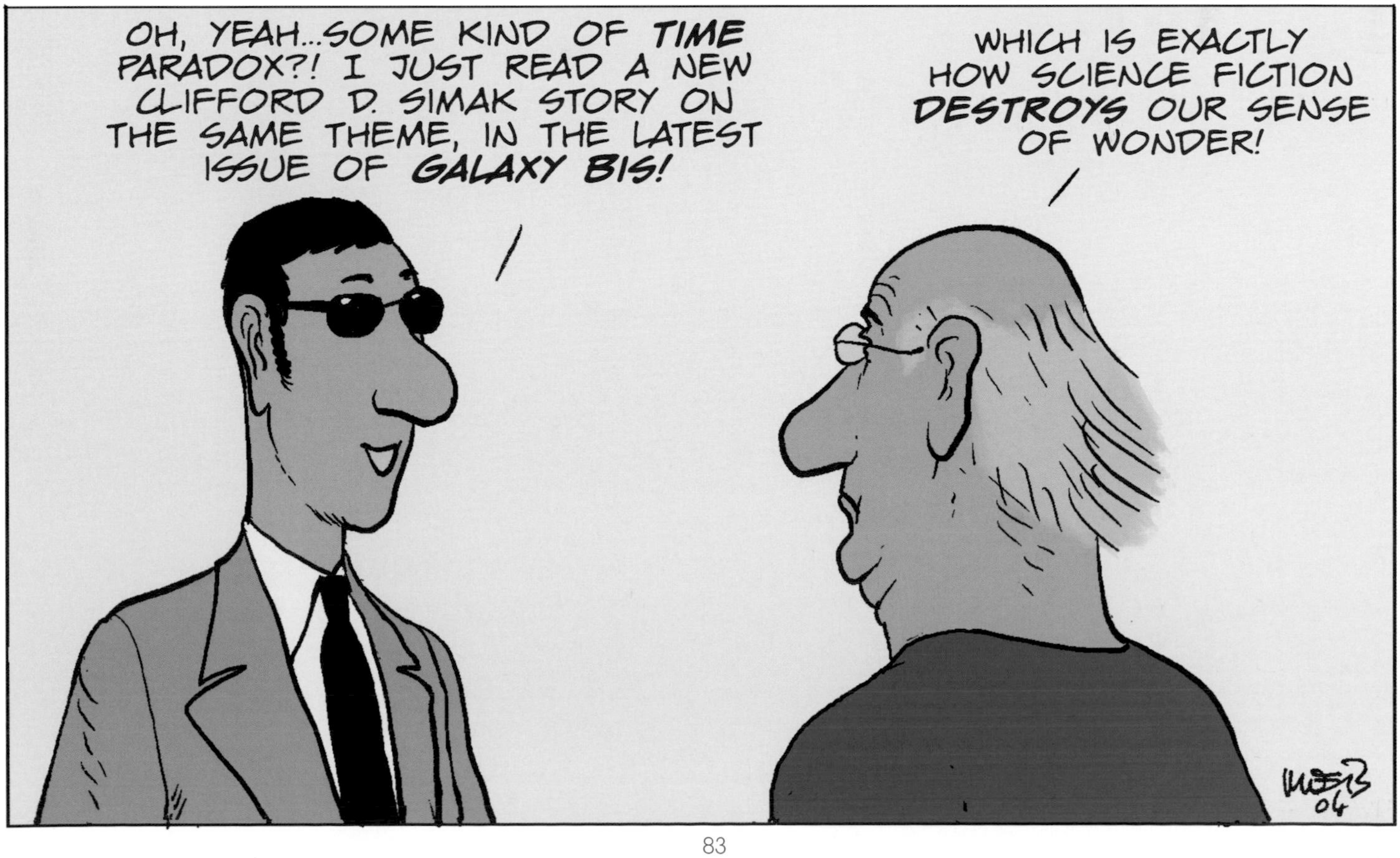
OH, YEAH...SOME KIND OF TIME PARADOX?! I JUST READ A NEW CLIFFORD D. SIMAK STORY ON THE SAME THEME, IN THE LATEST ISSUE OF GALAXY BIS!
WHICH IS EXACTLY HOW SCIENCE FICTION DESTROYS OUR SENSE OF WONDER!

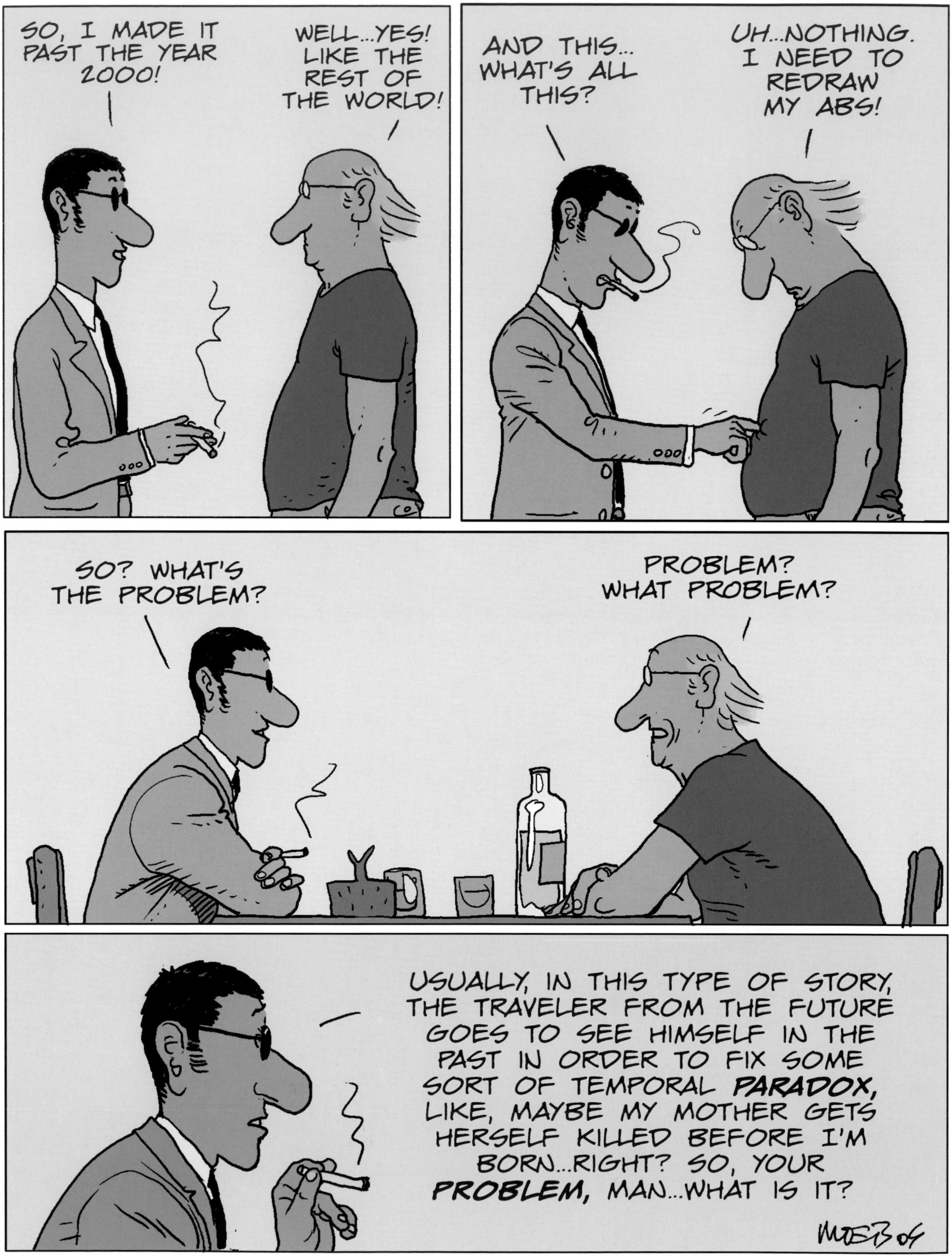
SO, I MADE IT PAST THE YEAR 2000!
WELL...YES! LIKE THE REST OF THE WORLD!
AND THIS... WHAT'S ALL THIS?
UH...NOTHING. I NEED TO REDRAW MY ABS!
SO? WHAT'S THE PROBLEM?
PROBLEM? WHAT PROBLEM?
USUALLY, IN THIS TYPE OF STORY, THE TRAVELER FROM THE FUTURE GOES TO SEE HIMSELF IN THE PAST IN ORDER TO FIX SOME SORT OF TEMPORAL **PARADOX,** LIKE, MAYBE MY MOTHER GETS HERSELF KILLED BEFORE I'M BORN...RIGHT? SO, YOUR **PROBLEM,** MAN...WHAT IS IT?

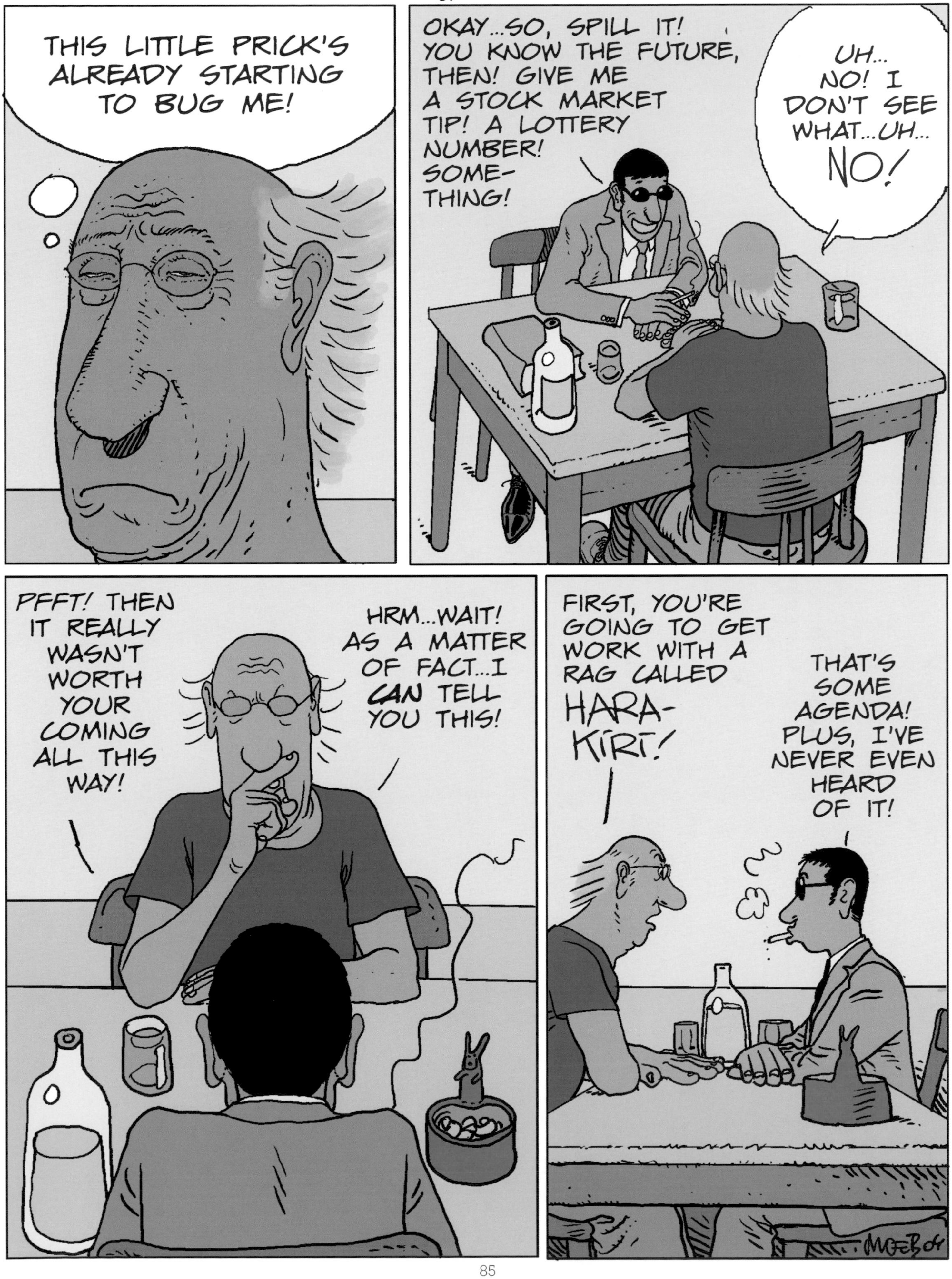
THIS LITTLE PRICK'S ALREADY STARTING TO BUG ME!
OKAY...SO, SPILL IT! YOU KNOW THE FUTURE, THEN! GIVE ME A STOCK MARKET TIP! A LOTTERY NUMBER! SOME-THING!
UH... NO! I DON'T SEE WHAT...UH... NO!
PFFT! THEN IT REALLY WASN'T WORTH YOUR COMING ALL THIS WAY!
HRM...WAIT! AS A MATTER OF FACT...I CAN TELL YOU THIS!
FIRST, YOU'RE GOING TO GET WORK WITH A RAG CALLED HARA-KIRI!
THAT'S SOME AGENDA! PLUS, I'VE NEVER EVEN HEARD OF IT!
MOEBIUS

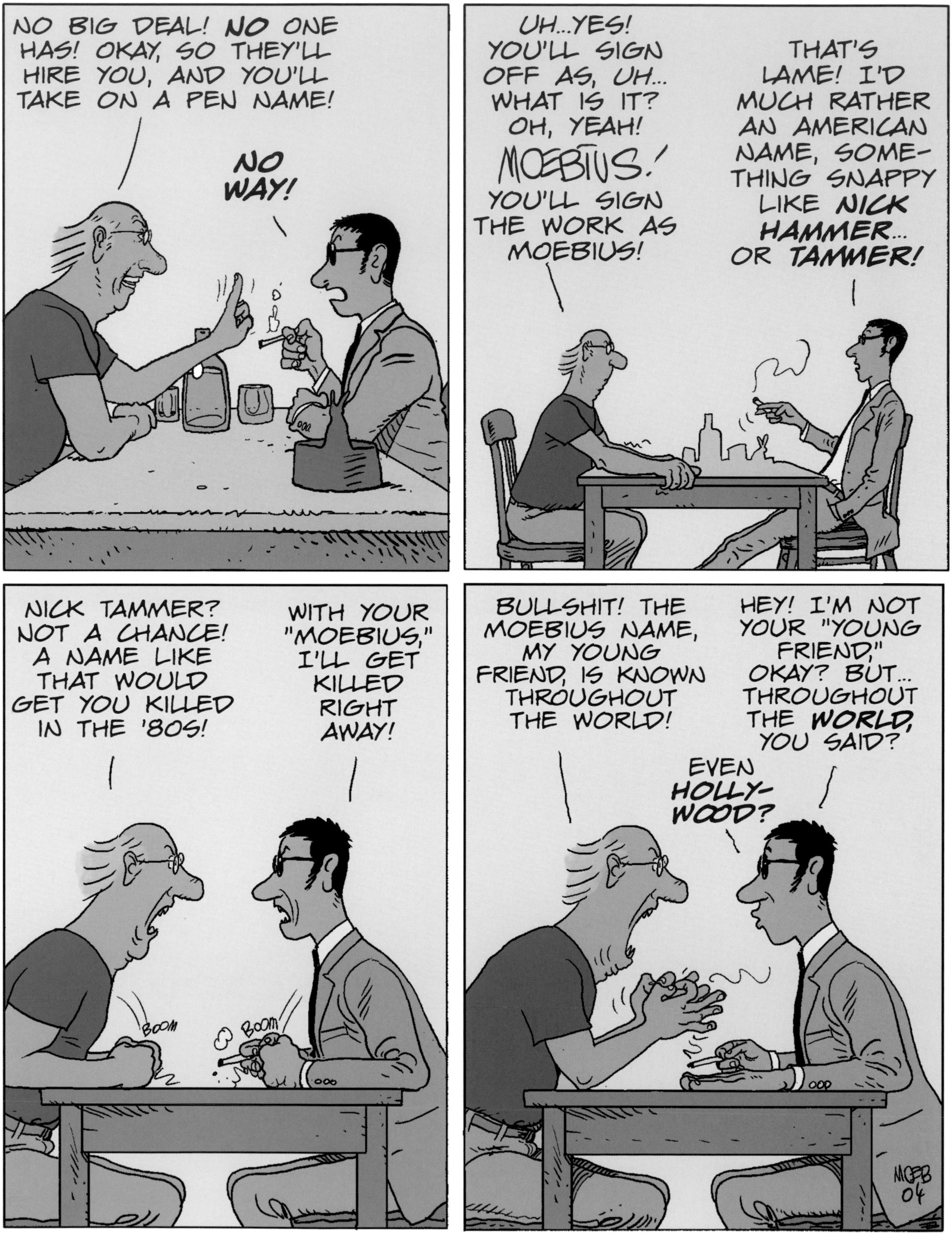
NO BIG DEAL! NO ONE HAS! OKAY, SO THEY'LL HIRE YOU, AND YOU'LL TAKE ON A PEN NAME!
NO WAY!
UH...YES! YOU'LL SIGN OFF AS, UH... WHAT IS IT? OH, YEAH! MOEBIUS! YOU'LL SIGN THE WORK AS MOEBIUS!
THAT'S LAME! I'D MUCH RATHER AN AMERICAN NAME, SOMETHING SNAPPY LIKE NICK HAMMER... OR TAMMER!
NICK TAMMER? NOT A CHANCE! A NAME LIKE THAT WOULD GET YOU KILLED IN THE '80S!
WITH YOUR "MOEBIUS," I'LL GET KILLED RIGHT AWAY!
BOOM
BOOM
BULLSHIT! THE MOEBIUS NAME, MY YOUNG FRIEND, IS KNOWN THROUGHOUT THE WORLD!
HEY! I'M NOT YOUR "YOUNG FRIEND," OKAY? BUT... THROUGHOUT THE WORLD, YOU SAID?
EVEN HOLLYWOOD?
MOEB 04

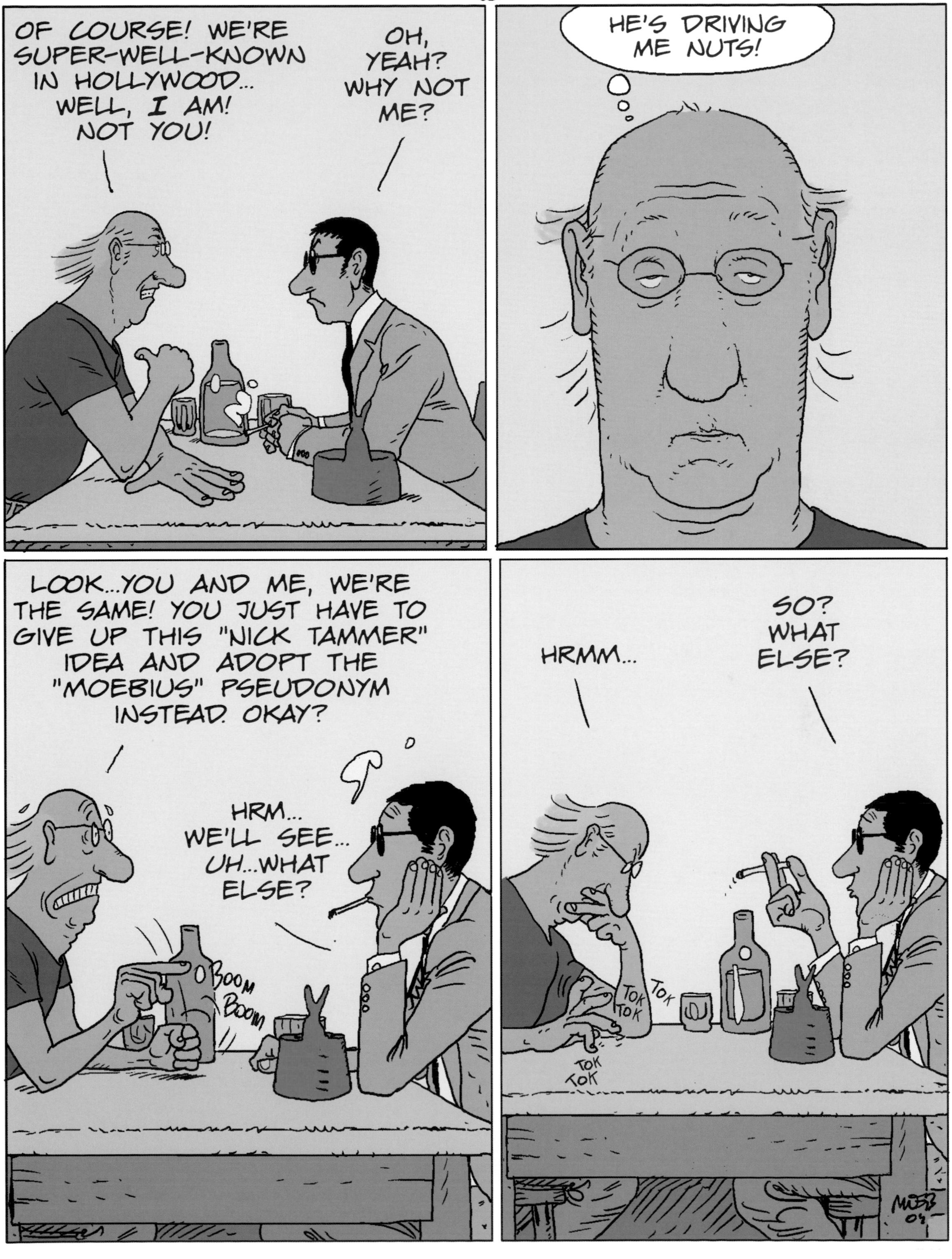
OF COURSE! WE'RE SUPER-WELL-KNOWN IN HOLLYWOOD... WELL, I AM! NOT YOU!
OH, YEAH? WHY NOT ME?
HE'S DRIVING ME NUTS!
LOOK...YOU AND ME, WE'RE THE SAME! YOU JUST HAVE TO GIVE UP THIS "NICK TAMMER" IDEA AND ADOPT THE "MOEBIUS" PSEUDONYM INSTEAD. OKAY?
HRM... WE'LL SEE... UH...WHAT ELSE?
BOOM BOOM
HRMM...
SO? WHAT ELSE?
TOK TOK TOK
TOK TOK

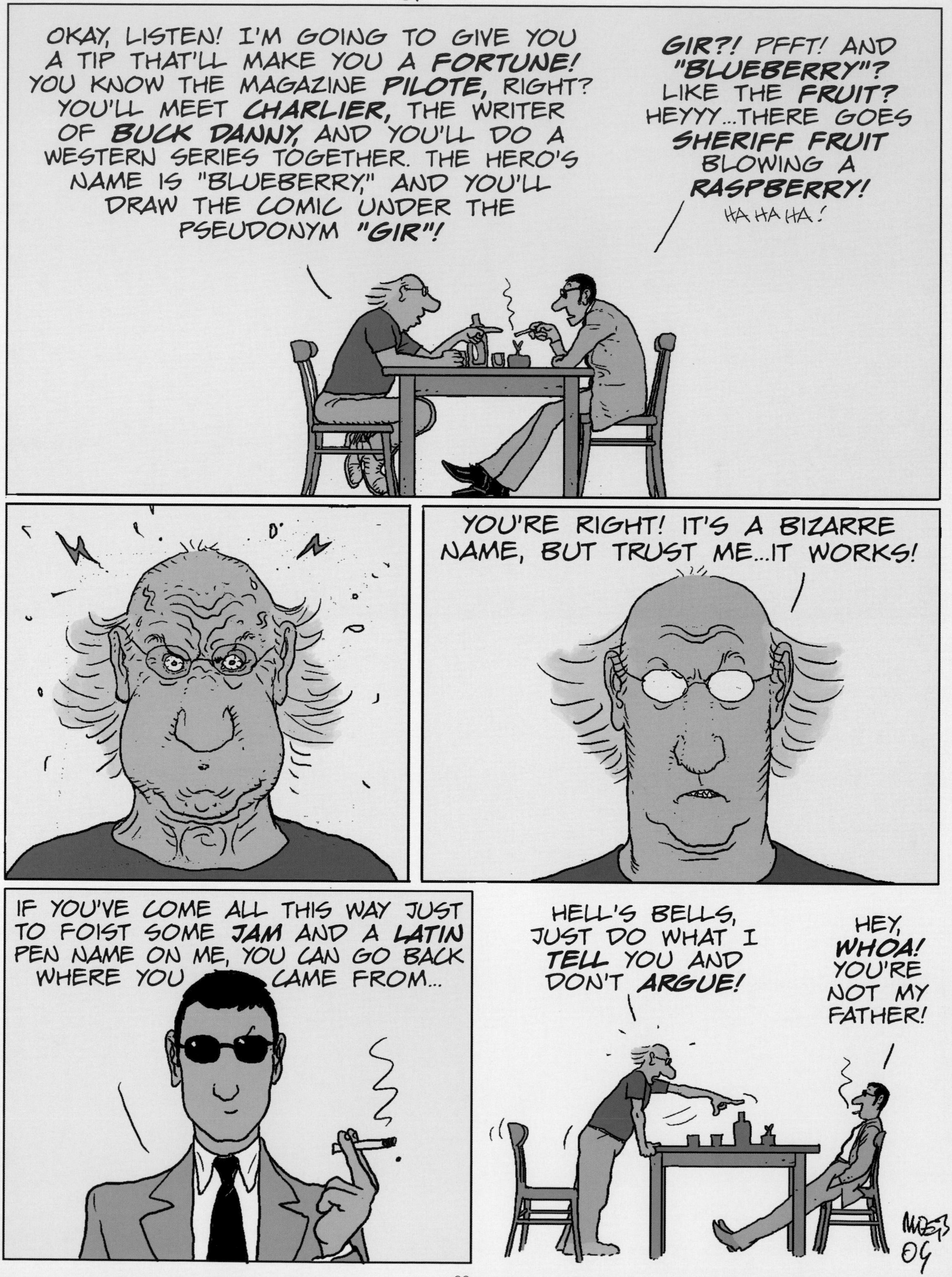
OKAY, LISTEN! I'M GOING TO GIVE YOU A TIP THAT'LL MAKE YOU A FORTUNE! YOU KNOW THE MAGAZINE PILOTE, RIGHT? YOU'LL MEET CHARLIER, THE WRITER OF BUCK DANNY, AND YOU'LL DO A WESTERN SERIES TOGETHER. THE HERO'S NAME IS "BLUEBERRY," AND YOU'LL DRAW THE COMIC UNDER THE PSEUDONYM "GIR"!
GIR?! PFFT! AND "BLUEBERRY"? LIKE THE FRUIT? HEYYY...THERE GOES SHERIFF FRUIT BLOWING A RASPBERRY!
HA HA HA!
YOU'RE RIGHT! IT'S A BIZARRE NAME, BUT TRUST ME...IT WORKS!
IF YOU'VE COME ALL THIS WAY JUST TO FOIST SOME JAM AND A LATIN PEN NAME ON ME, YOU CAN GO BACK WHERE YOU CAME FROM...
HELL'S BELLS, JUST DO WHAT I TELL YOU AND DON'T ARGUE!
HEY, WHOA! YOU'RE NOT MY FATHER!
MŒBIUS 09

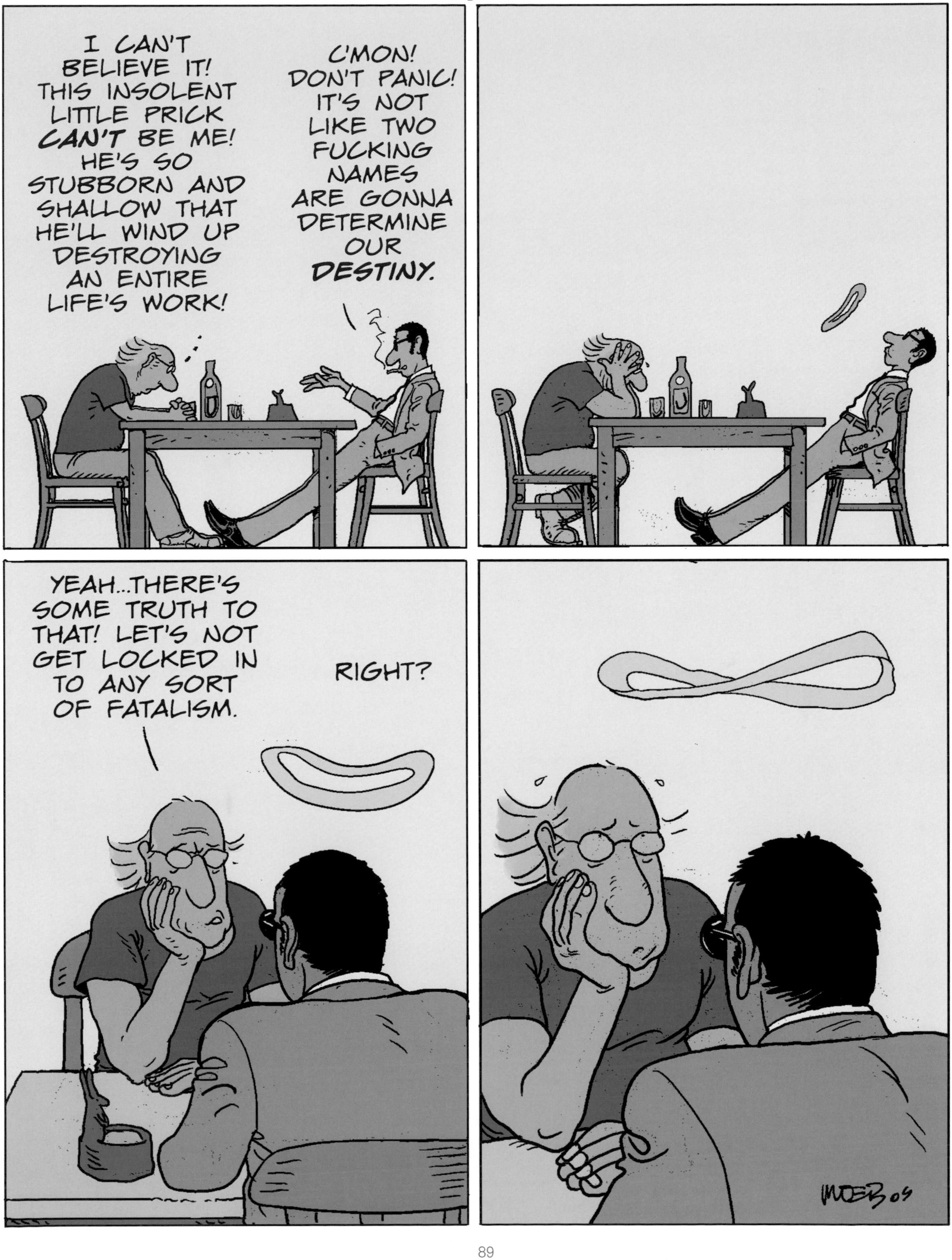
I CAN'T BELIEVE IT! THIS INSOLENT LITTLE PRICK CAN'T BE ME! HE'S SO STUBBORN AND SHALLOW THAT HE'LL WIND UP DESTROYING AN ENTIRE LIFE'S WORK!
C'MON! DON'T PANIC! IT'S NOT LIKE TWO FUCKING NAMES ARE GONNA DETERMINE OUR DESTINY.
YEAH...THERE'S SOME TRUTH TO THAT! LET'S NOT GET LOCKED IN TO ANY SORT OF FATALISM.
RIGHT?
MOEB 05

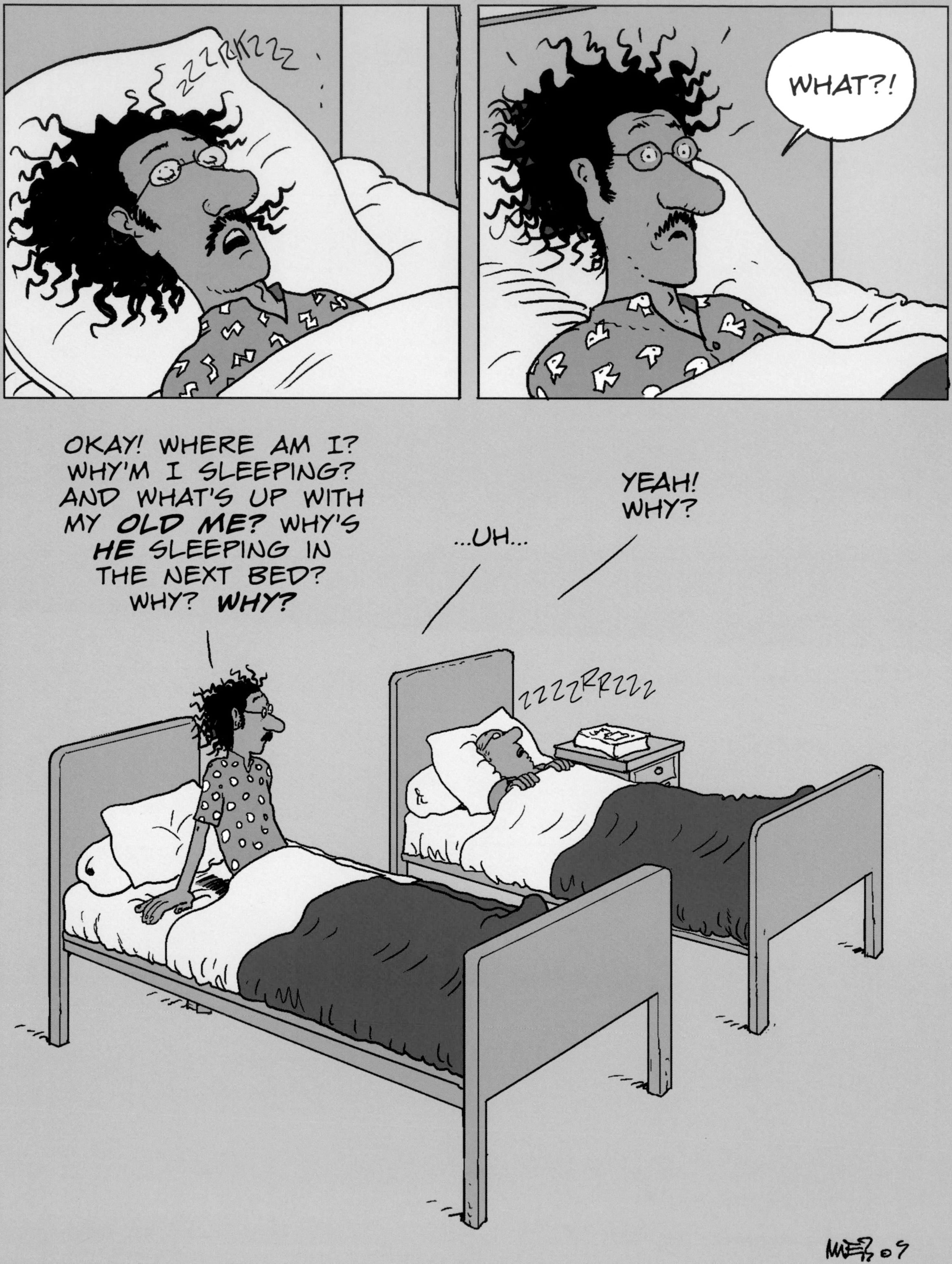
ZZZRRZZZ
WHAT?!
OKAY! WHERE AM I? WHY'M I SLEEPING? AND WHAT'S UP WITH MY OLD ME? WHY'S HE SLEEPING IN THE NEXT BED? WHY? WHY?
...UH...
YEAH! WHY?
ZZZZRRZZZ

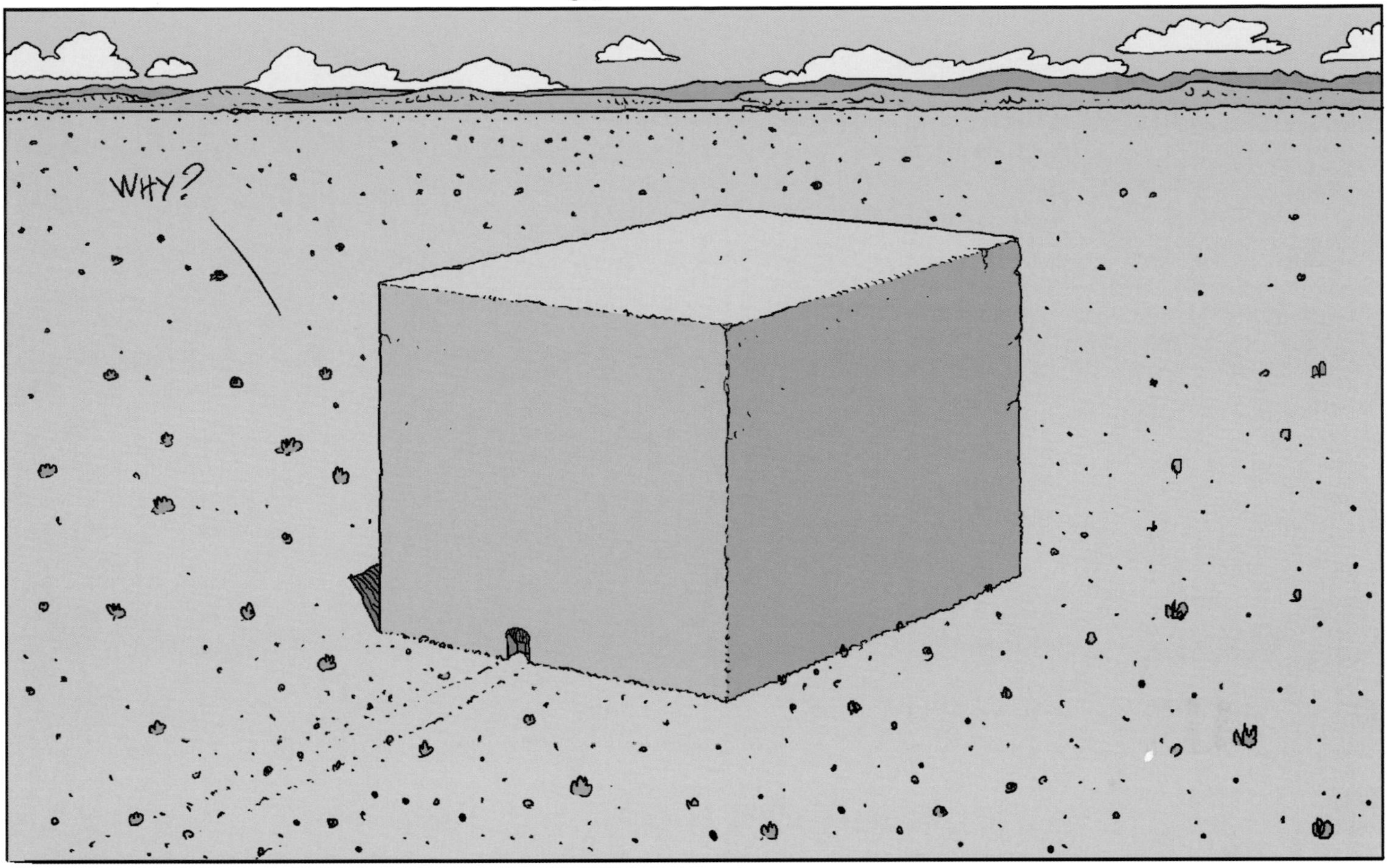
WHY?

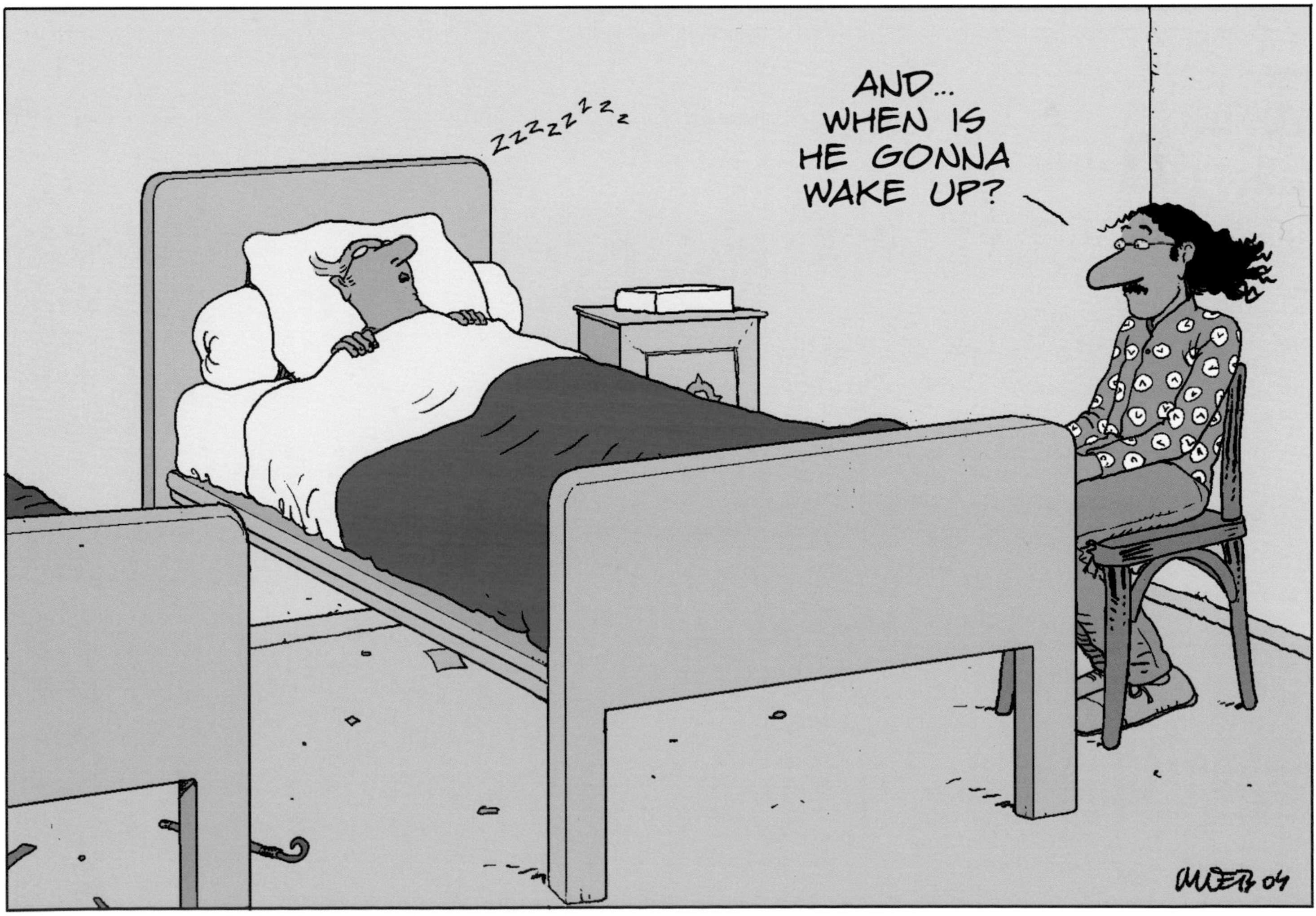
ZZZZZZZZZ
AND... WHEN IS HE GONNA WAKE UP?

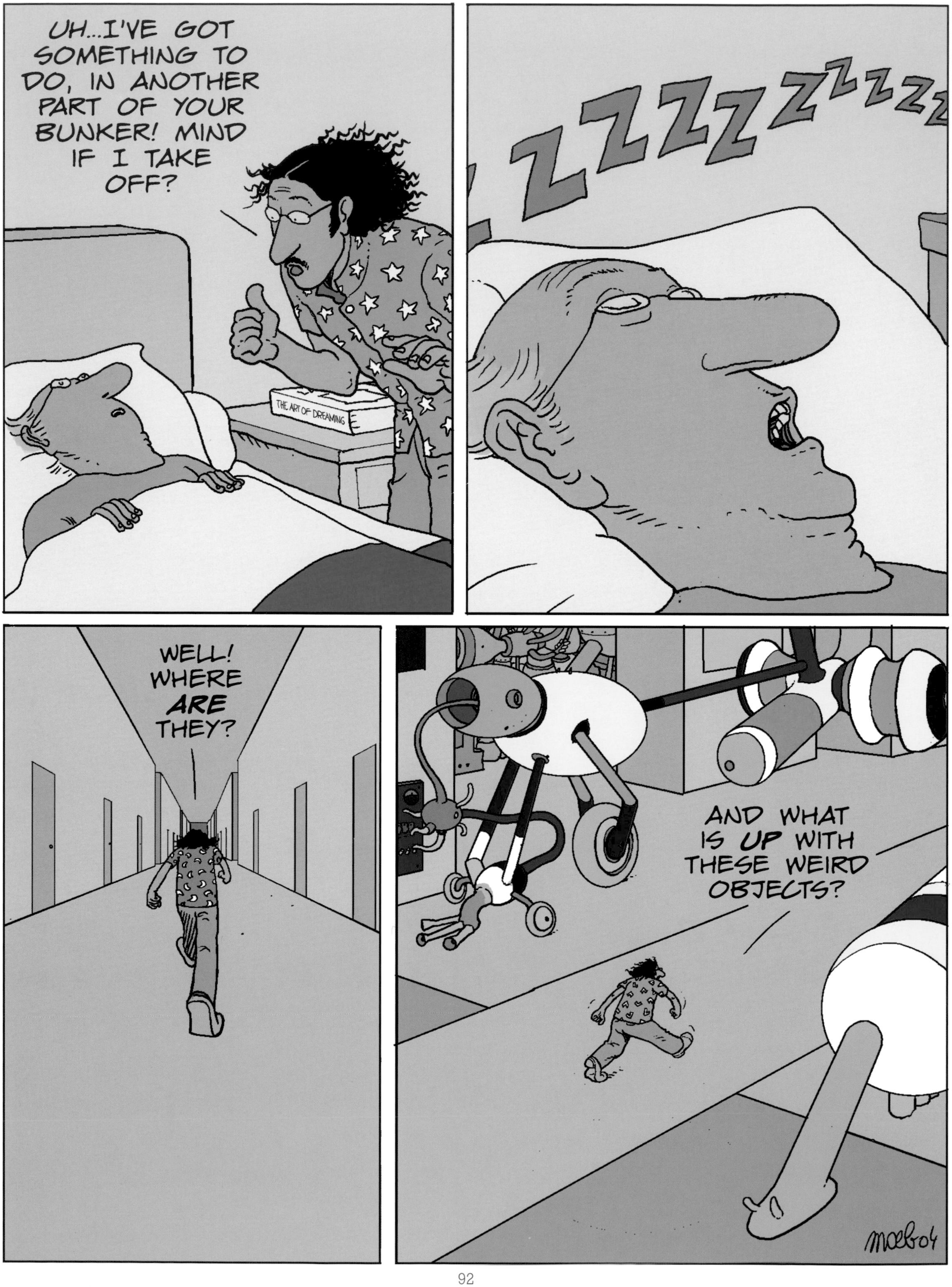
UH...I'VE GOT SOMETHING TO DO, IN ANOTHER PART OF YOUR BUNKER! MIND IF I TAKE OFF?
THE ART OF DREAMING
ZZZZZZZZZZZZ
WELL! WHERE ARE THEY?
AND WHAT IS UP WITH THESE WEIRD OBJECTS?
moeb04

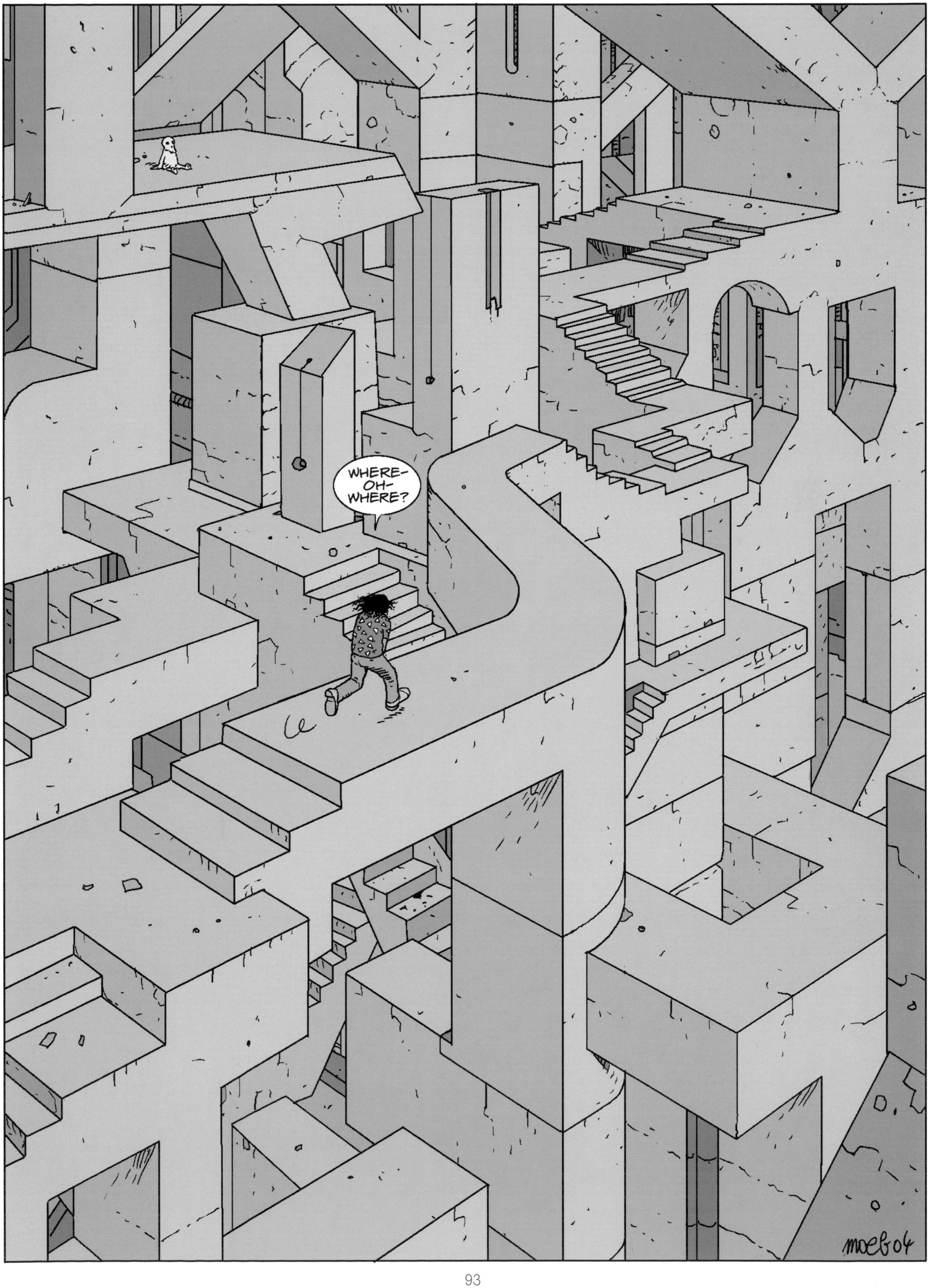
WHERE-
OH-
WHERE?
moeb 04

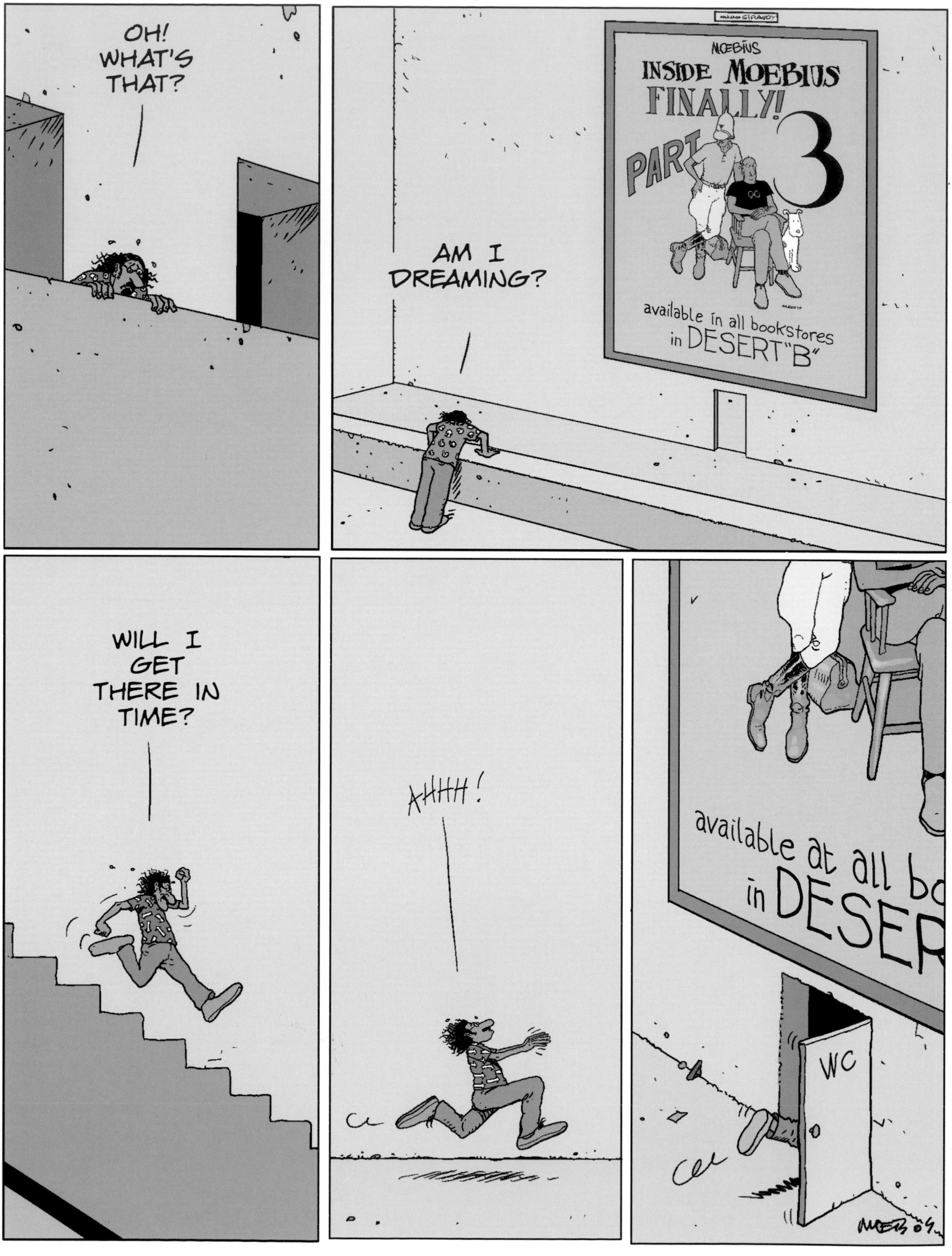
OH! WHAT'S THAT?
MŒBIUS
INSIDE MOEBIUS
FINALLY!
PART 3
available in all bookstores in DESERT "B"
AM I DREAMING?
WILL I GET THERE IN TIME?
AHHH!
available at all bo
in DESER
WC
MOEB 09

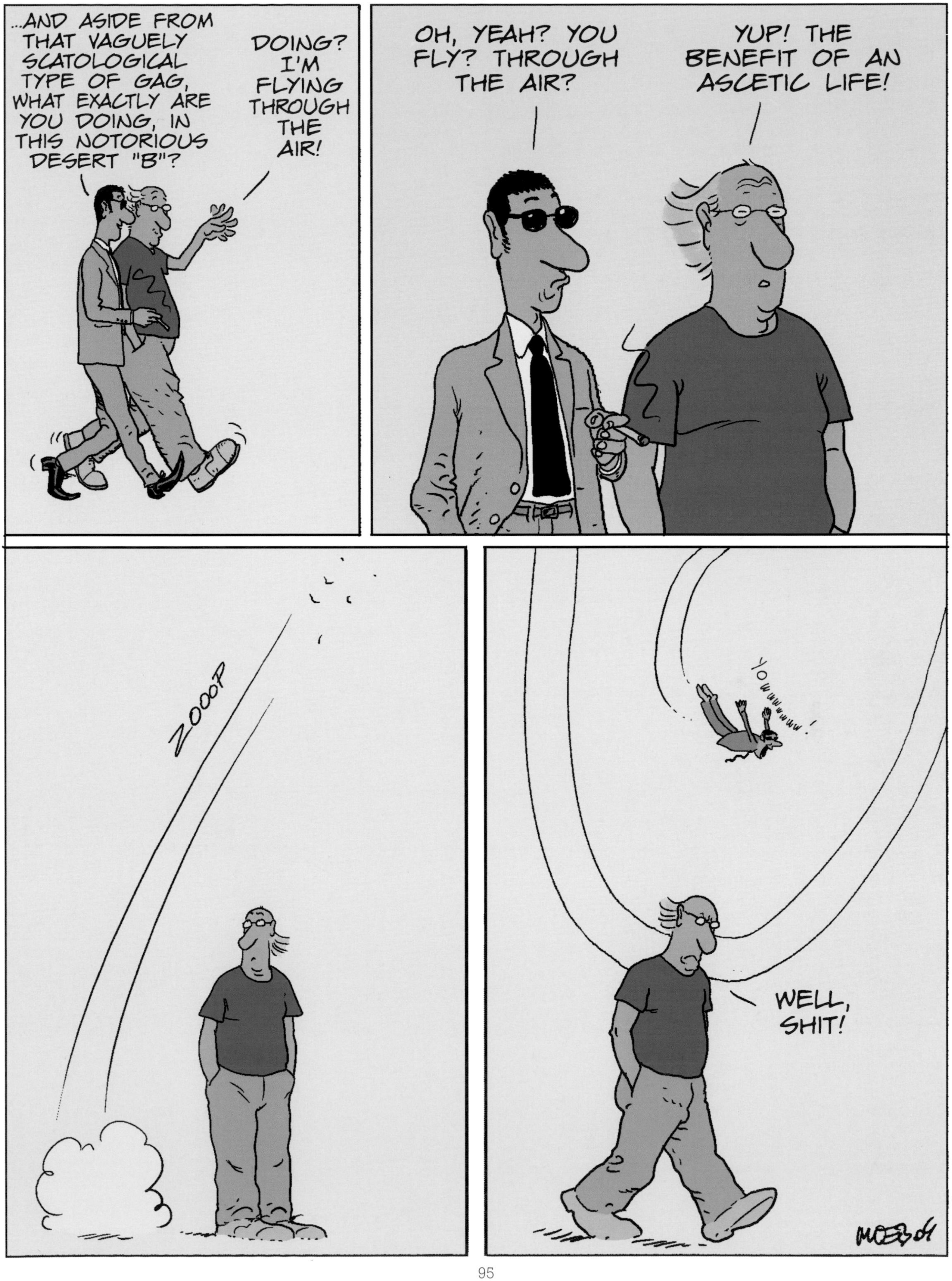
...AND ASIDE FROM THAT VAGUELY SCATOLOGICAL TYPE OF GAG, WHAT EXACTLY ARE YOU DOING, IN THIS NOTORIOUS DESERT "B"?
DOING? I'M FLYING THROUGH THE AIR!
OH, YEAH? YOU FLY? THROUGH THE AIR?
YUP! THE BENEFIT OF AN ASCETIC LIFE!
ZOOOP
YOWWWWWWWWW!
WELL, SHIT!
MOEB 01

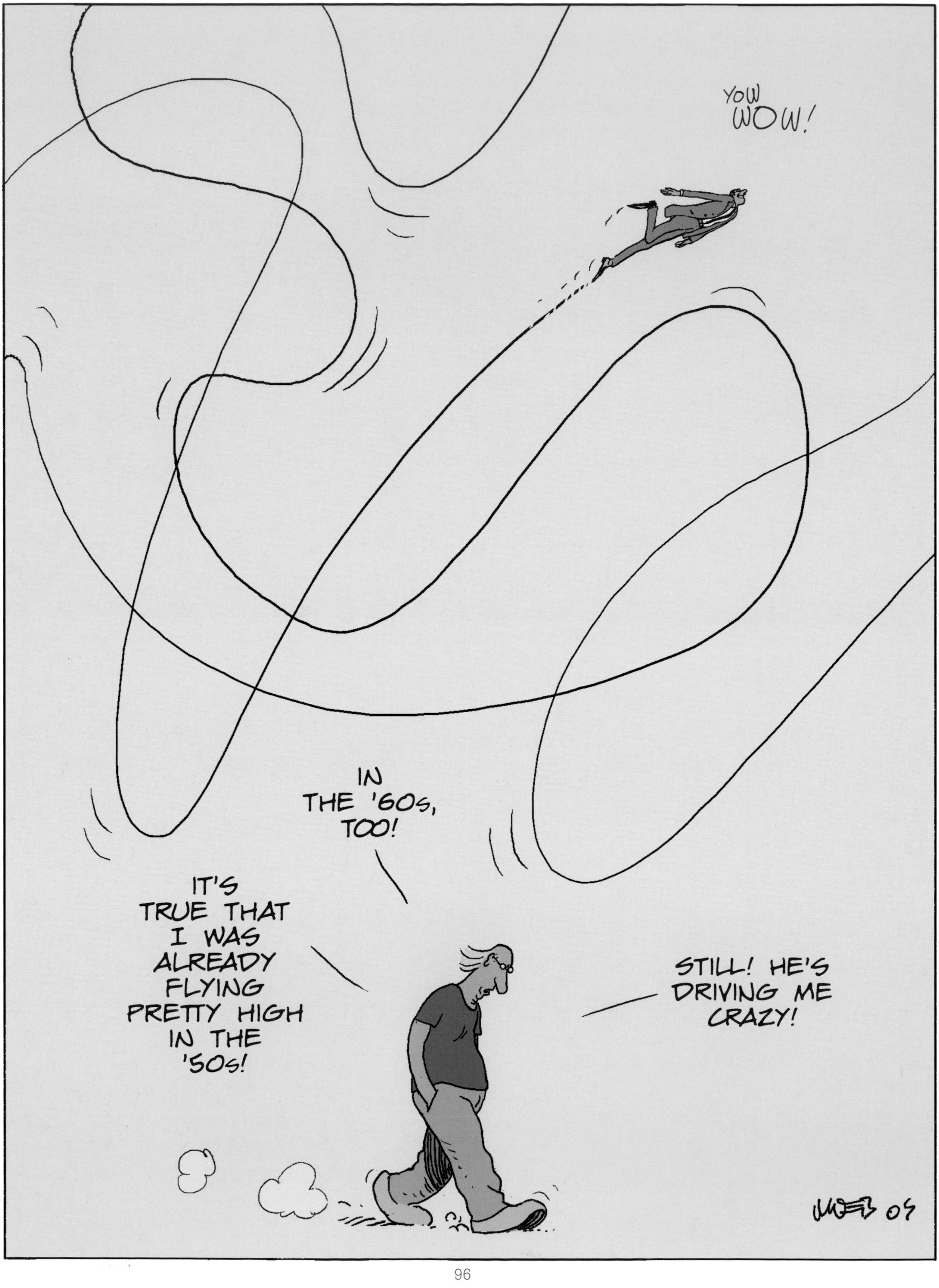
YOW WOW!
IN THE '60s, TOO!
IT'S TRUE THAT I WAS ALREADY FLYING PRETTY HIGH IN THE '50s!
STILL! HE'S DRIVING ME CRAZY!

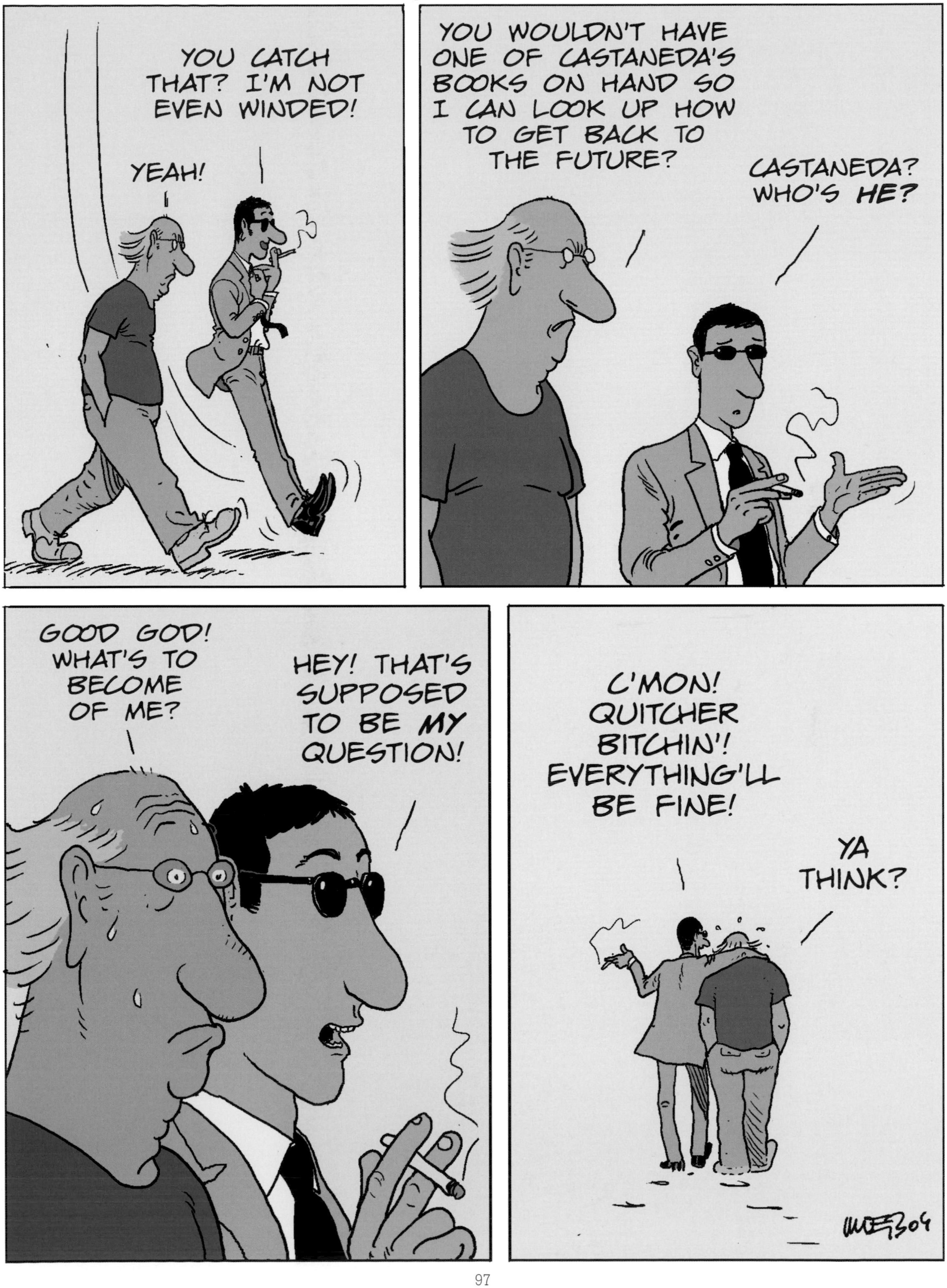
YOU CATCH THAT? I'M NOT EVEN WINDED!
YEAH!
YOU WOULDN'T HAVE ONE OF CASTANEDA'S BOOKS ON HAND SO I CAN LOOK UP HOW TO GET BACK TO THE FUTURE?
CASTANEDA? WHO'S **HE**?
GOOD GOD! WHAT'S TO BECOME OF ME?
HEY! THAT'S SUPPOSED TO BE **MY** QUESTION!
C'MON! QUITCHER BITCHIN'! EVERYTHING'LL BE FINE!
YA THINK?

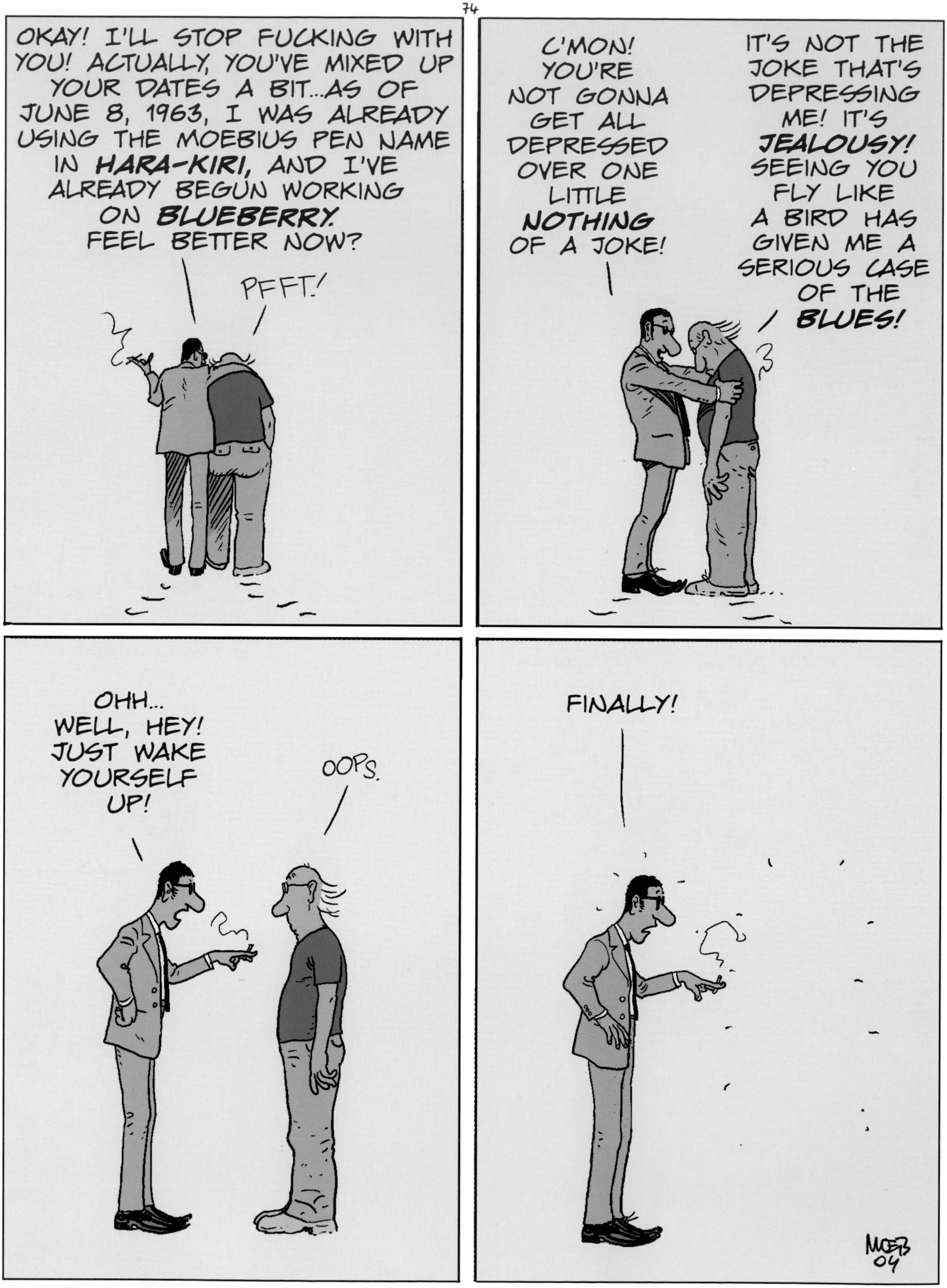
OKAY! I'LL STOP FUCKING WITH YOU! ACTUALLY, YOU'VE MIXED UP YOUR DATES A BIT...AS OF JUNE 8, 1963, I WAS ALREADY USING THE MOEBIUS PEN NAME IN HARA-KIRI, AND I'VE ALREADY BEGUN WORKING ON BLUEBERRY. FEEL BETTER NOW?
PFFT!
C'MON! YOU'RE NOT GONNA GET ALL DEPRESSED OVER ONE LITTLE NOTHING OF A JOKE!
IT'S NOT THE JOKE THAT'S DEPRESSING ME! IT'S JEALOUSY! SEEING YOU FLY LIKE A BIRD HAS GIVEN ME A SERIOUS CASE OF THE BLUES!
OHH... WELL, HEY! JUST WAKE YOURSELF UP!
OOPS.
FINALLY!
MOEB 04

75

WASTELAND

AN OBSESSIVE SEQUENCE OF HILARIOUS "GAGS" BY MOEB
(official release)

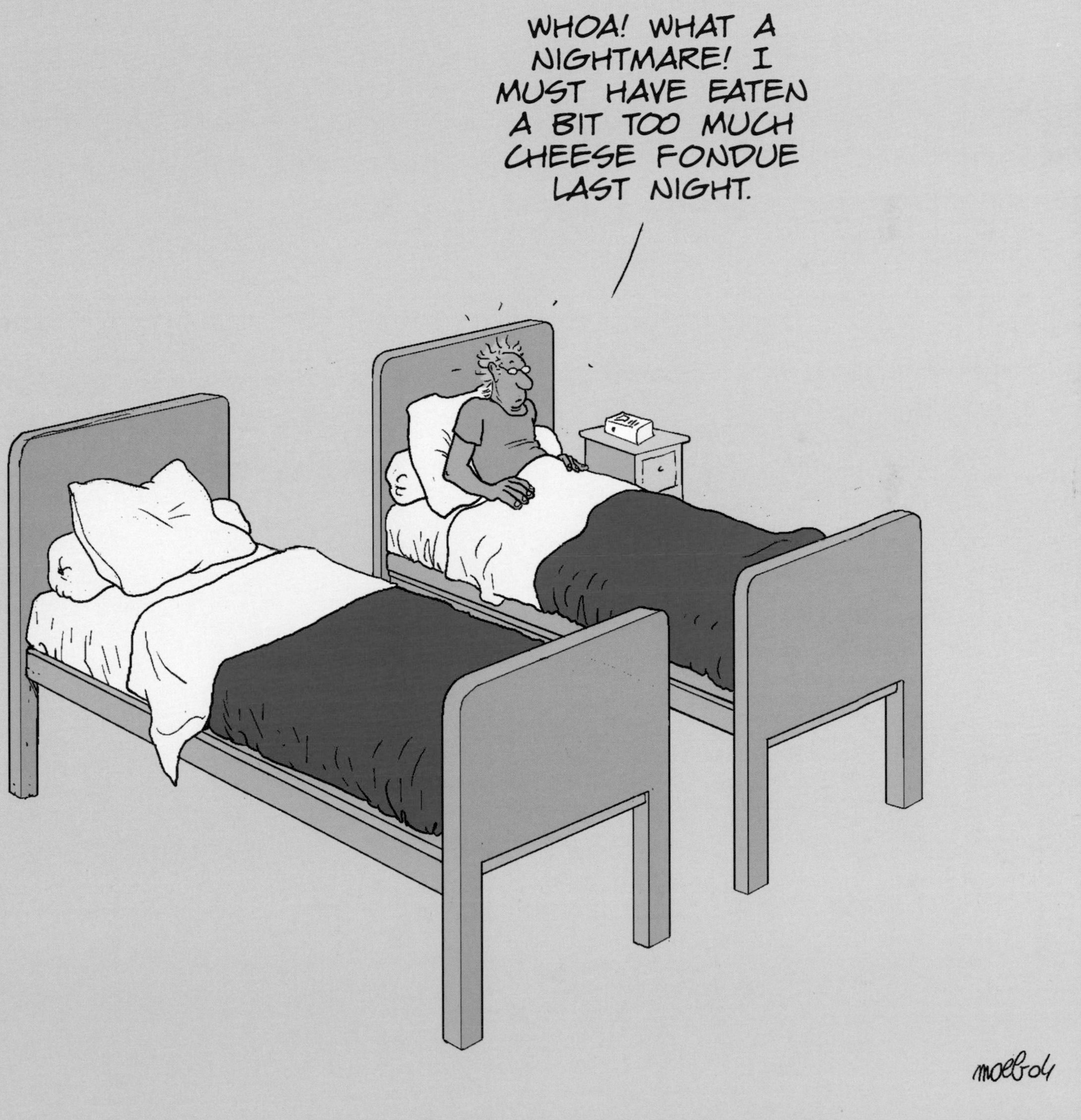
WHOA! WHAT A NIGHTMARE! I MUST HAVE EATEN A BIT TOO MUCH CHEESE FONDUE LAST NIGHT.
moeb 04

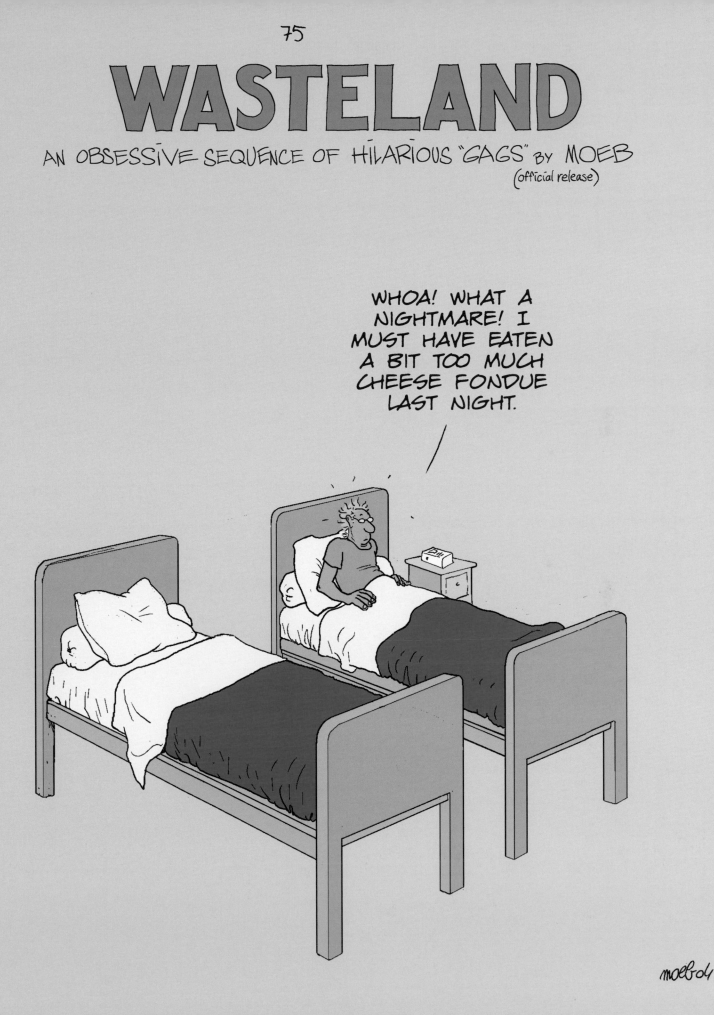

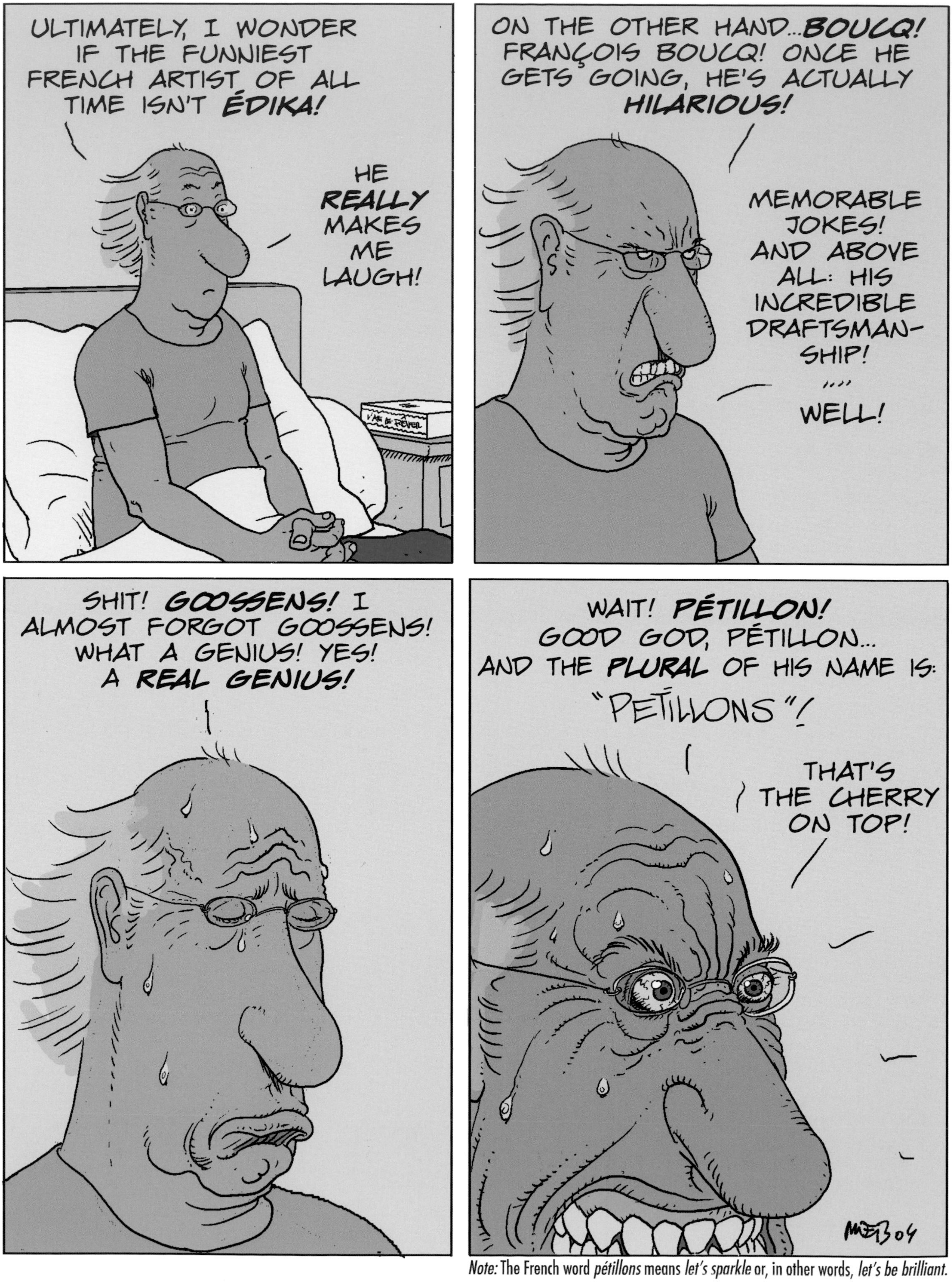
ULTIMATELY, I WONDER IF THE FUNNIEST FRENCH ARTIST OF ALL TIME ISN'T ÉDIKA!
HE REALLY MAKES ME LAUGH!
ON THE OTHER HAND...BOUCQ! FRANÇOIS BOUCQ! ONCE HE GETS GOING, HE'S ACTUALLY HILARIOUS!
MEMORABLE JOKES! AND ABOVE ALL: HIS INCREDIBLE DRAFTSMAN-SHIP!
....
WELL!
SHIT! GOOSSENS! I ALMOST FORGOT GOOSSENS! WHAT A GENIUS! YES! A REAL GENIUS!
WAIT! PÉTILLON! GOOD GOD, PÉTILLON... AND THE PLURAL OF HIS NAME IS:
"PETILLONS"!
THAT'S THE CHERRY ON TOP!

Note: The French word *pétillons* means *let's sparkle* or, in other words, *let's be brilliant.*

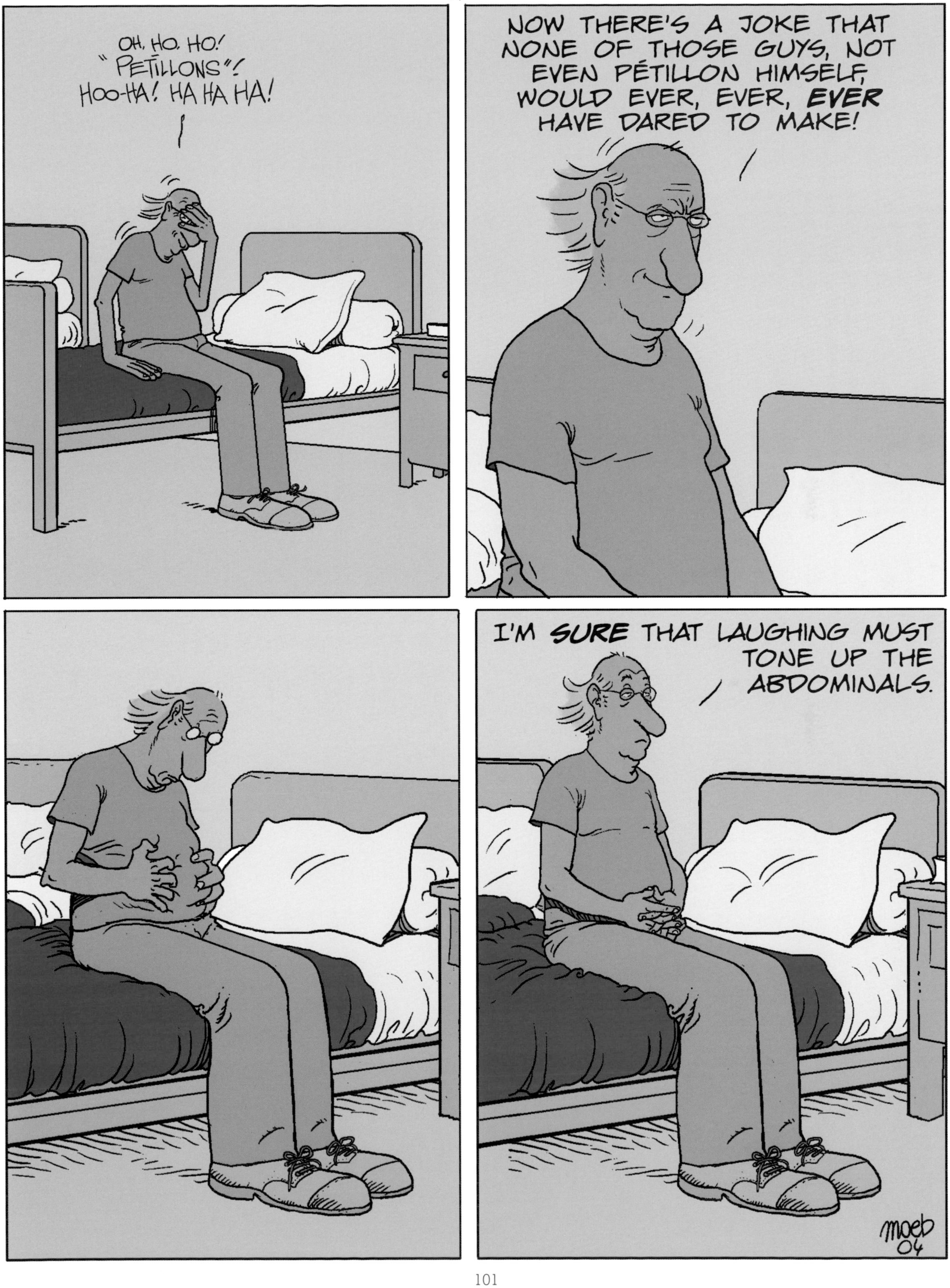
OH, HO, HO! "PETILLONS"! HOO-HA! HA HA HA!
NOW THERE'S A JOKE THAT NONE OF THOSE GUYS, NOT EVEN PÉTILLON HIMSELF, WOULD EVER, EVER, **EVER** HAVE DARED TO MAKE!
I'M **SURE** THAT LAUGHING MUST TONE UP THE ABDOMINALS.
moeb 04

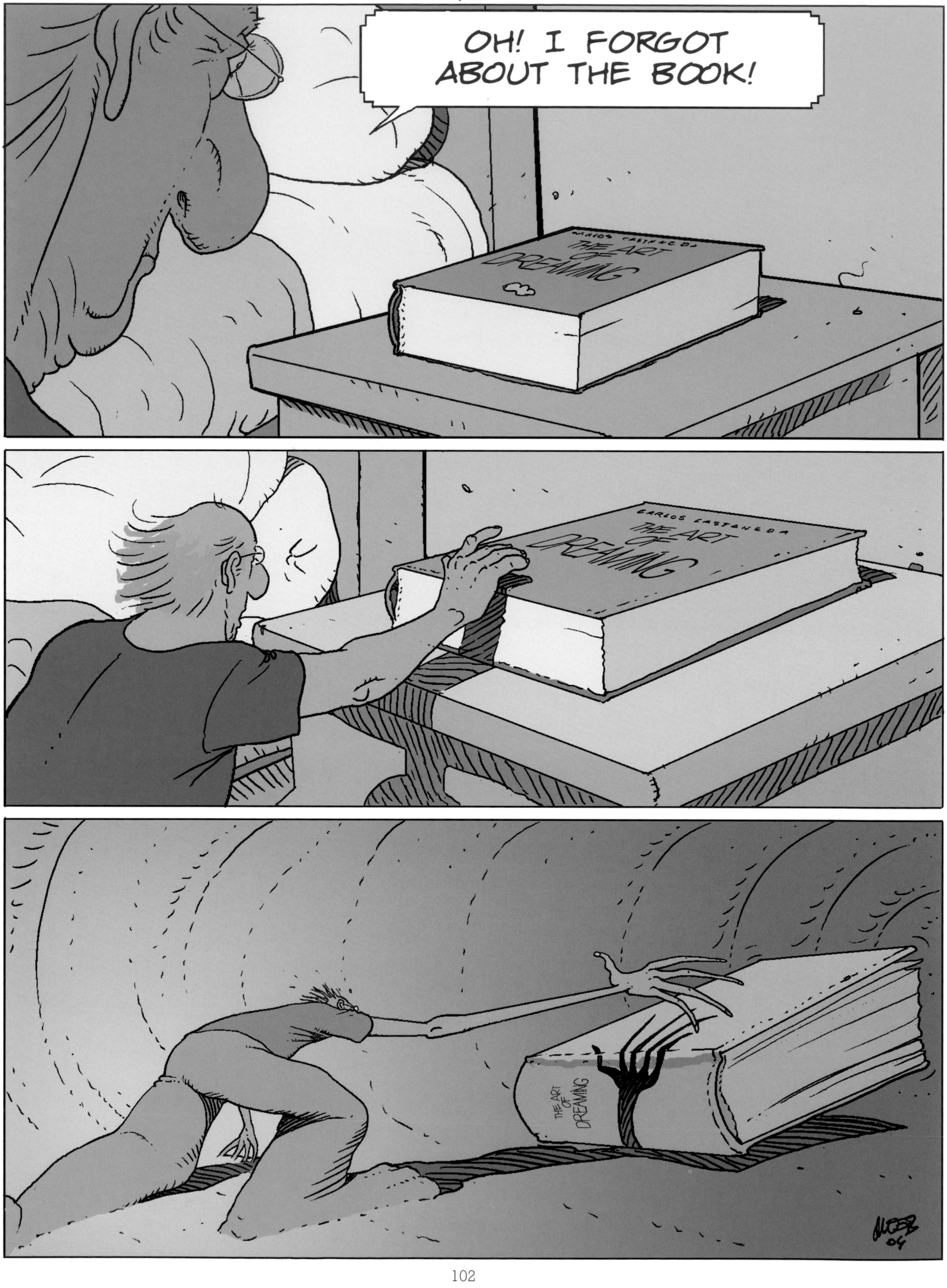
OH! I FORGOT ABOUT THE BOOK!
CARLOS CASTANEDA
THE ART OF DREAMING
THE ART OF DREAMING

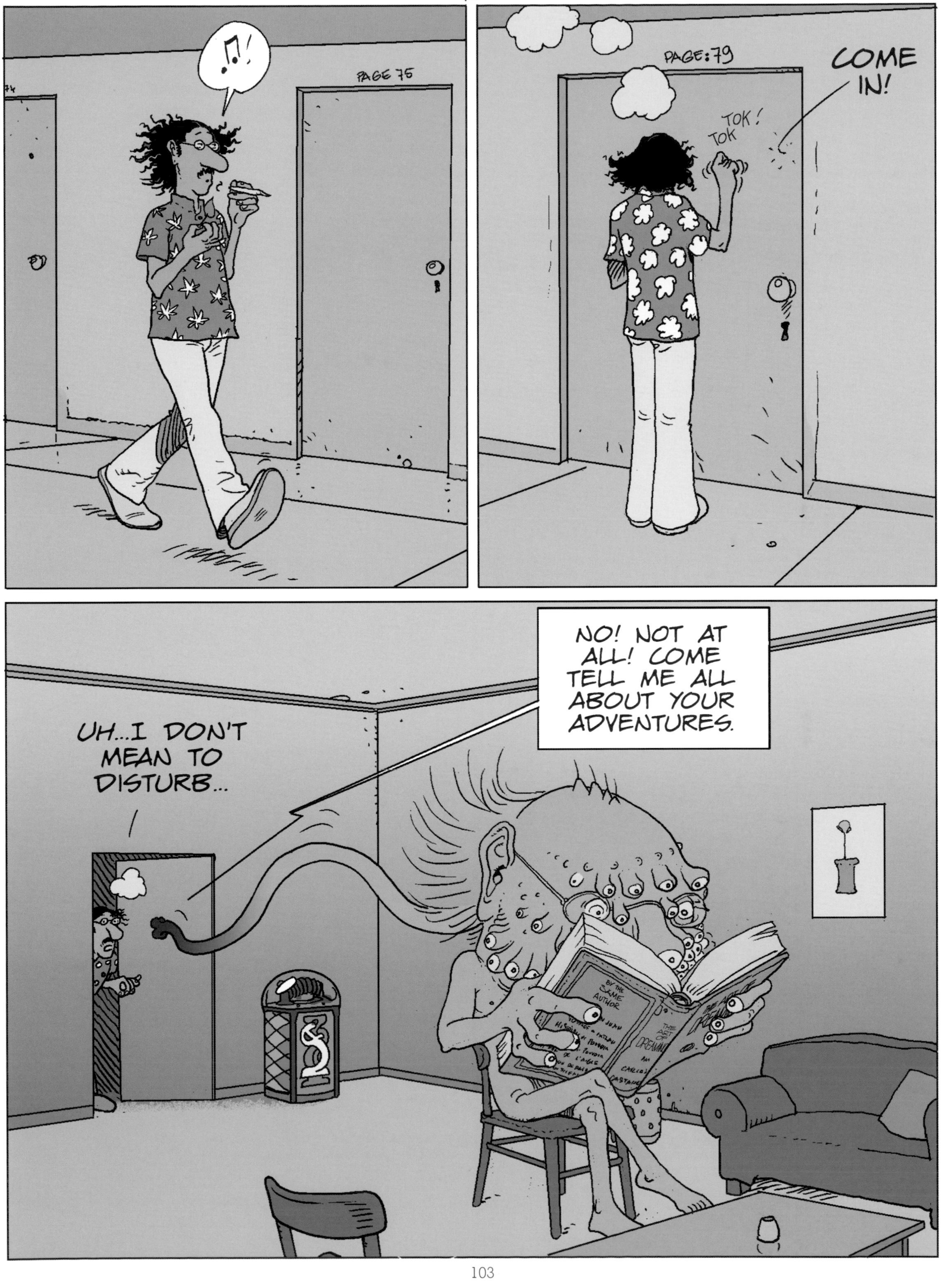
♫!
PAGE 75
PAGE: 79
TOK TOK!
COME IN!
UH...I DON'T MEAN TO DISTURB...
NO! NOT AT ALL! COME TELL ME ALL ABOUT YOUR ADVENTURES.
BY THE SAME AUTHOR
THE ART OF DREAMING

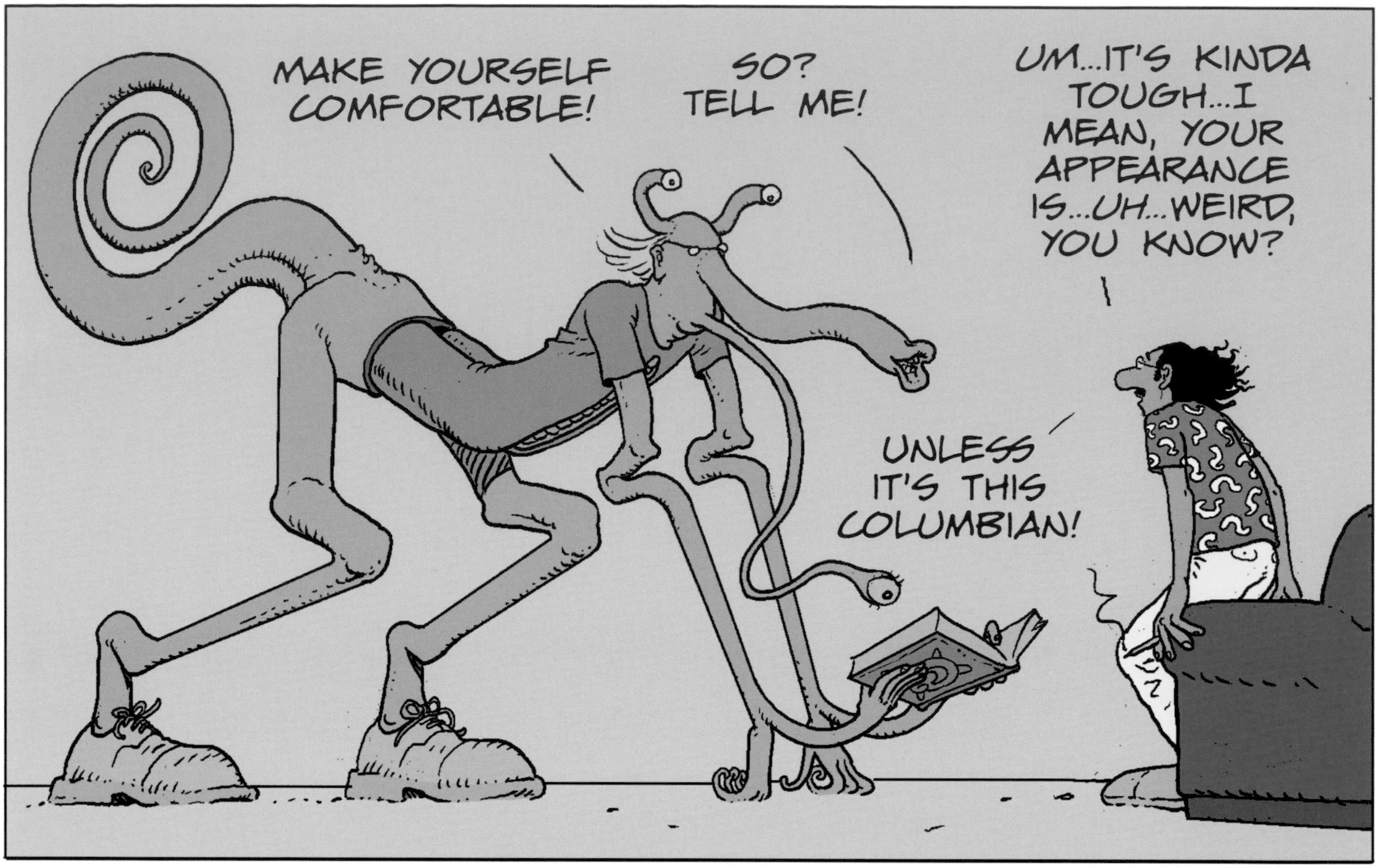
MAKE YOURSELF COMFORTABLE!
SO? TELL ME!
UM...IT'S KINDA TOUGH...I MEAN, YOUR APPEARANCE IS...UH...WEIRD, YOU KNOW?
UNLESS IT'S THIS COLUMBIAN!

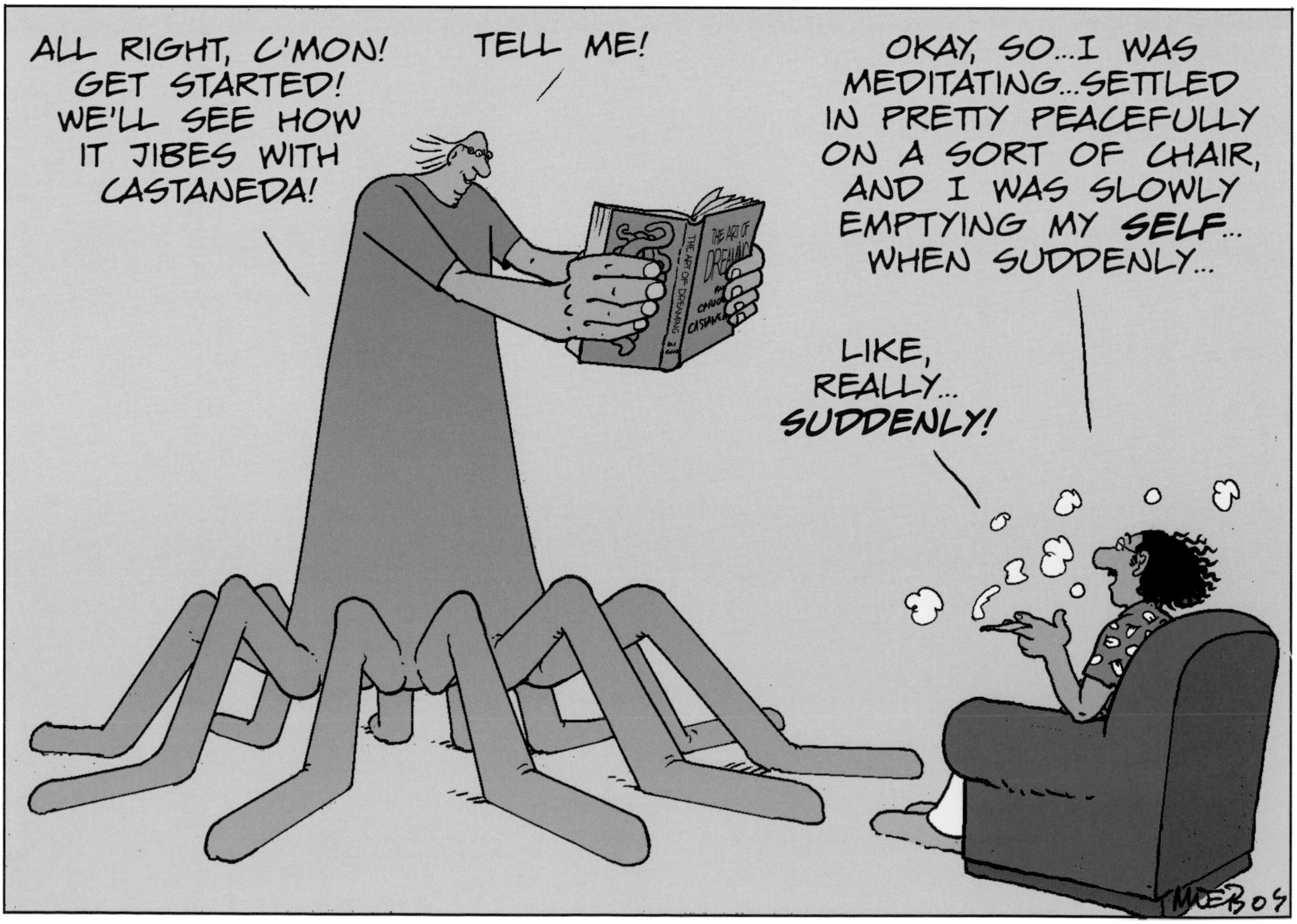
ALL RIGHT, C'MON! GET STARTED! WE'LL SEE HOW IT JIBES WITH CASTANEDA!
TELL ME!
OKAY, SO...I WAS MEDITATING...SETTLED IN PRETTY PEACEFULLY ON A SORT OF CHAIR, AND I WAS SLOWLY EMPTYING MY **SELF**... WHEN SUDDENLY...
LIKE, REALLY... **SUDDENLY!**
THE ART OF DREAMING
MOEBIUS

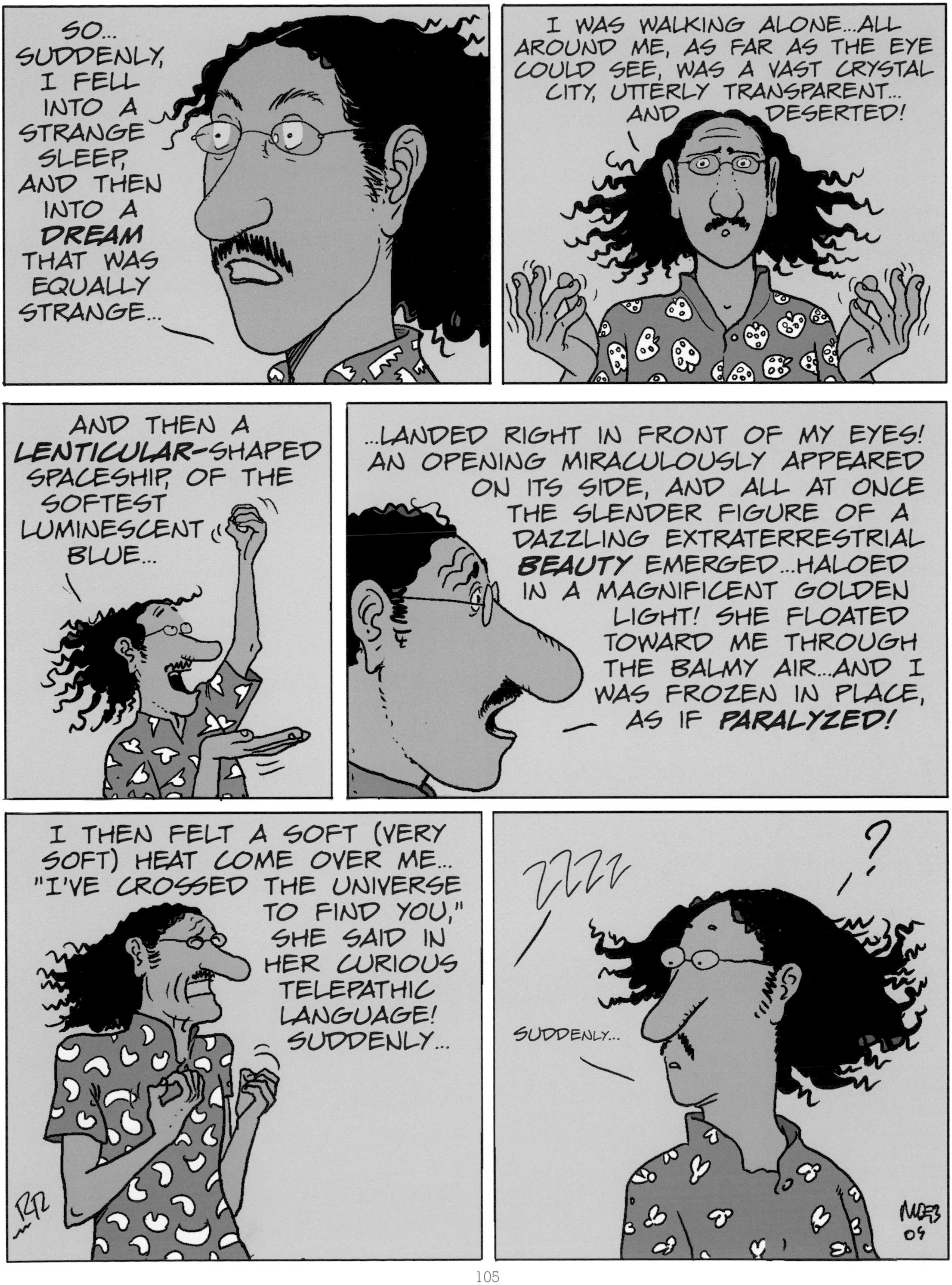
SO... SUDDENLY, I FELL INTO A STRANGE SLEEP, AND THEN INTO A DREAM THAT WAS EQUALLY STRANGE...
I WAS WALKING ALONE...ALL AROUND ME, AS FAR AS THE EYE COULD SEE, WAS A VAST CRYSTAL CITY, UTTERLY TRANSPARENT... AND DESERTED!
AND THEN A LENTICULAR-SHAPED SPACESHIP, OF THE SOFTEST LUMINESCENT BLUE...
...LANDED RIGHT IN FRONT OF MY EYES! AN OPENING MIRACULOUSLY APPEARED ON ITS SIDE, AND ALL AT ONCE THE SLENDER FIGURE OF A DAZZLING EXTRATERRESTRIAL BEAUTY EMERGED...HALOED IN A MAGNIFICENT GOLDEN LIGHT! SHE FLOATED TOWARD ME THROUGH THE BALMY AIR...AND I WAS FROZEN IN PLACE, AS IF PARALYZED!
I THEN FELT A SOFT (VERY SOFT) HEAT COME OVER ME... "I'VE CROSSED THE UNIVERSE TO FIND YOU," SHE SAID IN HER CURIOUS TELEPATHIC LANGUAGE! SUDDENLY...
ZZZZ
?
SUDDENLY...

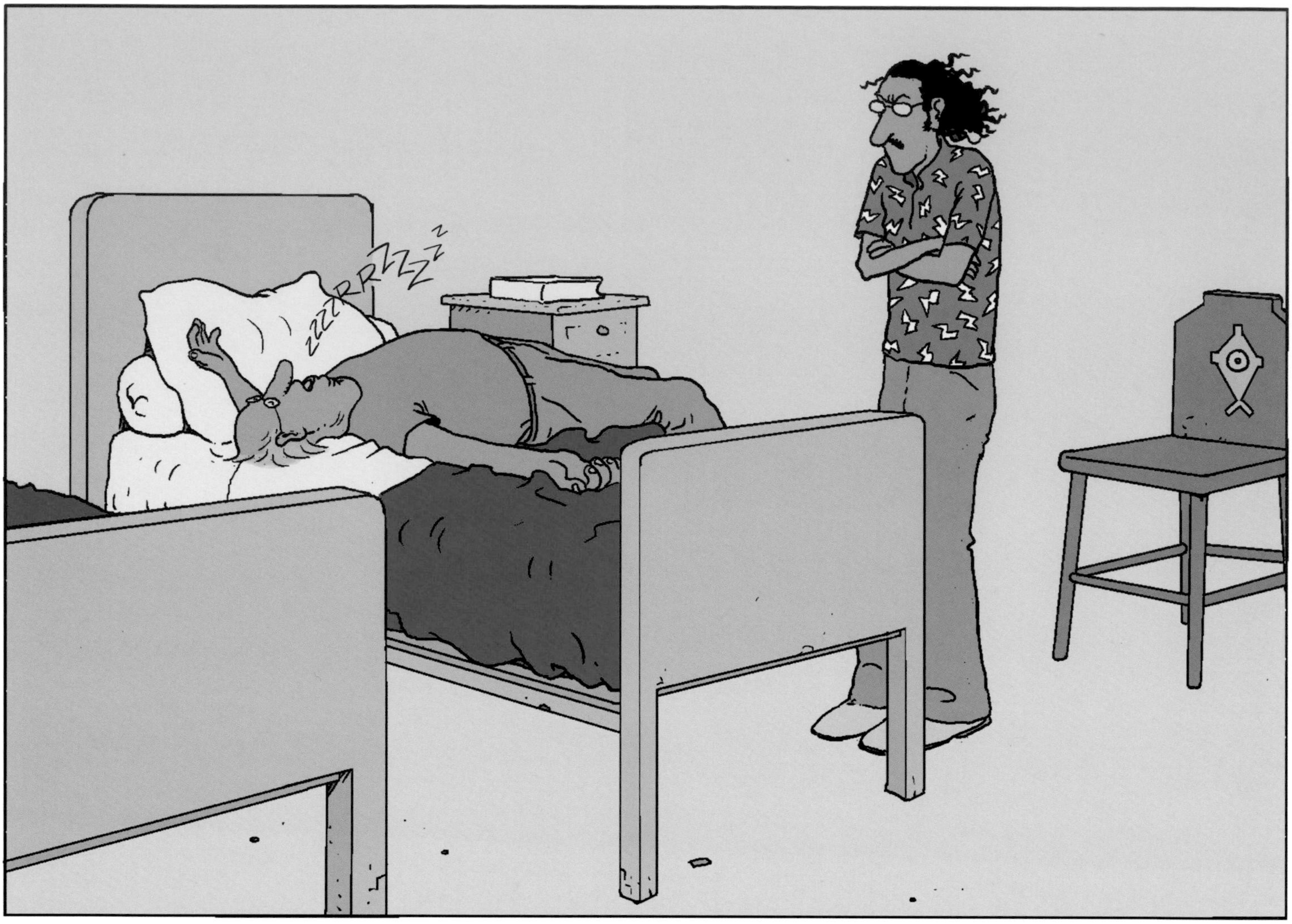
ZZZZRRZZZZZZ

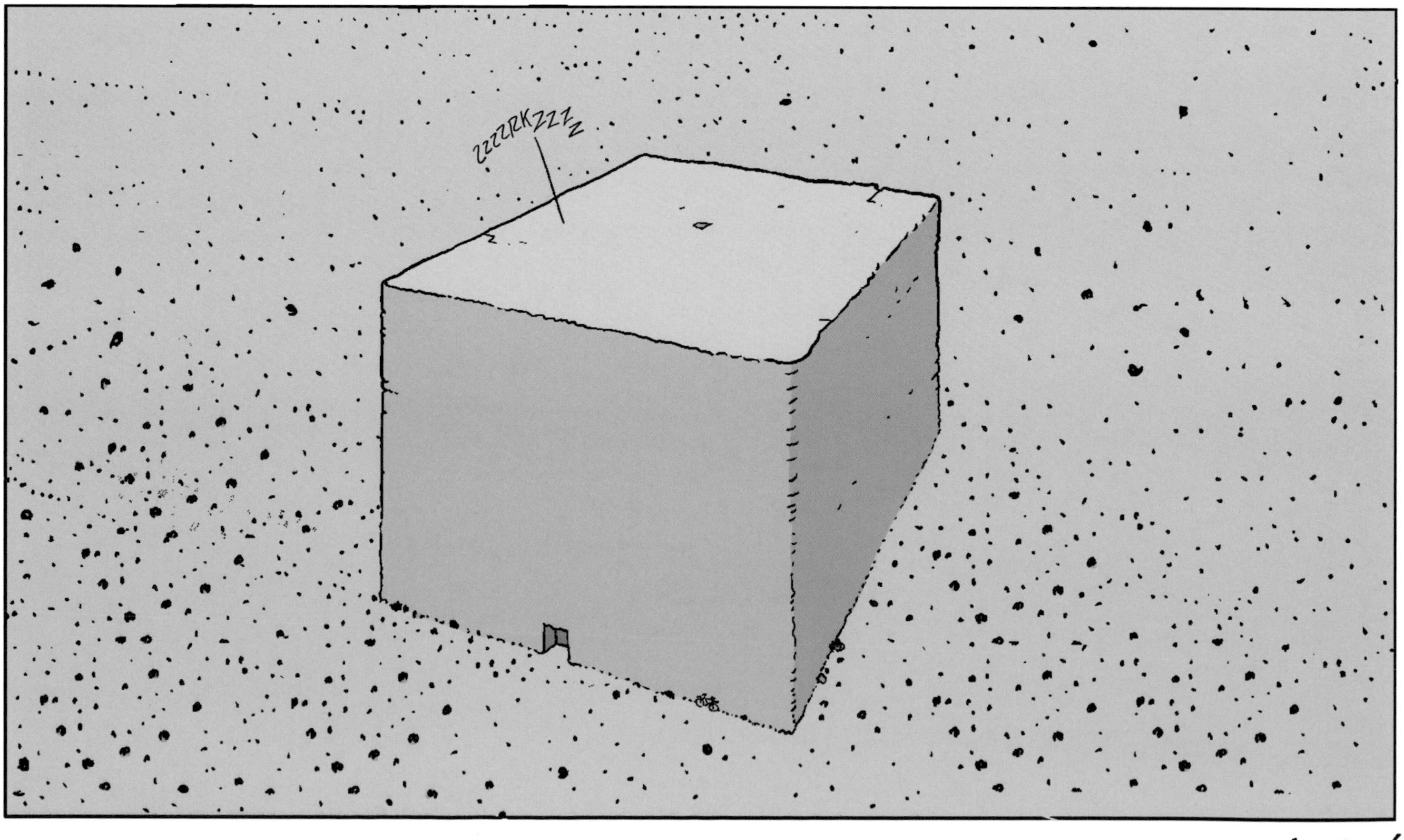
ZZZZRKZZZZ

MŒB 04

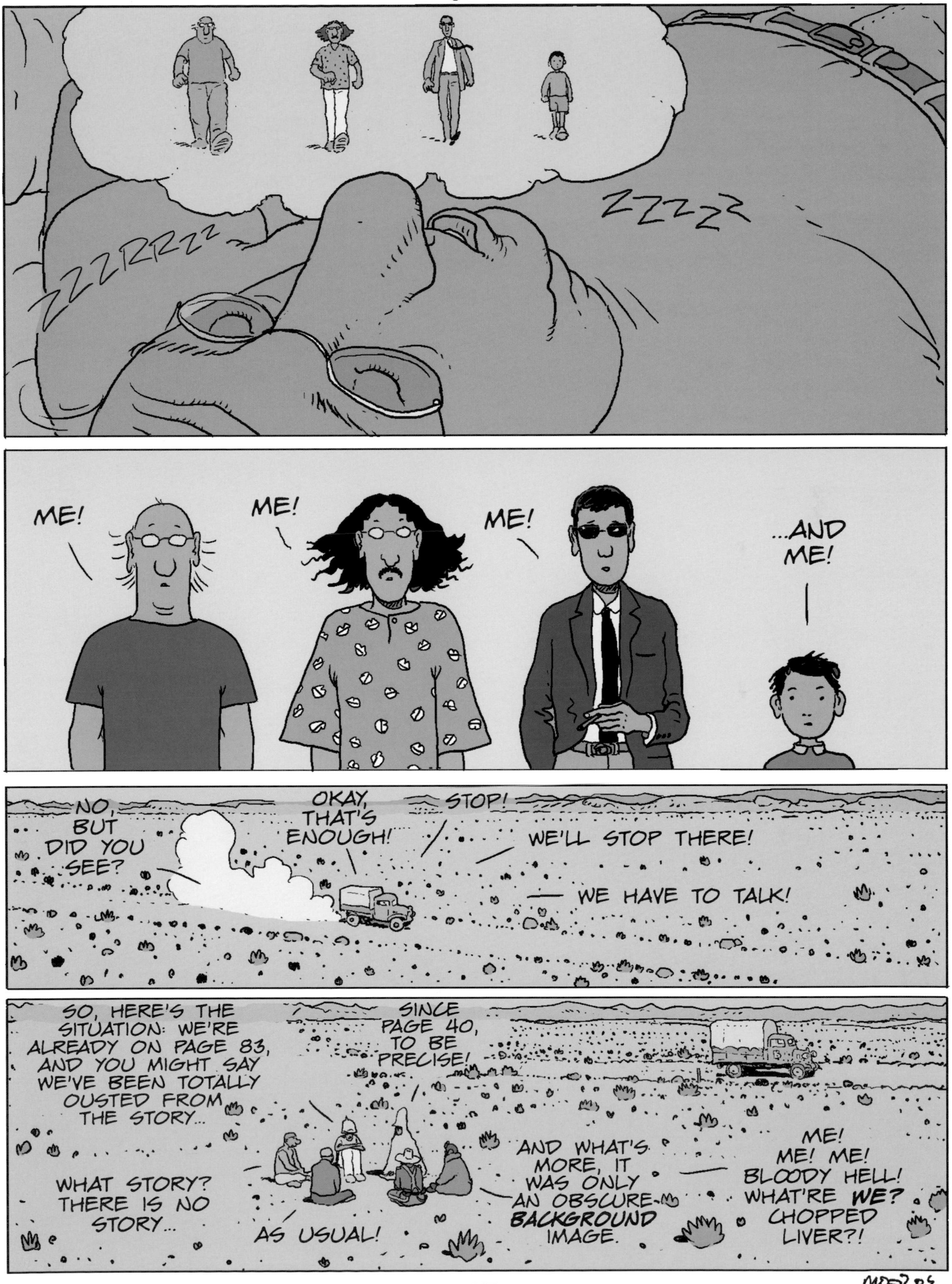
ZZZRRZZZ
ZZZZZ
ME!
ME!
ME!
...AND ME!
NO, BUT DID YOU SEE?
OKAY, THAT'S ENOUGH!
STOP!
WE'LL STOP THERE!
WE HAVE TO TALK!
SO, HERE'S THE SITUATION: WE'RE ALREADY ON PAGE 83, AND YOU MIGHT SAY WE'VE BEEN TOTALLY OUSTED FROM THE STORY...
SINCE PAGE 40, TO BE PRECISE!
WHAT STORY? THERE IS NO STORY...
AS USUAL!
AND WHAT'S MORE, IT WAS ONLY AN OBSCURE **BACKGROUND** IMAGE.
ME! ME! ME! BLOODY HELL! WHAT'RE **WE?** CHOPPED LIVER?!
MOEB 09

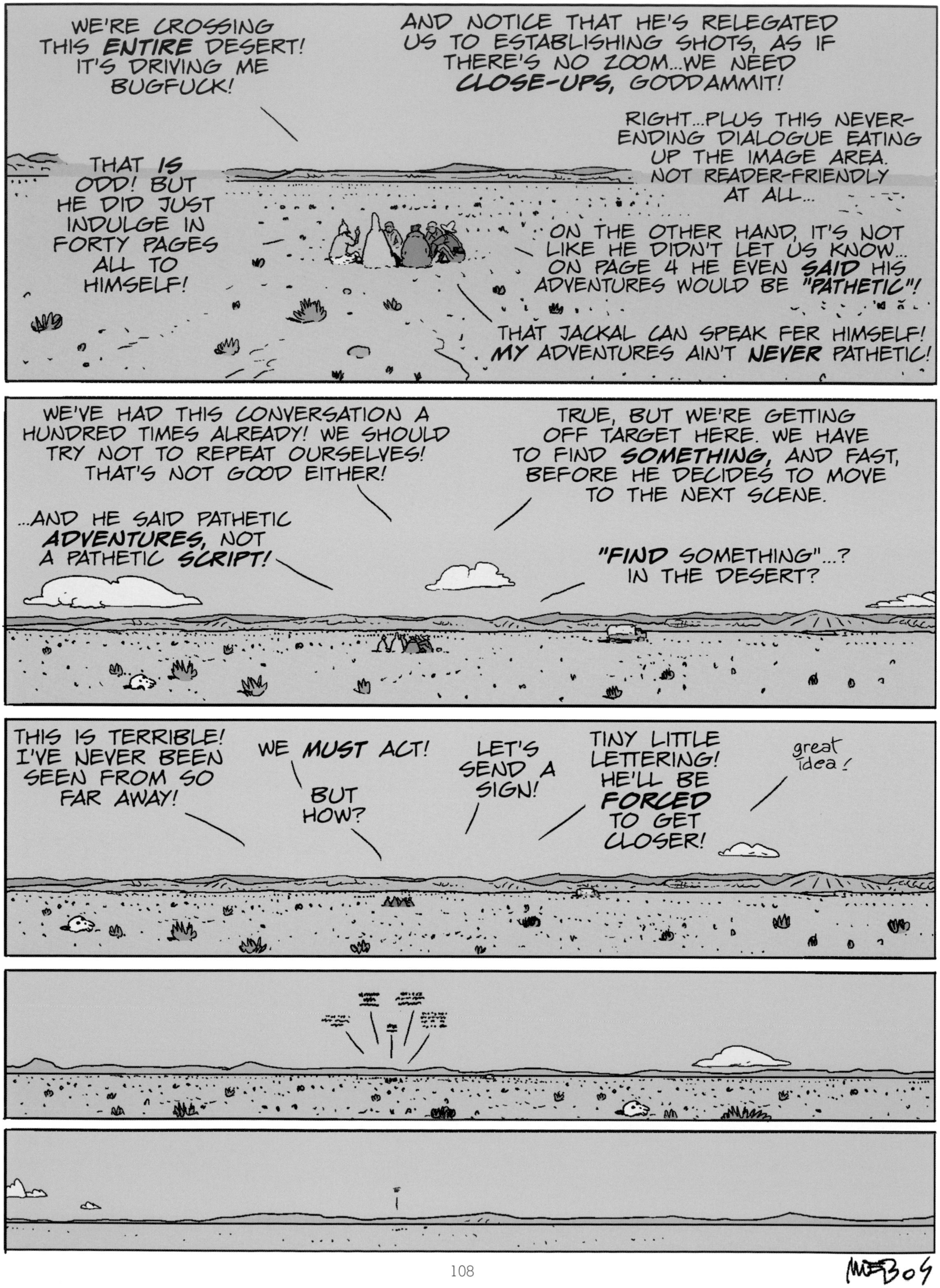
WE'RE CROSSING THIS ENTIRE DESERT! IT'S DRIVING ME BUGFUCK!
AND NOTICE THAT HE'S RELEGATED US TO ESTABLISHING SHOTS, AS IF THERE'S NO ZOOM...WE NEED CLOSE-UPS, GODDAMMIT!
RIGHT...PLUS THIS NEVER-ENDING DIALOGUE EATING UP THE IMAGE AREA. NOT READER-FRIENDLY AT ALL...
THAT IS ODD! BUT HE DID JUST INDULGE IN FORTY PAGES ALL TO HIMSELF!
ON THE OTHER HAND, IT'S NOT LIKE HE DIDN'T LET US KNOW... ON PAGE 4 HE EVEN SAID HIS ADVENTURES WOULD BE "PATHETIC"!
THAT JACKAL CAN SPEAK FER HIMSELF! MY ADVENTURES AIN'T NEVER PATHETIC!
WE'VE HAD THIS CONVERSATION A HUNDRED TIMES ALREADY! WE SHOULD TRY NOT TO REPEAT OURSELVES! THAT'S NOT GOOD EITHER!
TRUE, BUT WE'RE GETTING OFF TARGET HERE. WE HAVE TO FIND SOMETHING, AND FAST, BEFORE HE DECIDES TO MOVE TO THE NEXT SCENE.
...AND HE SAID PATHETIC ADVENTURES, NOT A PATHETIC SCRIPT!
"FIND SOMETHING"...? IN THE DESERT?
THIS IS TERRIBLE! I'VE NEVER BEEN SEEN FROM SO FAR AWAY!
WE MUST ACT!
BUT HOW?
LET'S SEND A SIGN!
TINY LITTLE LETTERING! HE'LL BE FORCED TO GET CLOSER!
great idea!

MŒBIUS

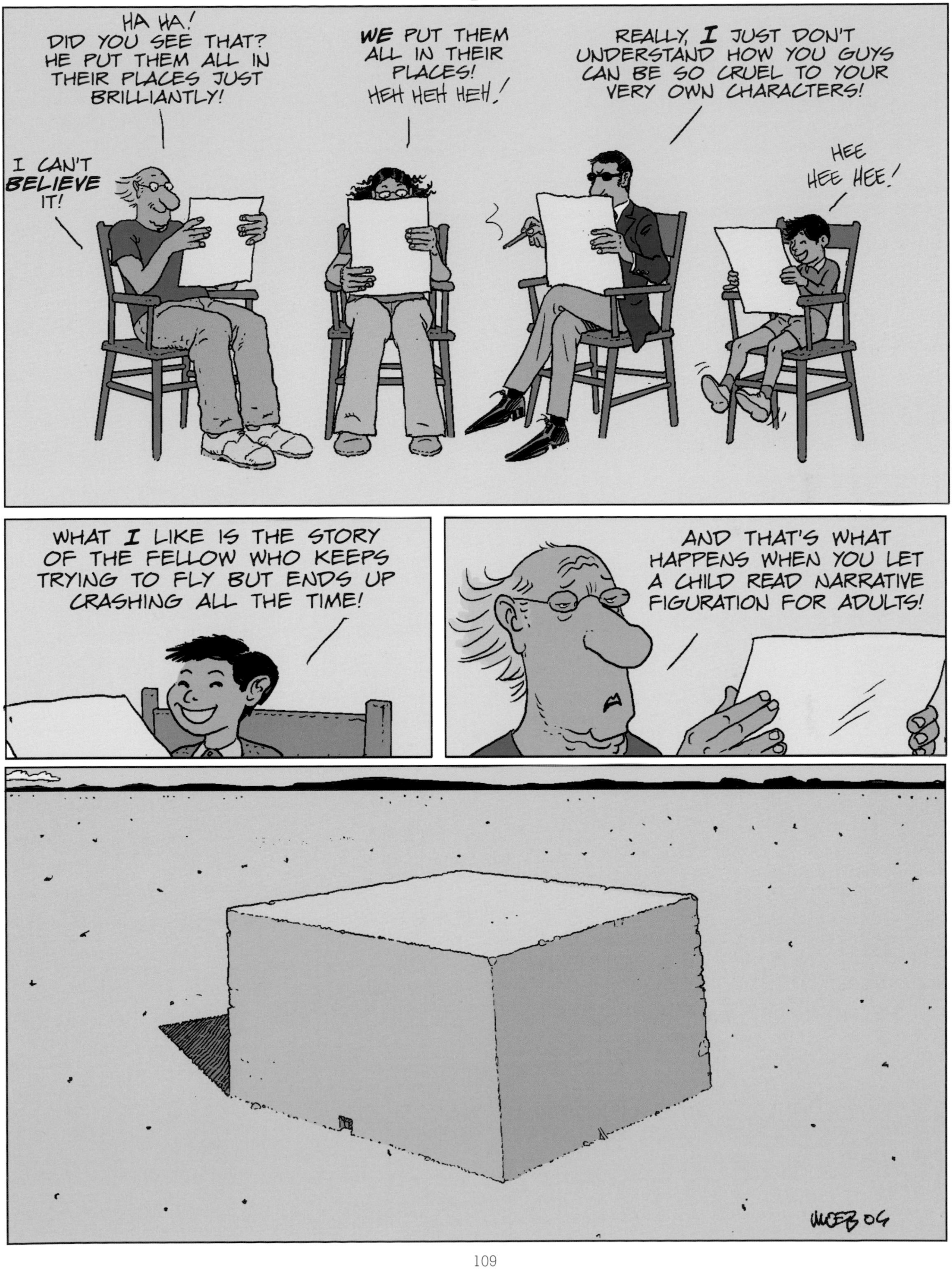
HA HA!
DID YOU SEE THAT? HE PUT THEM ALL IN THEIR PLACES JUST BRILLIANTLY!
I CAN'T BELIEVE IT!
WE PUT THEM ALL IN THEIR PLACES! HEH HEH HEH!
REALLY, I JUST DON'T UNDERSTAND HOW YOU GUYS CAN BE SO CRUEL TO YOUR VERY OWN CHARACTERS!
HEE HEE HEE!
WHAT I LIKE IS THE STORY OF THE FELLOW WHO KEEPS TRYING TO FLY BUT ENDS UP CRASHING ALL THE TIME!
AND THAT'S WHAT HAPPENS WHEN YOU LET A CHILD READ NARRATIVE FIGURATION FOR ADULTS!
MOEB 09

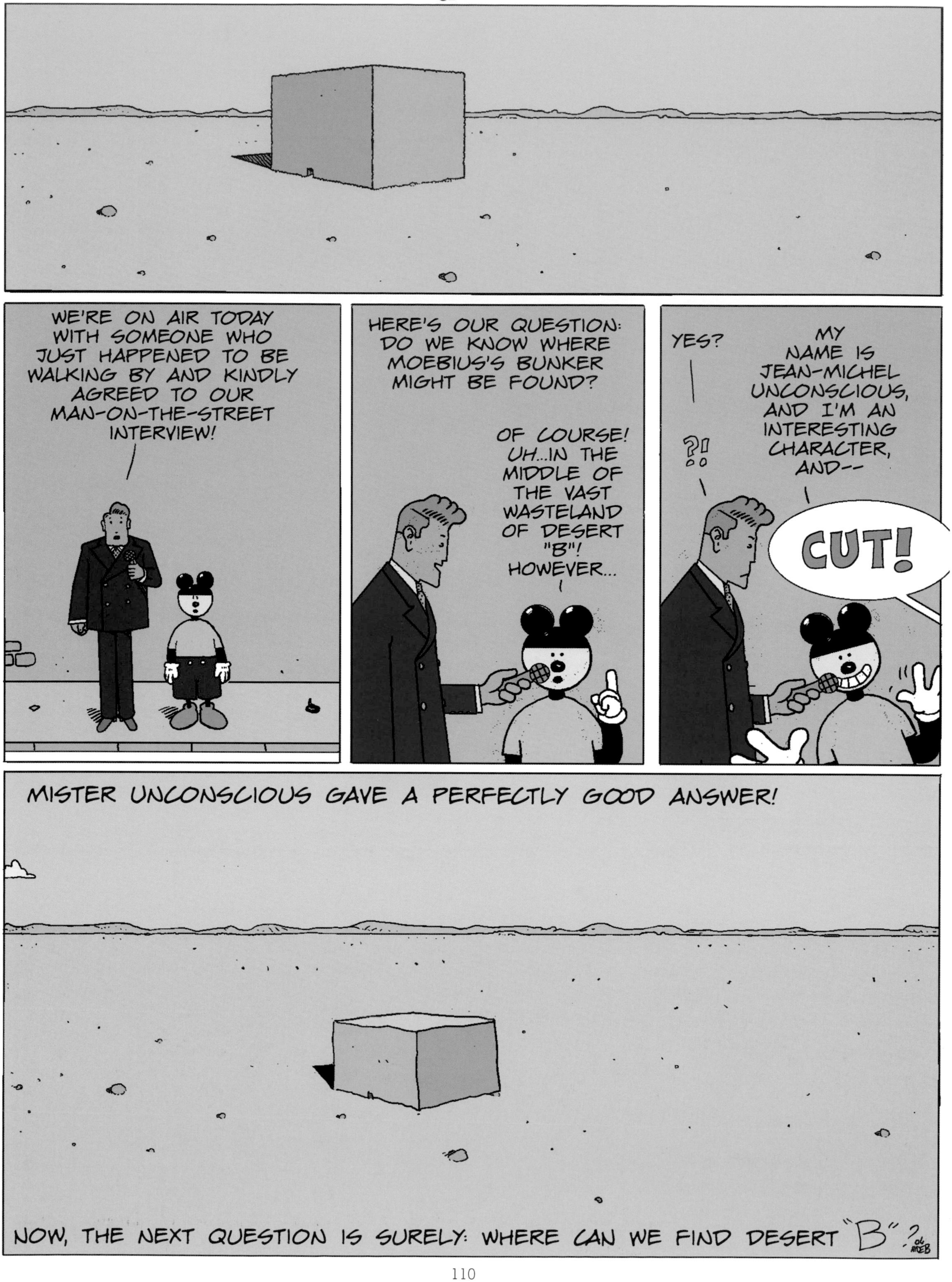
WE'RE ON AIR TODAY WITH SOMEONE WHO JUST HAPPENED TO BE WALKING BY AND KINDLY AGREED TO OUR MAN-ON-THE-STREET INTERVIEW!
HERE'S OUR QUESTION: DO WE KNOW WHERE MOEBIUS'S BUNKER MIGHT BE FOUND?
OF COURSE! UH...IN THE MIDDLE OF THE VAST WASTELAND OF DESERT "B"! HOWEVER...
YES?
?!
MY NAME IS JEAN-MICHEL UNCONSCIOUS, AND I'M AN INTERESTING CHARACTER, AND--
CUT!
MISTER UNCONSCIOUS GAVE A PERFECTLY GOOD ANSWER!
NOW, THE NEXT QUESTION IS SURELY: WHERE CAN WE FIND DESERT "B"?

AND FOR THAT, WE MUST ALL TAKE A SLIGHT STEP BACK.
JUST A BIT MORE, PLEASE...
MORE! GO ON! BACK AWAY!
STILL BACKING AWAY...
AH! WE'RE FINALLY BEGINNING TO IDENTIFY SOMETHING IN THE ART...
IT LOOKS DECIDEDLY LIKE SOME SORT OF RECTANGULAR SURFACE.
MŒB 04

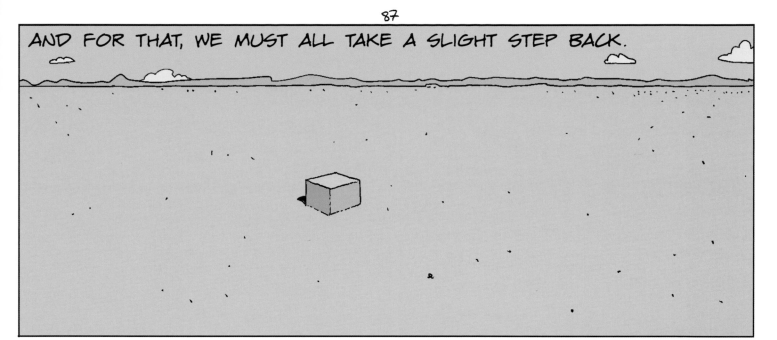

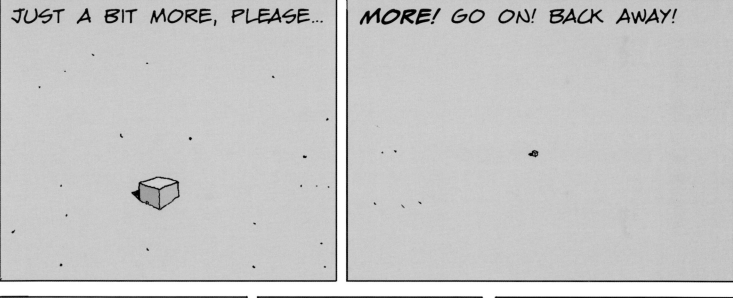

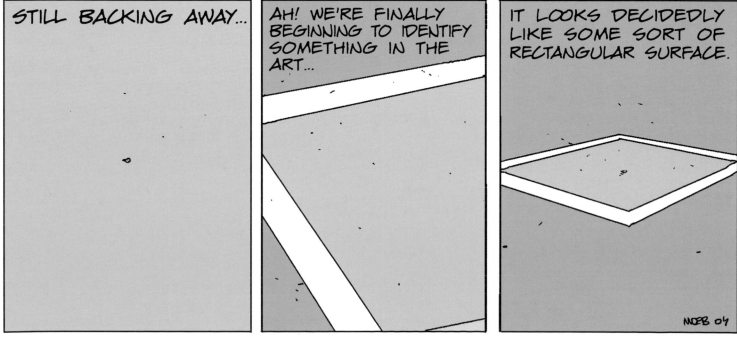

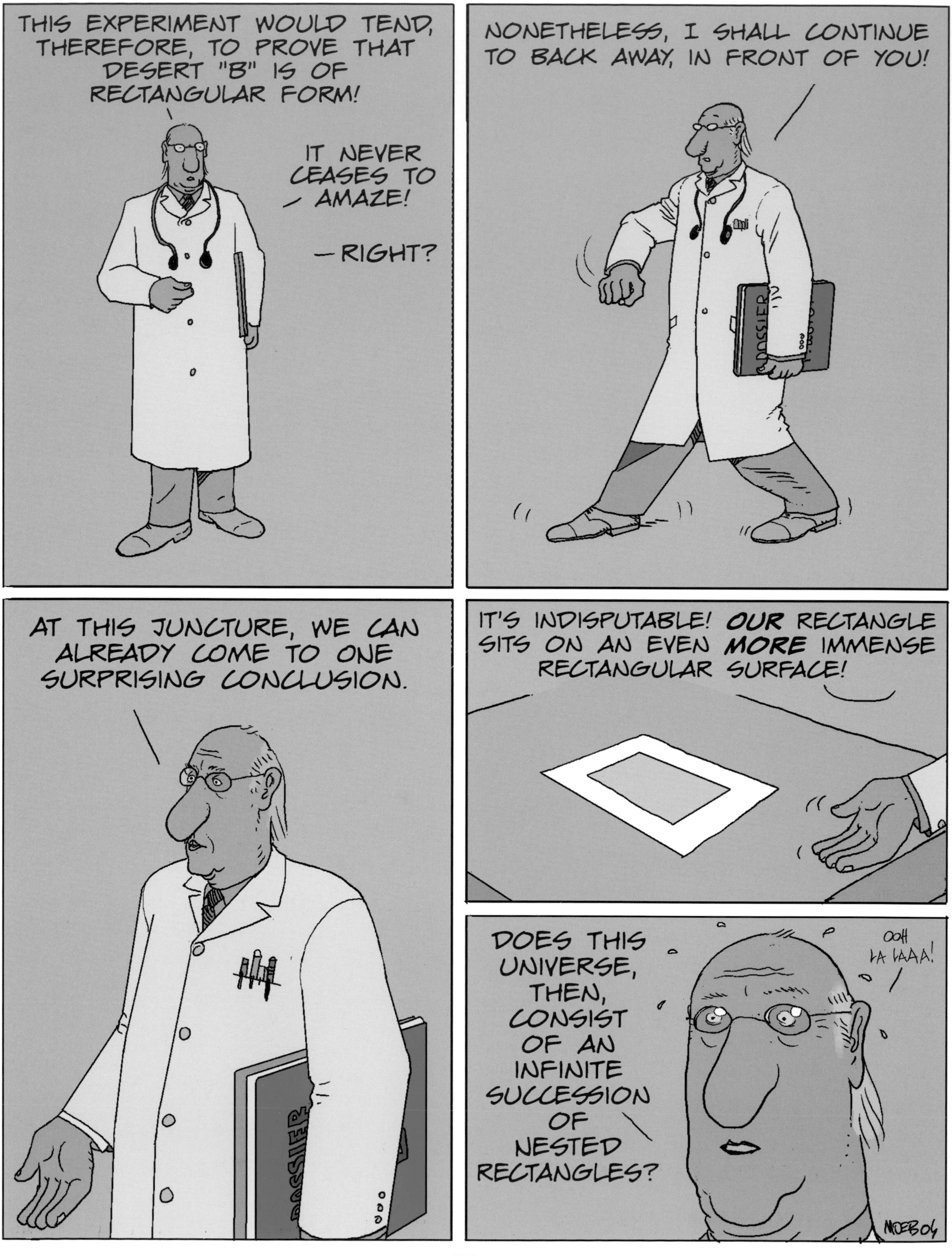
THIS EXPERIMENT WOULD TEND, THEREFORE, TO PROVE THAT DESERT "B" IS OF RECTANGULAR FORM!
IT NEVER CEASES TO AMAZE!
—RIGHT?
NONETHELESS, I SHALL CONTINUE TO BACK AWAY, IN FRONT OF YOU!
DOSSIER
AT THIS JUNCTURE, WE CAN ALREADY COME TO ONE SURPRISING CONCLUSION.
IT'S INDISPUTABLE! **OUR** RECTANGLE SITS ON AN EVEN **MORE** IMMENSE RECTANGULAR SURFACE!
DOES THIS UNIVERSE, THEN, CONSIST OF AN INFINITE SUCCESSION OF NESTED RECTANGLES?
OOH LA LAAA!
MOEB04

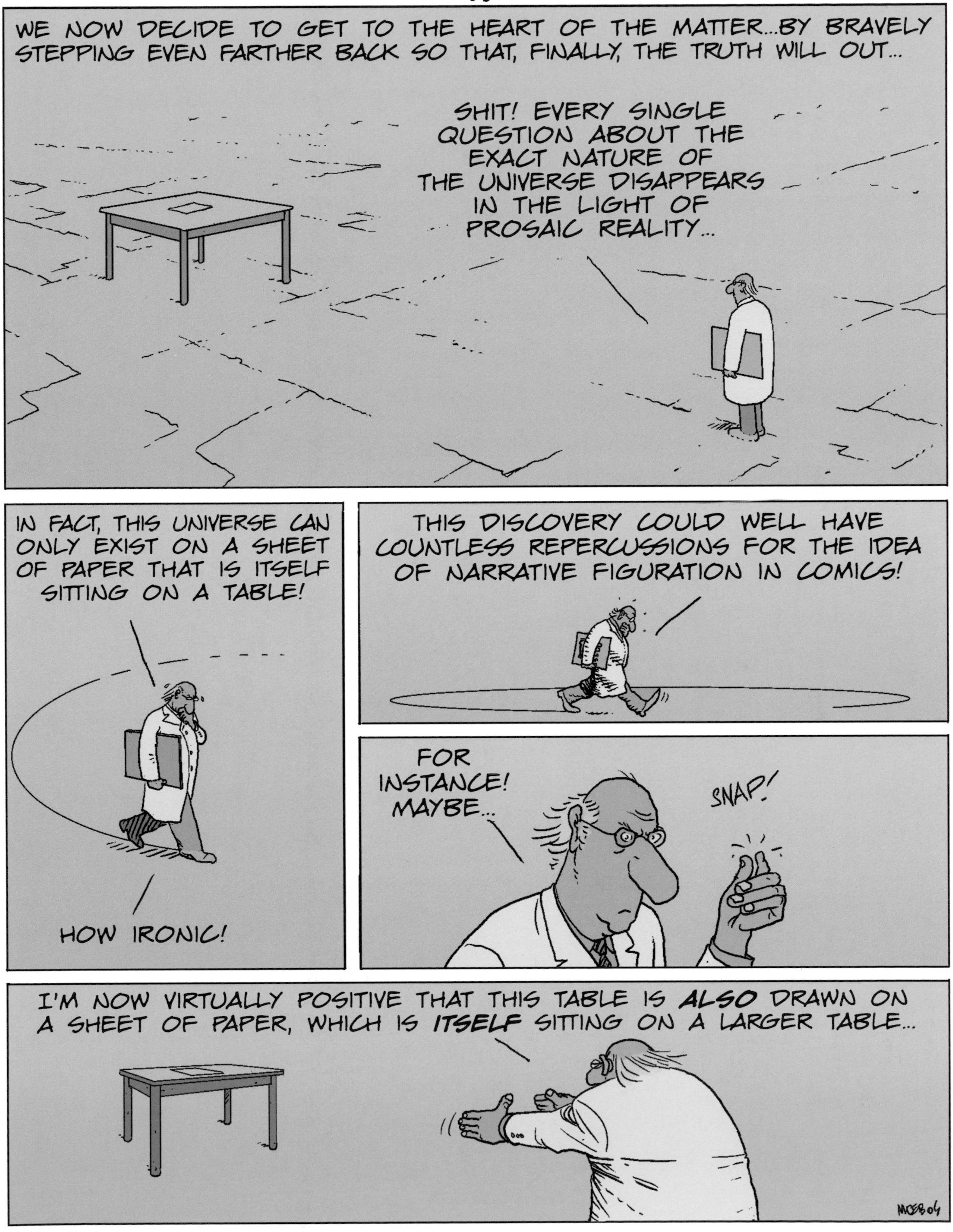
WE NOW DECIDE TO GET TO THE HEART OF THE MATTER...BY BRAVELY STEPPING EVEN FARTHER BACK SO THAT, FINALLY, THE TRUTH WILL OUT...
SHIT! EVERY SINGLE QUESTION ABOUT THE EXACT NATURE OF THE UNIVERSE DISAPPEARS IN THE LIGHT OF PROSAIC REALITY...
IN FACT, THIS UNIVERSE CAN ONLY EXIST ON A SHEET OF PAPER THAT IS ITSELF SITTING ON A TABLE!
HOW IRONIC!
THIS DISCOVERY COULD WELL HAVE COUNTLESS REPERCUSSIONS FOR THE IDEA OF NARRATIVE FIGURATION IN COMICS!
FOR INSTANCE! MAYBE...
SNAP!
I'M NOW VIRTUALLY POSITIVE THAT THIS TABLE IS **ALSO** DRAWN ON A SHEET OF PAPER, WHICH IS **ITSELF** SITTING ON A LARGER TABLE...
MOEB 04

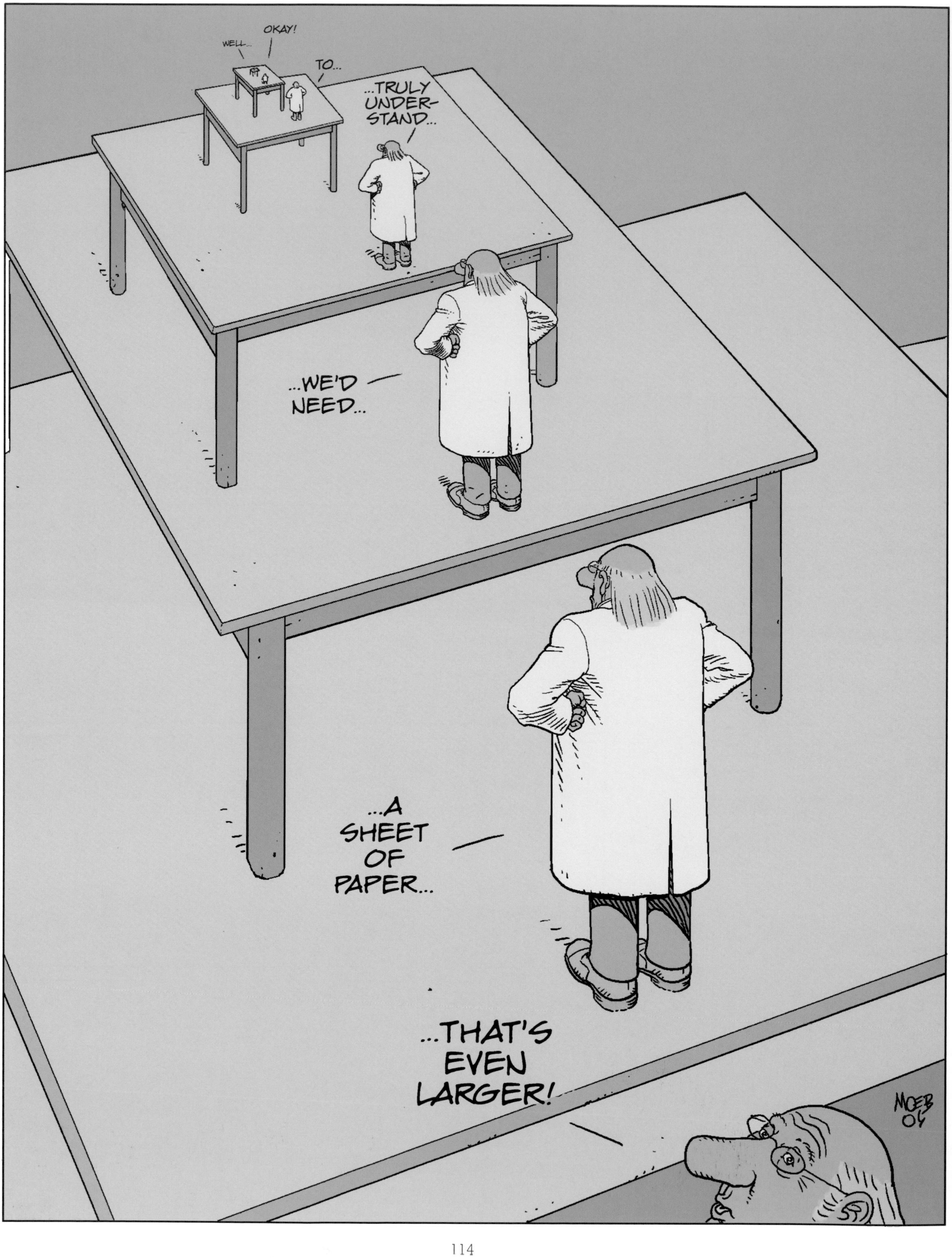
WELL...
OKAY!
TO...
...TRULY UNDER-STAND...
...WE'D NEED...
...A SHEET OF PAPER...
...THAT'S EVEN LARGER!
MOEB 04

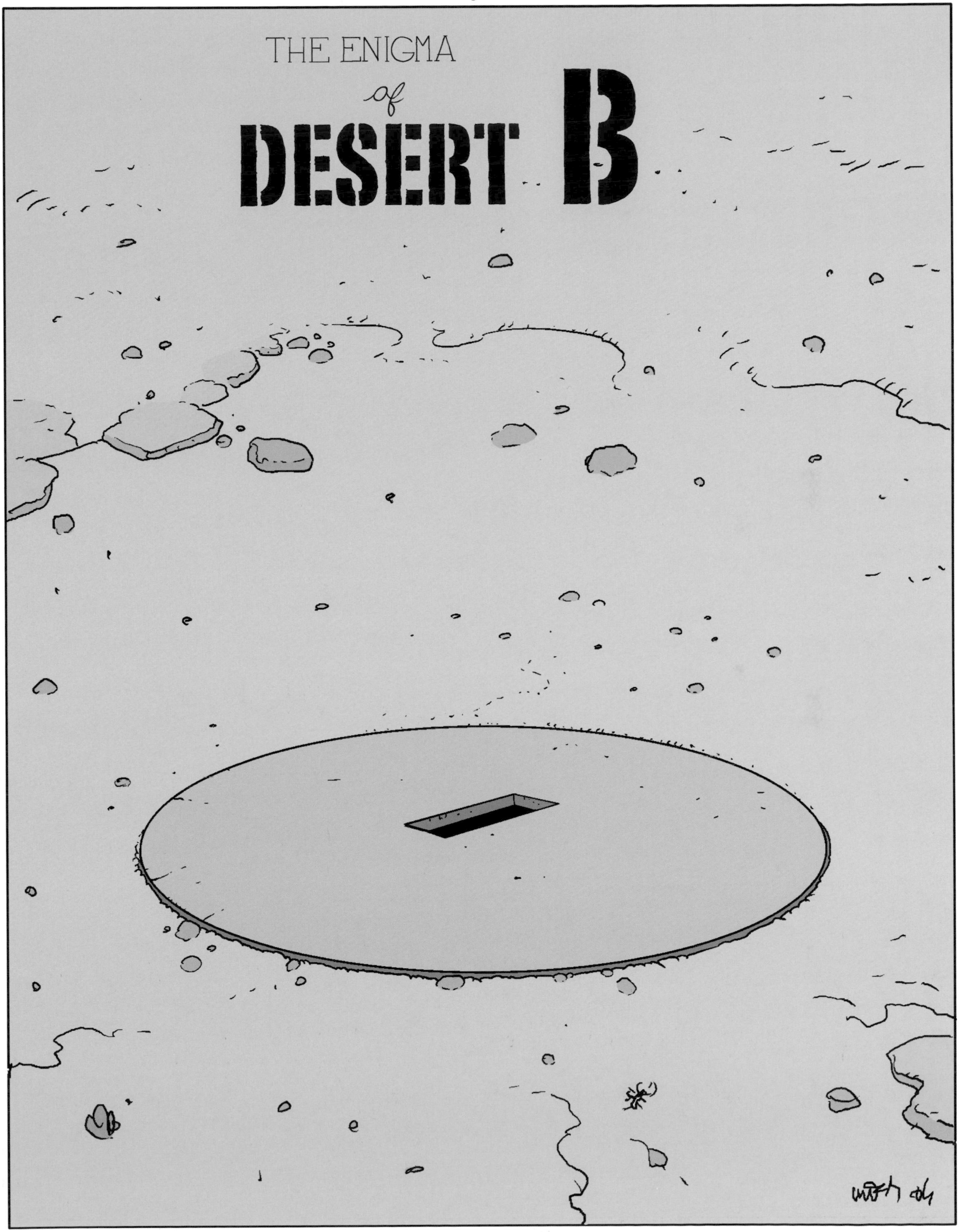
THE ENIGMA
of
DESERT B

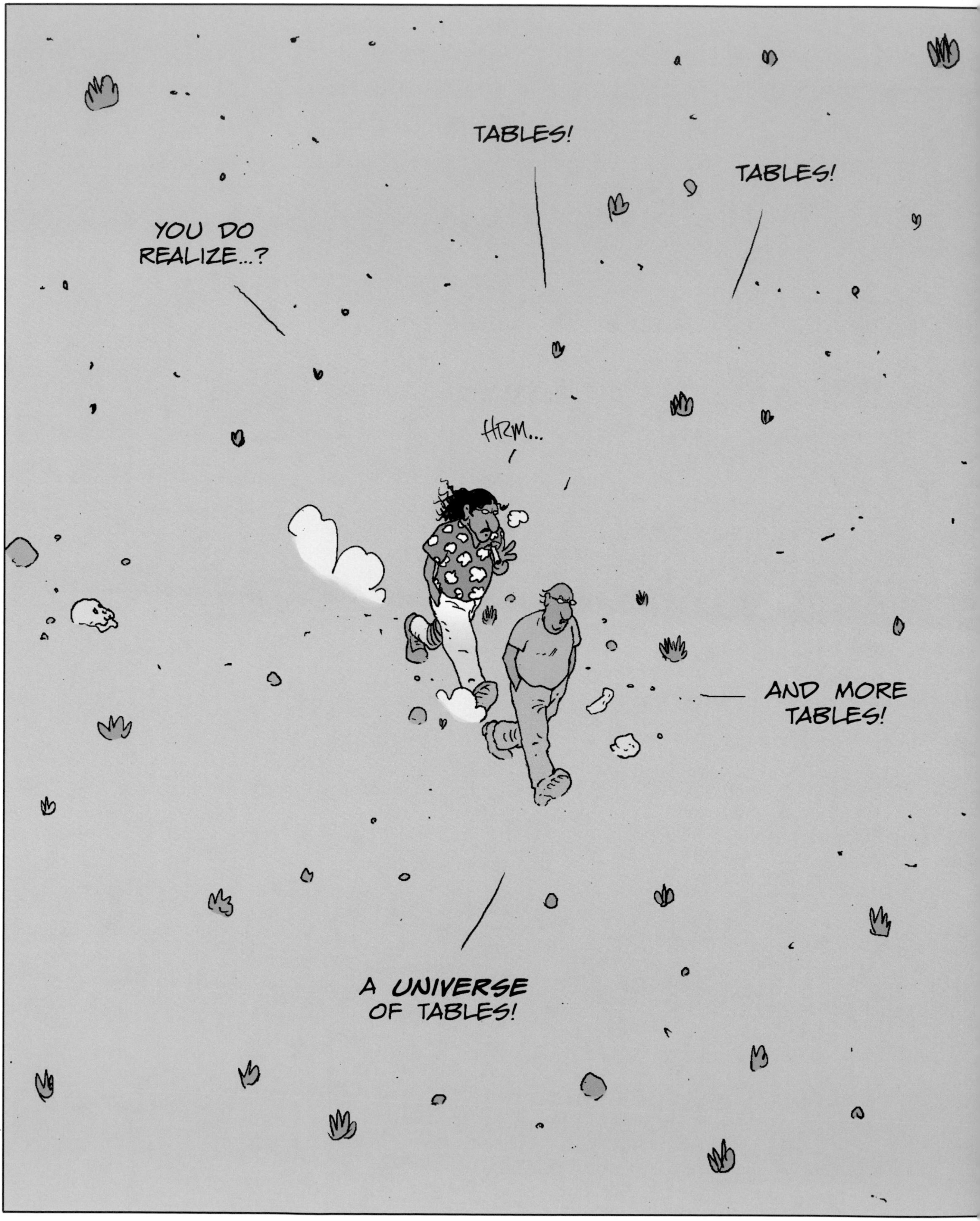
YOU DO REALIZE...?
TABLES!
TABLES!
AND MORE TABLES!
A UNIVERSE OF TABLES!
HRM...

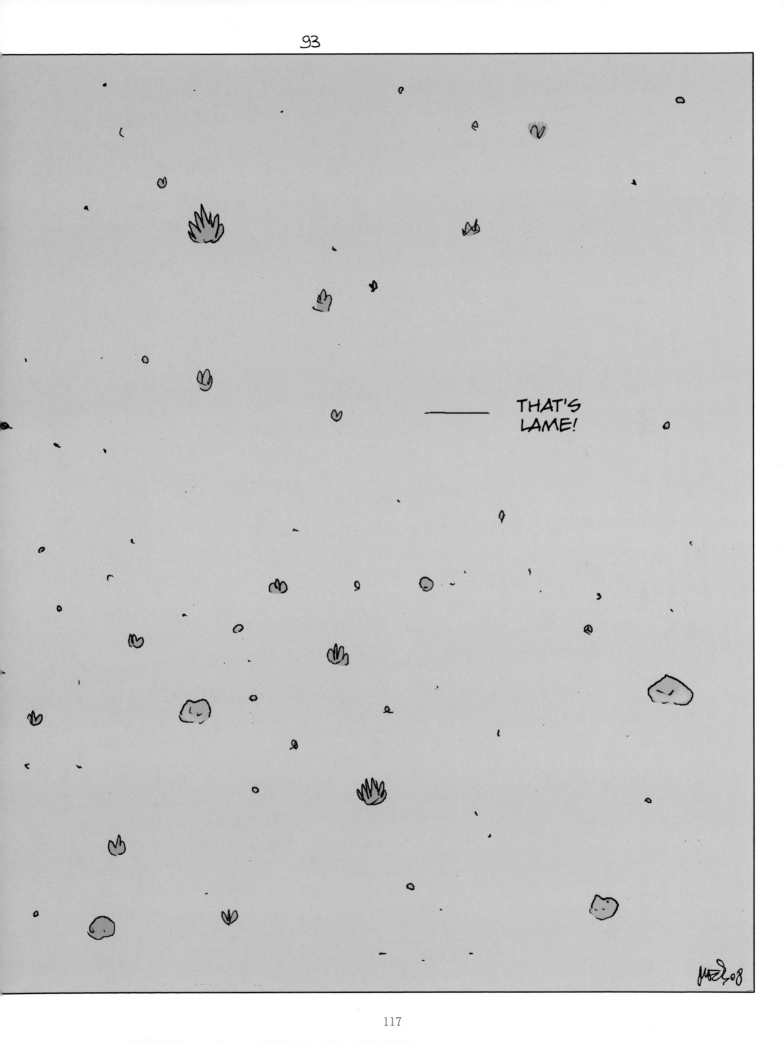

THAT'S
LAME!

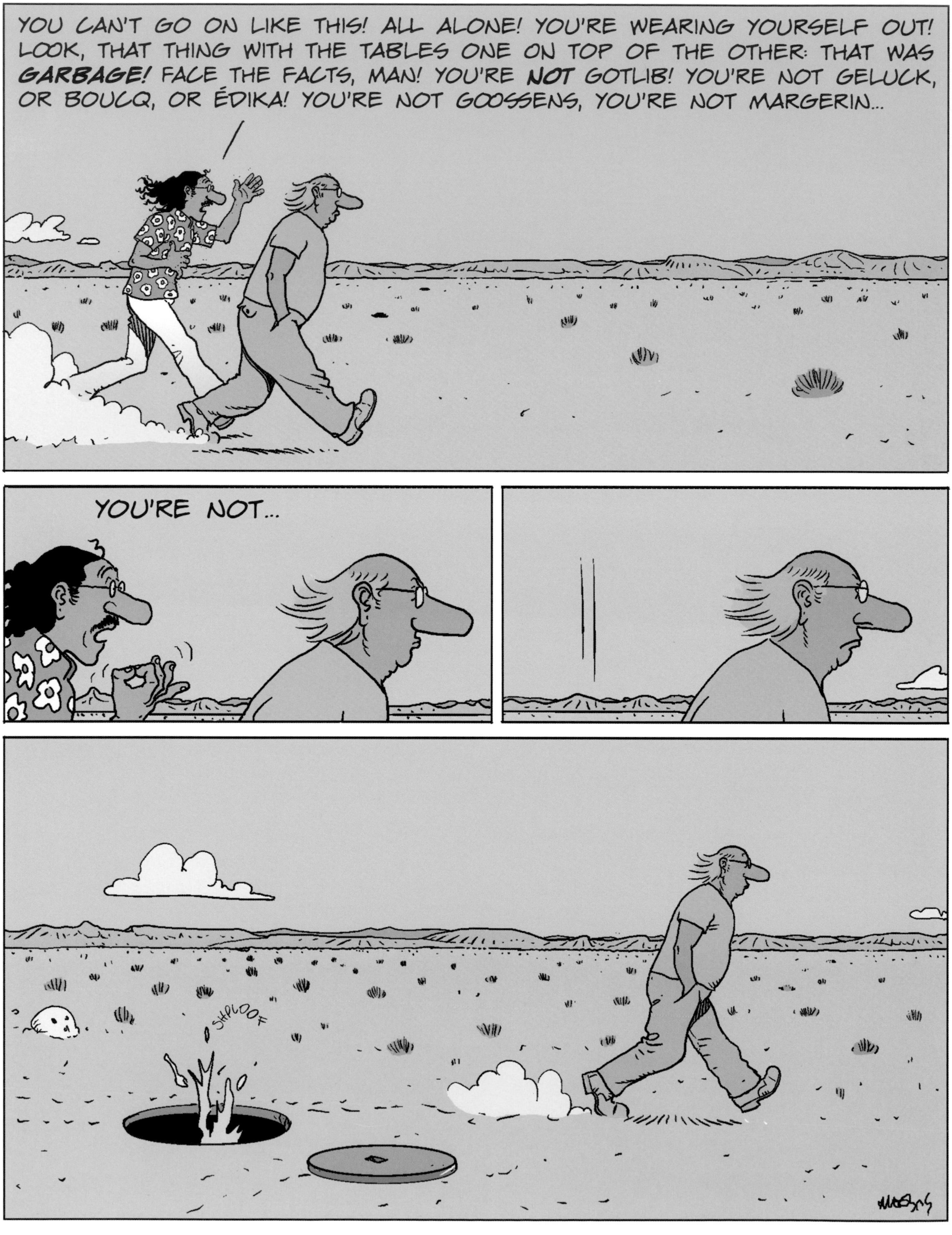
YOU CAN'T GO ON LIKE THIS! ALL ALONE! YOU'RE WEARING YOURSELF OUT! LOOK, THAT THING WITH THE TABLES ONE ON TOP OF THE OTHER: THAT WAS GARBAGE! FACE THE FACTS, MAN! YOU'RE NOT GOTLIB! YOU'RE NOT GELUCK, OR BOUCQ, OR ÉDIKA! YOU'RE NOT GOOSSENS, YOU'RE NOT MARGERIN...
YOU'RE NOT...
SHPLOOF

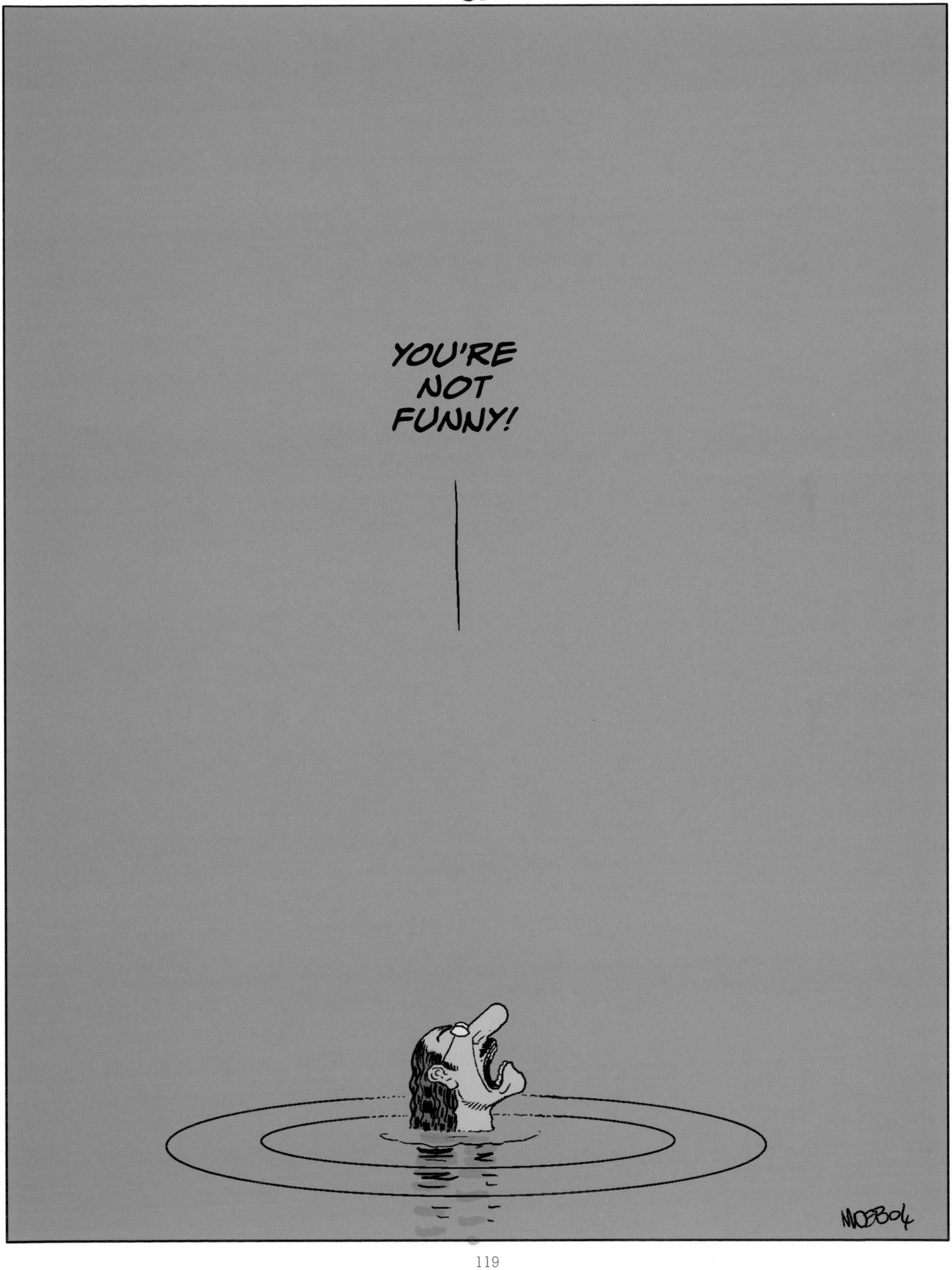
YOU'RE NOT FUNNY!
MOEBO4

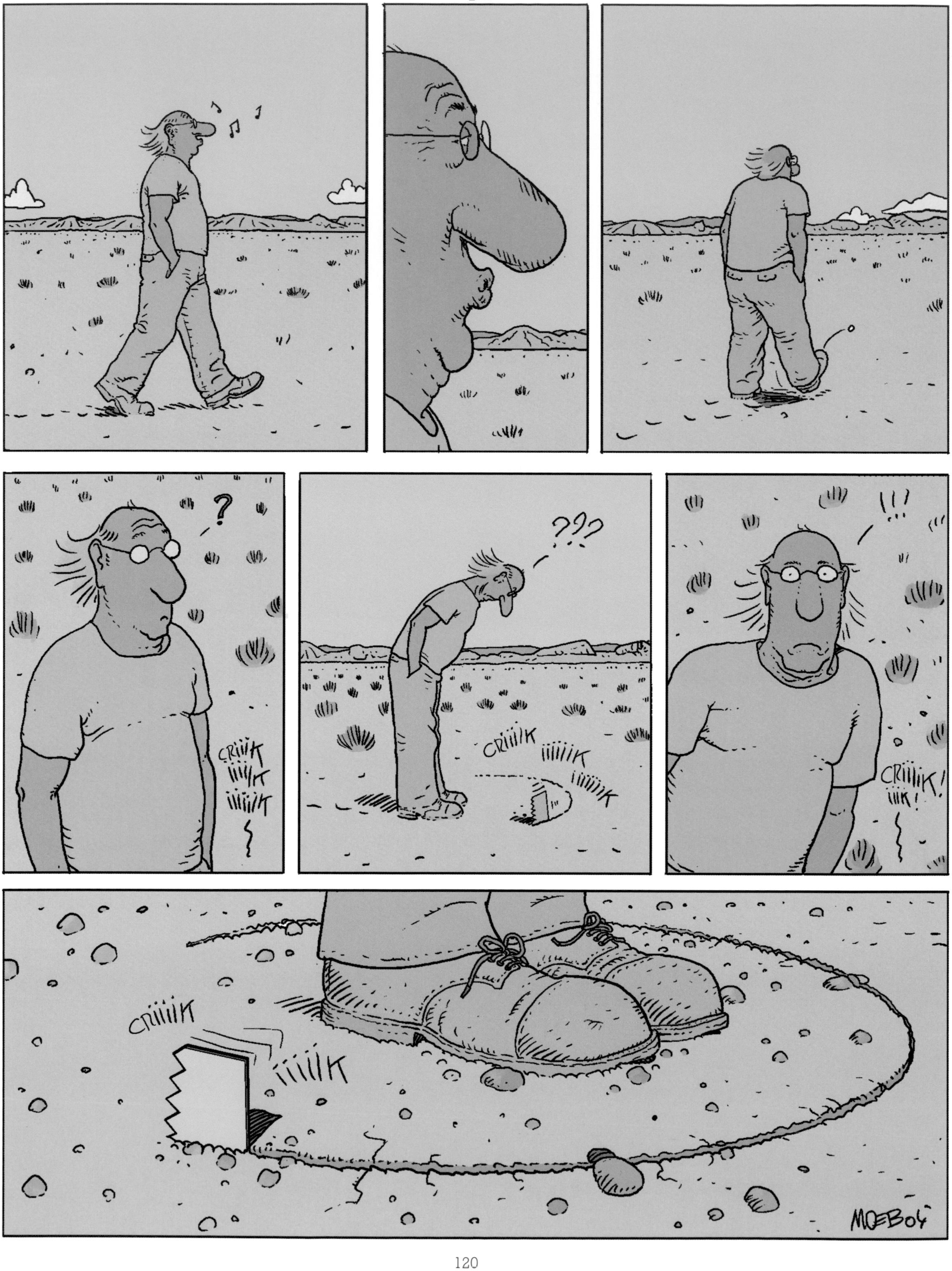
?
???
CRIIIIK
IIIIIIK
IIIIIIK
CRIIIIK
IIIIIIK
IIIIIIK
!!!
CRIIIIK!
IIIIK!
CRIIIIK
IIIIIK
MOEB04

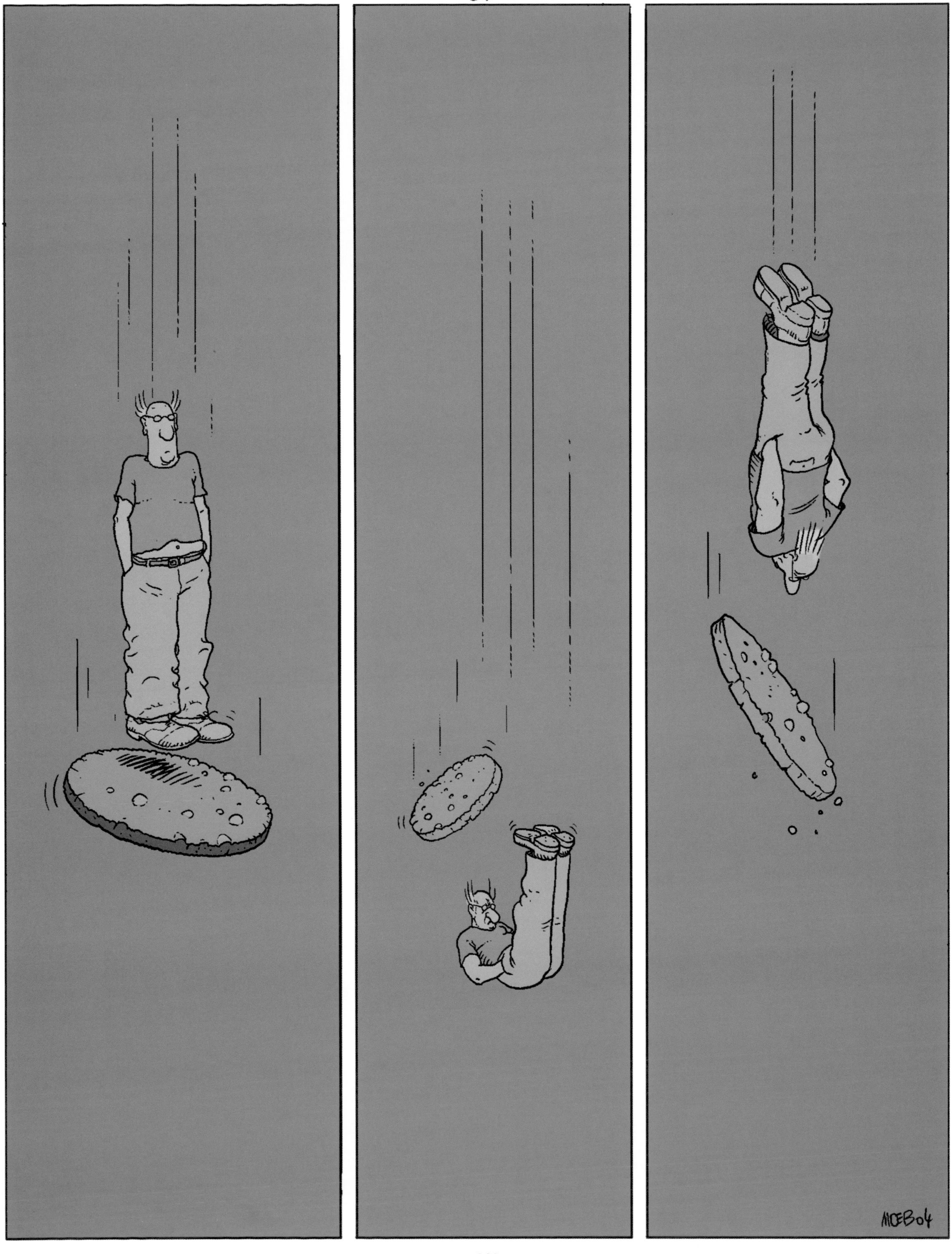
MŒB04

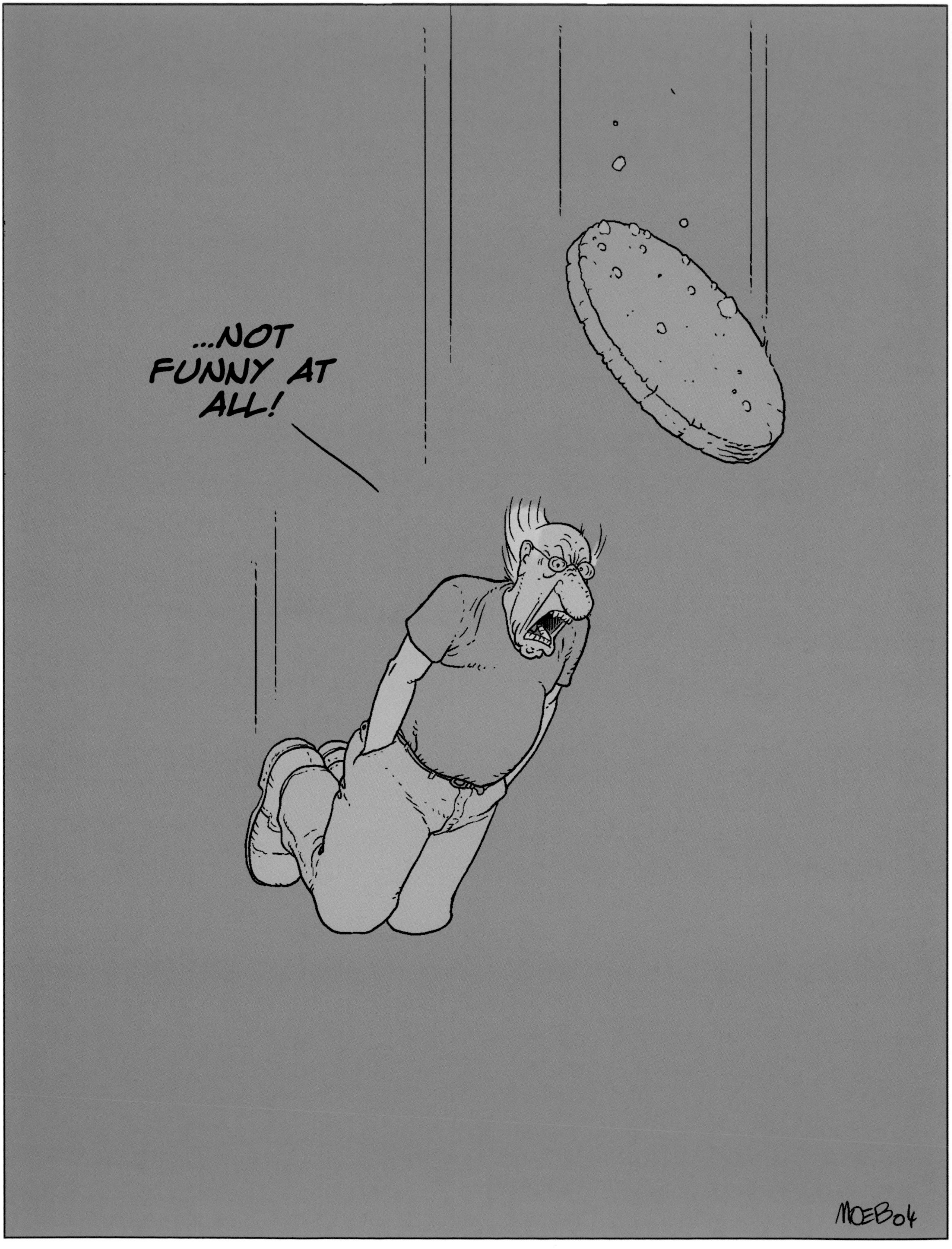
...NOT FUNNY AT ALL!
MOEB04

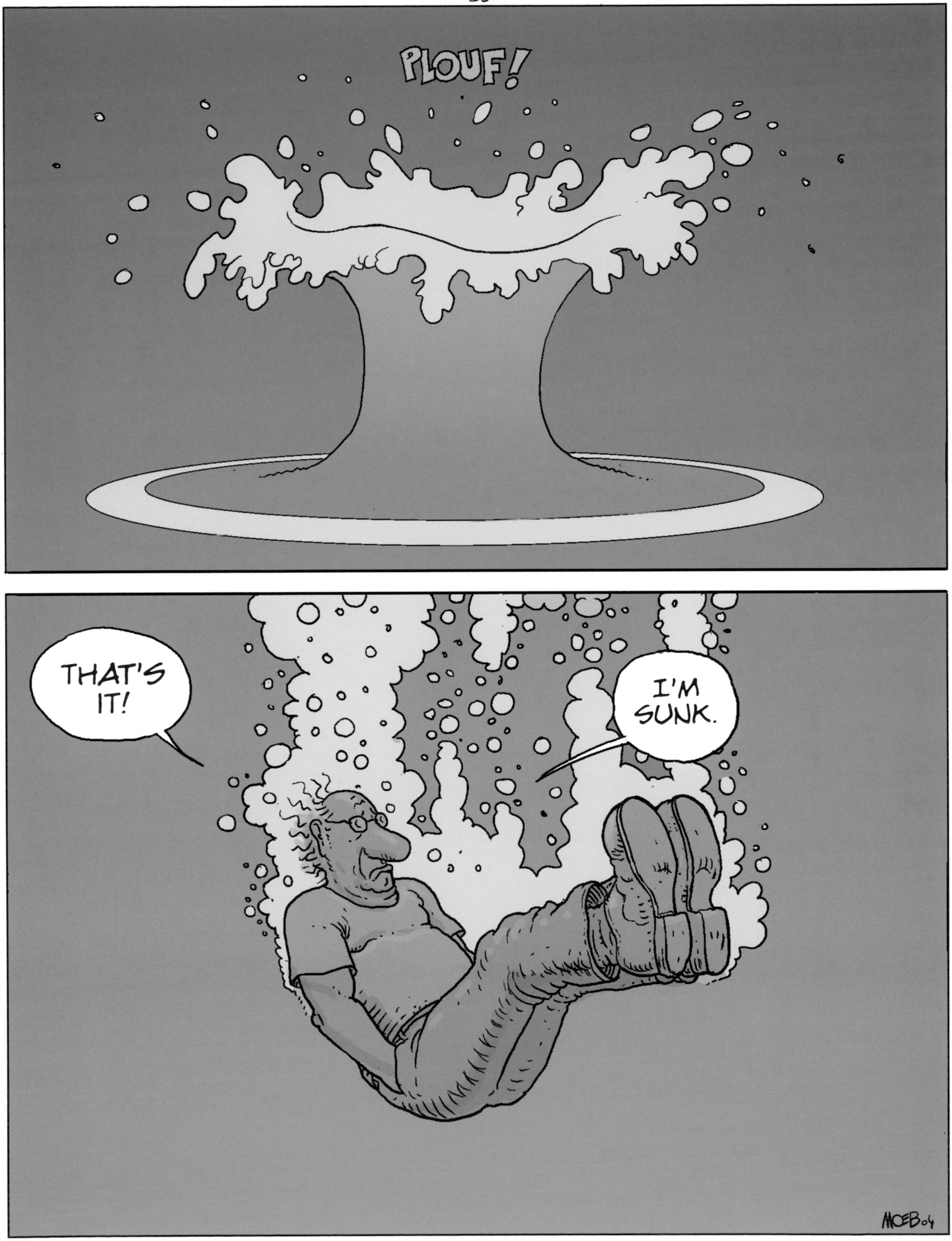
PLOUF!
THAT'S IT!
I'M SUNK.
MOEB 04

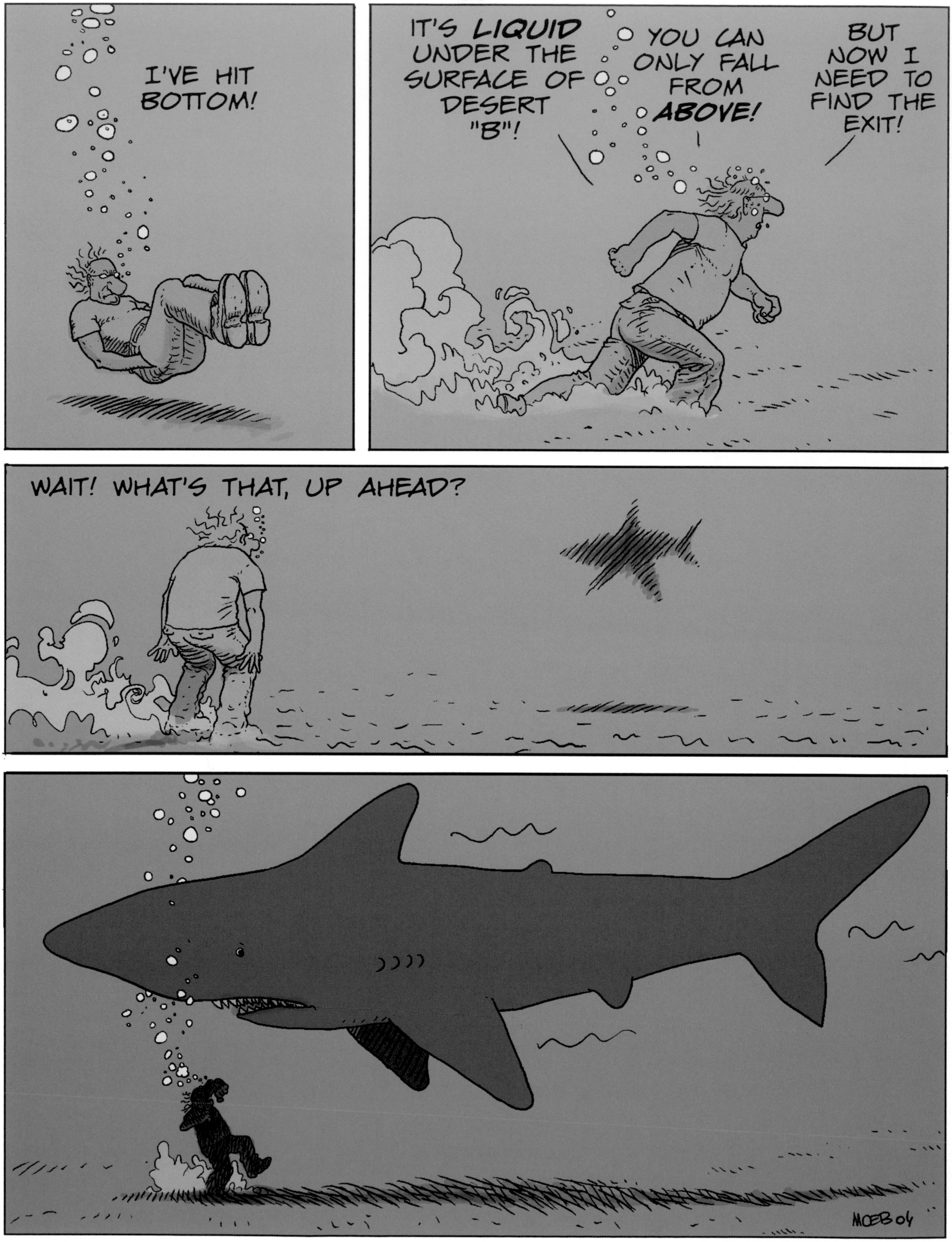
I'VE HIT BOTTOM!
IT'S LIQUID UNDER THE SURFACE OF DESERT "B"!
YOU CAN ONLY FALL FROM ABOVE!
BUT NOW I NEED TO FIND THE EXIT!
WAIT! WHAT'S THAT, UP AHEAD?
MOEB 04

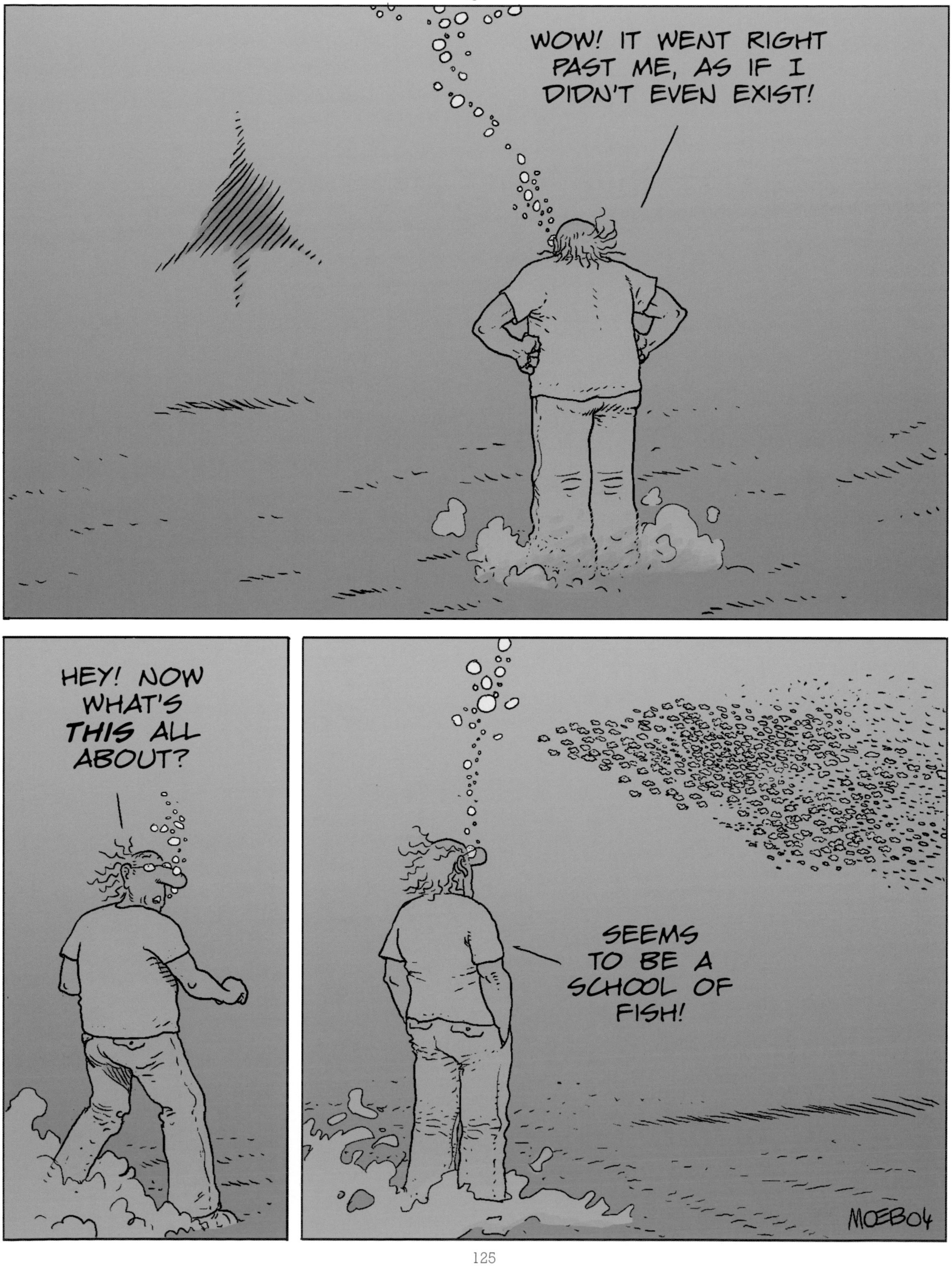

WOW! IT WENT RIGHT PAST ME, AS IF I DIDN'T EVEN EXIST!
HEY! NOW WHAT'S **THIS** ALL ABOUT?
SEEMS TO BE A SCHOOL OF FISH!
MOEB04

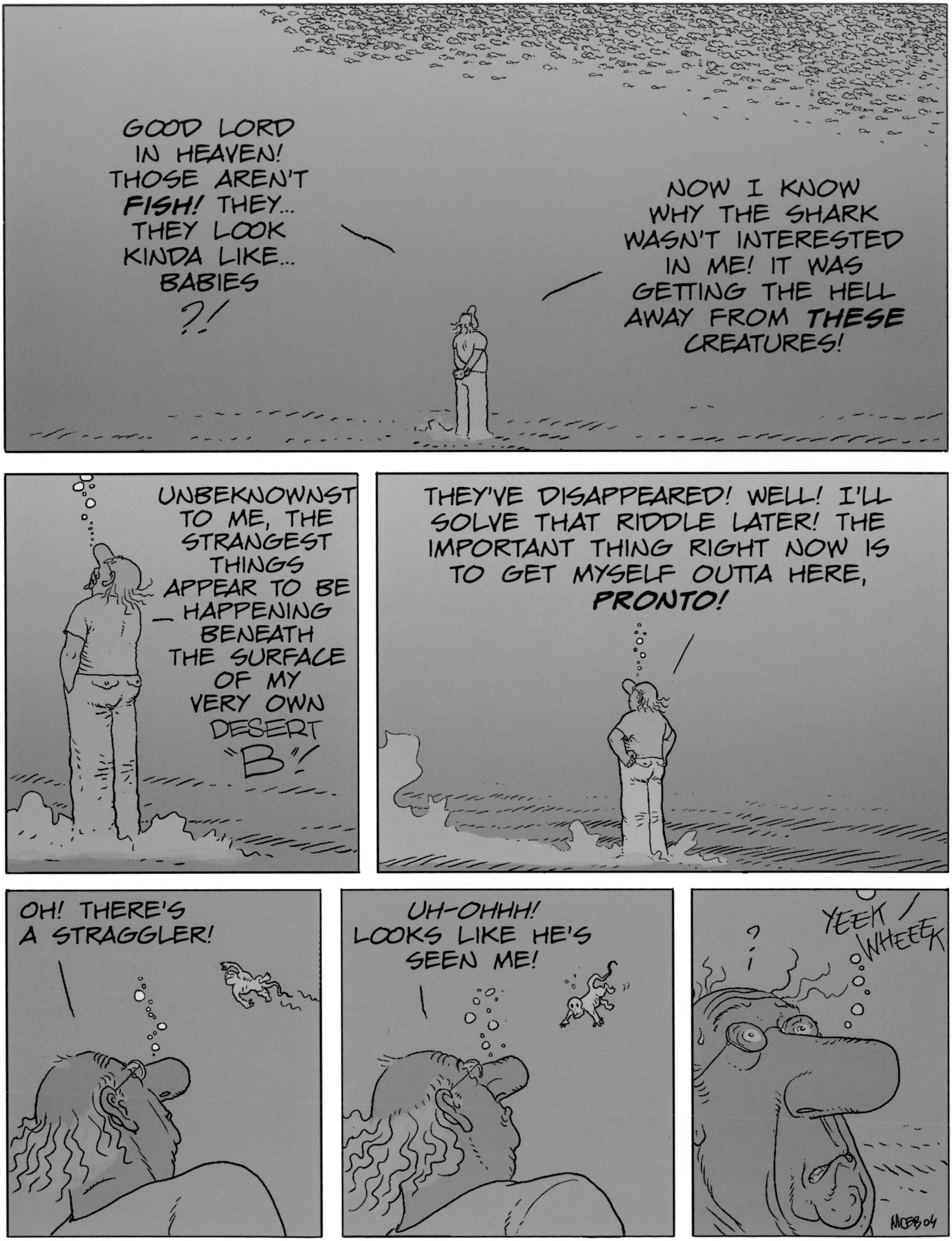
GOOD LORD IN HEAVEN! THOSE AREN'T FISH! THEY... THEY LOOK KINDA LIKE... BABIES ?!
NOW I KNOW WHY THE SHARK WASN'T INTERESTED IN ME! IT WAS GETTING THE HELL AWAY FROM THESE CREATURES!
UNBEKNOWNST TO ME, THE STRANGEST THINGS APPEAR TO BE HAPPENING BENEATH THE SURFACE OF MY VERY OWN DESERT "B"!
THEY'VE DISAPPEARED! WELL! I'LL SOLVE THAT RIDDLE LATER! THE IMPORTANT THING RIGHT NOW IS TO GET MYSELF OUTTA HERE, PRONTO!
OH! THERE'S A STRAGGLER!
UH-OHHH! LOOKS LIKE HE'S SEEN ME!
?
YEEK! WHEEEK
MŒB 04

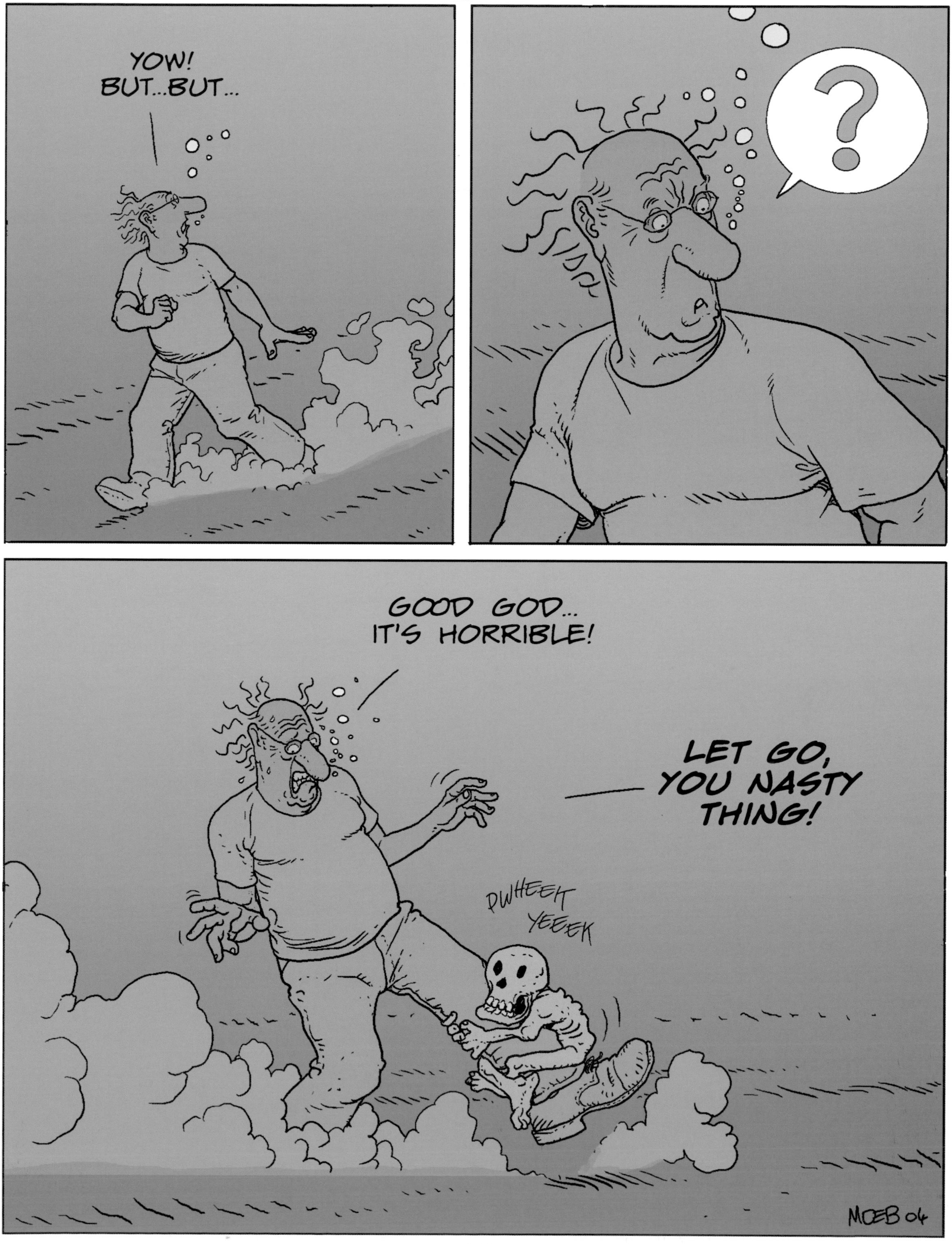
YOW!
BUT...BUT...
?
GOOD GOD...
IT'S HORRIBLE!
LET GO, YOU NASTY THING!
DWHEEK
YEEEK
MOEB 04

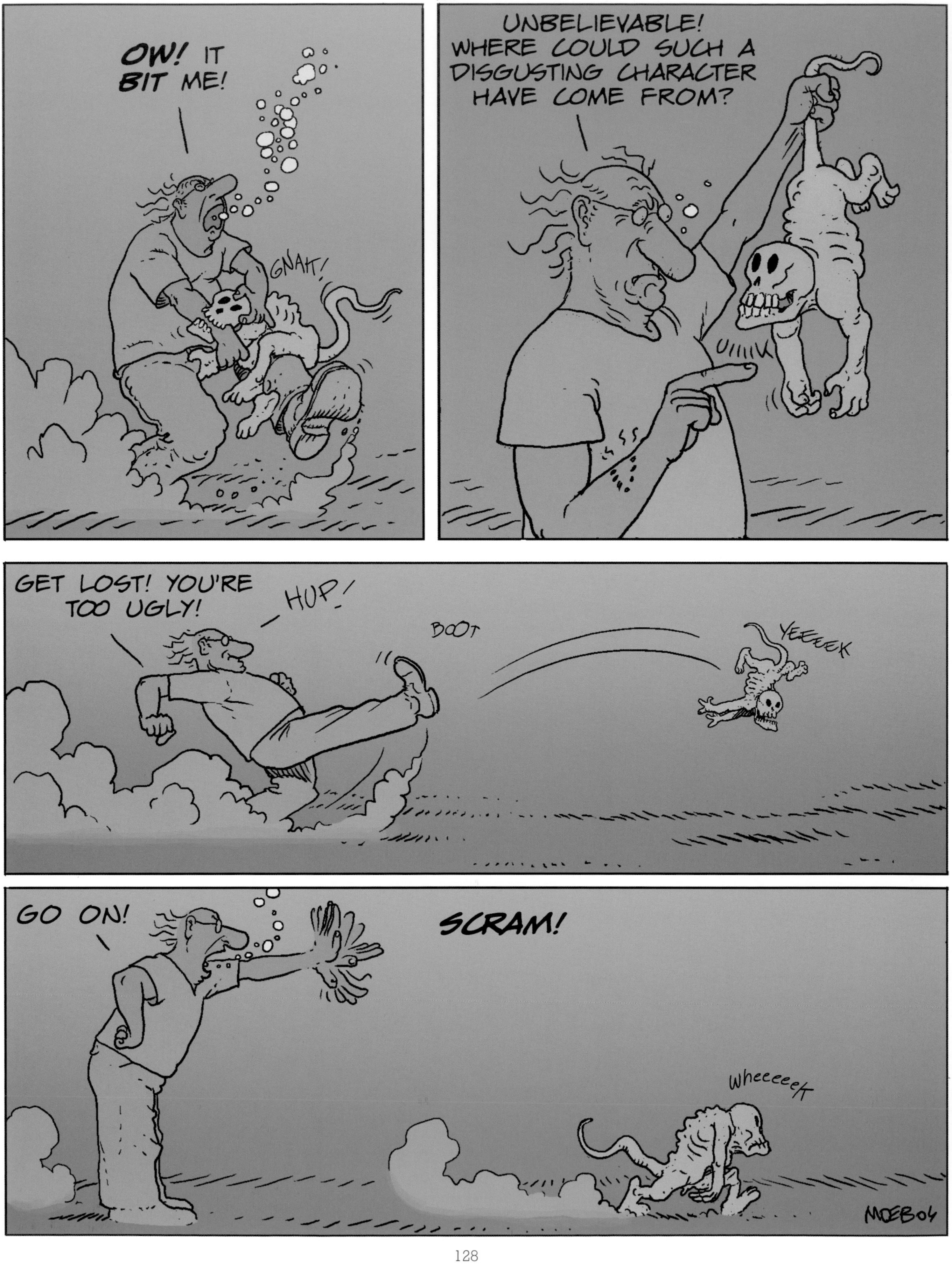
OW! IT BIT ME!
GNAK!
UNBELIEVABLE! WHERE COULD SUCH A DISGUSTING CHARACTER HAVE COME FROM?
GET LOST! YOU'RE TOO UGLY!
HUP!
BOOT
YEEEEK
GO ON!
SCRAM!
Wheeeeek
MOEB04

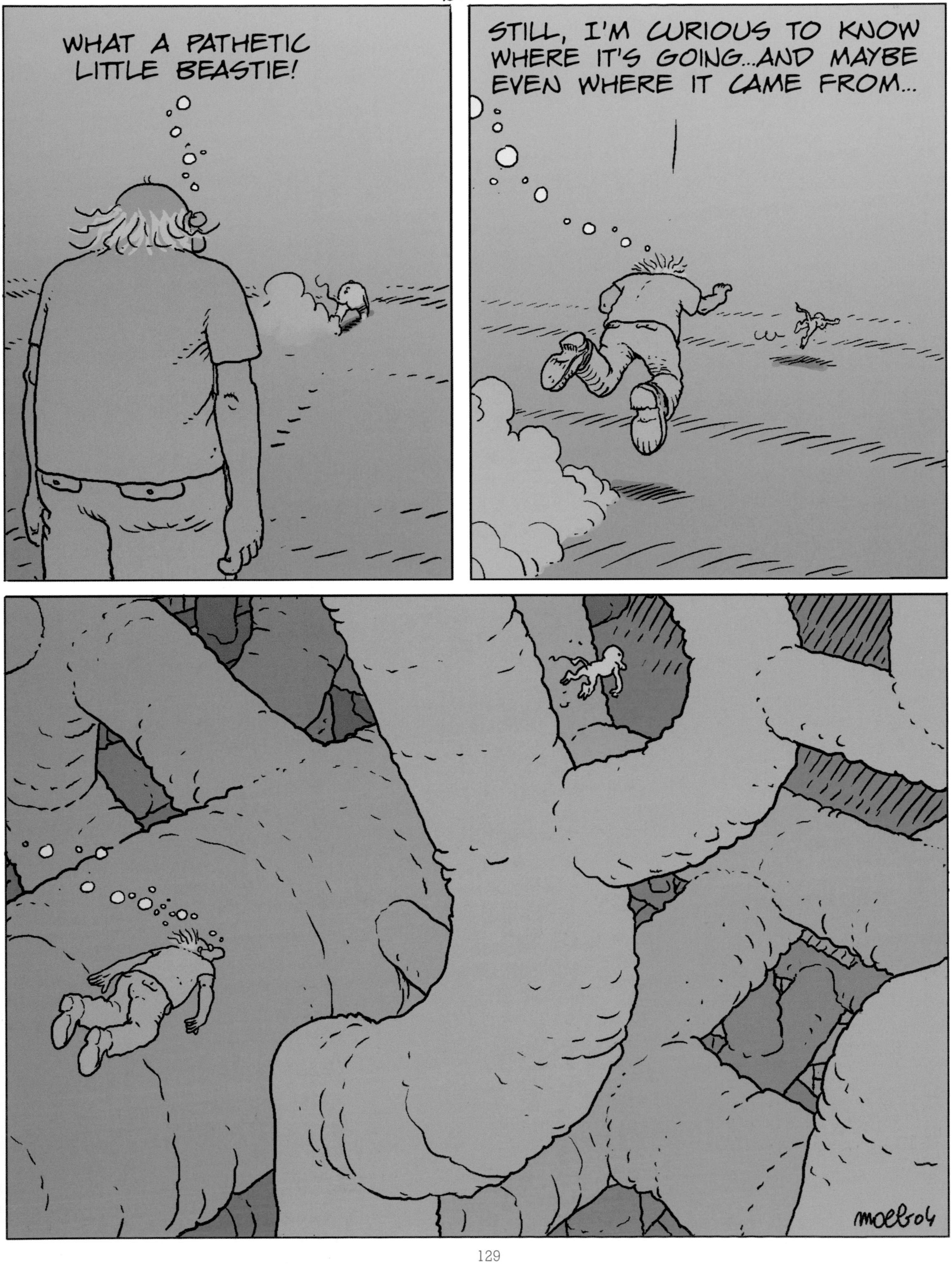
WHAT A PATHETIC LITTLE BEASTIE!
STILL, I'M CURIOUS TO KNOW WHERE IT'S GOING...AND MAYBE EVEN WHERE IT CAME FROM...
moeb04

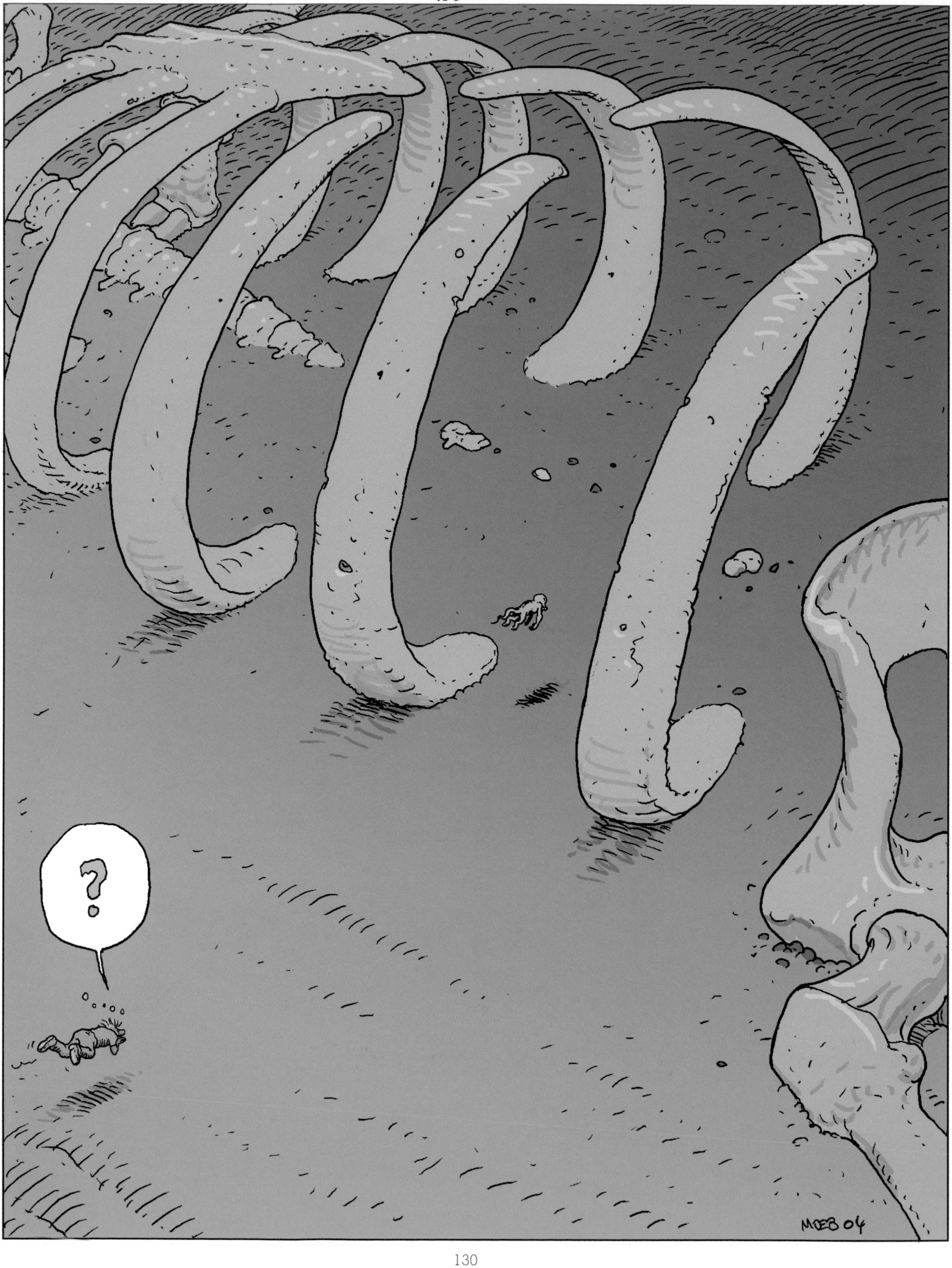
?
MOEB 04

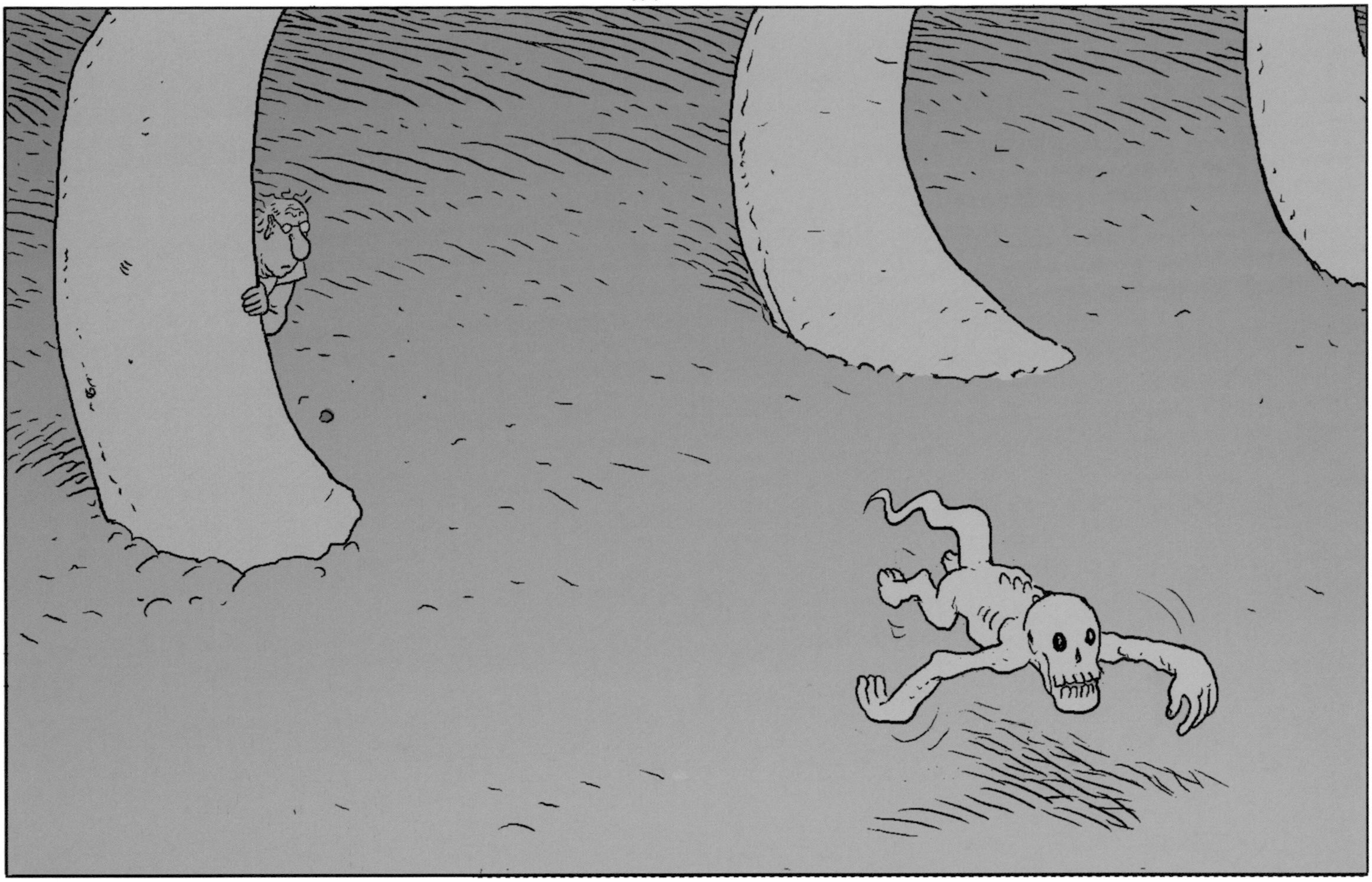

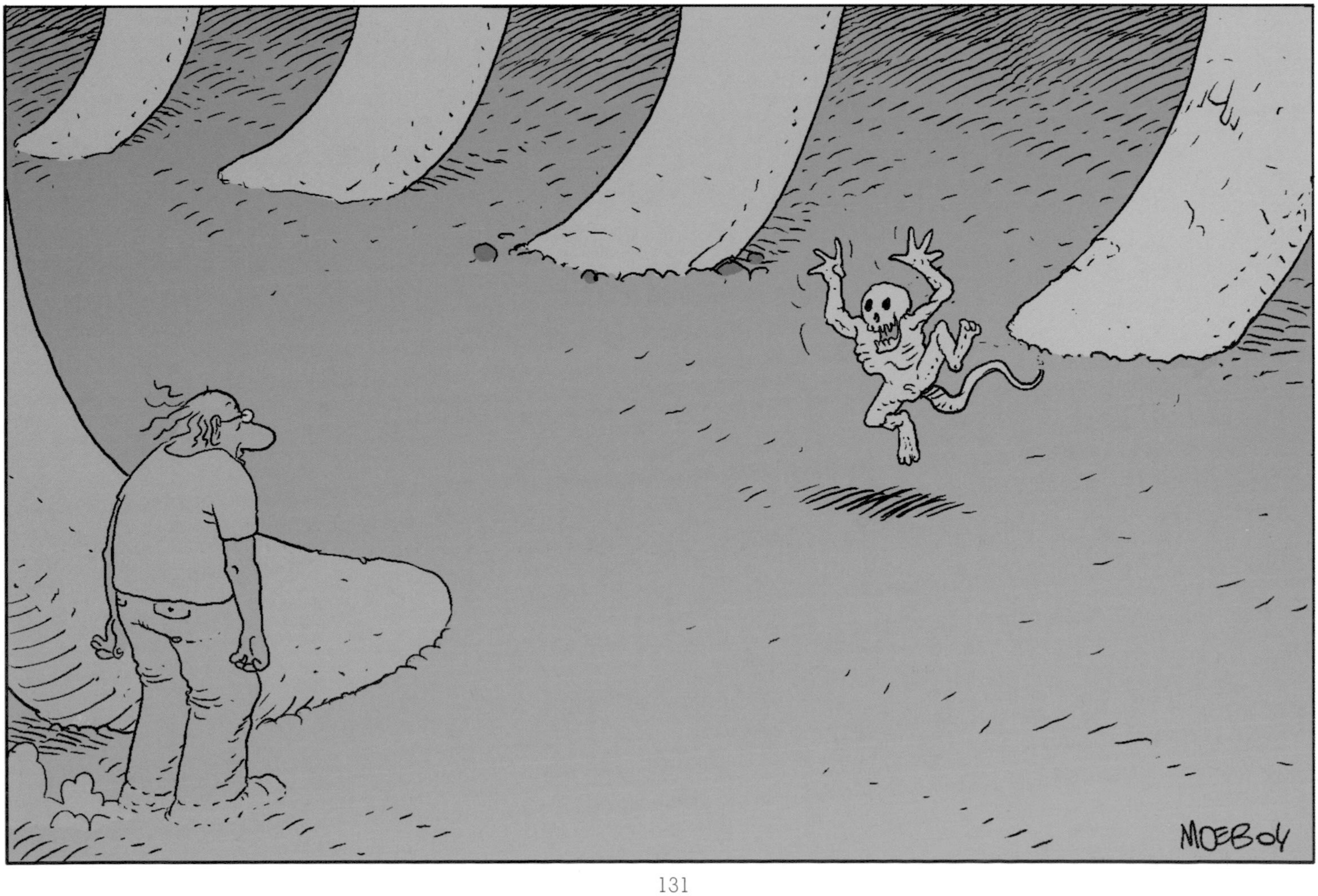
MOEB 04

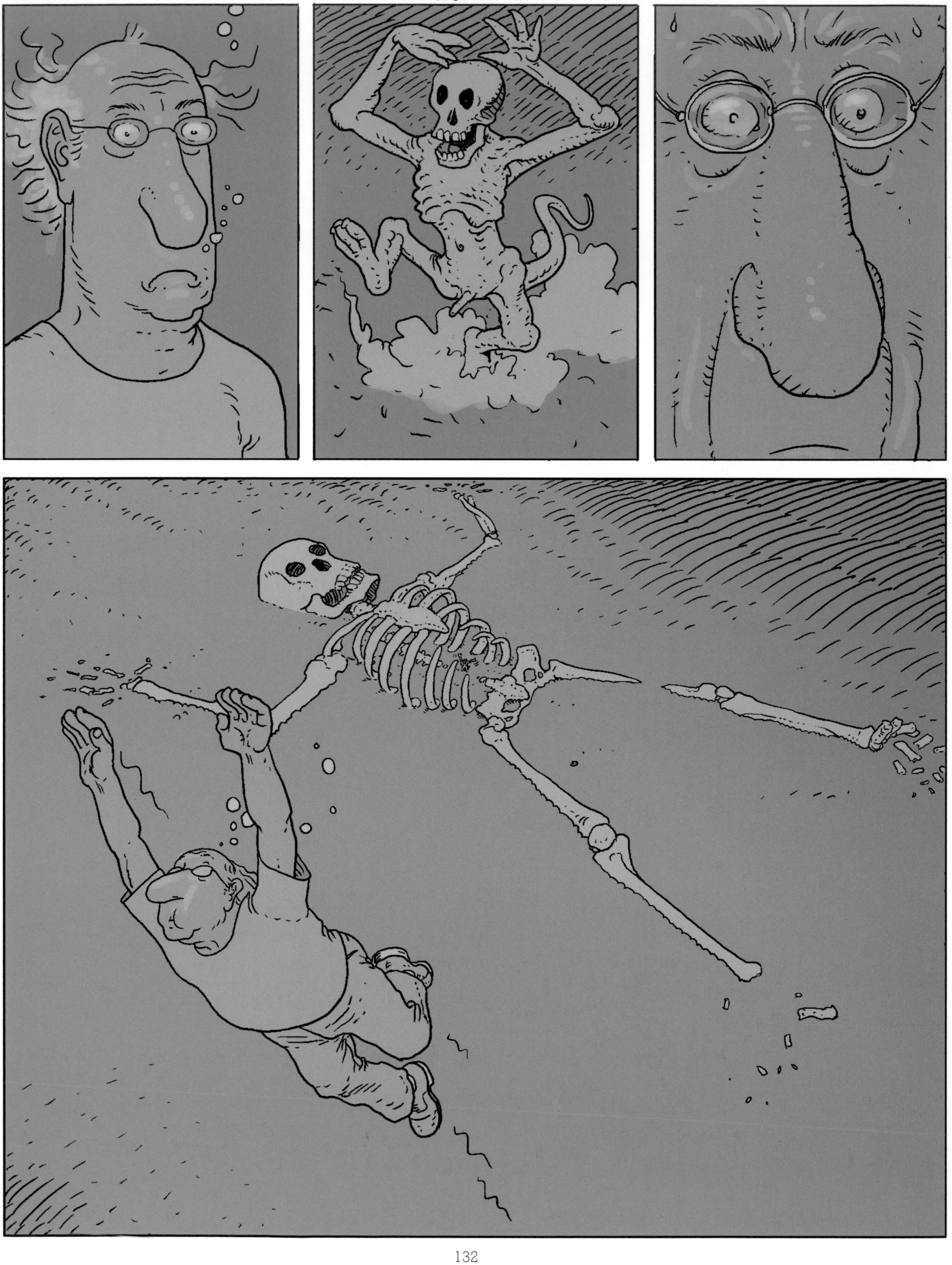

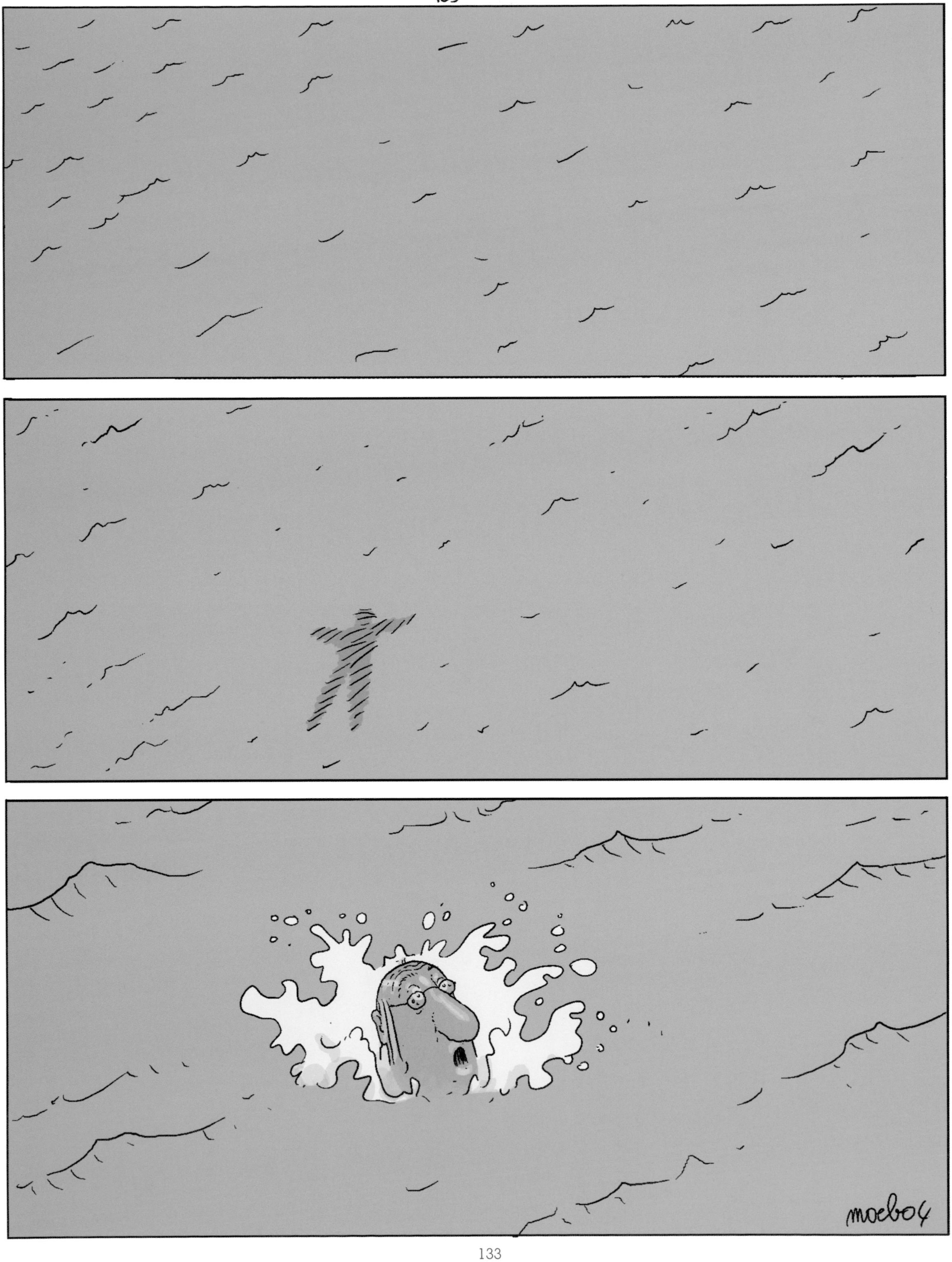
moebo4

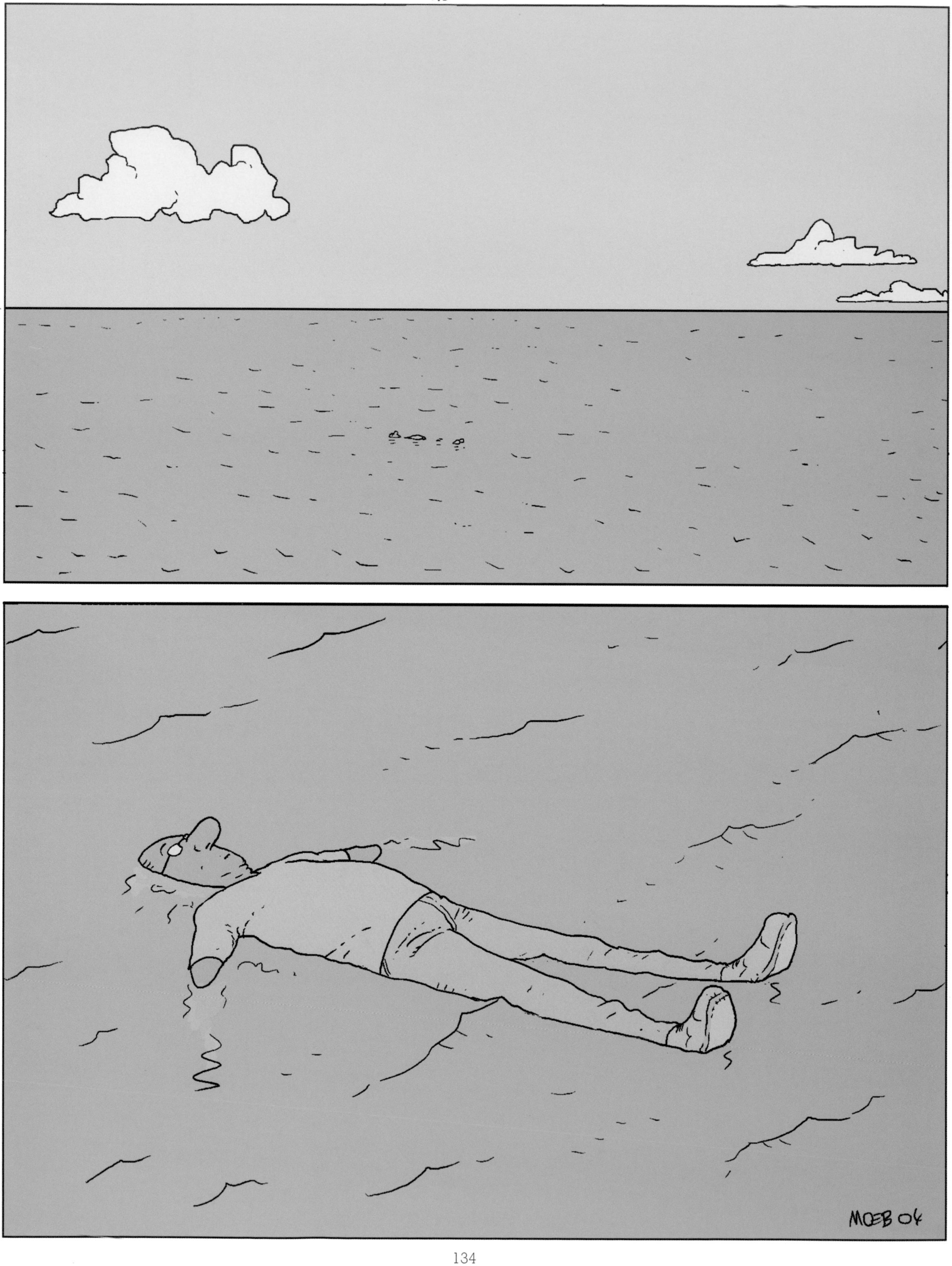
MOEB 04

III

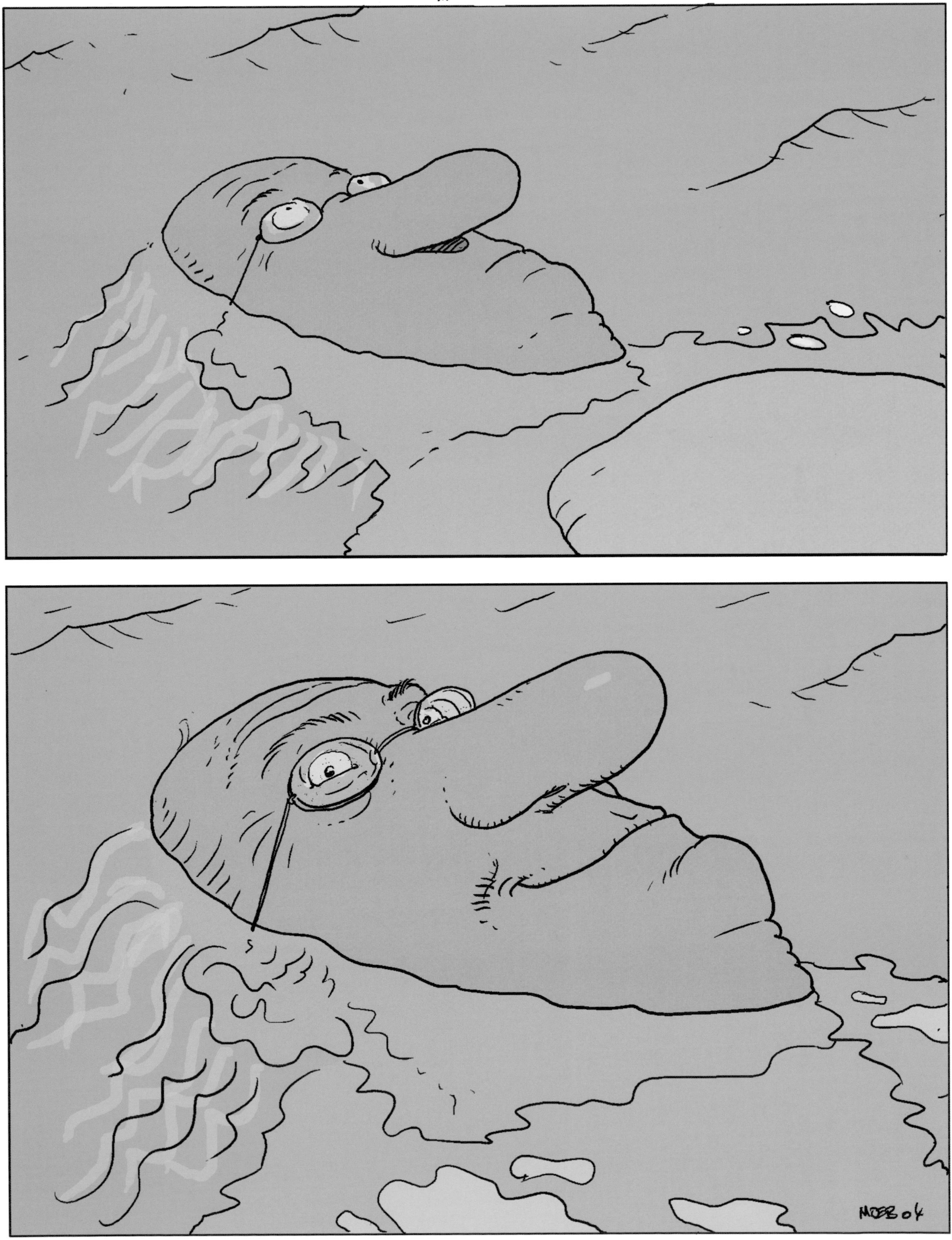

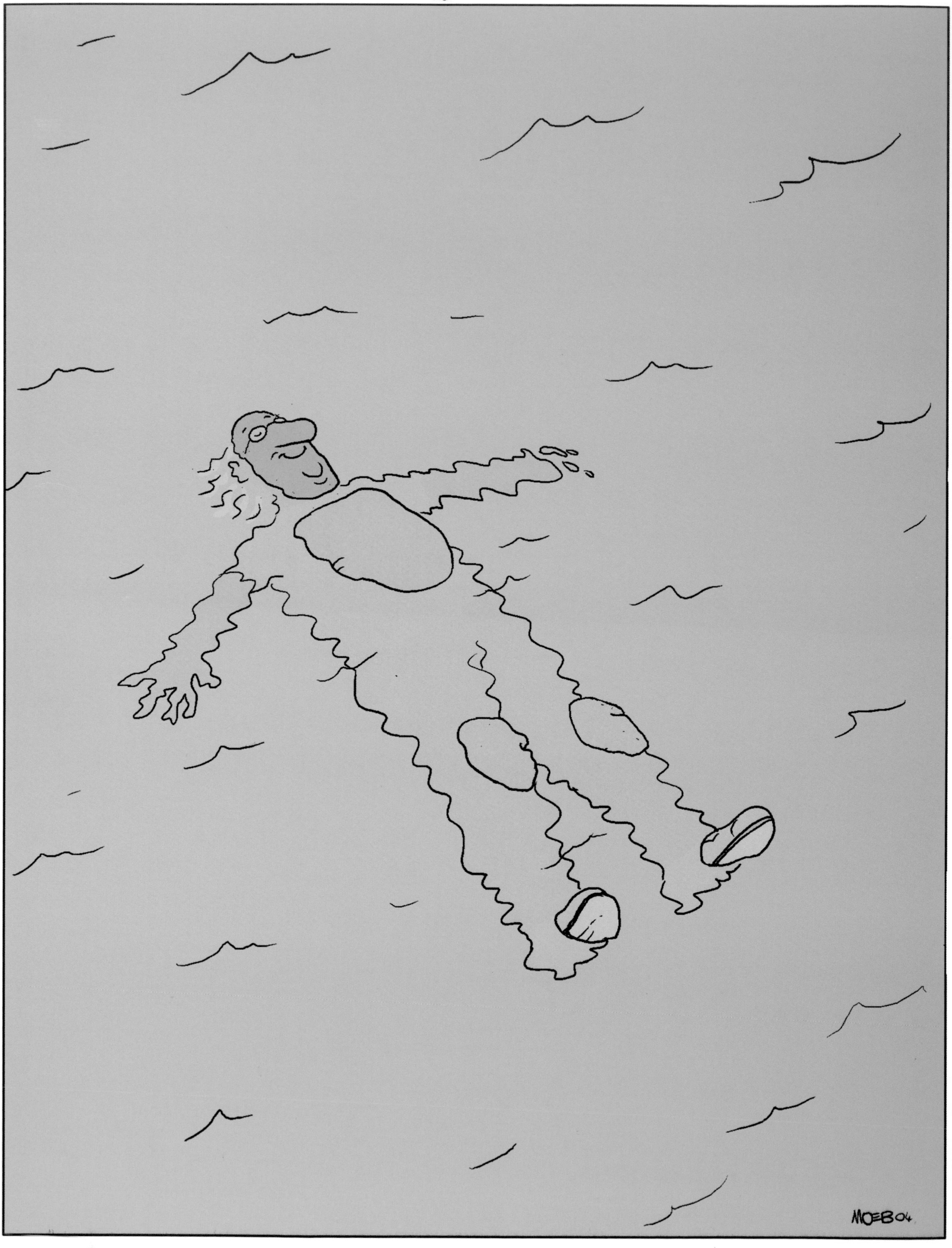
MOEB 04

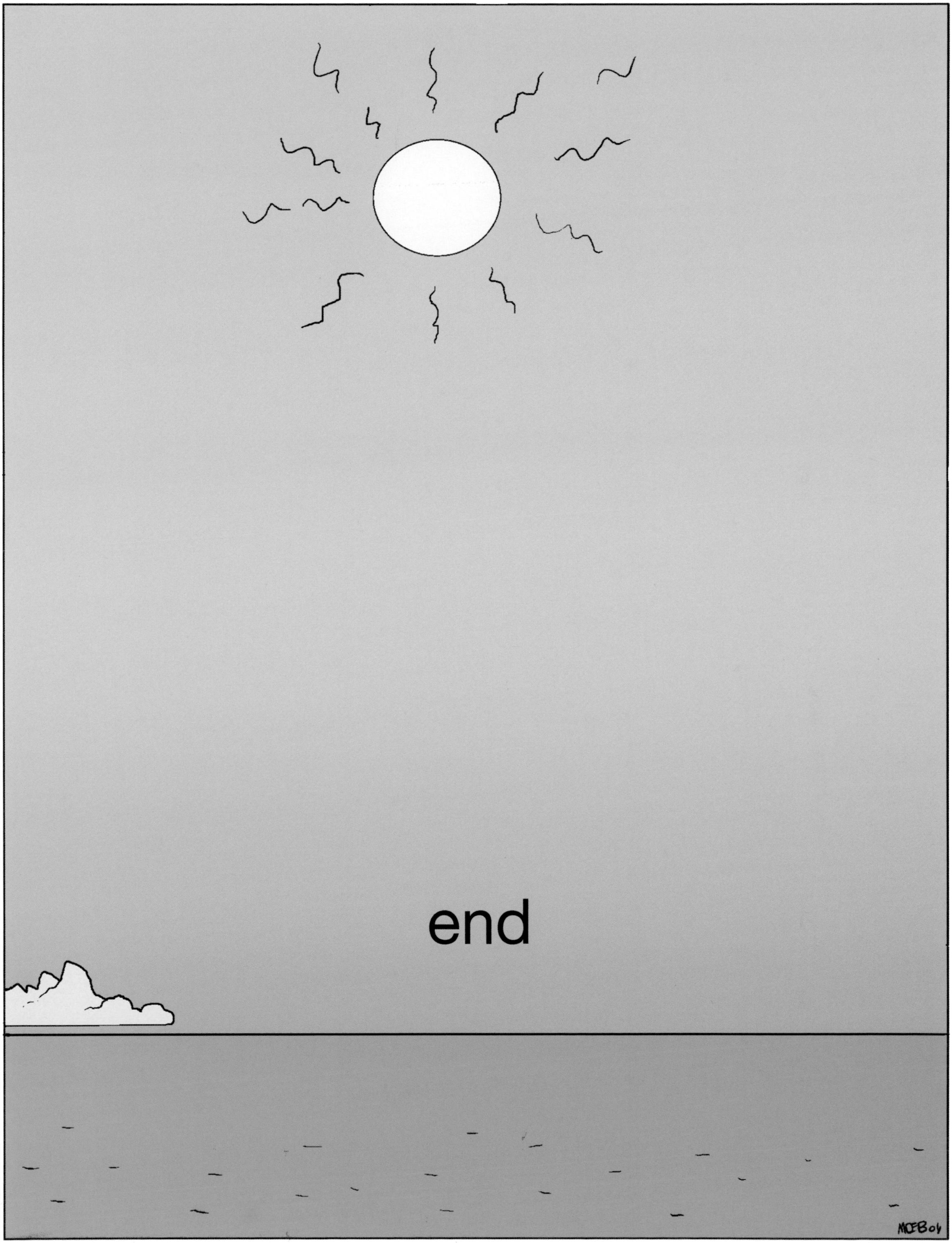
end

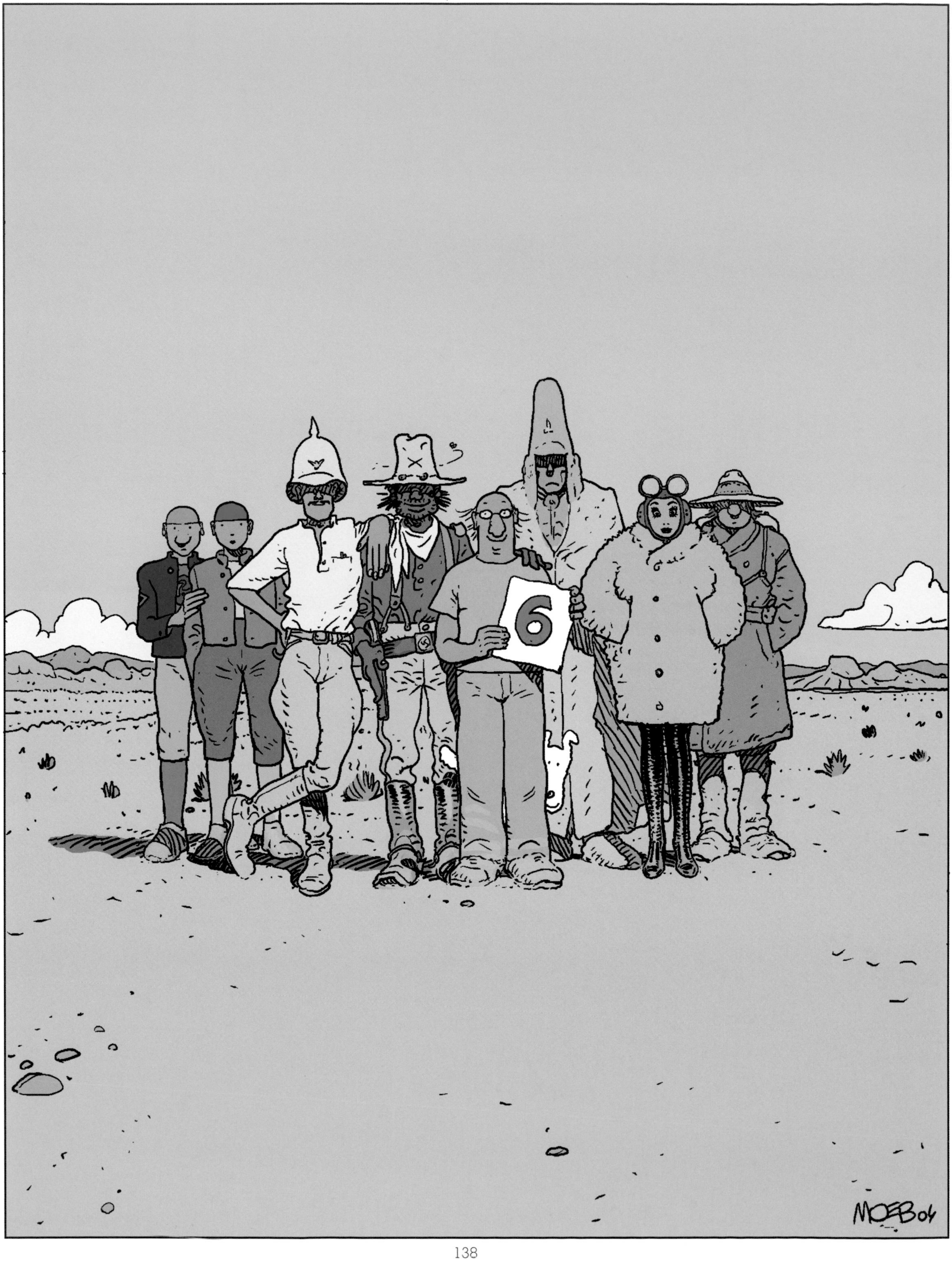
6
MOEB 04

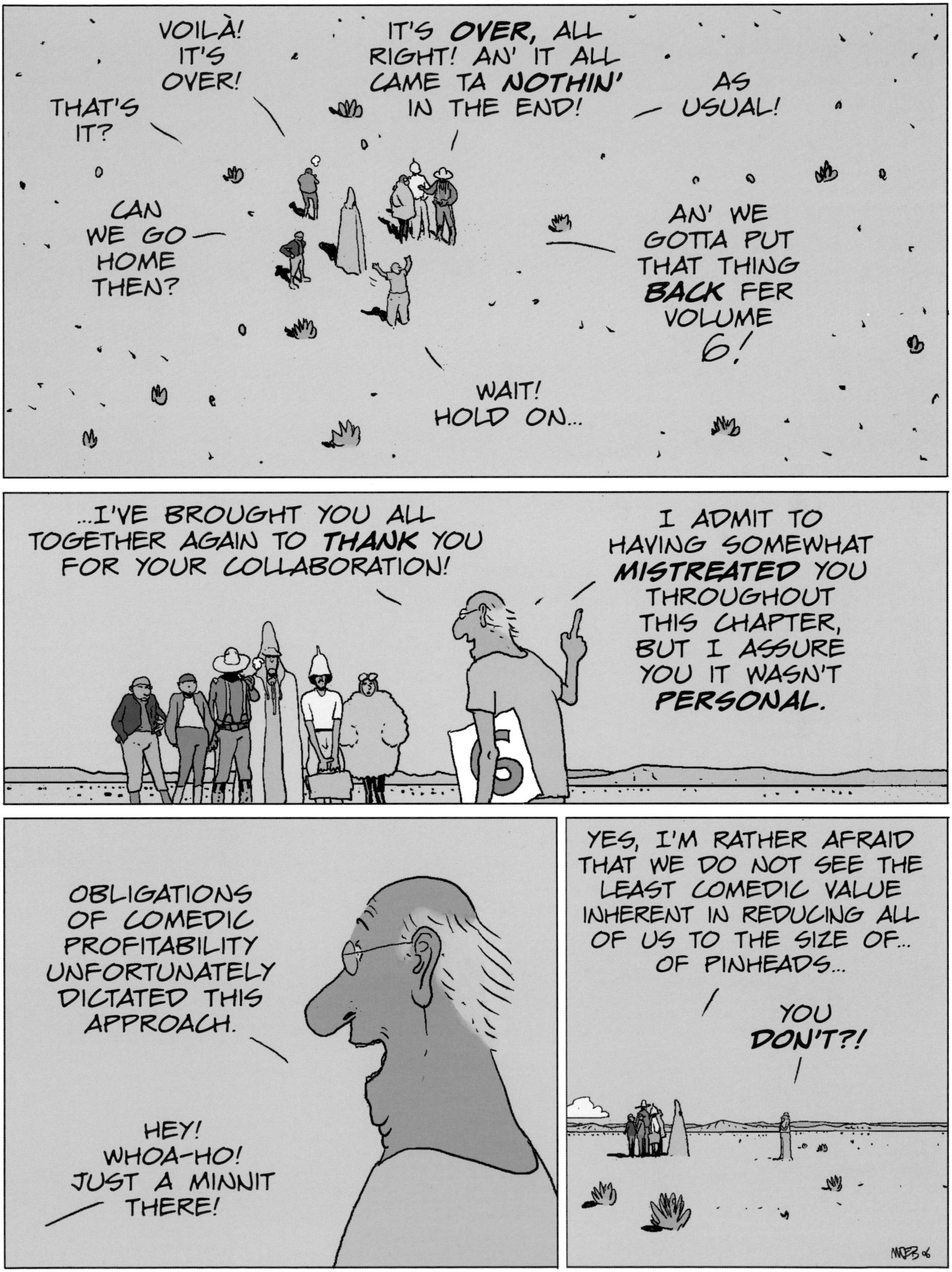
VOILÀ! IT'S OVER!
IT'S OVER, ALL RIGHT! AN' IT ALL CAME TA NOTHIN' IN THE END!
THAT'S IT?
AS USUAL!
CAN WE GO HOME THEN?
AN' WE GOTTA PUT THAT THING BACK FER VOLUME 6!
WAIT! HOLD ON...
...I'VE BROUGHT YOU ALL TOGETHER AGAIN TO THANK YOU FOR YOUR COLLABORATION!
I ADMIT TO HAVING SOMEWHAT MISTREATED YOU THROUGHOUT THIS CHAPTER, BUT I ASSURE YOU IT WASN'T PERSONAL.
6
OBLIGATIONS OF COMEDIC PROFITABILITY UNFORTUNATELY DICTATED THIS APPROACH.
HEY! WHOA-HO! JUST A MINNIT THERE!
YES, I'M RATHER AFRAID THAT WE DO NOT SEE THE LEAST COMEDIC VALUE INHERENT IN REDUCING ALL OF US TO THE SIZE OF... OF PINHEADS...
YOU DON'T?!
MŒB 06

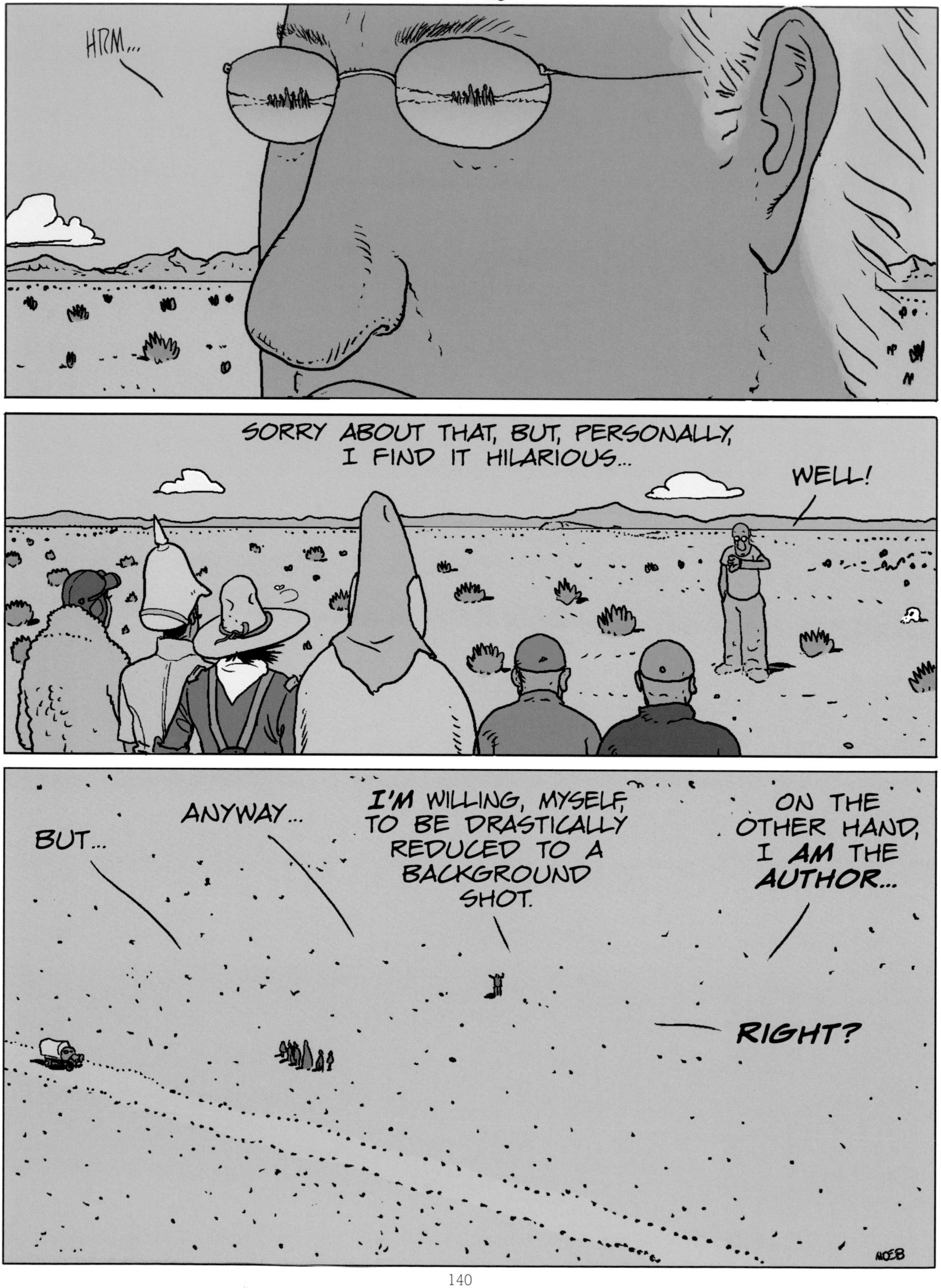
HRM...
SORRY ABOUT THAT, BUT, PERSONALLY, I FIND IT HILARIOUS...
WELL!
BUT...
ANYWAY...
I'M WILLING, MYSELF, TO BE DRASTICALLY REDUCED TO A BACKGROUND SHOT.
ON THE OTHER HAND, I AM THE AUTHOR...
RIGHT?
MOEB

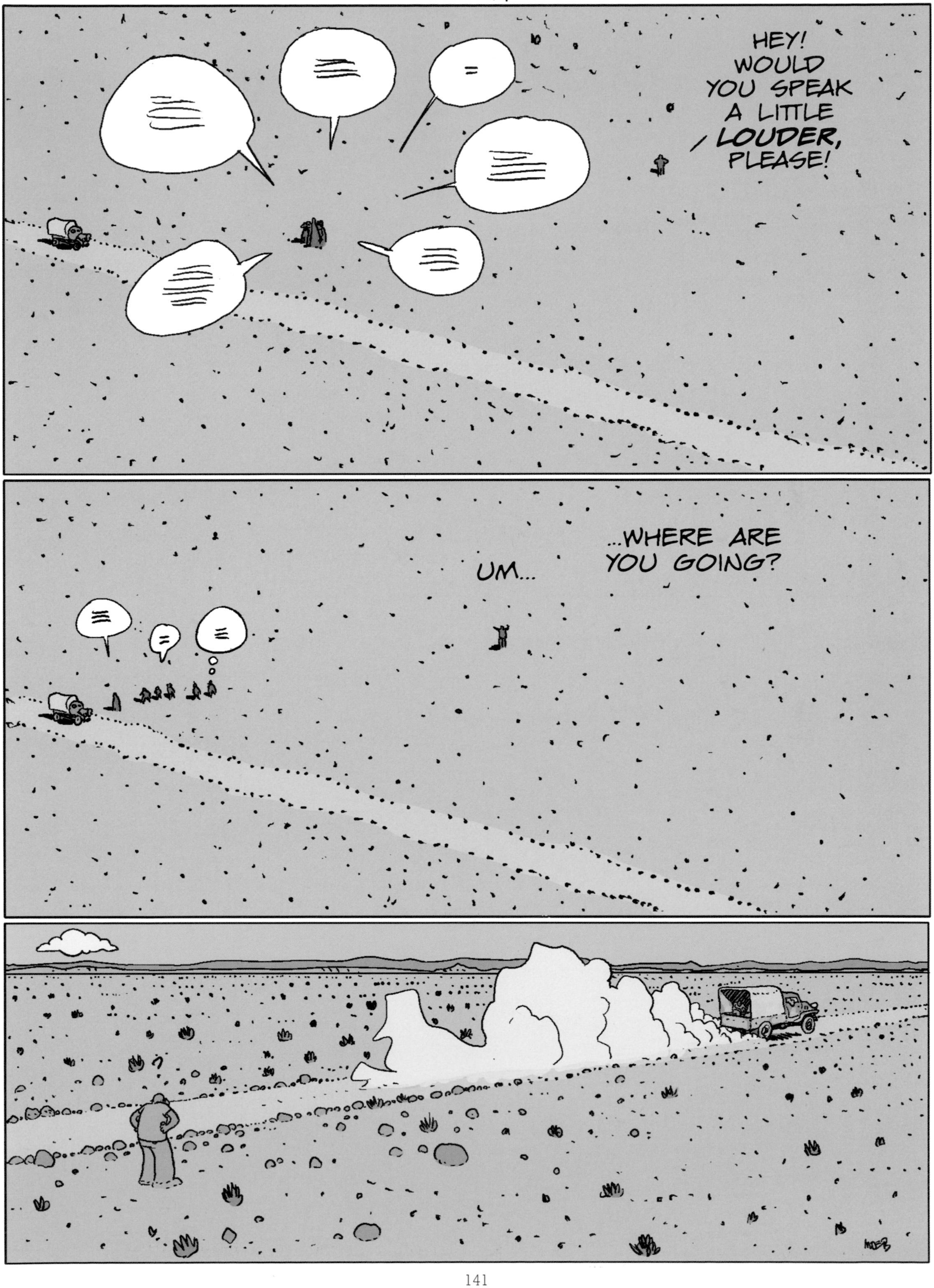
HEY! WOULD YOU SPEAK A LITTLE **LOUDER,** PLEASE!
UM...
...WHERE ARE YOU GOING?

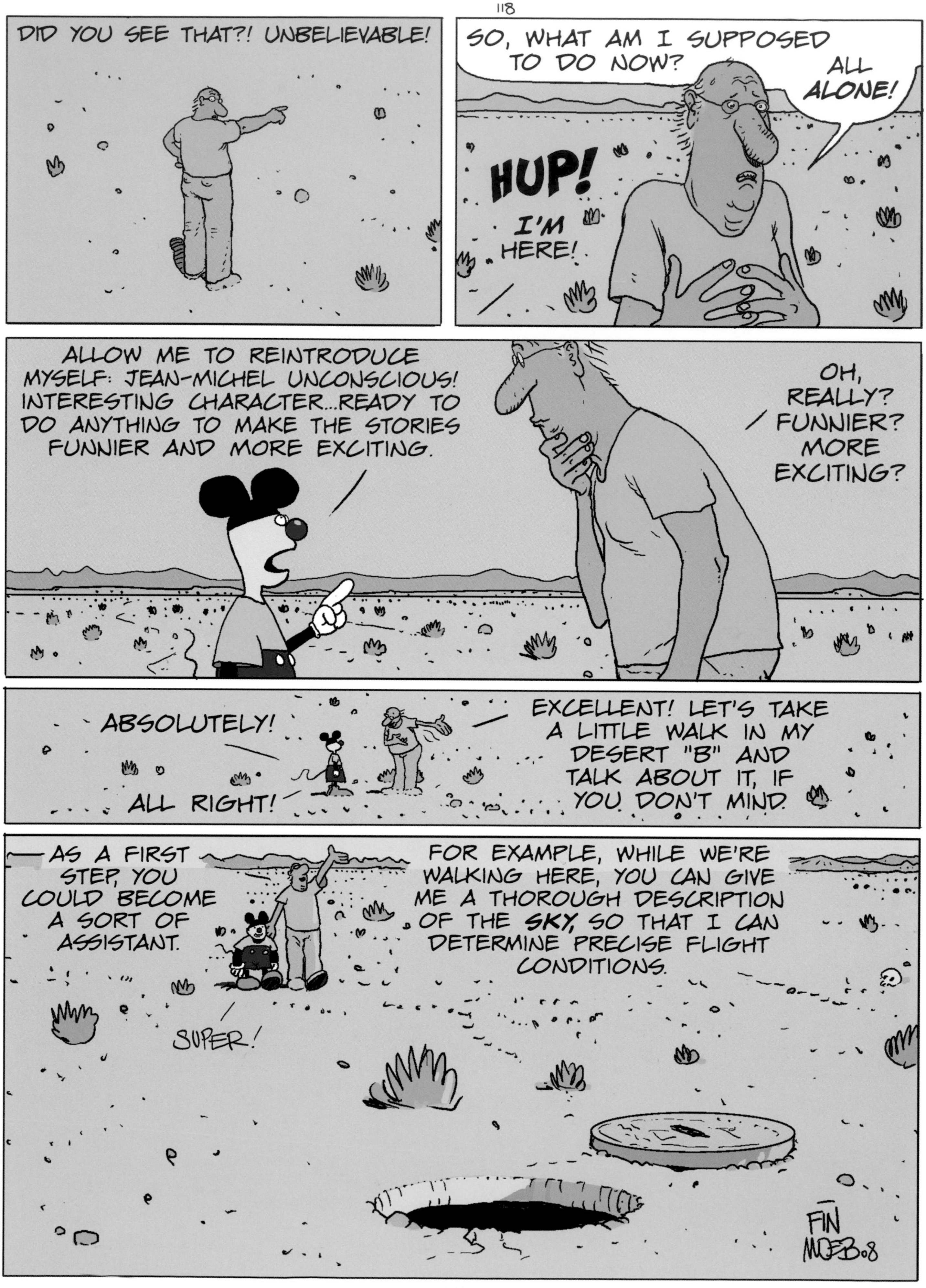
DID YOU SEE THAT?! UNBELIEVABLE!
SO, WHAT AM I SUPPOSED TO DO NOW?
ALL ALONE!
HUP!
I'M HERE!
ALLOW ME TO REINTRODUCE MYSELF: JEAN-MICHEL UNCONSCIOUS! INTERESTING CHARACTER...READY TO DO ANYTHING TO MAKE THE STORIES FUNNIER AND MORE EXCITING.
OH, REALLY? FUNNIER? MORE EXCITING?
ABSOLUTELY!
ALL RIGHT!
EXCELLENT! LET'S TAKE A LITTLE WALK IN MY DESERT "B" AND TALK ABOUT IT, IF YOU DON'T MIND.
AS A FIRST STEP, YOU COULD BECOME A SORT OF ASSISTANT.
FOR EXAMPLE, WHILE WE'RE WALKING HERE, YOU CAN GIVE ME A THOROUGH DESCRIPTION OF THE SKY, SO THAT I CAN DETERMINE PRECISE FLIGHT CONDITIONS.
SUPER!
FIN
MOEB.08

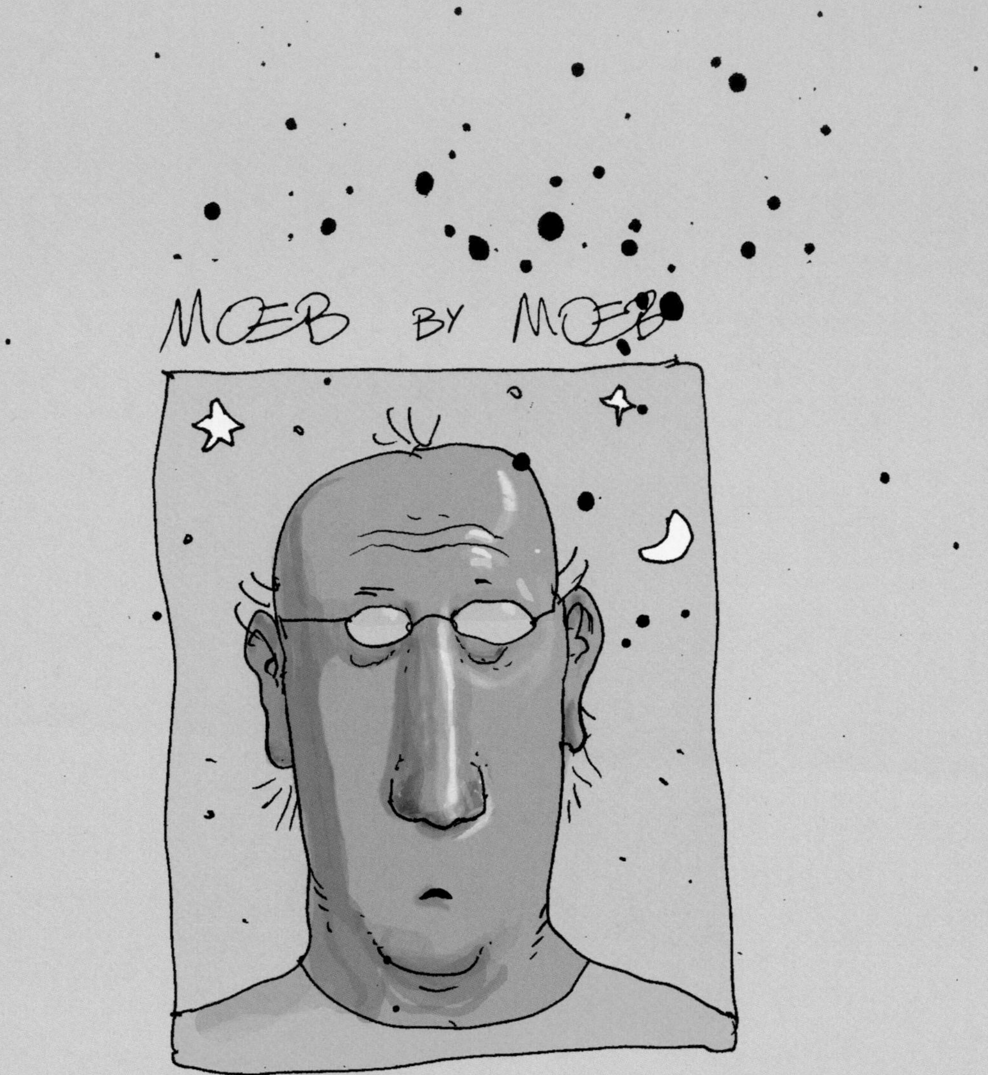
MOEB BY MOEB

INSIDE MOEBIUS SKETCHBOOK

N° 6

FIRST SECTION

INSIDE MOEBIUS
VOLUME 6

. . . Most of the time I put up a front!
I drew my stories in the guise of
enigmatic parables . . .

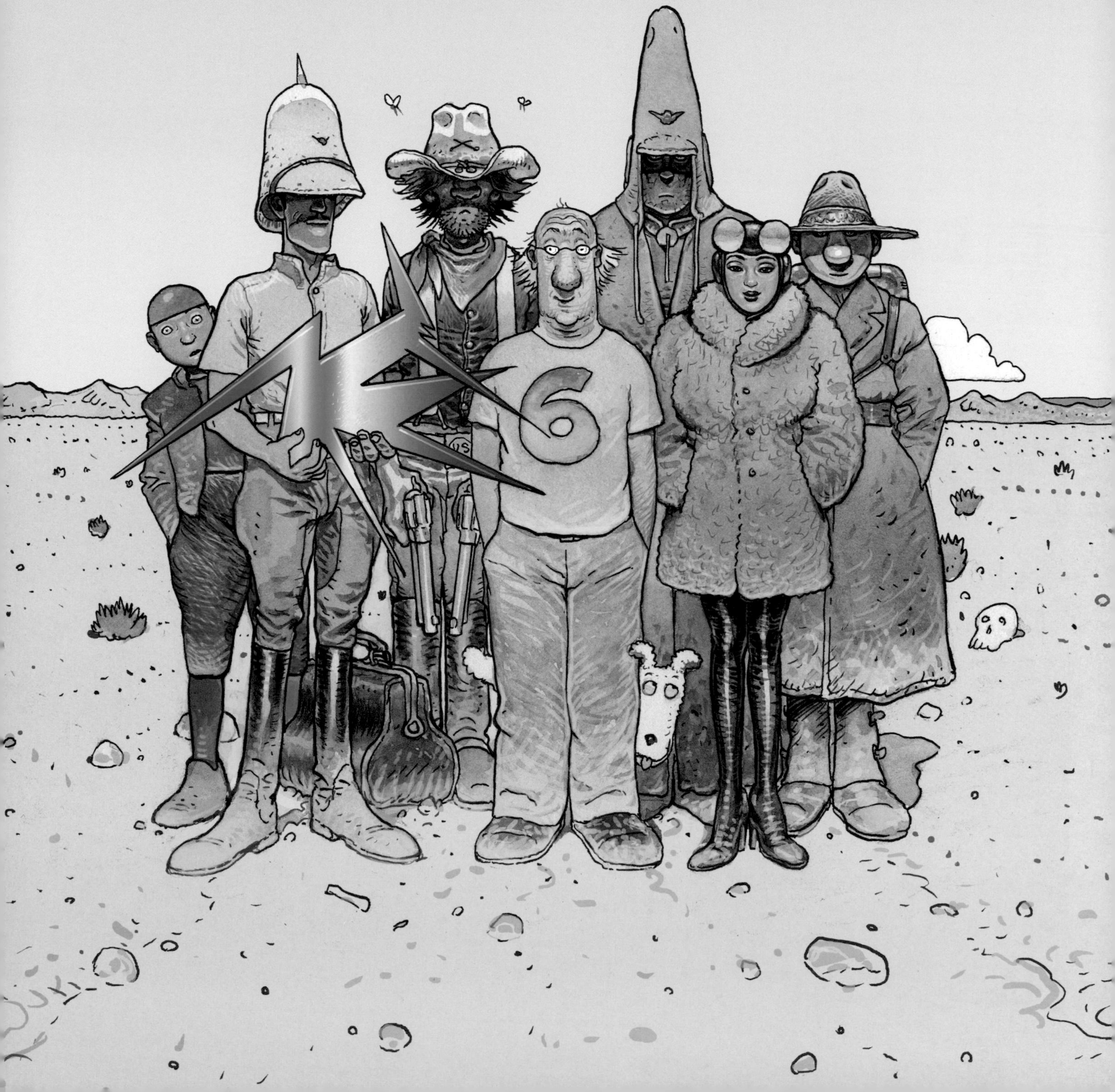

EXHAUSTED BY A SERIES OF **PATHETIC ADVENTURES,** MOEB BY MOEB TRIES TO RECOUP HIS ENERGY WITH A WELL-DESERVED REST IN HIS SINGLE BED AT THE CENTER OF THE SECRET BUNKER HE BUILT IN THE MOST **DESERTED** REGION OF DESERT "B."

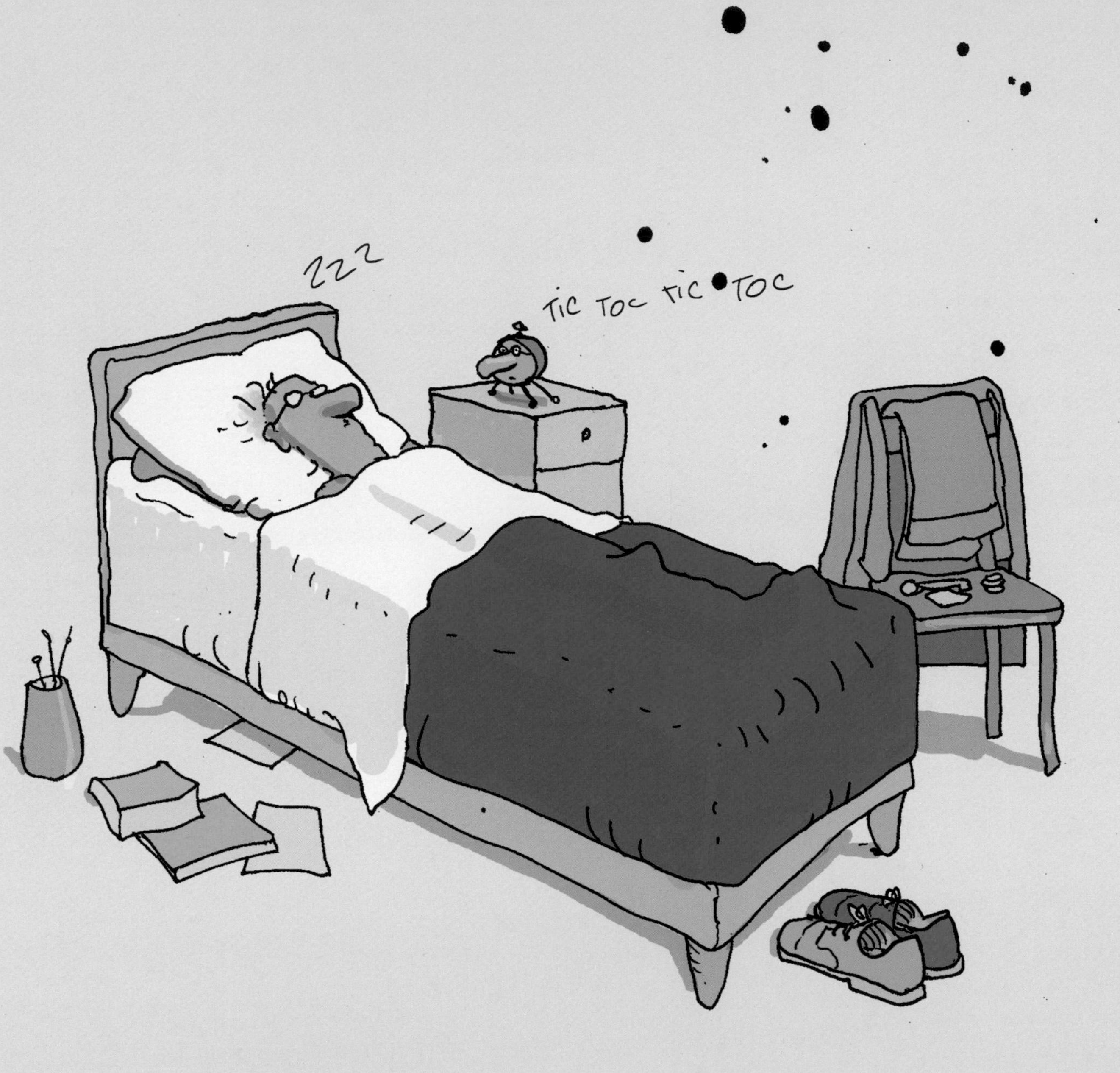
ZZZ
TIC TOC TIC TOC

BUT OBSESSIVE **DREAMS** RUN RELENTLESSLY THROUGH HIS CONSCIOUSNESS... LIKE DARK STORM CLOUDS IN A SERENE SKY...

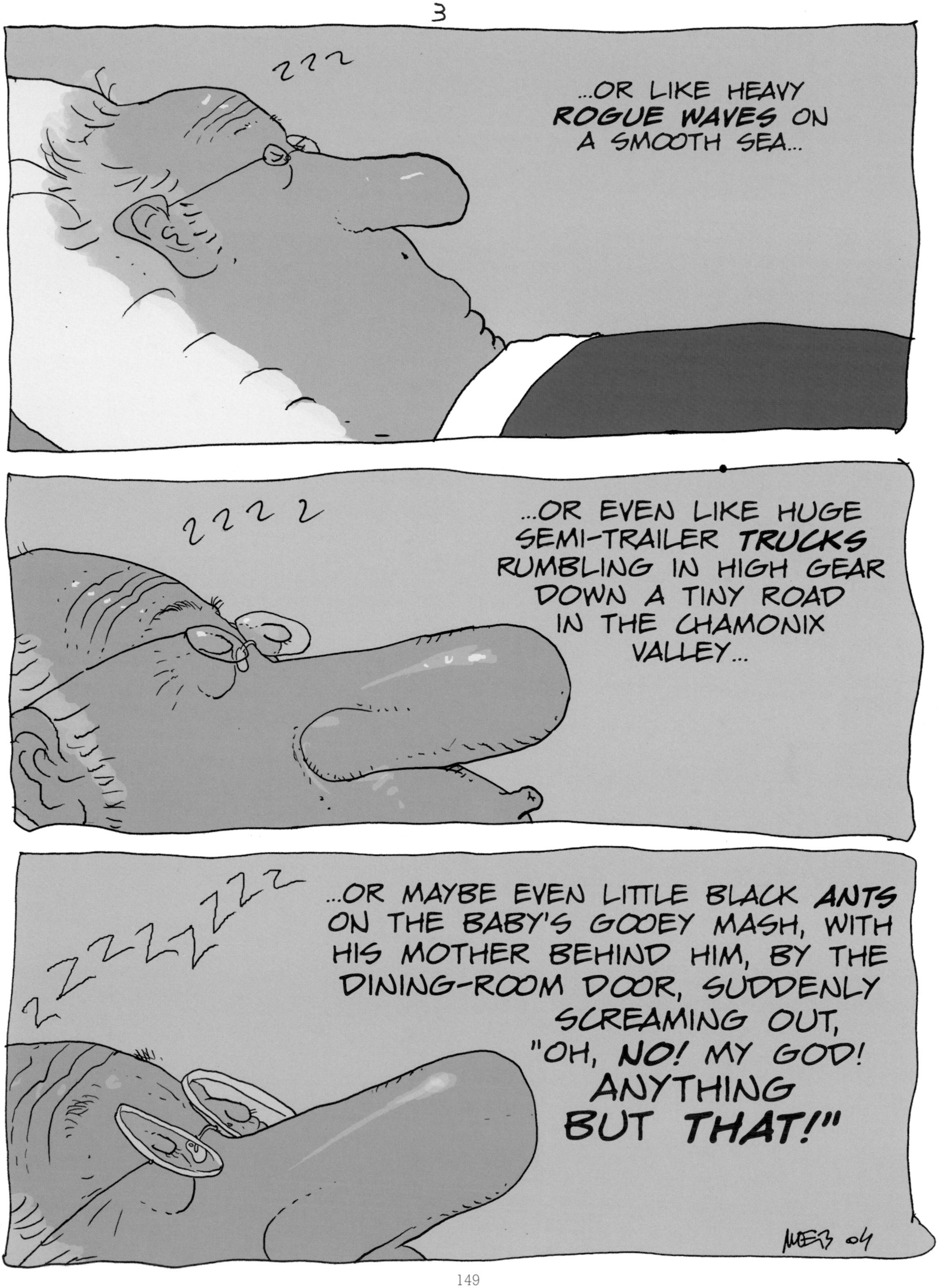
3
ZZZ
...OR LIKE HEAVY ROGUE WAVES ON A SMOOTH SEA...
ZZZZ
...OR EVEN LIKE HUGE SEMI-TRAILER TRUCKS RUMBLING IN HIGH GEAR DOWN A TINY ROAD IN THE CHAMONIX VALLEY...
ZZZZZZZZ
...OR MAYBE EVEN LITTLE BLACK ANTS ON THE BABY'S GOOEY MASH, WITH HIS MOTHER BEHIND HIM, BY THE DINING-ROOM DOOR, SUDDENLY SCREAMING OUT, "OH, NO! MY GOD! ANYTHING BUT THAT!"
MŒB 04

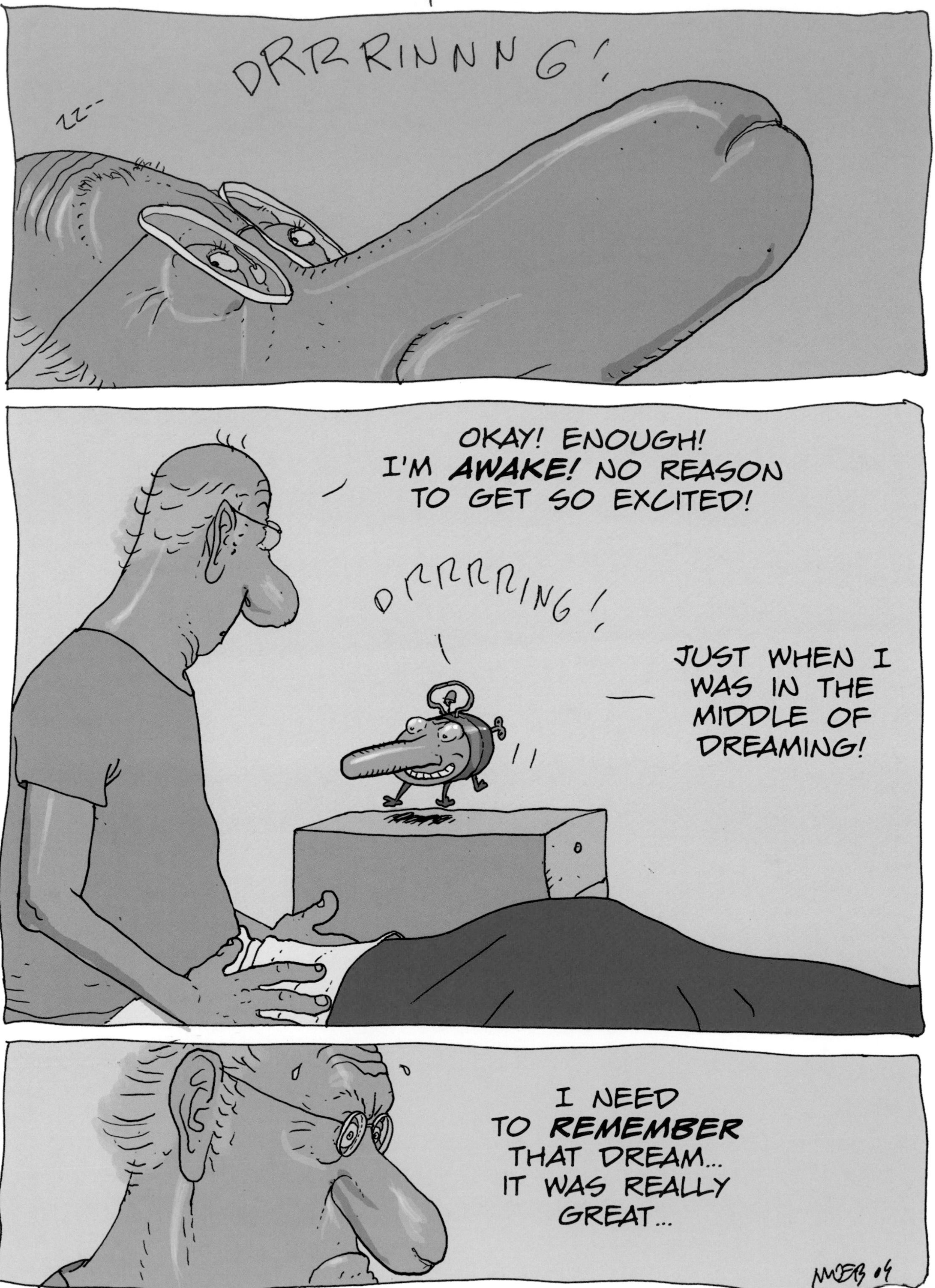
DRRRINNNG!
ZZ--
OKAY! ENOUGH! I'M AWAKE! NO REASON TO GET SO EXCITED!
DRRRRING!
JUST WHEN I WAS IN THE MIDDLE OF DREAMING!
I NEED TO REMEMBER THAT DREAM... IT WAS REALLY GREAT...
MOEB 04

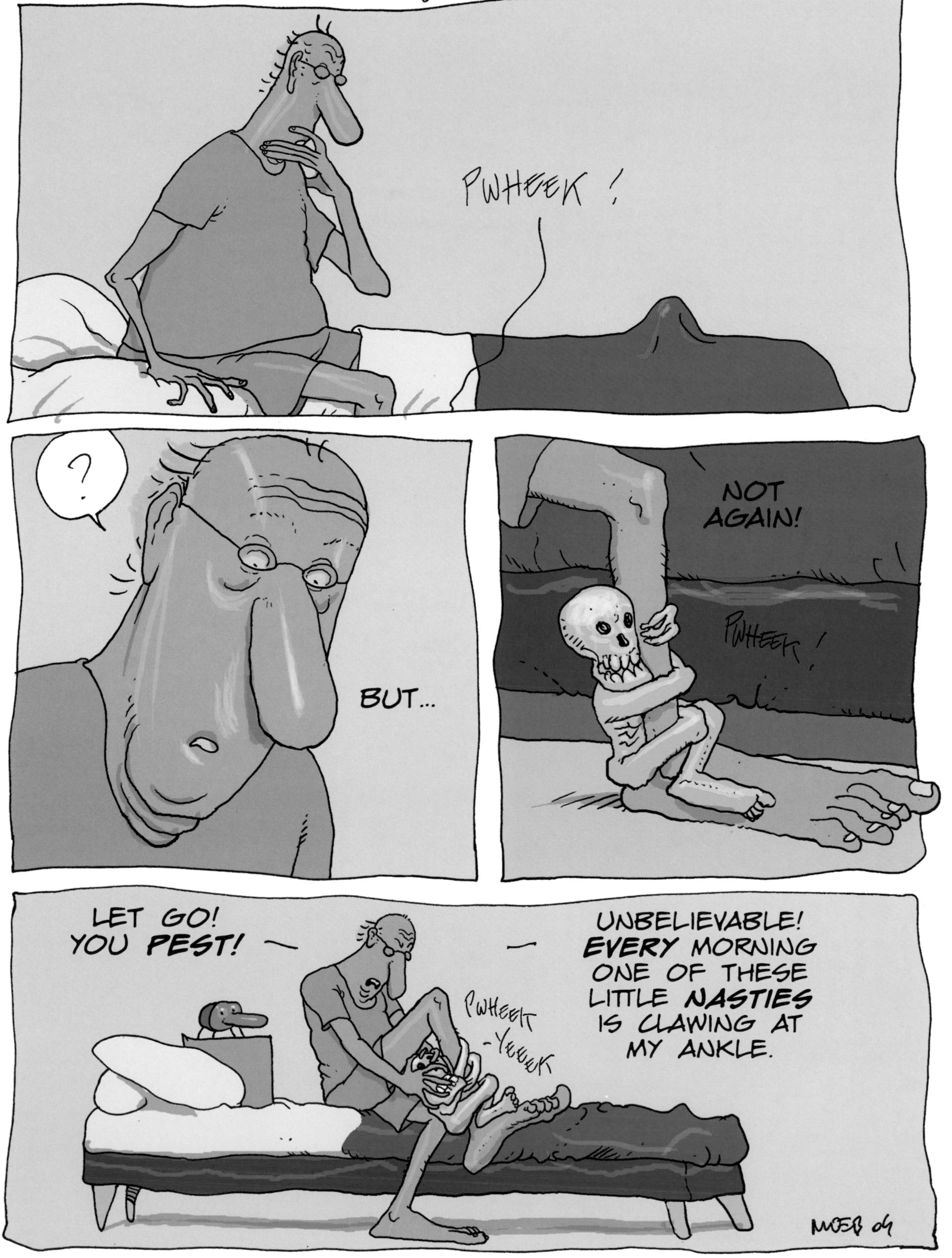
PWHEEK !
?
BUT...
NOT AGAIN!
PWHEEK !
LET GO! YOU PEST!
UNBELIEVABLE! EVERY MORNING ONE OF THESE LITTLE NASTIES IS CLAWING AT MY ANKLE.
PWHEEK
-YEEEK
MOEB 04

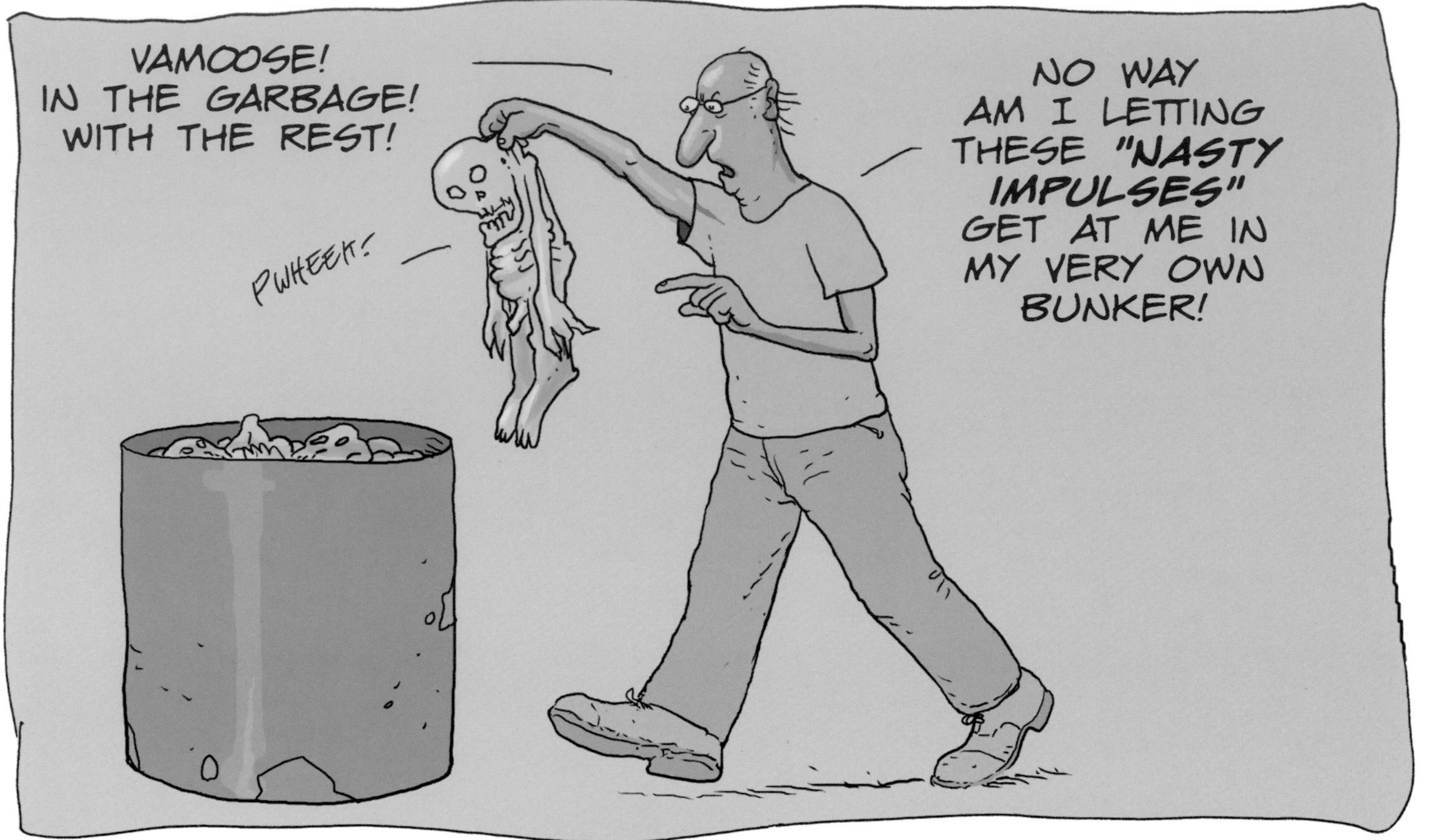
VAMOOSE! IN THE GARBAGE! WITH THE REST!
NO WAY AM I LETTING THESE "NASTY IMPULSES" GET AT ME IN MY VERY OWN BUNKER!
PWHEEK!

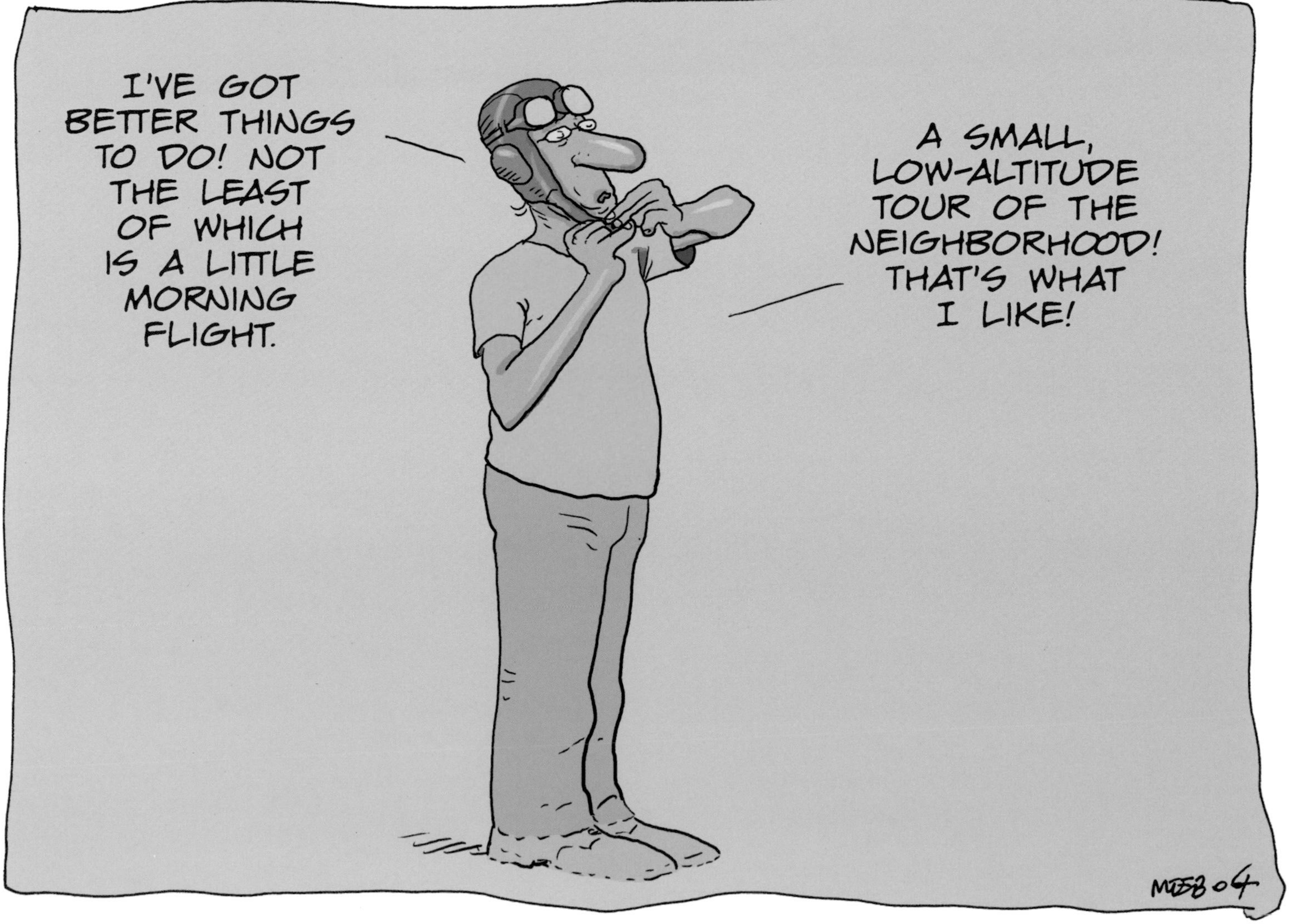
I'VE GOT BETTER THINGS TO DO! NOT THE LEAST OF WHICH IS A LITTLE MORNING FLIGHT.
A SMALL, LOW-ALTITUDE TOUR OF THE NEIGHBORHOOD! THAT'S WHAT I LIKE!
MJSB 04

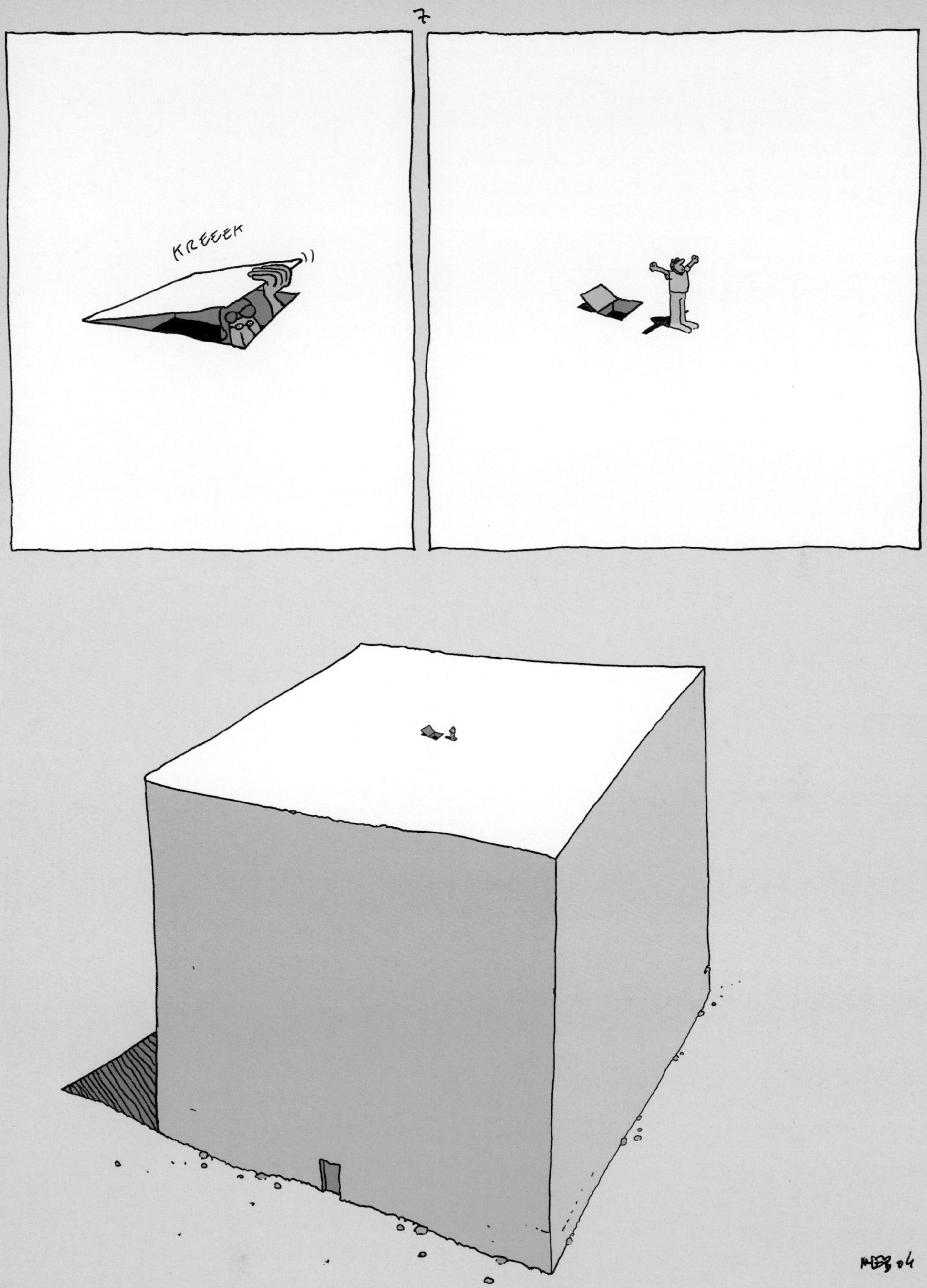
7
KREEEK

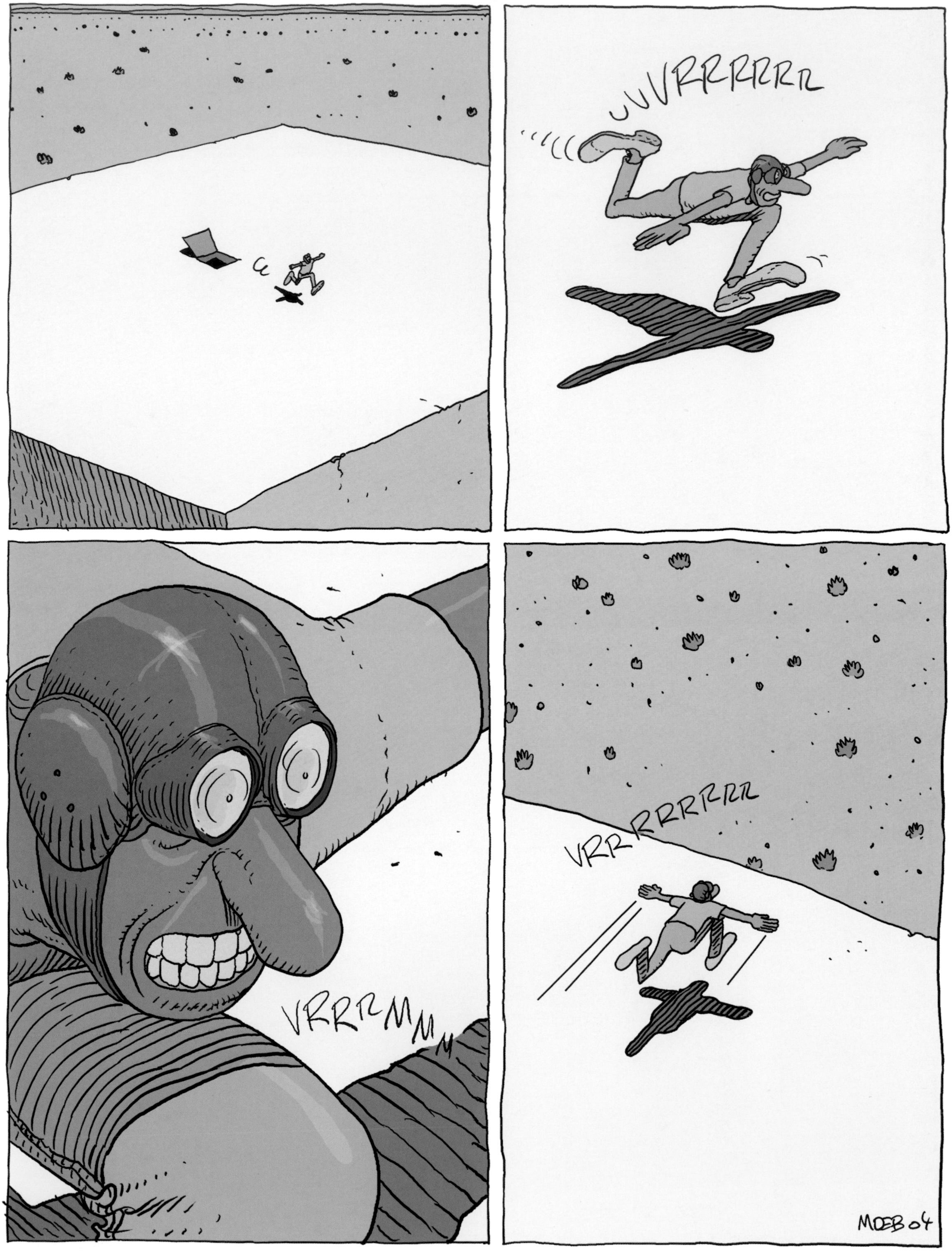
VVVRRRRRRR
VRRRMMM
VRRRRRRRRR
MOEB 04

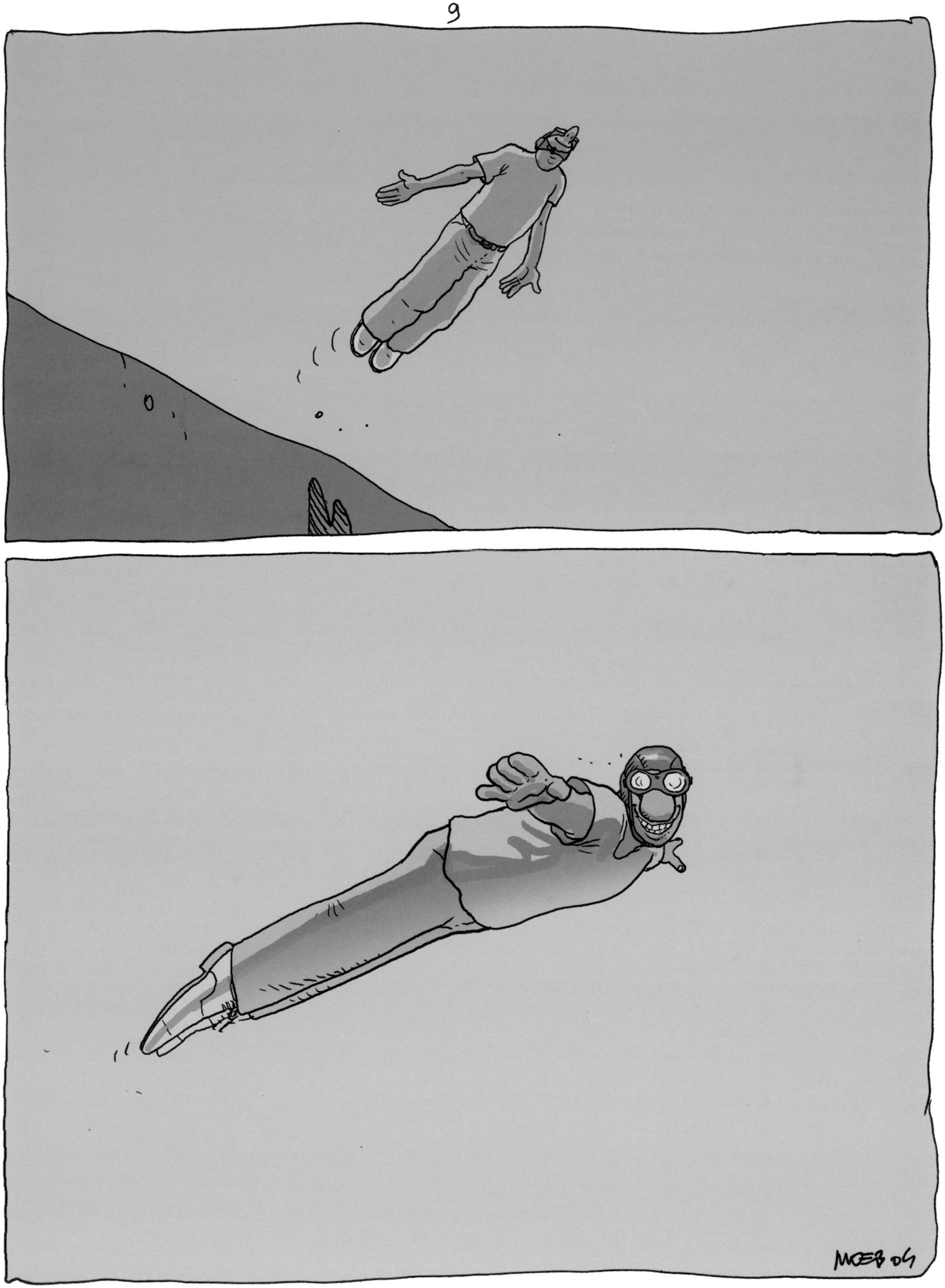

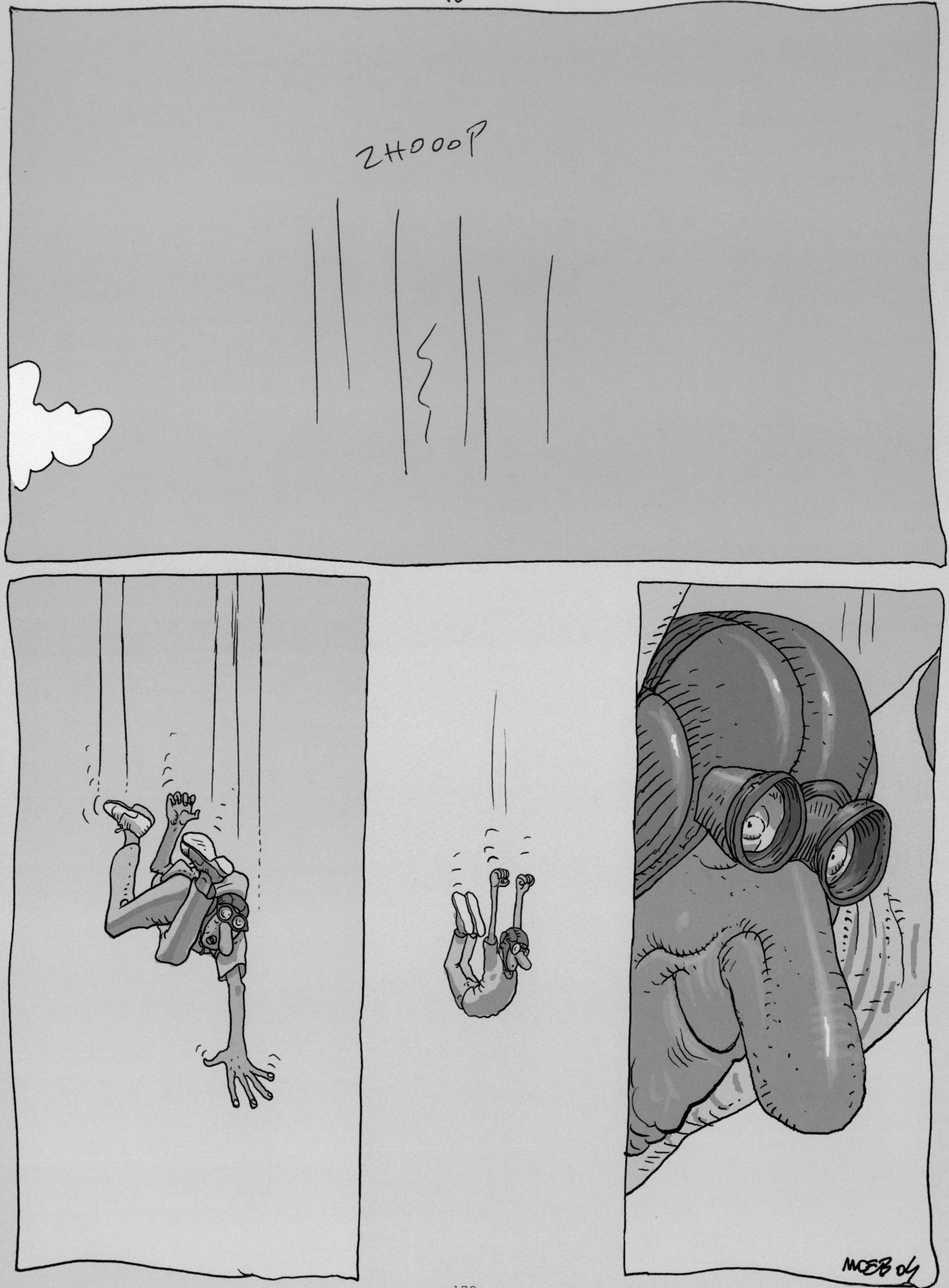
ZHOOOP
MOEB 04

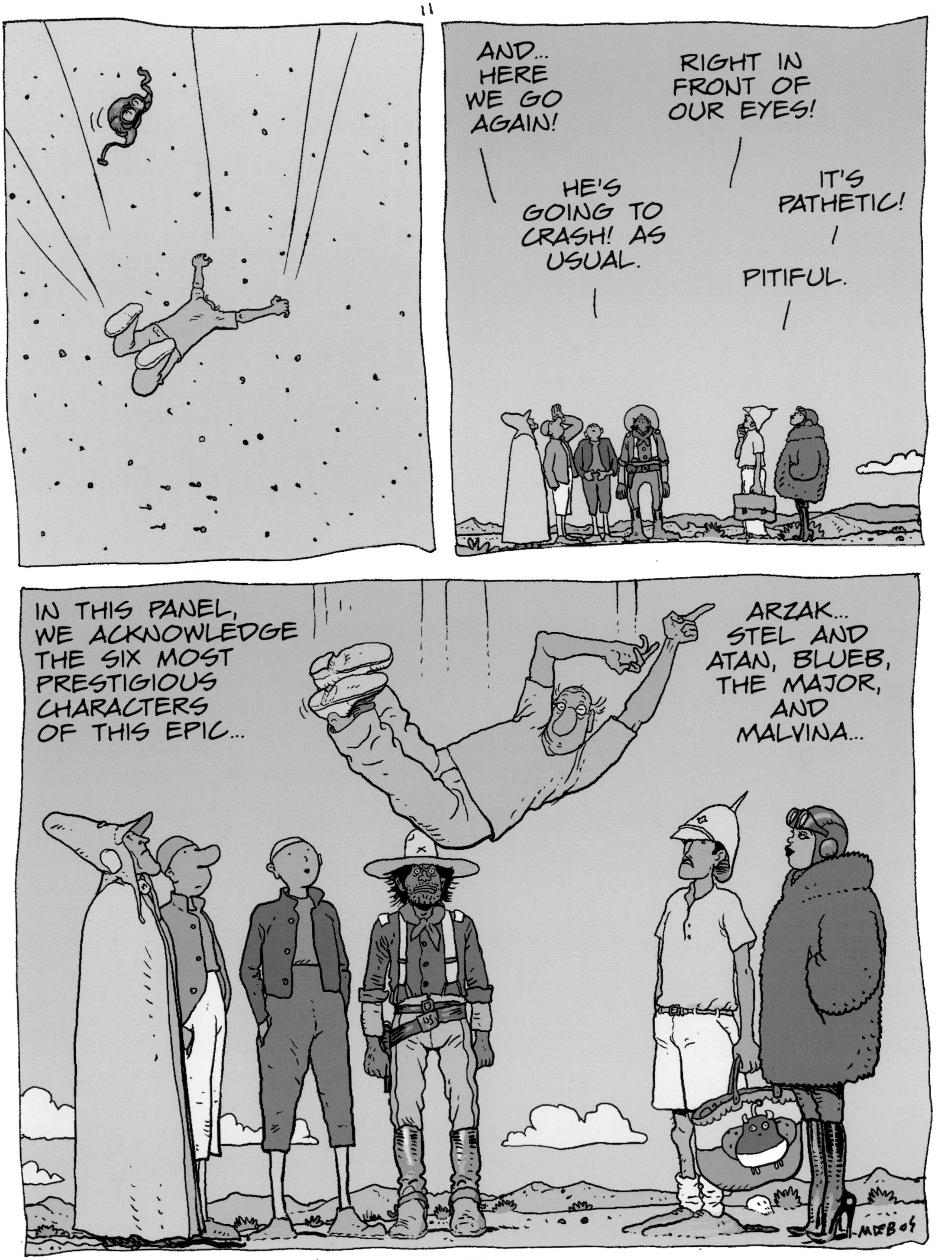
AND... HERE WE GO AGAIN!
RIGHT IN FRONT OF OUR EYES!
HE'S GOING TO CRASH! AS USUAL.
IT'S PATHETIC!
PITIFUL.
IN THIS PANEL, WE ACKNOWLEDGE THE SIX MOST PRESTIGIOUS CHARACTERS OF THIS EPIC...
ARZAK... STEL AND ATAN, BLUEB, THE MAJOR, AND MALVINA...

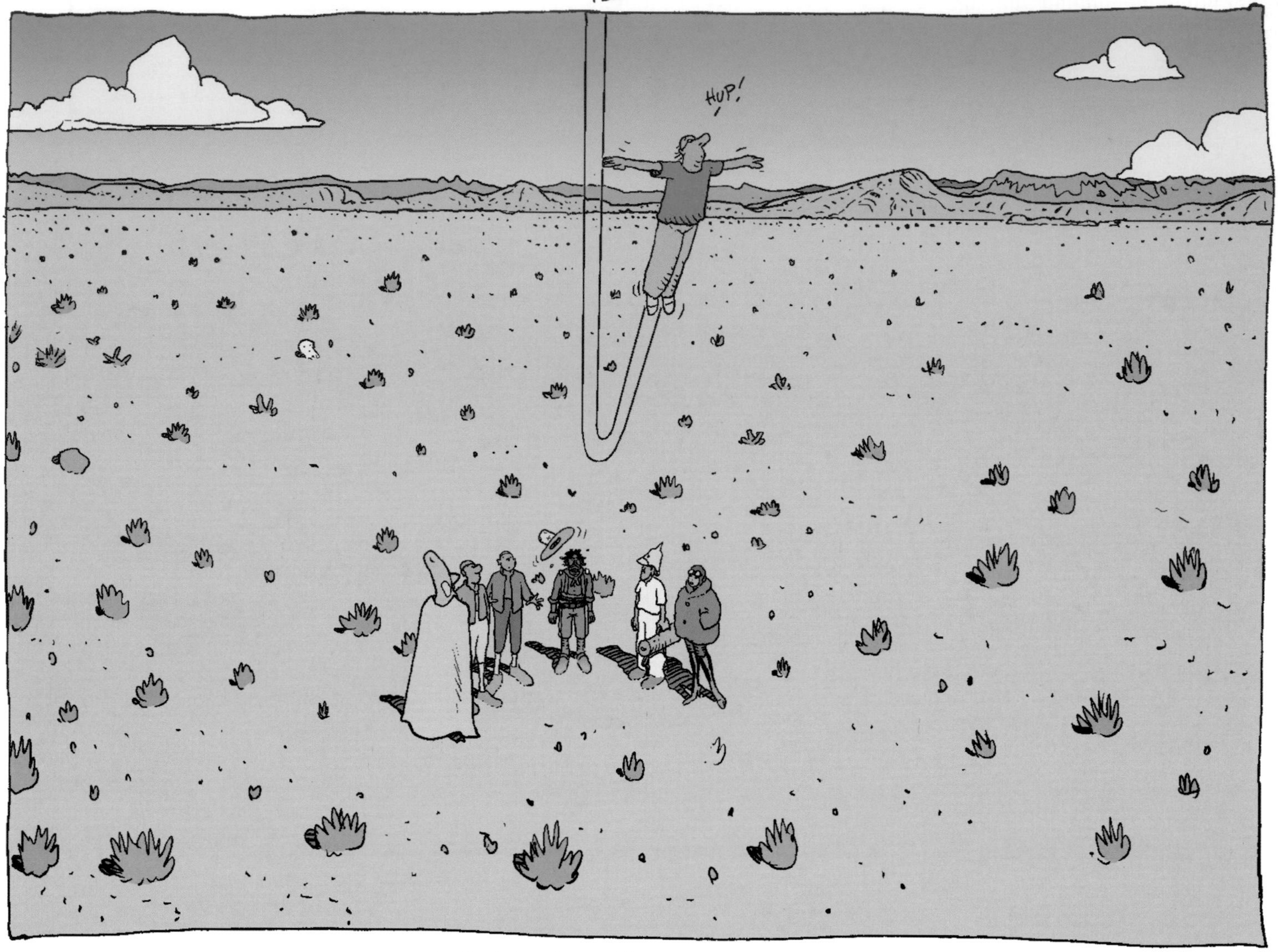
HUP!

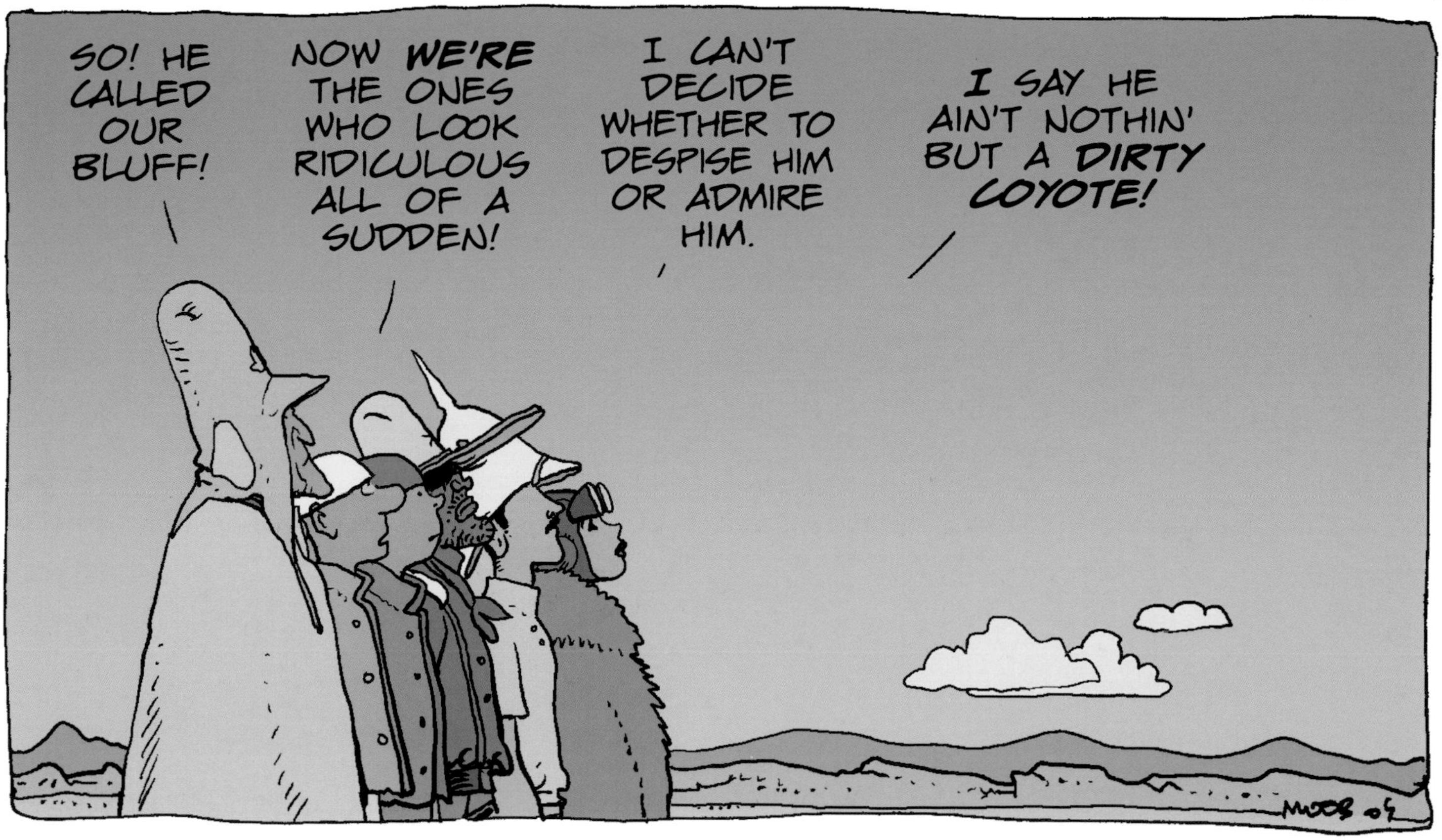
SO! HE CALLED OUR BLUFF!
NOW WE'RE THE ONES WHO LOOK RIDICULOUS ALL OF A SUDDEN!
I CAN'T DECIDE WHETHER TO DESPISE HIM OR ADMIRE HIM.
I SAY HE AIN'T NOTHIN' BUT A DIRTY COYOTE!

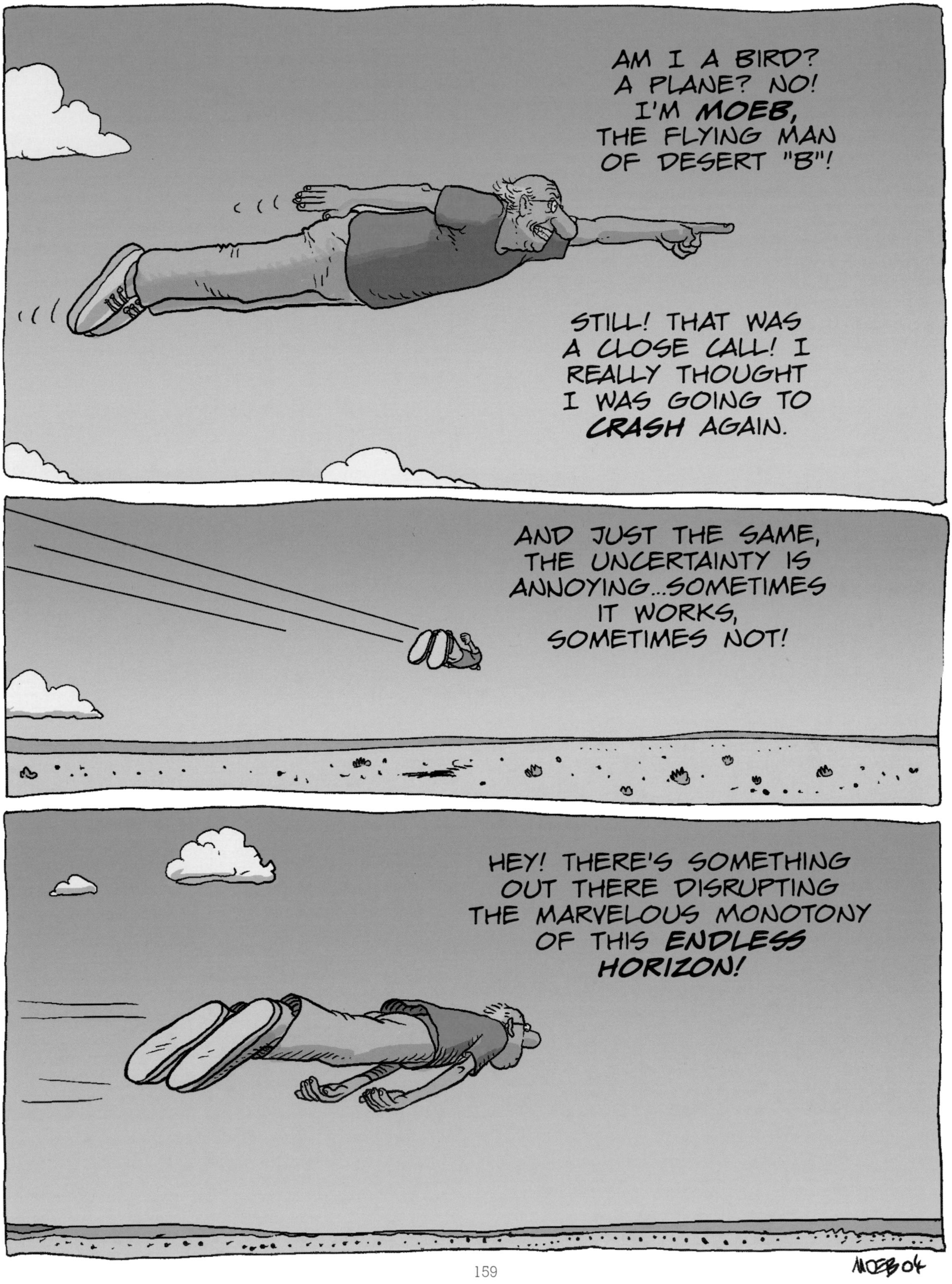
AM I A BIRD? A PLANE? NO! I'M MOEB, THE FLYING MAN OF DESERT "B"!
STILL! THAT WAS A CLOSE CALL! I REALLY THOUGHT I WAS GOING TO CRASH AGAIN.
AND JUST THE SAME, THE UNCERTAINTY IS ANNOYING...SOMETIMES IT WORKS, SOMETIMES NOT!
HEY! THERE'S SOMETHING OUT THERE DISRUPTING THE MARVELOUS MONOTONY OF THIS ENDLESS HORIZON!
MOEB 04

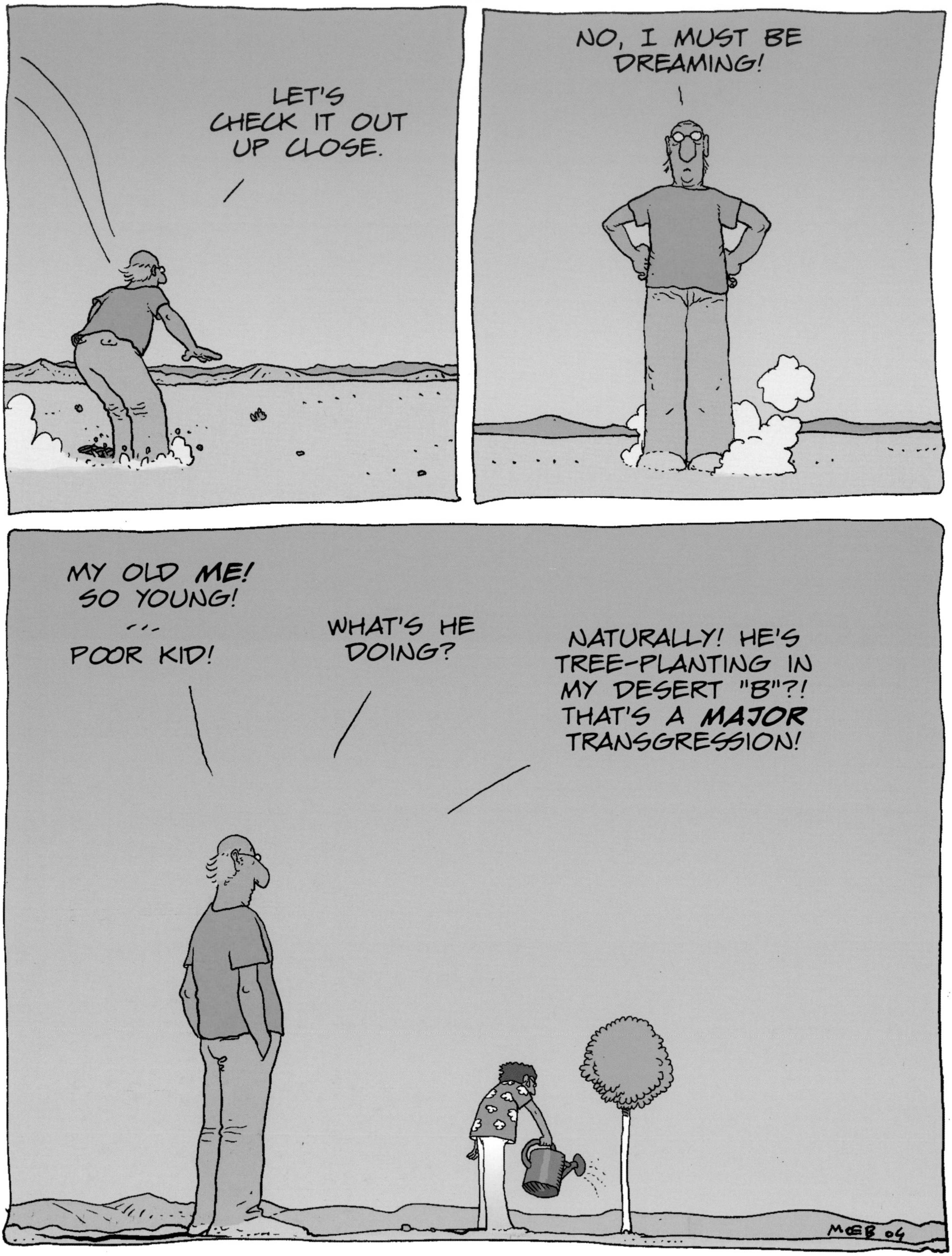
LET'S CHECK IT OUT UP CLOSE.
NO, I MUST BE DREAMING!
MY OLD ME! SO YOUNG!
...
POOR KID!
WHAT'S HE DOING?
NATURALLY! HE'S TREE-PLANTING IN MY DESERT "B"?! THAT'S A MAJOR TRANSGRESSION!
MŒB 04

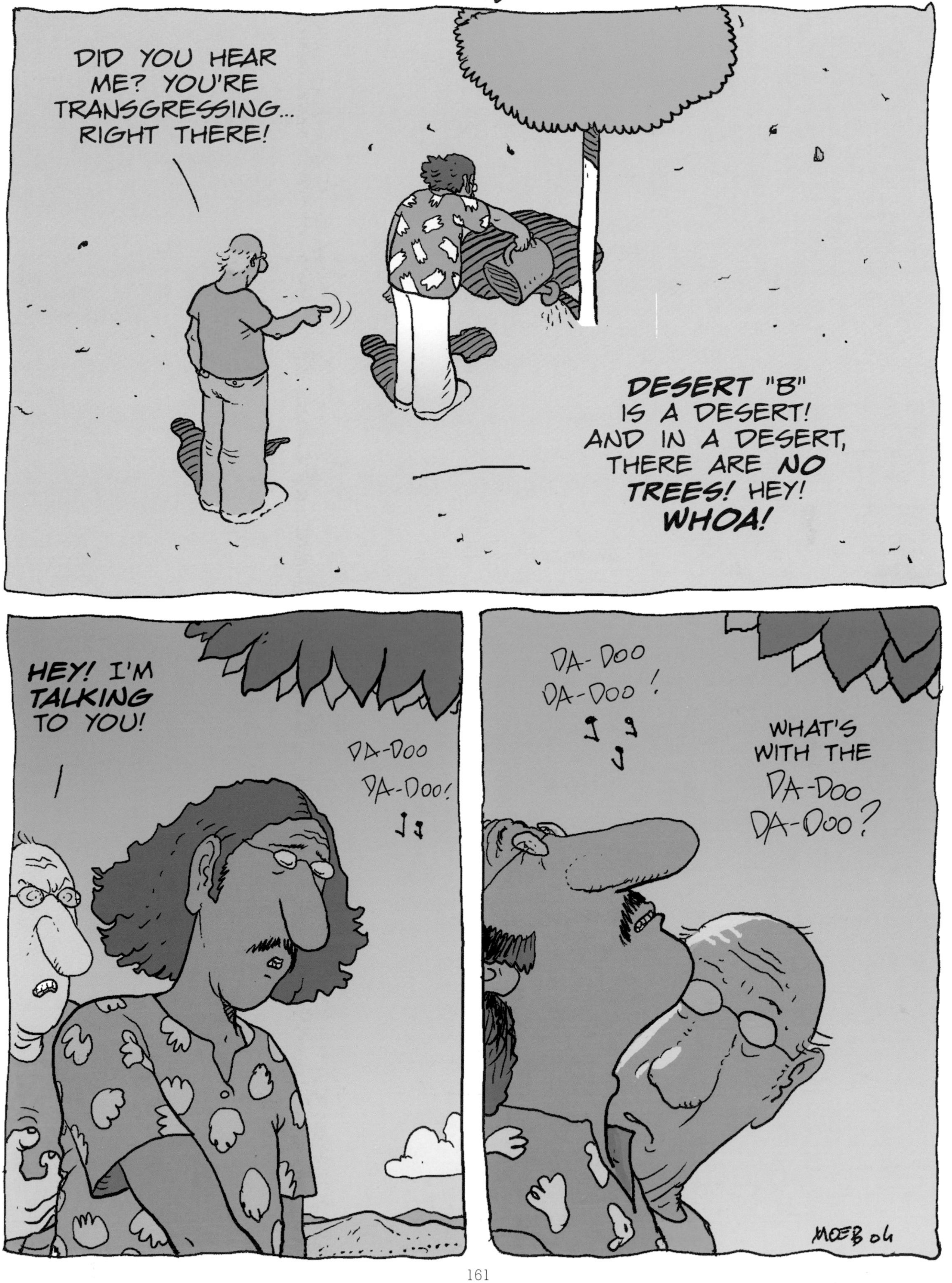
DID YOU HEAR ME? YOU'RE TRANSGRESSING... RIGHT THERE!
DESERT "B" IS A DESERT! AND IN A DESERT, THERE ARE NO TREES! HEY! WHOA!
HEY! I'M TALKING TO YOU!
DA-DOO DA-DOO!
DA-DOO DA-DOO!
WHAT'S WITH THE DA-DOO DA-DOO?
MOEB 04

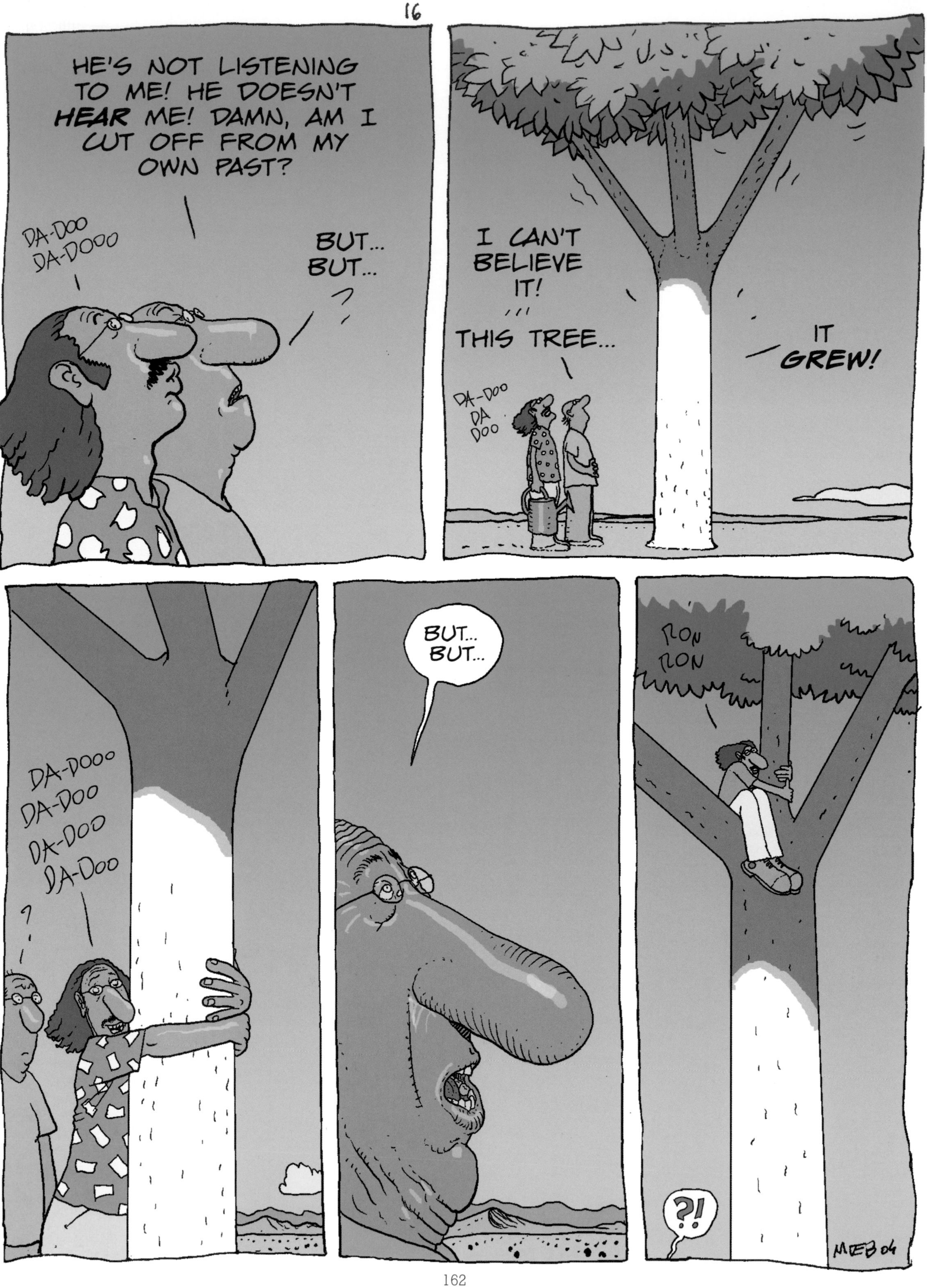
HE'S NOT LISTENING TO ME! HE DOESN'T **HEAR** ME! DAMN, AM I CUT OFF FROM MY OWN PAST?
DA-DOO DA-DOOO
BUT... BUT...
?
I CAN'T BELIEVE IT!
THIS TREE...
IT **GREW!**
DA-DOO DA DOO
DA-DOOO DA-DOO DA-DOO DA-DOO
?
BUT... BUT...
RON RON
?!
MEB 04

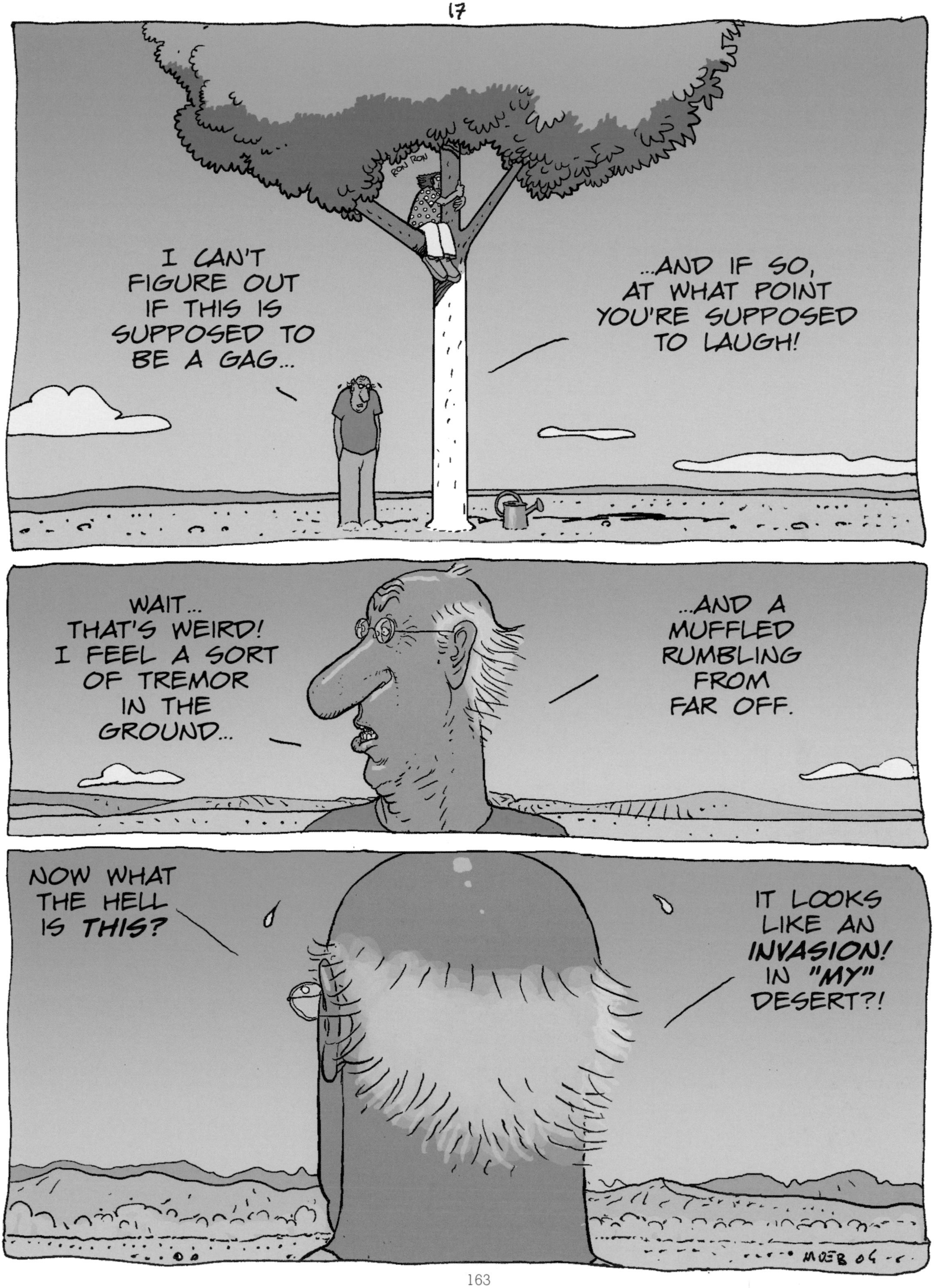
RON RON
I CAN'T FIGURE OUT IF THIS IS SUPPOSED TO BE A GAG...
...AND IF SO, AT WHAT POINT YOU'RE SUPPOSED TO LAUGH!
WAIT... THAT'S WEIRD! I FEEL A SORT OF TREMOR IN THE GROUND...
...AND A MUFFLED RUMBLING FROM FAR OFF.
NOW WHAT THE HELL IS *THIS?*
IT LOOKS LIKE AN *INVASION!* IN *"MY"* DESERT?!
MOEB 06

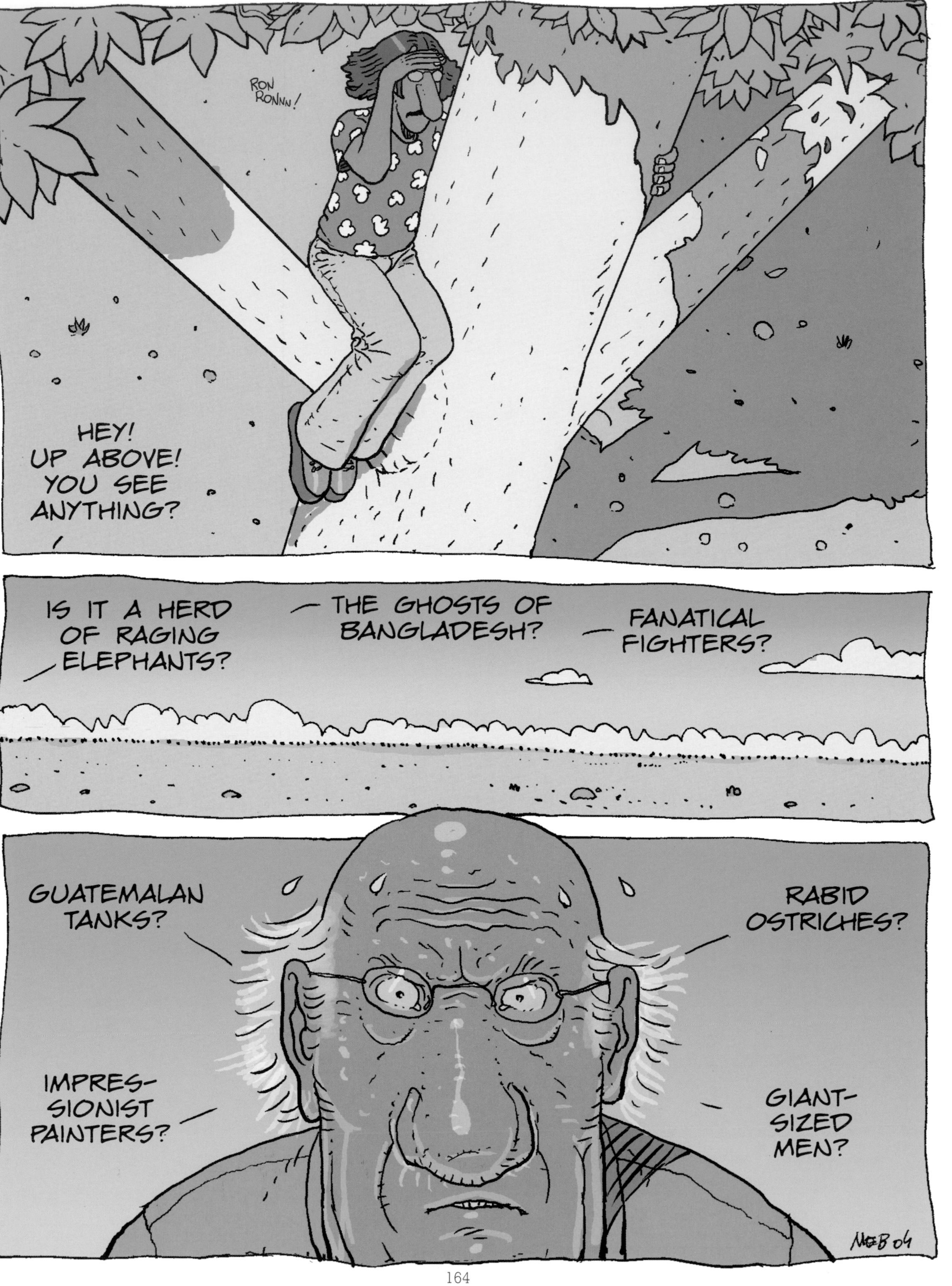
RON RONNN!
HEY! UP ABOVE! YOU SEE ANYTHING?
IS IT A HERD OF RAGING ELEPHANTS?
THE GHOSTS OF BANGLADESH?
FANATICAL FIGHTERS?
GUATEMALAN TANKS?
RABID OSTRICHES?
IMPRES-SIONIST PAINTERS?
GIANT-SIZED MEN?
MGB 04

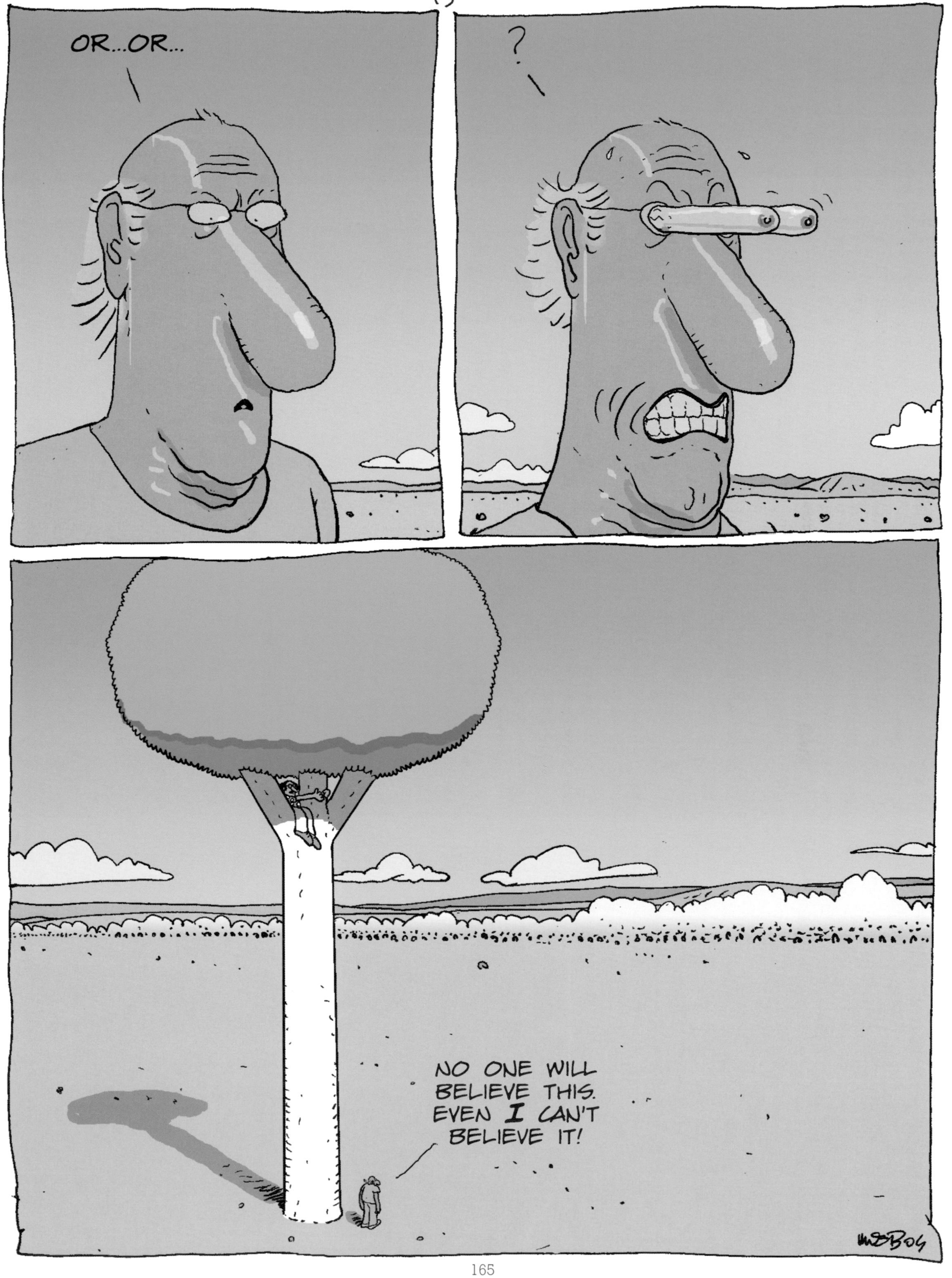
OR...OR...
?
NO ONE WILL BELIEVE THIS. EVEN **I** CAN'T BELIEVE IT!

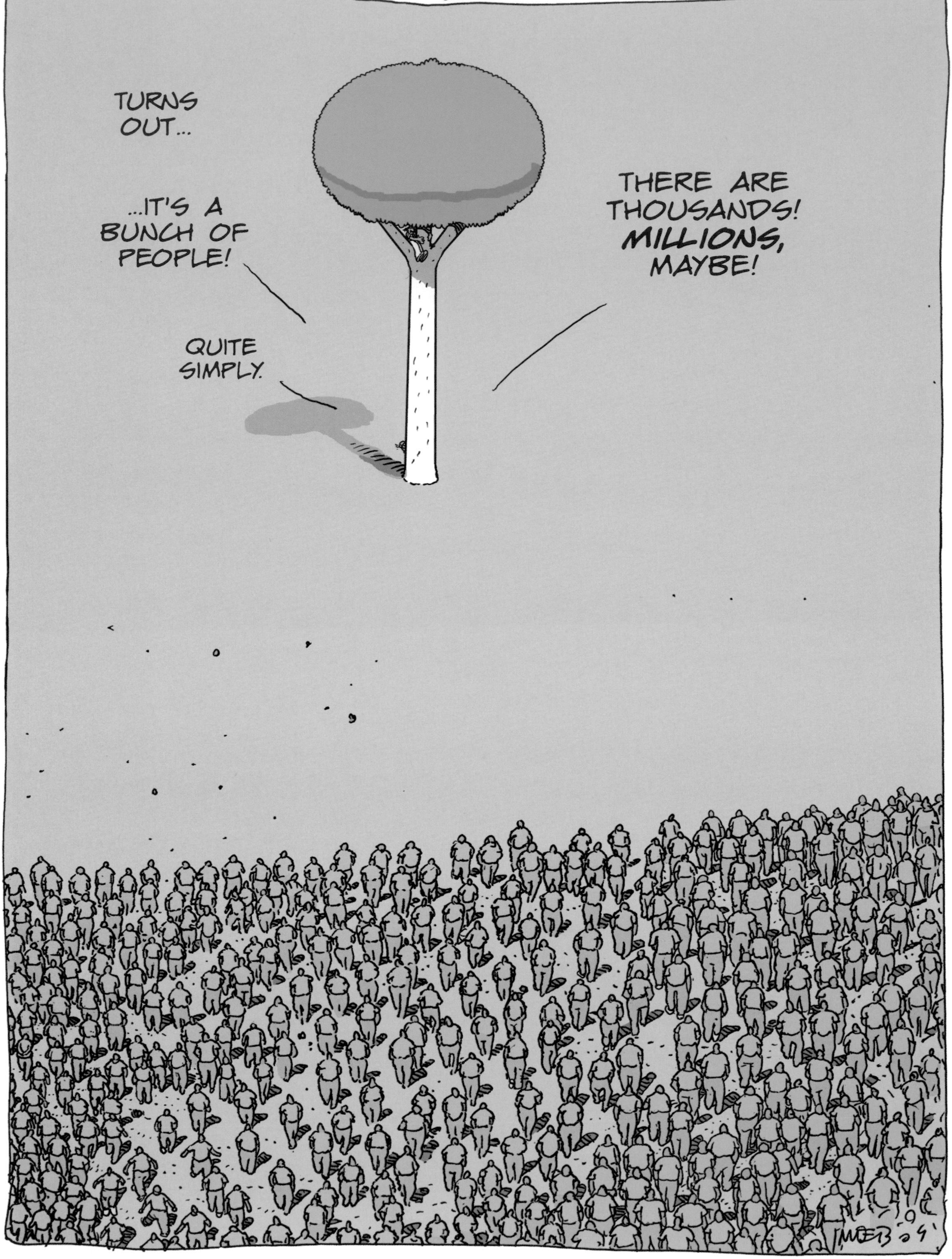
TURNS OUT...
...IT'S A BUNCH OF PEOPLE!
QUITE SIMPLY.
THERE ARE THOUSANDS! MILLIONS, MAYBE!

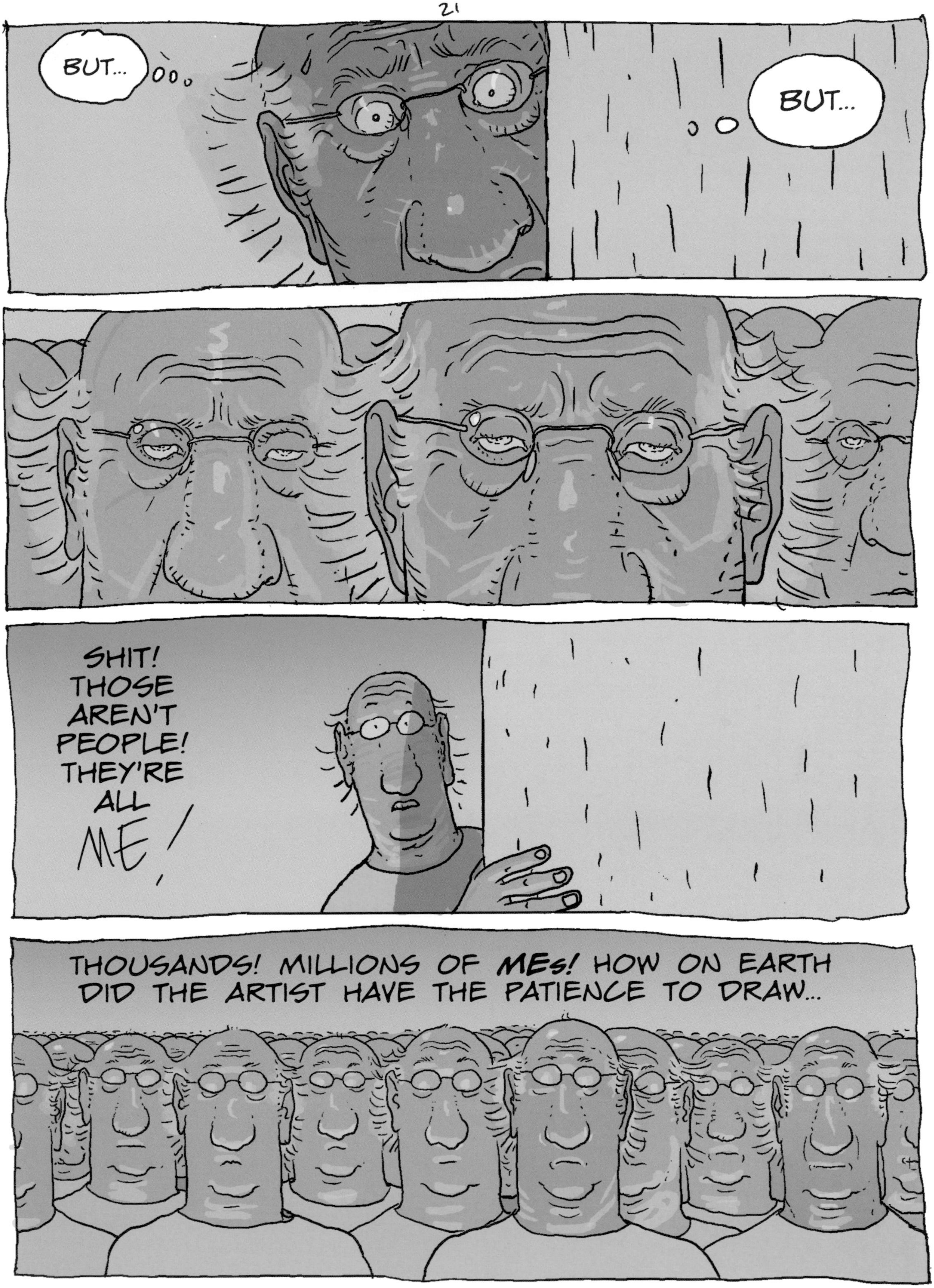
BUT...
BUT...
SHIT! THOSE AREN'T PEOPLE! THEY'RE ALL ME!
THOUSANDS! MILLIONS OF MEs! HOW ON EARTH DID THE ARTIST HAVE THE PATIENCE TO DRAW...

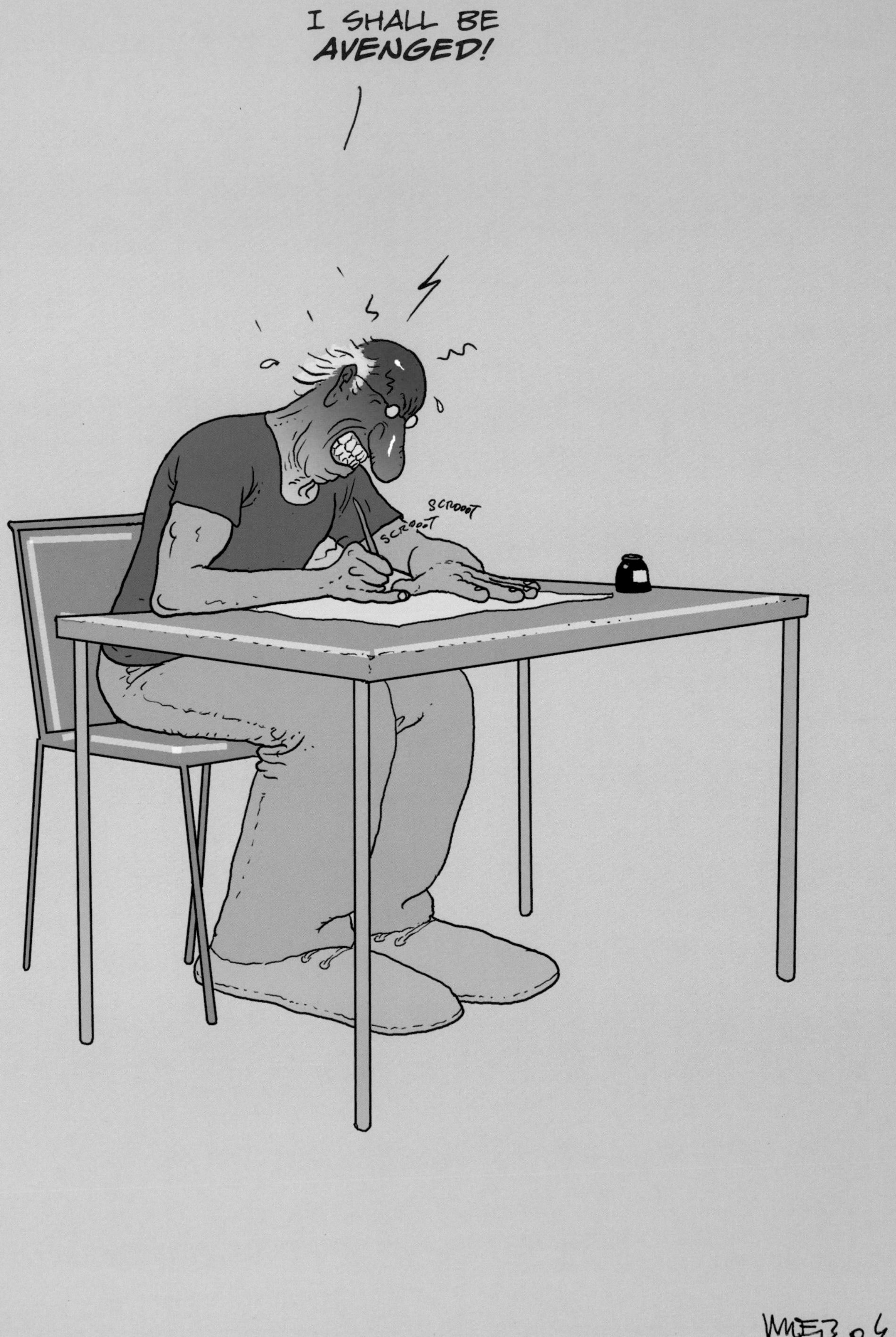
I SHALL BE
AVENGED!
SCROOOT
SCROOOT
MOEB 04

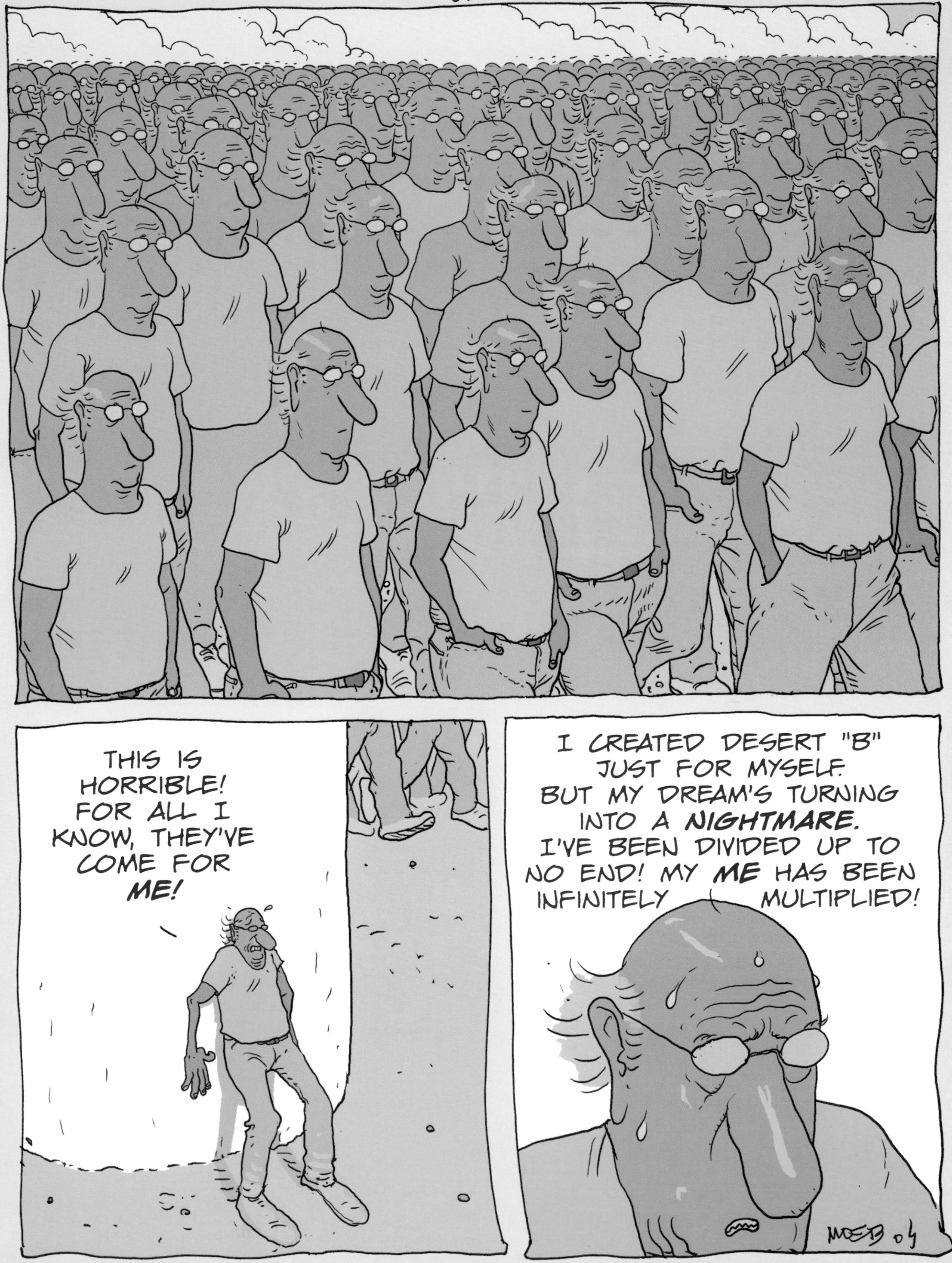
THIS IS HORRIBLE! FOR ALL I KNOW, THEY'VE COME FOR ME!
I CREATED DESERT "B" JUST FOR MYSELF. BUT MY DREAM'S TURNING INTO A NIGHTMARE. I'VE BEEN DIVIDED UP TO NO END! MY ME HAS BEEN INFINITELY MULTIPLIED!
MOEB 04

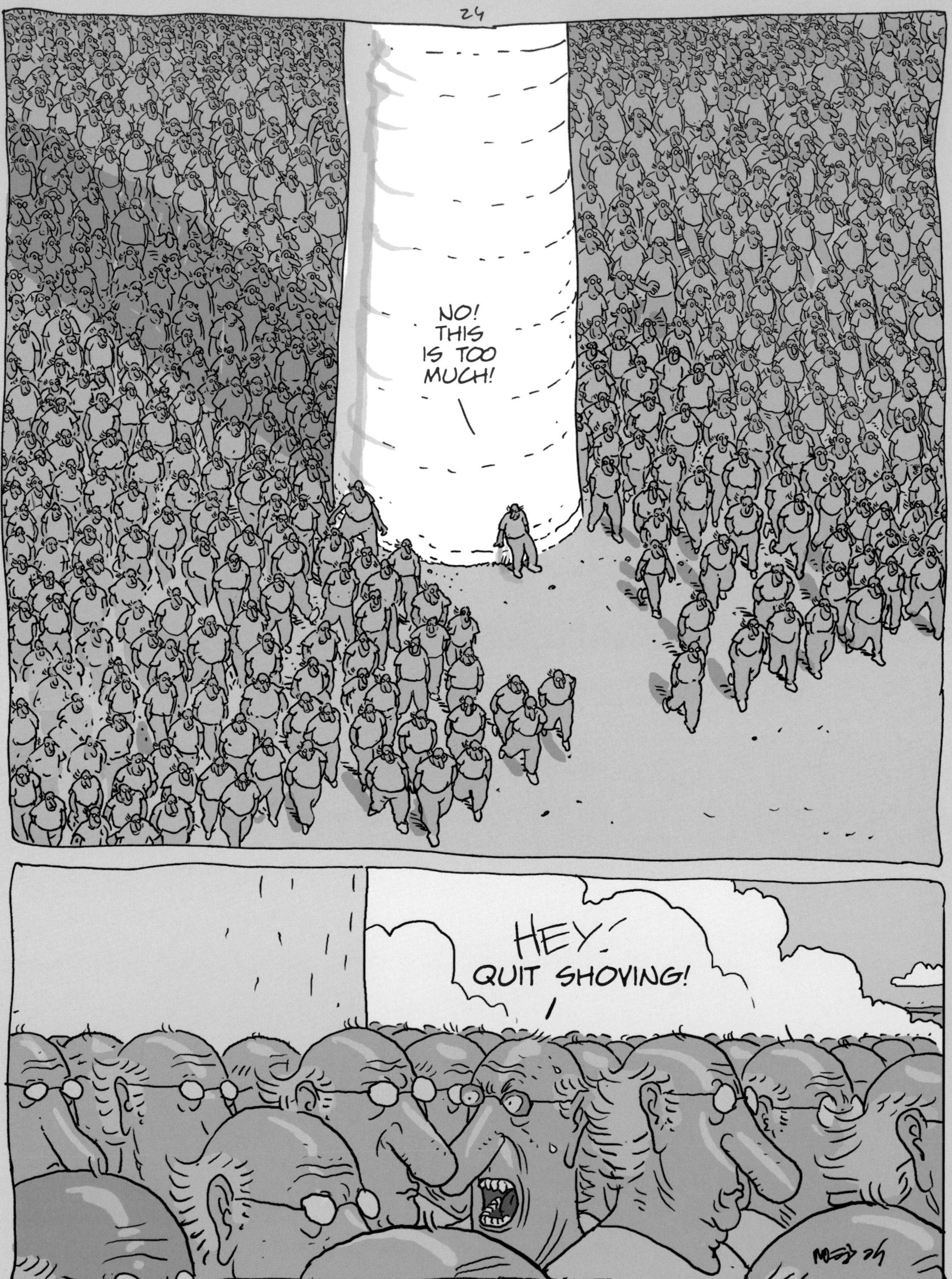
NO! THIS IS TOO MUCH!
HEY! QUIT SHOVING!

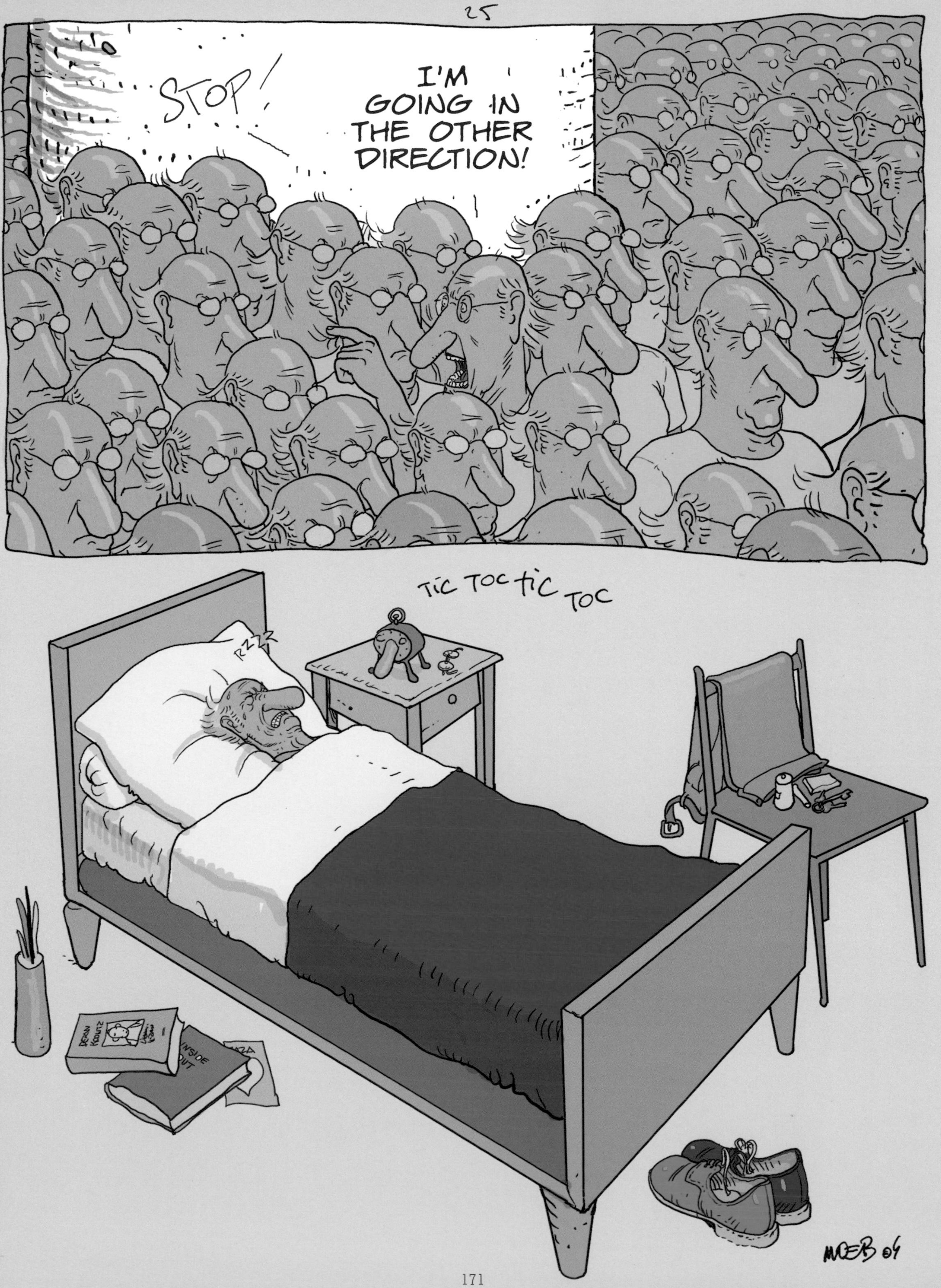

25
STOP!
I'M GOING IN THE OTHER DIRECTION!
TIC TOC TIC TOC
INSIDE OUT
MOEB 04

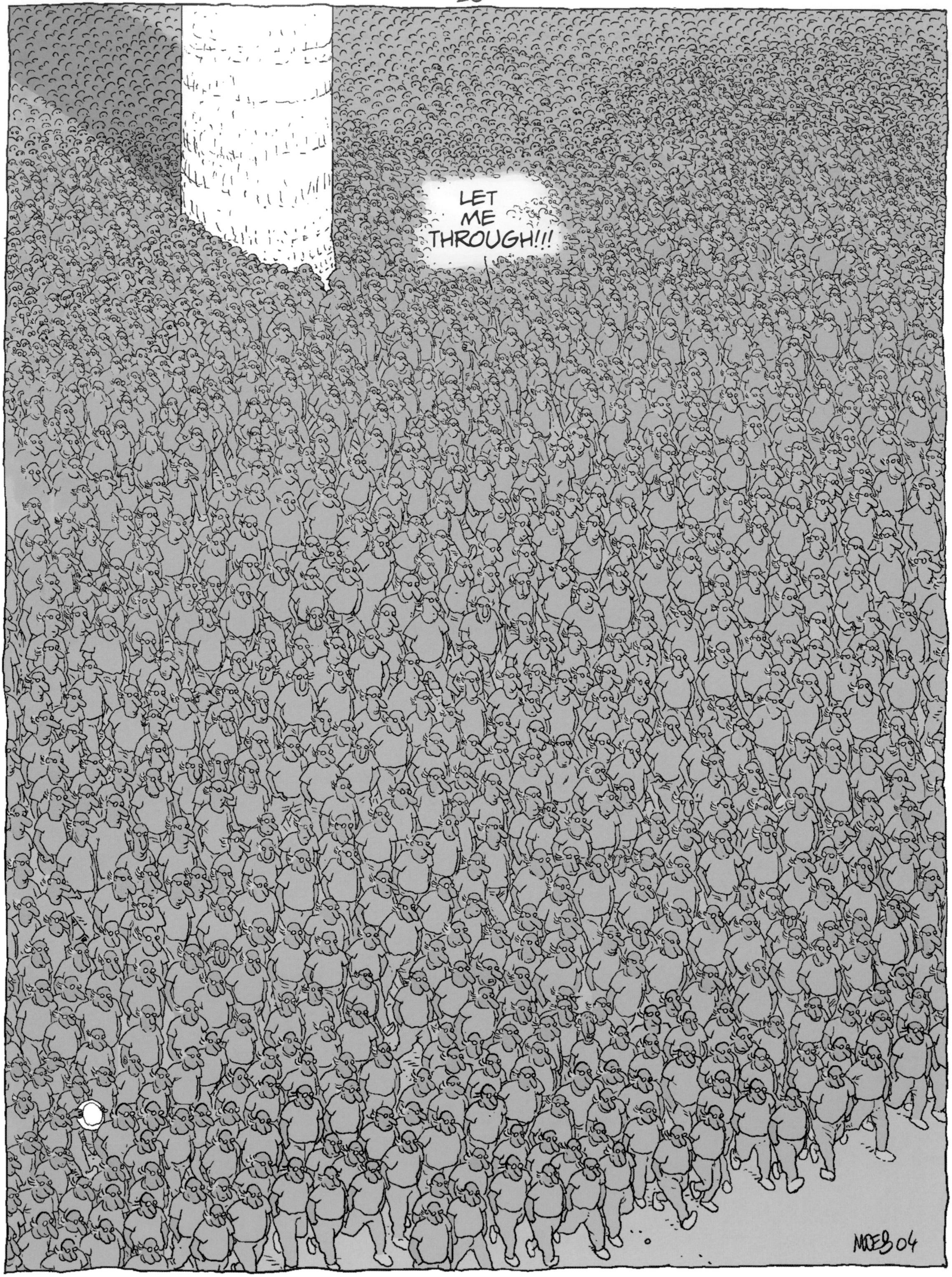
LET ME THROUGH!!!
MOEB 04

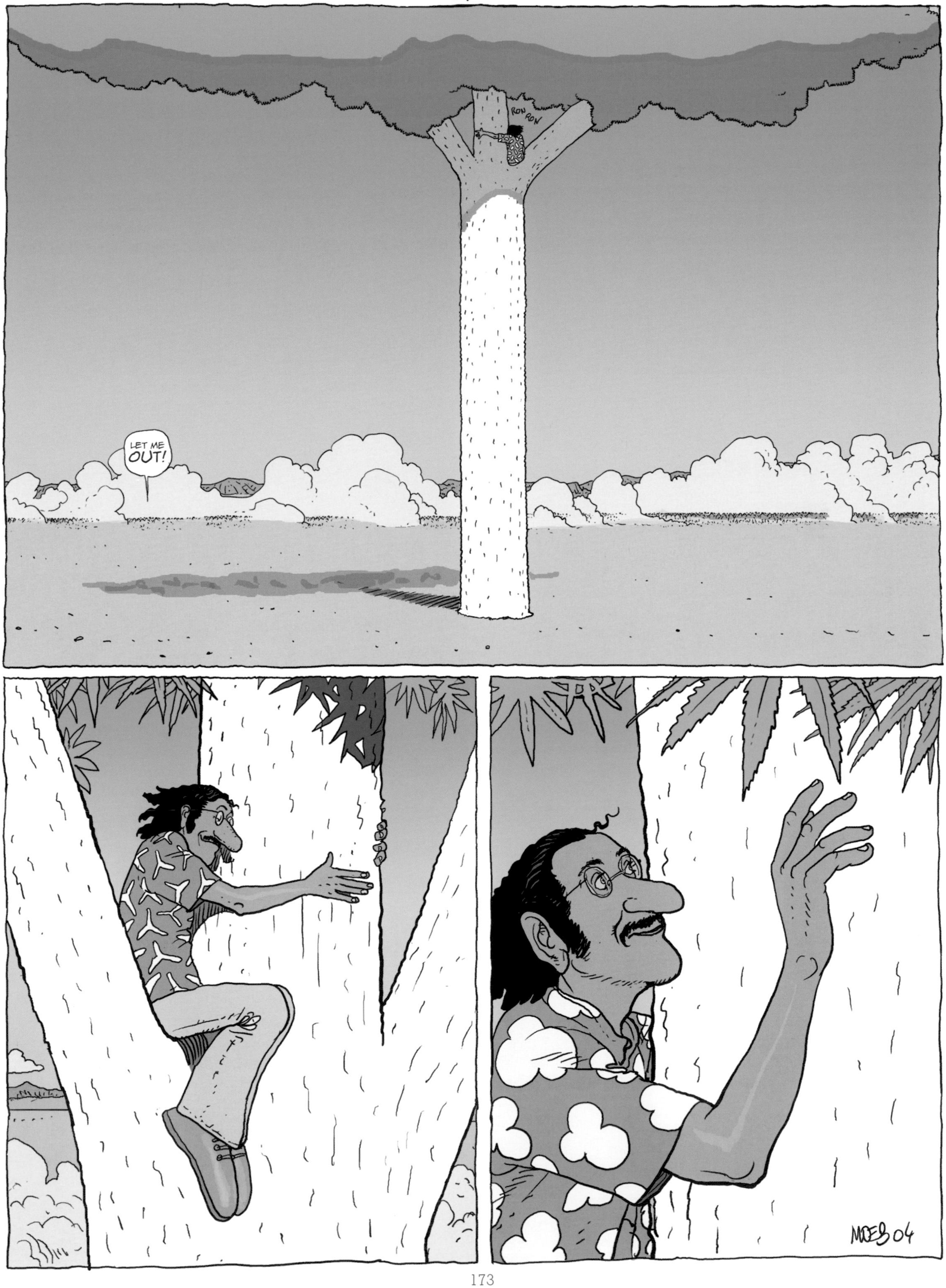
RON RON
LET ME OUT!
MOEB 04

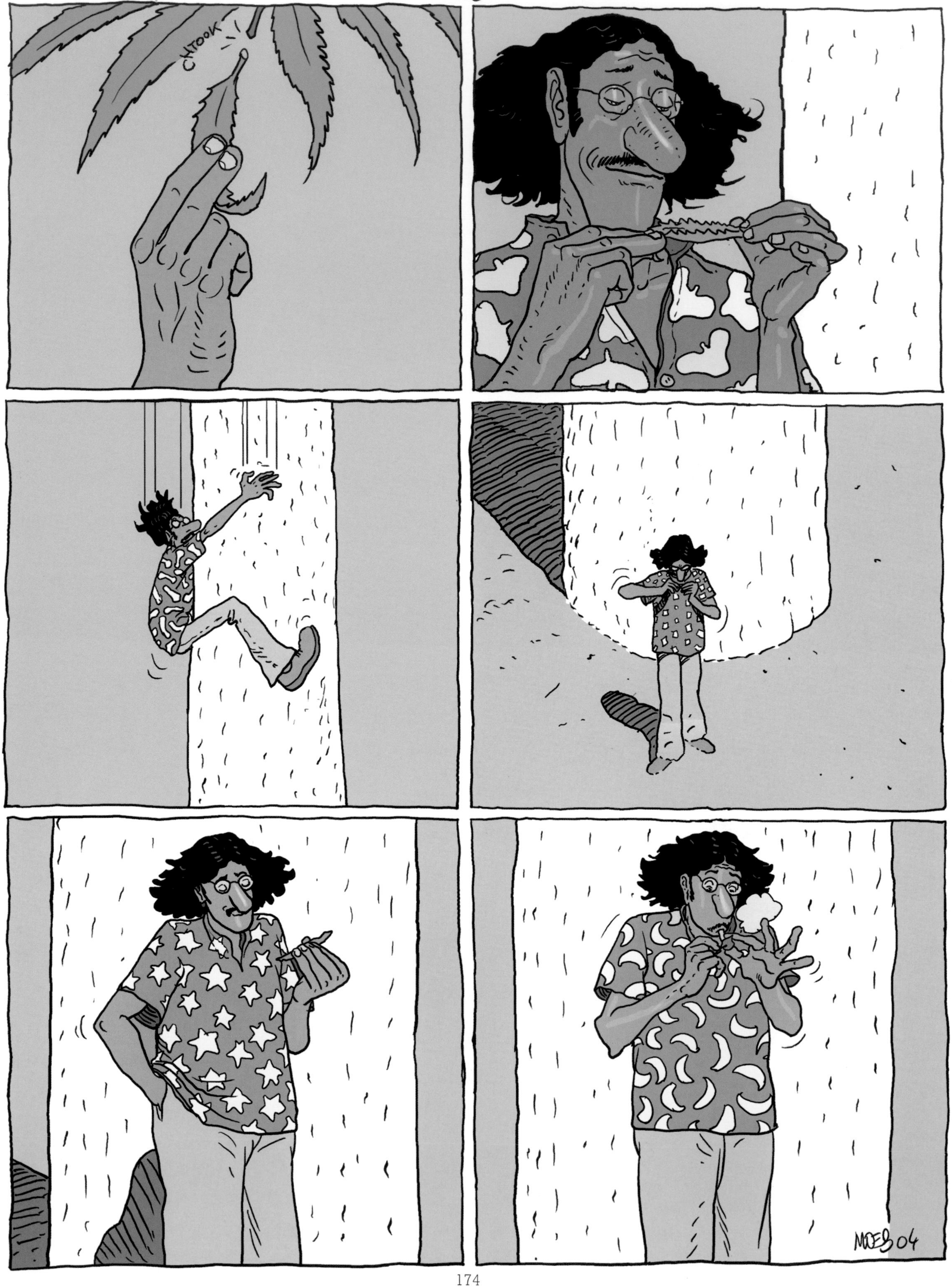
CHTOOK
MŒB 04

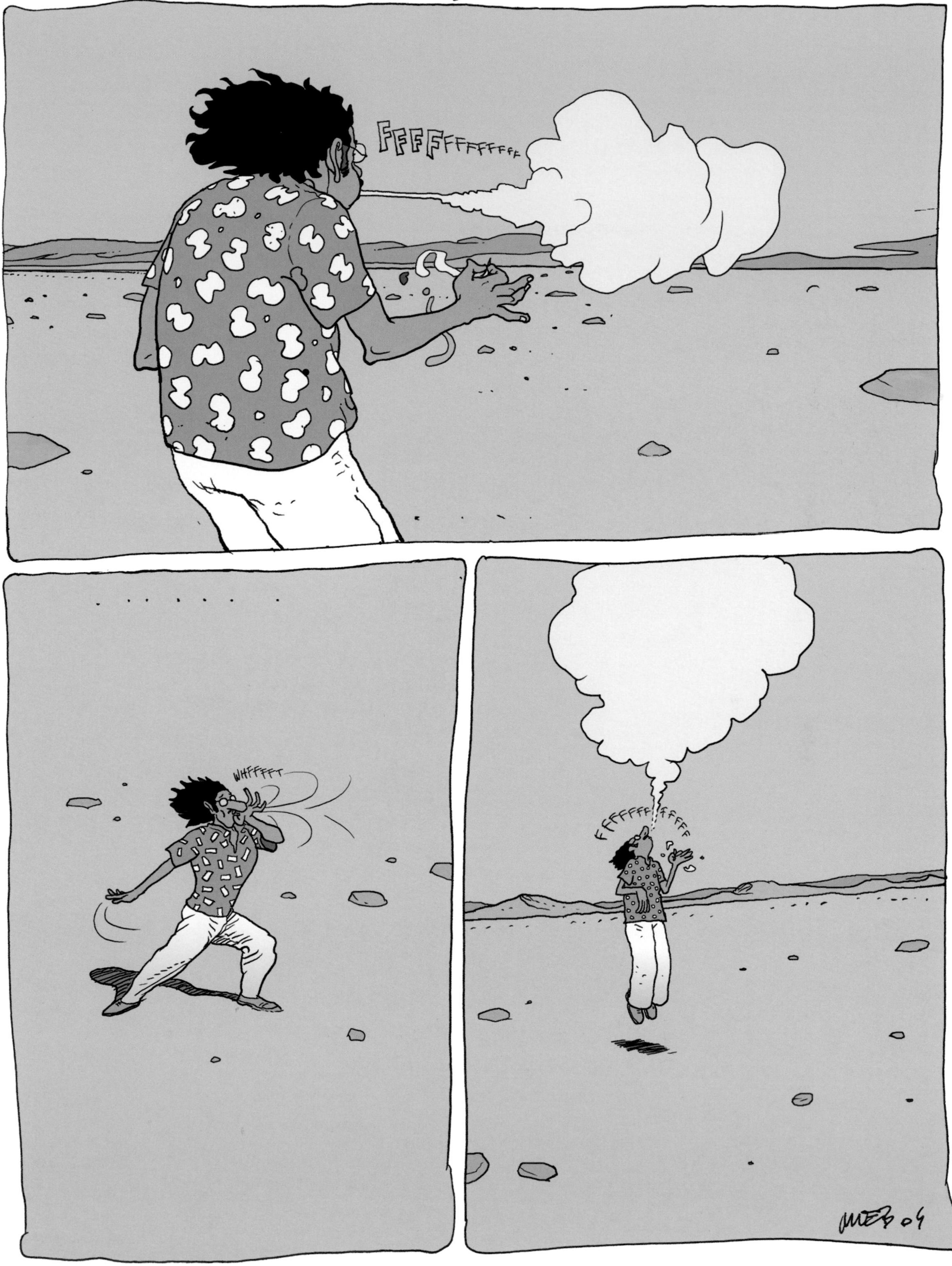
FFFFFFFFFFFF
WHFFFFT
FFFFFFFFFFFF

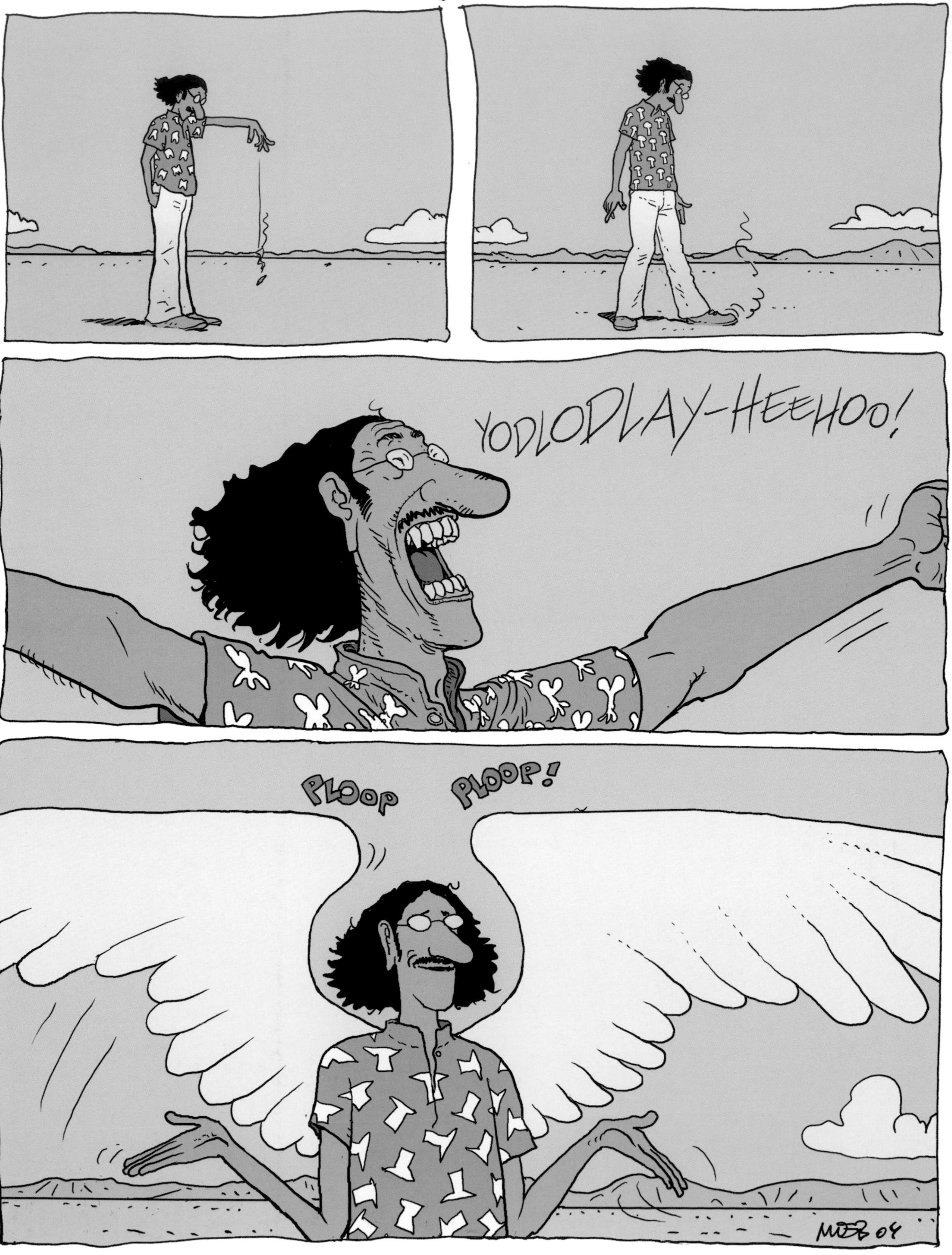
YODLODLAY-HEEHOO!
PLOOP
PLOOP!
MOEB 04

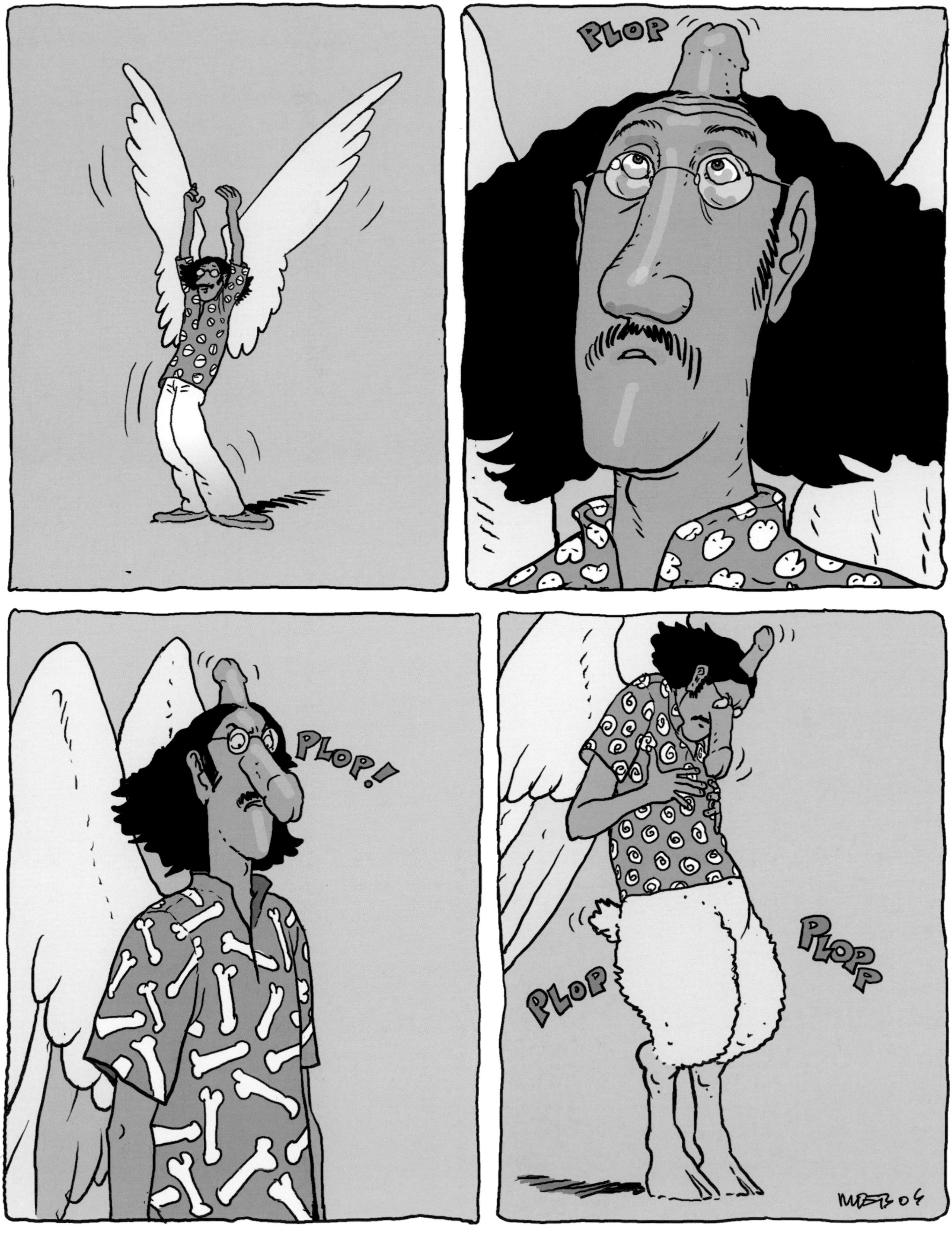
PLOP
PLOP!
PLOP
PLOPP
MB 04

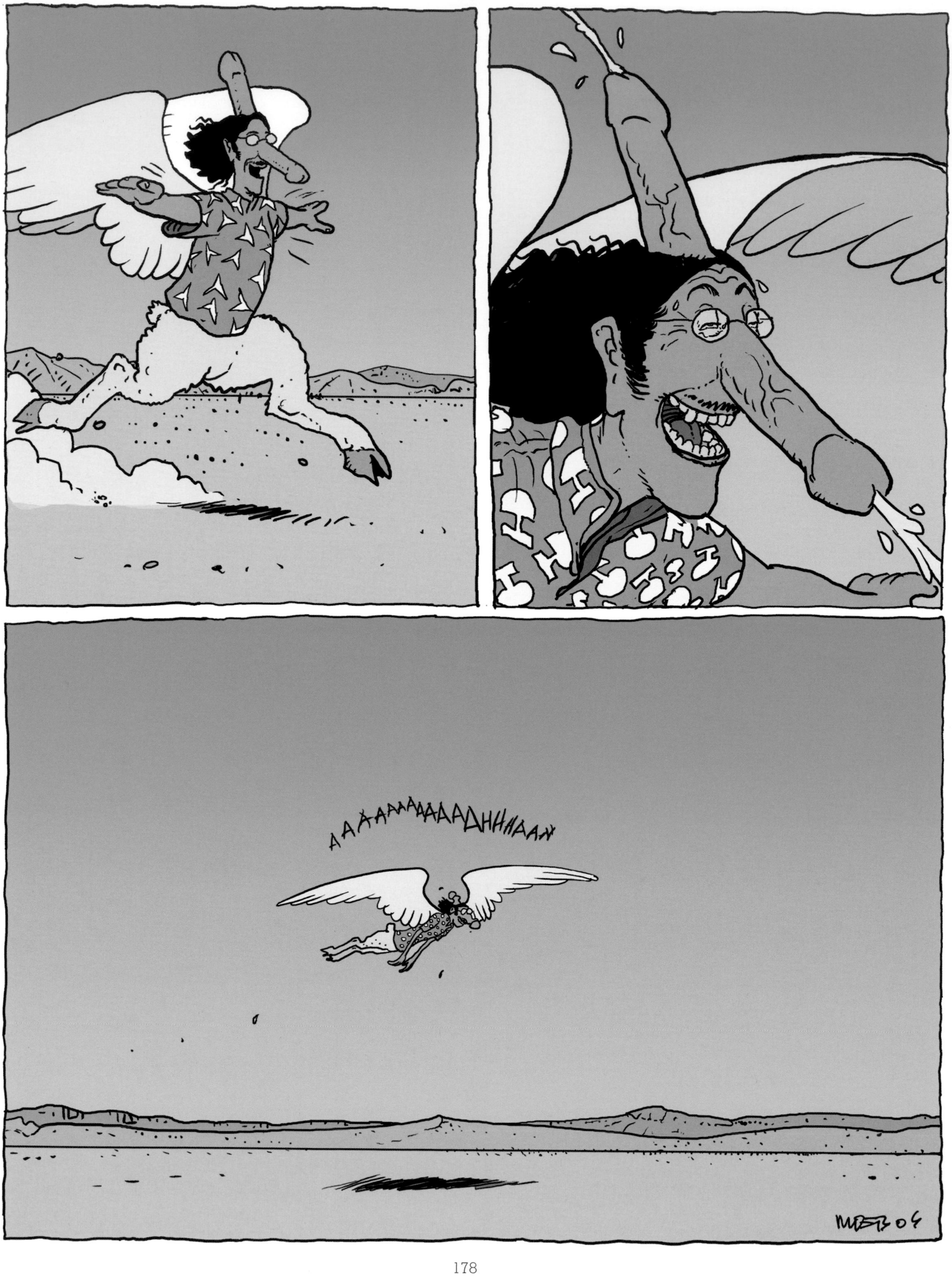
AAAAAAAAAAAAHHHAAN

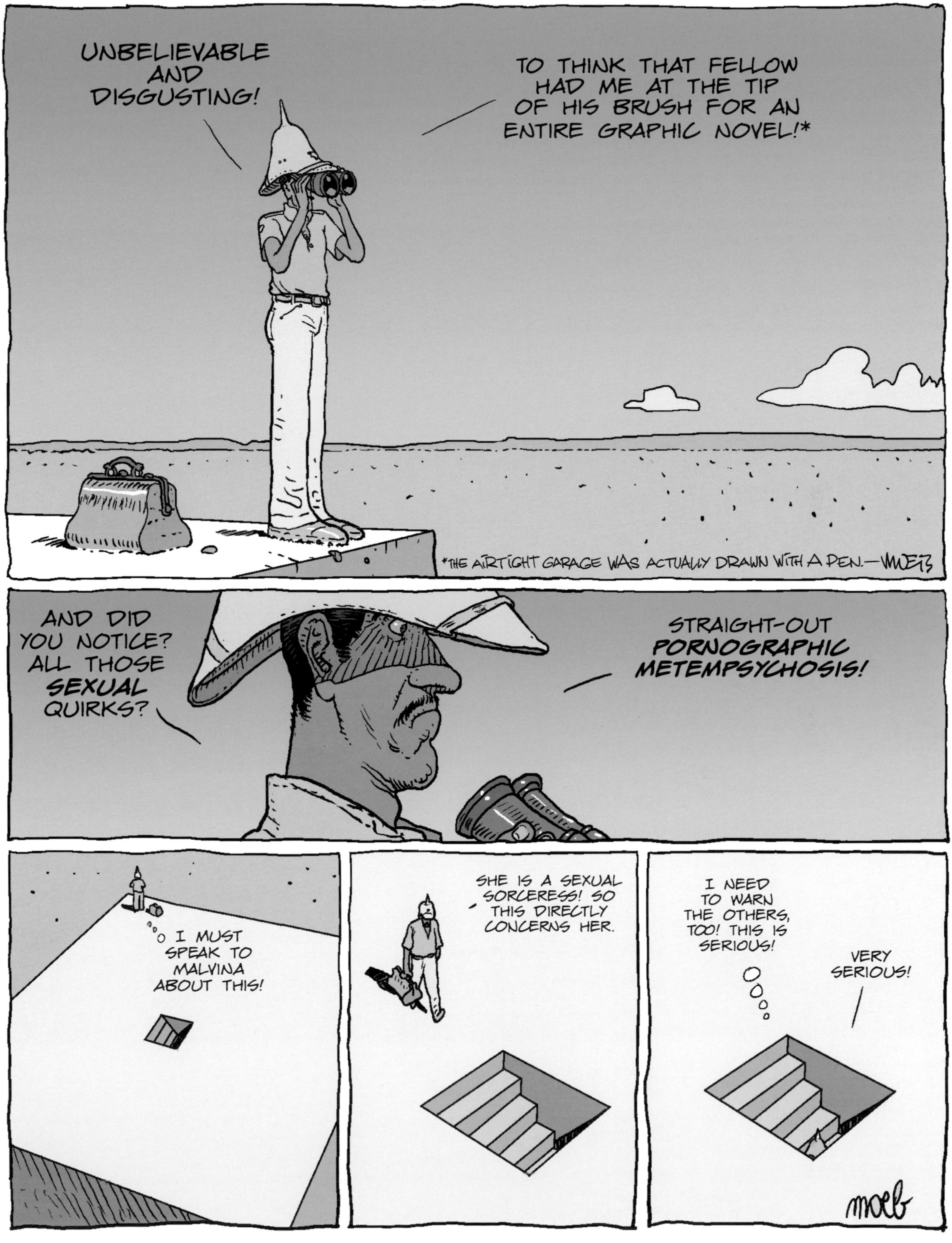
UNBELIEVABLE AND DISGUSTING!
TO THINK THAT FELLOW HAD ME AT THE TIP OF HIS BRUSH FOR AN ENTIRE GRAPHIC NOVEL!*
*THE AIRTIGHT GARAGE WAS ACTUALLY DRAWN WITH A PEN. —MOEB
AND DID YOU NOTICE? ALL THOSE SEXUAL QUIRKS?
STRAIGHT-OUT PORNOGRAPHIC METEMPSYCHOSIS!
I MUST SPEAK TO MALVINA ABOUT THIS!
SHE IS A SEXUAL SORCERESS! SO THIS DIRECTLY CONCERNS HER.
I NEED TO WARN THE OTHERS, TOO! THIS IS SERIOUS!
VERY SERIOUS!
moeb

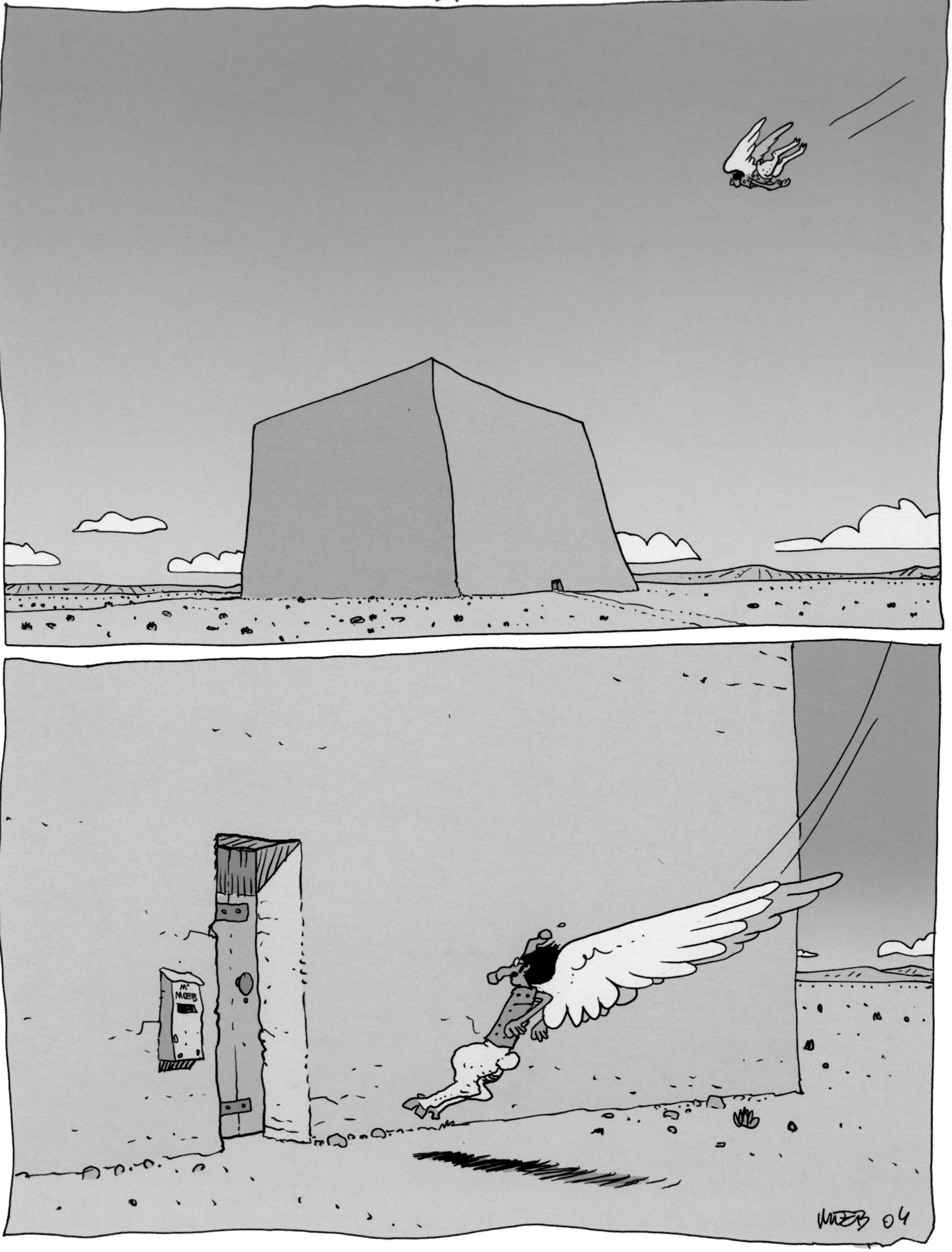
MOEB 04

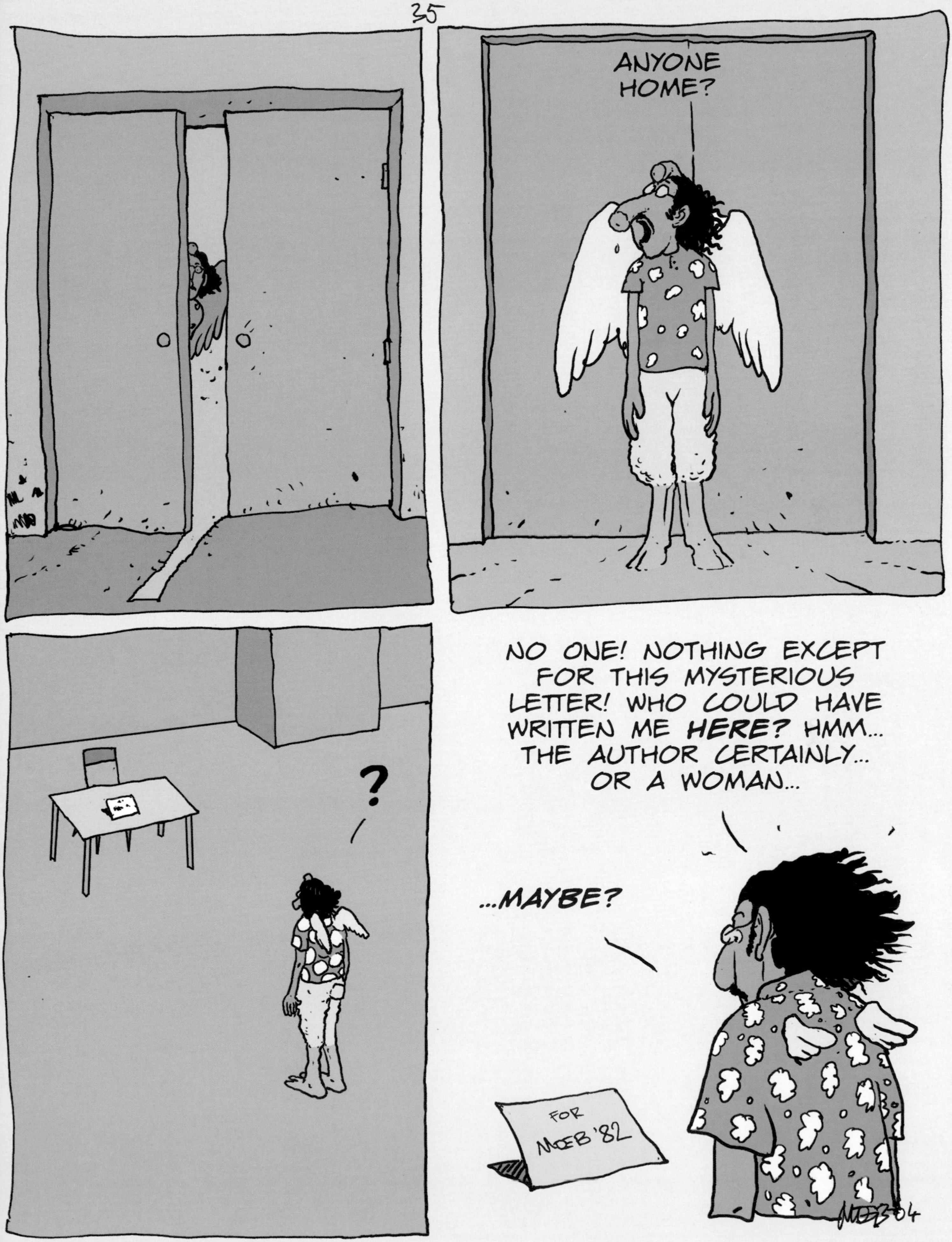
35
ANYONE HOME?
?
NO ONE! NOTHING EXCEPT FOR THIS MYSTERIOUS LETTER! WHO COULD HAVE WRITTEN ME HERE? HMM... THE AUTHOR CERTAINLY... OR A WOMAN...
...MAYBE?
FOR MOEB '82
MOEB '84

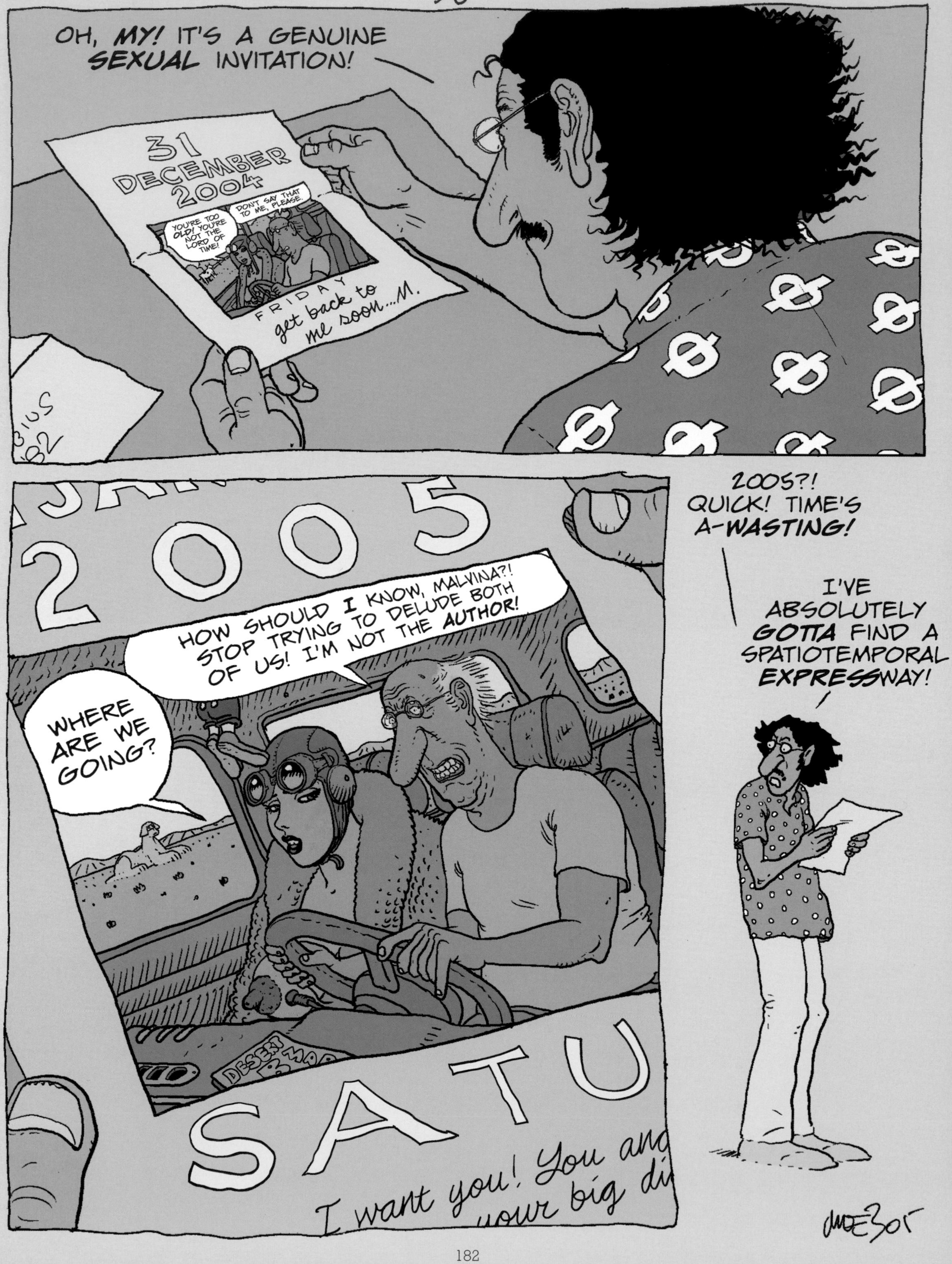
OH, MY! IT'S A GENUINE SEXUAL INVITATION!
31 DECEMBER 2004
YOU'RE TOO OLD! YOU'RE NOT THE LORD OF TIME!
DON'T SAY THAT TO ME, PLEASE.
FRIDAY
get back to me soon... M.
2005
HOW SHOULD I KNOW, MALVINA?! STOP TRYING TO DELUDE BOTH OF US! I'M NOT THE AUTHOR!
WHERE ARE WE GOING?
SATU
I want you! You and your big di
2005?! QUICK! TIME'S A-WASTING!
I'VE ABSOLUTELY GOTTA FIND A SPATIOTEMPORAL EXPRESSWAY!

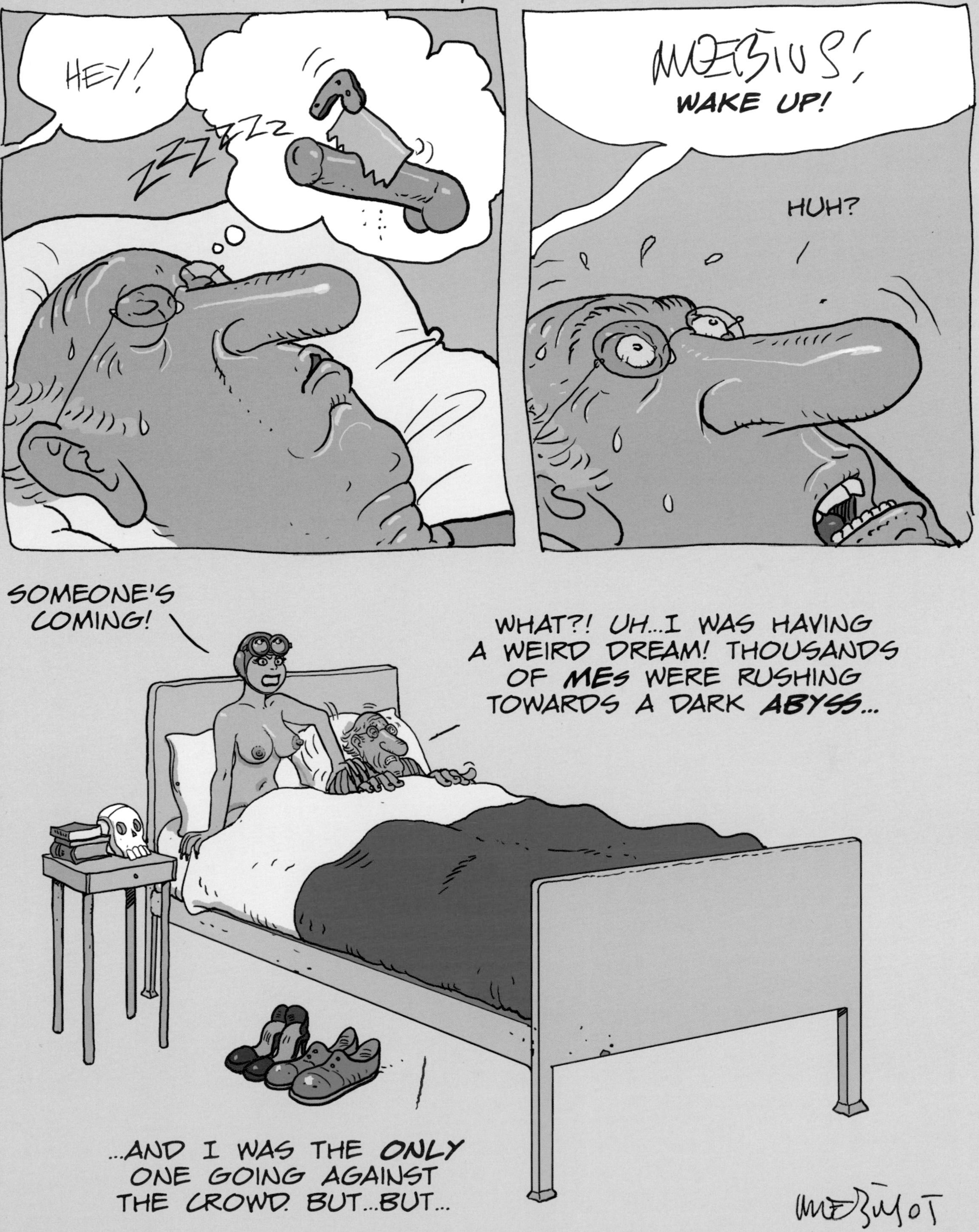
HEY!
ZZZZZZz
MOEBIUS! WAKE UP!
HUH?
SOMEONE'S COMING!
WHAT?! UH...I WAS HAVING A WEIRD DREAM! THOUSANDS OF MEs WERE RUSHING TOWARDS A DARK ABYSS...
...AND I WAS THE ONLY ONE GOING AGAINST THE CROWD. BUT...BUT...
MOEBIUS

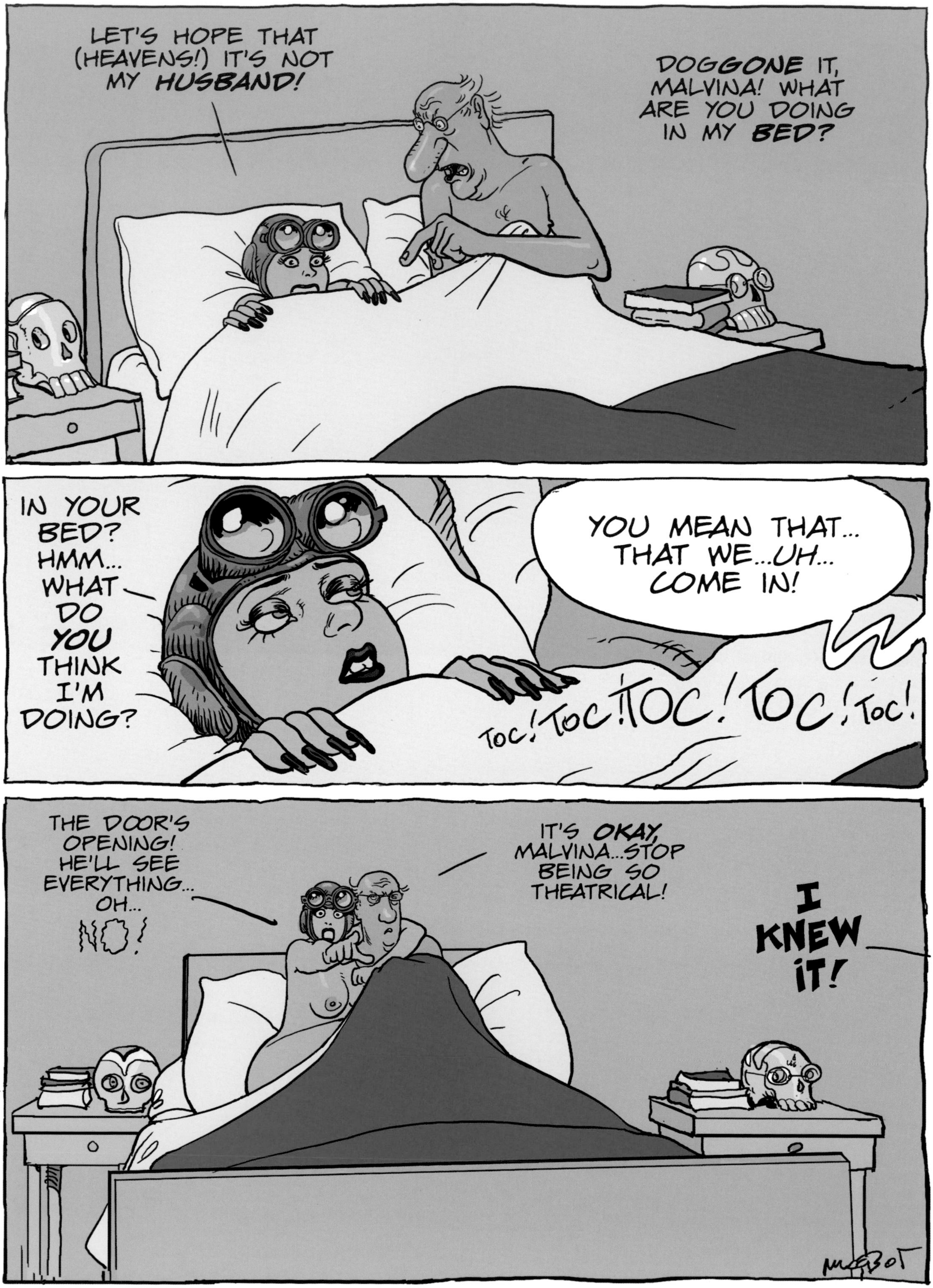
LET'S HOPE THAT (HEAVENS!) IT'S NOT MY HUSBAND!
DOGGONE IT, MALVINA! WHAT ARE YOU DOING IN MY BED?
IN YOUR BED? HMM... WHAT DO YOU THINK I'M DOING?
YOU MEAN THAT... THAT WE...UH... COME IN!
TOC! TOC! TOC! TOC! TOC!
THE DOOR'S OPENING! HE'LL SEE EVERYTHING... OH... NO!
IT'S OKAY, MALVINA...STOP BEING SO THEATRICAL!
I KNEW IT!

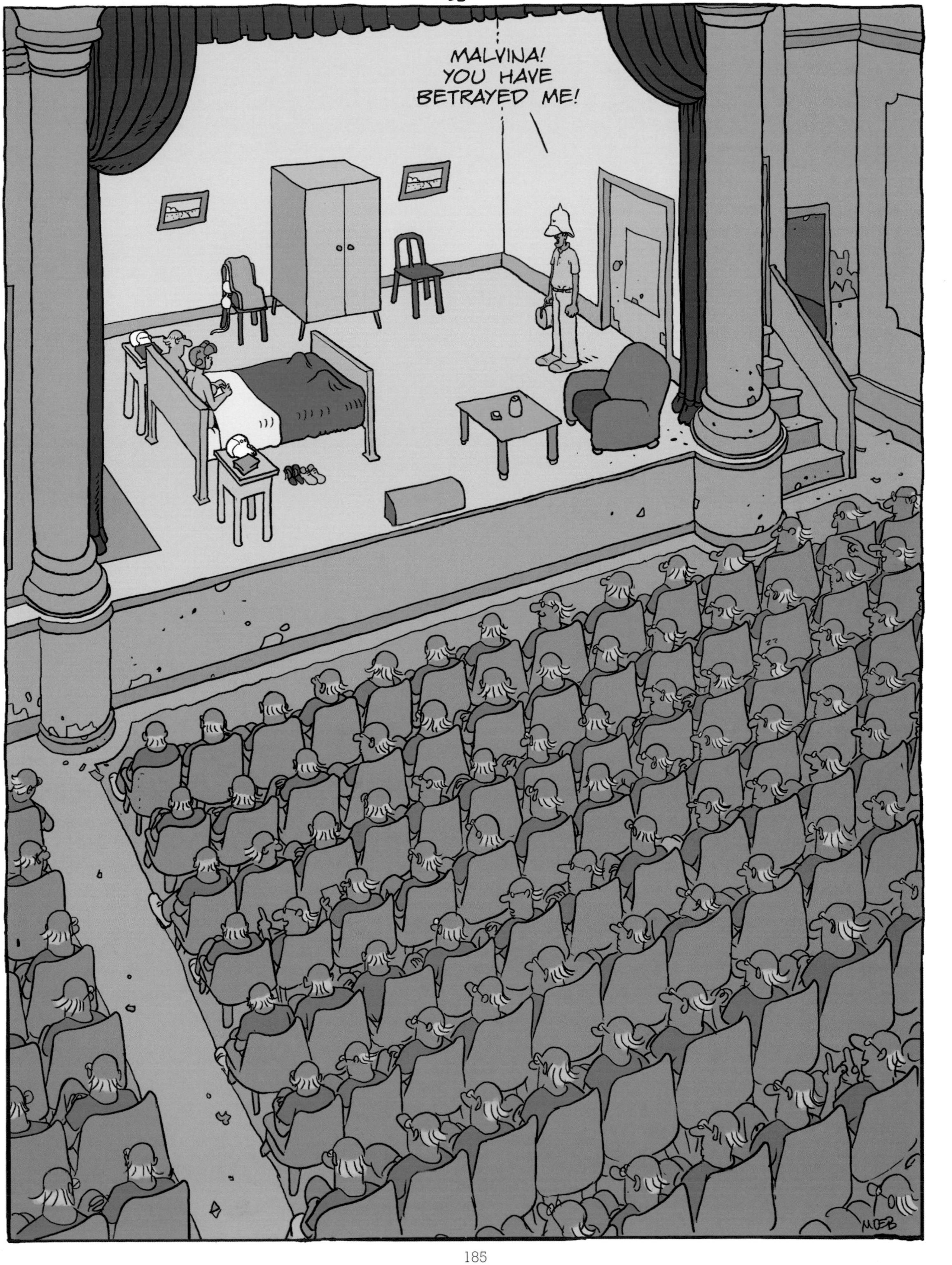
MALVINA! YOU HAVE BETRAYED ME!
MŒB

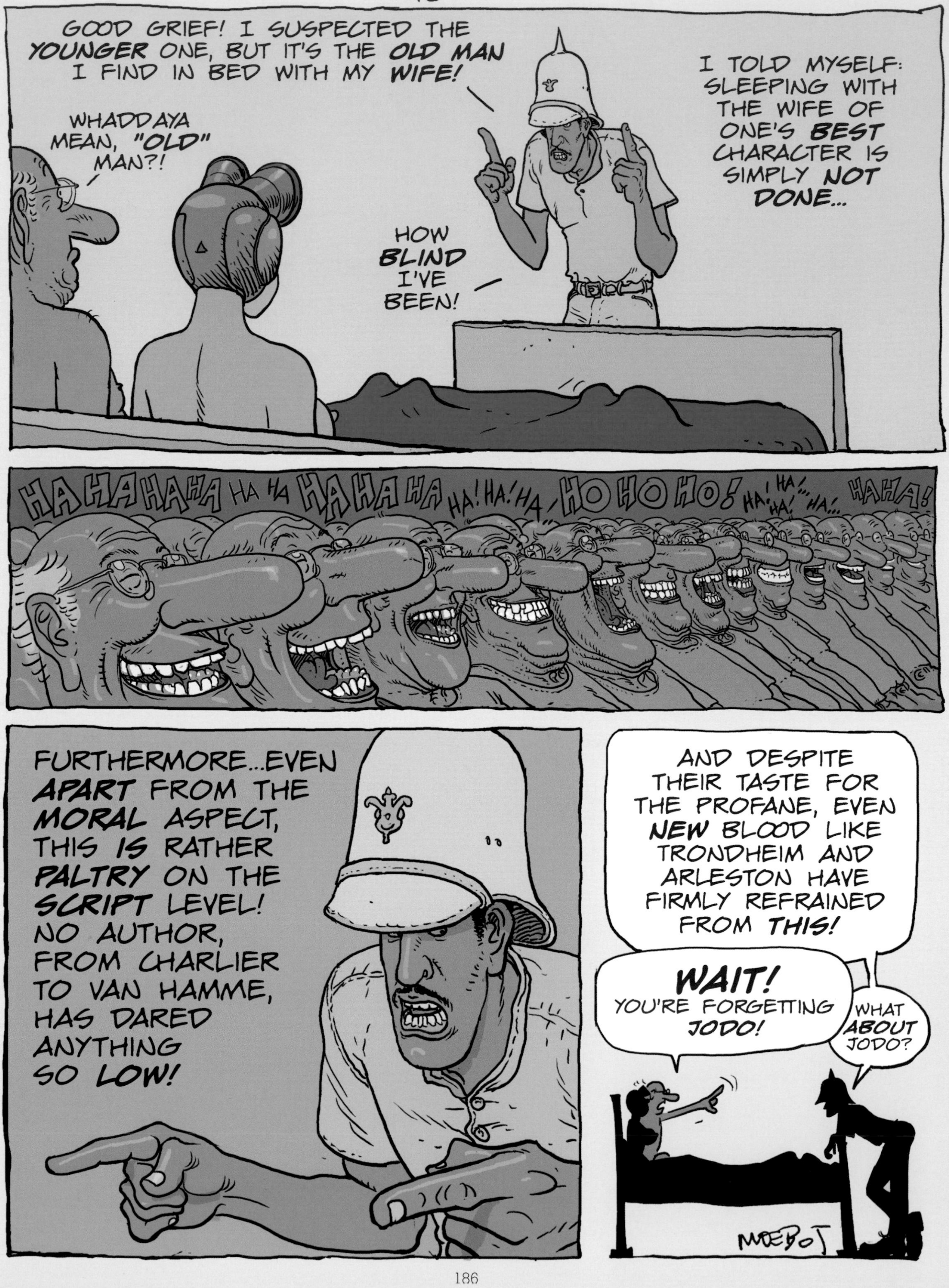
GOOD GRIEF! I SUSPECTED THE YOUNGER ONE, BUT IT'S THE OLD MAN I FIND IN BED WITH MY WIFE!
WHADDAYA MEAN, "OLD" MAN?!
I TOLD MYSELF: SLEEPING WITH THE WIFE OF ONE'S BEST CHARACTER IS SIMPLY NOT DONE...
HOW BLIND I'VE BEEN!
HAHAHAHA HA HA HAHAHA HA HA! HA! HA, HOHOHOHO! HA! HA! HA! HA! HAHA!
FURTHERMORE...EVEN APART FROM THE MORAL ASPECT, THIS IS RATHER PALTRY ON THE SCRIPT LEVEL! NO AUTHOR, FROM CHARLIER TO VAN HAMME, HAS DARED ANYTHING SO LOW!
AND DESPITE THEIR TASTE FOR THE PROFANE, EVEN NEW BLOOD LIKE TRONDHEIM AND ARLESTON HAVE FIRMLY REFRAINED FROM THIS!
WAIT! YOU'RE FORGETTING JODO!
WHAT ABOUT JODO?
MOEBIUS

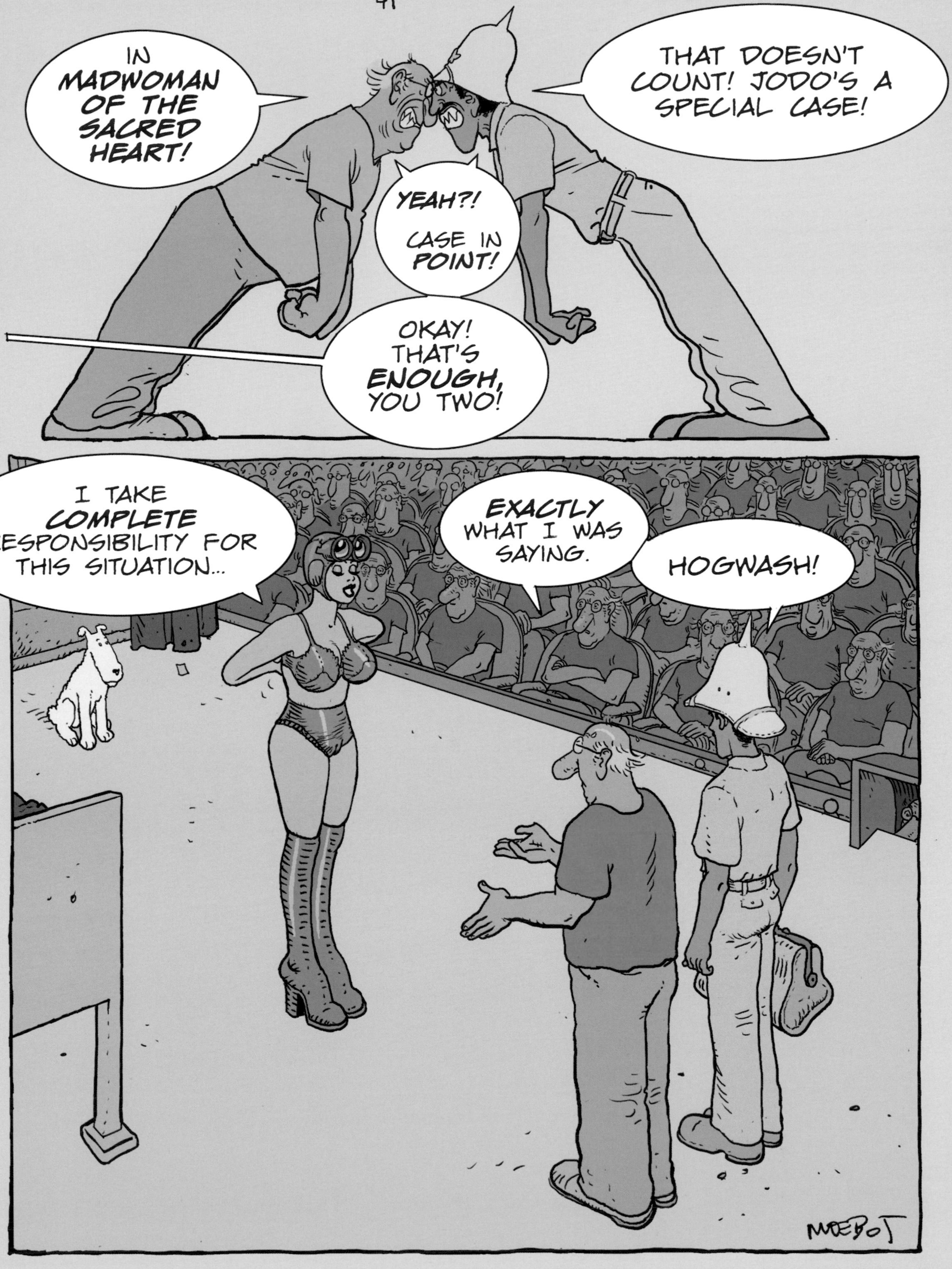
IN MADWOMAN OF THE SACRED HEART!
THAT DOESN'T COUNT! JODO'S A SPECIAL CASE!
YEAH?!
CASE IN POINT!
OKAY! THAT'S ENOUGH, YOU TWO!
I TAKE COMPLETE RESPONSIBILITY FOR THIS SITUATION...
EXACTLY WHAT I WAS SAYING.
HOGWASH!
MOEBOT

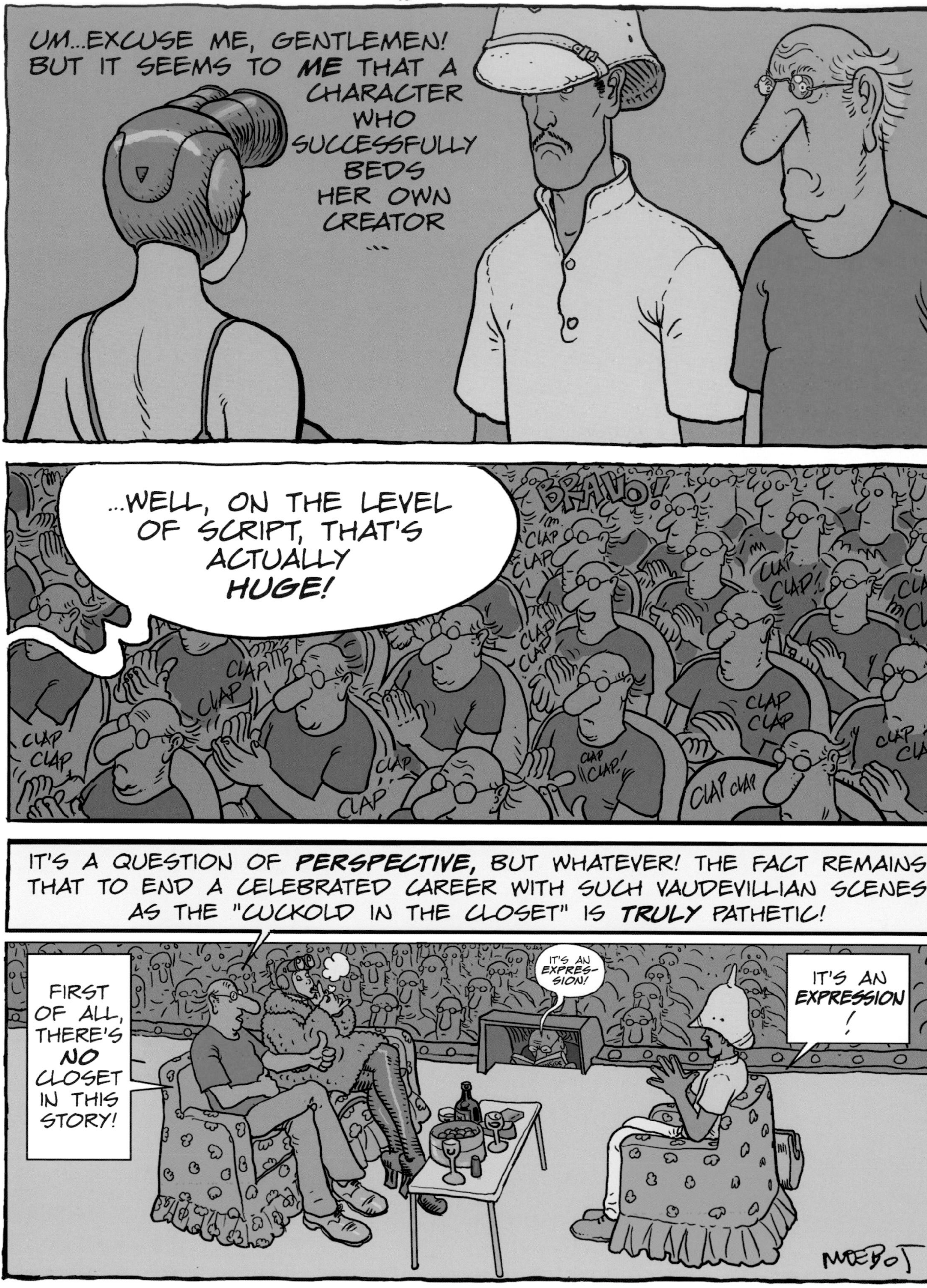
UM...EXCUSE ME, GENTLEMEN! BUT IT SEEMS TO ME THAT A CHARACTER WHO SUCCESSFULLY BEDS HER OWN CREATOR ...
...WELL, ON THE LEVEL OF SCRIPT, THAT'S ACTUALLY HUGE!
BRAVO!
CLAP CLAP
IT'S A QUESTION OF PERSPECTIVE, BUT WHATEVER! THE FACT REMAINS THAT TO END A CELEBRATED CAREER WITH SUCH VAUDEVILLIAN SCENES AS THE "CUCKOLD IN THE CLOSET" IS TRULY PATHETIC!
FIRST OF ALL, THERE'S NO CLOSET IN THIS STORY!
IT'S AN EXPRES-SION!
IT'S AN EXPRESSION !
MOEBIUS

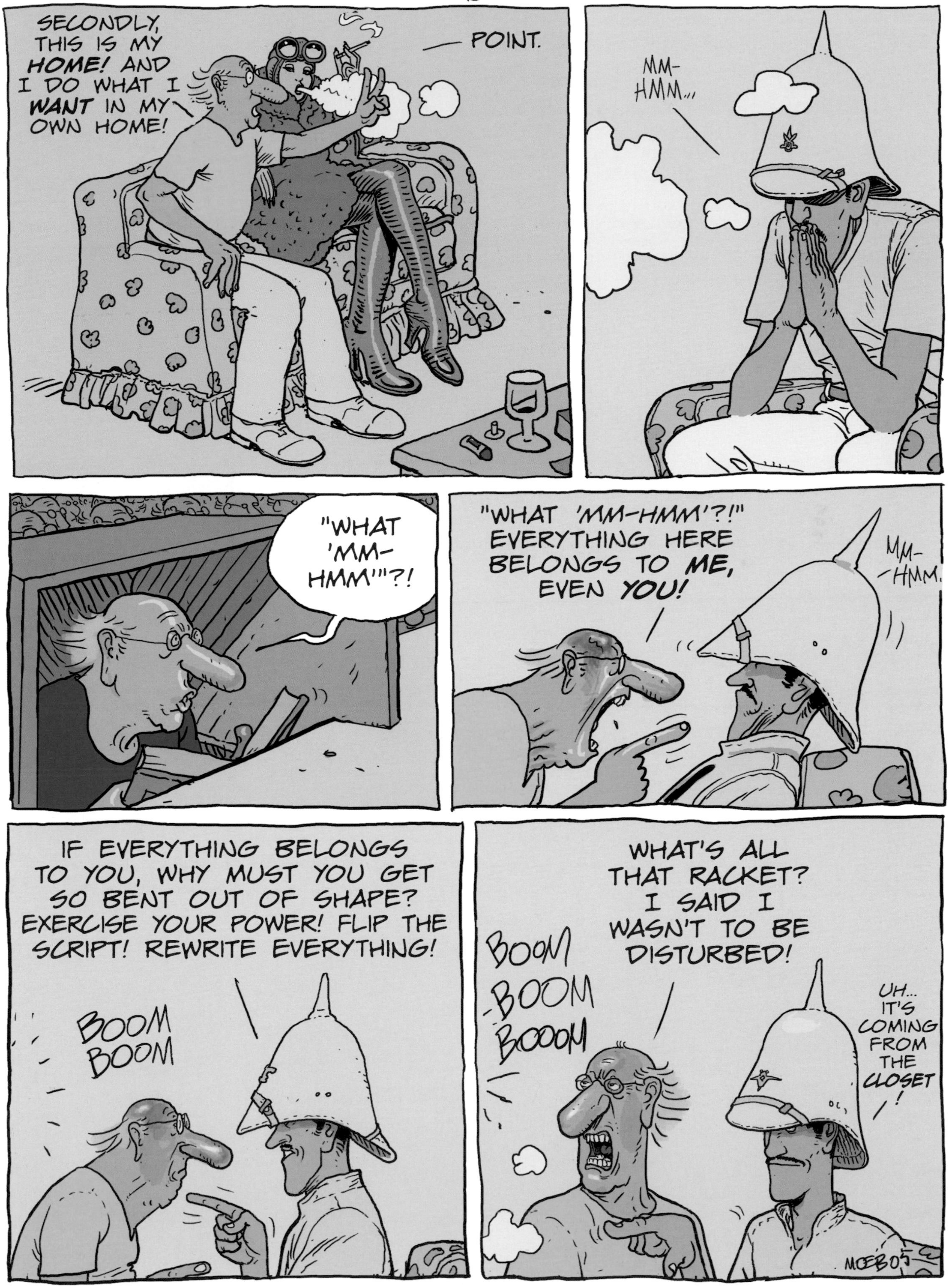
SECONDLY, THIS IS MY HOME! AND I DO WHAT I WANT IN MY OWN HOME!
— POINT.
MM-HMM...
"WHAT 'MM-HMM'"?!
"WHAT 'MM-HMM'?!" EVERYTHING HERE BELONGS TO ME, EVEN YOU!
MM--HMM.
IF EVERYTHING BELONGS TO YOU, WHY MUST YOU GET SO BENT OUT OF SHAPE? EXERCISE YOUR POWER! FLIP THE SCRIPT! REWRITE EVERYTHING!
BOOM BOOM
WHAT'S ALL THAT RACKET? I SAID I WASN'T TO BE DISTURBED!
BOOM BOOM BOOOM
UH... IT'S COMING FROM THE CLOSET!
MOEB05

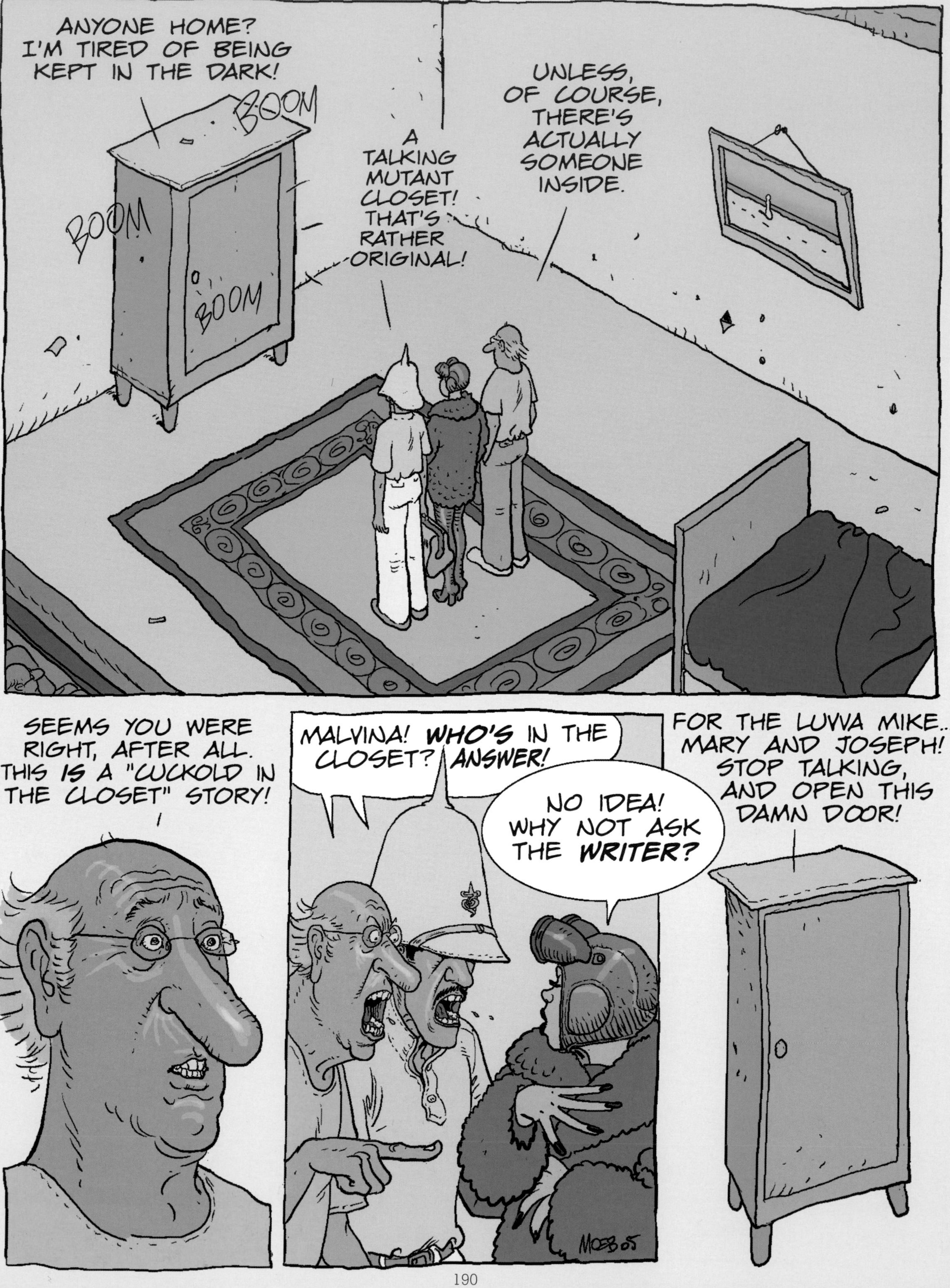
ANYONE HOME? I'M TIRED OF BEING KEPT IN THE DARK!
BOOM
BOOM
BOOM
A TALKING MUTANT CLOSET! THAT'S RATHER ORIGINAL!
UNLESS, OF COURSE, THERE'S ACTUALLY SOMEONE INSIDE.
SEEMS YOU WERE RIGHT, AFTER ALL. THIS **IS** A "CUCKOLD IN THE CLOSET" STORY!
MALVINA! **WHO'S** IN THE CLOSET? **ANSWER!**
NO IDEA! WHY NOT ASK THE **WRITER?**
FOR THE LUVVA MIKE... MARY AND JOSEPH! STOP TALKING, AND OPEN THIS DAMN DOOR!
MOEB 05

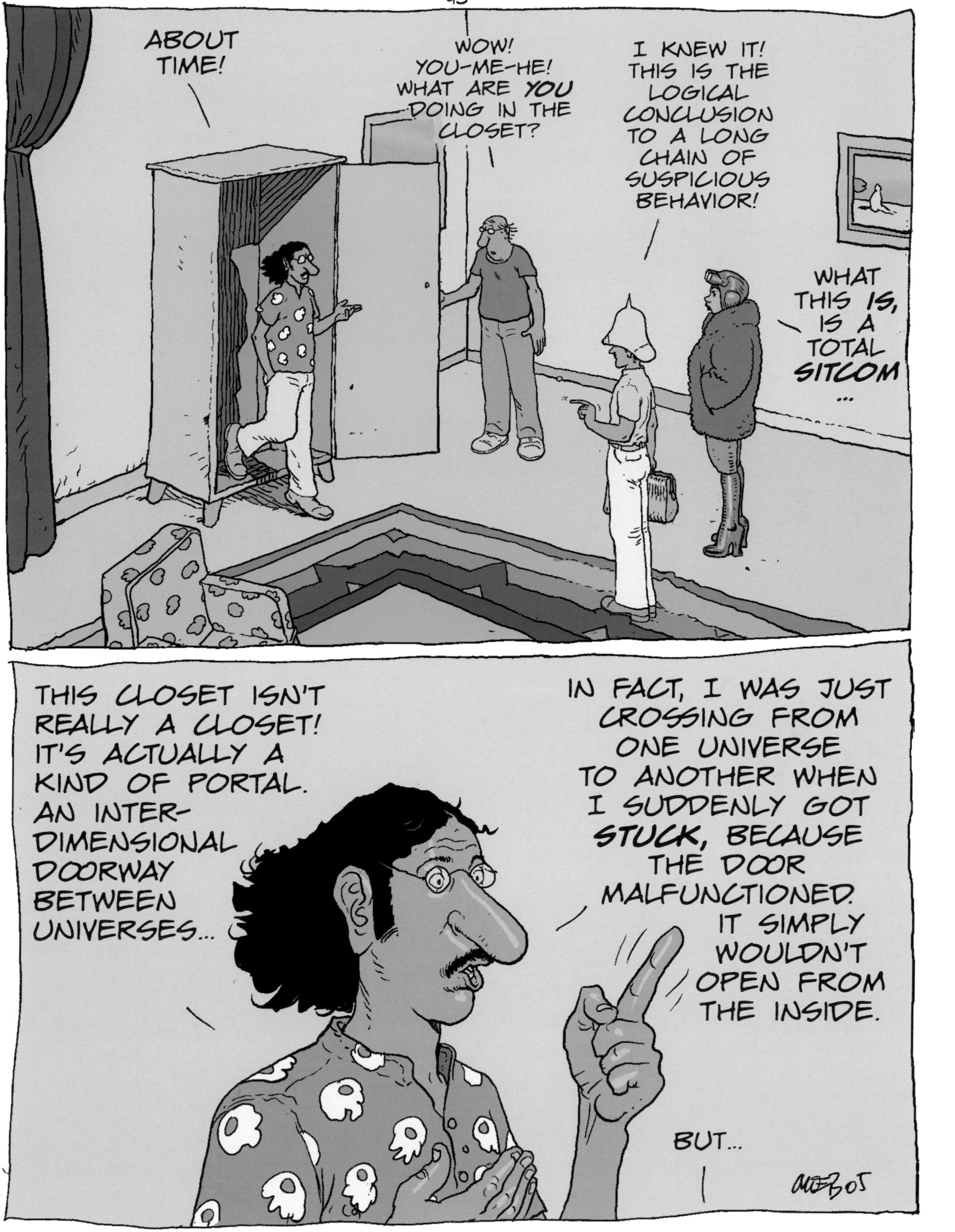
ABOUT TIME!
WOW! YOU-ME-HE! WHAT ARE YOU DOING IN THE CLOSET?
I KNEW IT! THIS IS THE LOGICAL CONCLUSION TO A LONG CHAIN OF SUSPICIOUS BEHAVIOR!
WHAT THIS IS, IS A TOTAL SITCOM ...
THIS CLOSET ISN'T REALLY A CLOSET! IT'S ACTUALLY A KIND OF PORTAL. AN INTER-DIMENSIONAL DOORWAY BETWEEN UNIVERSES...
IN FACT, I WAS JUST CROSSING FROM ONE UNIVERSE TO ANOTHER WHEN I SUDDENLY GOT STUCK, BECAUSE THE DOOR MALFUNCTIONED.
IT SIMPLY WOULDN'T OPEN FROM THE INSIDE.
BUT...

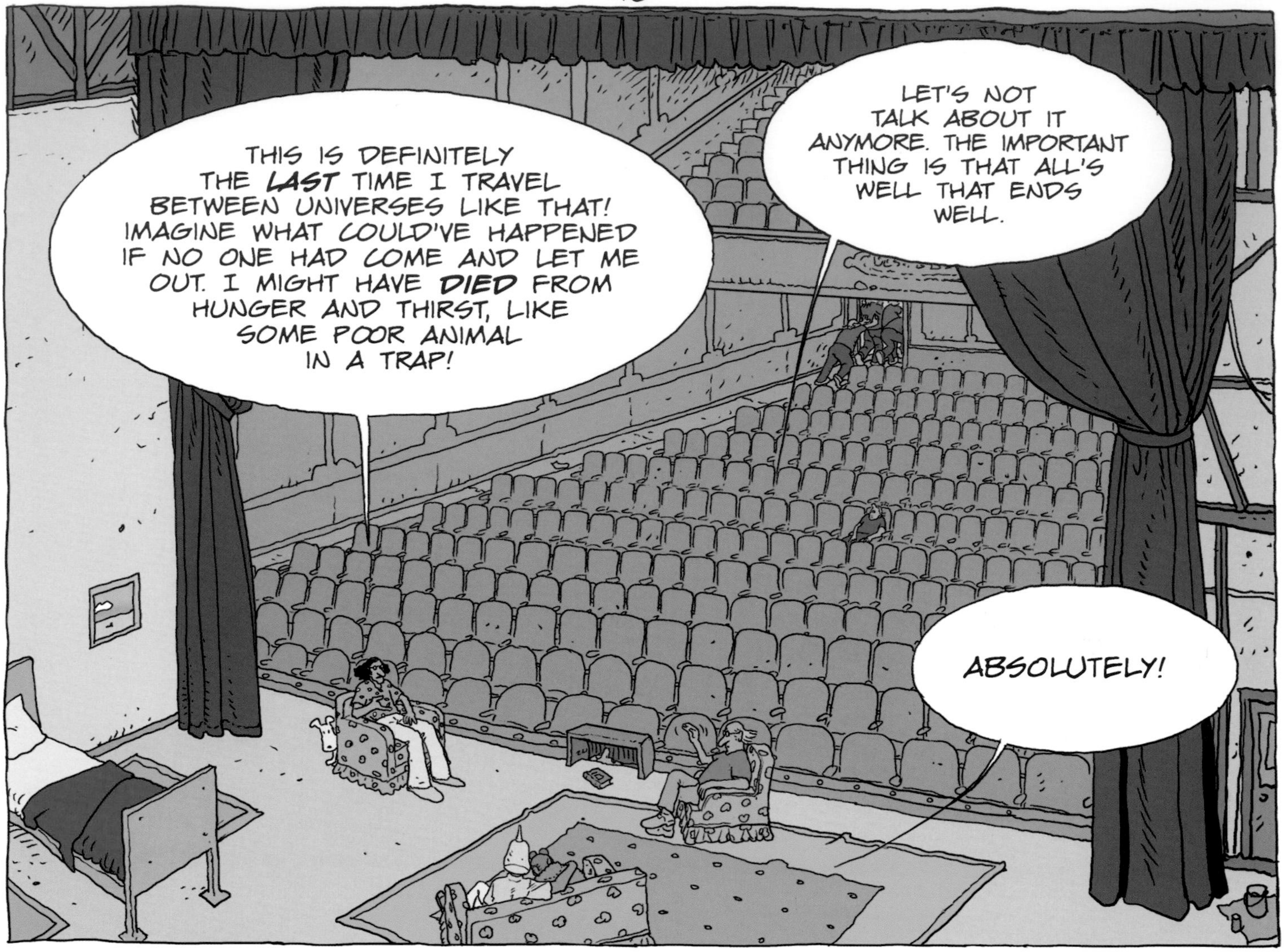
THIS IS DEFINITELY THE LAST TIME I TRAVEL BETWEEN UNIVERSES LIKE THAT! IMAGINE WHAT COULD'VE HAPPENED IF NO ONE HAD COME AND LET ME OUT. I MIGHT HAVE DIED FROM HUNGER AND THIRST, LIKE SOME POOR ANIMAL IN A TRAP!
LET'S NOT TALK ABOUT IT ANYMORE. THE IMPORTANT THING IS THAT ALL'S WELL THAT ENDS WELL.
ABSOLUTELY!

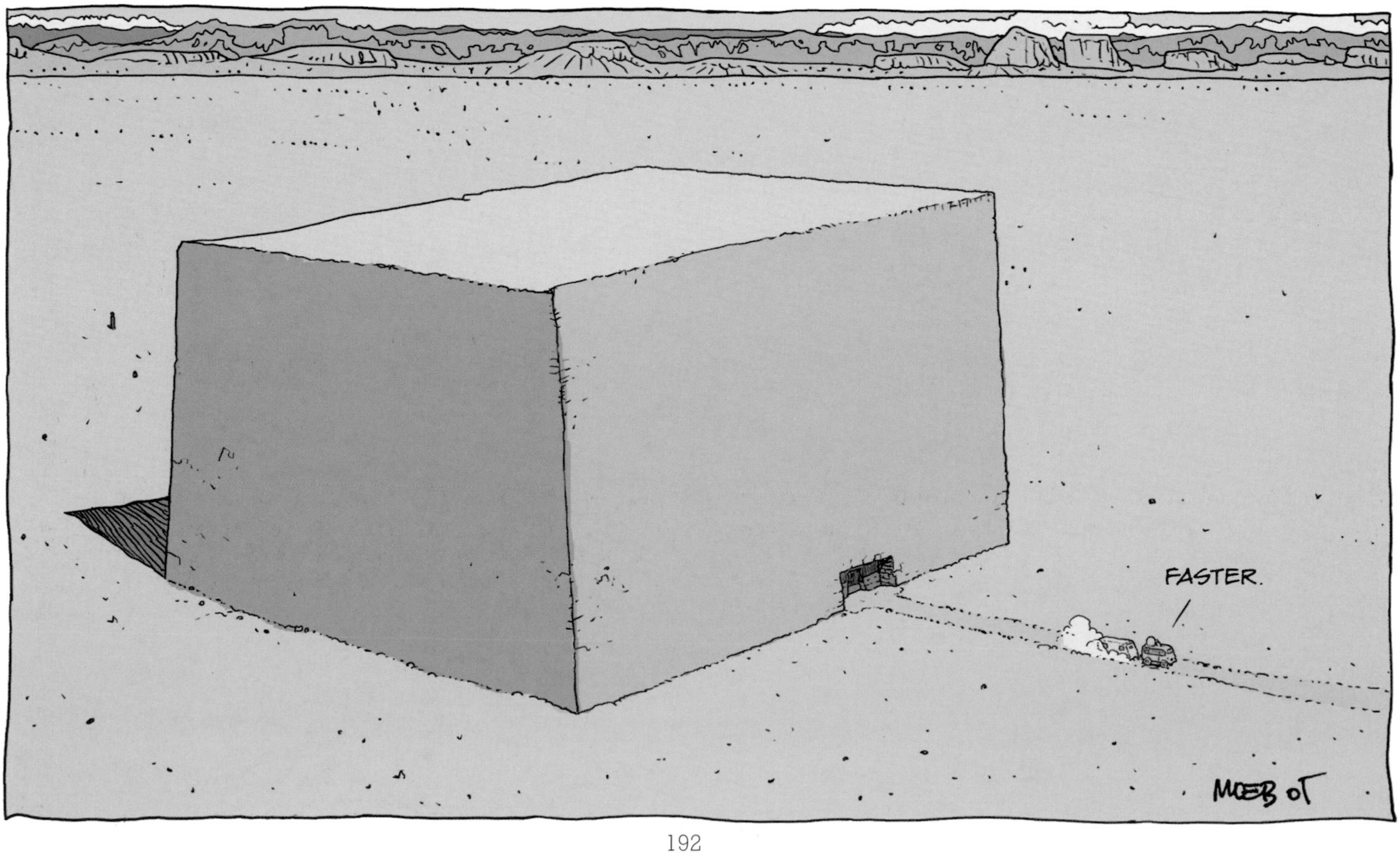
FASTER.
MOEBIUS

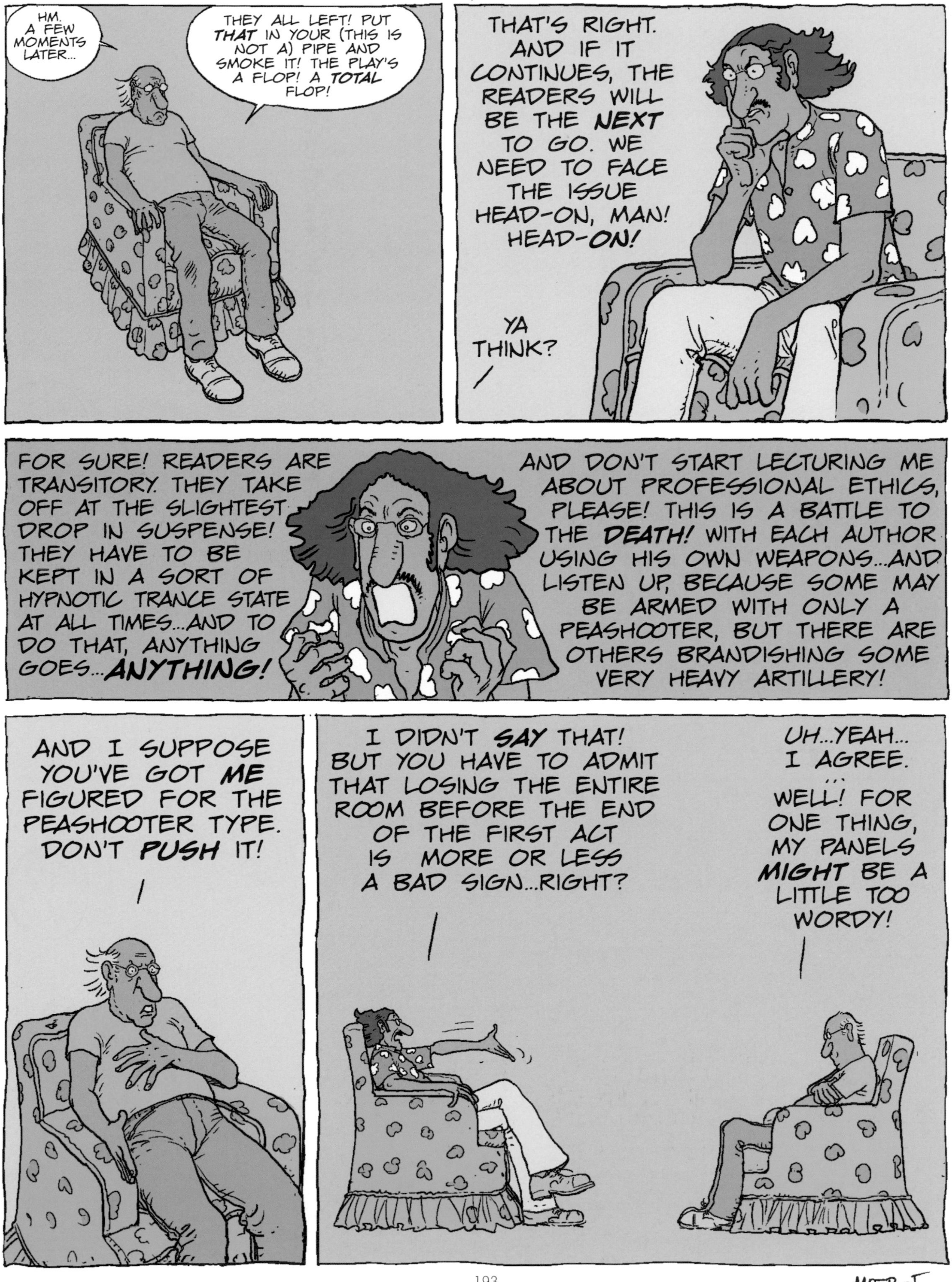
HM. A FEW MOMENTS LATER...
THEY ALL LEFT! PUT THAT IN YOUR (THIS IS NOT A) PIPE AND SMOKE IT! THE PLAY'S A FLOP! A TOTAL FLOP!
THAT'S RIGHT. AND IF IT CONTINUES, THE READERS WILL BE THE NEXT TO GO. WE NEED TO FACE THE ISSUE HEAD-ON, MAN! HEAD-ON!
YA THINK?
FOR SURE! READERS ARE TRANSITORY. THEY TAKE OFF AT THE SLIGHTEST DROP IN SUSPENSE! THEY HAVE TO BE KEPT IN A SORT OF HYPNOTIC TRANCE STATE AT ALL TIMES...AND TO DO THAT, ANYTHING GOES...ANYTHING!
AND DON'T START LECTURING ME ABOUT PROFESSIONAL ETHICS, PLEASE! THIS IS A BATTLE TO THE DEATH! WITH EACH AUTHOR USING HIS OWN WEAPONS...AND LISTEN UP, BECAUSE SOME MAY BE ARMED WITH ONLY A PEASHOOTER, BUT THERE ARE OTHERS BRANDISHING SOME VERY HEAVY ARTILLERY!
AND I SUPPOSE YOU'VE GOT ME FIGURED FOR THE PEASHOOTER TYPE. DON'T PUSH IT!
I DIDN'T SAY THAT! BUT YOU HAVE TO ADMIT THAT LOSING THE ENTIRE ROOM BEFORE THE END OF THE FIRST ACT IS MORE OR LESS A BAD SIGN...RIGHT?
UH...YEAH... I AGREE.
...
WELL! FOR ONE THING, MY PANELS MIGHT BE A LITTLE TOO WORDY!
MŒBIUS

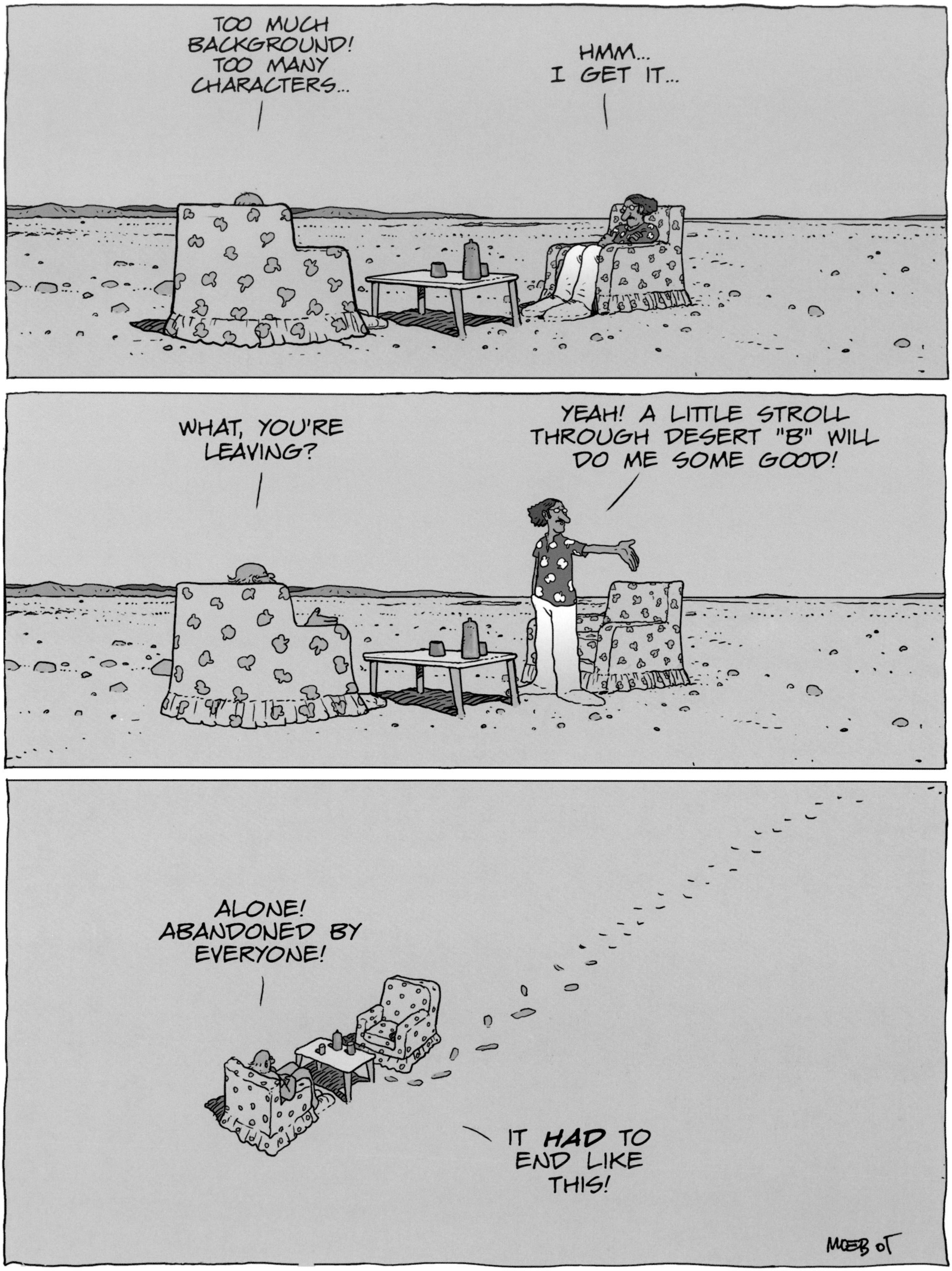
TOO MUCH BACKGROUND! TOO MANY CHARACTERS...
HMM... I GET IT...
WHAT, YOU'RE LEAVING?
YEAH! A LITTLE STROLL THROUGH DESERT "B" WILL DO ME SOME GOOD!
ALONE! ABANDONED BY EVERYONE!
IT **HAD** TO END LIKE THIS!
MOEB 07

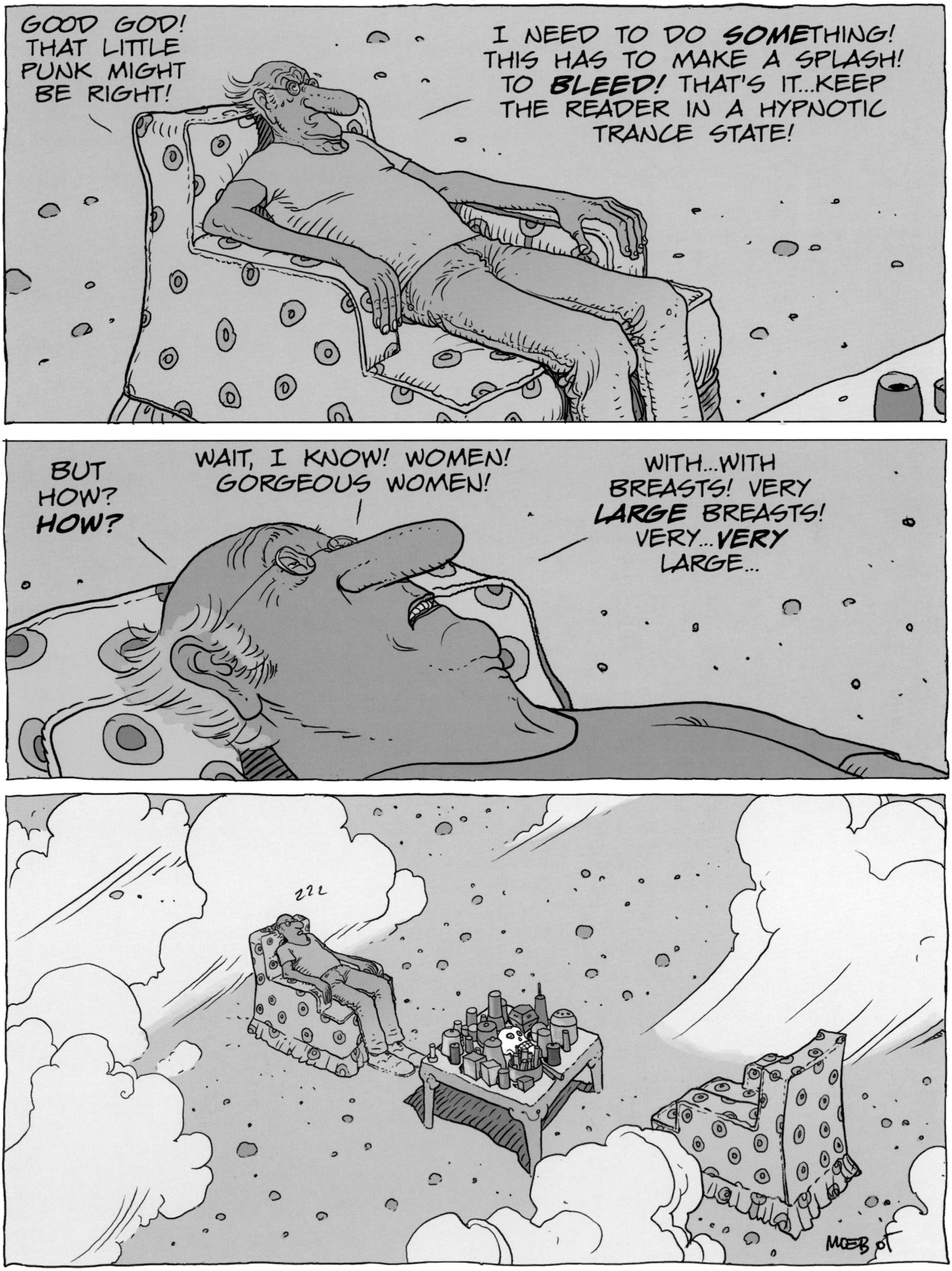
GOOD GOD! THAT LITTLE PUNK MIGHT BE RIGHT!
I NEED TO DO SOMETHING! THIS HAS TO MAKE A SPLASH! TO BLEED! THAT'S IT...KEEP THE READER IN A HYPNOTIC TRANCE STATE!
BUT HOW? HOW?
WAIT, I KNOW! WOMEN! GORGEOUS WOMEN!
WITH...WITH BREASTS! VERY LARGE BREASTS! VERY...VERY LARGE...
ZZZ
MOEB 07

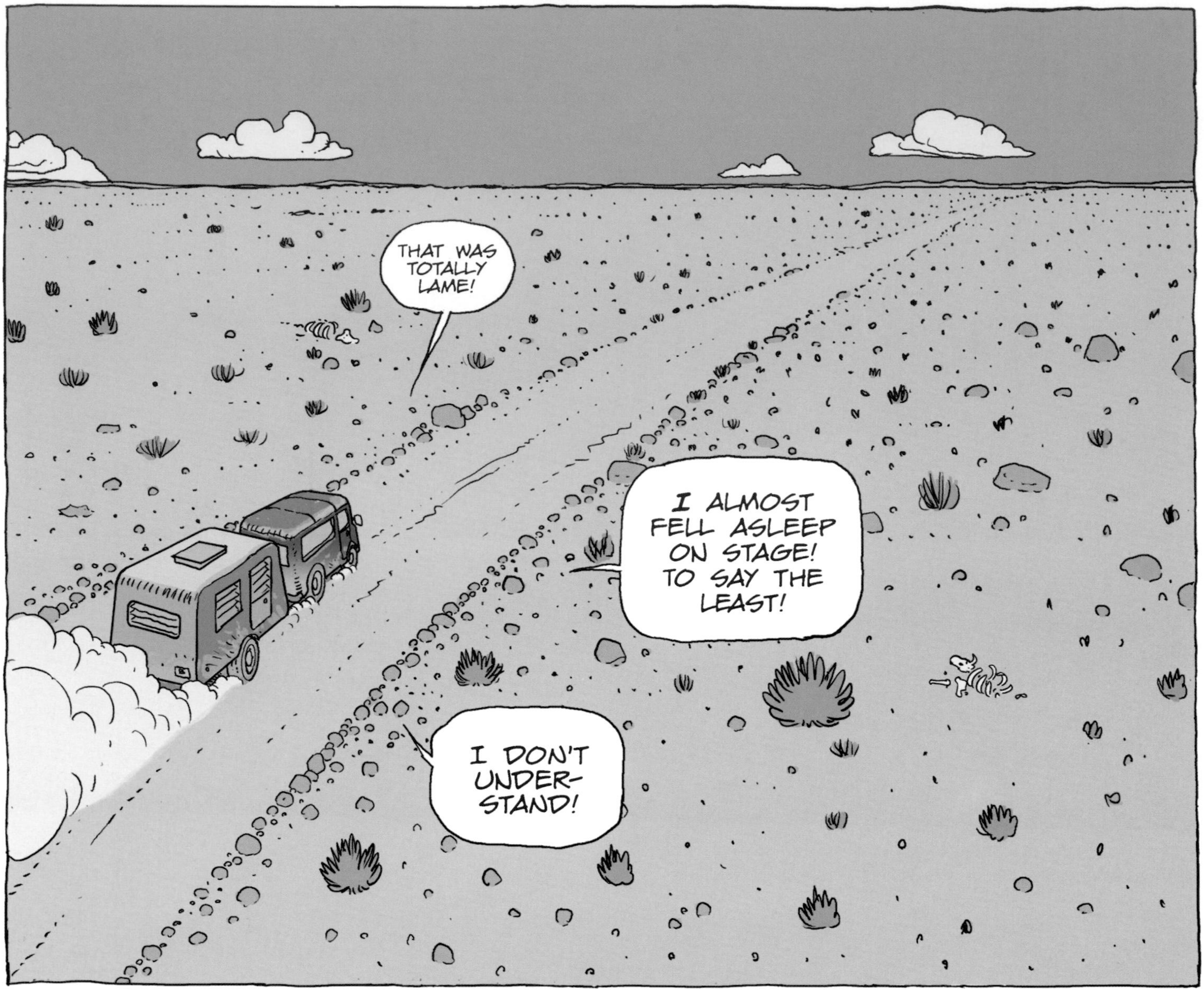
THAT WAS TOTALLY LAME!
I ALMOST FELL ASLEEP ON STAGE! TO SAY THE LEAST!
I DON'T UNDER- STAND!

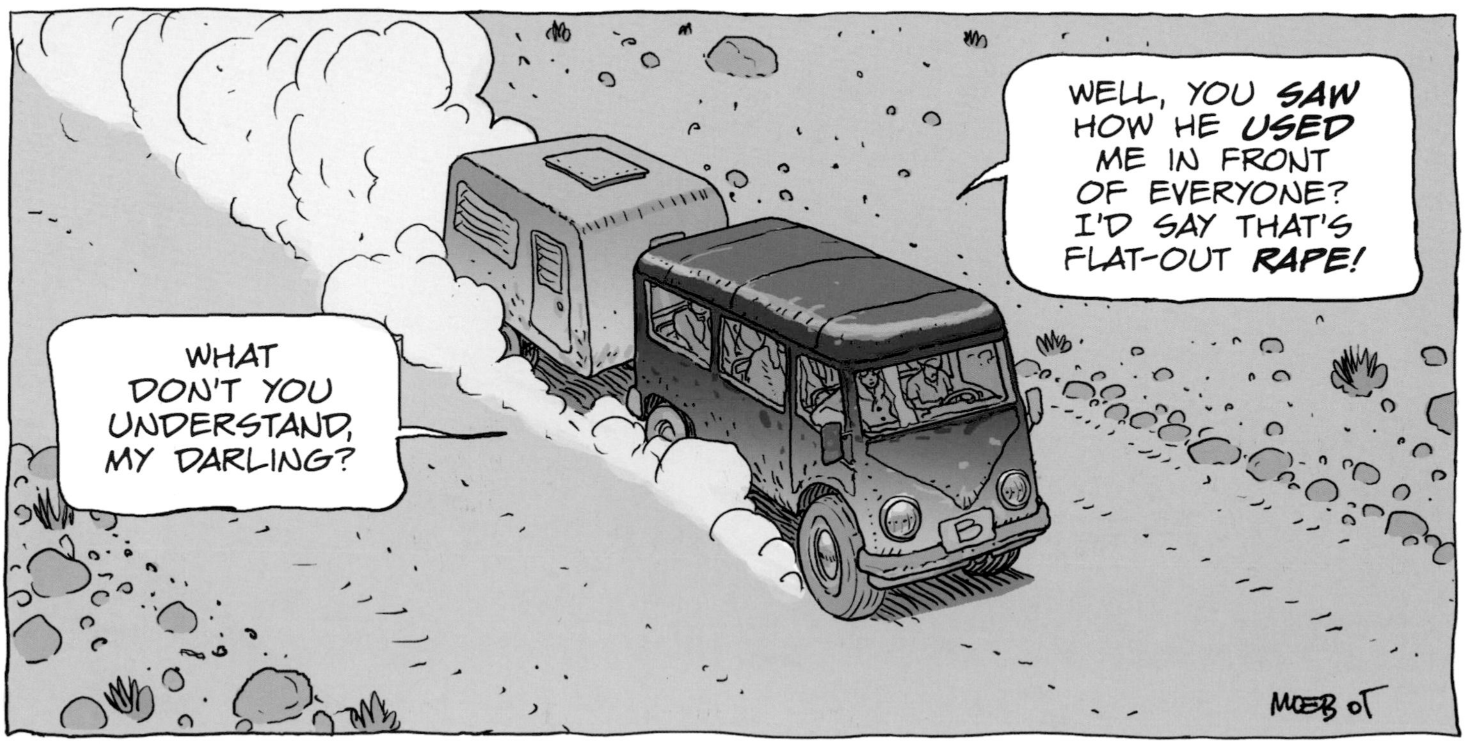
WELL, YOU SAW HOW HE USED ME IN FRONT OF EVERYONE? I'D SAY THAT'S FLAT-OUT RAPE!
WHAT DON'T YOU UNDERSTAND, MY DARLING?
MOEB 07

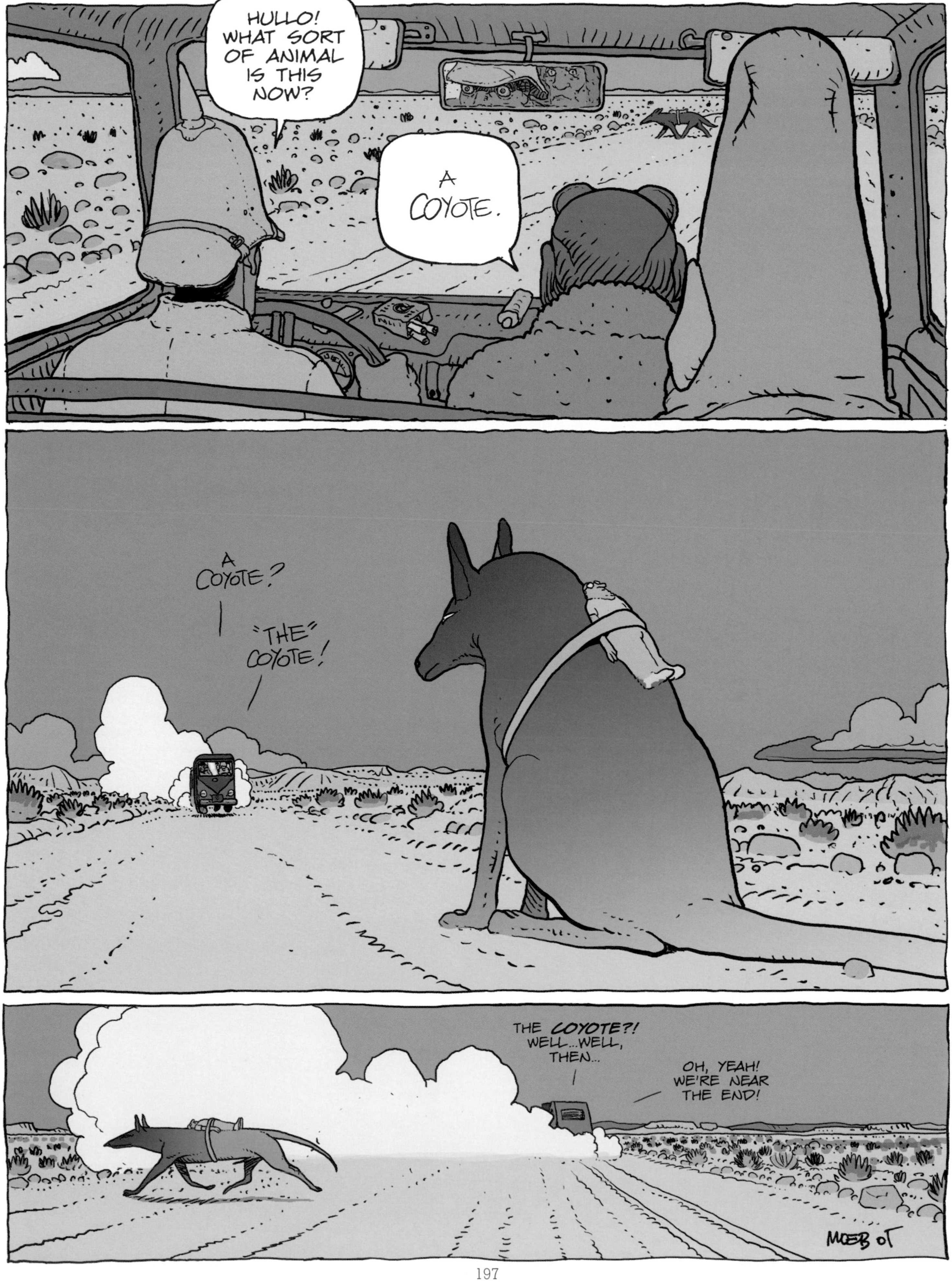
HULLO! WHAT SORT OF ANIMAL IS THIS NOW?
A COYOTE.
A COYOTE?
"THE" COYOTE!
THE COYOTE?! WELL...WELL, THEN...
OH, YEAH! WE'RE NEAR THE END!
MŒB 07

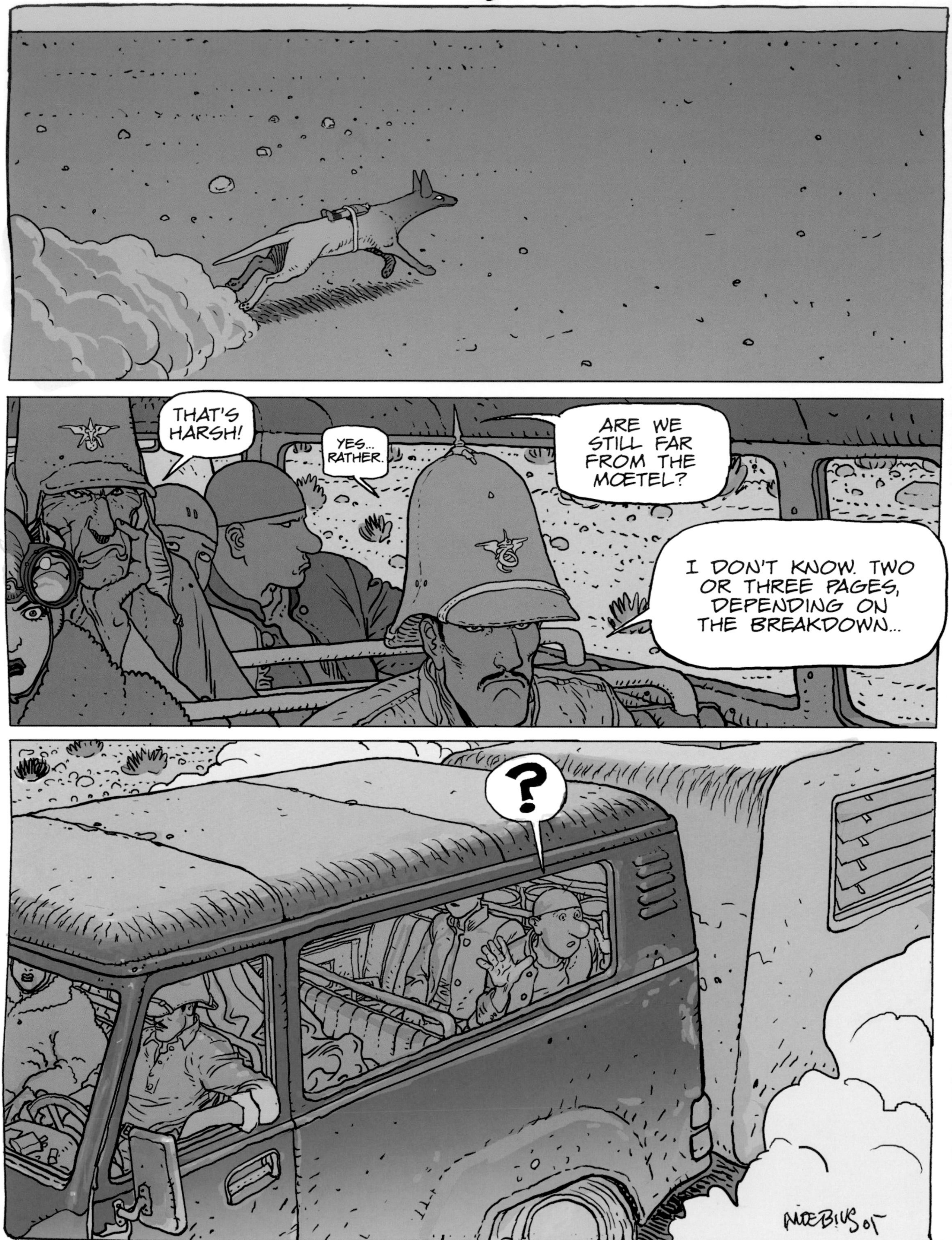
THAT'S HARSH!
YES... RATHER.
ARE WE STILL FAR FROM THE MOETEL?
I DON'T KNOW. TWO OR THREE PAGES, DEPENDING ON THE BREAKDOWN...
?
MOEBIUS 05

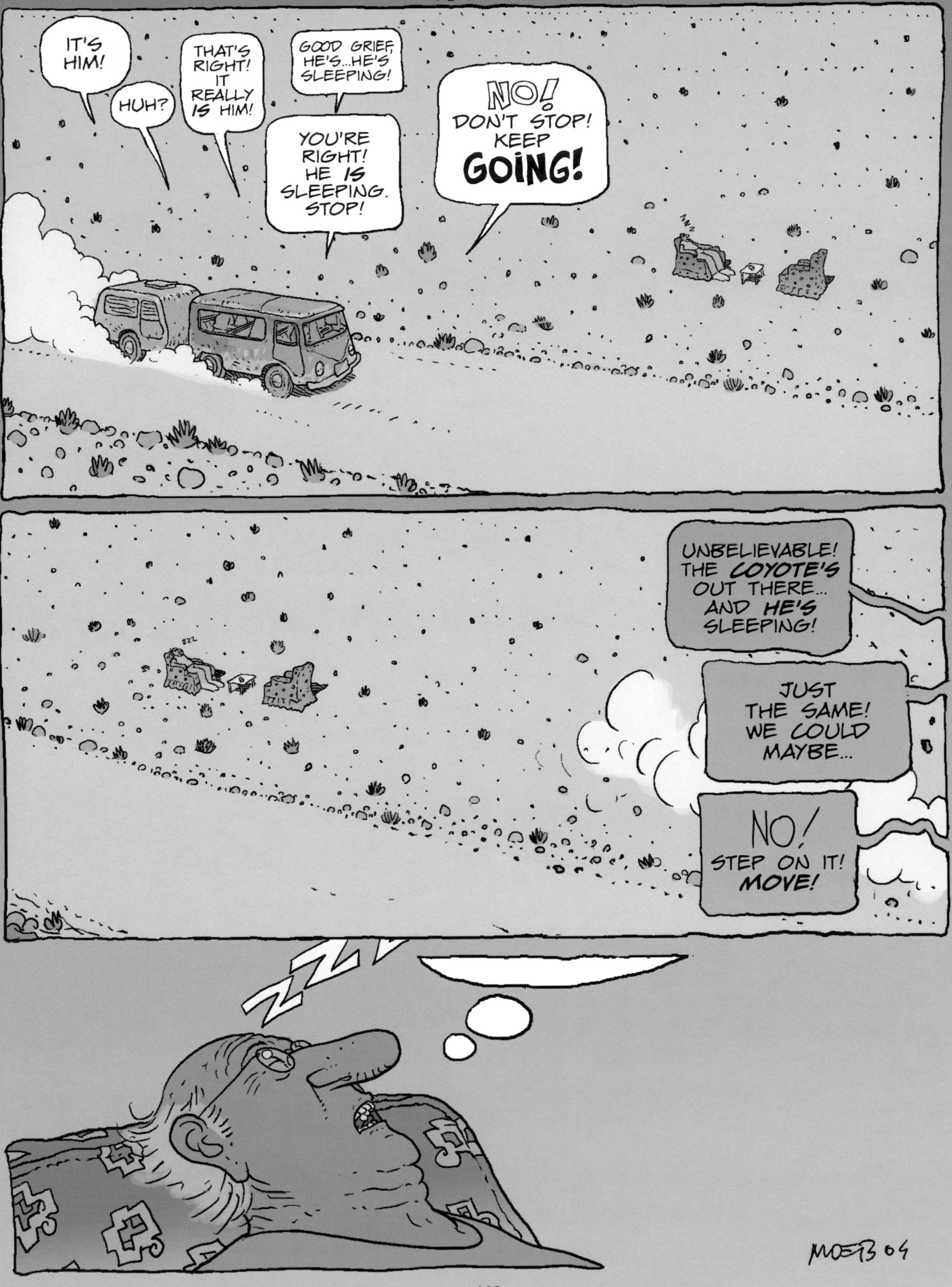
IT'S HIM!
HUH?
THAT'S RIGHT! IT REALLY IS HIM!
GOOD GRIEF, HE'S...HE'S SLEEPING!
YOU'RE RIGHT! HE IS SLEEPING. STOP!
NO! DON'T STOP! KEEP GOING!
UNBELIEVABLE! THE COYOTE'S OUT THERE... AND HE'S SLEEPING!
JUST THE SAME! WE COULD MAYBE...
NO! STEP ON IT! MOVE!
MOEB 04

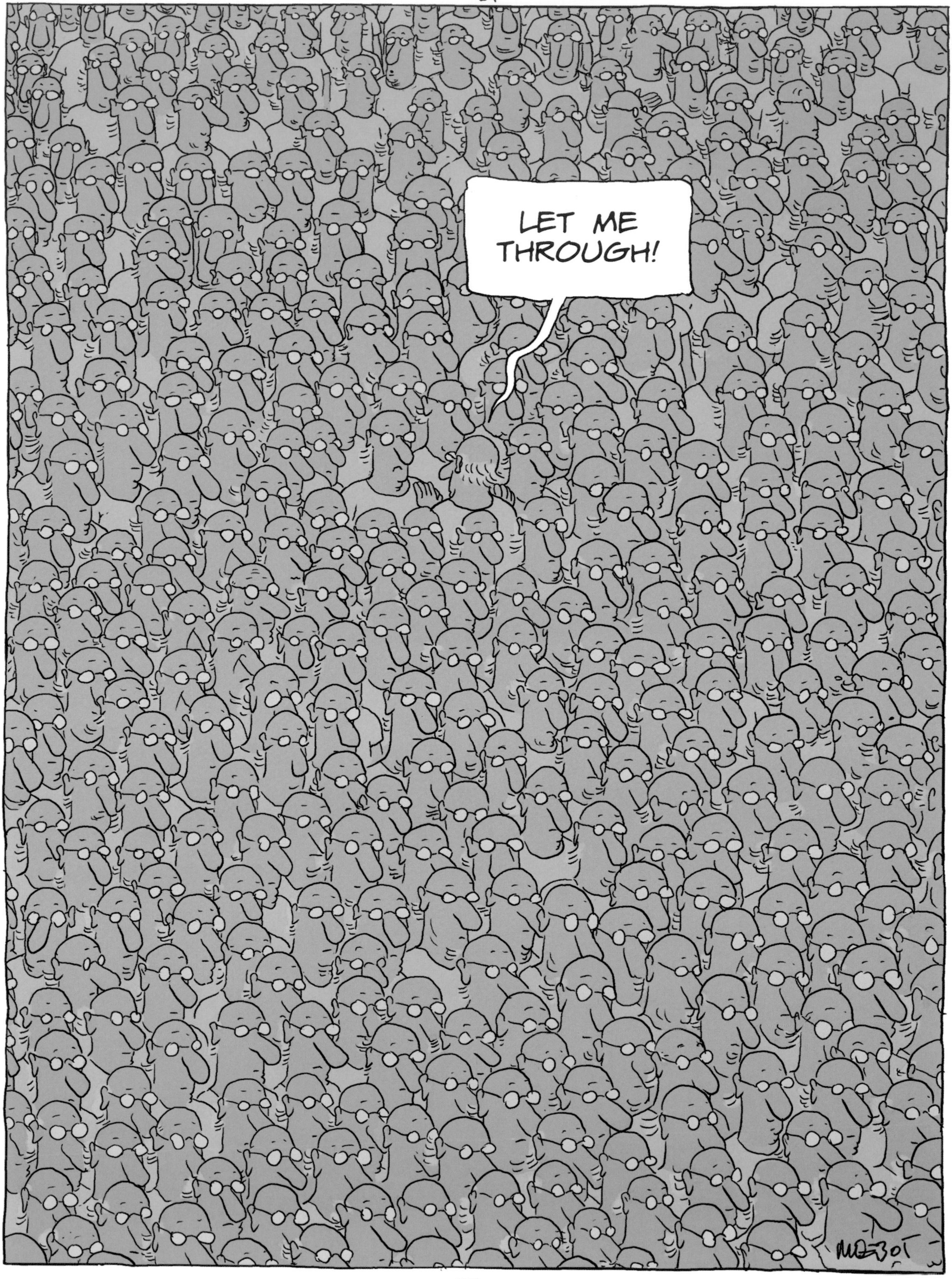
LET ME THROUGH!

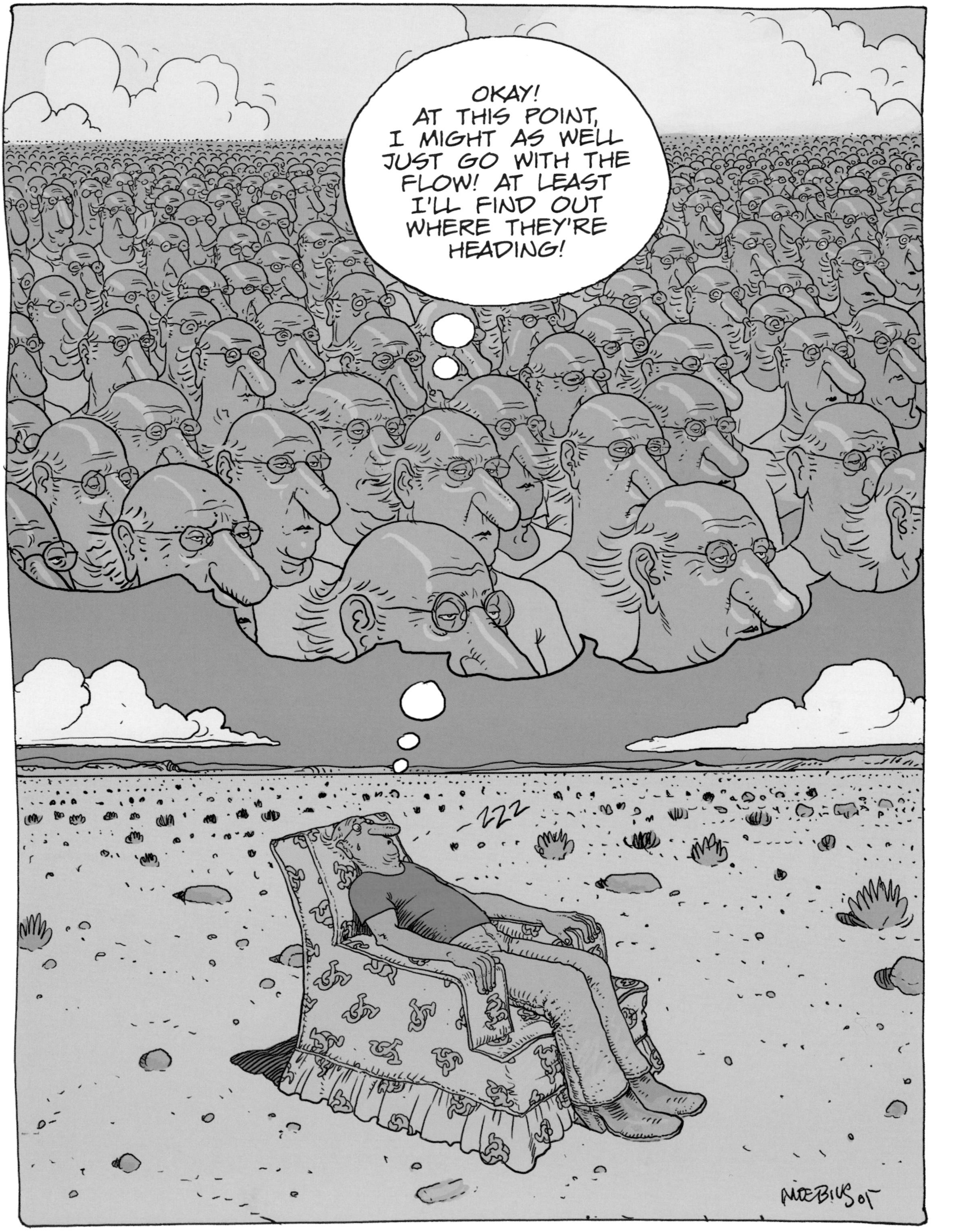
OKAY! AT THIS POINT, I MIGHT AS WELL JUST GO WITH THE FLOW! AT LEAST I'LL FIND OUT WHERE THEY'RE HEADING!
ZZZ
MOEBIUS 05

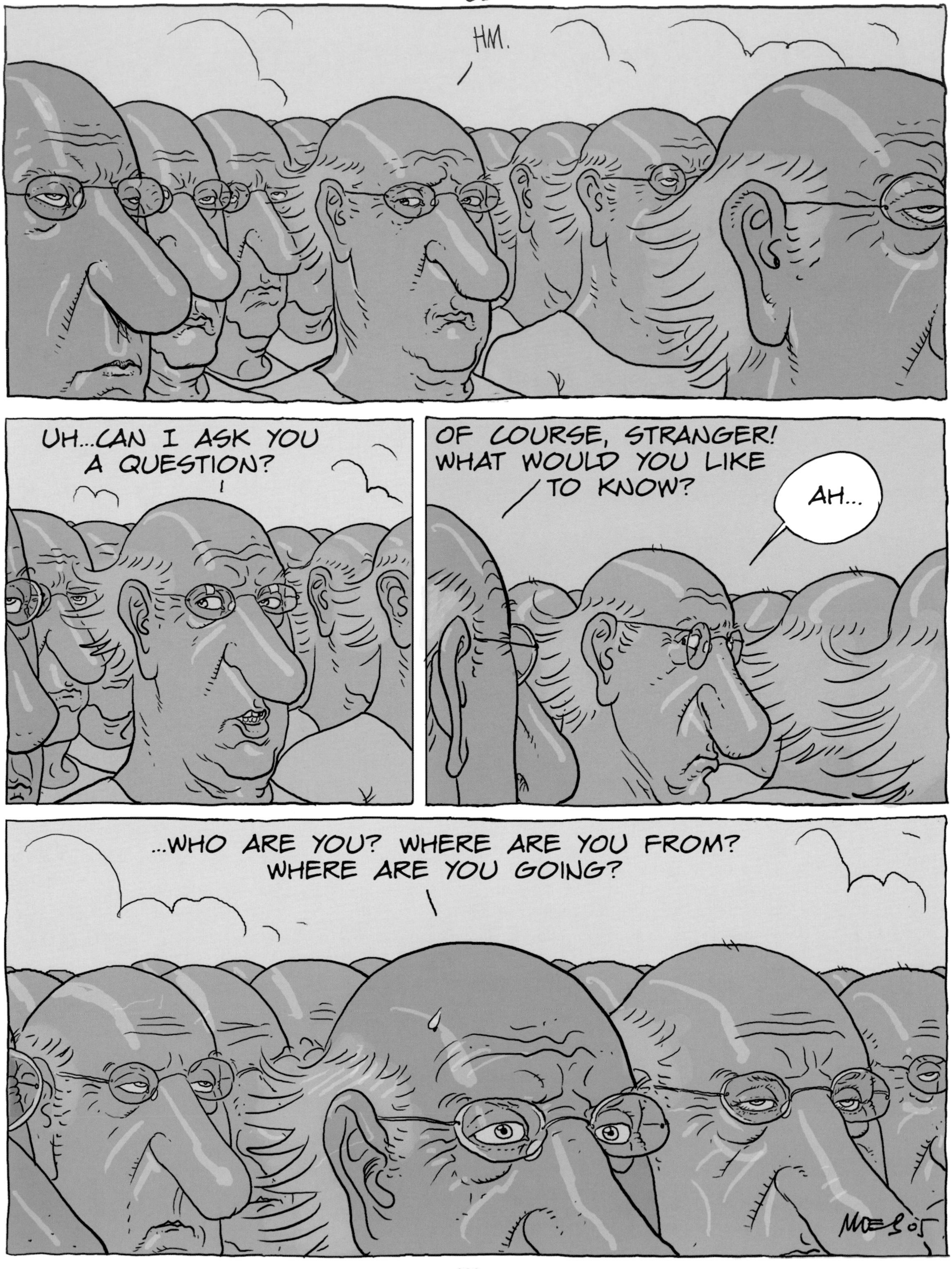
HM.
UH...CAN I ASK YOU A QUESTION?
OF COURSE, STRANGER! WHAT WOULD YOU LIKE TO KNOW?
AH...
...WHO ARE YOU? WHERE ARE YOU FROM? WHERE ARE YOU GOING?
MOEB '05

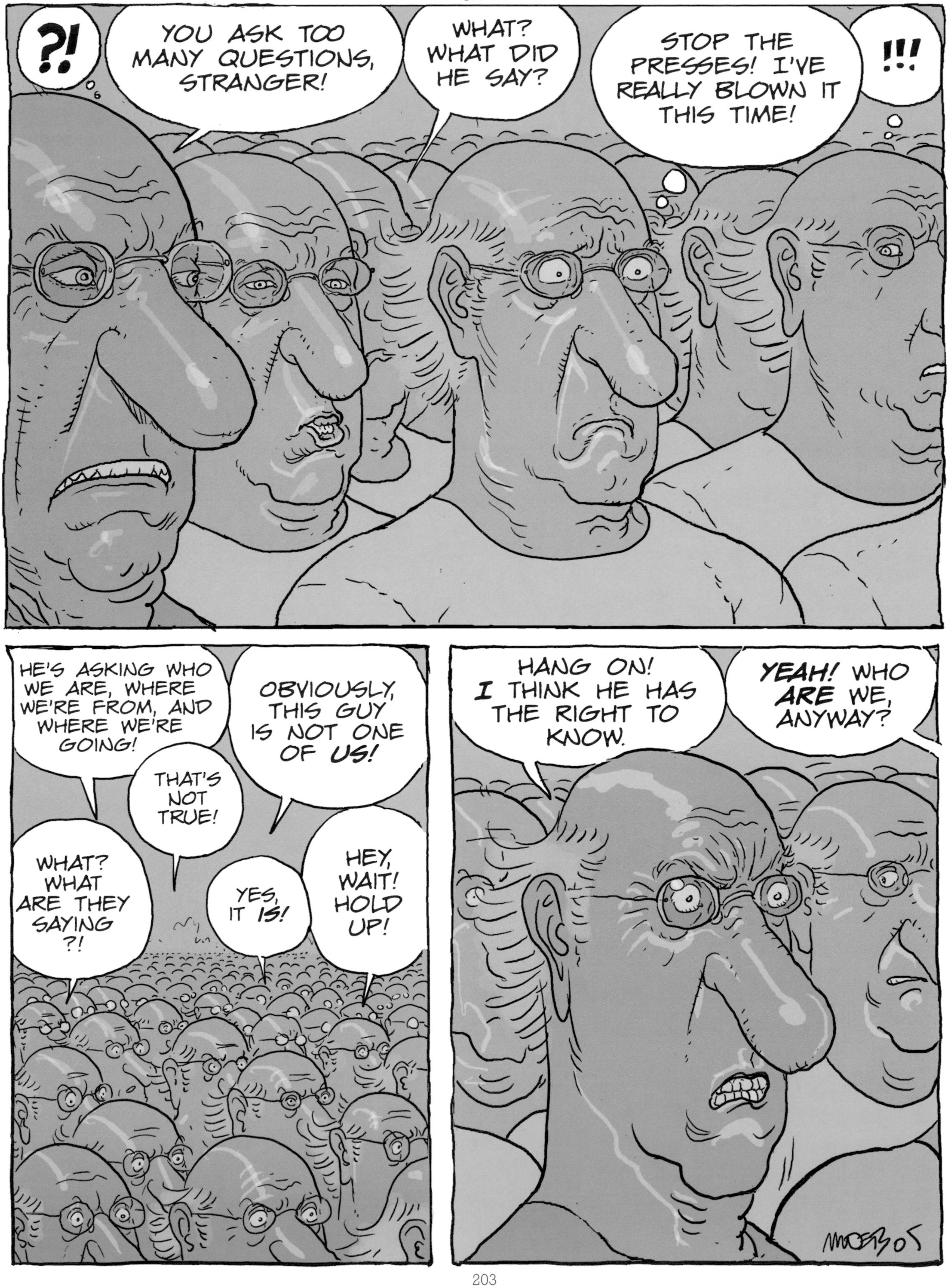
?!
YOU ASK TOO MANY QUESTIONS, STRANGER!
WHAT? WHAT DID HE SAY?
STOP THE PRESSES! I'VE REALLY BLOWN IT THIS TIME!
!!!
HE'S ASKING WHO WE ARE, WHERE WE'RE FROM, AND WHERE WE'RE GOING!
OBVIOUSLY, THIS GUY IS NOT ONE OF *US*!
THAT'S NOT TRUE!
WHAT? WHAT ARE THEY SAYING ?!
YES, IT *IS*!
HEY, WAIT! HOLD UP!
HANG ON! *I* THINK HE HAS THE RIGHT TO KNOW.
YEAH! WHO *ARE* WE, ANYWAY?
MOEBIUS 05

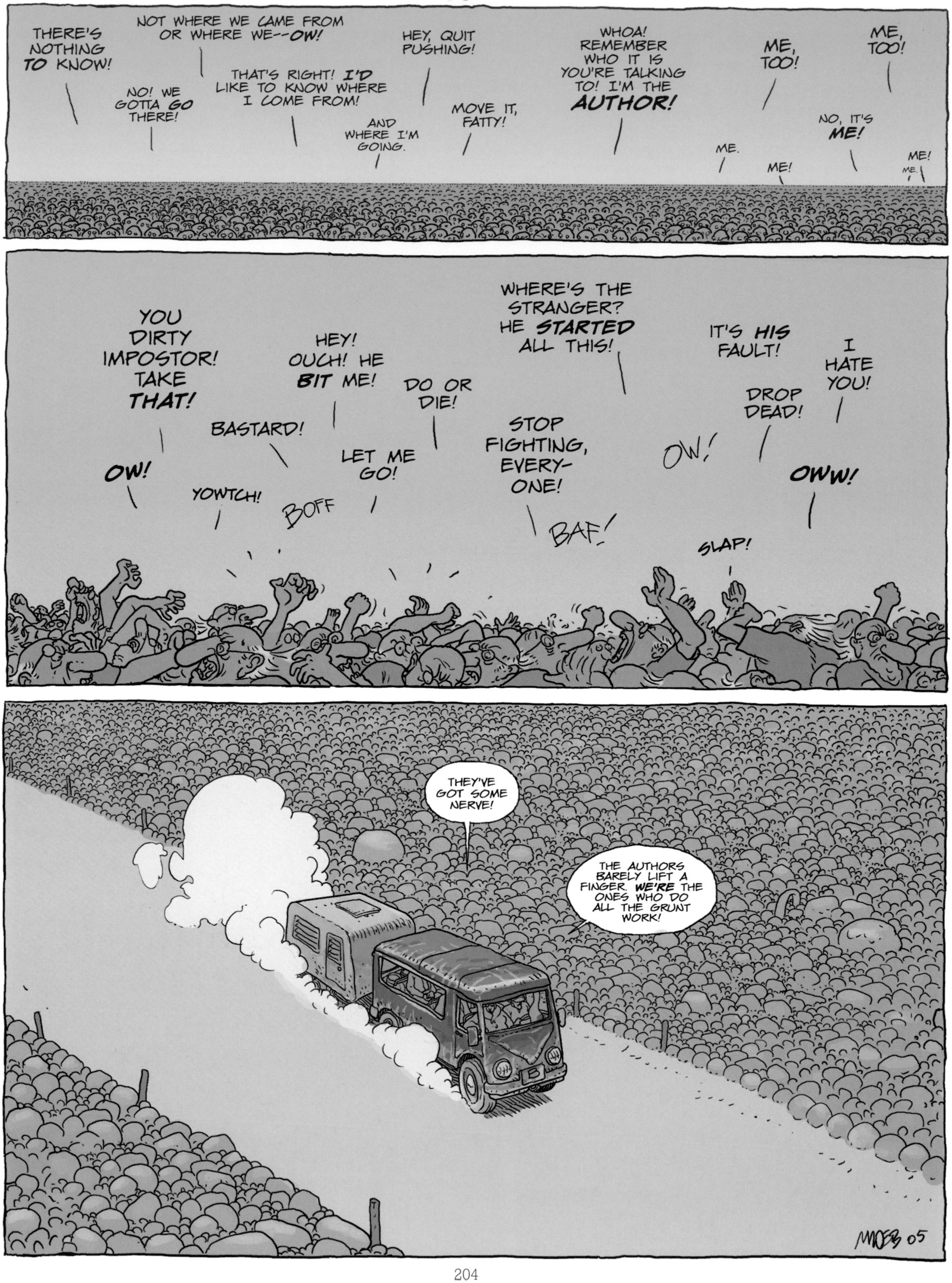
THERE'S NOTHING TO KNOW!
NOT WHERE WE CAME FROM OR WHERE WE--OW!
NO! WE GOTTA GO THERE!
THAT'S RIGHT! I'D LIKE TO KNOW WHERE I COME FROM!
AND WHERE I'M GOING.
HEY, QUIT PUSHING!
MOVE IT, FATTY!
WHOA! REMEMBER WHO IT IS YOU'RE TALKING TO! I'M THE AUTHOR!
ME.
ME, TOO!
ME!
NO, IT'S ME!
ME, TOO!
ME!
ME.
YOU DIRTY IMPOSTOR! TAKE THAT!
OW!
BASTARD!
YOWTCH!
HEY! OUCH! HE BIT ME!
BOFF
DO OR DIE!
LET ME GO!
WHERE'S THE STRANGER? HE STARTED ALL THIS!
STOP FIGHTING, EVERY-ONE!
BAF!
OW!
IT'S HIS FAULT!
DROP DEAD!
SLAP!
I HATE YOU!
OWW!
THEY'VE GOT SOME NERVE!
THE AUTHORS BARELY LIFT A FINGER. WE'RE THE ONES WHO DO ALL THE GRUNT WORK!
MOEB 05

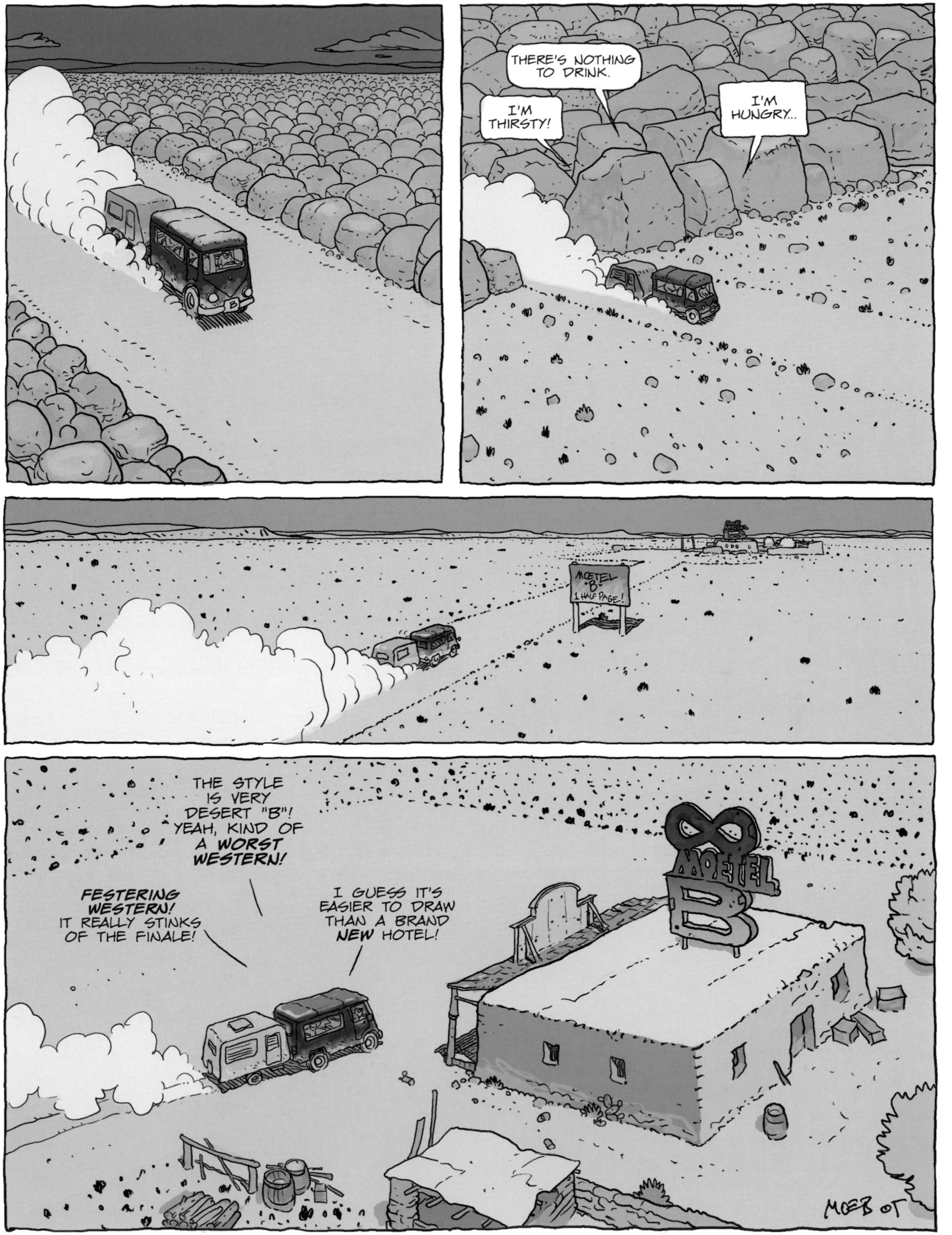
I'M THIRSTY!
THERE'S NOTHING TO DRINK.
I'M HUNGRY...
MOETEL "B" 1 HALF PAGE!
THE STYLE IS VERY DESERT "B"! YEAH, KIND OF A **WORST WESTERN!**
FESTERING WESTERN! IT REALLY STINKS OF THE FINALE!
I GUESS IT'S EASIER TO DRAW THAN A BRAND **NEW** HOTEL!
MOETEL B
MOEB 07

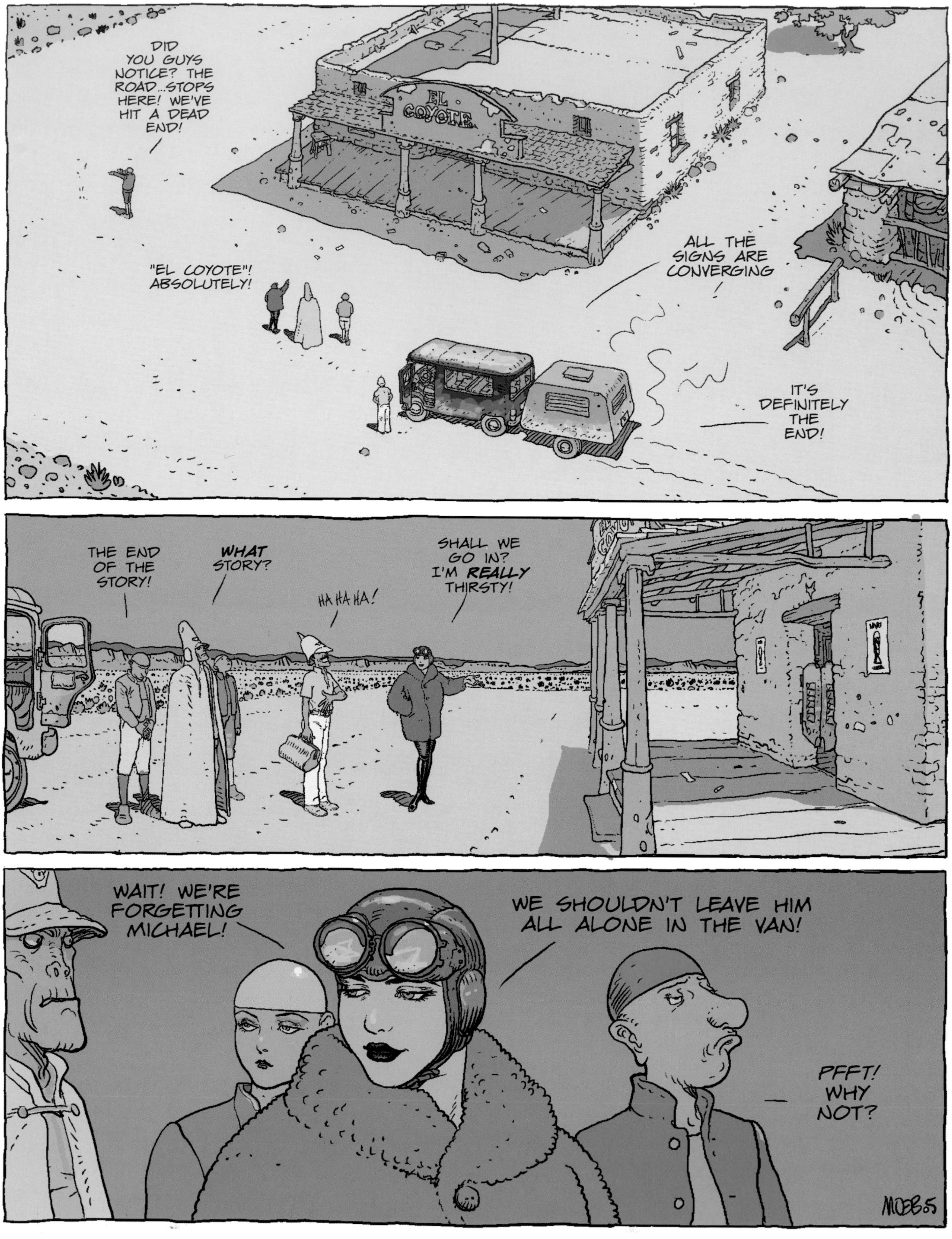
DID YOU GUYS NOTICE? THE ROAD...STOPS HERE! WE'VE HIT A DEAD END!
EL COYOTE
"EL COYOTE"! ABSOLUTELY!
ALL THE SIGNS ARE CONVERGING!
IT'S DEFINITELY THE END!
THE END OF THE STORY!
WHAT STORY?
HA HA HA!
SHALL WE GO IN? I'M REALLY THIRSTY!
WAIT! WE'RE FORGETTING MICHAEL!
WE SHOULDN'T LEAVE HIM ALL ALONE IN THE VAN!
PFFT! WHY NOT?
MOEB.05

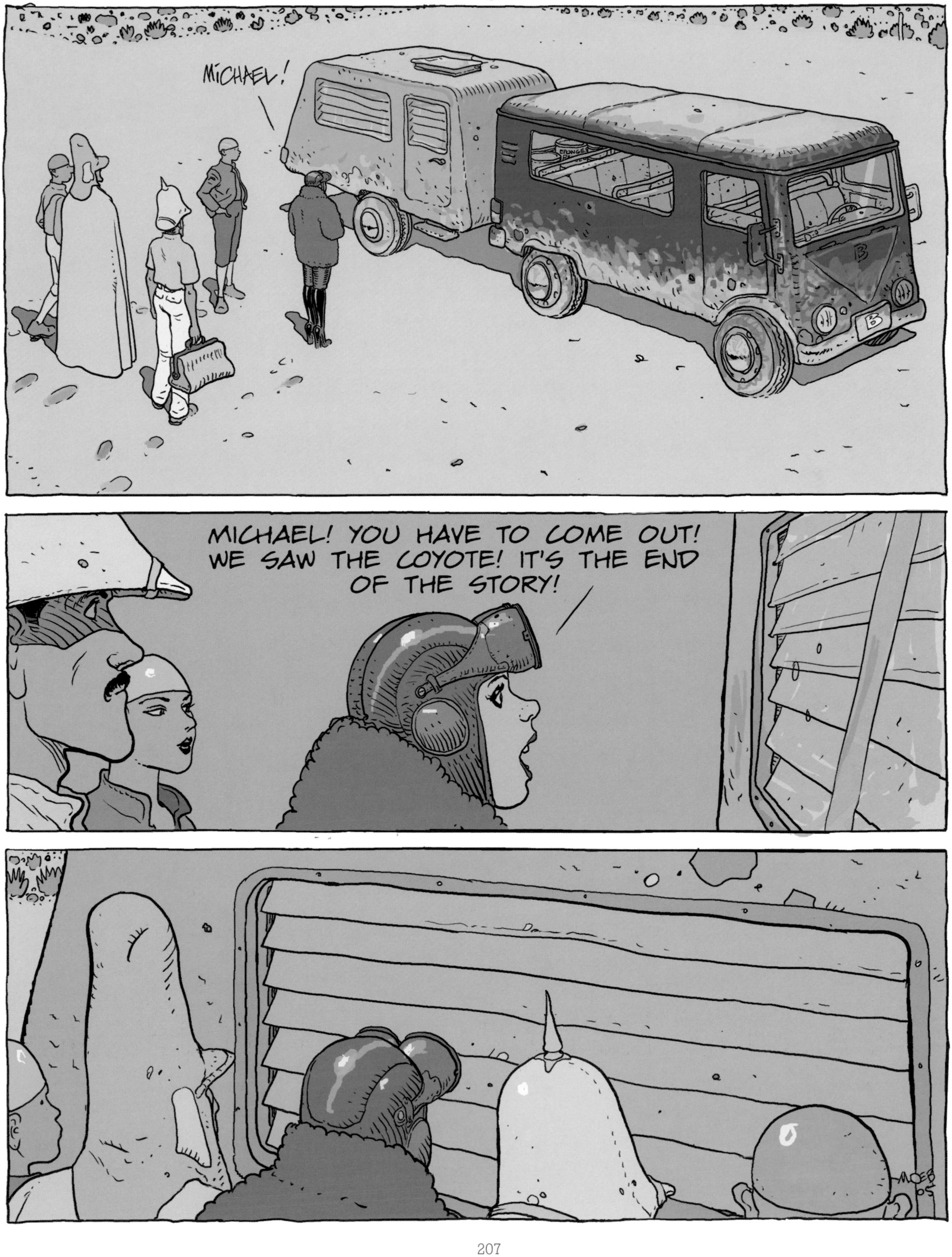
MICHAEL!
MICHAEL! YOU HAVE TO COME OUT! WE SAW THE COYOTE! IT'S THE END OF THE STORY!
MOEB 05

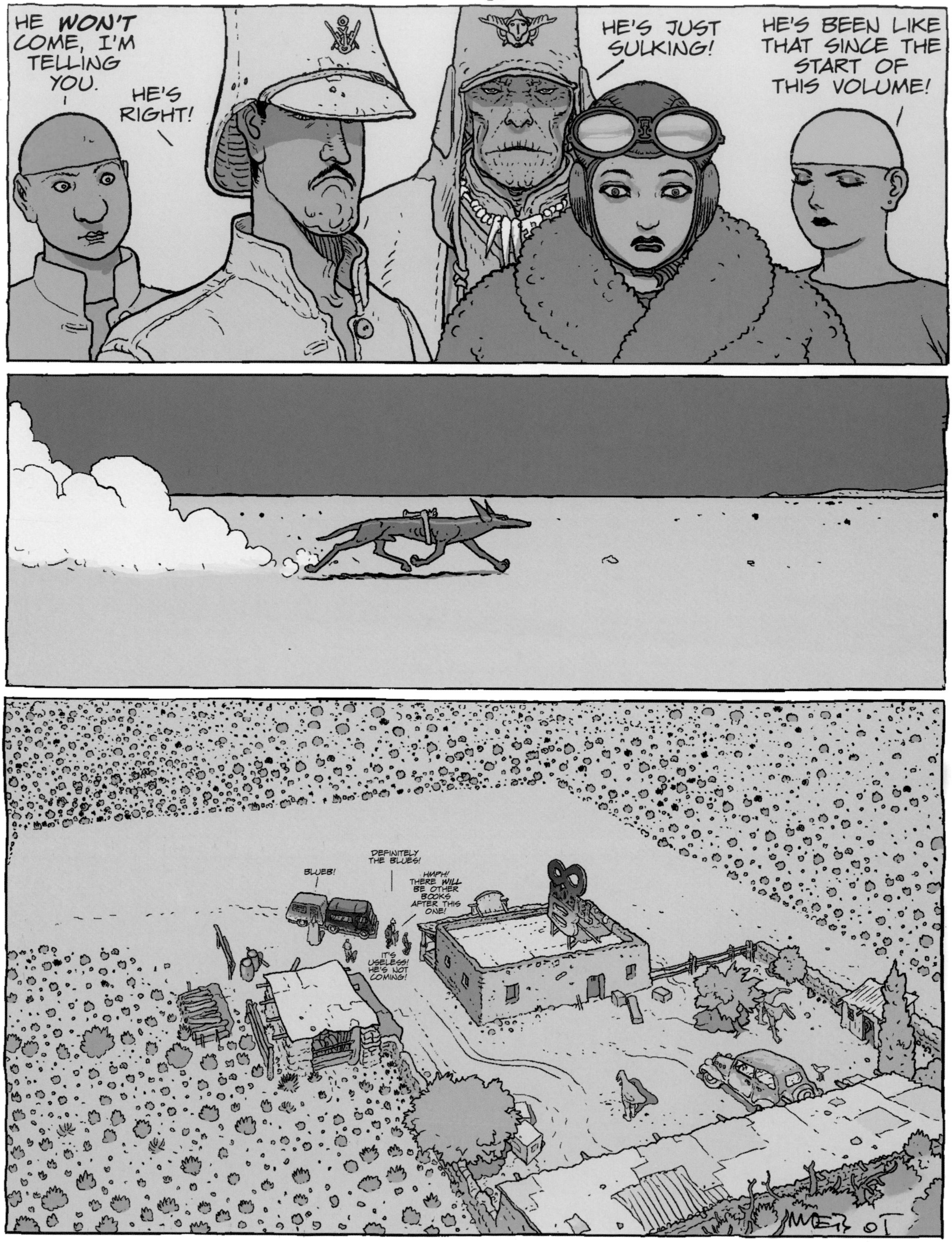
HE **WON'T** COME, I'M TELLING YOU.
HE'S RIGHT!
HE'S JUST SULKING!
HE'S BEEN LIKE THAT SINCE THE START OF THIS VOLUME!
BLUEB!
DEFINITELY THE BLUES!
HMPH! THERE *WILL* BE OTHER BOOKS AFTER THIS ONE!
IT'S USELESS! HE'S NOT COMING!
MŒBIUS 07

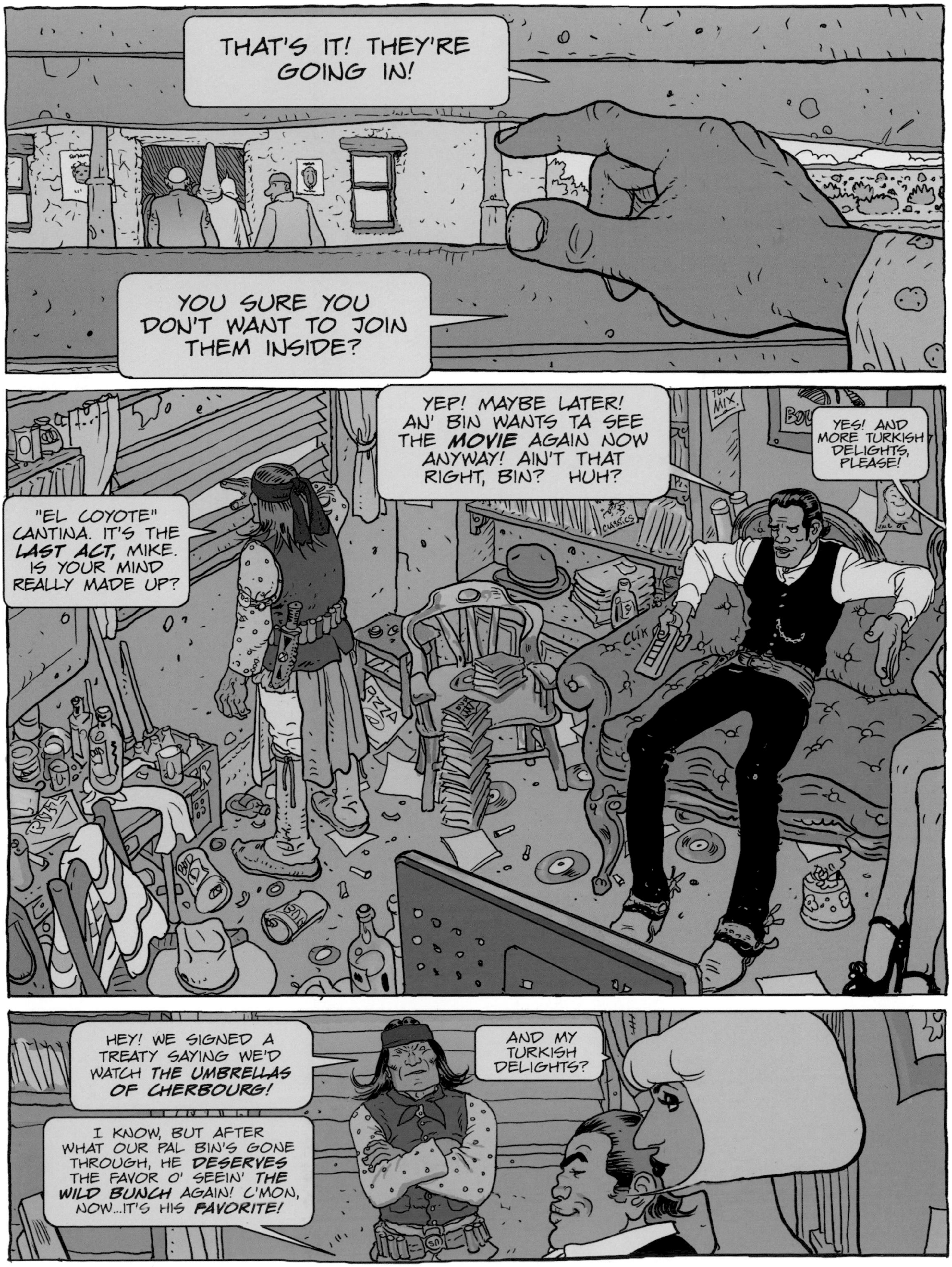
THAT'S IT! THEY'RE GOING IN!
YOU SURE YOU DON'T WANT TO JOIN THEM INSIDE?
YEP! MAYBE LATER! AN' BIN WANTS TA SEE THE MOVIE AGAIN NOW ANYWAY! AIN'T THAT RIGHT, BIN? HUH?
YES! AND MORE TURKISH DELIGHTS, PLEASE!
"EL COYOTE" CANTINA. IT'S THE LAST ACT, MIKE. IS YOUR MIND REALLY MADE UP?
CLIK
HEY! WE SIGNED A TREATY SAYING WE'D WATCH THE UMBRELLAS OF CHERBOURG!
AND MY TURKISH DELIGHTS?
I KNOW, BUT AFTER WHAT OUR PAL BIN'S GONE THROUGH, HE DESERVES THE FAVOR O' SEEIN' THE WILD BUNCH AGAIN! C'MON, NOW...IT'S HIS FAVORITE!

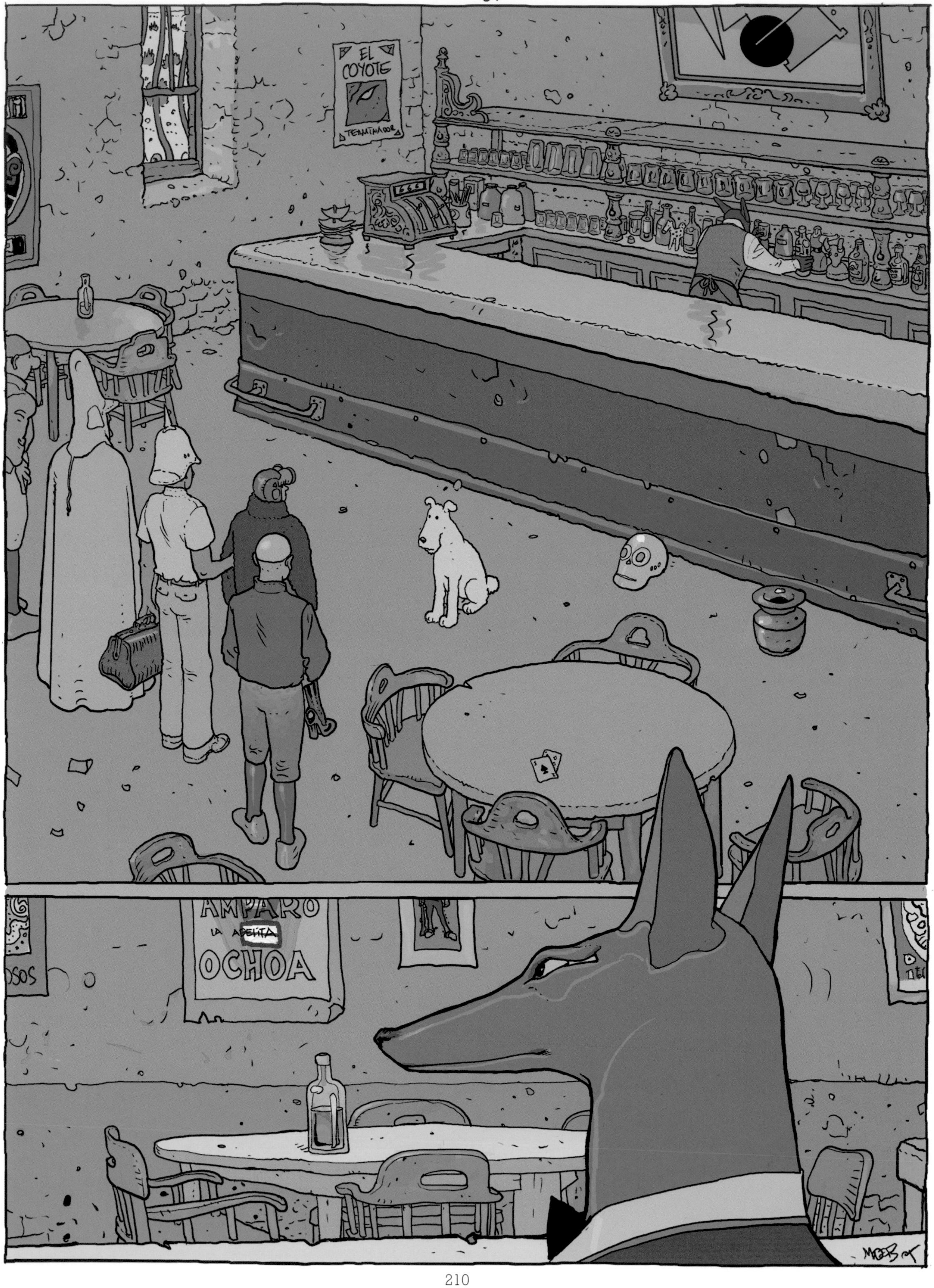
EL COYOTE
TERMINADOR
666
AMPARO
LA ADELITA
OCHOA

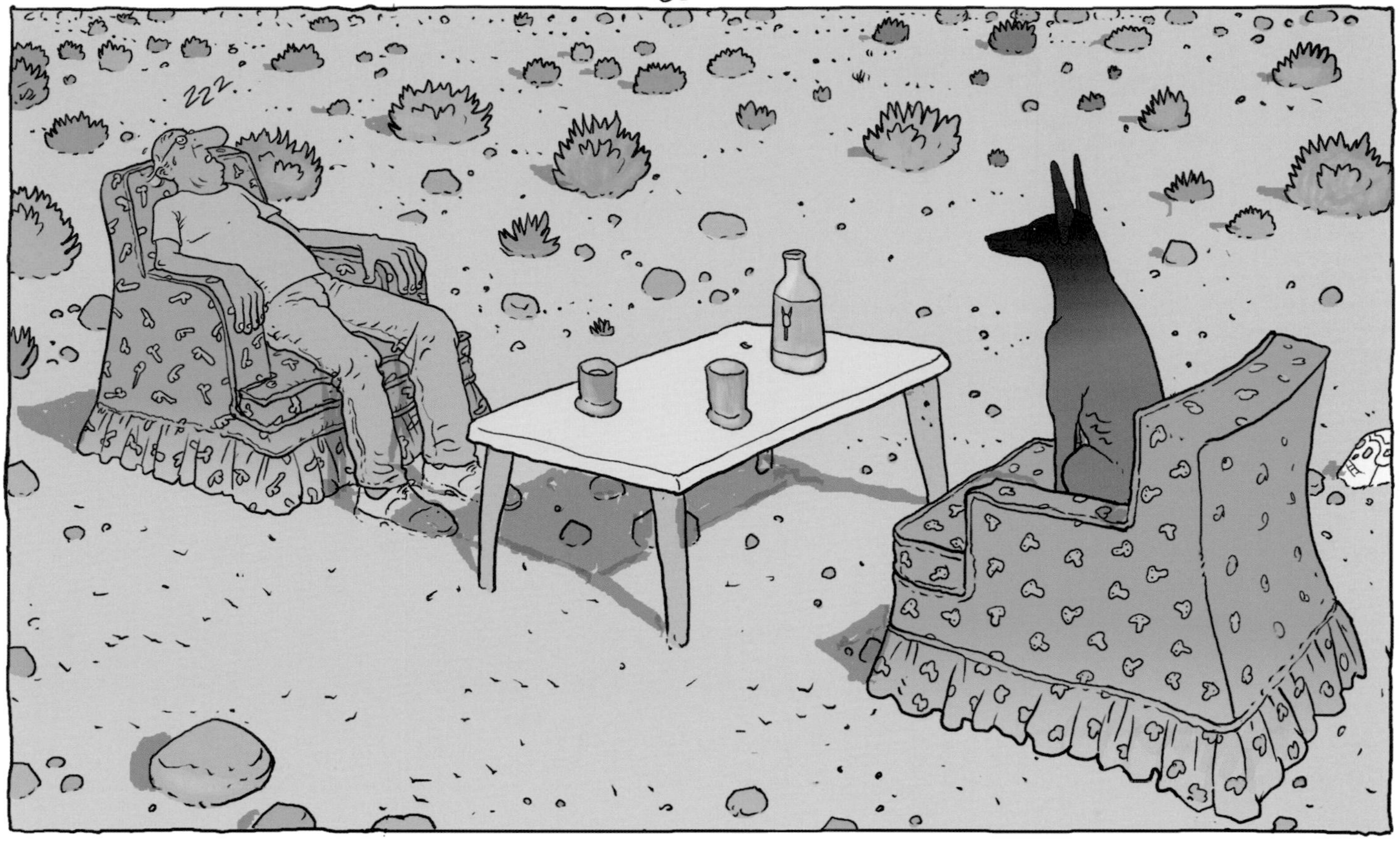
ZZZ

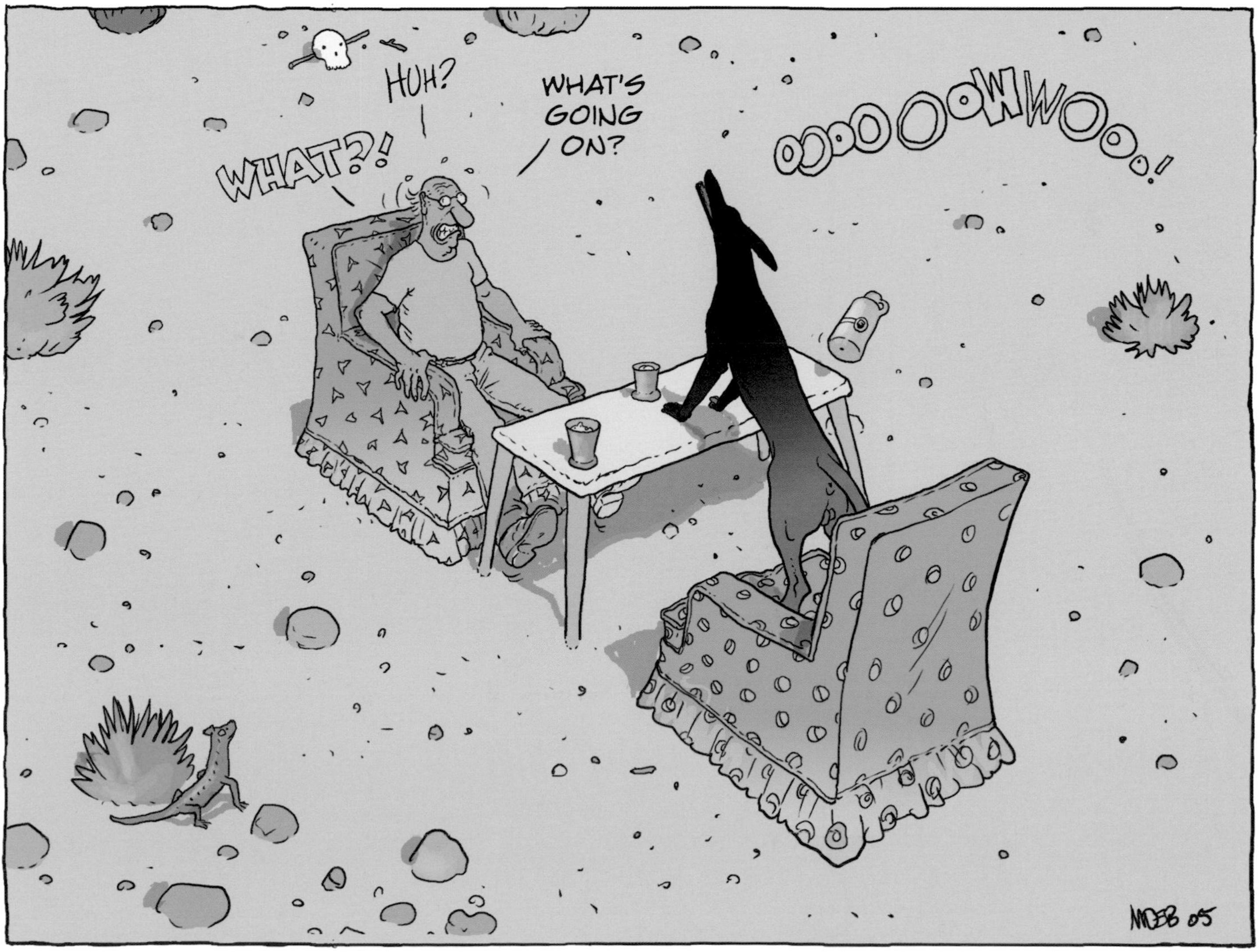
WHAT?!
HUH?
WHAT'S GOING ON?
OOOOOOWWOOO!
MOEB 05

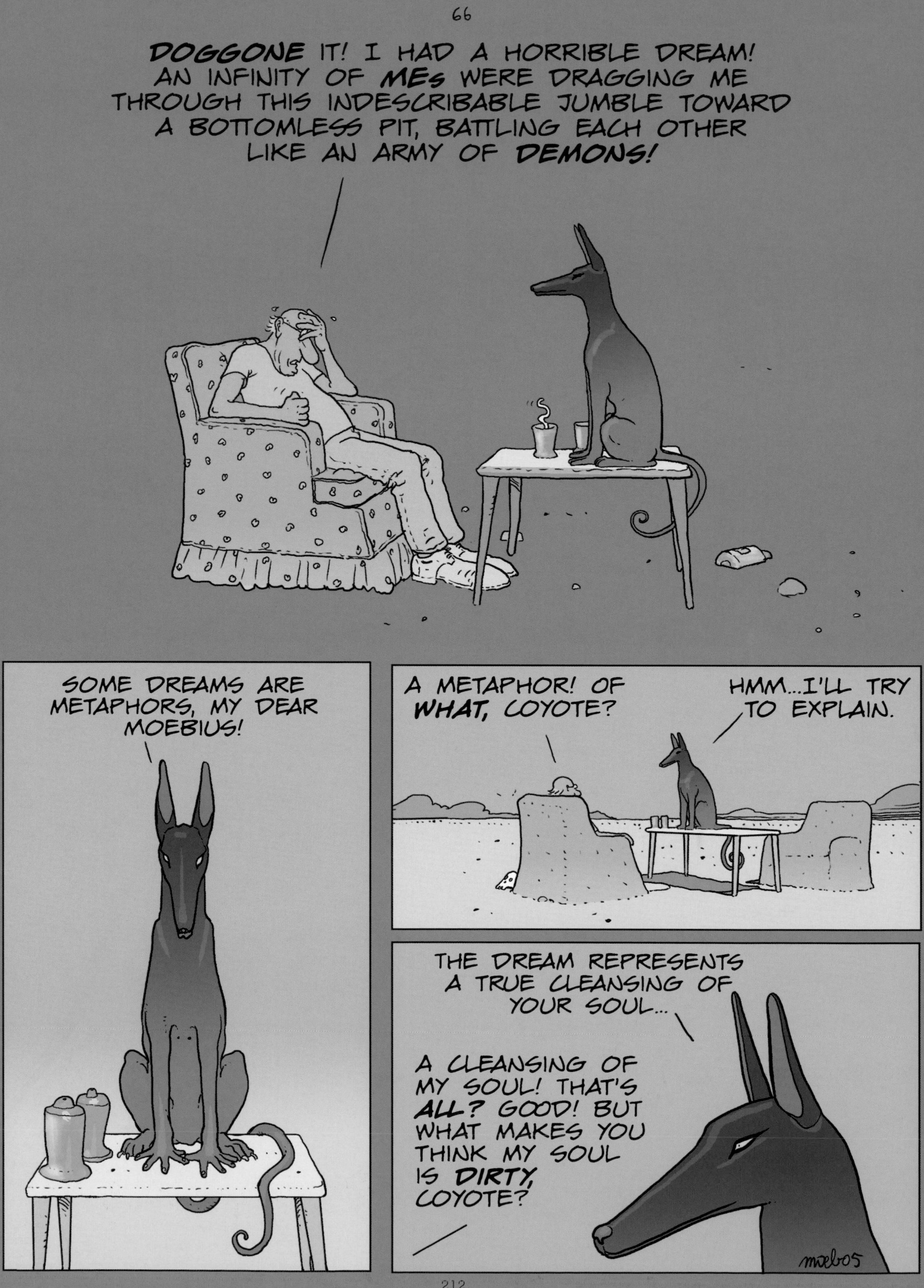
66
DOGGONE IT! I HAD A HORRIBLE DREAM! AN INFINITY OF MEs WERE DRAGGING ME THROUGH THIS INDESCRIBABLE JUMBLE TOWARD A BOTTOMLESS PIT, BATTLING EACH OTHER LIKE AN ARMY OF DEMONS!
SOME DREAMS ARE METAPHORS, MY DEAR MOEBIUS!
A METAPHOR! OF WHAT, COYOTE?
HMM...I'LL TRY TO EXPLAIN.
THE DREAM REPRESENTS A TRUE CLEANSING OF YOUR SOUL...
A CLEANSING OF MY SOUL! THAT'S ALL? GOOD! BUT WHAT MAKES YOU THINK MY SOUL IS DIRTY, COYOTE?
moebius

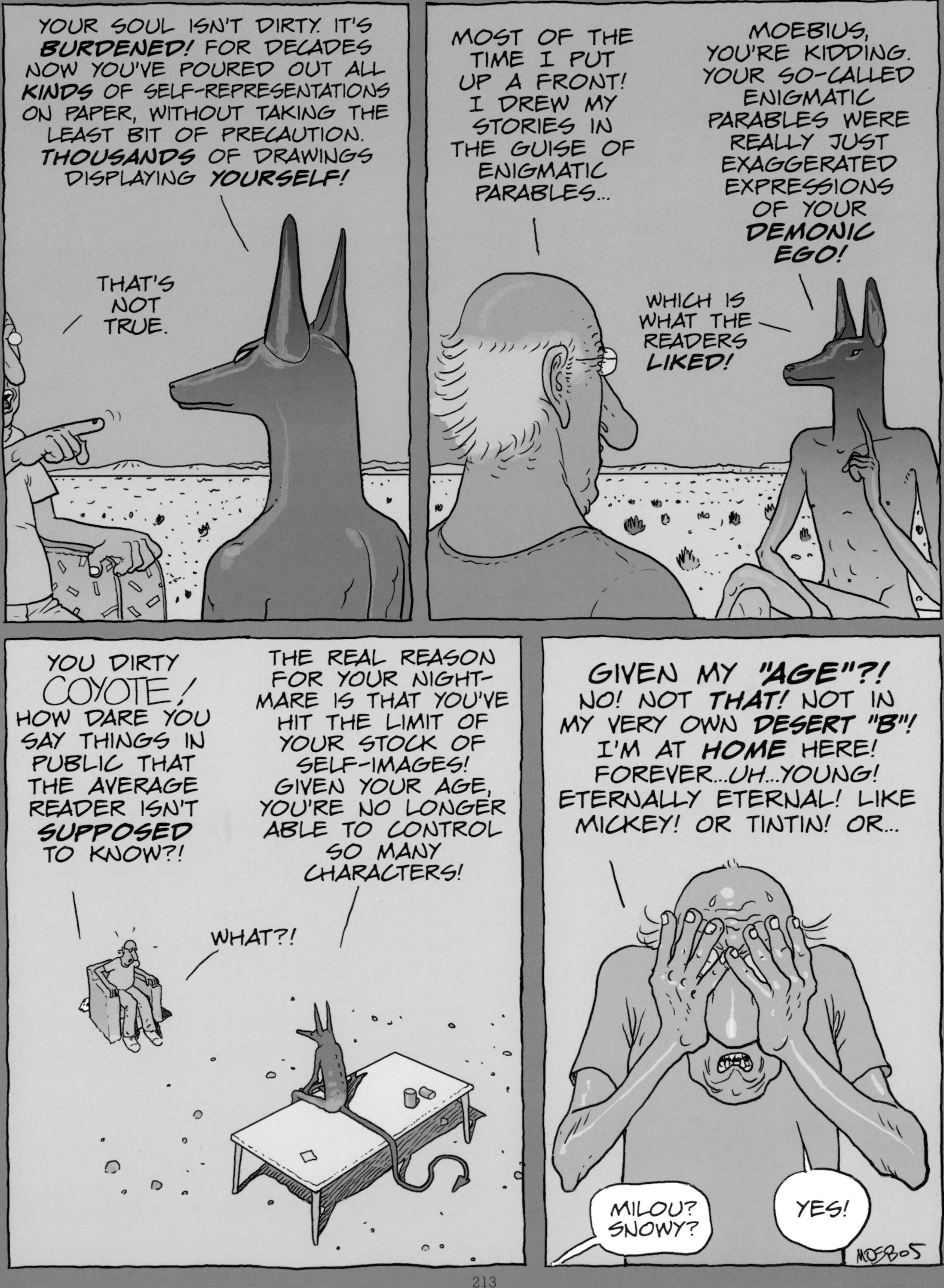
YOUR SOUL ISN'T DIRTY. IT'S BURDENED! FOR DECADES NOW YOU'VE POURED OUT ALL KINDS OF SELF-REPRESENTATIONS ON PAPER, WITHOUT TAKING THE LEAST BIT OF PRECAUTION. THOUSANDS OF DRAWINGS DISPLAYING YOURSELF!
THAT'S NOT TRUE.
MOST OF THE TIME I PUT UP A FRONT! I DREW MY STORIES IN THE GUISE OF ENIGMATIC PARABLES...
MOEBIUS, YOU'RE KIDDING. YOUR SO-CALLED ENIGMATIC PARABLES WERE REALLY JUST EXAGGERATED EXPRESSIONS OF YOUR DEMONIC EGO!
WHICH IS WHAT THE READERS LIKED!
YOU DIRTY COYOTE! HOW DARE YOU SAY THINGS IN PUBLIC THAT THE AVERAGE READER ISN'T SUPPOSED TO KNOW?!
THE REAL REASON FOR YOUR NIGHT-MARE IS THAT YOU'VE HIT THE LIMIT OF YOUR STOCK OF SELF-IMAGES! GIVEN YOUR AGE, YOU'RE NO LONGER ABLE TO CONTROL SO MANY CHARACTERS!
WHAT?!
GIVEN MY "AGE"?! NO! NOT THAT! NOT IN MY VERY OWN DESERT "B"! I'M AT HOME HERE! FOREVER...UH...YOUNG! ETERNALLY ETERNAL! LIKE MICKEY! OR TINTIN! OR...
MILOU? SNOWY?
YES!
MOEB 05

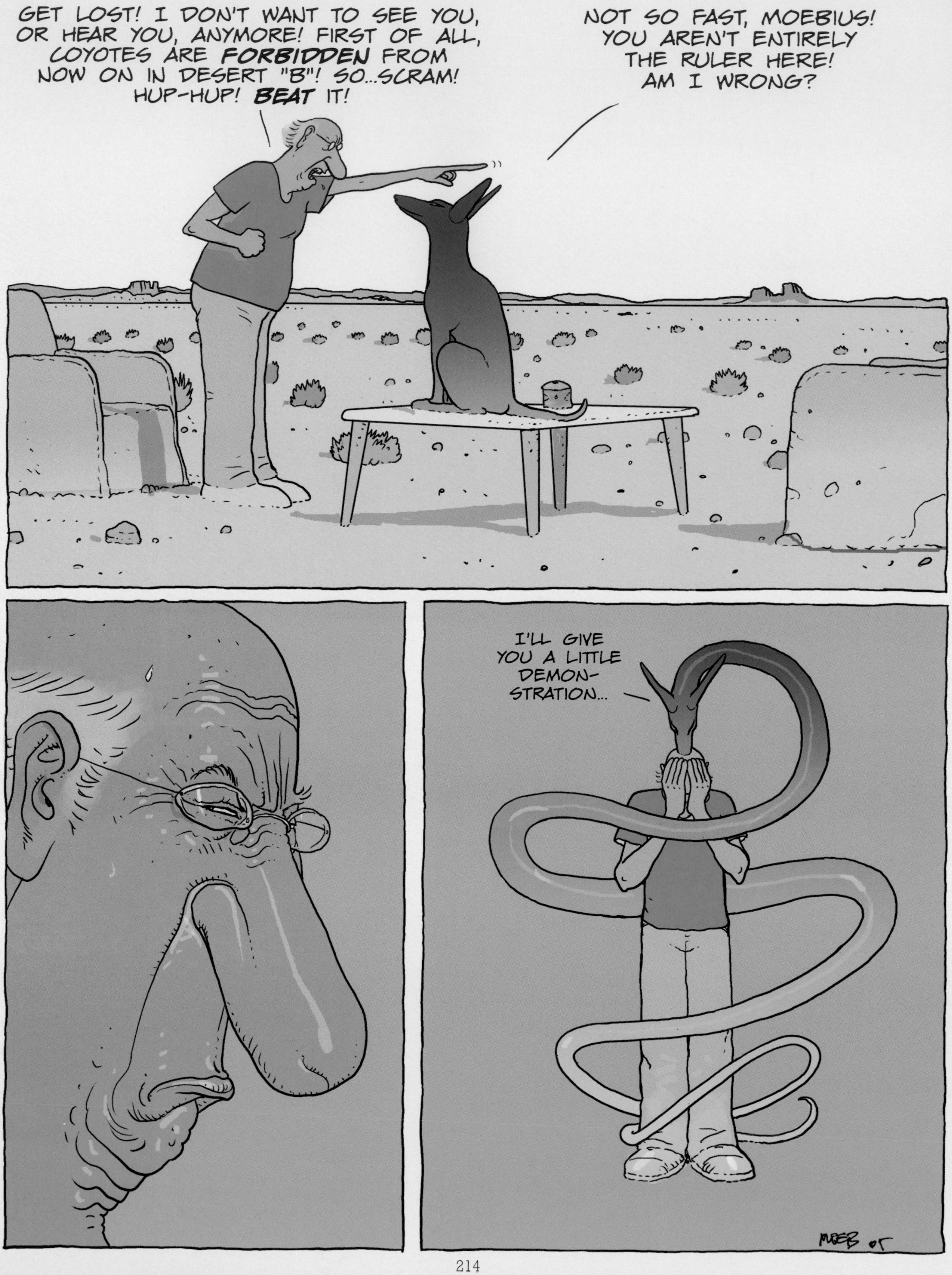
GET LOST! I DON'T WANT TO SEE YOU, OR HEAR YOU, ANYMORE! FIRST OF ALL, COYOTES ARE **FORBIDDEN** FROM NOW ON IN DESERT "B"! SO...SCRAM! HUP-HUP! **BEAT** IT!
NOT SO FAST, MOEBIUS! YOU AREN'T ENTIRELY THE RULER HERE! AM I WRONG?
I'LL GIVE YOU A LITTLE DEMON-STRATION...
MOEB 05

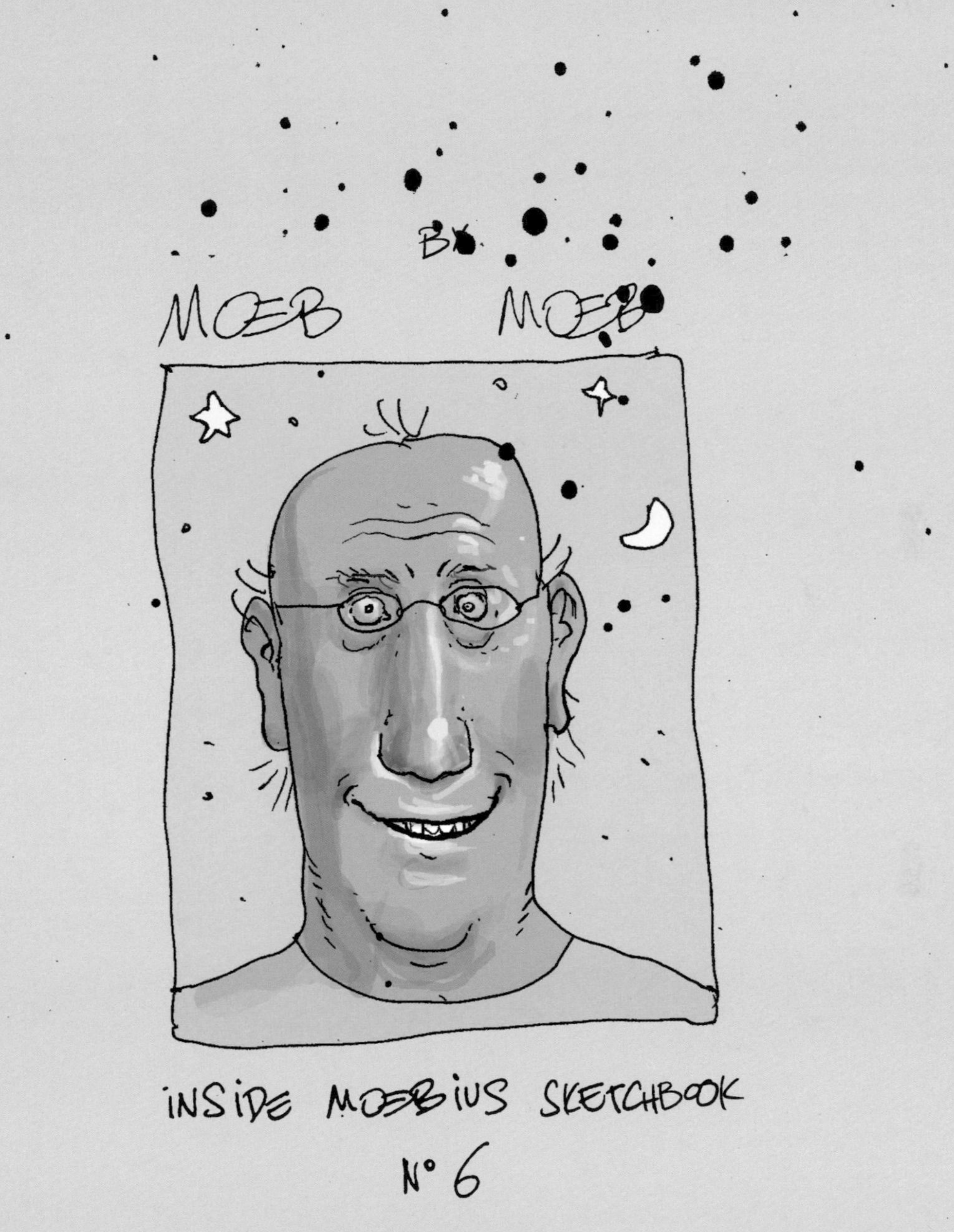
BY
MOEB MOEB
INSIDE MOEBIUS SKETCHBOOK
N° 6

SECOND SECTION

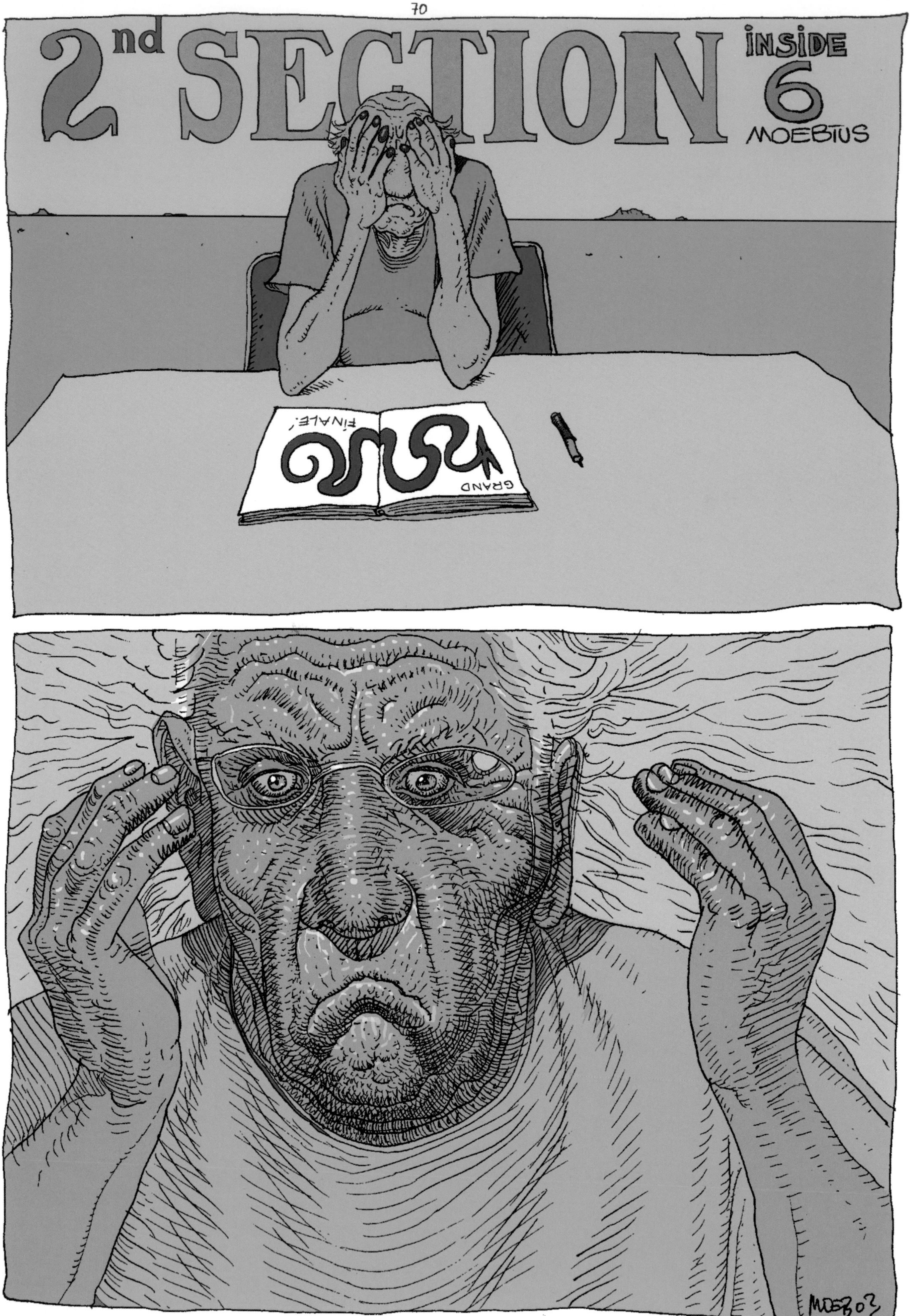
2nd SECTION
INSIDE
6
MOEBIUS
GRAND
FINALE!
MOEBIUS 03

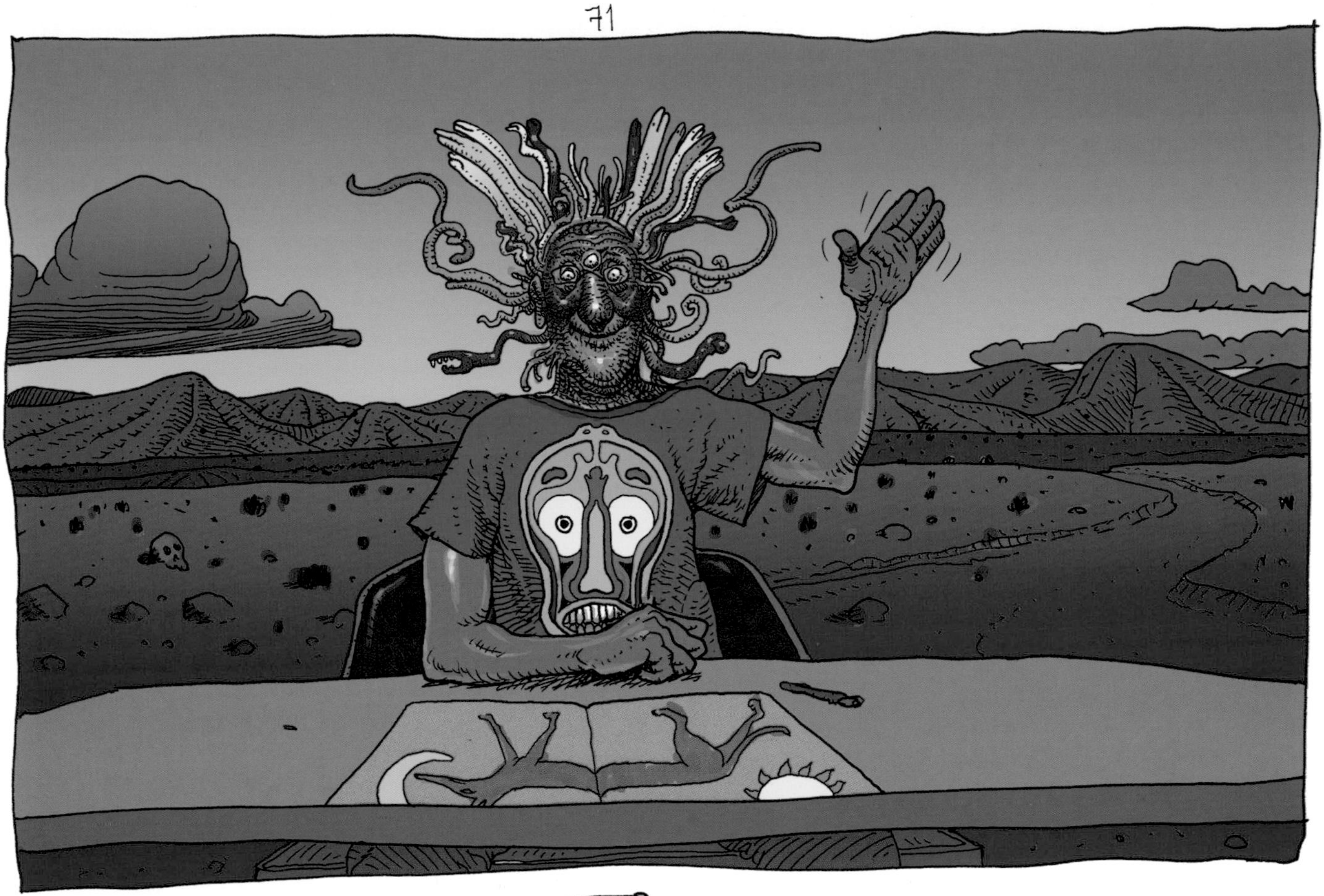

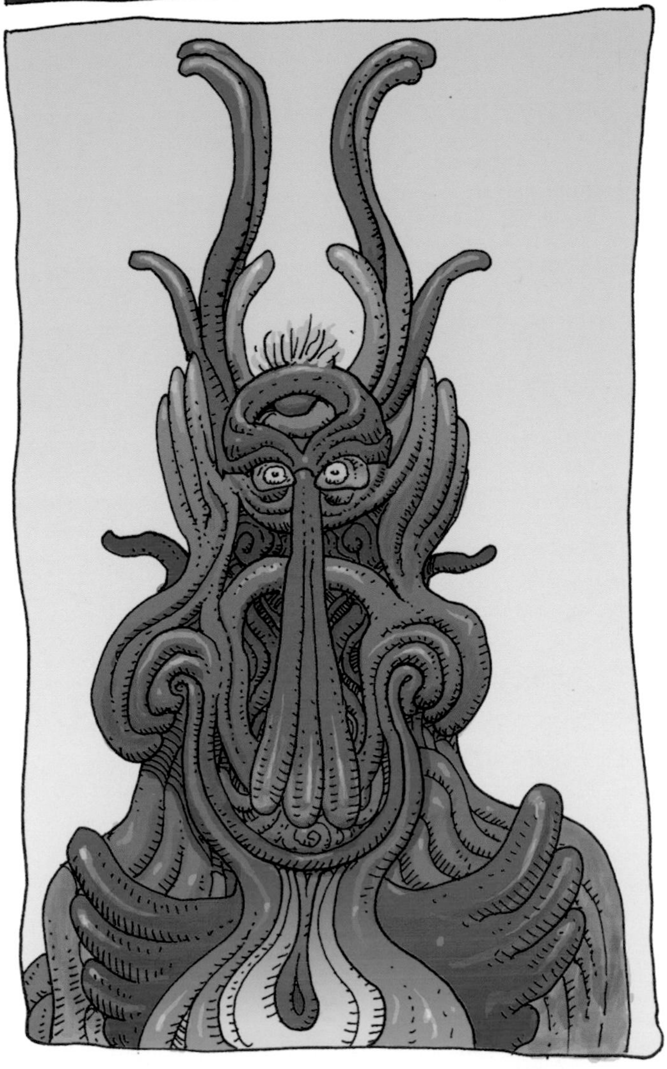

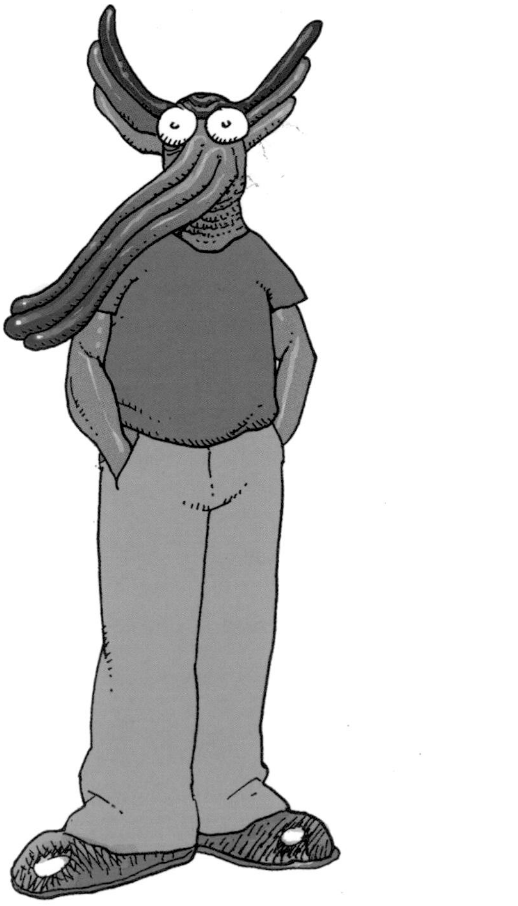

MOEB06

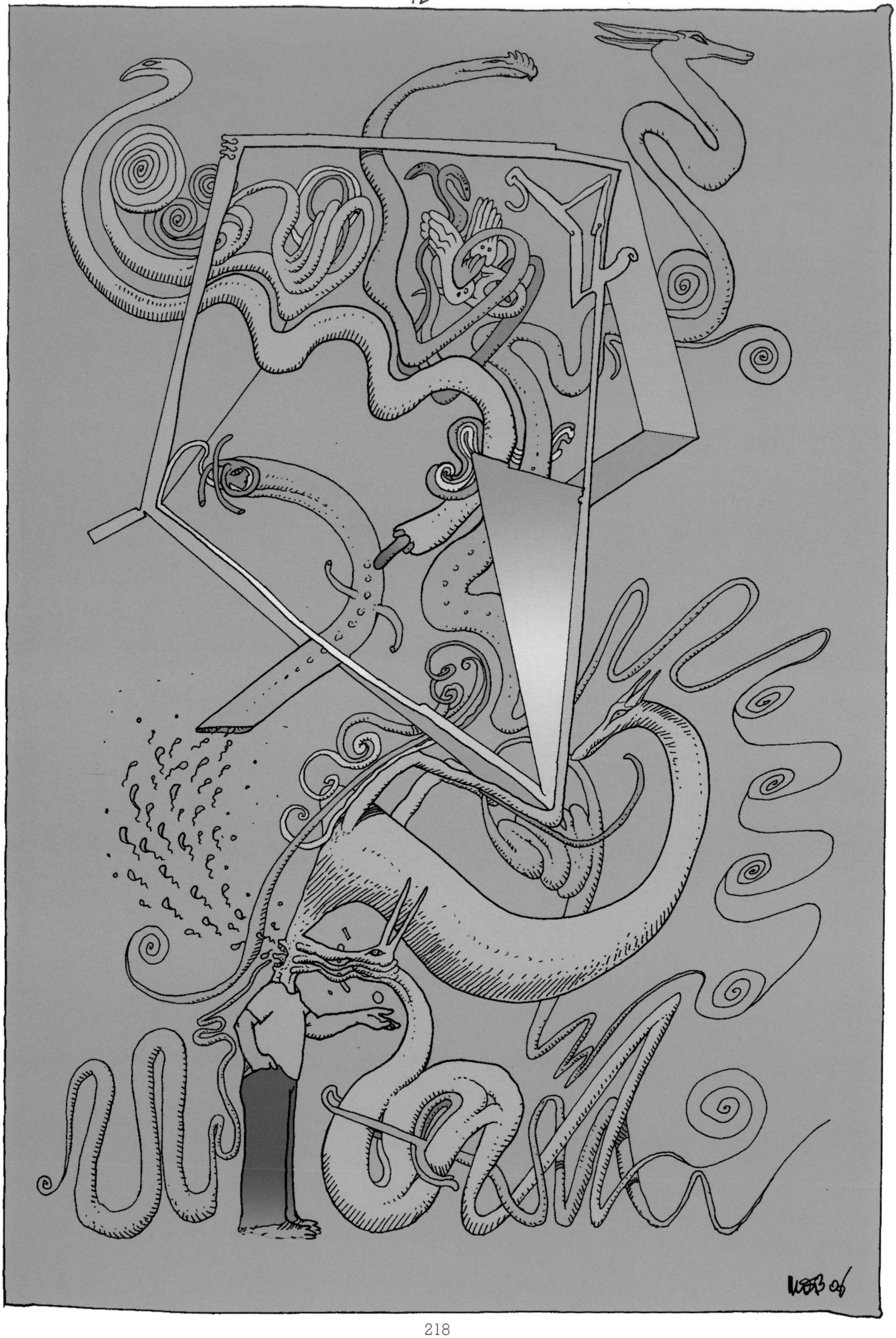

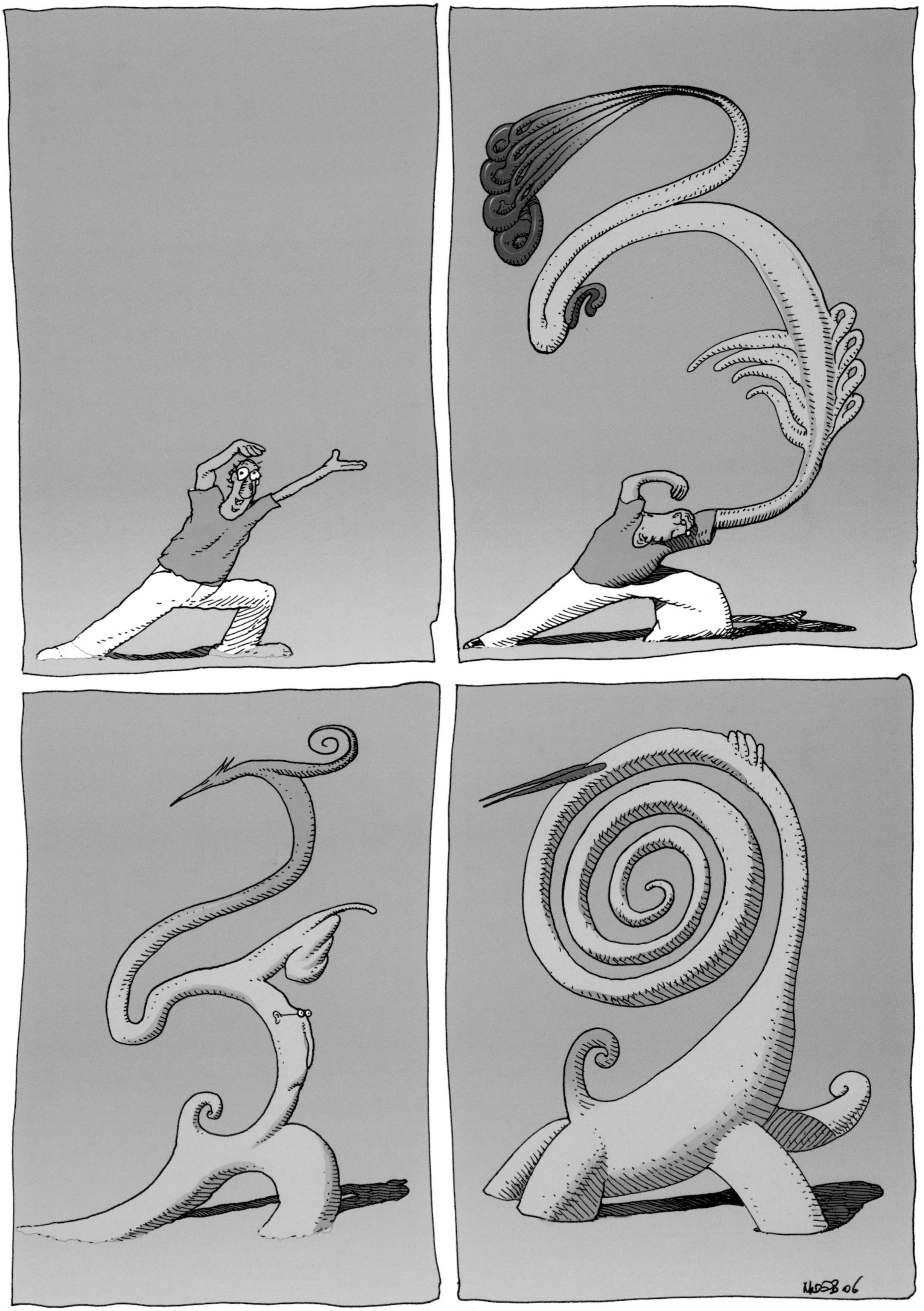

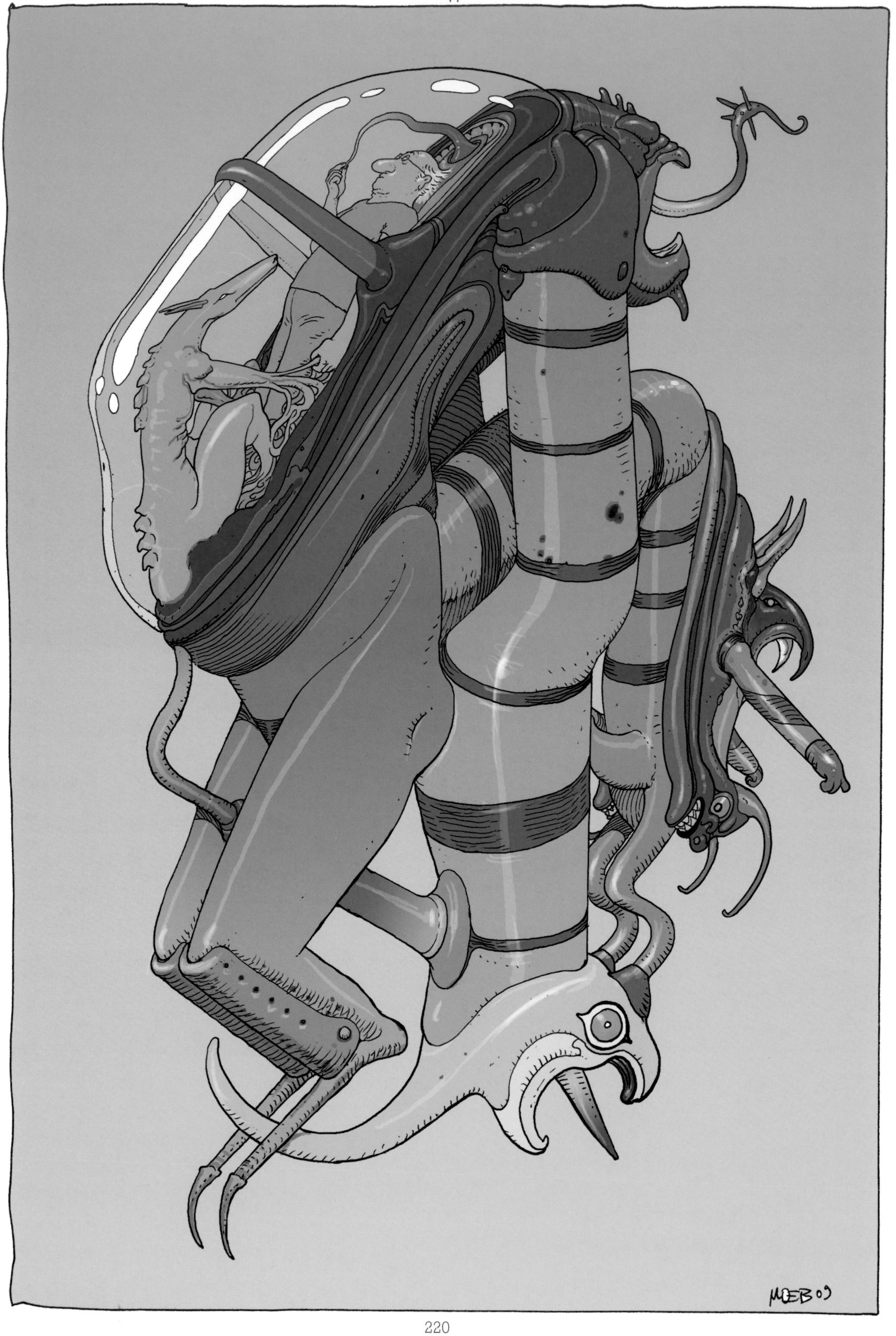
MŒB 09

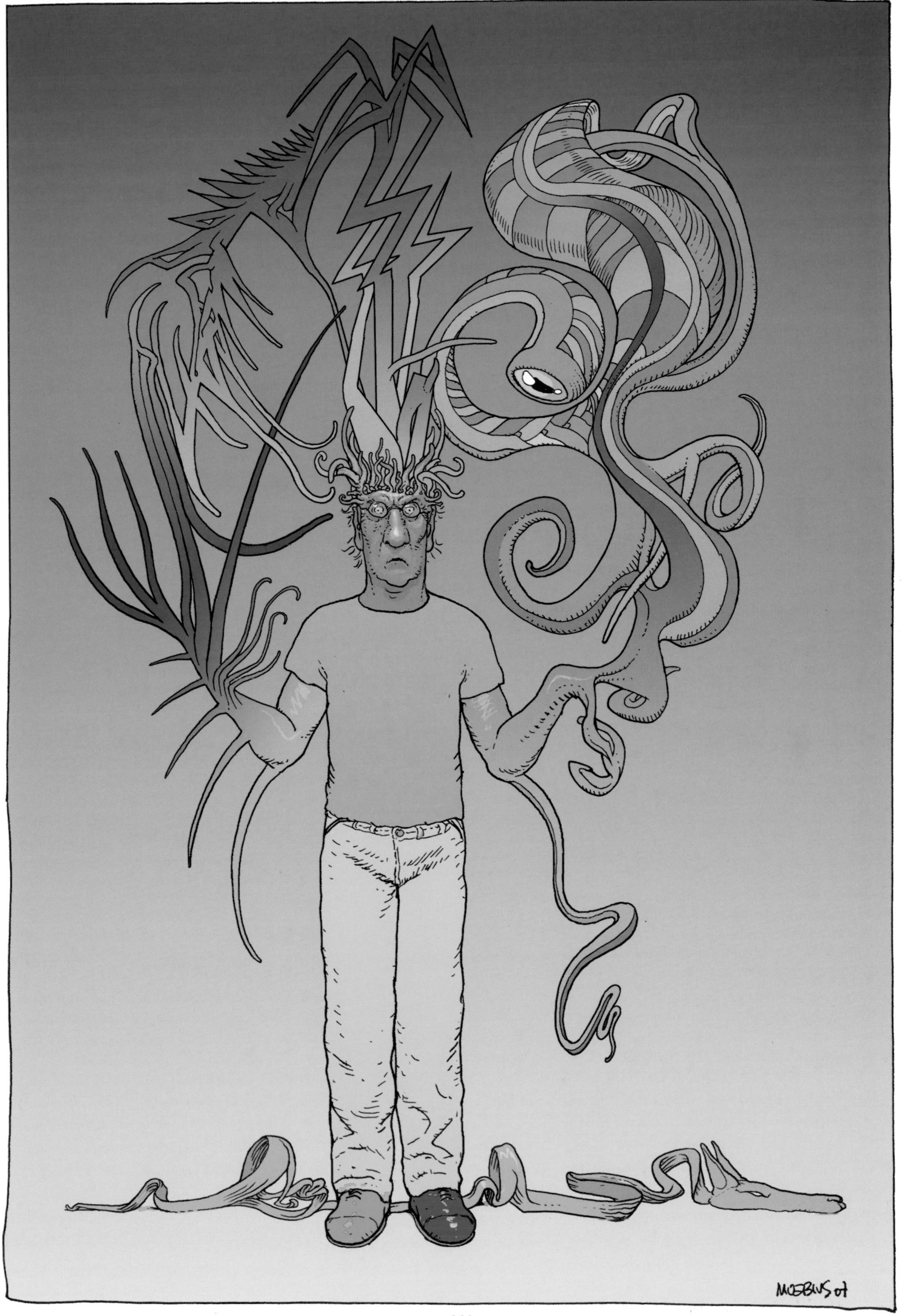
MOEBIUS 07

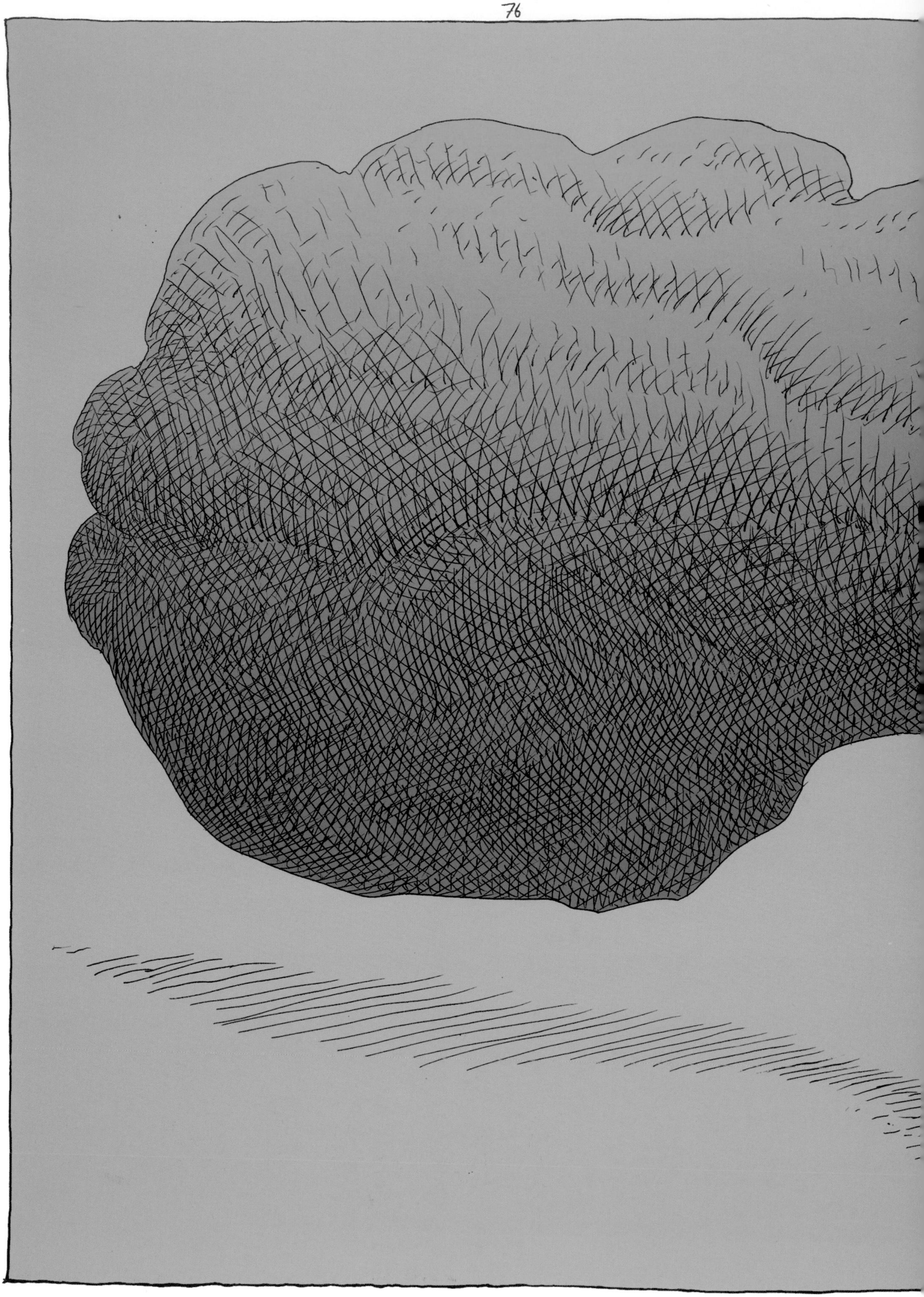

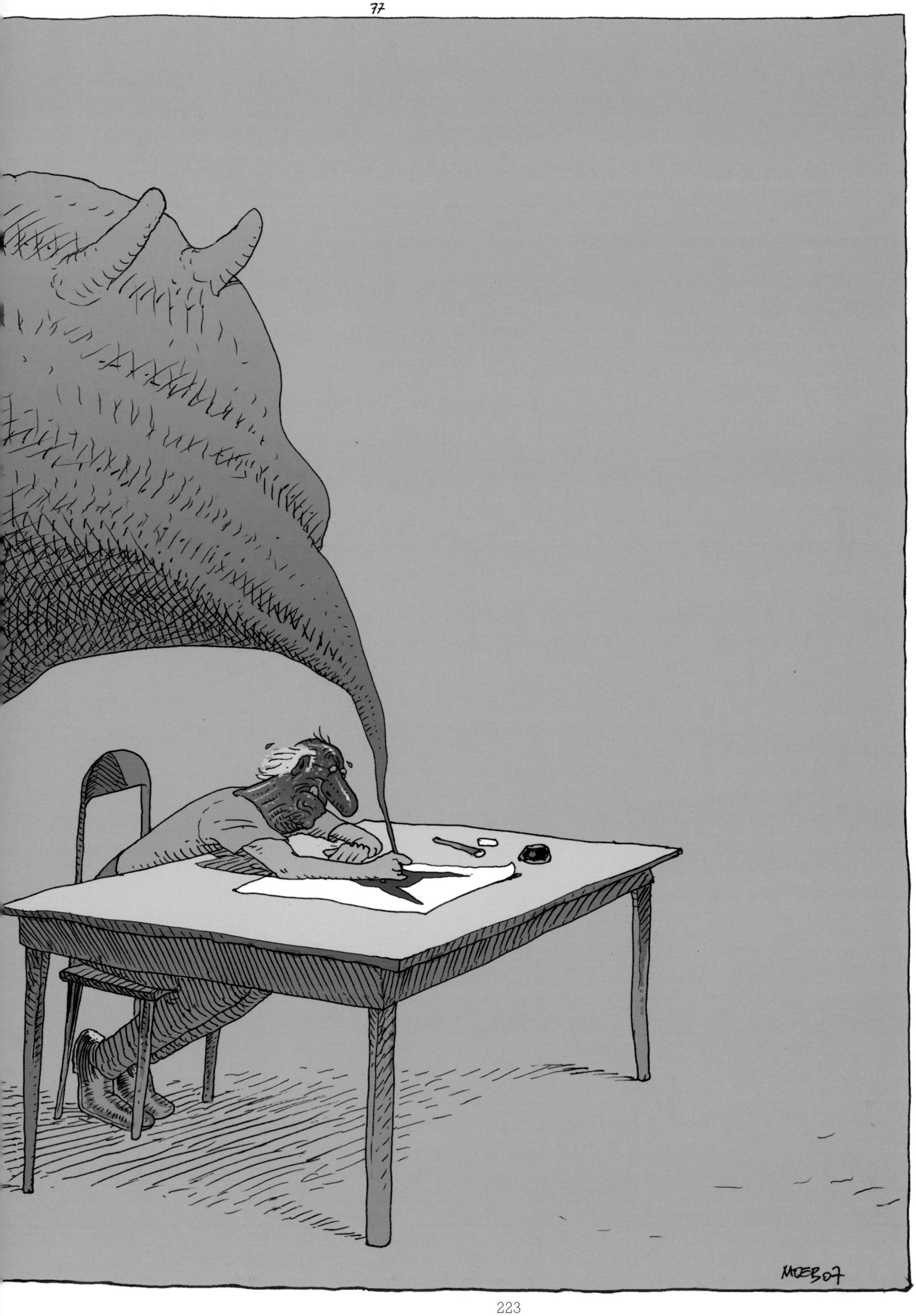
MŒB07

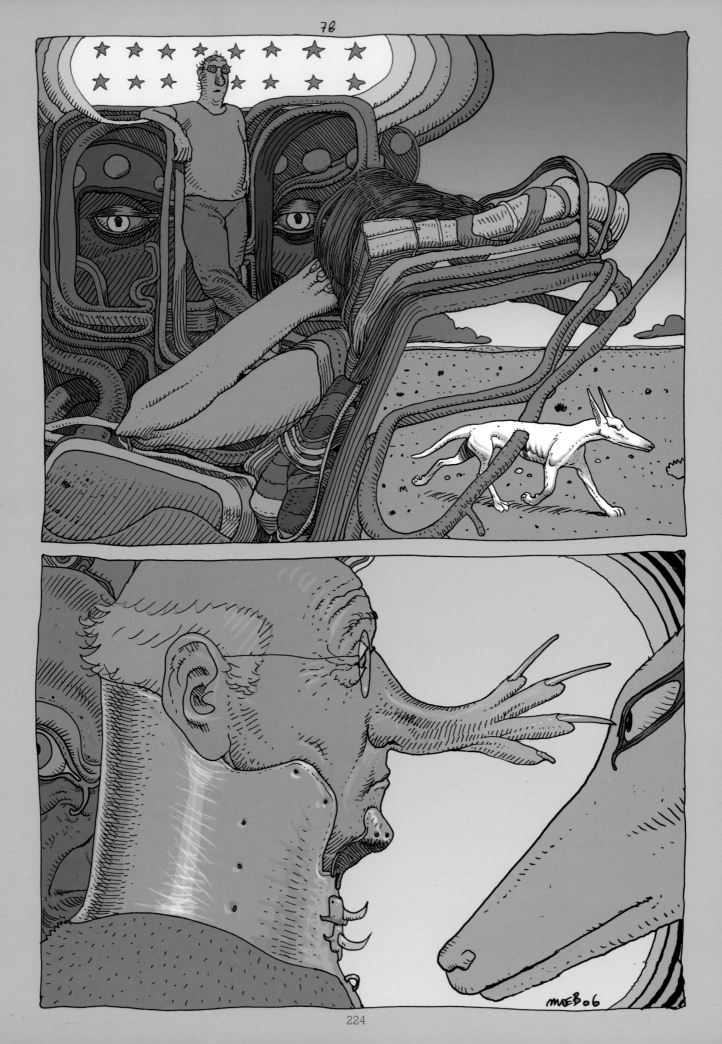

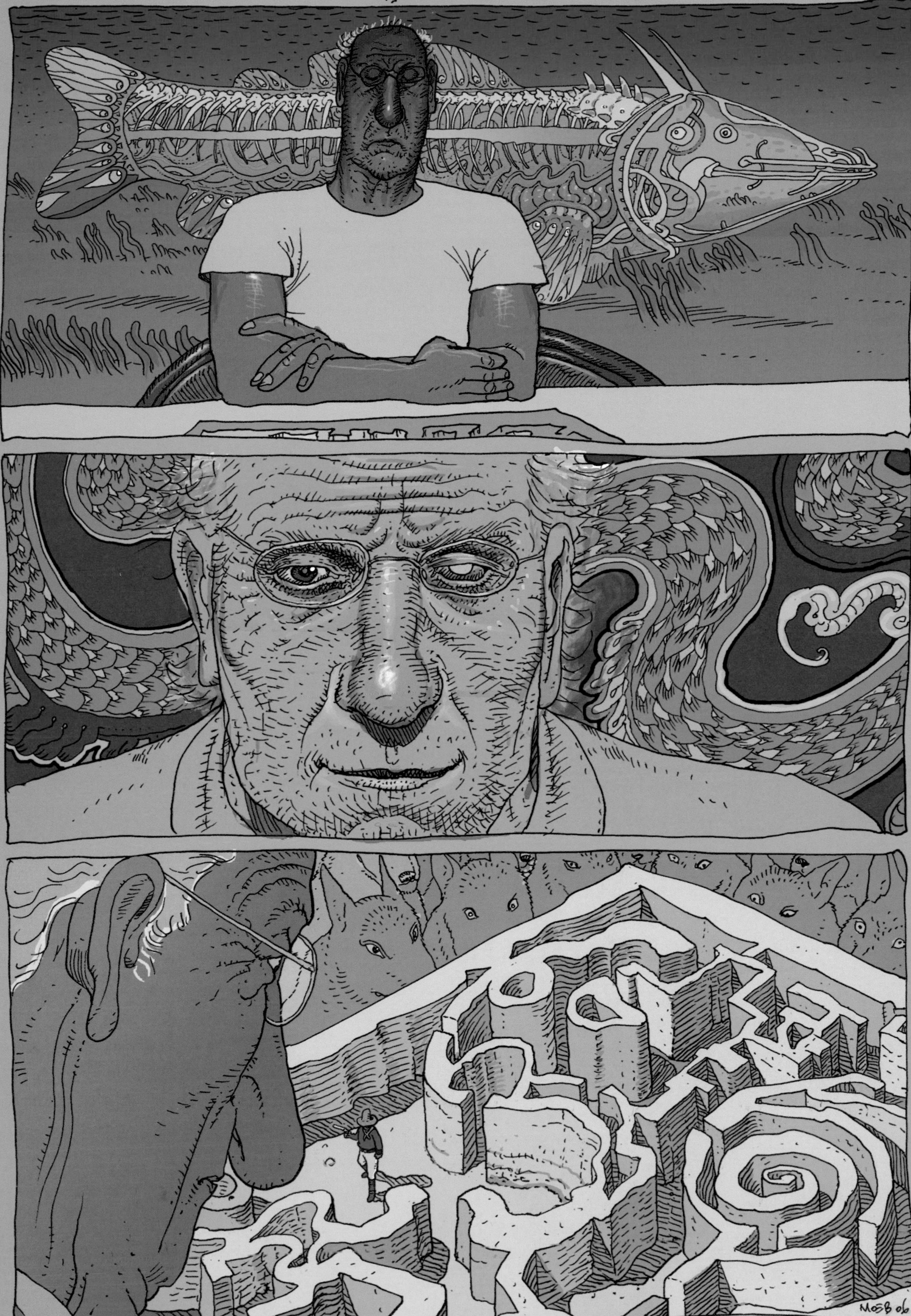
MœB 06

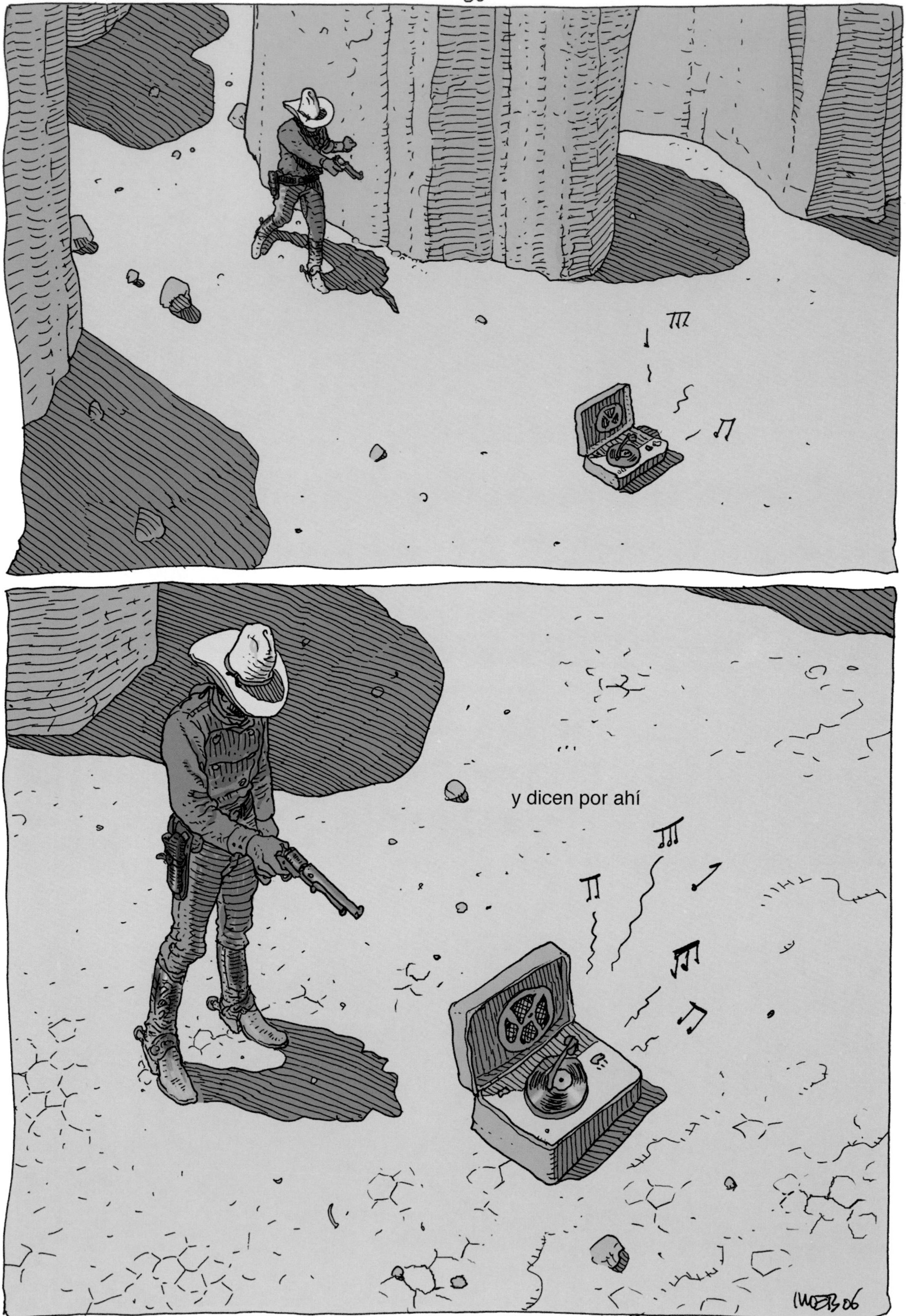
y dicen por ahí
MŒBIUS 06

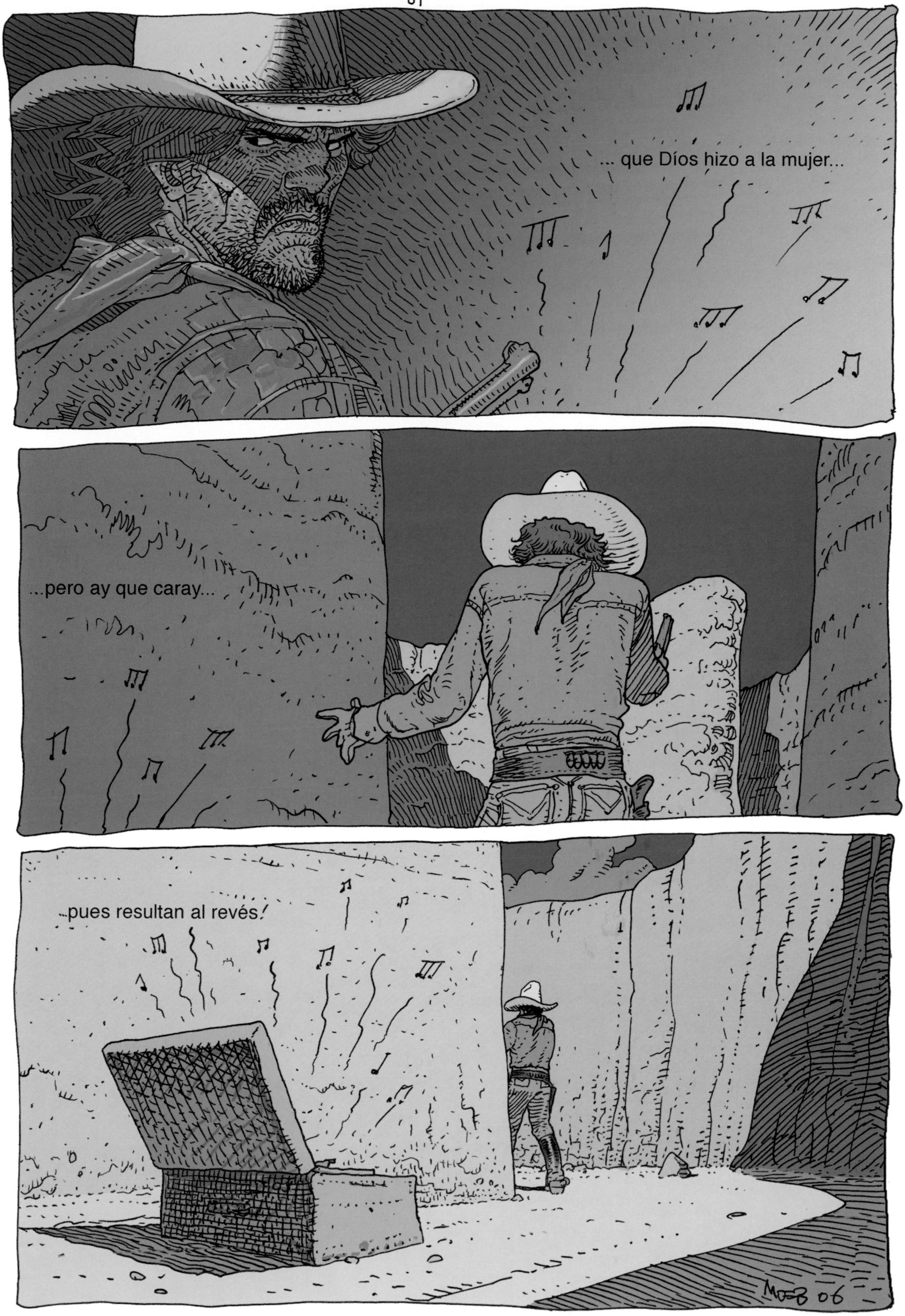
... que Díos hizo a la mujer...
...pero ay que caray...
..pues resultan al revés.
MOEB 06

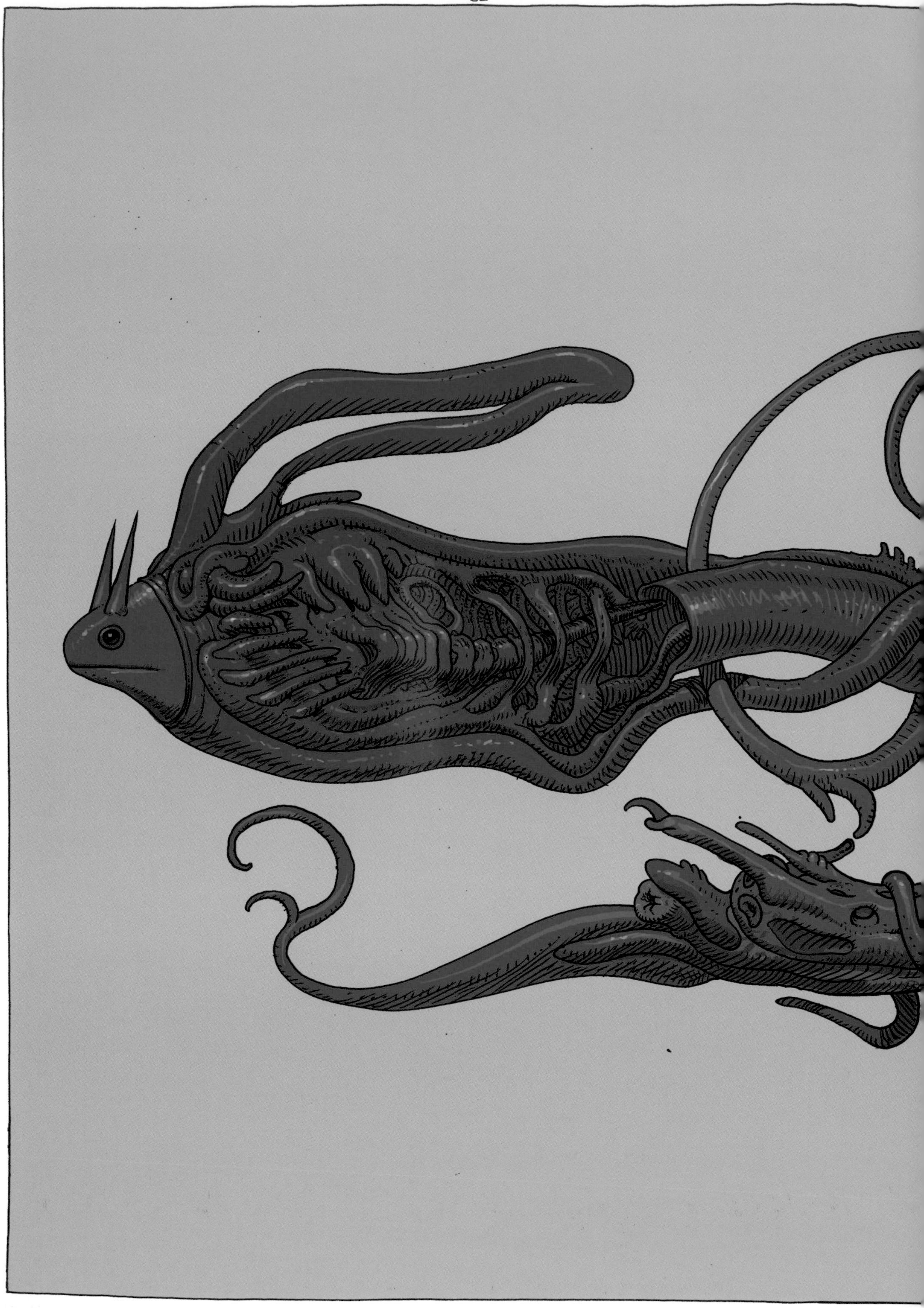

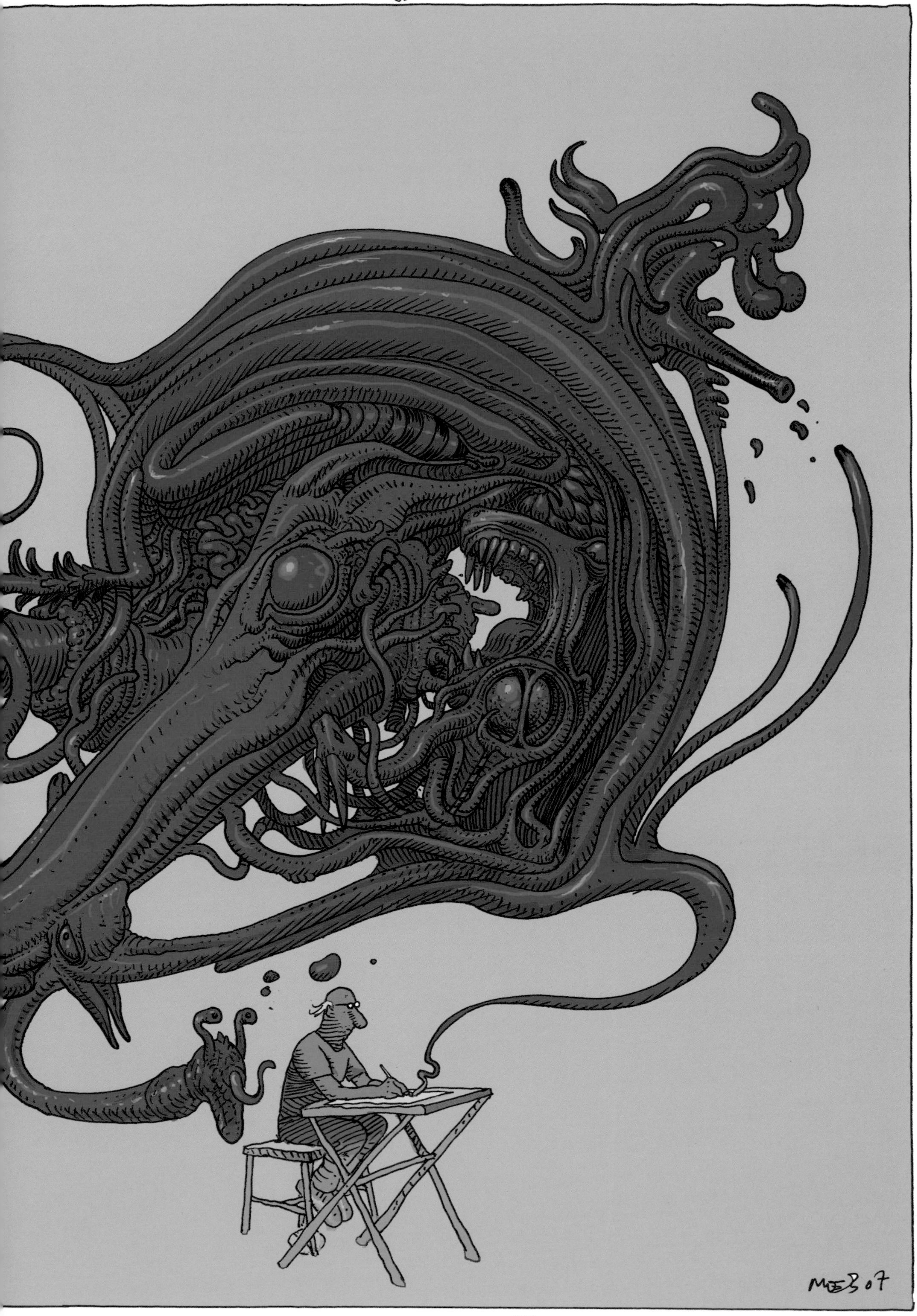

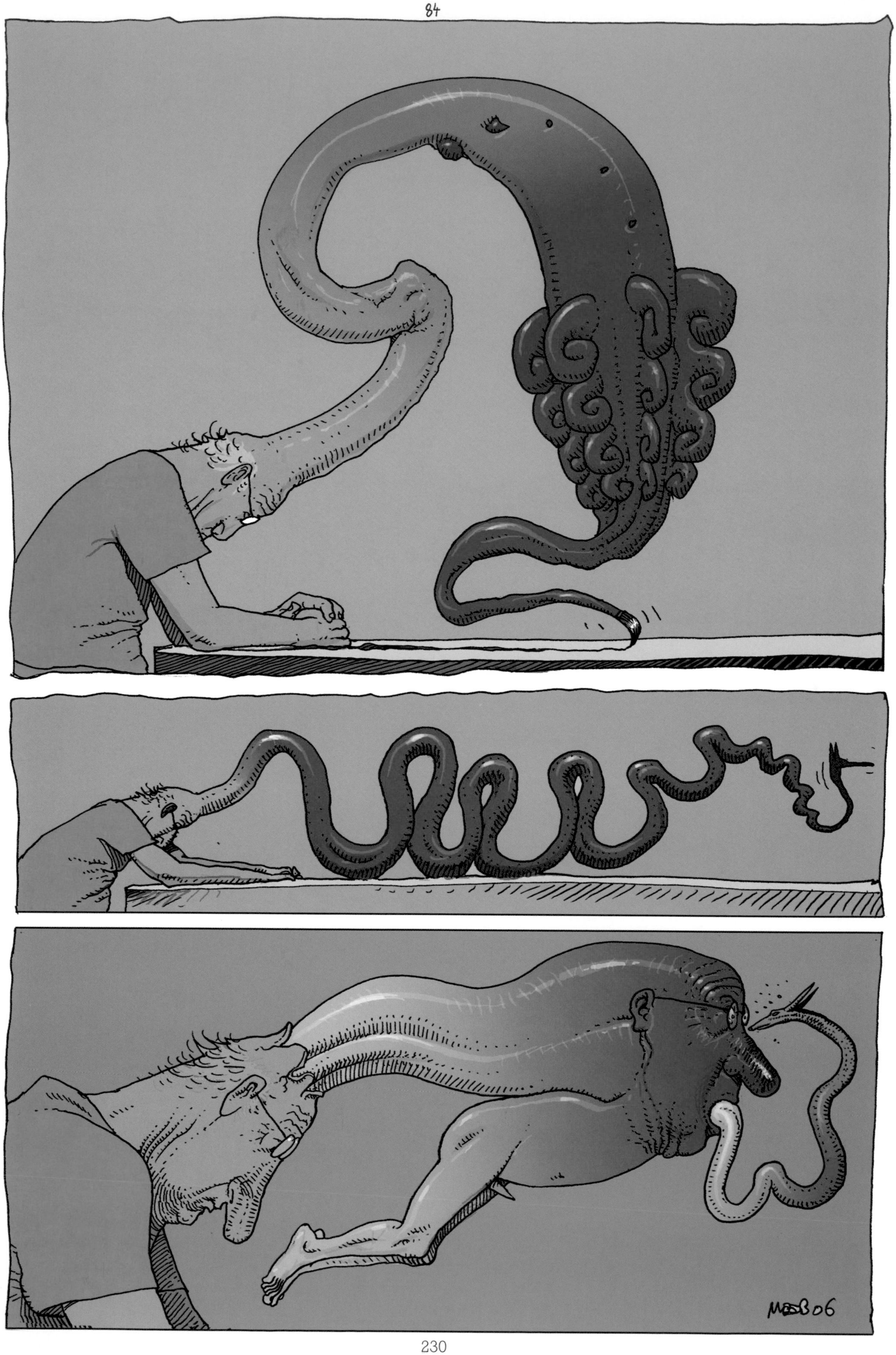
MŒB 06

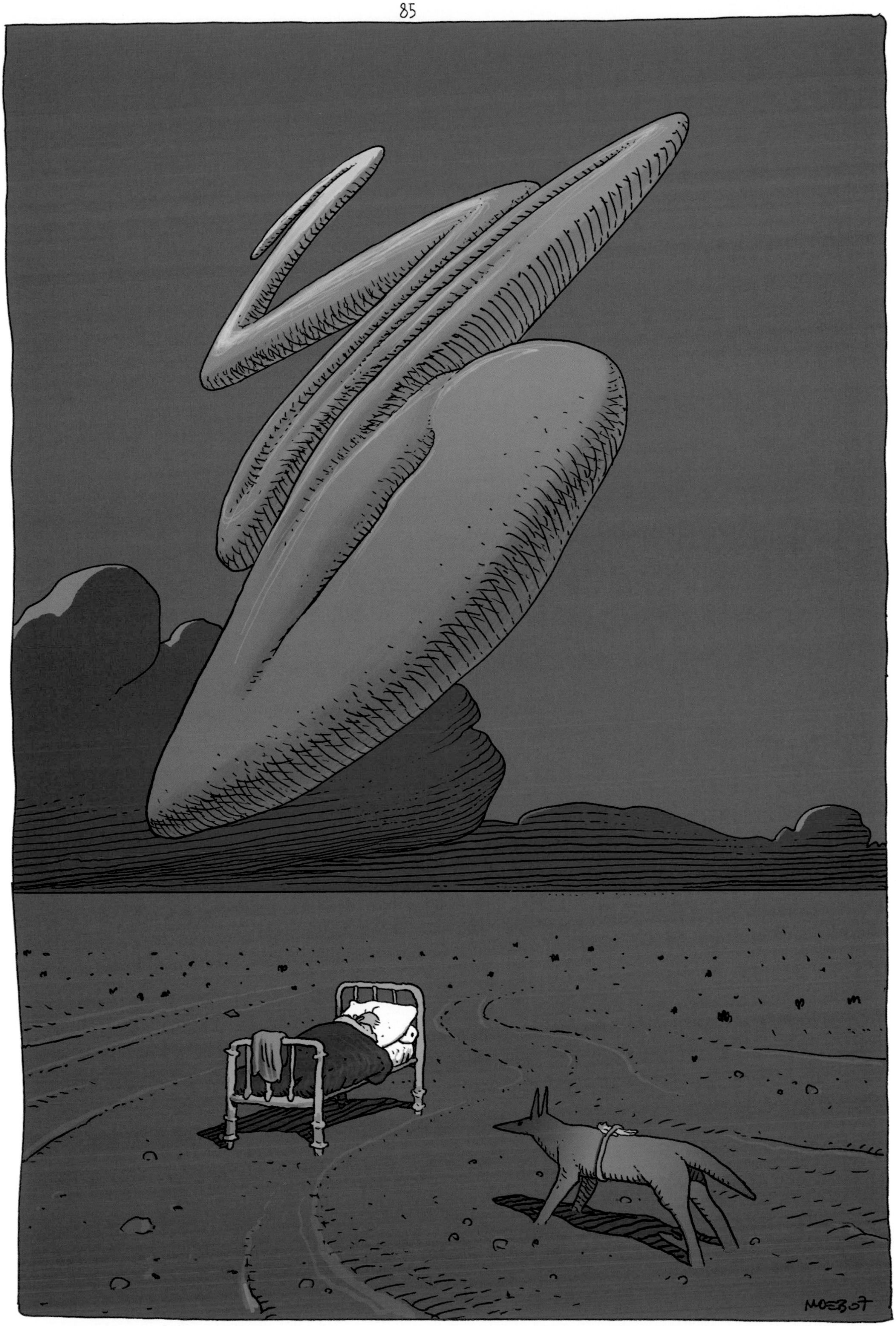
MOEB07

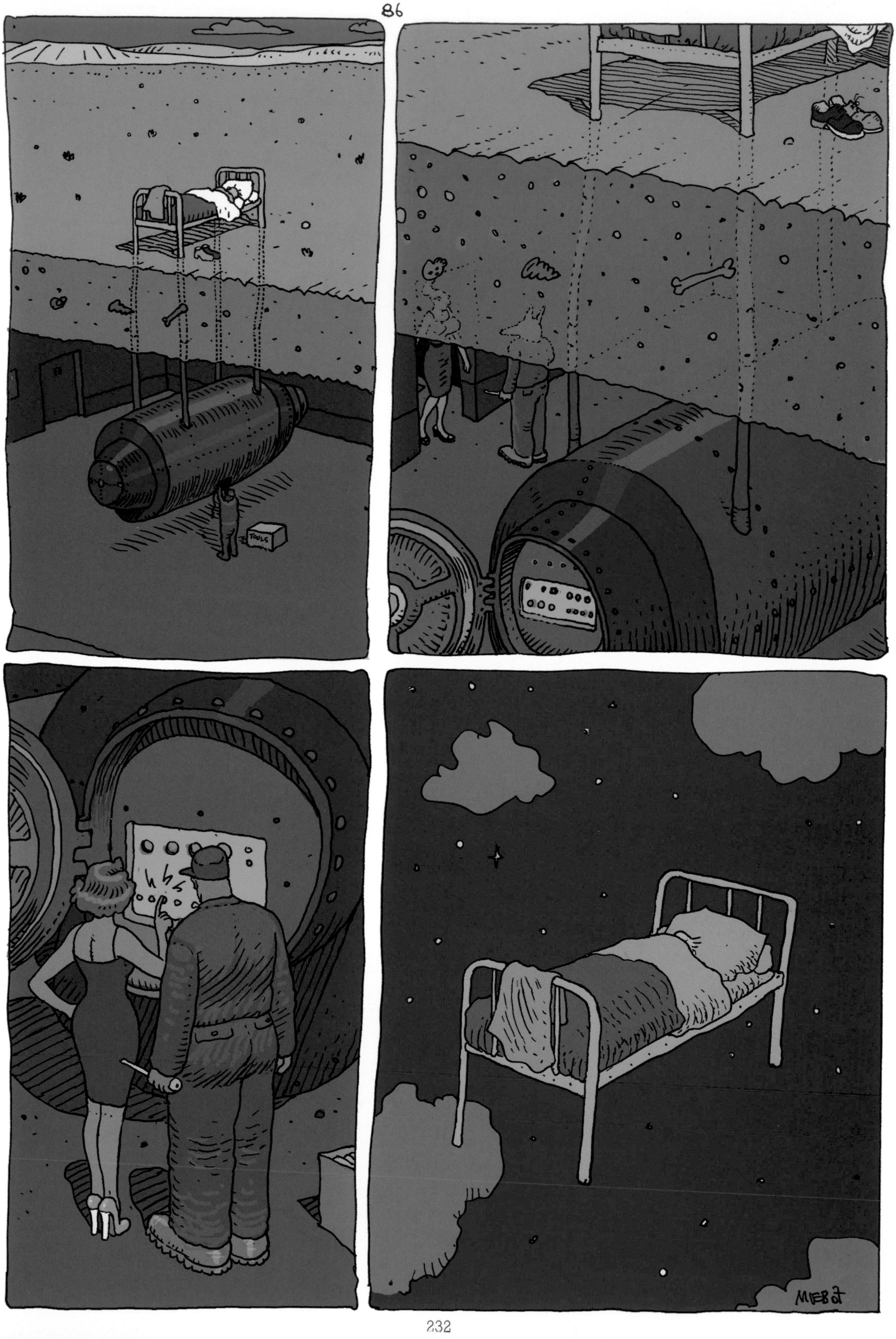
TOOLS

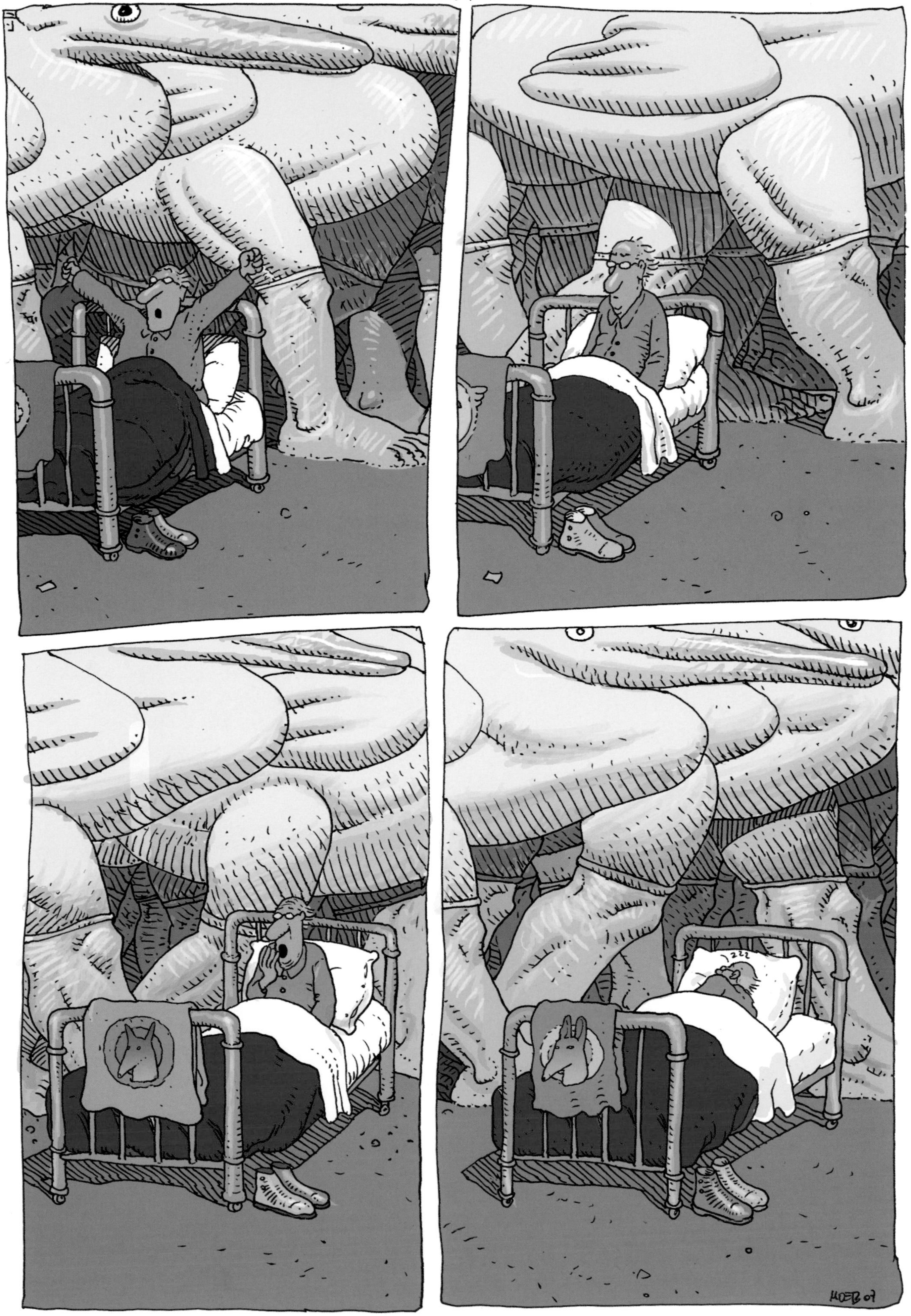
zzz

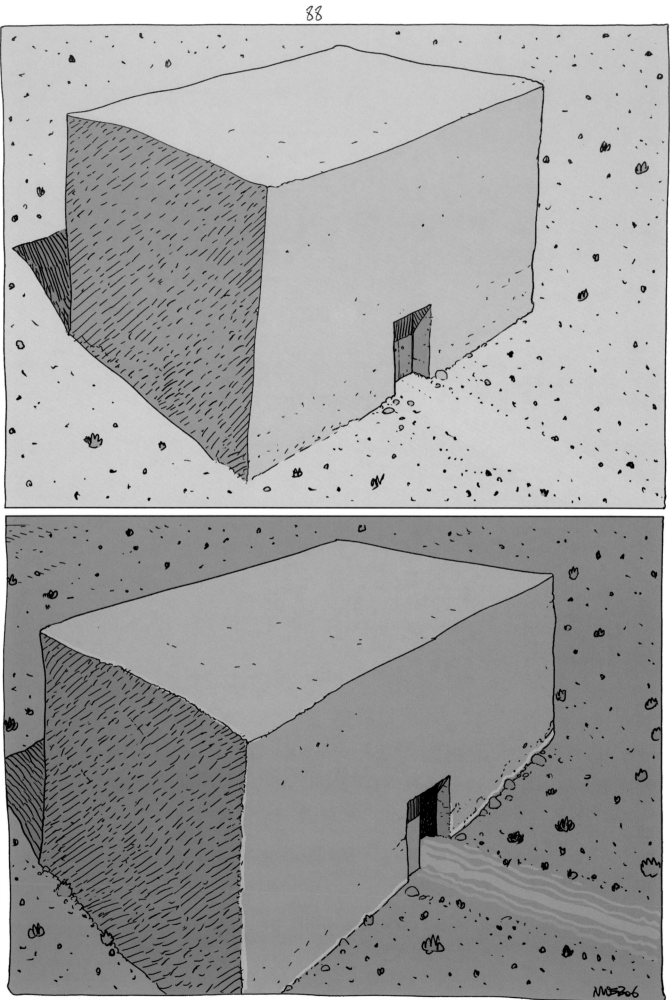

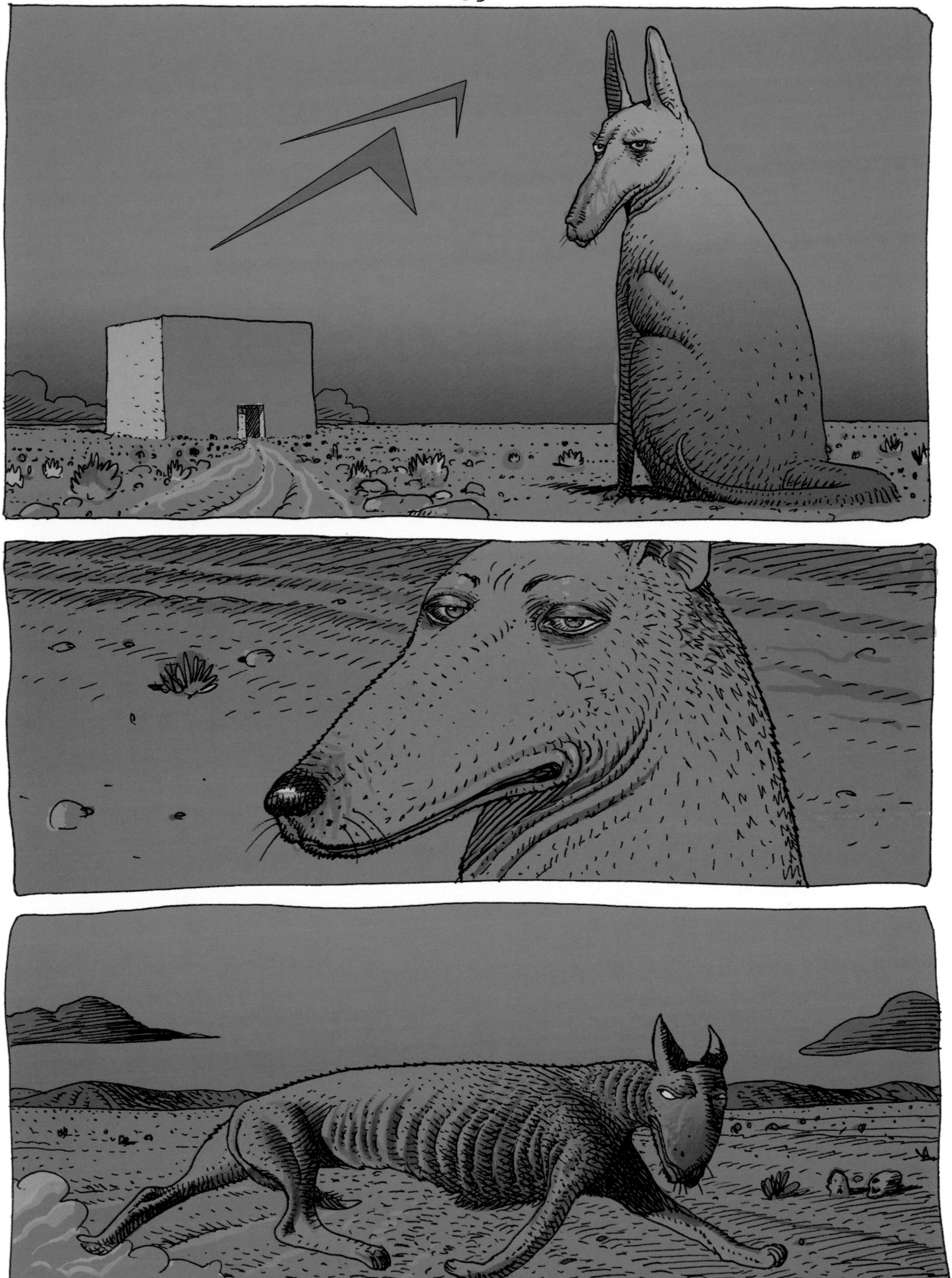
MOEBIUS 06

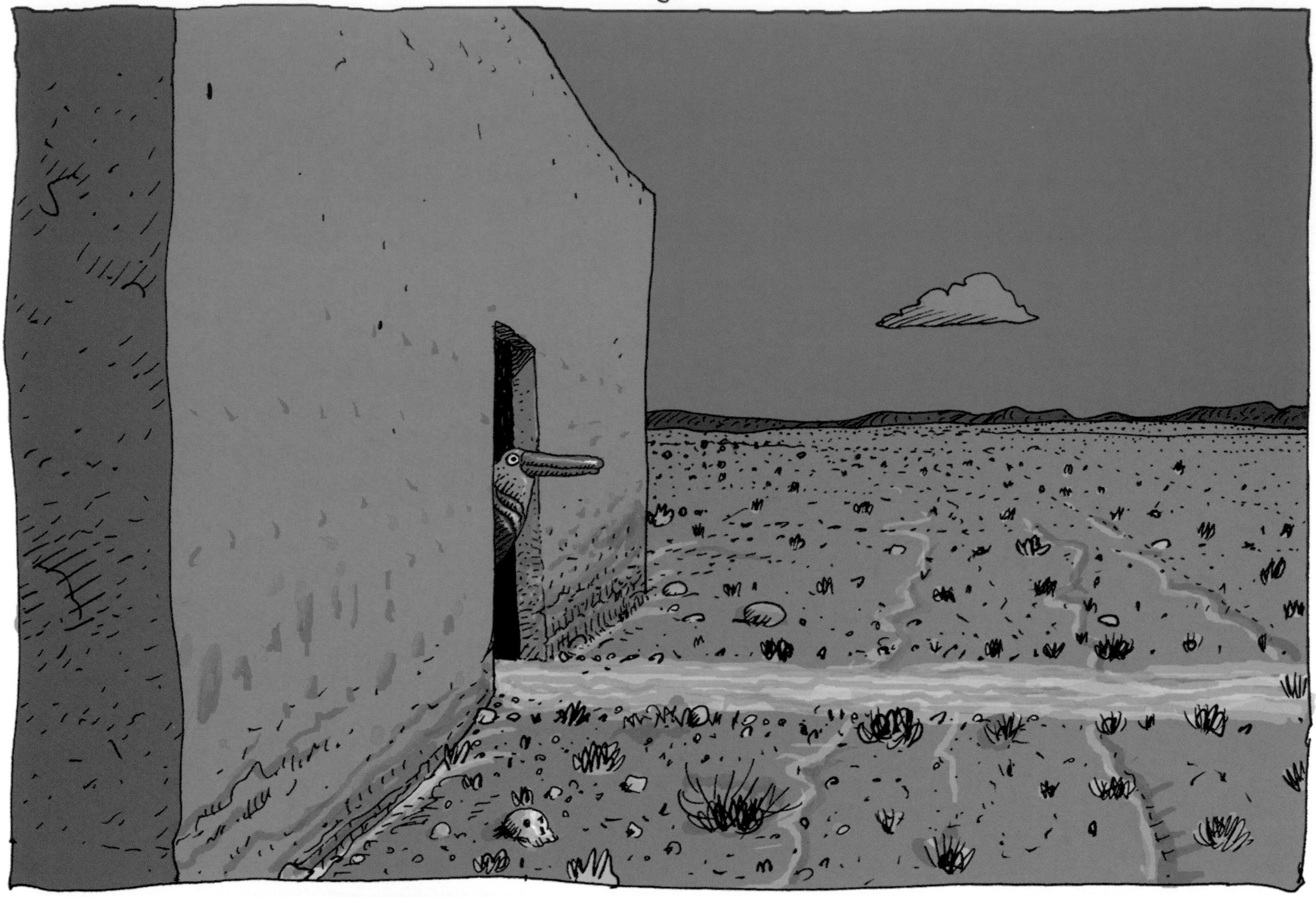

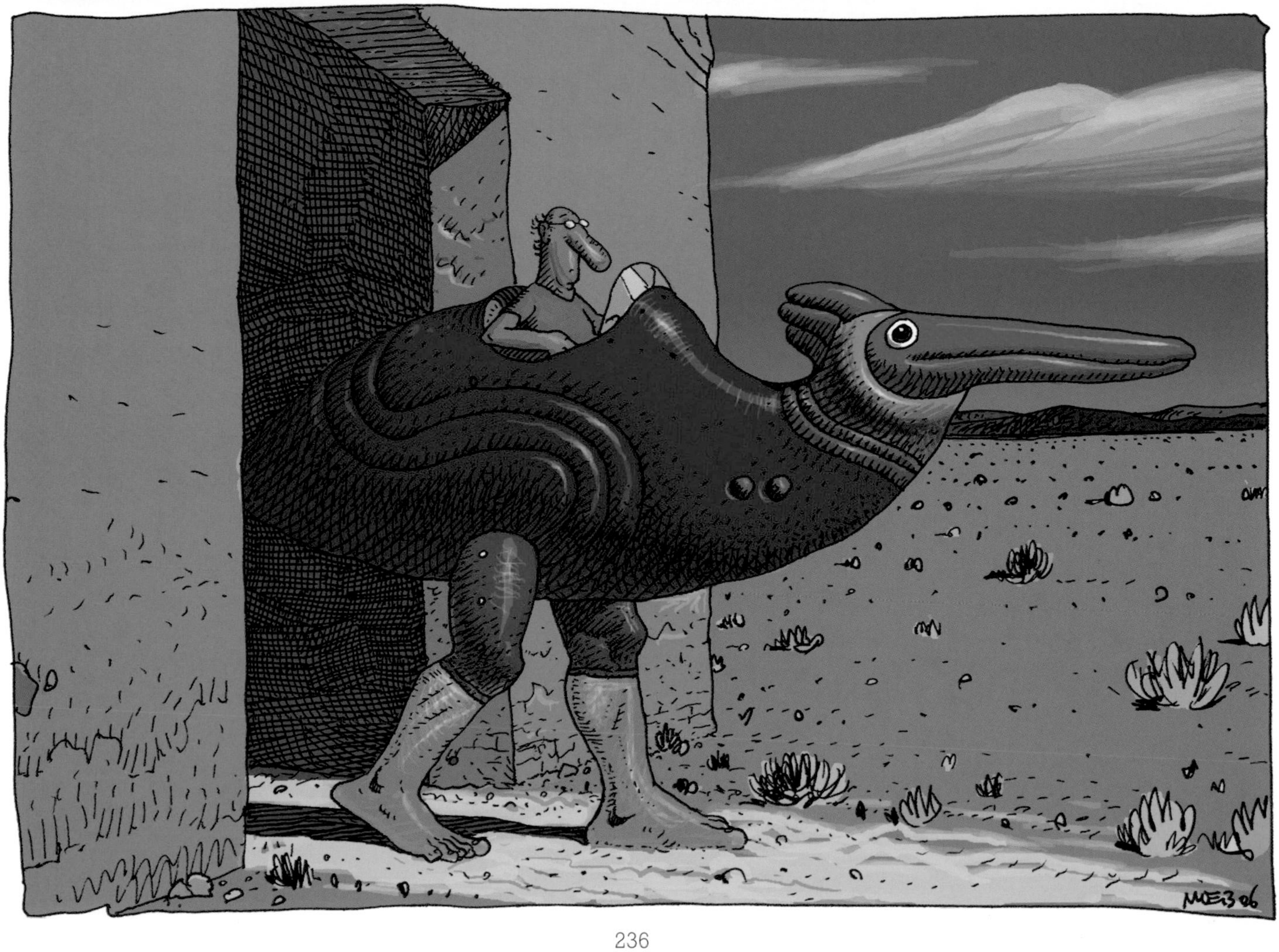

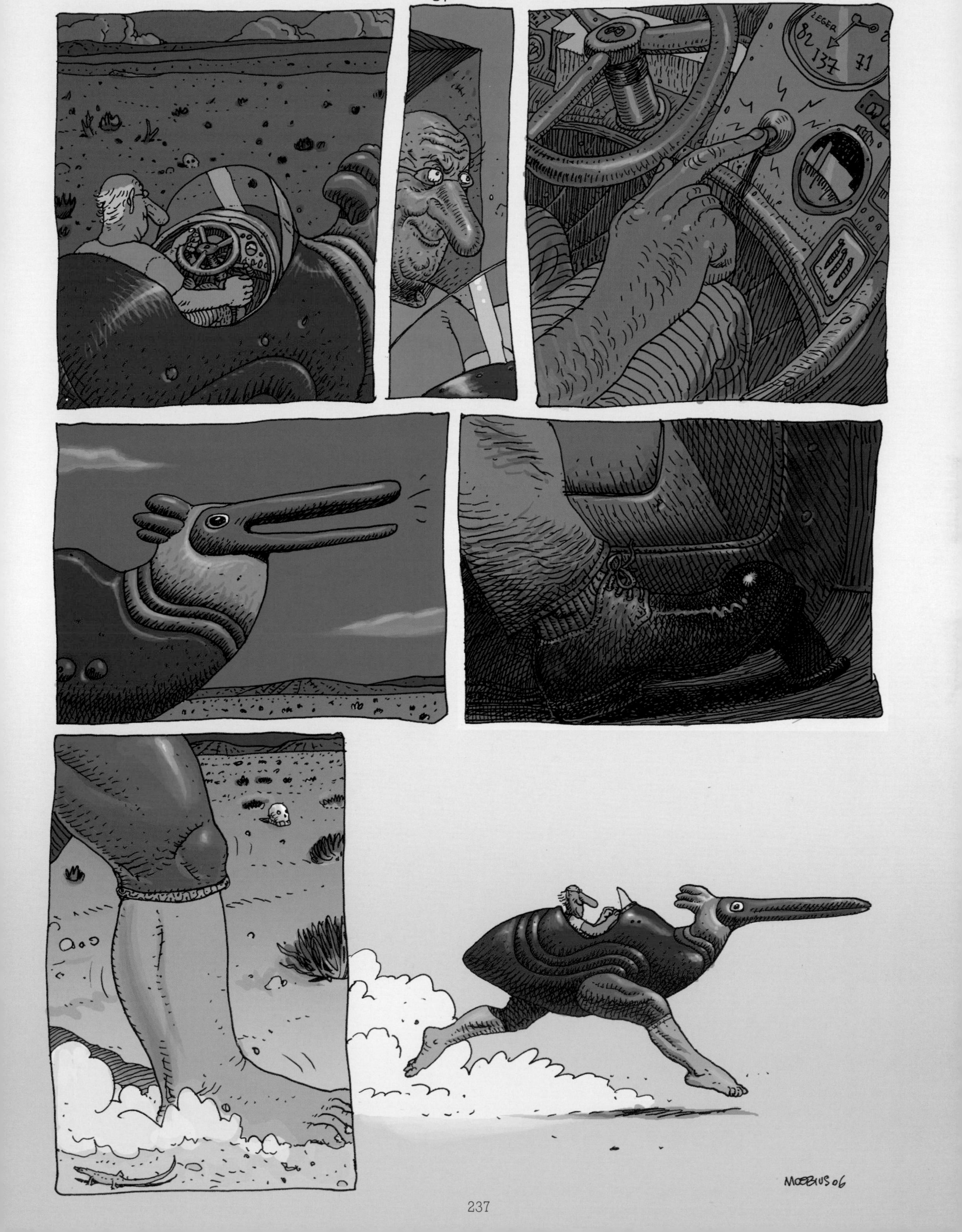
MOEBIUS 06

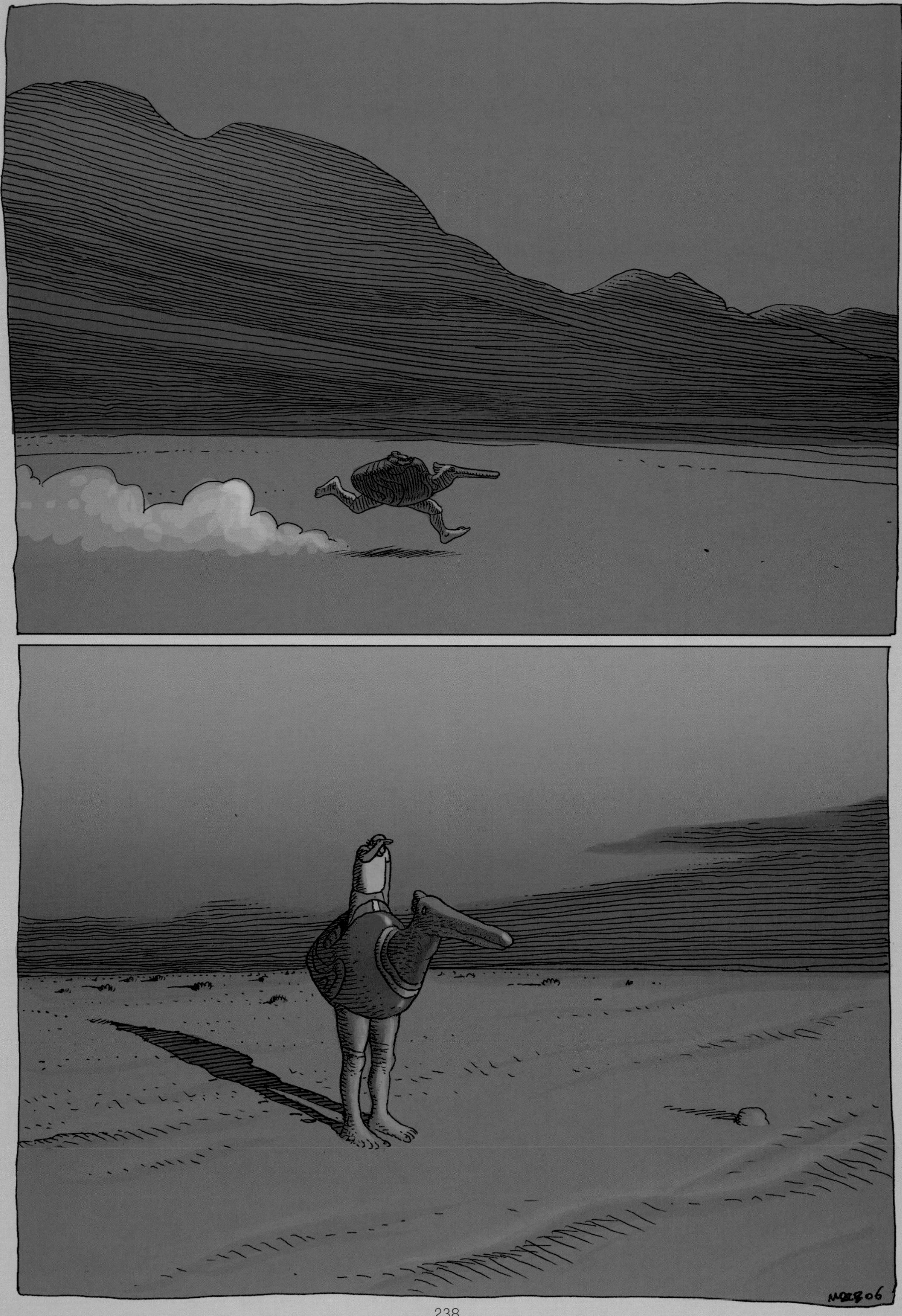

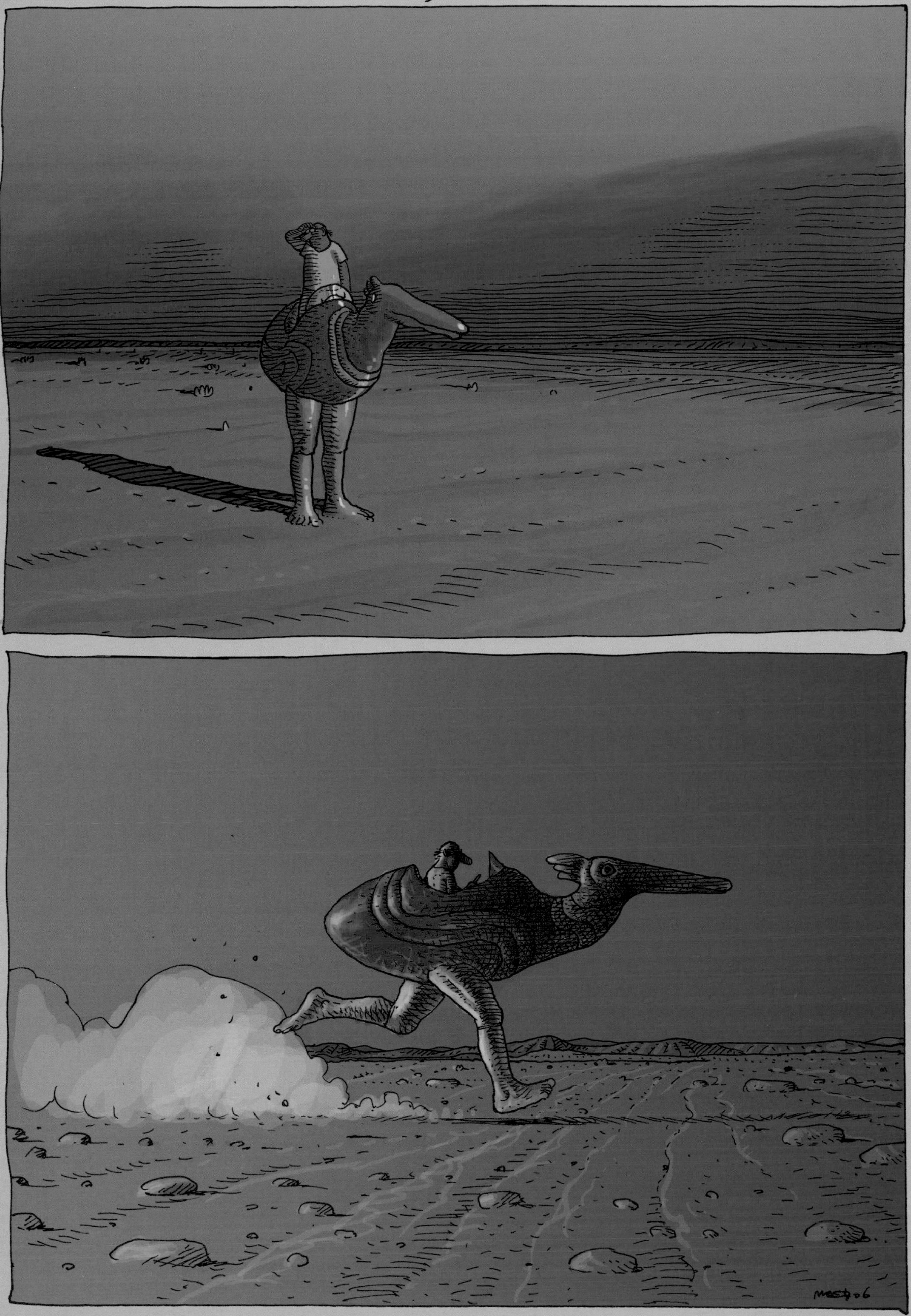

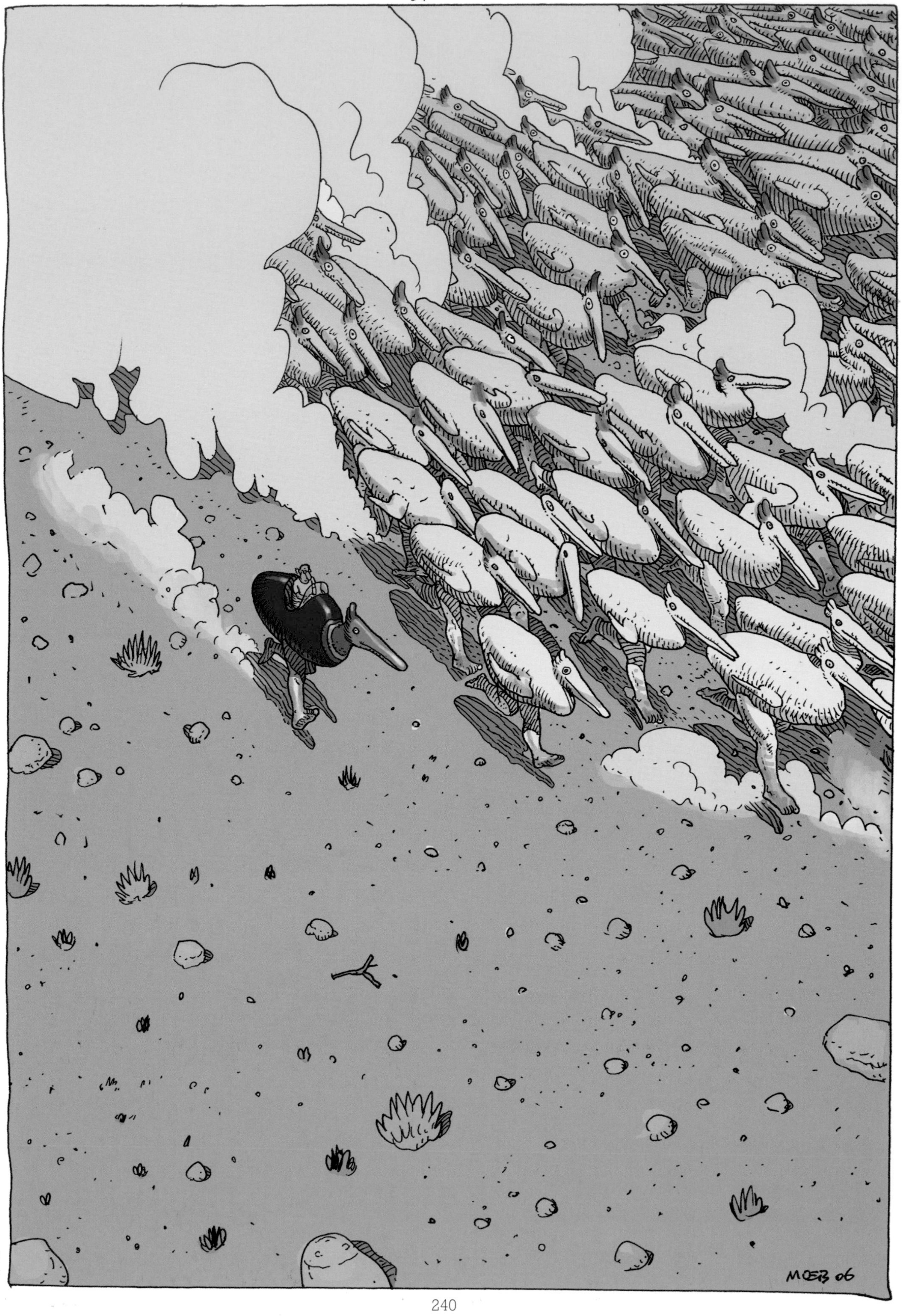
MOEB 06

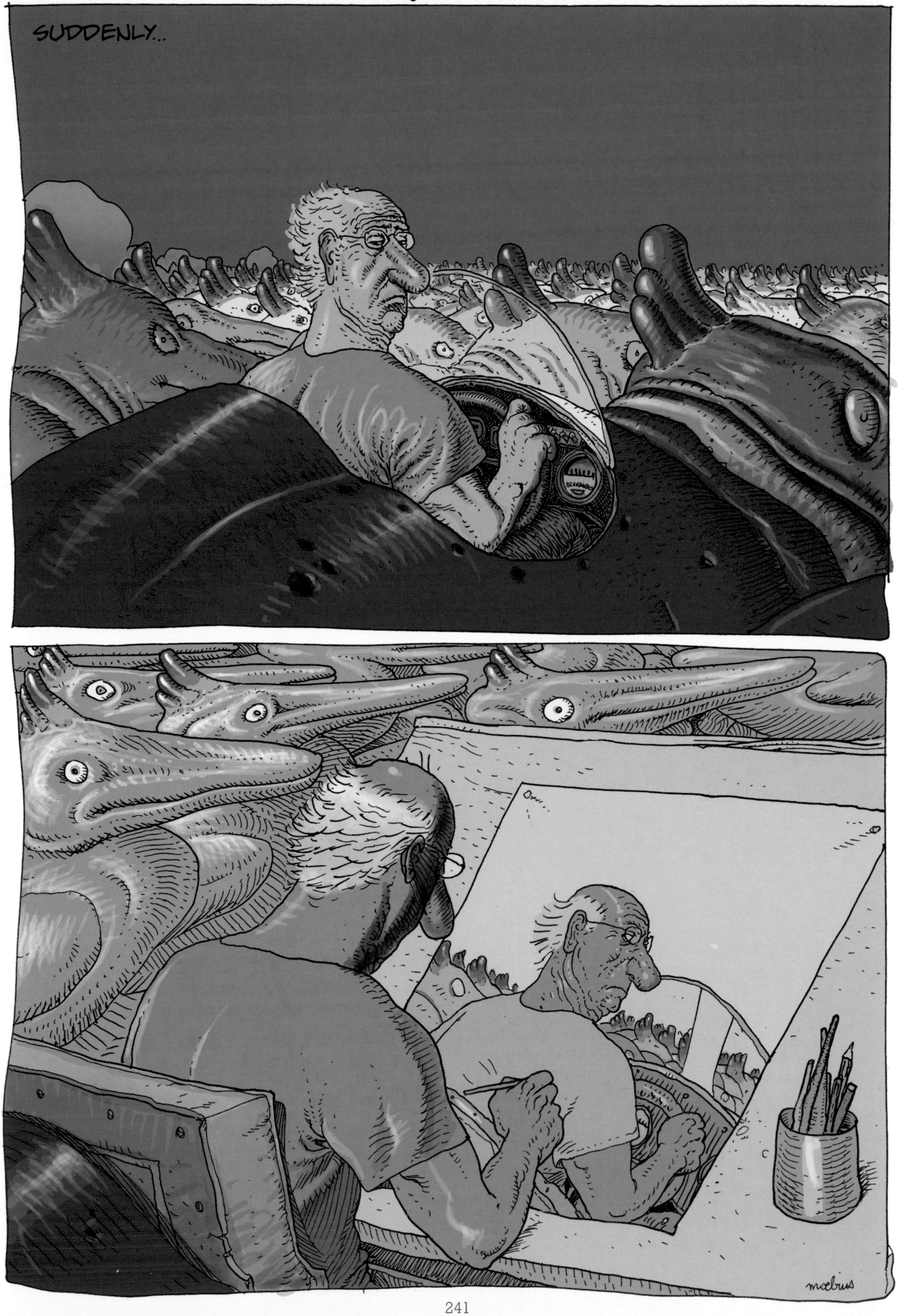
SUDDENLY…
moebius

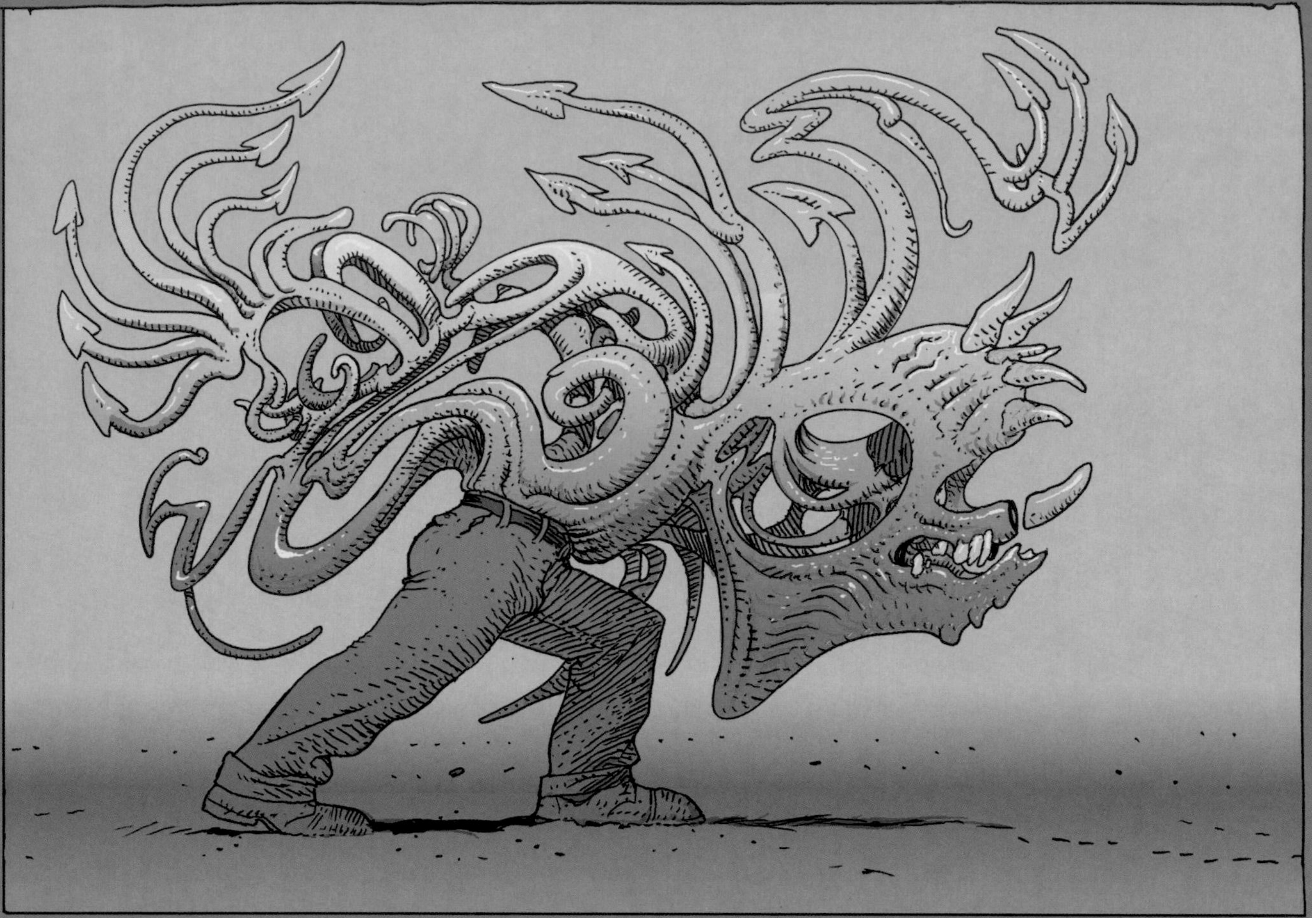

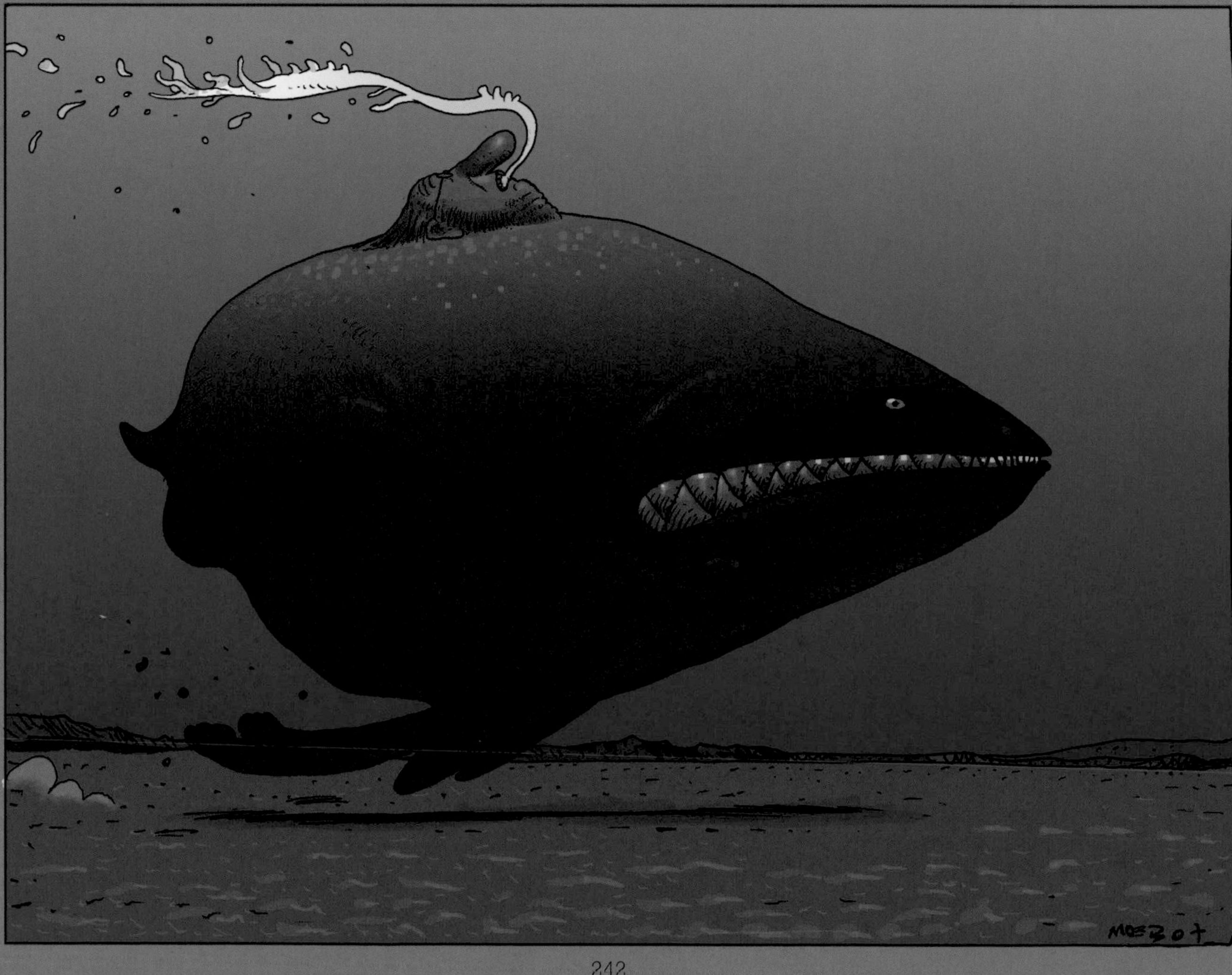
MOEB07

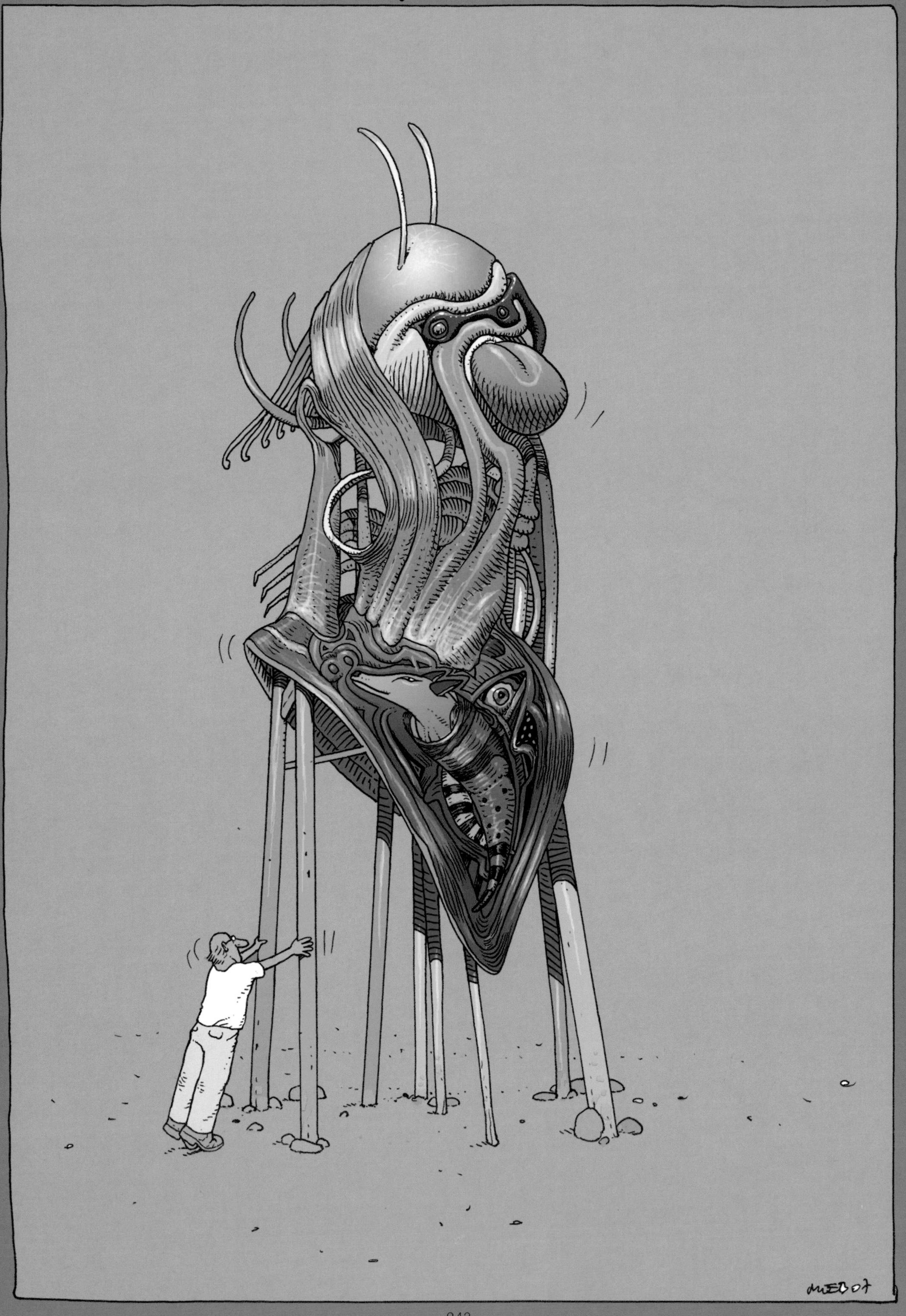

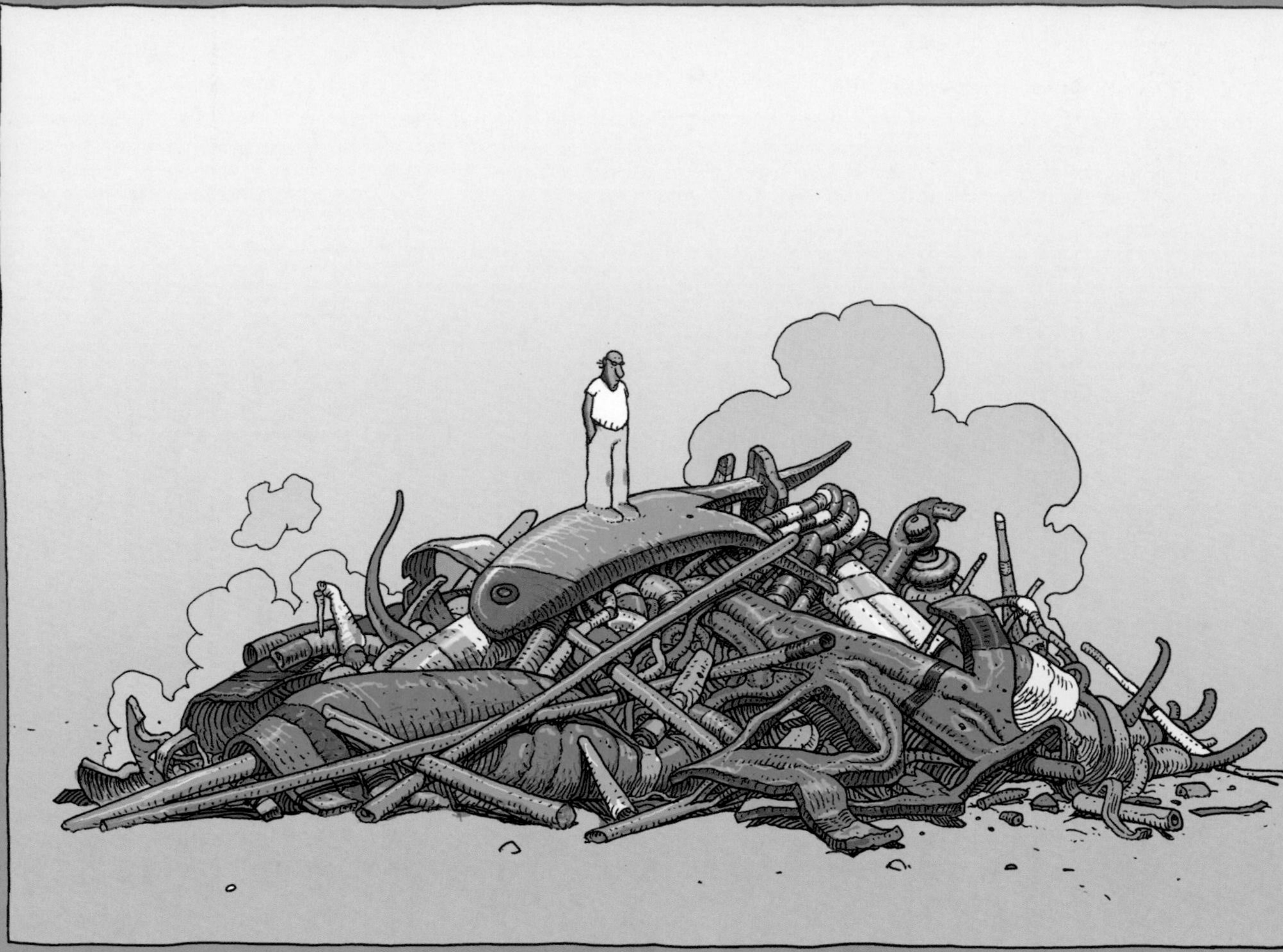

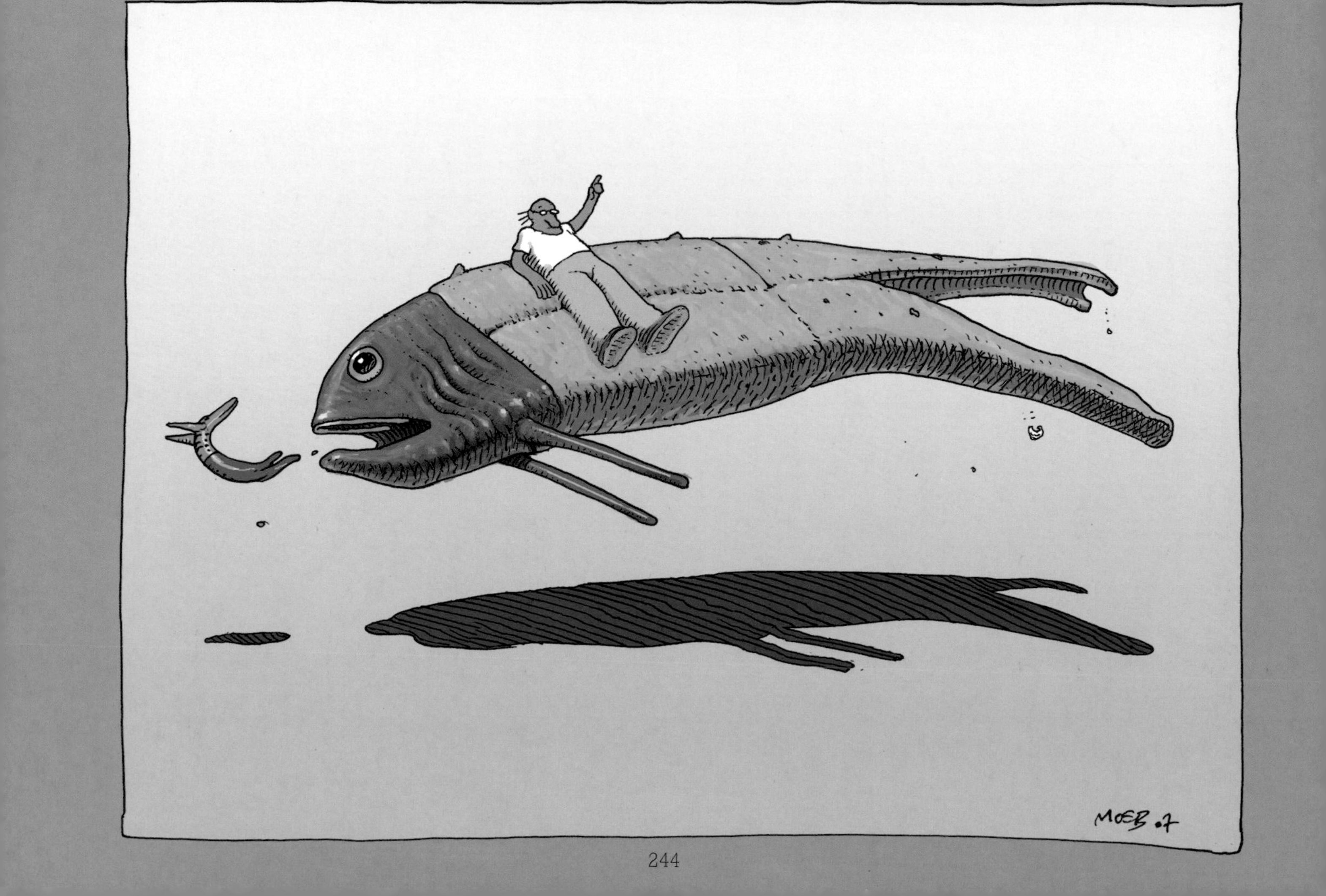
MOEB .07

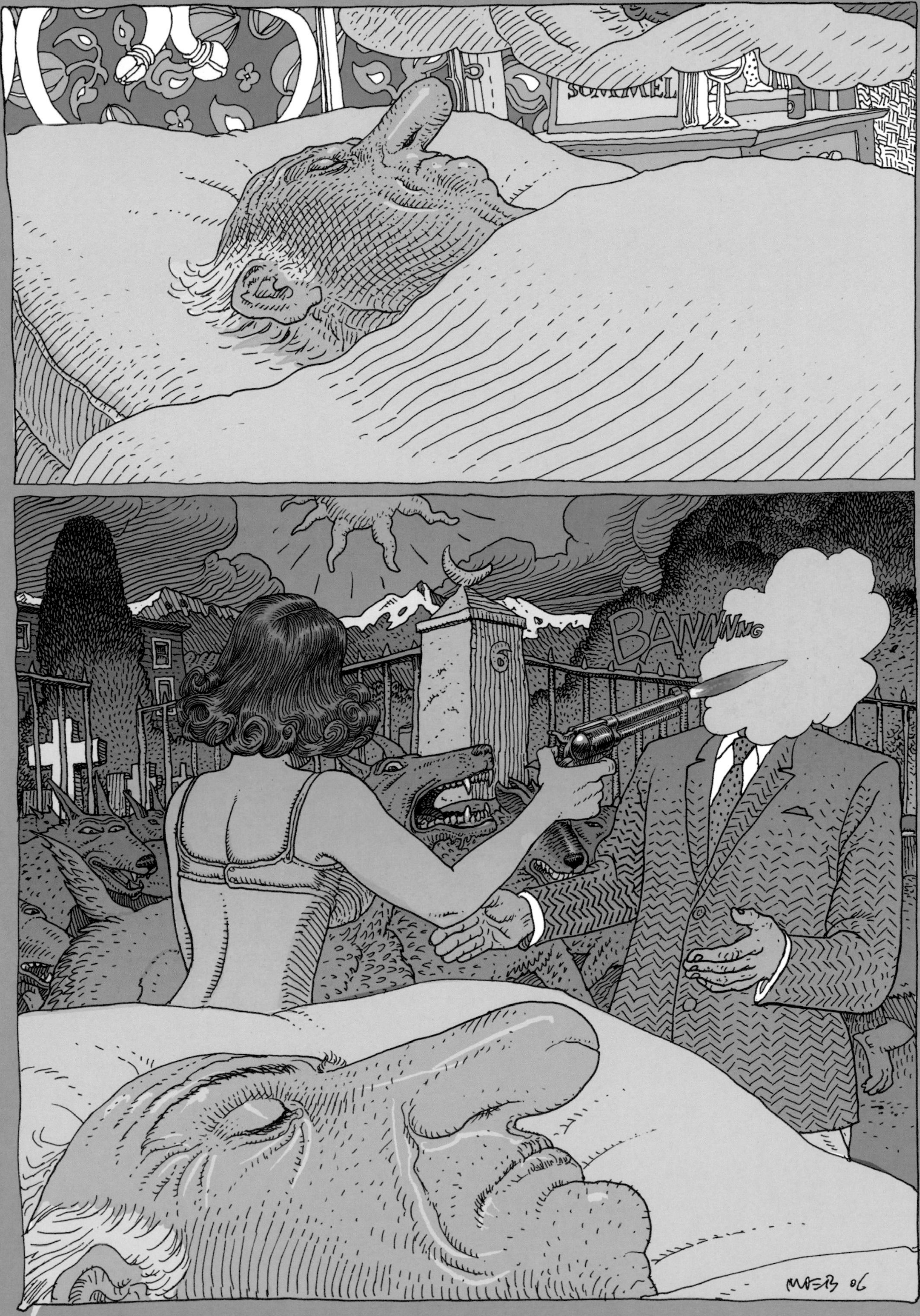
SOMMEL
6
BANNNNNG
MŒBIUS 06

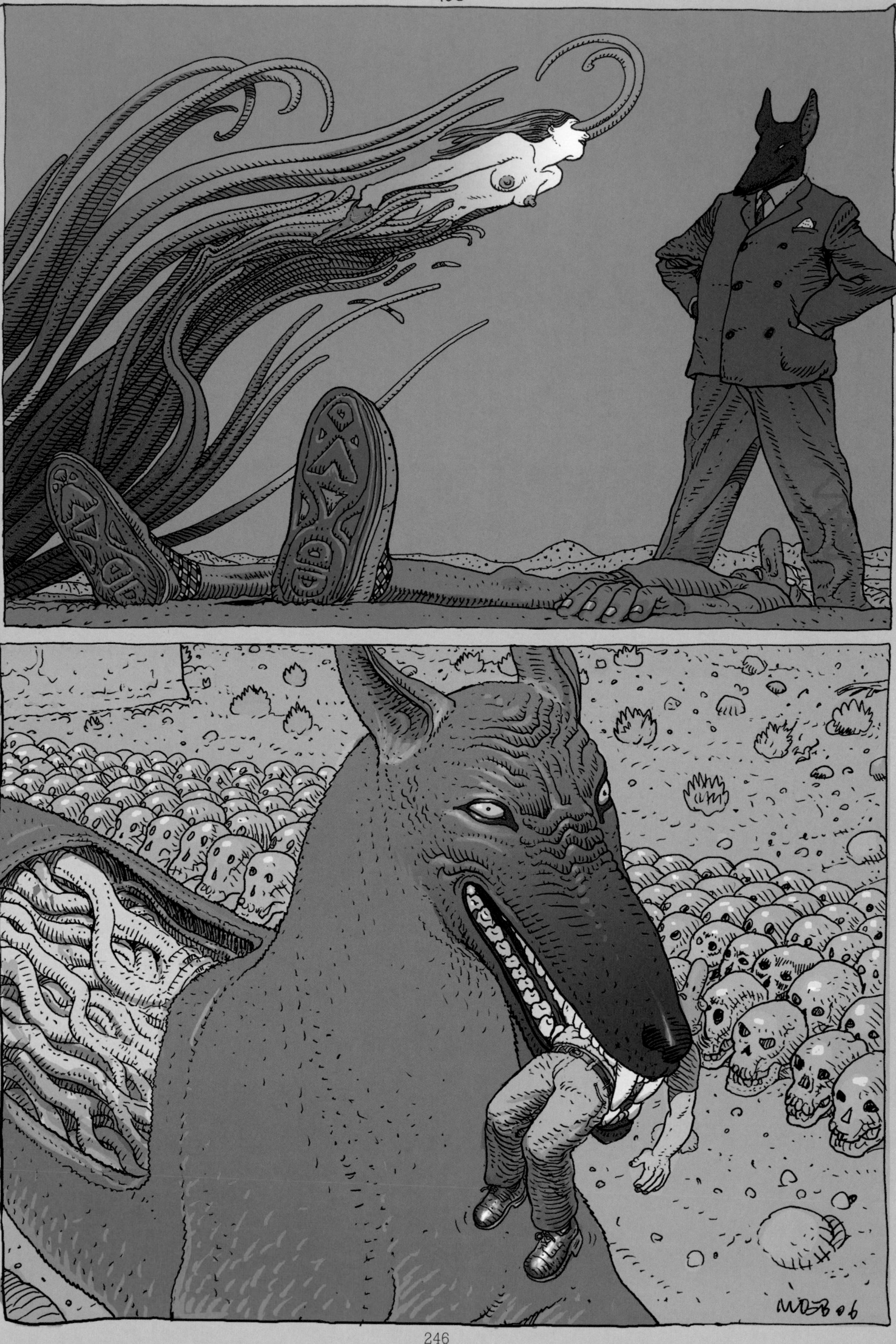

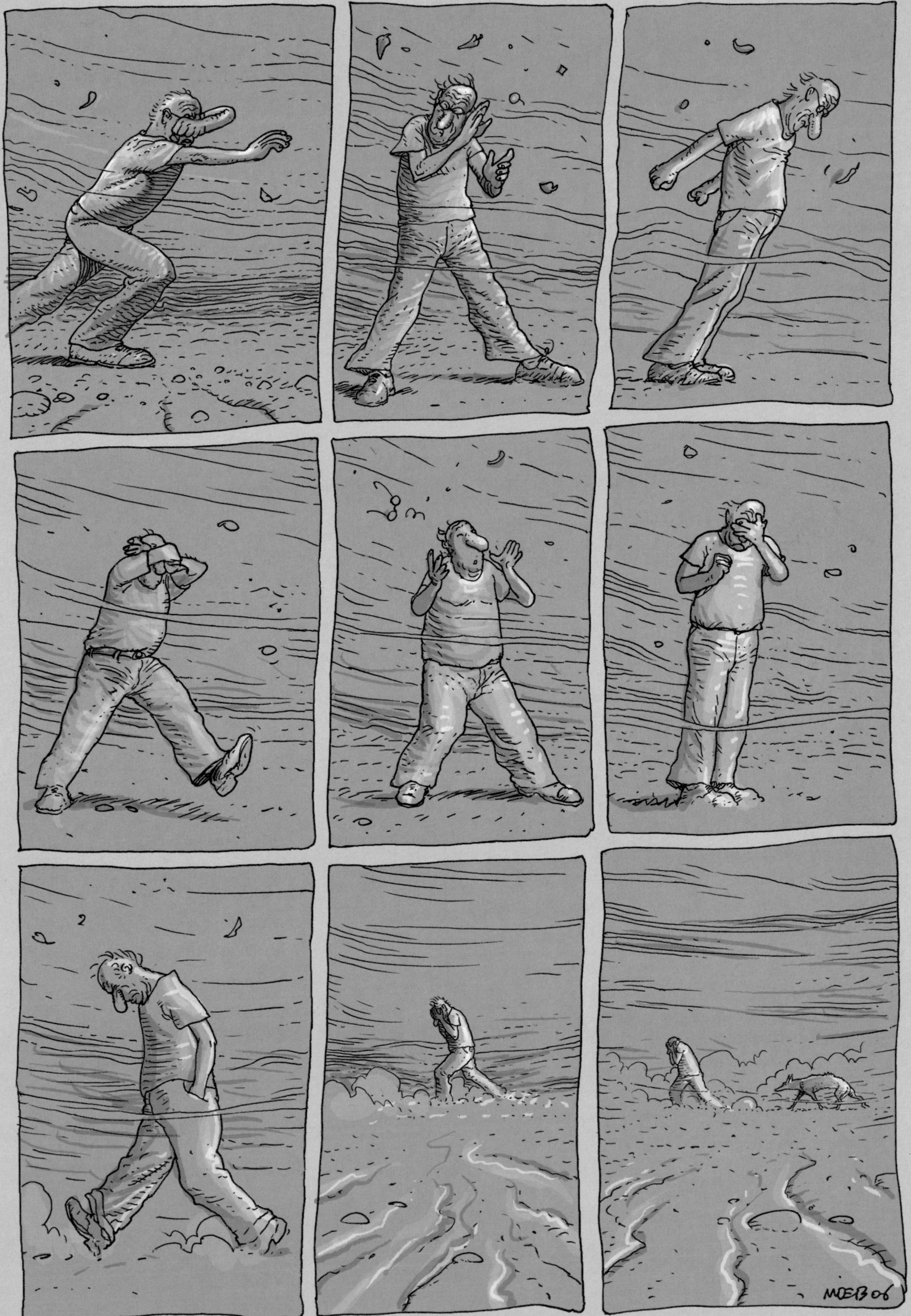

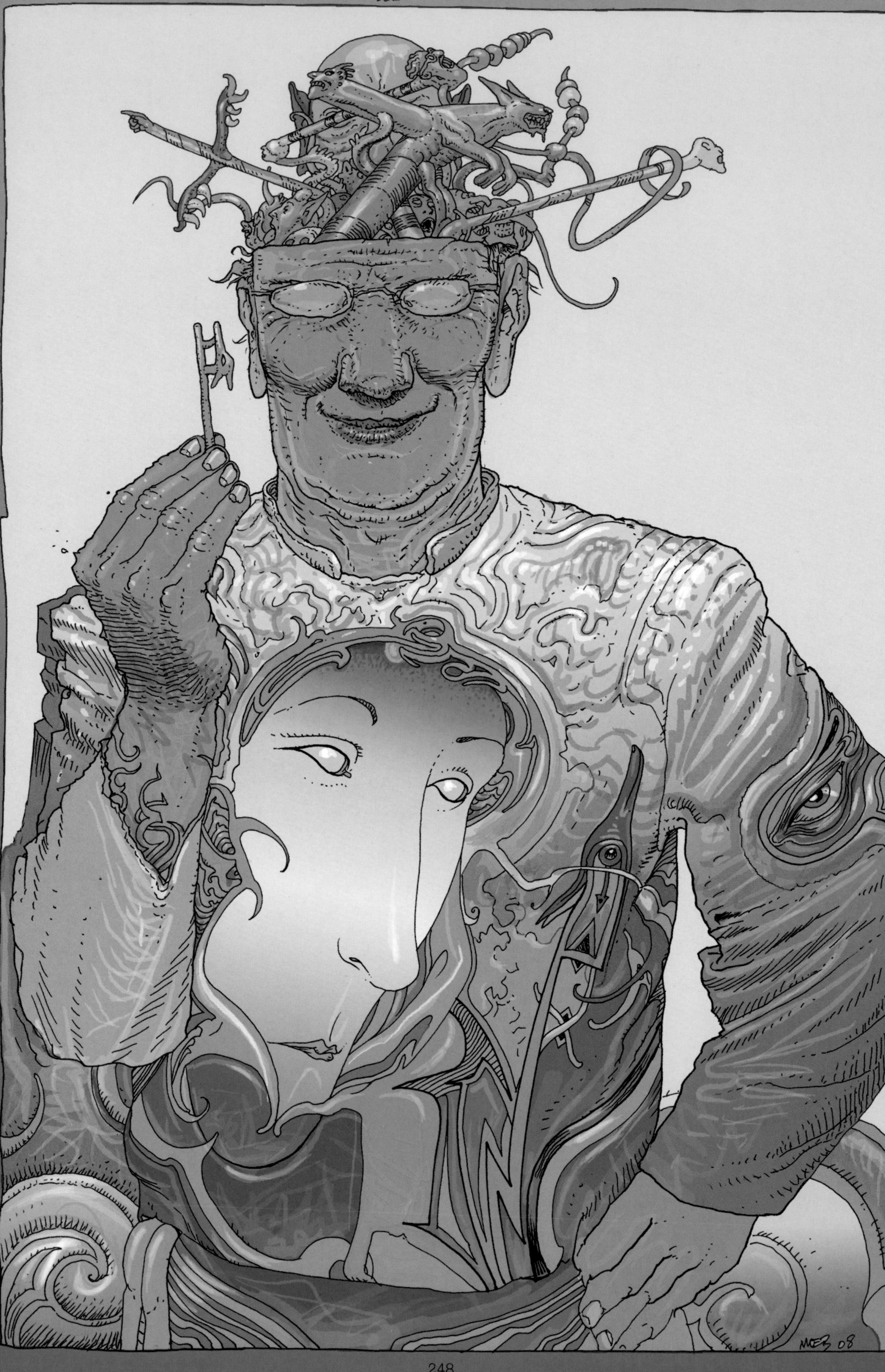
MŒB 08

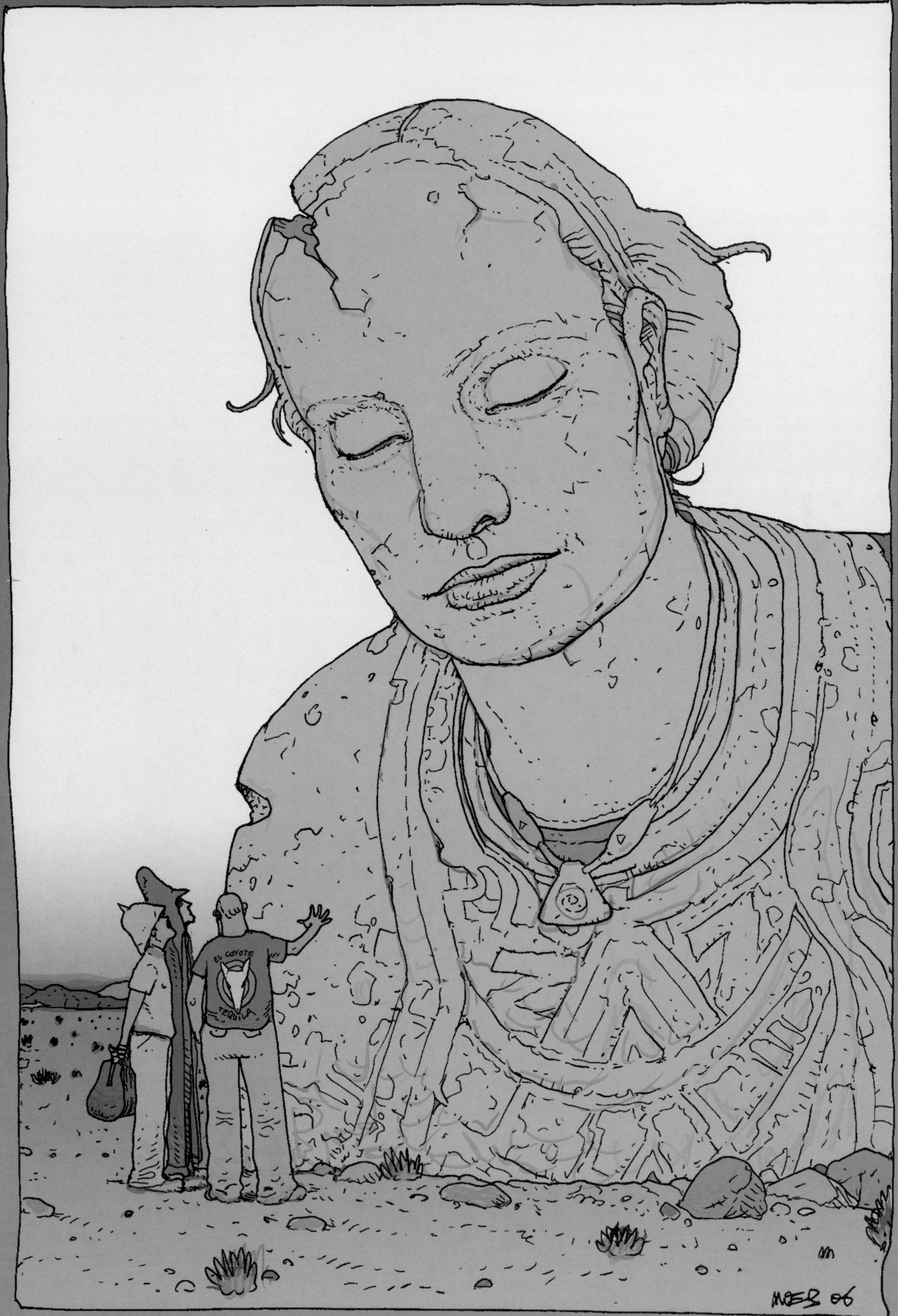
EL COYOTE
TEQUILA
MŒBIUS 06

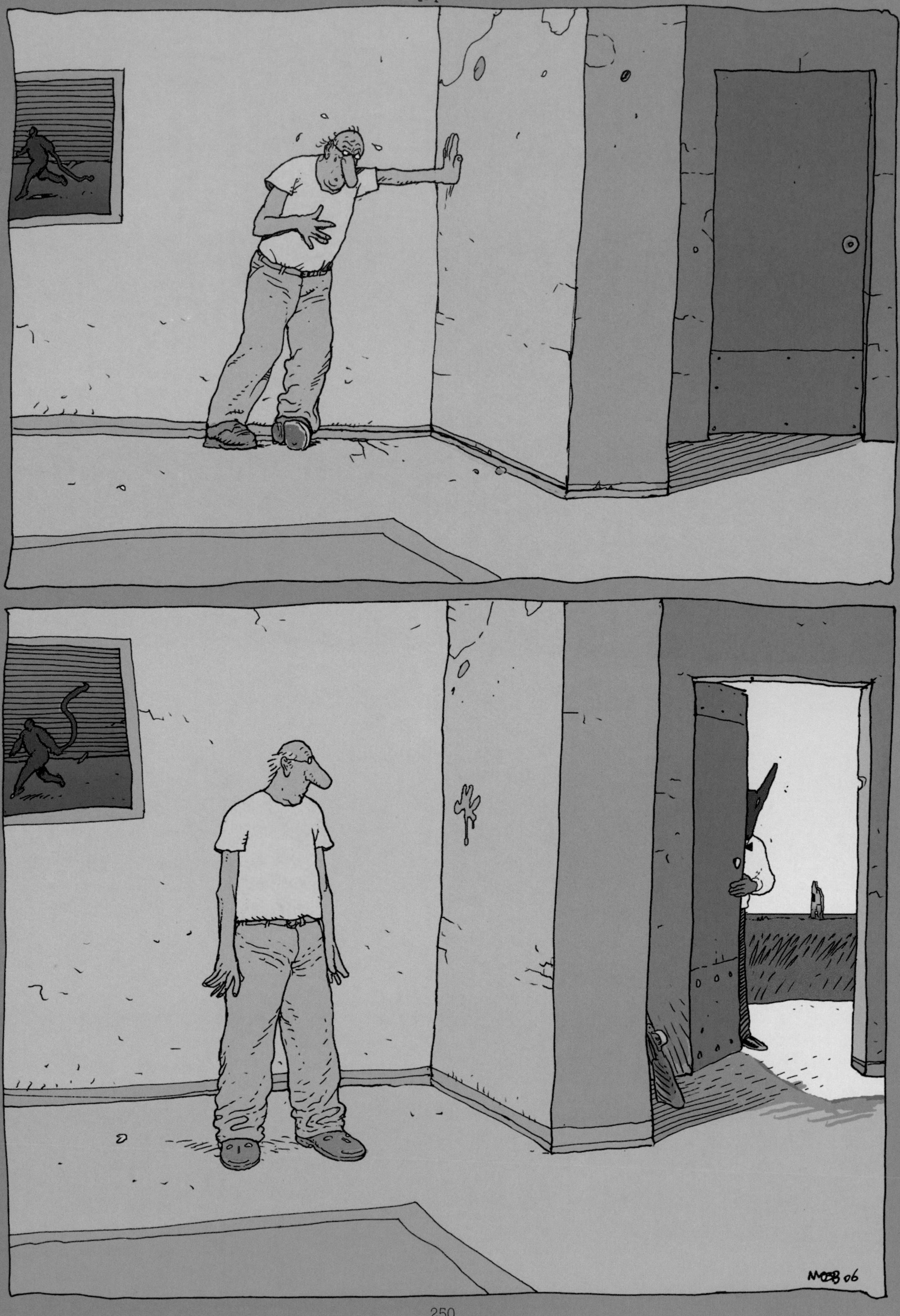
MŒB 06

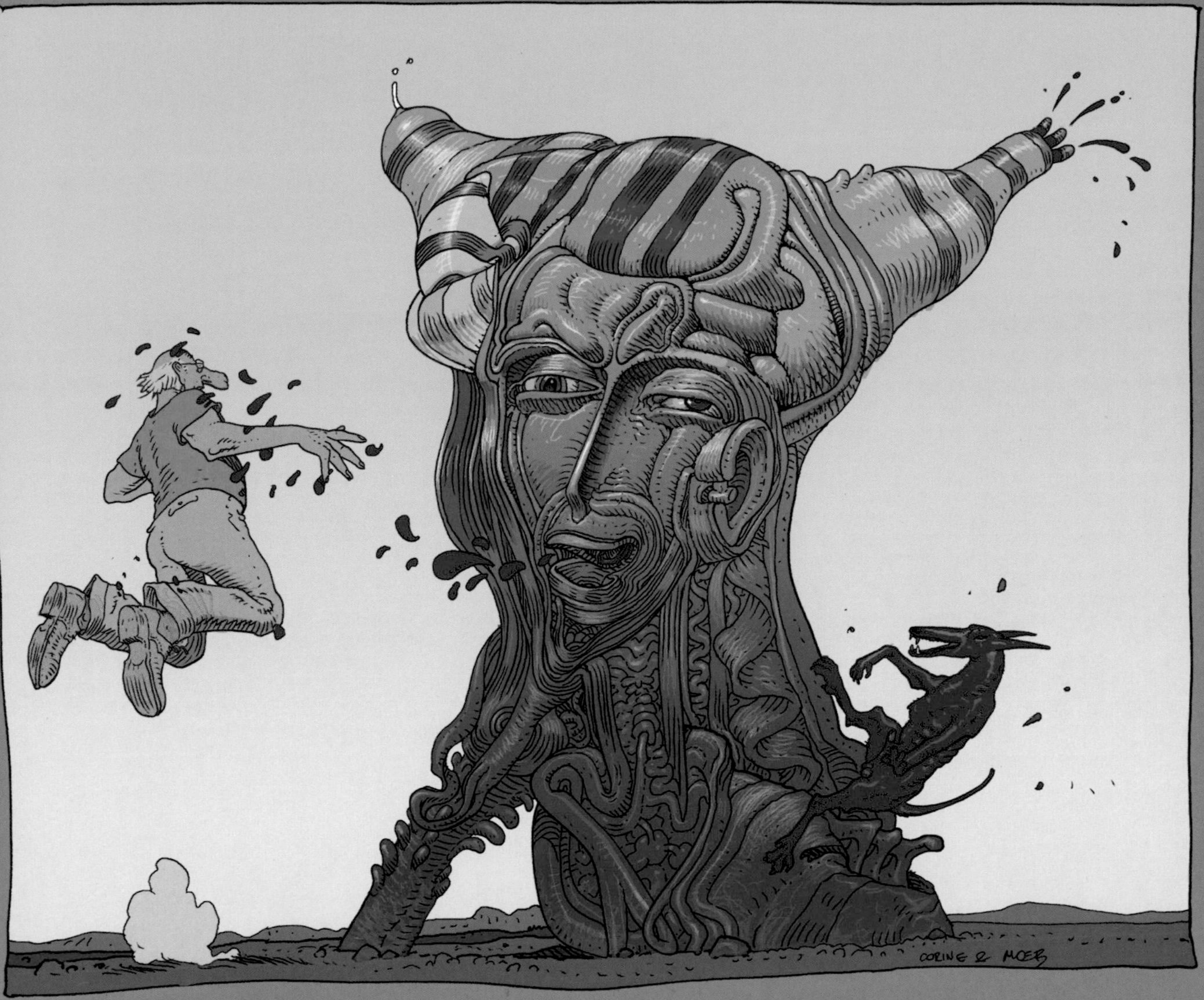
CORINE & MOEB

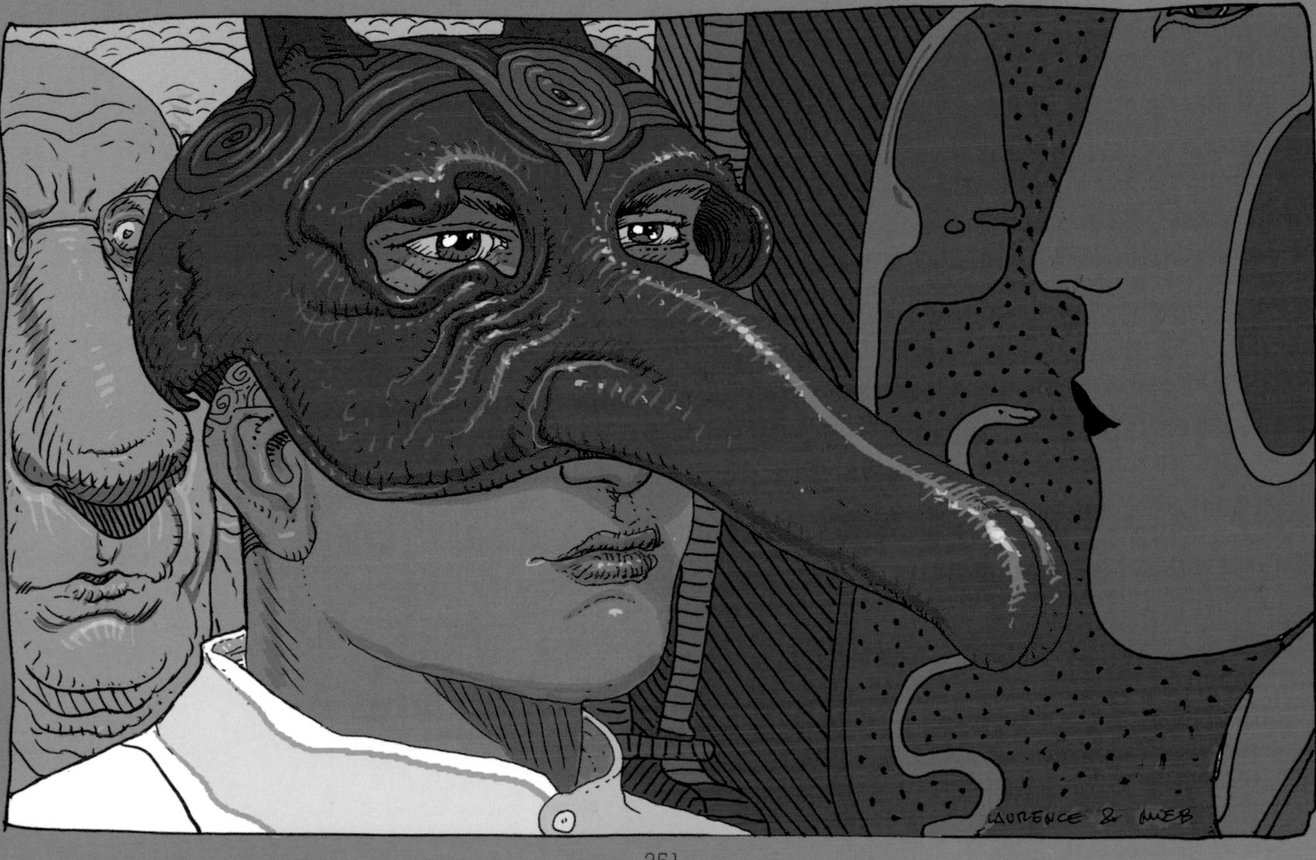
LAURENCE & MOEB

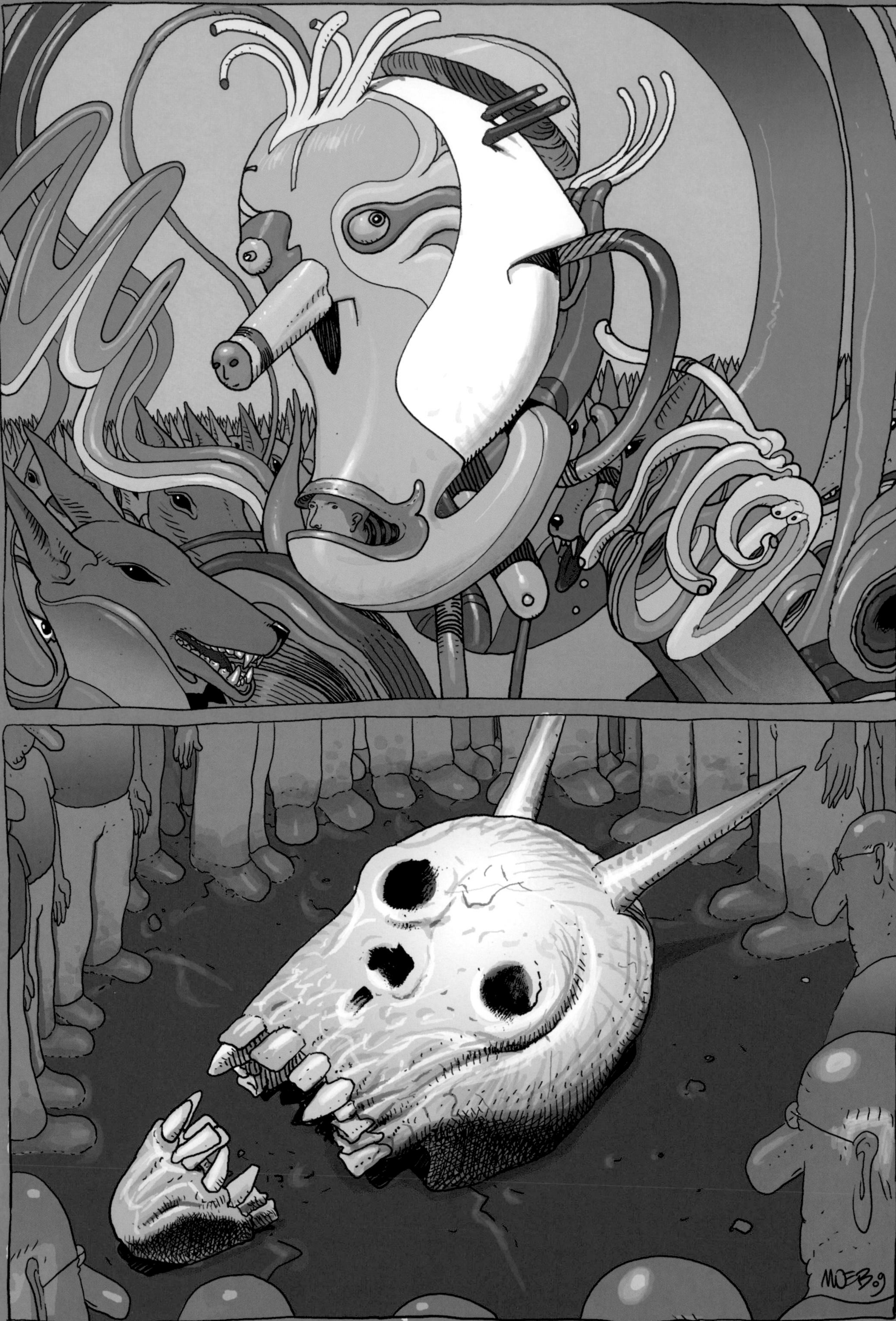
MOEB.09

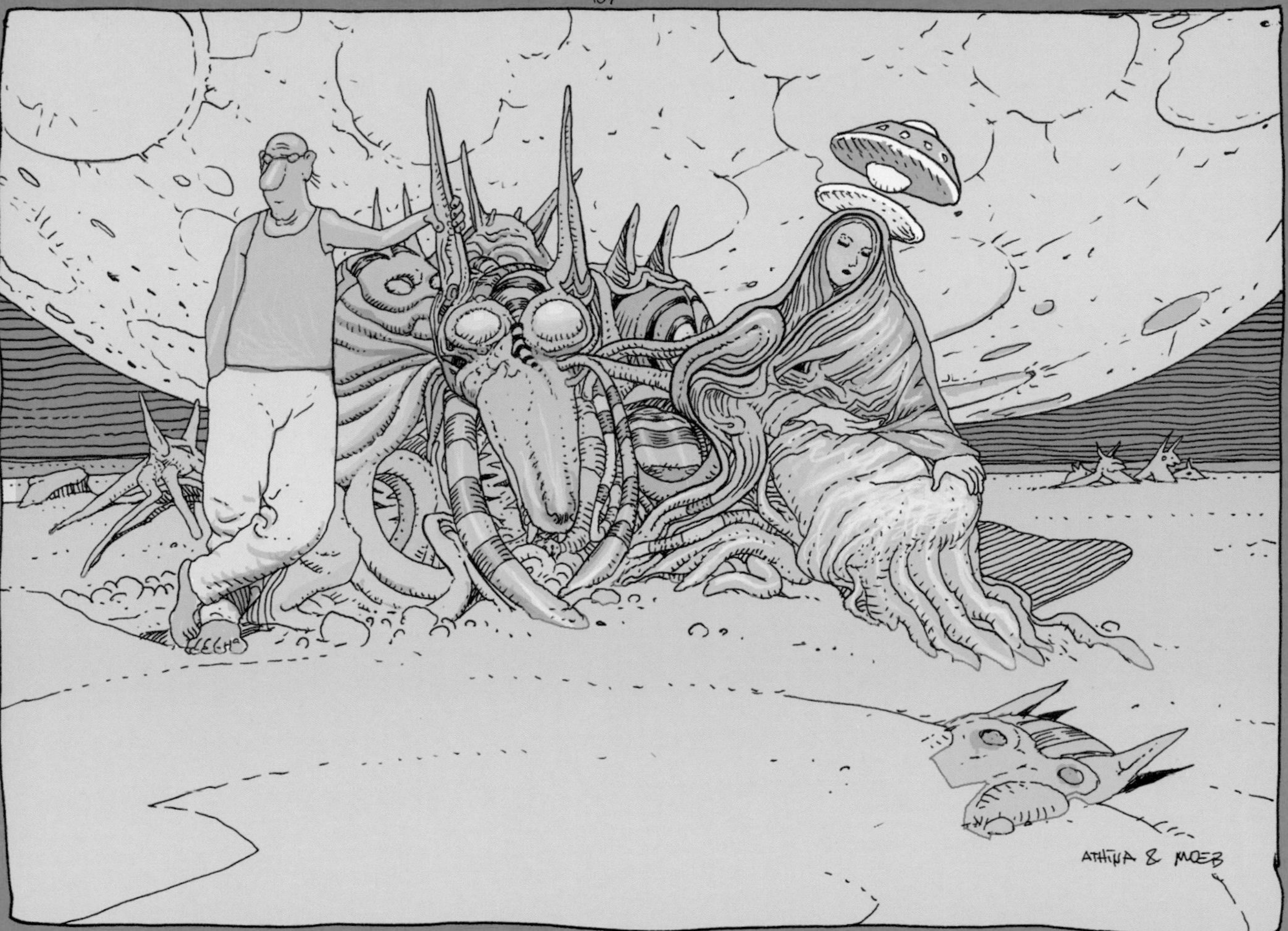
ATHINA & MOEB

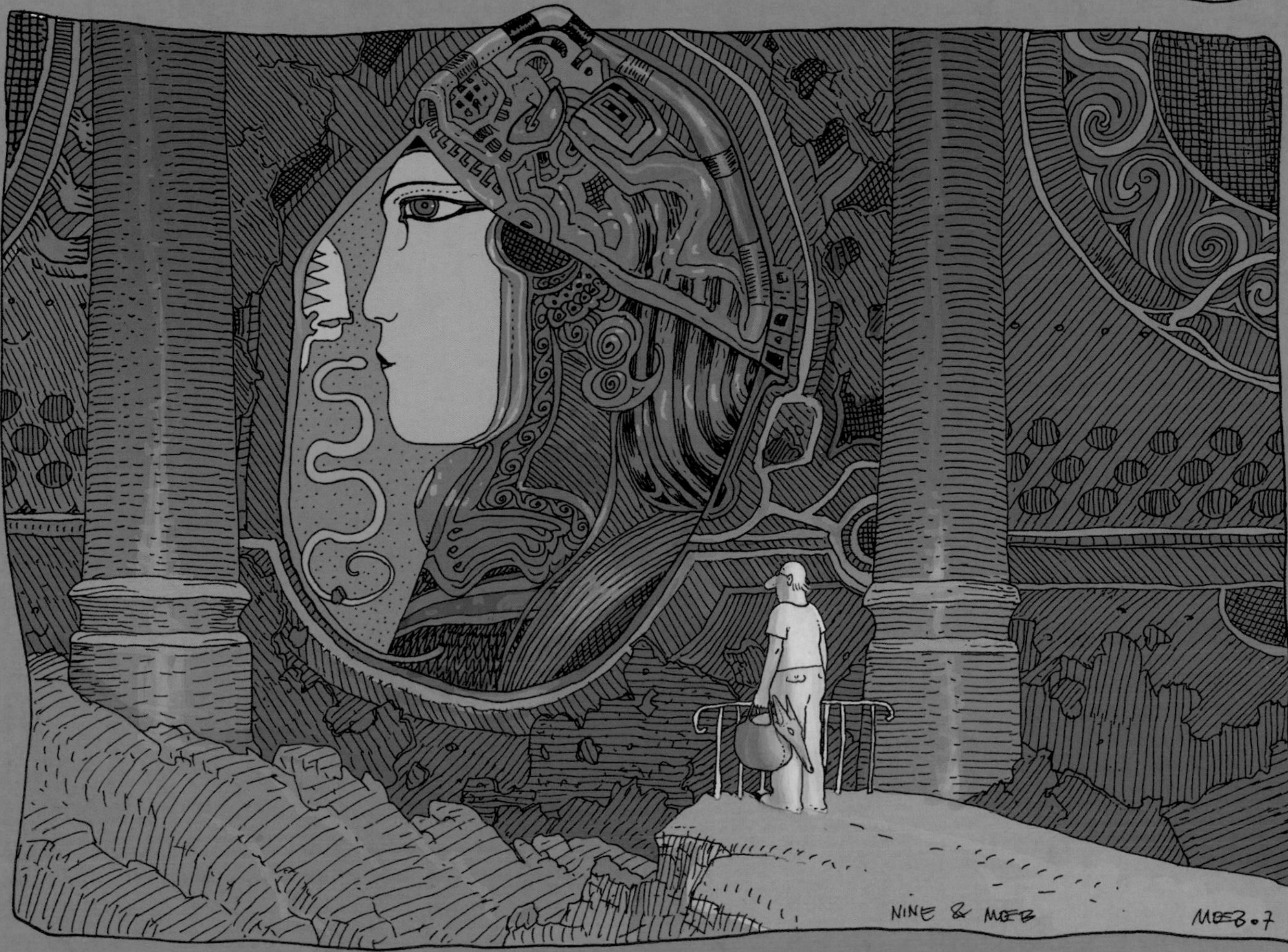
NINE & MOEB
MOEB.07

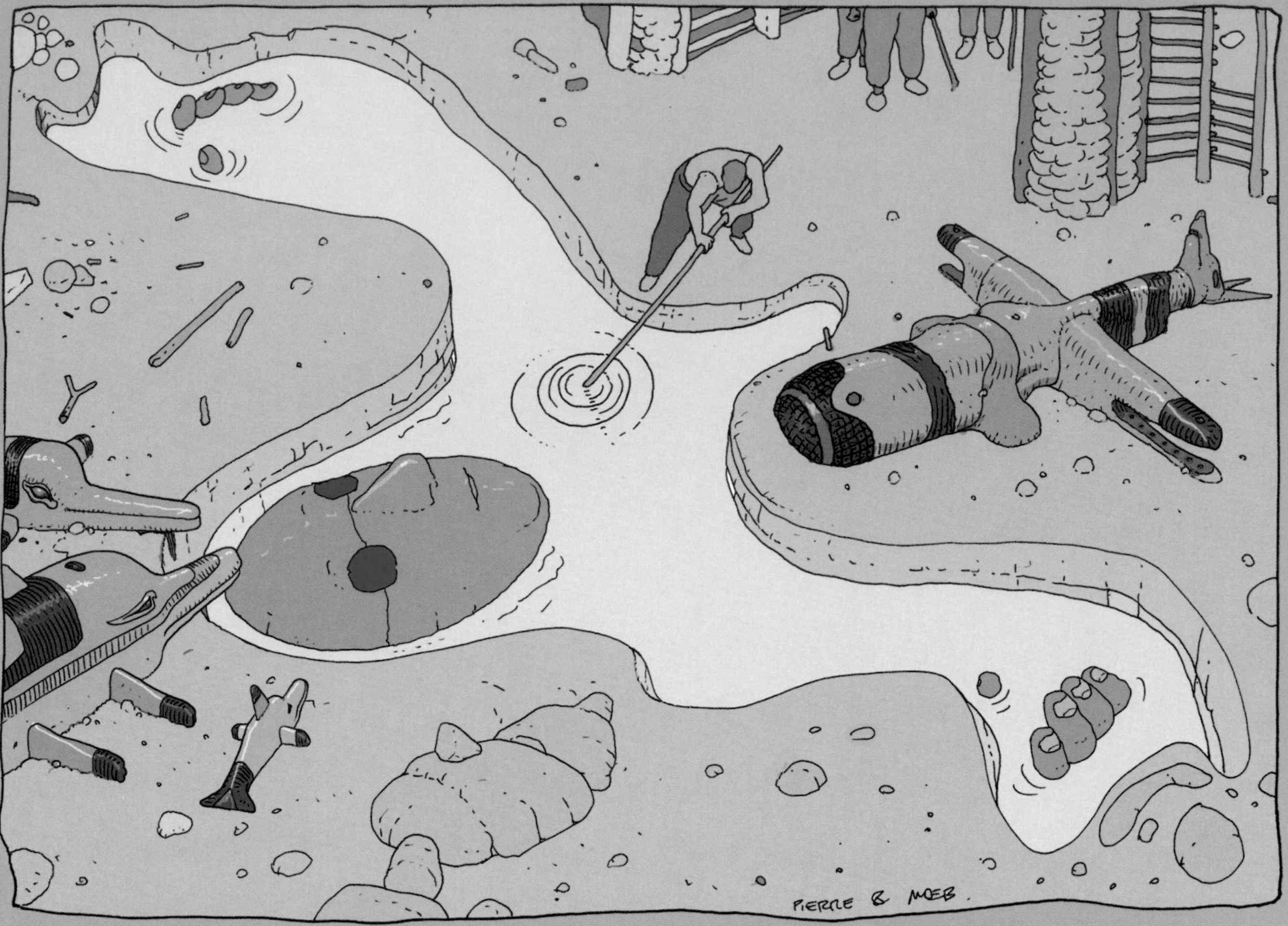
PIERRE & MOEB

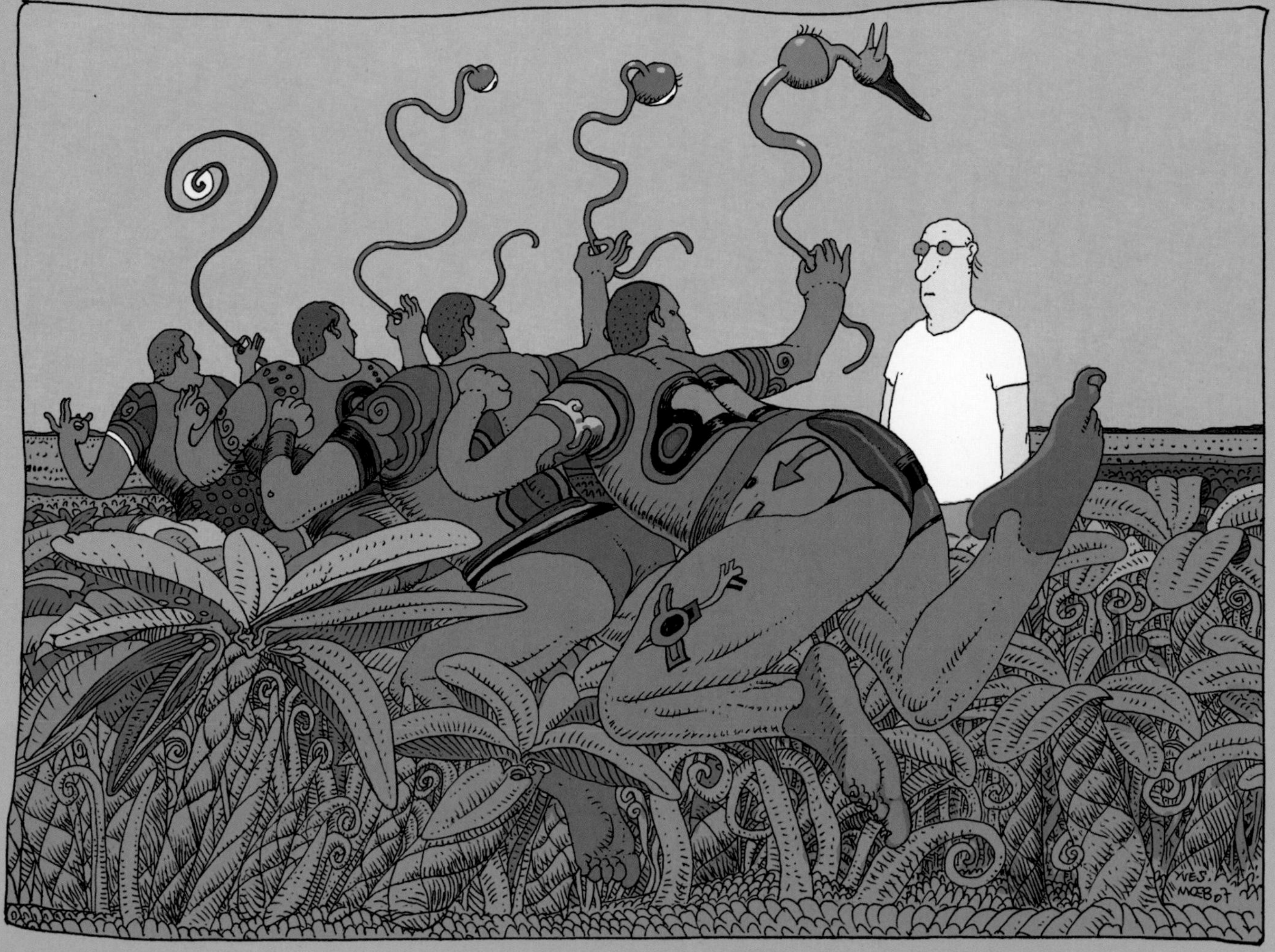
YVES
MOEB 07

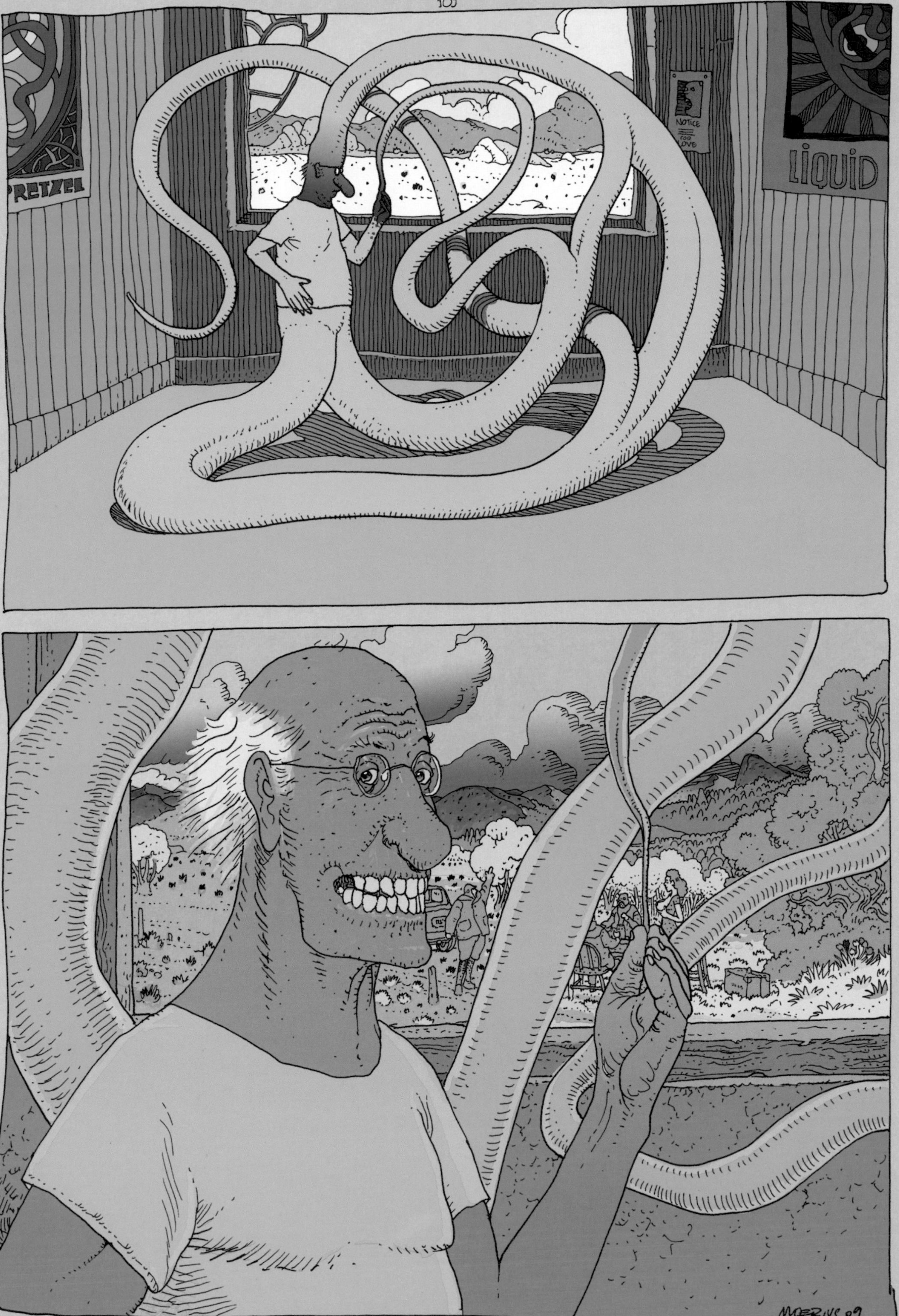
PRETZEL
NOTICE
FOR LOVE
LIQUID
MOEBIUS 09

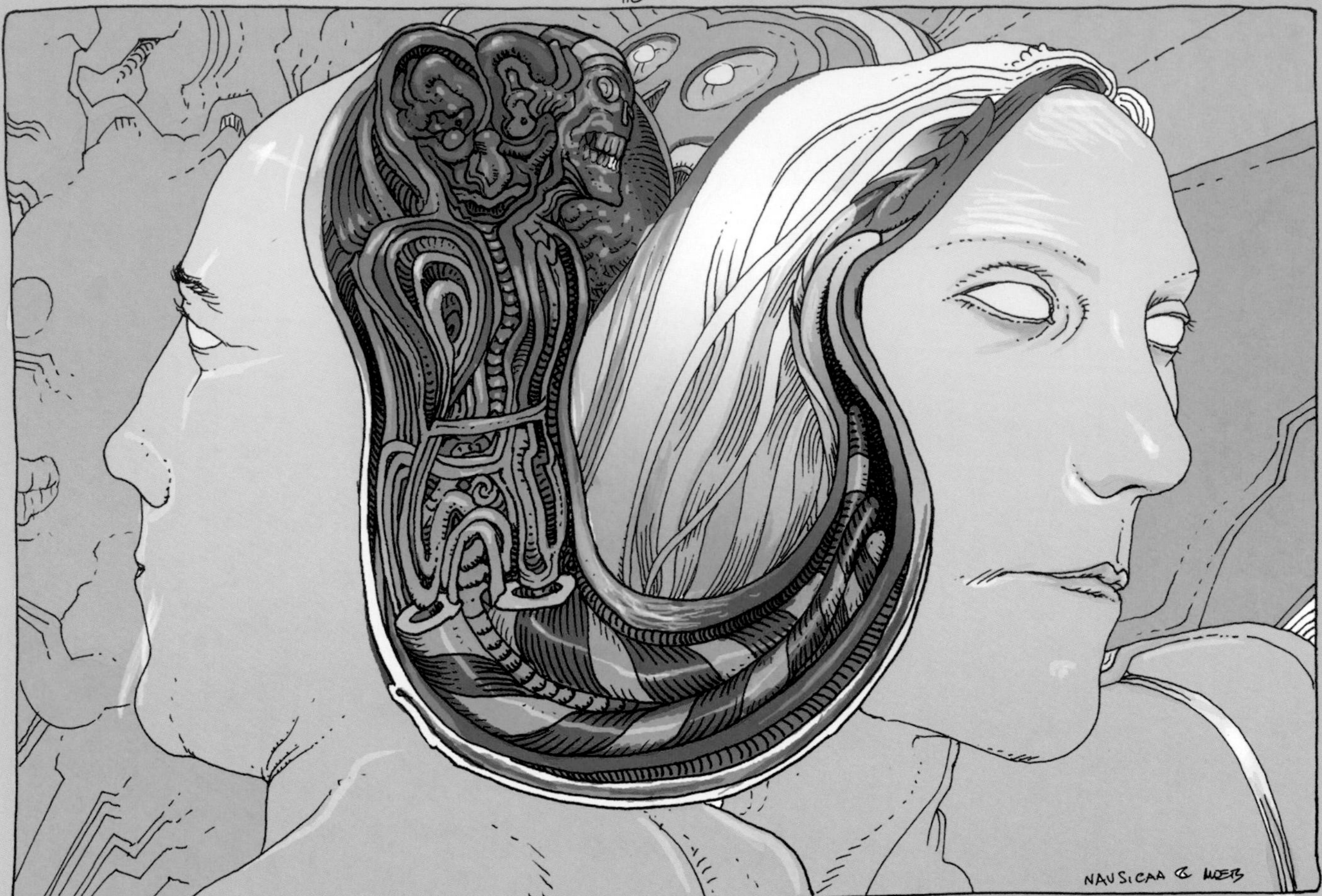
NAUSICAA © MOEB

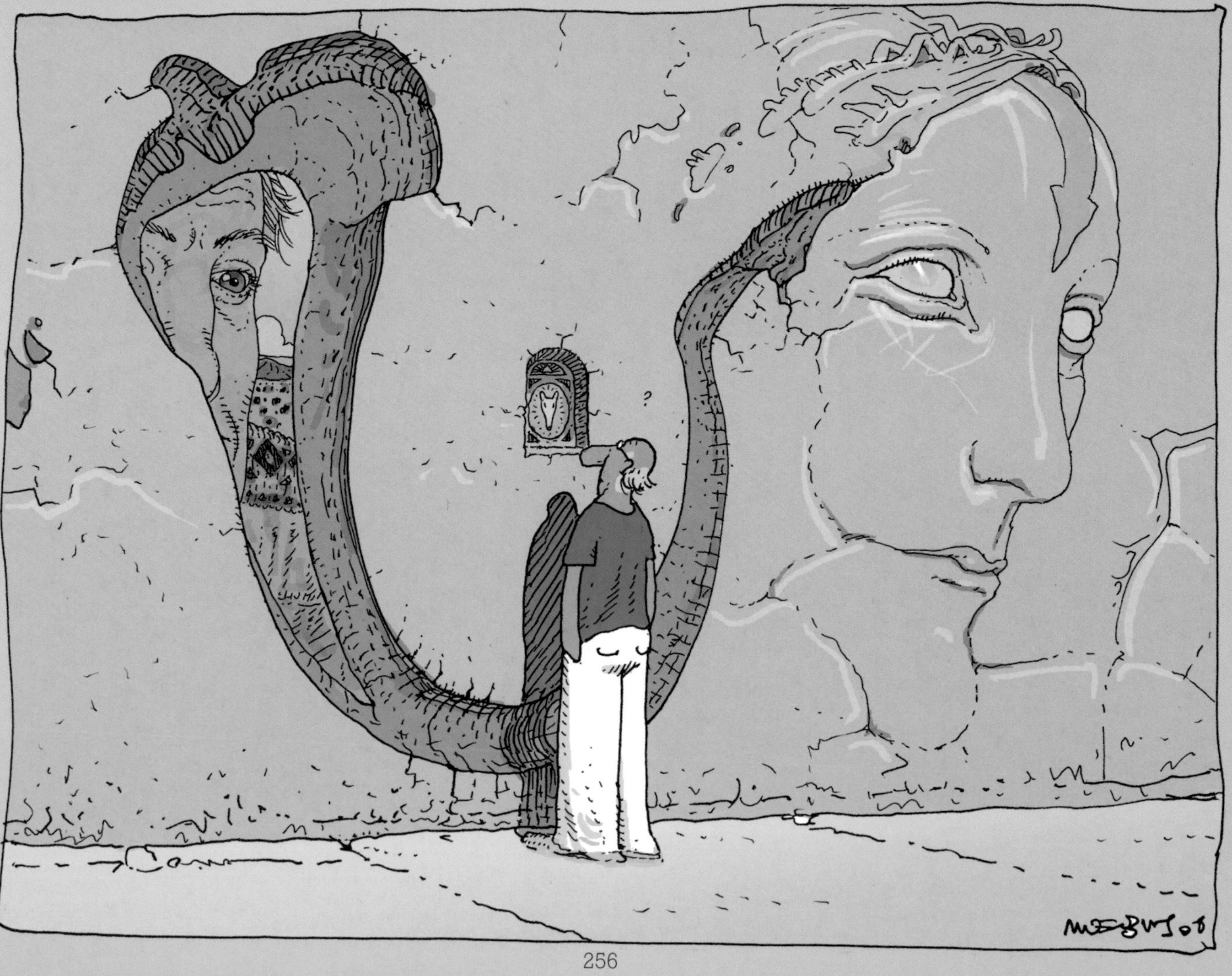
MOEBIUS 08

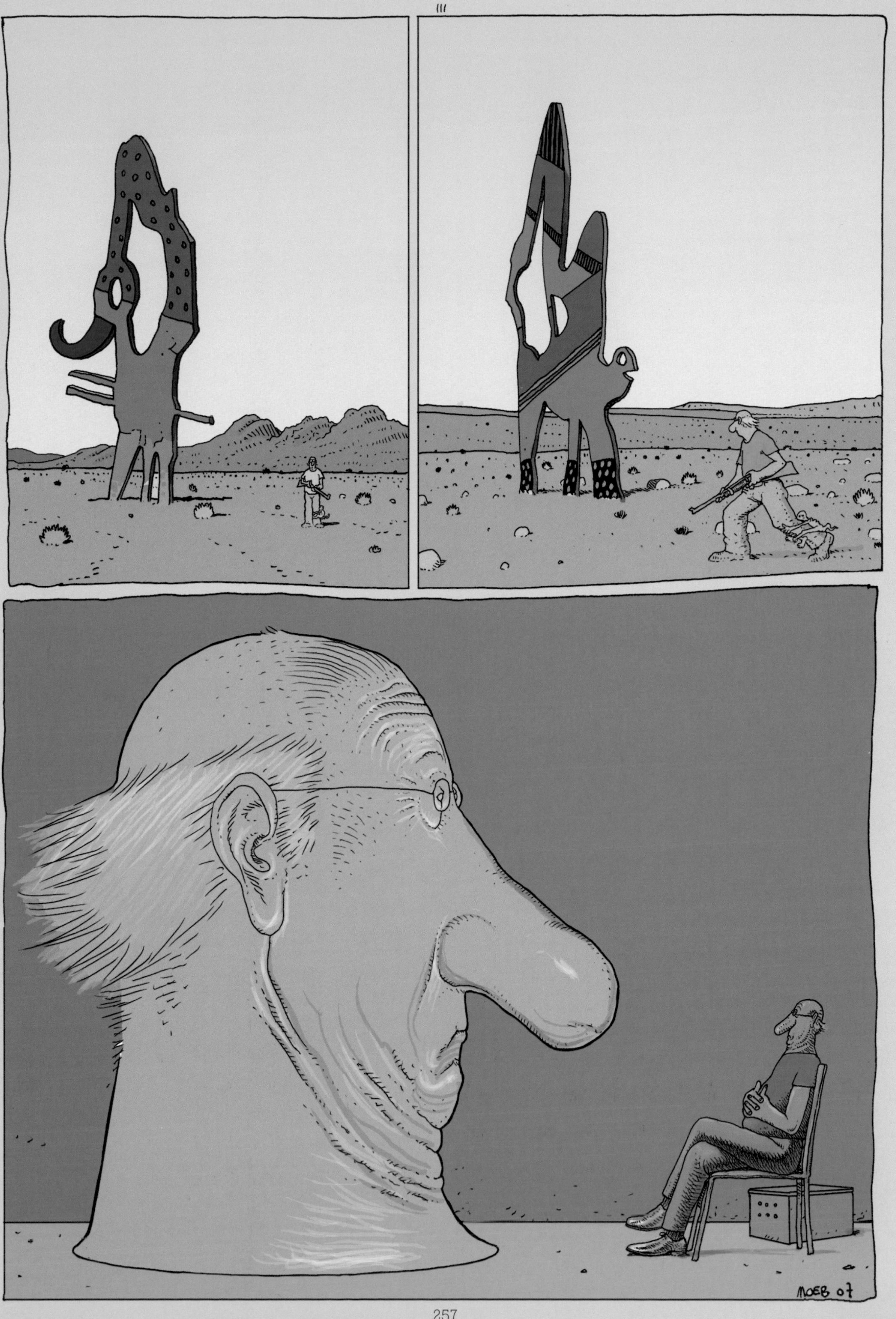
MOEB 07

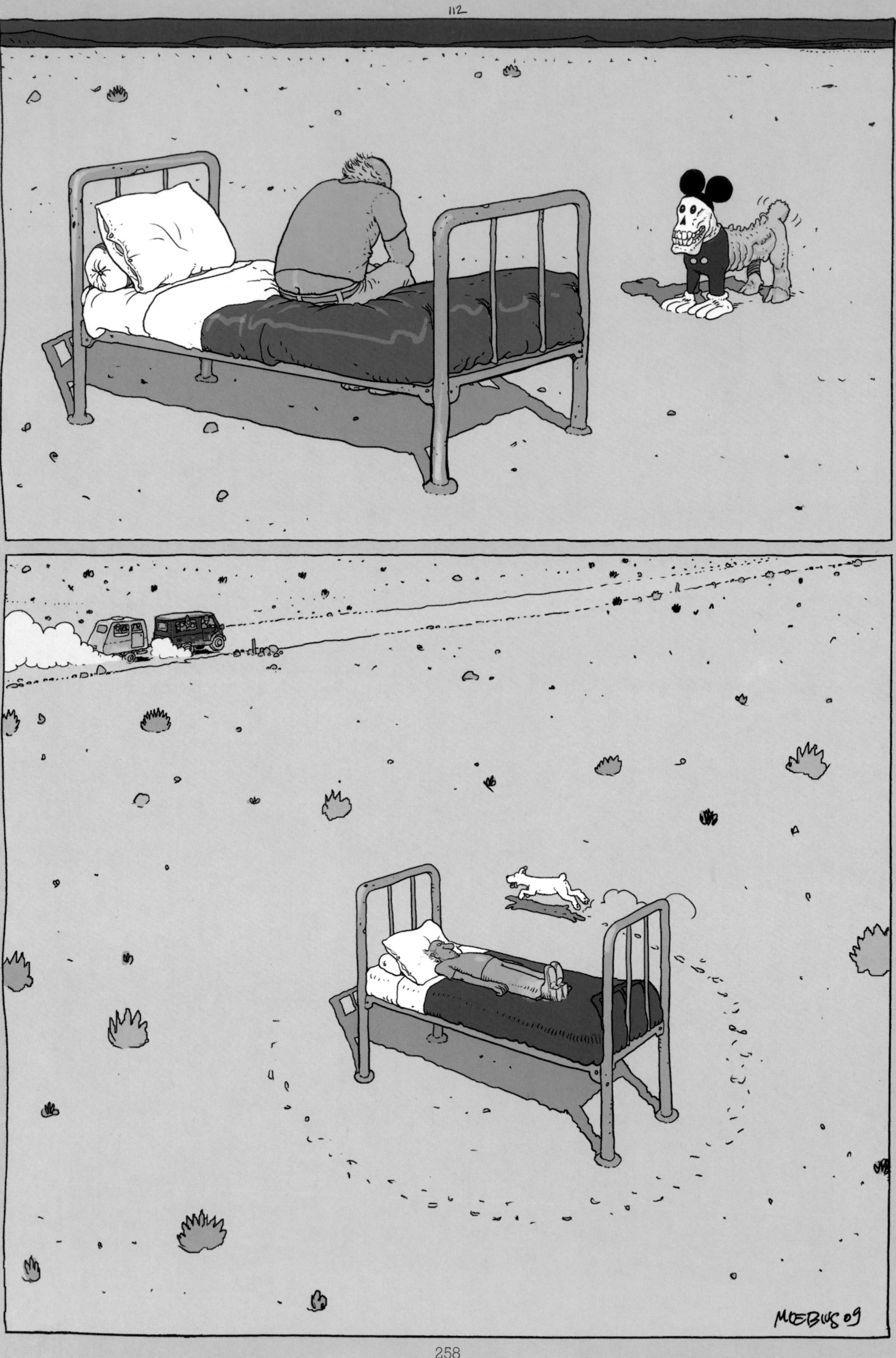
112
MŒBIUS 09

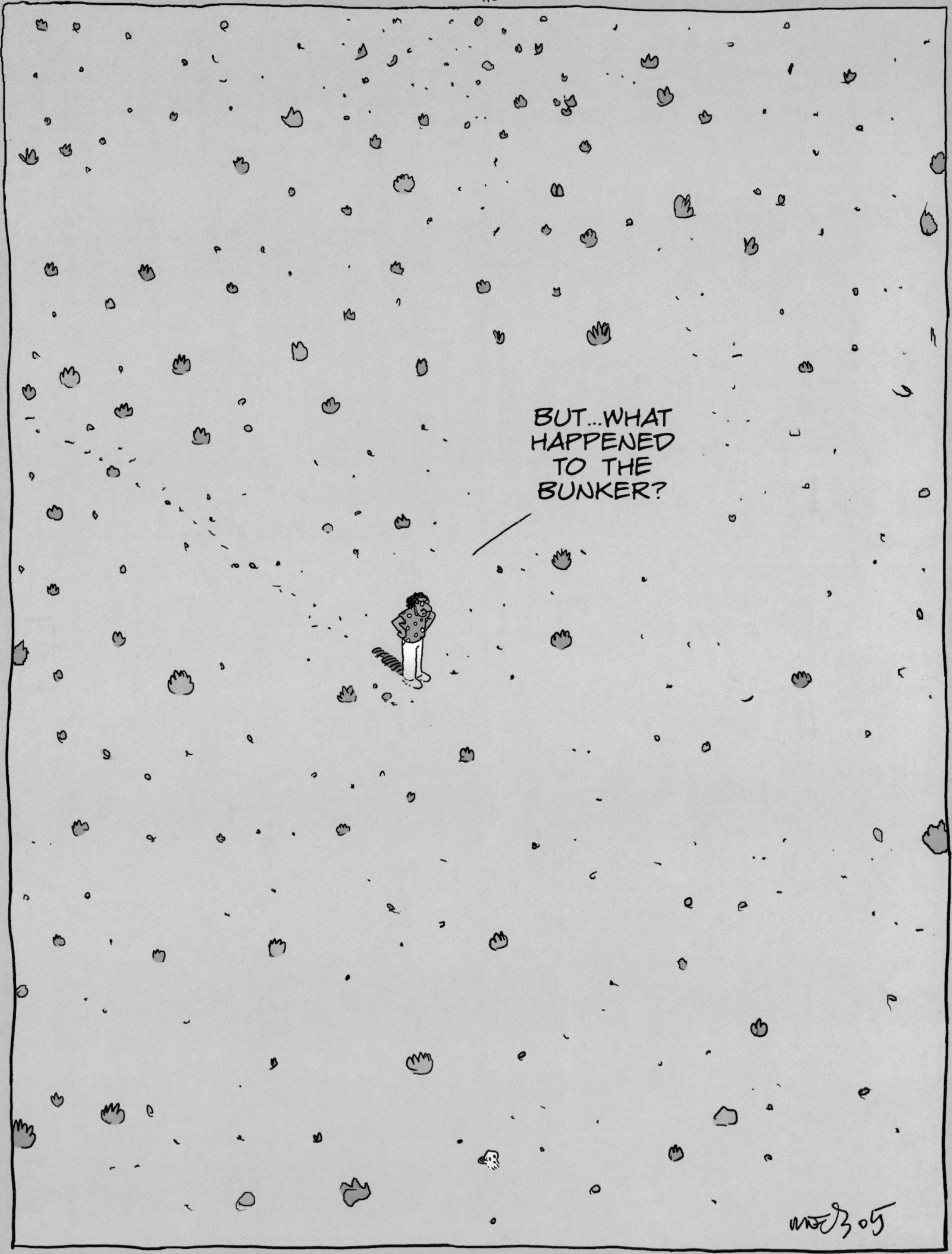
BUT...WHAT HAPPENED TO THE BUNKER?

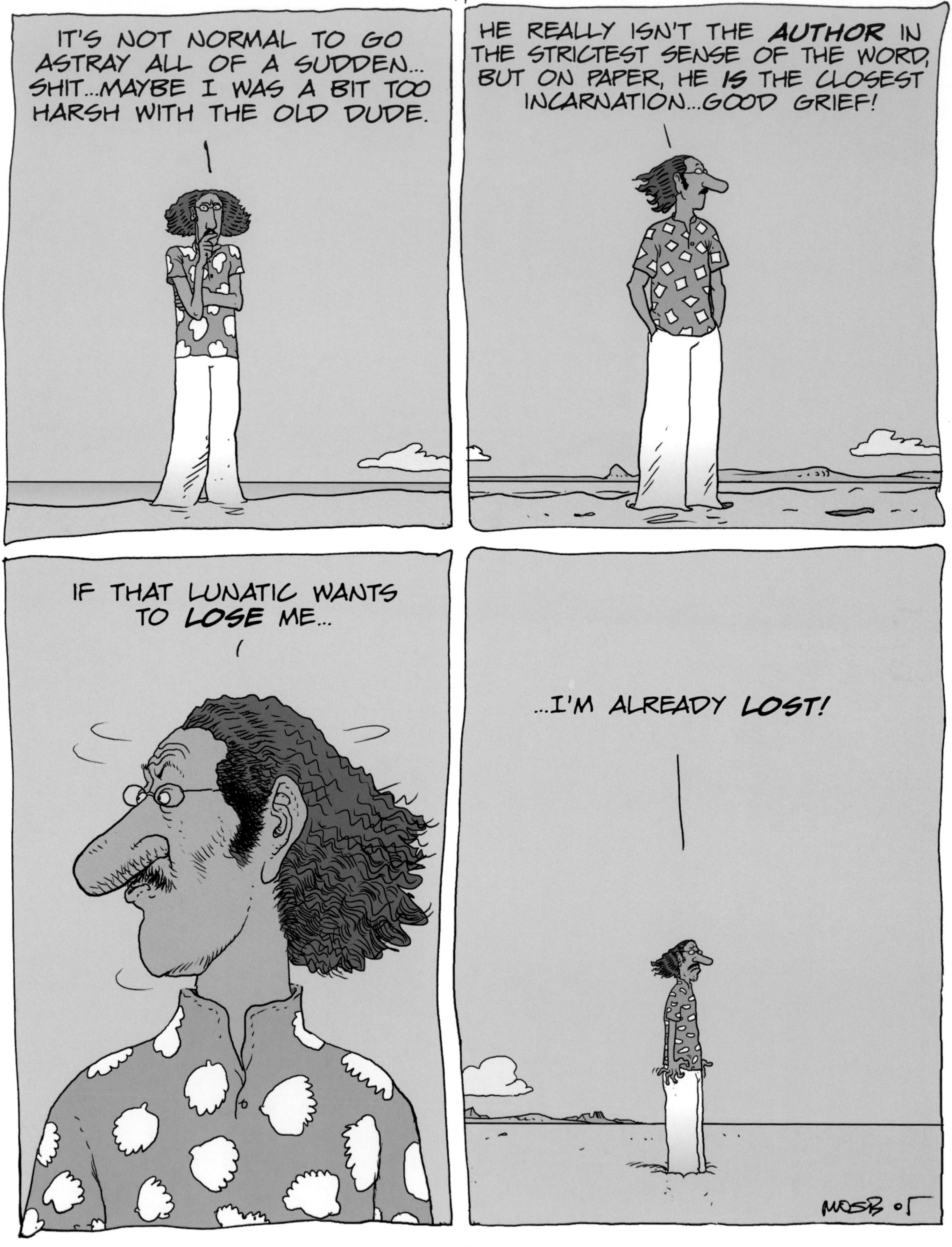
IT'S NOT NORMAL TO GO ASTRAY ALL OF A SUDDEN... SHIT...MAYBE I WAS A BIT TOO HARSH WITH THE OLD DUDE.
HE REALLY ISN'T THE **AUTHOR** IN THE STRICTEST SENSE OF THE WORD, BUT ON PAPER, HE **IS** THE CLOSEST INCARNATION...GOOD GRIEF!
IF THAT LUNATIC WANTS TO **LOSE** ME...
...I'M ALREADY **LOST!**
MŒBIUS 05

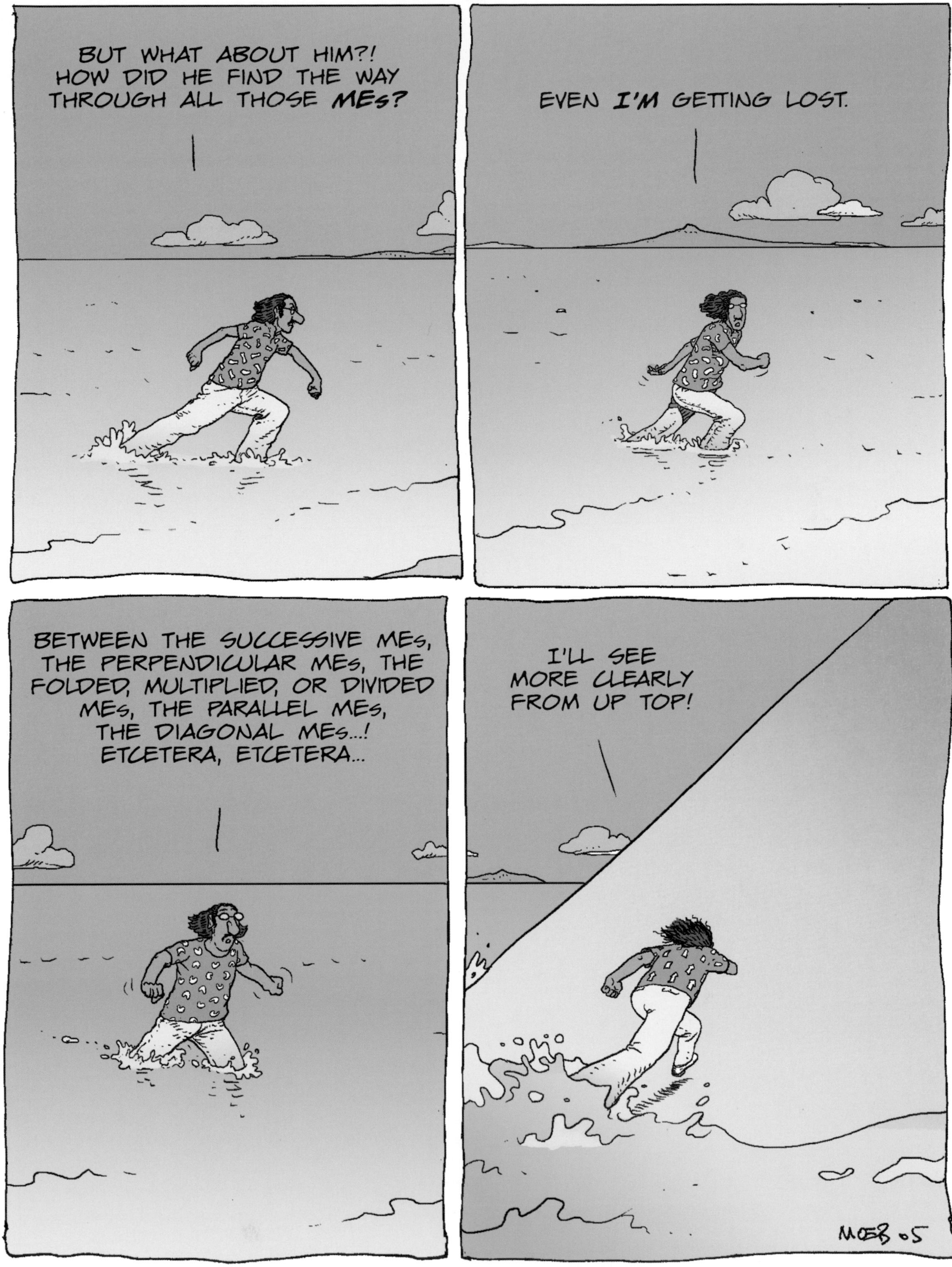
BUT WHAT ABOUT HIM?! HOW DID HE FIND THE WAY THROUGH ALL THOSE MEs?
EVEN I'M GETTING LOST.
BETWEEN THE SUCCESSIVE MEs, THE PERPENDICULAR MEs, THE FOLDED, MULTIPLIED, OR DIVIDED MEs, THE PARALLEL MEs, THE DIAGONAL MEs...! ETCETERA, ETCETERA...
I'LL SEE MORE CLEARLY FROM UP TOP!
MŒB .05

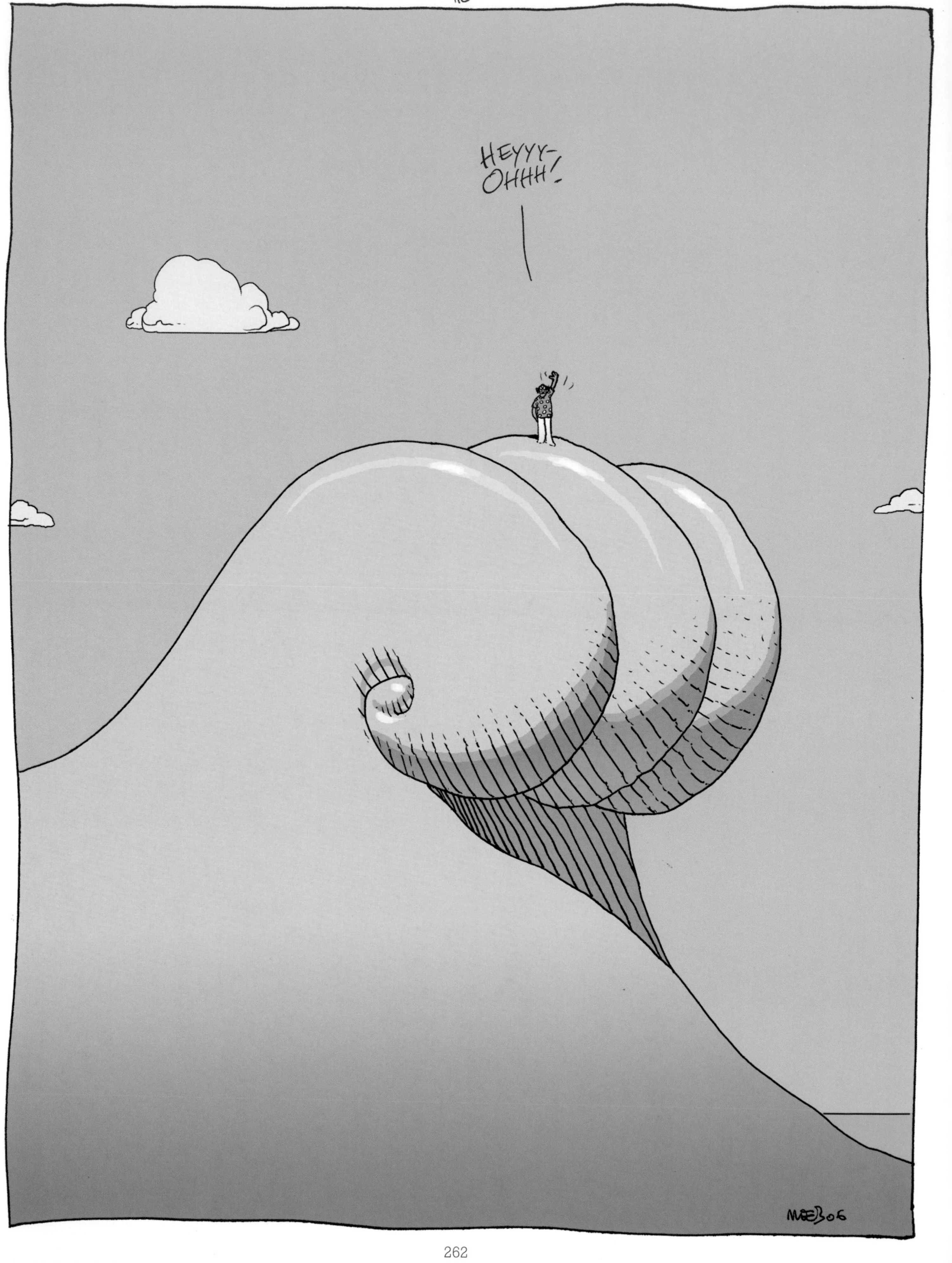
HEYYY-
OHHH!
MOEB06

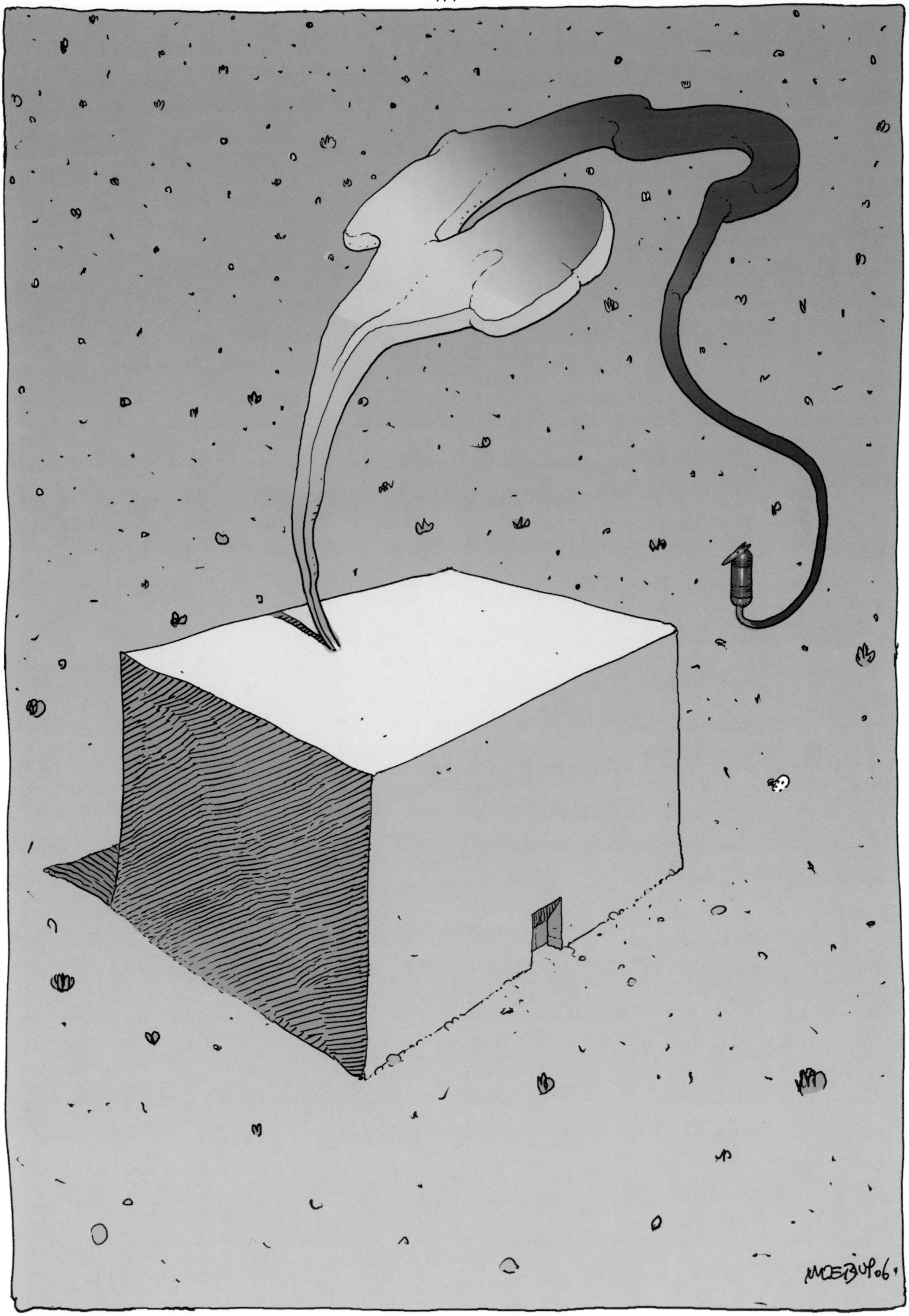

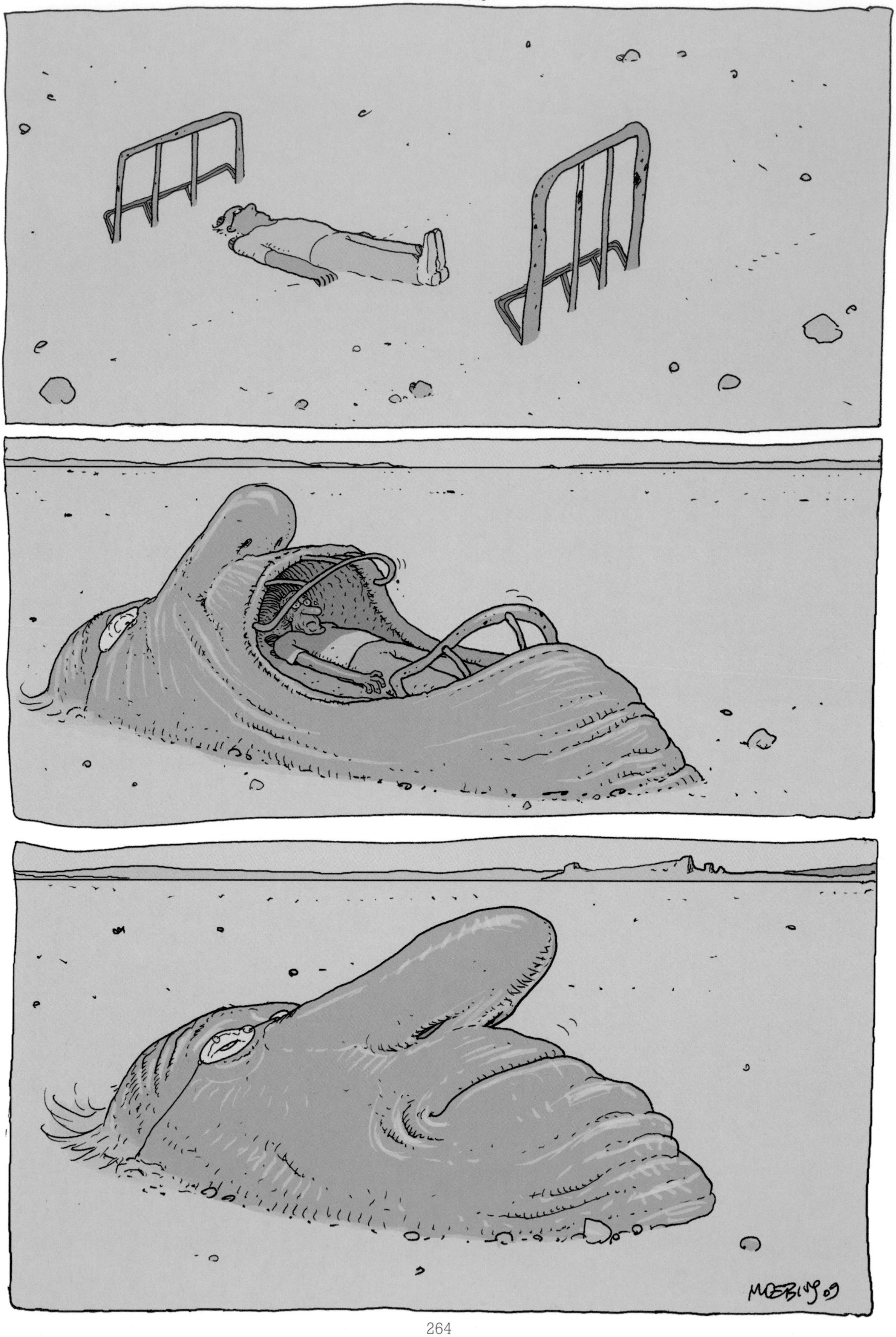
MOEBIUS 09

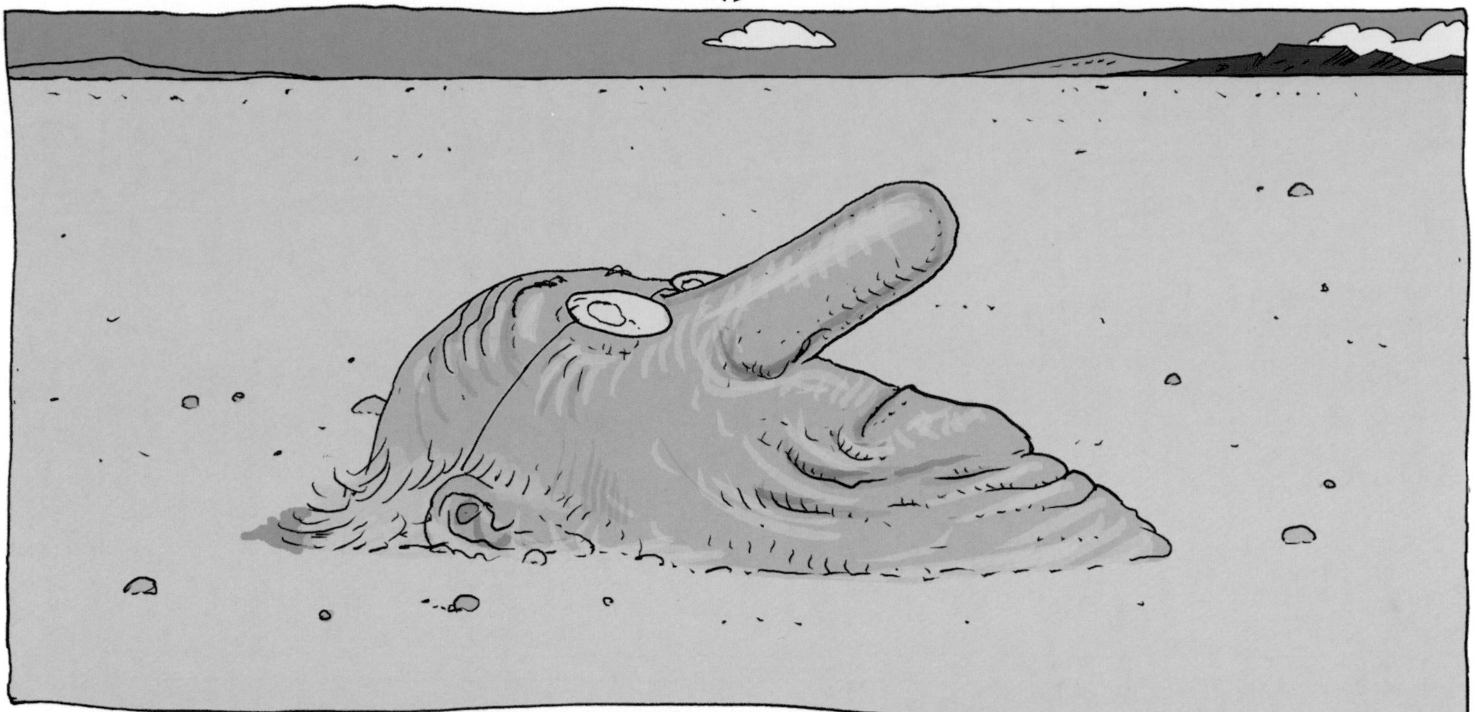

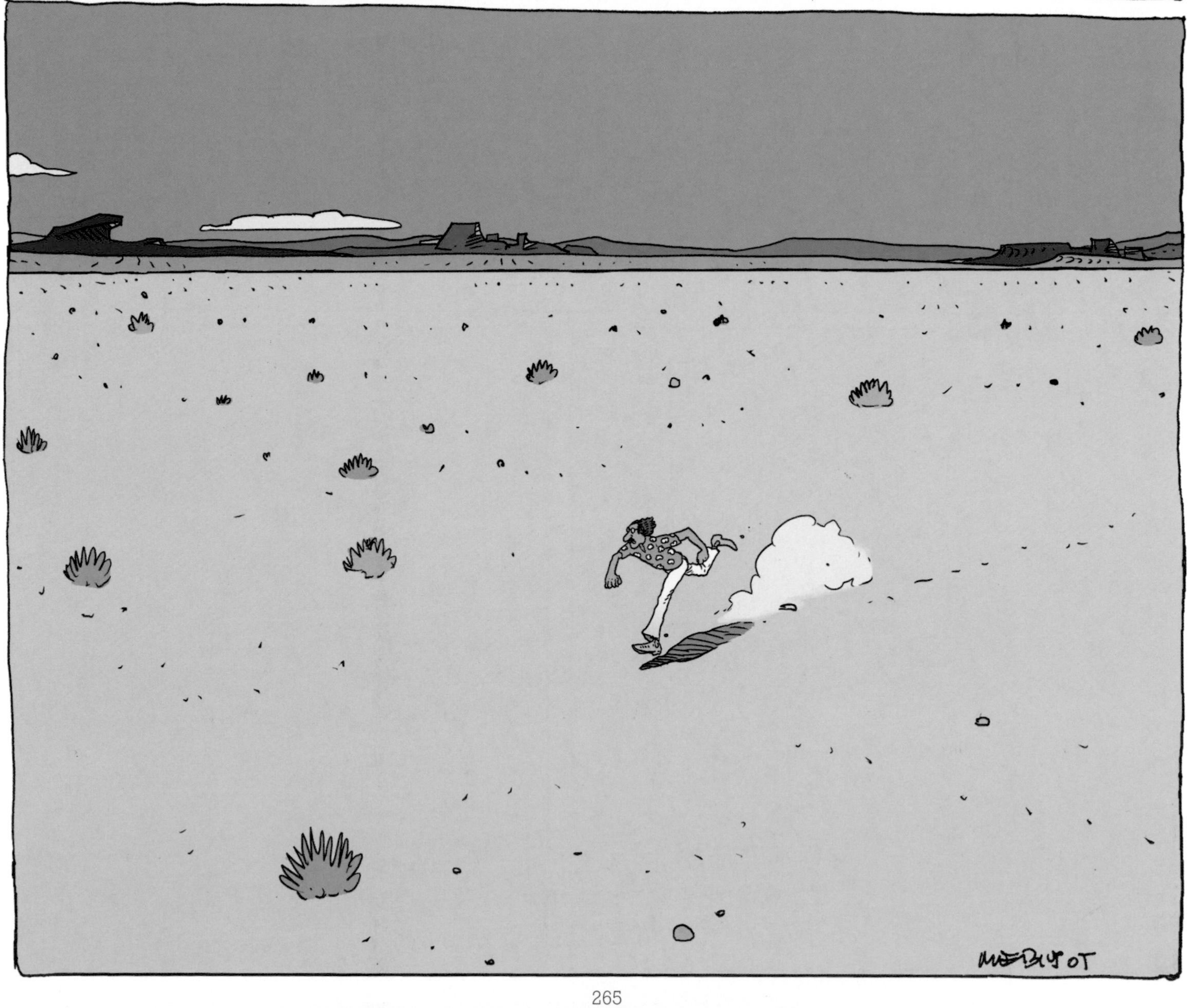

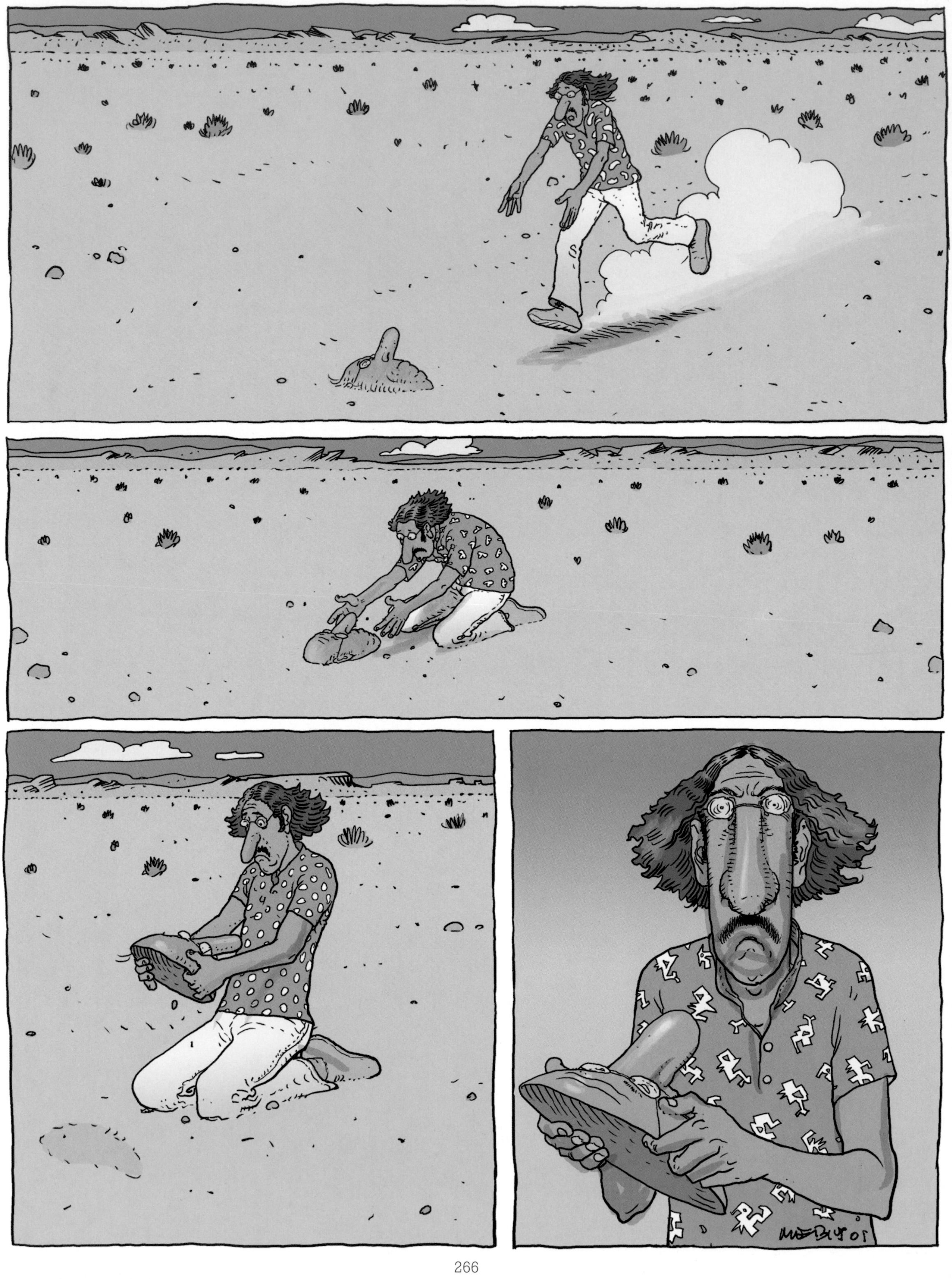

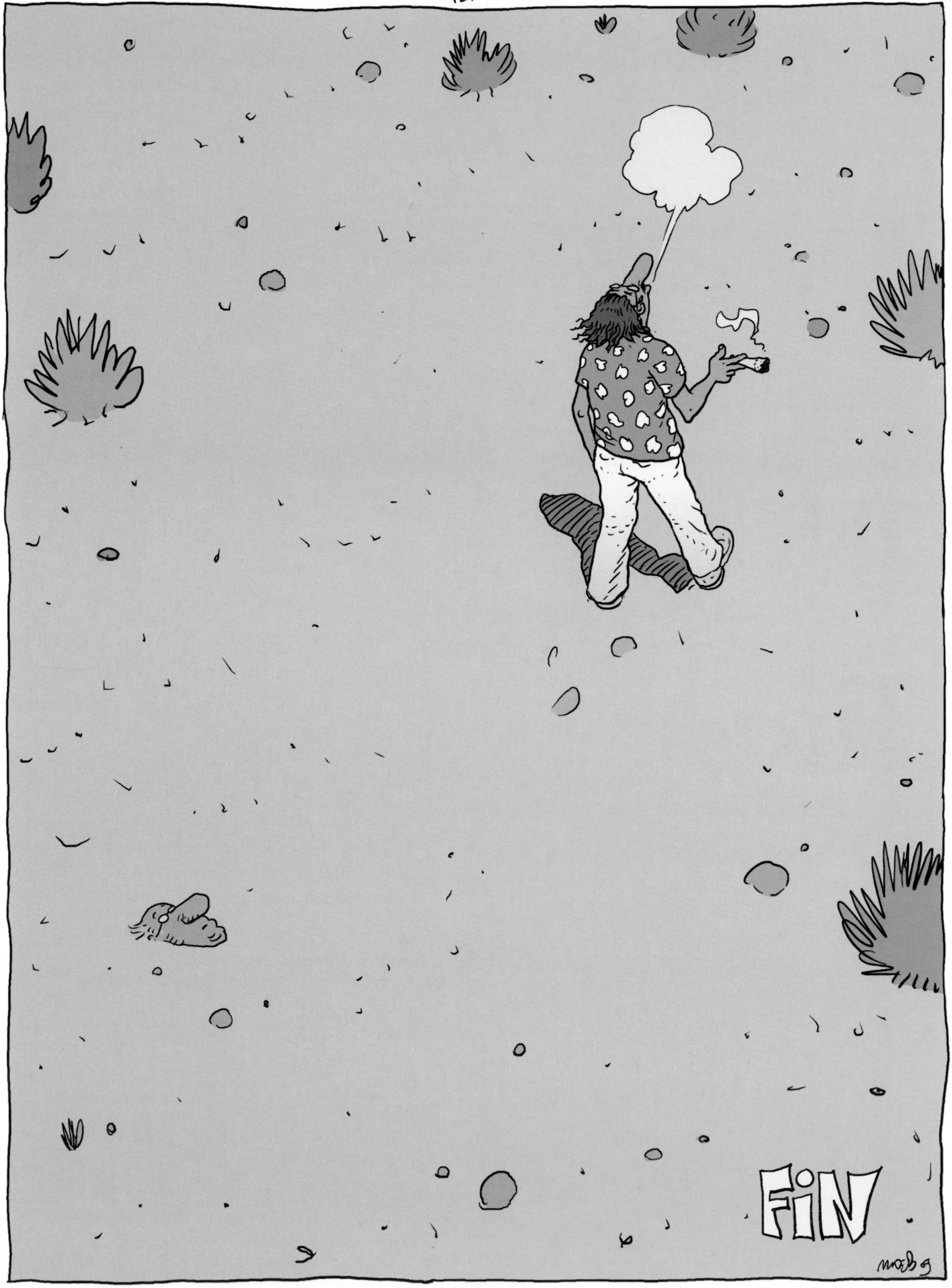
FiN
MOEB 09

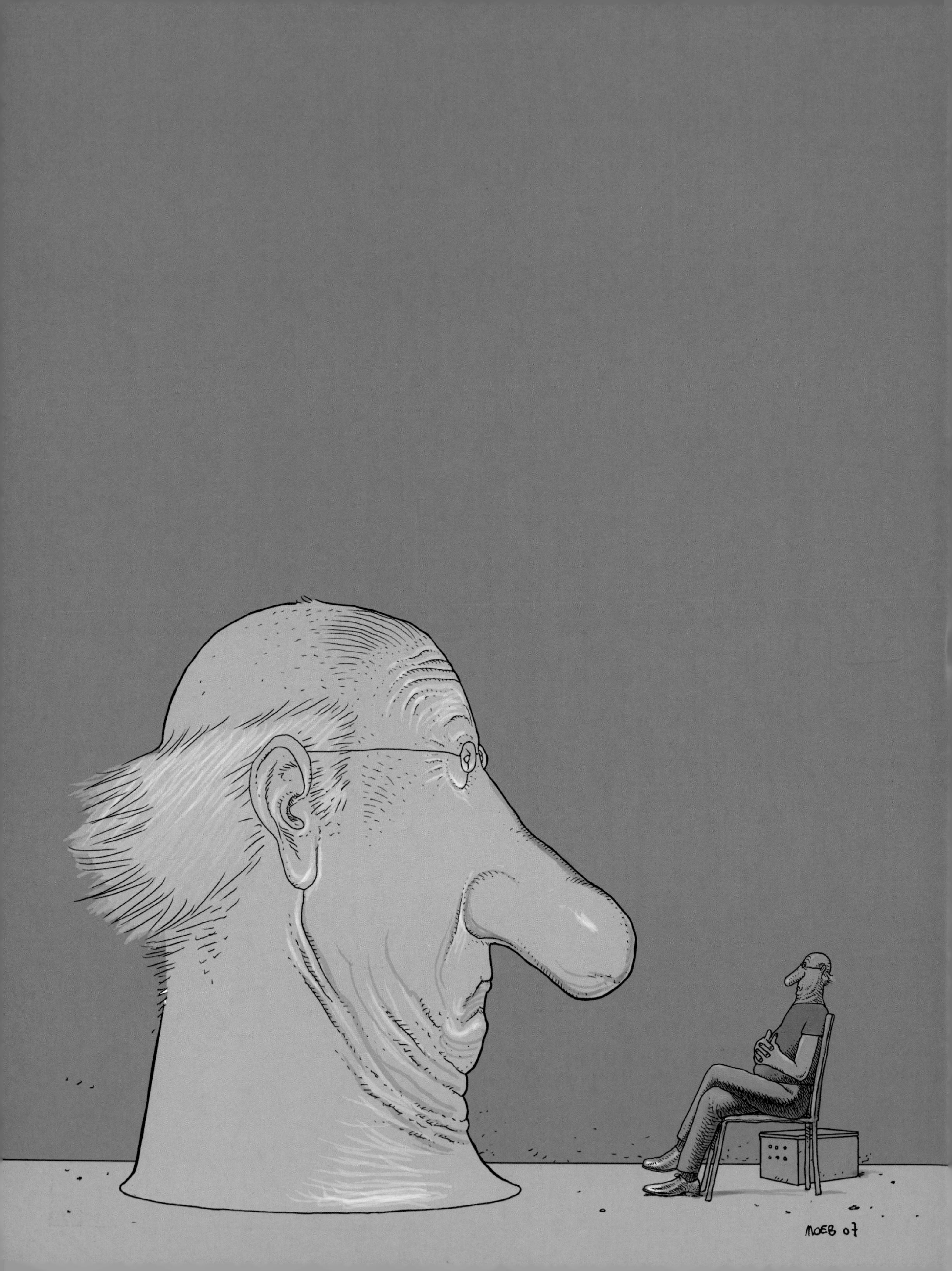
MOEB 07